ALSO BY ALAN TAYLOR

*Liberty Men and Great Proprietors: The Revolutionary
Settlement on the Maine Frontier, 1760–1820*
(1990)

WILLIAM COOPER'S TOWN

Recipient of the
1995 New York State Historical Association
Manuscript Award

WILLIAM COOPER'S TOWN

*Power and Persuasion
on the Frontier of the
Early American Republic*

ALAN TAYLOR

*Alfred A. Knopf
New York
1995*

THIS IS A BORZOI BOOK
PUBLISHED BY ALFRED A. KNOPF, INC.

Grateful acknowledgment is made to the following for permission to reprint
previously published material:
Harvard University Press: Excerpts from *The Letters and Journals of James Fenimore
Cooper,* vols. I–VI, 1960–1968, edited by James Franklin Beard. Vols. I and II,
copyright © 1960 by the President and Fellows of Harvard College. Vols. III and
IV, copyright © 1964 by the President and Fellows of Harvard College. Vols. V
and VI, copyright © 1968 by the President and Fellows of Harvard College.
Reprinted by permission of Harvard University Press.
State University of New York Press: Excerpts from *The Pioneers* by James Fenimore
Cooper. Copyright © 1980 by State University of New York. Reprinted by
permission of State University of New York Press.

Library of Congress Cataloging-in-Publication Data
Taylor, Alan, [date]
William Cooper's town : power and
persuasion on the frontier of the early
American republic / Alan Taylor.
p.   cm.
Includes bibliographical references (p.   ) and index.
ISBN 0-394-58054-0
1. Cooperstown (N.Y.)—History. 2. Cooper,
James Fenimore, 1789–1851. Pioneers. I. Title.
F129.C77T38   1995
974.7'74—dc20   95-21748   CIP

Manufactured in the United States of America
First Edition

For Shelley and Peter,
Erik and Evan

and

in memory of
Paul Fenimore Cooper, Jr.

Contents

Illustrations follow page 278.

WILLIAM
COOPER'S
TOWN

INTRODUCTION

T HE DEATH OF JUDGE WILLIAM
Cooper in late 1809 dismayed his
friend Miers Fisher, who, on June 13,
1810, wrote a moving letter of tribute addressed to the judge's sons. Fisher was a
pious Quaker, a former mayor of Philadelphia, and a wealthy lawyer who had become Cooper's partner in frontier land
speculations. Despite early poverty and
limited education, Cooper had risen to become the preeminent landlord, presiding
judge, and U.S. congressman of Otsego

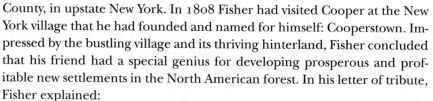

*"The enterprise of Judge Temple is tam-
ing the very forests!" exclaimed Elizabeth, throwing off the covering, and
partly rising in the bed. "How rapidly
is civilization treading on the footsteps
of nature!" she continued, as her eye
glanced over not only the comforts, but
the luxuries of her apartment, and her
ear again listened to the distant, but
often repeated howls from the lake.*

—*James Fenimore Cooper,*
The Pioneers, 212

County, in upstate New York. In 1808 Fisher had visited Cooper at the New
York village that he had founded and named for himself: Cooperstown. Impressed by the bustling village and its thriving hinterland, Fisher concluded
that his friend had a special genius for developing prosperous and profitable new settlements in the North American forest. In his letter of tribute,
Fisher explained:

> He was a man to whom my mind bore a most cordial friendship, founded on
> esteem & of whose Life I wished to know more than a seven years acquain-
> tance afforded, in order that I might write a history of the wonderful dispen-
> sations of Providence in enabling a great mind to emerge from Obscurity &
> to display a benevolent use of Talents more exalted than Bonaparte or any of
> his predecessors of conquering memory; their ambition laid waste the fruitful
> fields & turn'd the Gardens of Europe & Asia to Desarts—thy father's great
> mind converted the savage wilds of America to fruitful fields & he lived to see
> the unborn generations of his first settlers enjoying Peace, Liberty & Safety
> under their own cultivated Settlements; But I sat down to write a Letter not a
> History!

To make sense of Judge Cooper, Fisher had to narrate Cooper's life as part
of the larger history of his time and nation. Cooper's remarkable rise from
humble origins to riches and influence represented the opportunity, equality, and mobility that became so celebrated in the early American Republic.

And as a frontier promoter and landlord, he worked at the heart of the great phenomenon of his place in time—the conquest, resettlement, and transformation of the North American forest.[1]

But William Cooper was a controversial as well as a commanding figure. Many former friends, as well as old rivals, eventually concluded that his cunning at speculation and political intrigue exceeded the bounds of genteel respectability. Even Miers Fisher began to suspect that Cooper had cheated him by secretly hoarding the best lands in one of their joint purchases. Pained by the dawning suspicion, in 1815 he wrote, "From the opinion I had entertained of the Integrity of William Cooper, I . . . shall be very sorry to find myself deceived for I had rather submit to that [deception] than discover a personal advantage to myself in the misconduct of one whom I deemed an honest man & my friend."[2]

William Cooper became rich, powerful, and famous by attaching himself to his nation's rapid population growth and territorial expansion at the frontier margins. He benefited from the recent Revolutionary War, which had dispossessed the native inhabitants of New York, the Iroquois tribes. Devastated by American raids in 1779 and abandoned by their British allies in 1783, the Iroquois had to surrender almost all of their homeland. Their domains passed first to land speculators such as William Cooper and then to thousands of settlers whose new farms steadily obliterated the marks of their Indian predecessors. When Miers Fisher insisted that the "savage wilds" had been converted by Cooper's peaceful enterprise, he erased the role of conquest in the settlement of North America. From the Indian perspective Cooper and his settlers were Bonapartes whose ambitions laid waste the fruitful fields of the Iroquois.[3]

Slow to develop as a colony, New York became the most dynamic state in the newly independent American Republic. During the four decades that followed the end of the war in 1783, thousands of Yankees flocked from crowded New England into upstate New York to replace the Iroquois. New York's population quadrupled from 340,120 in 1790 to 1,372,812 in 1820. In 1790 New York had been the nation's fifth state in population, lagging behind Virginia, Massachusetts, Pennsylvania, and North Carolina. By 1820 New York had become the most populous state in the nation—as well as the leader in manufacturing and banking capital and in commercial exports. Most of the Yankees settled in the hills and valleys of northern, central, and western New York—dramatically shifting the distribution of the state's population; in 1785 three-fourths of New Yorkers still lived in the Hudson valley or along the Atlantic coast; in 1820 three-fourths of the state's people lived in the newer counties to the north and west of Albany. The new nation's explosive expansion exceeded in pace and extent the experience of any preceding American generation, and New York was the vanguard state of the developing nation. As the aggressive and energetic developer of fron-

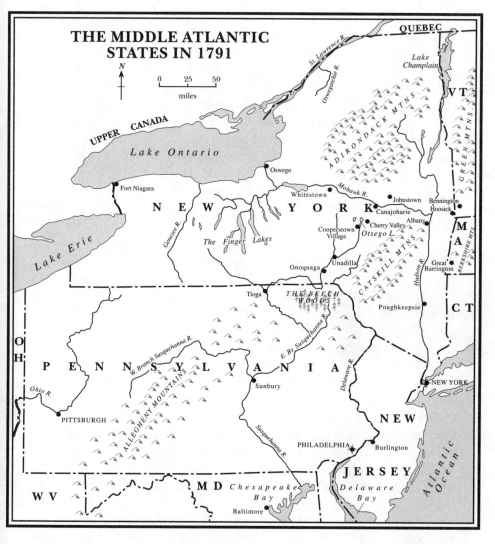

THE MIDDLE ATLANTIC
STATES IN 1791

N

0   25   50
miles

MAP 1

tier settlements in central New York, William Cooper played a leading role
in that state's rapid demographic and commercial expansion.[4]

During the 1780s and 1790s the American Revolution played out its social implications in Cooperstown and the hundreds of other new settlements that proliferated in the backcountry newly conquered from the
natives. The combination of centrifugal expansion and revolutionary legacy
opened to question the values and institutions of the colonial past, permitting the emergence of a more dynamic and competitive social order. The
many new settlements were the cockpits for contentious struggles over the
distribution of new property and new political offices. Because the competitors cloaked themselves in conflicting interpretations of the recent

Revolution, those struggles served to define the meaning of that social upheaval.[5]

Exploiting the social flux wrought by the Revolution and by the rapid creation of new frontier communities, Cooper became rich and influential through his aggressive land speculations. Honoring that new wealth and influence, the New York legislature created Otsego County in 1791, and the governor named Cooper the presiding judge of its courts—despite his scant education, colloquial speech, and rough manners. Three years later he secured election to the U.S. Congress, winning a remarkable 84 percent of the vote in his home county. Cooper tried to complete his social ascent by remaking himself in the image of the gentlemen who had presided over colonial America's older, more stable communities. Although a great beneficiary of the revolutionary upheaval, Cooper joined with like-minded leading men of the Federalist persuasion determined to contain and limit the egalitarian implications of the recent revolution.[6]

The Federalists underestimated the enduring potential of the American Revolution to legitimate upstarts unwilling or unable to achieve or endure genteel authority. Cooper did not recognize that the many new communities of frontier migrants would sustain a more open and uninhibited competition for wealth and power that he could never control. During the late 1790s Cooper was challenged simultaneously from within his own party by more genteel men who disdained his rough edges and from without by rural democrats who saw him as a would-be aristocrat. Only partially successful at genteel reinvention, he was vulnerable to calumny and ridicule from both the common and the polite. By trying and failing to become a polished gentleman, Cooper only hastened the collapse of his public authority. Unable to silence his critics, in late 1799 he resigned as a judge and announced his retirement from Congress. In part because of his blunders, Cooper's Federalist party suffered catastrophic defeats in the national and state elections of 1800 and 1801. Dishonored by defeat, William Cooper never again held a political or judicial post. Political power in America instead passed to a new class of professional politicians, who made a show of their democratic love for the people. Cooper's decline revealed how the revolutionary legacy and frontier expansion interacted to corrode the unity of social, political, cultural, and economic authority exercised by the colonial and Federalist elites.[7]

After his political downfall Cooper invested his hopes in his children, arranging and paying for their education in the manners and arts of gentility. He prepared them to complete his ascent by winning acceptance among the most prestigious families in New York. They would, he hoped, restore the public authority that he had temporarily grasped during the 1790s. Dying in late 1809, William Cooper seemed in his will to endow his children with a great fortune and social preeminence. However, their inheritance proved fatally compromised by faulty land titles and burdensome debts that, in the years 1819–1824, culminated in foreclosures that virtually wiped out the family fortune. As his inheritance vanished, James Fenimore Cooper, the youngest son, became a novelist, publishing his first novel in 1820 and his third, *The Pioneers*, in 1823.[8]

In *The Pioneers* the novelist tried to revive and reclaim his lost property and position in an imagined place: Templeton. Set in the Otsego country of the 1790s, the novel vividly evokes a frontier community in conflict over who should own its resources and who should govern the people. Richly descriptive, *The Pioneers* offers an intensely reimagined past as an act of reverie and repossession. In an 1850 introduction to the novel, Cooper noted, "The face of the country, the climate as it was found by the whites, and the manners of the settlers, are described with a minuteness for which the Author has no other apology than the force of his own recollections." The novelist indulged his pleasing memories and exorcised his painful ones.[9]

In particular Cooper wrestled with the contradictions and mysteries of his father's character. Impelled by powerful and difficult memories, Cooper cast his father as the novel's Judge Marmaduke Temple, the founder, developer, and ruler of the frontier village of Templeton. Judge Temple is a man of good intentions but loose scruples, of expansive vision but flawed manners, of benevolent paternalism but blundering execution. Temple falls just short of the full gentility and true self-discipline needed to maintain his authority over Templeton's fractious and greedy settlers.[10]

The Pioneers secured James Fenimore Cooper's reputation as the first great and popular novelist in the United States and the premier literary spokesman for his generation. The novel also jogged the memory of former President John Adams, who had known William Cooper as a congressman during the 1790s. In 1824 Adams wrote to a friend in upstate New York, "I understand [that] your New York novelist has been in Boston, and I am quite affronted with him that he did not call upon me. I knew and respected his Father who was indeed one of the great Pioneers."[11]

William Cooper's development of Cooperstown and his son's creation of Templeton were different stages of a common effort, over two generations, to create, sustain, and justify a wealthy and powerful estate in the rapidly changing American Republic. Both generations tried to achieve a unity of social, economic, political, and cultural preeminence idealized in colonial America but at odds with the legacy of the American Revolution. William Cooper sought that unity as the "father" of the real community of Cooperstown; in the wake of his failure, his son sought the same in the imaginary frontier village of Templeton. In the real village of Cooperstown, the father built—and then lost—an estate of wealth and power that the son tried to recover in the imaginary village of Templeton.

By treating William Cooper's career and his son's most powerful novel as parts of a whole, *William Cooper's Town* is a hybrid of three usually distinct genres: biography, social history, and literary analysis. First, it is a biography of Judge William Cooper, with particular emphasis on his relationships with his family and with important allies and rivals. Second, this book is a social history—a community study of Cooperstown, New York, and its Otsego County hinterland from the village's founding in 1786 by William Cooper to the publication of *The Pioneers* by his son in early 1823. The analysis and narrative consider hundreds of settlers and villagers whose lives and aspirations interacted with those of the Cooper family. Unlike many community studies that are relentlessly local, this book examines the play within Otsego of regional, national, and international forces. These include the conflicts between natives and colonists, rebels and Loyalists for possession of the land; the competition of diverse social visions meant to shape the human re-occupation of Otsego; the environmental struggle by settlers to remake the forest into a more reassuring and profitable landscape dominated by privately owned farms; the influence of the transatlantic market over the investments and labors of land speculators and common settlers; the partisan battles between Federalists and Republicans to control the new American Republic; the heated competition of diverse Protestant denominations for the souls of the frontier people; and the struggle by American writers and publishers to create a profitable and distinctive national literature and historical memory. The subject is not simply William Cooper's village (Cooperstown) but its surrounding township (Otsego), county (also named Otsego), state (New York), and nation (the United States)—as well as its transatlantic, Anglo-American cultural and economic context. My quarry is not the elusive essence and operation of "community" but the local ramifications of institutions and movements that affected the nation.

Third, I reassess the production and meanings of *The Pioneers,* in which the novelist recoded in fiction his childhood memories of the frontier village of Cooperstown. My book reappropriates the world of *The Pioneers* to reexamine the frontier community as the setting for the reordering and reimagining of American society in the late eighteenth and early nineteenth centuries. My narrative builds both upon *The Pioneers* as a source and toward it as the culmination of the Coopers' efforts to achieve wealth and authority. There is a shift in the ballast of the three elements as the story moves forward in time, for William Cooper preceded the creation of Cooperstown in 1786; as it grew in size and diversity, the community increasingly escaped from his control at the turn of the century; and James Fenimore Cooper wrote *The Pioneers* in 1822 to reassert his family's claims to preeminence.

By describing in detail a family and their place, I mean to reveal the interplay of frontier settlement, political struggles, and narrative making in the early American Republic. I want to see how Americans resolved their revolution through the competitive construction of new property, new power, and new stories in the many frontier communities. The economic, political, and cultural processes of construction occurred simultaneously and interdependently. No single process can be privileged as autonomous, prior, primary, and exclusively determinative of the other two. People made property, power, and stories reciprocally and all at once (although, as author, I will often have to attend more closely to one at a time in a given section or chapter). William and James Fenimore Cooper were enmeshed in all three constructions. My fundamental premise, derived from the philosopher David Carr and the historian William Cronon, is that narratives have power because they are woven into life, not simply imposed upon a chaotic experience after the fact.[12]

Part 1

ASCENT

Chapter One

FRIEND BILLY

O N NOVEMBER 12, 1774, A YOUNG couple seeking a marriage license appeared before "his Excellency William Franklin, Esqr., Governor of the Province of New Jersey." The illegitimate son and talented protégé of Benjamin Franklin, William Franklin had been a royal governor for nearly twelve years. Wealthy and well connected, he dwelled in a magnificent three-story mansion beside the Delaware River in Willingboro near Burlington, then one of New Jersey's two provincial capitals. With the help of his friends George Croghan and Sir William Johnson, Franklin had acquired thousands of acres of frontier land near Otsego Lake in central New York. The young man

The posterity of Marmaduke . . . had descended to a point, below which, in this happy country, it is barely possible for honesty, intellect, and sobriety to fall. . . . It was the father of our new acquaintance, the Judge, who first began to re-ascend the scale of society; and in this undertaking he was not a little assisted by a marriage, which aided in furnishing the means of educating his only son, in a rather better manner than the low state of the common schools in Pennsylvania could promise; or than had been the practice in the family, for the two or three preceding generations.

—*James Fenimore Cooper,* The Pioneers, *31*

at the door was a penurious and ill-educated wheelwright named William Cooper. A month short of his twentieth birthday, Cooper lived across the river in Byberry, Pennsylvania. His intended bride, Elizabeth Fenimore, was the daughter of a prosperous Quaker farmer in Willingboro. Neither man could have known, or would have guessed, that a decade later Cooper would wrest away Franklin's lands to become a rich and powerful man in an independent American republic.[1]

In 1774 young William Cooper knew the ways of gentility and power only from a respectful distance. In eighteenth-century America a fundamental divide separated the genteel, or polite, few from the common many who had to work with their hands as farmers, artisans, sailors, or day laborers. Taking their cue from the hierarchical social order in Great Britain, most colonists conceded that public authority should be exercised by men such as William Franklin, who claimed to be the "better sort." The phrase referred to an elite who combined superior wealth with polished manners, classical learning, and a reputation for honor and integrity. Colonial leaders presumed, and most common folk accepted, that social, political, and cultural authority should be united in an order of gentlemen. Artisans and common farmers could vote and hold local offices as surveyors of roads or viewers of fences—offices that bore little honor and no pay but some manual labor. However, it was presumptuous for any man without the attributes of gentility to seek the more prestigious and lucrative public offices at the county or provincial level, as sheriffs, justices, judges, assemblymen, and councillors. Gentlemen also enjoyed privileged access to immense grants of frontier lands that augmented and perpetuated their interests and estates. To obtain title to new farms, common colonists had to pay wealthy speculators, who had exploited their political connections to secure vast tracts on the frontier from royal governors and their councils. In Otsego the would-be settler had to buy land from a William Franklin, George Croghan, or Sir William Johnson. Settlers' payments to landlords reinforced the inequality of wealth and power.[2]

Cultural acceptance, rather than formal law, underlay the ideal of genteel authority in eighteenth-century America. For lack of a legally established aristocracy, claims to genteel superiority in America depended on public acceptance. By giving or withholding deference, the public played a key role in defining who enjoyed genteel prestige. An American was a gentleman only if other people, common as well as genteel, publicly conceded that he had crossed—by breeding, education, and acquisition—that critical but subtle line separating the genteel few from the common many.[3]

Wealth was necessary but not sufficient for genteel authority. The acquisition of property was the easiest and, usually, the first attainment of the upwardly mobile. The man who achieved new wealth ordinarily lagged in his accumulation of the other attributes of gentility: polished manners, urbane tastes, literary knowledge, and legal sophistication. Indeed, social mobility was vaguely suspect as subversive of a recognized, respected, and stable social hierarchy. The self-made man was vulnerable to the biting epithet "mushroom gentleman"—one who had sprung up overnight from the dung. A man of new wealth needed the approval of those already accepted by themselves and by others as possessing the full range of gentility. Colonists of new wealth hastened to complete their portfolios of genteel ways by retraining themselves to speak, walk, gesture, dress, pose, and think like aristocrats. Prestige and high office rewarded those who succeeded, while those who fell short reaped ridicule. Nothing was considered more foolish, more fit for satire, than the upstart who assumed airs he could not master.[4]

Benjamin Franklin had thoroughly reinvented himself as a gentleman to complete his ascent from obscurity and poverty as a journeyman printer in mid-eighteenth-century Philadelphia. He became a wealthy publisher and civic promoter partly through his discipline, genius, and hard work and, partly, by winning the patronage of leading gentlemen, initially in Philadelphia and subsequently in London. His wealth accumulated, Franklin retired from his printing business at age forty-two to cultivate the manners, perfect the learning, and pursue the political and scientific avocations of a benevolent and public-spirited gentleman. Franklin lived lavishly, acquiring a coach, fine clothes, and a circle of powerful new friends. (Years later, during the American Revolution, he would create and perform his new, and politically useful, role as the simple, self-made American.)

Recognizing the importance of an heir and protégé to his own further ascent, Franklin endowed his son with the means and the attributes of gentility. William Franklin grew up accustomed to the wealth, education, and genteel patrons that his father had won through persistent effort and performance. A private tutor, a classical academy, and the law school of the Middle Temple in London completed young Franklin's education in the knowledge and manners of gentility. Father and son toured England and the Continent, received everywhere by gentlemen of learning and power. Pushed forward by his father, William caught the eye of Lord Bute, the British king's principal adviser, who arranged the young man's appointment as the royal governor of New Jersey in 1763. The appointment was a tribute both to William's promise as a courtier and to his father's ascent to gentility. A dozen years later, when William clung to the British cause during the American Revolution and broke with his father, it became apparent that Benjamin had been all too successful at making an aristocrat of his son.[5]

The Franklins' success was rare and remarkable for the mid-eighteenth century. The social mobility of ambitious tradesmen and farmers into positions of wealth and prestige had been more common in the preceding century, when society had been more fluid, populations smaller, and the economic opportunities greater. During the middle decades of the eighteenth century, the colonies became more crowded, stable, and stratified— more like the mother country. This "Anglicization" gradually concentrated wealth and high office in the hands of an increasingly class-conscious elite. The consolidation of a gentry class inhibited the access of common men to property and power. Although the middling order of yeomen farmers and master artisans remained conspicuously large and prosperous relative to its counterpart in England, there was a gradual but pronounced trend toward social polarization. Growing numbers of poor men and women spent their entire lives as laborers, seamen, cottagers, or tenant farmers without any power or much property. Given the social trends, in 1774 it seemed impossible that a young wheelwright would become wealthy and powerful at the expense of the royal governor of New Jersey. But over the ensuing decade the American Revolution would challenge the gentry's power throughout the colonies and unravel the estates of the particular gentlemen who

claimed Otsego. By the mid-1780s Cooper had accumulated enough property and connections to seek wealth and leadership in the new American
Republic by bidding for control of the Otsego Patent.[6]

ASCENT 🦢

William Cooper began life in social obscurity in a provincial corner of the
British empire. Born December 2, 1754, in a log house in Smithfield (now
Somerton), on the outskirts of Philadelphia, he was the third child and second son of Hannah (Hibbs) and James Cooper, a Quaker farmer of limited
means ("exceedingly poor," according to one account). William's early education was almost entirely manual; he never learned to write grammati-
cally or to spell consistently. In 1789 he apologized to a correspondent: "P.S.
Thee will at all times be Pleasd to excuse bad Spelling as I was Never Larnt
to write nor Cypher but have taking [them] up my Selfe." Surviving letters
from his brothers indicate that they enjoyed more schooling; apparently
James and Hannah Cooper did not regard William as their most promising
or favored son. None of his three brothers and four sisters prospered, and
all but one eventually relied on William's charity—evidence of just how remarkable his own ascent was.[7]

By the time he turned seventeen, Cooper had three brothers and four sisters—too many for all to inherit a share in the small family farm. A Cooper
family tradition maintains that as an adolescent he quarreled with his father
and ran away from home to become a wheelwright. Either as a runaway or
by his father's placement, Cooper became an apprentice and then a journeyman wheelwright in Byberry, a northern suburb of Philadelphia on the
heavily traveled road heading northeast toward Trenton Ferry and New
York City. His prospects seemed bleak in 1776, when he first appeared on
the Byberry tax rolls as a wheelwright without any taxable property. Making
and repairing wagons and their wheels was hard, dirty, backbreaking
work—no genteel business and no path to riches. Although wanting in material assets, Cooper displayed a bold self-confidence. Impatient with the
constraints that birth and circumstances had initially placed on his own
prospects, he acted quickly and decisively, insisting that first impressions
"were always the best."[8]

Tall, strong, and a bit stout, William Cooper had a powerful physical presence and a winning personality. His bright eyes and rich, melodious voice
also commanded attention. In describing Marmaduke Temple, James Fenimore Cooper remembered his father as "of a large stature" with "a fine
manly face, and particularly a pair of expressive, large blue eyes, that
promised extraordinary intellect, covert humour, and great benevolence."
Despite his lack of schooling, William delighted in playing with words; he

loved to banter, to tell stories and jokes, to compose and sing songs, and to write funny or sentimental poems. Hearty, gregarious, talkative, generous, humorous, and charming, he made friends easily. In 1786 a Philadelphia merchant affectionately addressed Cooper as "Friend Billy." His generous bonhomie shines in the note he sent to his friend John Porteous in 1798: "My dear Friend, . . . I am building a Large house. When done I will have all my old friends for one week to warme it. At the Head of the list [stands] *John Porteous* whos friendship and Generosity, I have so often Experienced and who will always be considered as the best of men by his Friend, William Cooper." One day, almost twenty-five years after his father's death, James Fenimore Cooper passed an old house that had belonged to a family friend. He wrote, "I enjoyed this walk exceedingly. It recalled my noble looking, warm-hearted, witty father, with his deep laugh, sweet voice and fine rich eye, as he used to lighten the way, with his anecdote and fun."[9]

Cooper began his ascent from poverty on November 13, 1774, by marrying Elizabeth Fenimore, the daughter of a well-to-do Quaker farmer. Surviving documents indicate neither how nor when the couple met. Family tradition maintains that Richard Fenimore opposed his daughter's marriage to so poor and young a husband, which would explain their civil ceremony (Quaker practice required parental approval for a couple to marry within the unity). Two weeks shy of his twentieth birthday, Cooper married unusually young; he was more than a year short of the legal age when young men could first make binding contracts for themselves; he was two and a half years younger than his bride. She came from a much wealthier family. In 1774 her father was the second richest taxpayer (of sixty-eight) in Willingboro Township, located on the southwestern edge of Burlington City. He owned 500 acres and twenty horses and cattle—an especially large and prosperous farm for such an old (first settled by English folk in the 1670s), fertile, and populous county. It could not have reassured Elizabeth's father to hear his new son-in-law declare "that he was poor and she must shift for herself."[10]

Richard Fenimore may have soaked his anger in alcohol. In August of 1775 (nine months after the marriage), the overseers of the Burlington Monthly Meeting charged Fenimore "with taking strong drink to excess, with prophane Swearing and other reproachful Conduct for which they have unsuccessfully treated with him." Finding him "in a situation unfit to be spoke with," the overseers were "discouraged by his disorderly conduct from paying him another visit." But it is also possible that Richard Fenimore's personal crisis had long been simmering and perhaps accounted for Elizabeth's haste to leave his household.[11]

Whatever her other attractions, Elizabeth Fenimore's potential inheritance would have been alluring to a penurious and ambitious young wheelwright—especially as she had no brother to serve as a Fenimore male heir.

Richard Fenimore had to anticipate passing on his property to a grandson born to one of his three daughters. It is suggestive that Elizabeth and William married suddenly and without parental approval within a week of her sister Rachel's more orderly marriage within meeting to John Heaton. Had William Cooper applied his considerable charm to persuade Elizabeth that they could and should win a race to provide a grandson? If so, William and Elizabeth did win, as they quickly conceived a son, born on August 12, 1775—exactly nine months after their marriage—and named Richard Fenimore Cooper. In any event, Richard Fenimore did favor his first grandson and namesake with the largest bequest of land given in his will drafted in April 1789.[12]

At first the new couple, their son, and then their first daughter, Hannah (born in 1777 and named in honor of both their mothers), lived in Byberry, where William continued to ply his trade. About 1778 the Coopers moved to Willingboro and began to draw upon the Fenimore estate. Apparently mollified, Richard Fenimore seems to have given William Cooper at least 168 acres at a crossroads three miles southwest of Burlington City. Rather than farm the land or set up there as a wheelwright, William Cooper established a store and probably a tavern and developed a small commercial hamlet of a dozen buildings that he dubbed Coopertown—a little forerunner of his New York venture. Not satisfied with his ascent from wheelwright to country storekeeper and real estate developer, Cooper gambled that he could also succeed at the more competitive, but potentially more lucrative, mercantile business of Burlington City, the trading center for the county. By the spring of 1782 he had moved into the city and established a store.[13]

Founded by English Quakers in 1677 and dominated by their descendants, Burlington had the look and feel of an old, entrenched community. Described in 1788 by a visitor as "a pretty little town," it had a grid of streets laid out around the axis of two broad main streets—High and Market—intersecting at right angles. The main streets were flanked by tall, thick shade trees, small shops, narrow brick town houses, and the occasional mansion of a weighty Friend or Anglican gentleman. Wooden fences enclosed neat gardens. The public buildings included two substantial Quaker meetinghouses, an Anglican church, library, market house, and courthouse. More than a century old, Burlington differed markedly from the rough new settlements proliferating two hundred miles away to the north and the west.[14]

Although an economic satellite of the international entrepôt of Philadelphia, Burlington was an important regional trading town. Consisting of about two hundred houses, it was the largest urban center in New Jersey. The surrounding countryside was fertile and dotted with the substantial barns, sheds, houses, and fences of prosperous old farms. Burlington County was proverbial for the quality of its cheese and its pork. The farmers carted their produce and drove their livestock into the city to dicker with the merchants in the central market, located at the juncture of Market and High streets. In their riverside warehouses the traders assembled cargoes and packed them into flat-bottomed riverboats for shipment twenty miles down the Delaware to Philadelphia's merchants, who exported the valley's surplus to market in Europe and the West Indies.[15]

Another family tradition insists that William Cooper early rebelled against his Quaker heritage and was expelled by his monthly meeting for nonattendance. The records of the Byberry Preparatory Meeting and its superintending Abington Monthly Meeting are mute; they contain no references to William Cooper, either as a member or as a recusant. Nor did he ever join the Meeting in Burlington. He came of age at a time when many young Quakers found the world more alluring than the rigorous adherence to a plain style demanded by the increasingly separatist Quaker meetings. It seems that Cooper settled into a halfway status as a "wet Quaker"—one who occasionally attended weekly meetings for worship but did not submit to the monthly and quarterly meetings for discipline; one who preserved some aspects of the plain style while adopting many of the fashions and manners of the secular world.[16]

Certainly, much in William Cooper's colorful character and worldly behavior violated the plain principles of his parents' faith. His boisterous delight in wrestling and horse racing put him at odds with the Quaker aversion to activities that did not "improve the time." His playfulness with words clashed with the Quaker determination to avoid all trifling conversation in favor of the plain truth spoken without ostentation. Contrary to Quaker precepts of orderly caution in business, William Cooper sold alcohol as a storekeeper; accepted and tendered paper money; and was careless in his record keeping, maddeningly slow to pay many of his debts, and recklessly bold in his land speculations. Later in life, after he became rich and moved to Cooperstown, Cooper ignored Quaker teaching by pursuing a political career, by acquiring slaves to serve as domestic servants, by sending his sons to college, and by erecting an impressive mansion.[17]

Uninterested in spirituality, William Cooper did not participate in the meditative Quaker search for the Inner Light. He praised religion only as it benefited the social morals and material prosperity of a community, and he detected God only as the creator of the material world and its natural laws. Reluctant to name God, Cooper spoke of the Supreme Being as his senior partner in the work of settling and developing the frontier. "I . . . hope I shall be kept within the Bounds of Providential feer [of He] whome I Look too as the finisher of all my workes," he remarked in 1789. In *A Guide in the Wilderness,* Cooper described his deist's epiphany at Niagara Falls: "before this majestic image of eternal power, the soul is fixed in awe and reverence—the voice of a companion is irksome—self is forgot—full of the idea of Almighty power—though terrible, delightful—sense dwells upon the image—thought wanders obscurely after something which it cannot grasp, and the beholder is lost in exstacy as I am in description!" A thorough materialist, Cooper often insisted that he believed only what he could see, measure, and buy or sell. A confirmed utilitarian, he quickly shook off the sublime impact of Niagara Falls to calculate: "That most attractive and gratifying object of human curiosity, the falls of Niagara, would of itself create a thoroughfare, and the product of the tolls on the turnpikes and canal-gates would raise a revenue sufficient in a very short time to requite the undertakers."[18]

He never belonged to a church, very much like Marmaduke Temple, whom Mrs. Holister charges with "carelessness about his sowl. It's nather a Methodie, nor a Papish, nor a Prasbetyrian, that he is, but jist nothing at all." When visiting Philadelphia, Cooper frequently called on Henry and Elizabeth Drinker, pious and prestigious Friends, for breakfast, dinner, supper, tea, or a night's lodging—but only once did he accompany Henry Drinker to a Quaker meeting. Sometimes Cooper was publicly indiscreet about his doubts, leading his political rivals to charge atheism and blasphemy. In 1796 a foe insisted, "The man who rails at religion, ought not to enjoy our confidence. Is it not notorious, that Judge Cooper said to some people who he saw coming out of a house of worship—That he would sooner see them come out of a whore-house?"[19]

Despite his early rejection of Quaker authority and Quaker spirituality, William Cooper remained a Friend in many of his ways and values. Like Marmaduke Temple, Cooper was "quite the quaker in externals." He favored dark colors, especially black, in his clothing. In 1793, despite having become a politician and slaveowner, Cooper still thought of himself as a Friend, for when called upon to swear to an affidavit, he insisted on the alternative of affirming—"being one of the people called Quakers," the court clerk recorded. In his correspondence, until the mid-1790s, he numbered the months and days to avoid their pagan names, and he signed himself "Friend Cooper." In letters and speech he often used *thee* and *thou*, very much like Marmaduke Temple, who "when much interested or agitated," spoke "the language of his youth." He disliked religious establishments and spoke out against war, and he sought utilitarian knowledge that would make men happier and more prosperous. Although (like Marmaduke Temple) he kept a few slaves, in 1792 Cooper praised an antislavery pamphlet sent to him by Benjamin Rush: "I am still quaker Enuff to Esteem the Christian Spirit it manifest in the writer and have no Doubt in the next generation that Plan will be adopted." Late in life, while founding a new settlement in northern New York, Cooper took along a book by William Penn, the Quaker founder of Pennsylvania: "Penn's [book] I Read myself almost dayley. Nither Solon nor Lycurgus was greater than he." But Cooper admired

Penn's Quaker benevolence and paternalism as the leader of settlers rather than his Quaker spirituality as a seeker after salvation.[20]

William Cooper remained "quaker Enuff" to enjoy the patronage and partnership of wealthy and prestigious Quakers, known as "weighty Friends," who economically and culturally dominated Burlington. To succeed in his own mind, William Cooper had to impress the weighty Friends who valued material accumulation if it also benefited the community. Successful as a storekeeper, he accumulated civic responsibilities and important friends. According to his store ledger listing the credit accounts of six esquires, Burlington's leading men frequented Cooper's store. Beginning in 1783 Cooper served on three criminal trial juries and one grand jury—further marks of his acceptance as a substantial citizen. In the summer of 1787 he played a leading role in a meeting of Burlington merchants convened to protest a new state excise tax. In 1786–87 he won a seat on the City Council, and he was the overseer of the poor in 1787 and 1788. Cooper had risen from poverty to assume public responsibility for those still in need.[21]

His family also grew over the course of the 1780s. In 1778 William and Elizabeth Cooper moved to Burlington with two young children—three-year-old Richard Fenimore and one-year-old Hannah. During the next eleven years the Coopers celebrated the births of eight children but mourned the early deaths of three. Born on March 7, 1779, Ann Cooper soon died. Twins Isaac and Abraham followed on May 6, 1781, but only the first survived infancy. On February 24, 1784, another daughter assumed the name Ann and, as the longest lived of the children, kept it for the next eighty-six years. Elizabeth gave birth to another set of twins on January 4, 1786—a girl and a boy; one took her name and the other assumed her husband's. The daughter soon died, but William Jr. survived childhood. Two more sons followed, Samuel in May of 1787 and James, the future novelist, on September 15, 1789 (he did not add the middle name Fenimore until 1827).[22]

Elizabeth bore an increasing burden as the births and deaths mounted, a burden compounded by her husband's frequent and prolonged absences in pursuit of his distant land speculations. William departed for central New York to secure the Otsego Patent in the depth of winter just days after Elizabeth gave birth to her second set of twins—and about the time one of them died. When we get a little clearer picture of Elizabeth in the 1790s, she is a profoundly unhappy woman. Her alienation and morbidity may have their roots in the burdens and traumas of the preceding decade. William Cooper's life during the 1780s is a narrative of increasing success in the public sphere; Elizabeth Cooper's story—virtually lost to us—is far more private and far less happy.

BOOKS 🖋

The Library Company of Burlington, the town's preeminent social club and cultural institution, played a critical role in William Cooper's ascent. Founded by weighty Friends and wealthy Anglicans in 1757, the Library Company was the seventh oldest subscription library in the colonies. The charter members had included William Franklin and several members of the Smith family—the weightiest Friends in Burlington. Cooper secured membership in January 1780, when he was twenty-five years old. That admission was a critical watershed in Cooper's life, demarking his subsequent pursuit of gentility from his previous life of hard labor and limited prospects. As a member Cooper became familiar with the town's most prestigious and best-read men, and he gained access to the worldly knowledge contained in 1,400 volumes written by "the most highly approved antient and modern authors." Worth in excess of £500, the collection was far too large and expensive for any one citizen of Burlington to own. The directors promised that the library gave "young people an opportunity of becoming acquainted with the sentiments of those great men in all ages, who have been celebrated for their learning and abilities, of storing their minds with ideas, which through life may be highly serviceable to them, and it affords a rational entertainment to all." The member would "not only improve the mind, but mend the heart." Beginning with his £3.13.0 admission fee and continuing by dues of ten shillings a year, Cooper bought access to the books and networks necessary for his gradual reinvention as a gentleman. Virtually uneducated when he came to Burlington, Cooper used the Library Company as his school to cultivate the knowledge, mores, and manners of a William Franklin and a Richard Smith. The circulation records indicate that he early read, and later returned to, *The Preceptor: Containing a General Course of Education, Wherein the First Principles of Polite Learning are Laid Down in a Way Most Suitable for Trying the Genius and Advancing the Instruction of Youth*—a sign that Cooper was a purposeful reader seeking a crash course in gentility.[23]

The Library Company's circulation records survive for Cooper's first nine years as a member, documenting his increasingly ambitious program of self-education. As a reader Cooper began slowly, checking out only six volumes in 1780, ten in 1781, and seventeen in 1782. Thereafter, he picked up the pace, withdrawing forty-two volumes in 1783—more than the combined total of his first three years. He became the Library Company's most diligent reader, appearing on most Sunday afternoons, the one time in the week when the library opened (see Table 1). During the period 1783–1788 Cooper averaged forty-six volumes a year. By March 7, 1789, when the surviving circulation records break, Cooper had withdrawn a total of 319 volumes—a major effort for a man who began with bare literacy and who, at the same time, had to meet the increasing demands of his growing family, expanding store, and complicated land speculations. Yet no other member read so much so quickly. He must have burned a lot of midnight oil and skimmed much that he checked out. Cooper was in a hurry to catch up to the well-educated gentlemen who dominated the civic, economic, and cultural life of Burlington.[24]

A 1748 novel by the Scotsman Tobias Smollett, *The Adventures of Roderick Random,* had a special appeal to Cooper. It was one of the two books he checked out on his first day as a member, and it was the only novel that he withdrew twice, returning for it seven years later. Bawdy, earthy, and sometimes scatalogical, *Roderick Random* was considered coarse, low, and indecent by highbrow, moralizing critics. It was certainly a long march from the exemplary, pious biographies read by orthodox Friends. Consequently, the novel suggests the common bedrock of Cooper's taste as he began to expand his mind. In the eighteenth century novels offered readers a vicarious opportunity to experience the tests of achieving and preserving gentility. Cooper may have readily identified with the protagonist and narrator, a penurious but persistent young man alienated from his family and obliged to make his way in a world preoccupied with money. Rendered vulnerable to hypocrites by his early poverty, Random becomes obsessed with acquiring and counting money. He wins friends and patrons by dint of wit and reading: "logick I made no account of; but above all things, I valued myself on my taste in the *Belle Lettre,* and a talent for poetry, which had already produced some morceaus, that brought me a great deal of reputation. These qualifications added to a good face and shape, acquired the esteem and acquaintance of the most considerable people in town." William Cooper could have said exactly the same of his tastes, talents, and progress in Burlington during the 1780s. Random's ultimate ascent to gentility and wealth would have reassured Cooper, then in such suspense at the prospects of his own risky speculations.[25]

Cooper's priorities can be measured by comparing the distribution of his readings with the proportion of titles in the categories defined by the Library Company's catalog. For example, Cooper checked out 10 volumes of novels—3 percent of the 319 volumes he withdrew over the course of the decade; according to the catalogue, novels accounted for 4 percent of the library's overall holdings. In other words, Cooper read novels in a proportion roughly representative of their distribution in the library. What categories did Cooper concentrate in? Over the decade he read disproportionately in "Voyages and Travels," "Poetry," and "Polite Literature, or Belles Lettres." His preferences followed closely the example set by the fictional Roderick Random. Conversely, Cooper especially neglected

"Miscellanies and Drama," "Physic, Philology, Arts & Sciences," and "Sermons and Divinity" (see Table 2).[26]

His selections reveal a worldly mind engaged in a conscious effort to transcend his provincial origins and outlook. Cooper sought that borderland where the imaginative and the tangible intersected, where a narrator conducted the mind's eye to alien places that were ostensibly real but distant in space and time from Burlington. Preferring rich description to weighty analysis, Cooper avoided anything abstract, theoretical, metaphysical, or spiritual—especially the library's extensive collection of sermons and religious commentaries. Even his rare and tentative forays into the religious literature attest to the limits of his interest; twice he checked out the Bible, indicating that he did not own the ubiquitous book of eighteenth-century America. Reading selectively even within his favorite categories (such as "Voyages and Travels"), Cooper borrowed neither the *Journal of the Reverend John Wesley* nor Rev. George Whitefield's *Voyage from Georgia to Gibralter.*[27]

During his first five years (1780–1784), he concentrated on books that quickly and easily widened his comprehended world in space and time, reading mostly histories, biographies, and travelogues (see Table 3). These books vicariously transported the former wheelwright and rustic Quaker to Louisiana and Siberia, South America and Hungary, Barbados and Greenland, Persia and Scotland, England and Arabia, Sweden and Gambia, Germany and Kamchatka, Senegal and Russia, Switzerland and Lake Superior, ancient Rome and the court of Louis XIV—places he had never seen and would never visit as a body. Eager for concise and diverse samples, he especially liked multivolume compilations of biographies, histories, and travels: Horace Walpole's *Anecdotes of Painting in England, with Some Account of the Principal Artists* (1762), John Hackett's *Select and Remarkable Epitaphs, Lives, &c.,* John Campbell's *Lives of British Admirals, and Other Eminent Seamen* (1744), the *Biographia Britannica; or the Lives of the Most Eminent Persons who have Flourished in Great Britain and Ireland From the Earliest Ages Down to the Present Times* (1747), Thomas Birch's *The Heads of Illustrious Persons of Great Britain; with their Lives, and Characters* (1743–1751), Thomas Salmon's *Modern History, or Present State of All Nations* (1739), and Tobias Smollett's *Compendium of Voyages* (1757). Preferring narratives of ostensible facts to avowed fictions, he initially read few collections of poetry, fewer novels, and no plays. The aging and Anglocentric nature of the library's holdings also shaped Cooper's reading. He withdrew mostly volumes published in Great Britain a generation earlier; he read almost nothing published after 1780 and next to nothing published in the United States. There was an old-fashioned, backward-looking quality to the gentility that Cooper acquired as a reader in Burlington on the fringes of the cosmopolitan world ruled by London's example.[28]

After 1784 Cooper broadened the range as he escalated the volume of his reading. Although he continued to withdraw many histories, biographies, and travelogues, they assumed a smaller proportion of his overall reading as he turned primarily to "Poetry" and "Polite Literature, or Belles Lettres" (see Table 3). In poetry his taste ran to epic rather than to the romantic or the sublime. Cooper especially loved Alexander Pope's vivid translations of Homer's *Iliad* and *Odyssey*, checking out one or the other (or both) on no less than thirteen occasions over a six-year period. In "Belles Lettres" Cooper doted on Jonathan Swift's *Collected Works*, reading and sometimes rereading seven volumes, and he made a disciplined march through the back volumes of *The London Magazine,* from 1734 through 1782. On forty-seven occasions he withdrew at least one, and usually two or three, volumes of *The London Magazine.* He returned to some volumes, especially for the late 1770s and early 1780s, three, four, even five times. He read no other work with such diligence and frequency, as if it uniquely contained the master key to gentility. As a smattering of brief, diverse pieces of satire, criticism, poetry, sketches, and travels, *The London Magazine* perfectly suited Cooper's eclectic and impatient ambition as a reader.[29]

In part the shift in Cooper's reading after 1784 reflects both an exhaustion of his favorite travel and history books and a continuing maturation of his abilities as a reader. But it is probably not accidental that Cooper's turn coincided with his ambitious acquisition of the Otsego Patent in 1785–86. Thereafter he had more reason to believe that he could claim gentility if his mores and manners could but keep pace with his increased wealth. In mid-decade Cooper became a more ambitious reader as he began to feel that his acquisition of a genteel mind was at once more feasible and more urgent.

Cooper's peculiarly diligent and increasingly ambitious reading bemused his fellow members. Noting the striking contrasts between his humble origins and his lofty ambitions, between his boisterous manners and his genteel reading, the members bestowed joking sobriquets that the librarian began to enter next to Cooper's name in the circulation records. On June 19, 1784, he became "Sir William Cooper, Knight and Baronet." In subsequent entries he was "Cooper the Learned," "Counsellor Cooper," and "William Cooper, Esq."—all spoofs of a man who was neither a knight nor learned, neither a lawyer nor (yet) a squire. No other member was so honored with nicknames in the records during the 1780s, indicating that they deemed Cooper a unique and colorful character. The joking titles grew more frequent and elaborate immediately after he secured the Otsego Patent and probably boasted to his friends in Burlington of his cunning exploits at the controversial auction. One entry dubbed him "Sir William Cooper, Lord Proprietor."[30]

The sobriquets hint at inside, shared jokes of the sort that accumulate around someone adept at poking fun at himself and others, someone at once popular and a bit laughable. But at the same time the members showed growing confidence in Cooper's abilities and integrity. They elected him one of their ten directors in 1786 and their treasurer a year later. As treasurer he collected their dues and paid for the candles, firewood, house rent, and the librarian's fee.[31]

However, no sooner had Cooper secured the respect of the other members than he began to neglect his duties as treasurer, missing four of the five Library Company meetings held in 1788. His absence was especially inopportune because that year the company erected its own building on a city lot donated by Joseph Bloomfield. For want of their absent treasurer, the Library Company had to rely on a special committee to supervise expenditures and construction. Cooper also missed the spring meeting in 1789, when the Library Company elected a new treasurer, Robert Smith. At the same time Cooper became sloppy with the borrowed books, incurring his first fine at the end of 1787 and two pointed (and unusual) rebukes in the circulation records for 1788. He returned one volume of *The London Magazine* with a missing cover and a second that had been "basely abused." Cooper's absences and carelessness probably both stemmed from his increasing preoccupation with his newly acquired lands in distant upstate New York. In a small way his neglect as treasurer and subscriber prefigured a repetitive pattern in his life: time and again he would take on more responsibility than he could manage, disappointing those who expected too much from him. Eager for approbation, he found it difficult to say no when prestigious men entrusted him with too many responsibilities.[32]

POLITICS 🦂

During the 1780s Cooper also received a political education in Burlington. He became a leading citizen in a Quaker community that had opposed the recent American Revolution. In general, colonial Quakers had prospered within the British empire, and they believed that it was their duty to avoid war and to accept and obey existing authorities as divinely established. In particular, Burlington's leading men saw no reason for revolution, because they were so prosperous and influential under New Jersey's colonial regime. Along with Perth Amboy in the east, Burlington served as one of New Jersey's two colonial capitols. An oligarchy, primarily composed of learned and weighty Friends (especially the Smiths), dominated the politics of Burlington City and County. Burlington's elite controlled New Jersey's colonial assembly through an alliance with Gov. William Franklin and the leading gentlemen of Perth Amboy. Moreover, the Quakers and their Anglican allies disliked and distrusted the Yankee and Scotch-Irish Presbyterians who were the most zealous revolutionaries. Remaining under the relatively tolerant British empire seemed preferable to living in an independent republic run by bigoted Presbyterians who had, in the past, persecuted Quakers.[33]

The revolutionaries regarded the Quakers either as covert Loyalists or as selfish hypocrites unwilling to shoulder their share of the dangers and costs to secure American liberties. In New Jersey and Pennsylvania the Whigs jailed Quaker leaders, confiscated Quaker movable property in lieu of taxes and militia service, and disenfranchised Friends by requiring voters, jurors, and officeholders to take oaths of allegiance to their state and to the Continental Congress. The war's physical destruction briefly came to Burlington in December 1776, when Hessian troops temporarily occupied the town; the Quaker town fathers were willing to collaborate, but Whig gunboats in the river cannonaded the town, damaging its buildings and obliging the Hessians to withdraw. Whig militia then landed to harass and plunder suspected Loyalists among the townspeople.[34]

During the 1780s the revolutionary contest persisted at Burlington County's polling places every October. The Quaker and Anglican oligarchy of Burlington City struggled to regain, and Whig militiamen to retain, control of the county's annually elected sheriff, county clerk, governor's councillor, and legislative assemblymen. Reviving their colonial practices, the Quaker-Anglican party tried to dominate the clerks and inspectors who determined who could vote and who would be rejected as unqualified. The Whigs countered with armed intimidation of their opponents and enforcement of the oaths that disenfranchised the wartime Loyalists and neutrals. Although a majority in the state, Whigs were a minority in Burlington County. Rare in and around Burlington City, the Whigs abounded in the smaller, poorer, and more isolated towns on the county periphery. Declaring their opponents to be Loyalists, the Whig militia officers justified intimidation as necessary to counter their foes' "great Ambition to . . . Rule what they have in Vain attempted to Destroy." It was "as necesary in Peace to Guard against the private, as it was in War against the declared Enemies of our Country." In 1782 and 1784 the Quaker-Anglican party controlled the ballot boxes and won the elections, whereas armed Whigs intimidated the opposition to prevail in 1783 and 1785. The Quaker-Anglican party finally triumphed in Burlington County in 1788, after the state legislature eliminated the oath of allegiance as a qualification to vote.[35]

In 1789 Burlington's Quaker-Anglican party asserted its renewed control of the county, as part of the Federalist coalition that triumphed in New Jersey's first congressional campaign. Disgusted by the anti-Loyalist and paper-money policies of the state of New Jersey, Burlington's leaders welcomed the stronger federal government promised by the Constitution of 1787. In 1789 New Jersey's voters chose their four congressmen at large, rather than from individual districts. The Federalists counted on western New Jersey's voters to overcome the strong lead that the Antifederalist candidates built in the eastern counties. The Federalists shrewdly exploited the election law,

which stipulated that the polls should open on February 11 but left the closing date to the discretion of each county's clerks and inspectors. In Burlington County the Federalists controlled the ballot box and did not close the
polling until March 4, three weeks after it commenced. By prolonging and
controlling the polling in Burlington County, the Federalists overcame the
early Antifederalist lead built in the eastern counties. They swept their entire congressional slate into office over the outraged protests of their out-
witted opponents.[36]

William Cooper got caught up in these contentious elections, almost certainly on the side of the Quaker-Anglican party. His name appears on both
of the Burlington County voting lists that survive for 1783 and 1787. A
Quaker-Anglican protest petition listed Cooper as one of the witnesses who
could describe the intimidation practiced by the Whigs—evidently because
he was one of the Quaker voters forcibly debarred from voting by the militia in 1783. Cooper was present in Burlington in February of 1789, but the
evidence does not indicate whether he played any role in that campaign.
However, his close friend and associate Richard R. Smith, the son of Richard
Smith, was a Federalist clerk of the election. Moreover, there was no reason
for an ambitious young Quaker to buck both the town fathers and the overwhelming majority in the county in order to support a slate associated with
the hated Presbyterians of eastern New Jersey. At the Burlington elections
of the 1780s, Cooper saw that victory went to those who enlisted the greatest number of leading gentlemen and those who physically controlled the
polling places. During the 1790s in Otsego he would practice the political
arts he had learned in Burlington during the 1780s.[37]

OPPORTUNITY 🕯

In the mid-1780s Cooper's modest success in Burlington as a local land
speculator, city storekeeper, and active citizen whetted his ambition. He remained alert to promising speculations that might elevate his fortune and
standing into the top ranks of American society. As a leading member of the
Library Company, Cooper became familiar with several men who, as shareholders in "the Burlington Company" had speculated in frontier lands in
central New York. He learned that they owned a mortgage on the "Otsego
Patent," a potentially valuable but legally tangled tract of 29,350 acres located beside Otsego Lake at the headwaters of the Susquehanna River. Acquisition of such a substantial tract in the path of the westward migration of
New Englanders could enrich whoever obtained title and retailed farms to
settlers. However, the Burlington Company faced daunting competition
from rival claimants, including William Franklin, the former royal governor
who had fled newly independent America for exile in England. Despairing

of untangling the web of conflicting claims that clouded their title, the elderly members of the Burlington Company were prepared to sell their shares to a younger, more vigorous aspirant. Intrigued by the opportunity, William Cooper rode northward to investigate the Otsego country of central New York in the fall of 1785.

Chapter Two

VISIONS

I N THE FALL OF 1785 WILLIAM COOPER first saw the land around Otsego Lake that would make him wealthy, powerful, and famous. Journeying northward, he left behind the well-settled landscape of prosperous farms that surrounded Burlington. He crossed New Jersey and ascended the Hudson River to Albany, the jumping-off point for the new frontier settlements to the north and west. Turning westward, Cooper ascended the broad but shallow and fast-running Mohawk River. Reaching the town of Canajoharie on the south bank, he left his boat and mounted a horse. Heading southwest, he rode uphill through a dense forest along a tortuous path filled with rocks, stumps, roots, mud holes, and fallen trees. A year earlier another traveler had characterized that route as "the worst road in the world, all hills and marshes, mud up to the axles of the wagons." Cooper crossed the watershed between the Mohawk valley to the north and the many small tributaries that ran southwest to gather into the Susquehanna River, which flowed southward toward Chesapeake Bay. Passing through the frontier village of Cherry Valley, he approached his goal, "the rough and hilly country of Otsego, where there existed not an inhabitant, nor any trace of a road."[2]

Leave to Caesar the boast of having destroyed two million of men; let yours be that of having cut down two million of trees. He made men disappear from the fruitful soils where they were born; your labours made a new and happier race appear where none before had been.

— William Sampson, to William Cooper, 1807[1]

The work of water and ice on former mountains, Otsego was a land of lofty, rolling hills set amidst fast-running streams at an elevation that varied from 1,000 to 2,000 feet above sea level. It had been scoured and gouged by the glaciers that advanced toward the south when the earth had cooled during the last Ice Age, then melted in their retreat back to the north when the planet warmed again about 12,000 years ago. The retreating glaciers left a landscape of elongated hills and ridges pointing from the northeast toward the southwest and rounded on their tops. As the glaciers retreated vegetation reclaimed the land, eventually covering the hills and valleys with a thick forest of tall trees. Copious rainfall, in excess of forty inches annually, poured over the land and filled rapid streams, which cut deep valleys between the hills and ridges as they flowed southwestward and fell into the Susquehanna River. "The whole Country is well watered by Creeks, Brooks & Springs," remarked one visitor. Beginning in Otsego Lake, the Susquehanna was, for its first twenty miles, a narrow and crooked stream obstructed by dead, fallen trees. Thereafter the accumulated tributaries gradually widened it into "a broad shoal river, usually made up of long stretches of slack water and short rapids." Shad could ascend from the ocean every spring to spawn and die in the lakes (until men dammed the river). Because the streams carried off the precipitation so rapidly, Otsego had few and small swamps and only two large lakes. Both Canadarago (or Schuyler's) and Otsego lakes lay in the region's northern tier at the head-waters of the Susquehanna.[3]

The abundant flow of water over the hilly landscape produced an unevenly distributed soil in Otsego. On the flat, low-lying lands beside the larger streams, the runoff slowed and detritus accumulated, creating thicker layers of dark humus derived from the hillsides exposed to erosion. Otsego's richest lands were these alluvial soils beside the Susquehanna and the larger tributary streams: the Schenevus, Cherry Valley, Oaks, Otego, Butternuts, and Unadilla. The traveler Richard Smith considered the Otego valley floor "one of the finest Bottoms in the World." However, most of the Otsego country consisted of rolling uplands, where the topsoil was thinner as a result of the erosion that enriched the bottoms.[4]

The varying soils and microenvironments of Otsego's uneven, elevated landscape produced a diverse forest—a mosaic of mixed plant communities. Towering up to 150, and even 200, feet, the hemlocks and white pines were concentrated on the highest and the lowest lands: on the steepest slopes and in the swamps—wherever soils were sandier and nutrient poor. Along the more gradual slopes an occasional clump of white pines or hemlocks appeared, surrounded and outnumbered by a mix of deciduous hardwoods: maples, beech, butternuts, elm, wild cherry, basswood, linden, birch, chestnut, and white, red, and black oaks. Hardwoods probably constituted three-fifths of the region's forest, and the softwoods (hemlock and pine) made up the balance. Maple and beech were the two most numerous types of hardwood trees.[5]

THE WASTE OF CREATION

In *A Guide in the Wilderness*, Cooper recalled his first visit to Otsego. He remembered having felt like a new Adam in a new creation—utterly removed from human society, from manmade structures, from any cultural inheri-

tance. He believed that he had plunged into a timeless, wild land of pure
nature still waiting for people to come and remake it, to improve it for their
comfort and profit:

> *I was alone three hundred miles from home, without bread, meat, or food of any
> kind; fire and fishing tackle were my only means of subsistence. I caught trout
> in the brook, and roasted them on the ashes. My horse fed on the grass that grew
> by the edge of the waters. I laid me down to sleep in my watch-coat, nothing but
> the melancholy Wilderness around me. In this way I explored the country,
> formed my plans of future settlement, and meditated upon the spot where a
> place of trade or village should afterwards be established.*

Climbing a mountain west of Cherry Valley, Cooper gazed westward upon
Otsego Lake and the beginning of the Susquehanna; for the first time, he
saw the site of Cooperstown. Moved by the scene, he named the eminence
Mount Vision and, over the years, repeated his story of solitary discovery.
Thereafter Mount Vision assumed a special importance in the Cooper family memory. In his novels set in Otsego, James Fenimore Cooper recurrently
employed the view from Mount Vision as a symbolic vantage point for as-
sessing the troubled evolution of the community below.[6]

In *The Pioneers*, Marmaduke Temple recalls William Cooper's vision as his
own. Following a deer path, Temple remembers riding west from Cherry
Valley to the summit of a mountain

> *that I have since called Mount Vision; for the sight that there met my eyes seemed
> to me as the deceptions of a dream. The fire had run over the pinnacle, and, in
> a great measure, laid open the view. The leaves were fallen, and I mounted a
> tree, and sat for an hour looking on the silent wilderness. Not an opening was
> to be seen in the boundless forest, except where the lake lay, like a mirror of glass.
> The water was covered by myriads of the wild-fowl that migrate with the changes
> in the season; and, while in my situation on the branch of the beech, I saw a
> bear, with her cubs, descend to the shore to drink. I had met many deer, gliding
> through the woods, in my journey; but not the vestige of a man could I trace
> during my progress, nor from my elevated observatory. No clearing, no hut,
> none of the winding roads that are now to be seen, were there; nothing but
> mountains rising behind mountains, and the valley, with its surface of
> branches, enlivened here and there with the faded foliage of some tree.*[7]

In addition to this opening description of Otsego before settlement, *A Guide
in the Wilderness* and *The Pioneers* share a culminating depiction of the transformed landscape wrought by Cooper and his settlers. Although Otsego was
"the roughest land in all the state, and the most difficult of cultivation of all that
has been settled," William Cooper boasted in 1807:

> *It maintains at present eight thousand souls, with schools, academies,
> churches, meeting-houses, turnpike roads, and a market town. It annually*

yields to commerce large droves of fine oxen, great quantities of wheat and other grain, abundance of pork, pot ash in barrels, and other provisions; merchants with large capitals, and all kinds of useful mechanics reside upon it; the waters are stocked with fish, the air is salubrious, and the country [is] thriving and happy.

His son concurred, celebrating the Otsego of 1823 as a county of "neat and comfortable farms, with every indication of wealth about them," and of "beautiful and thriving villages" sustaining the academies and schoolhouses of "a moral and reflecting people."[8]

The two contrasting landscapes, of discovery and of settlement, served as framing devices to locate and define William Cooper's achievements and his son's inheritance. These distinct opening and closing scenes give heroic meaning to William Cooper as the developer who made the first landscape give way to the second. Following his discovery he founded the village of Cooperstown at the foot of the lake where the bear and her cubs drank. He recruited and assisted the settlers whose labor felled the forest and created farms filled with crops, livestock, barns, fences, and homes. He made thousands of humans happy by obliging nature to serve commerce; converting nature's waste into marketable commodities generated the profits to build substantial homes and found the public institutions of a civilized people. In 1807 he reflected, "I am now descending into the vale of life, and I must acknowledge that I look back with self complacency upon what I have done, and am proud of having been an instrument in reclaiming such large and fruitful tracts from the waste of creation." By executing the "plans" he had projected onto the forest in 1785, Cooper completed a divine task left undone by the Creator.[9]

Cooper described his life's work in the prevailing myth of his time—the late eighteenth and early nineteenth centuries—and of his people, the Americans of European ancestry, Protestant faith, and commercial ambitions who had invaded North America and were rapidly remaking its landscape to suit their own interests and expectations. Their myth of the second creation emerged out of the extraordinary economic and demographic success enjoyed by the Americans as they conquered and occupied the continent. The participants in New York's phenomenal growth delighted in hearing their accomplishments magnified and celebrated. The mythmakers of conquest drew two sharp and related distinctions: between the natives and the newcomers, and between the before and after landscapes of white settlement. The settlers entered a landscape that they called pure nature (or "wilderness") and that they insisted was a dangerous adversary they were destined to conquer. In a 1795 speech to the leading settlers of Whitestown (a new settlement about fifty miles from Cooperstown), the Reverend Francis Adrian Van der Kemp explained that they had "transformed the gloomy forests into meadows and corn fields" to "enrich ourselves and our fellow citizens with the fruits of our toils. What pleasure! what raptures we enjoy in the contemplation of a cleared, fenced acre of the first crop of corn, wheat or grass that ever covered that spot, since the creation!" In 1796 Elihu Phinney, editor of the Cooperstown newspaper, boasted of "the rapid progress of improvement, by which a vast Wilderness, where lately the Bear, the Wolf, and the Panther prowled thro' the forest, had been converted into rich towns and beautiful villages, where the eye is delighted with the view of elegant mansions, and the ear regaled by 'the busy hum of men.' "[10]

In recounting his vision, William Cooper erased all of the land's previous owners and users: the Indians who had dwelled on the land for centuries, the white hunter-squatters who replaced them, and a generation of land speculators who had preceded Cooper. He implied that no predecessor, Indian or white, had owned or worked the land. In fact, Cooperstown was not the first vision projected onto the land at the foot of Otsego Lake; Cooper's town supplanted and obliterated the vestiges of four previous communities: the Indian school of Moses the Mohawk, the New Jerusalem of Rev. John Christopher Hartwick, the estate of Col. George Croghan, and the cabins of some hunter-squatters. Restoring the Indians, squatters, and colonial landlords, as James Fenimore Cooper did in *The Pioneers*, imparts a very different cast to William Cooper's story, shifting his ownership and development of Otsego from the beginning to the midst of a history of conquest and settlement.[11]

INDIANS

The substantial ruins of extensive fortified villages scattered on hilltops throughout the Iroquois country belied the notion that the Indians had never truly occupied or owned the land. These had been constructed between about A.D. 1000 and 1500 by the Iroquois as they developed horticulture and tribal polities. They abandoned the fortified villages during the seventeenth century, when they proved to be deathtraps; their inhabitants were vulnerable to attacking Europeans and, especially, to disease pathogens that afflicted crowded populations. As their number shrank from war and disease, the survivors moved into smaller, more decentralized villages strung along riverbanks. The new villages were easier to flee from when danger approached or epidemics spread. Assuming that the Iroquois had always lived in small, dispersed, riverside villages, Americans were mystified by the abandoned earthworks. In west-central New York, William Cooper found "vast fortresses or intrenched camps, sometimes covering ten acres in space; surrounded by ditches and guarded by pit-falls, artfully contrived." One of these ruins could be found in the Otsego Country at

Unadilla beside the upper Susquehanna; in 1796 an impressed traveler described the triangular earthwork there as a "very formidable place of defence." The ideological solution to these inconvenient vestiges was to deny that the Iroquois had made them and instead to credit some other distinct but unknown, vanished, and far more ancient people—perhaps the legendary lost tribes of Israel. American leaders would only credit the Iroquois with having destroyed the fortified villages and their apparently civilized inhabitants. This solution recast the ruins into a further indictment of the Iroquois as barbarians: as the destroyers, rather than the creators, of civilized works.[12]

Although they no longer lived in fortified villages, the eighteenth-century Iroquois were far from the wild men of the forest depicted by the Americans. Like any human population, the natives could not live in nature without affecting it. They obtained most of their diet not from hunting and gathering but from an agriculture that was more productive per acre than that of the white settlers. Most of the Indians' domain remained a forest, but they cleared and cultivated impressive fields along the river bottoms. Their well-tended and flourishing crops of maize, beans, squashes, and pumpkins were the envy of encroaching settlers. Iroquois women cultivated and harvested these crops, while their men were warriors and hunters. Because Americans defined a culture in terms of what men did, they would not recognize the agricultural accomplishments of the Iroquois but instead categorized them as a savage race of hunter-warriors. White men dismissed what Indian women created as anomalous.[13]

Far from living in timeless, primitive isolation, the Iroquois had been in increasing contact with white explorers, traders, soldiers, missionaries, and farmers since the early seventeenth century. They had developed an extensive and sophisticated diplomacy with other tribes and with the representatives of the French and British empires. The Iroquois had also bent their economic activities to obtain European trade goods that, by the eighteenth century, had become their necessities. Their men hunted to secure pelts to sell to traders as well as to obtain meat for their families; the pelts procured guns, gunpowder, knives, axes, hoes, hatchets, clothing, jewelry, kettles, horses, and alcohol. In 1769 Richard Smith, a Quaker traveler with paternalistic notions about Indians, was shocked to discover that they could drive hard bargains for their labor and commodities. They were, he complained, "extortionate and very apt to ask high Prices especially when they perceive a Necessity for their Assistance. Perhaps they learned this from the Dutch."[14]

The cultural synthesis of Indian and European ways was apparent in Onoquaga (or Oquaga), the largest Indian town on the Susquehanna. Located southwest of Otsego in what are now the towns of Afton and Windsor, in Broome County, Onoquaga was a cluster of villages on both sides of the river. Its mixed population came primarily from the Tuscarora, Mohawk, and Oneida tribes of the Iroquois confederation. But Onoquaga also drew in diverse Indian refugees who had been dispossessed of their homelands further south and east: Shawnee, Nanticoke, Conoy, Delaware, Tutelo, and Mohican. The Onoquagans had borrowed and adapted much of the material culture and some of the agricultural methods of their powerful and numerous white neighbors. Some of the villagers continued to live in the traditional multifamily longhouses constructed of bark laid over a framework of poles, but most had adopted single-family log cabins. The better cabins even had stone chimneys and glass windows—amenities beyond the means of the poorest white settlers. The village also included a Christian graveyard and "a considerable large building" that doubled as a garrison house and a Presbyterian church.[15]

On the eve of the American Revolution, Onoquaga demonstrated the possibilities of peaceful accommodation and cultural adaptation. Its people were not primitives, unchanged from their ancestors who had first cast eyes on the Europeans. Richard Smith concluded, "Having often visited the whites, their manners seem to differ little from those of our lower Class of People." In 1775 John Hector St. John de Crevecoeur visited Onoquaga and praised the "neat and warm habitations" and the "great deal of industry" manifest in the well-cultivated fields. He concluded, "They were greatly civilized and received me with their usual hospitality." In 1778 Lt. Col. William Butler observed, "It was the finest Indian town I ever saw; on both sides [of] the River there was about 40 good houses, square logs, shingles & stone Chimneys, good Floors, glass Windows, &c., &c."[16]

In 1765 some Mohawks from Onoquaga established a satellite village at the foot of Lake Otsego. When food became scarce that spring in Onoquaga, a Christian Mohawk teacher, aptly named Moses, and his students removed to the future site of Cooperstown, where they subsisted on Lake Otsego's abundant fish. Hoping to make their new settlement permanent, Moses and his students sought agricultural techniques and milling technology from their white neighbors. Moses had studied at the famous charity school for Indians conducted in Lebanon, Connecticut, by Rev. Eleazar Wheelock, a Congregationalist. In July the Indians at Lake Otsego wrote to ask Wheelock for assistance "in setting up husbandry by sending a number of white people to live with us who, when they come, should build us mills, teach us husbandry, and furnish us with tools for husbandry." They hastened to add that they meant to retain the land for their own people: "We would have you understand, Brethren, that we have no thoughts of selling our Land to any that come to live among us; for if we should sell a little Land to any, by & by they would want to buy a little more and so our Land would go by Inches till we should have none to live upon." Receiving only a letter of encouragement and a missionary from Wheelock, Moses and his students returned to Onoquaga in September 1765. Although Moses failed to establish an enduring community at Otsego Lake, Indians continued to so-journ in the region for hunting, fishing, and gathering.[17]

Subsequently, American travelers, settlers, and surveyors found abundant evidence that they were not the first people to use Otsego. The newcomers discovered the stones and sticks of recently abandoned fishing encampments along the lake and streams. Around the lake they found numerous stone or lead sinkers from the nets the Indians had drawn through the lake waters to catch trout and whitefish. The settlers appropriated and repaired the stone dams and the weirs woven from branches and placed in the streams by Indians to trap migrating fish. At certain spots along the streams and the river, sojourning Iroquois families had also cleared garden plots and planted orchards. In 1768, at the juncture of Otego Creek with the Susquehanna, the surveyor Robert Picken found an "Old Field, formerly an Indian Castle, near a mile long, very fine land." In 1769 Richard Smith noted Indian graves beside Schenevus Stream: "One of them was a flat Pyramid of about 3 feet high trenched round, another was platted like a tomb and a third something like our Form." William Cooper reported that his settlers unearthed "many stone-axes, leaden pipes, spears of flint, [and] vessels of pottery." In addition to the earthworks of an ancient Indian town, Unadilla had a large cairn of stones that the settlers called "the Indian monument." In the woods surveyors encountered brush heaped for hundreds of yards in a line to serve as "deer fences" for funnelling driven animals toward waiting hunters. In 1773 at Otego Stream a Mohawk named Cornelius told Richard Smith that the Indians were "making a deer fence from the Susquehanna into the woods 6 or 8 miles from us."[18]

No unchanged forest primeval, Otsego also bore the marks of the fires annually set by Indian hunters. They set fires to drive deer downwind into ambushes and to reshape the forest itself: the fires reduced the brush that obstructed vision and pursuit; and by opening up the forest floor to more sunlight, they encouraged grasses and berries that increased the number and health of the region's deer herds. Because the oldest, tallest, toughest trees could endure the annual ground fires through the brush and fallen deadwood, the Indians had given shape to a forest of substantial, well-spaced trees with a high canopy of leafy branches and a rich ground strata of annual plants, but in the middle there was only a minimal subcanopy of smaller trees and perennial shrubs. In the Otego valley, Richard Smith noted, "The underbrush here, as in many other Places, is not very thick," and "one may almost ride in a chair [i.e., a carriage]." Descending the Susquehanna from Unadilla to Onoquaga in June of 1769, Smith "saw some Indians setting Fire to the woods. . . . The upland hereabouts has been burnt & looks something like a settled Country." From the summit of Mount Vision, William Cooper viewed a forest that was in part a human construct; indeed, an Indian fire probably created the opening that permitted

Cooper to examine a land he misperceived as untouched by humanity.[19]

Because the Iroquois sited their villages and encampments so well—in locales that combined fertile soil, abundant wood, and water—the first white
settlers and speculators scanned the landscape for signs of Indian occupation as evidence of the very best lands. White settlements ordinarily began
on lands that Indians had already cleared and planted with corn, beans,
pumpkins, and apple trees. In stark contrast to their ideologues, who justified conquest by denying all marks of Indian ownership and use, the pragmatic settlers and surveyors eagerly sought and followed those signs.
Settlers did not move into a vacuum; instead they built upward and expanded outward from the works of their predecessors. By covering the land
with their own fields and structures, Otsego's settlers gradually obliterated
the marks that another people had preceded them. In 1850 Susan Fenimore Cooper, the novelist's daughter, could insist that, except for Council
Rock, a partially submerged boulder at Lake Otsego's outlet, "the red man
has left no mark here, on hill or dale, lake or stream."[20]

The myth of the settlers as second creators accelerated this obliteration
of the Indian presence. The American newcomers saw the forest environment of New York through the lens of their own anticipations as second creators. Their minds superimposed a future landscape: a habit of projection
which ensured that the land would be changed. In 1779 Lt. Robert Parker
paused in the midst of the American invasion of the Iroquois homeland to
write in his journal:

> But here let us leave the busy army for a moment and suffer our imaginations
> to run at large through these delightful wilds, & figure to ourselves the open-
> ing prospects of future greatness . . . & that we may yet behold with a pleasing
> admiration those deserts that have so long been the habitation of beasts of prey
> & a safe asylum for our savage enemies, converted into fruitful fields, covered
> with all the richest productions of agriculture, amply rewarding the industrious
> husbandman by a golden harvest; the spacious plains abounding with flocks
> & herds to supply his necessary wants. These Lakes & Rivers that have for
> ages past rolled in sacred silence along their wonted course, unknown to Chris-
> tian nations, produce spacious cities & guilded spires, rising on their banks,
> affording a safe retreat for the virtuous few that disdains to live in affluence at
> the expense of their liberties. The fish, too, that have so long enjoyed a peaceful
> habitation in these transparent regions, may yet become subservient to the in-
> habitants of this delightful country.

In contrast to the supposedly indolent savages who suffered so much nature
to remain wild and free, the conquerors would render every resource and
every form of life—even the rivers and their fish—"subservient." Lieutenant Parker betrayed no sense of the irony that he penned these sentiments as his invading army destroyed the impressive agricultural villages of
the Iroquois.[21]

By telling themselves stories of their renewed creation of a wasteland, the victorious Americans erased from memory the accomplishments of the Indians. The newcomers cast the natives as closer to wolves and bears than to civilized human beings. Prone to categorize into stark dichotomies, the leading Americans defined the Indians as solitary, idle, selfish, unchanging, unimproving and unimprovable, heathen savages who lived by hunting and fishing alone. American leaders then defined their own people in stark contrast, as industrious Christians dedicated to agriculture, innovation, and civil institutions. James Kent, the leading jurist in New York, proclaimed that because "the cultivation of the soil was an obligation imposed by nature upon mankind," the Americans had justly dispossessed the Indians, who were merely "rude tribes, which had not advanced from the hunter state" and had "no right to complain, if a nation of cultivators puts in a claim for a part." Adrian Van der Kemp nullified the Indians by virtually expunging their vestiges from the land. "We may consider ourselves . . . as the Aborigenes of the land," he insisted, because "our copper-coloured neighbors . . . scarce leave behind them any traces of their former residence—than here and there, their hunting and fishing encampments—here and there a wooden trap—here and there a burned or pealed tree. We may consider ourselves, as the creators of our increasing fields and meadows, as the embellishers of this new world—as the Patriarchs of a numberless people, yet in Nature's womb."[22]

The story that Indians were wild beings who made no mark on the land had a self-fulfilling quality. The definition of Indians as timeless, unchangeable savages both inspired and took renewed power from the physical destruction of the Iroquois peoples. The myth justified brutal conquest; defeat rendered the surviving Indians ever closer to the description of them as miserably inconsequential. The thoroughness with which the American Revolutionary armies destroyed the crops and villages of the Iroquois revealed a determination to obliterate all signs that the Iroquois had exercised dominion over the land, all signs that they were an agricultural people. As a result of epidemic diseases, warfare, environmental changes, and the consequent hunger, the Iroquois died faster than they could reproduce. By the mid-1790s the Iroquois population of New York had declined to 3,500, about a third of their number just thirty years earlier. Most of the survivors were destitute, demoralized, and confined to reservations— small portions of their homeland all located well to the west of Otsego. For a generation after the natives had been routed, Otsego's settlers taught their children to dread and detest Indians. Henry Clarke Wright recalled that no child was "allowed to grow up in that region, without imbibing more or less hatred and horror of the Indians. Tales of Indian cruelties were in the mouths of all mothers and nurses."[23]

After the American Revolution, small groups of Iroquois and Mohicans returned to Otsego in the warm months to hunt and fish; to sell venison, fish, brooms, medicines, bark or willow baskets, and deerskin moccasins to whites; or to importune for gifts of food. According to local tradition, one wandering Mohican basket maker and hunter named Captain John served as the model for Chingachgook, the lone Indian in *The Pioneers*. Numerous in the last years of the eighteenth century, the Indian visitors dwindled to a few by the middle of the next century. In 1850 Susan Fenimore Cooper remarked, "Now they come very seldom, and singly, or in families, craving permission to build a shanty of boughs or boards, in order to ply their trade of basket-makers." To white eyes, the sojourning Indians seemed a debauched and pathetic sight. Although famous for portraying the Indian as a noble savage in his fictions, James Fenimore Cooper regarded the heroic native as extinct in New York by the 1820s. In *Notions of the Americans*, he characterized New York's Indians as "all alike, a stunted, dirty and degraded race." However, during a visit to an Indian encampment outside Cooperstown, Susan Fenimore Cooper noted that "when aroused" they displayed "the poetical, figurative speech, and the dignified, impressive gesture of their race. The contrast between the degraded aspect they bear every day, and these sudden instinctive flashes, is very striking."[24]

THE NEW JERUSALEM

Nor was William Cooper the first white man to project his vision, his plans onto the forested landscape of the Otsego country. Thirty years earlier an eccentric and itinerant Lutheran clergyman, John Christopher Hartwick, had acquired 21,500 acres south of the lake to serve as the site for his utopian community. Dedicating his land to "*my Heirs*, Jesus Christ, the son of God and man," Hartwick meant to establish "a regular Town, close built & to be called New Jerusalem" centered on a seminary that would train missionaries to preach among the "red or Black Heathens" who were "yet in a State of Barbarity & Thorns to our eyes & Pricks in our Sides."[25]

Born in 1714 in the German duchy of Saxe-Gotha, Hartwick had been educated for the Lutheran ministry at Halle, a leading pietistical seminary. In 1746 he emigrated to America to serve as a missionary among the Germans settled around Rhinebeck in the Hudson valley. Hartwick quickly concluded that he had left civilization behind and moved to the wild margins where unwary Christians were degenerating into the barbarism of their Indian neighbors. In a letter home to his superiors in Germany, Hartwick reported, "There are many opportunities here for temptation and willingness to sin. There is great ignorance; and freethinking and indifference to religion contribute also. To sum it up, the situation is desperate."[26]

Appalled at the lax morality and loose doctrines of his new neighbors,

Hartwick tried to impose a strict discipline. In the process he alienated most of his parishioners and his Lutheran ministerial colleagues in the province of New York. They complained,

> *He is too austere in his manner and often does not speak to the people. He maintains no regularity at divine service, begins one or two hours late, makes the people sing long hymns, and preaches so long that the people who live far away have to ride home late at night and thus neglect their cattle. He is head-strong and stubborn and will let no one say anything to him or give him advice, saying that he had not come here to learn from them but to teach them.*

In January 1750 three hostile Lutheran ministers went to Rhinebeck to depose Hartwick before his assembled congregation. The leader of the delegation was Rev. Wilhelm Christoph Berkenmeyer, the leading Lutheran minister in the Hudson valley. The confrontation became violent as Hartwick literally clung to his pulpit in the face of his foes and the enraged parishioners. According to Hartwick, they attacked him "with fists, tore off my wig, hit me in the face and wanted forcefully to drag me out of the church."[27]

Rousted from his parish, Hartwick found refuge in Pennsylvania where he found a patron in Rev. Henry M. Muhlenberg, who appreciated his piety, zeal, and learning. Muhlenberg "saw through the faults, which clung to him, to the excellent grounding in doctrine which he possessed." But Muhlenberg concluded that, like many other young ministers newly arrived from Europe, Hartwick had mishandled his difficult new position: "They start out vigorously and use European standards which do not always fit the complicated conditions of America." Muhlenberg had learned that "what was needed was not great learning, but rather . . . faithful patience and concern."[28]

Unlike the shrewd and influential Muhlenberg, Hartwick stubbornly refused to adapt to his new society. Instead of adjusting to his assertive parishioners, Hartwick was determined to discipline them. When offered other ministerial positions, he insisted that the laity first sign a covenant that "they would forswear shooting, horse-racing, boozing, and dancing." In vain Muhlenberg cautioned Hartwick "that one should first lay a foundation of true Christianity in the hearts of the people and then build from the inside to the outside." On the contrary, Hartwick believed that people could not develop Christian hearts until their behavior was strictly controlled. He held common people to a higher standard than he felt obliged to keep. In 1759 a magistrate in Hackensack, New Jersey, opposed Hartwick's appointment there because "he did not have the talent for visiting and attracting people, which after all, was necessary in view of the conditions in the scattered congregations; he would rather go fishing and bird-hunting." Intensely misogynistic, Hartwick would cross streets or leap fences to avoid women; he never married. Stubborn and imperious, he delivered sermons that exceeded two hours in length and exhausted his audience; but whenever he heard another minister preach, Hartwick would quickly "become annoyed, shuffle his feet, cough, or make motions for him to stop." Unable to find parishioners who would accept his dictation for long, Hartwick roamed from parish to parish up and down the Atlantic seaboard from Virginia to Maine. According to Muhlenberg, congregations repeatedly complained that Hartwick "was too hot-tempered and strict, and said that they did not want him as their preacher any longer." For long interludes he lived off the charity of Muhlenberg and his sons. Because Hartwick rarely bathed or changed his clothes, he was a difficult guest.[29]

Hartwick blamed his travails on the dispersed pattern of settlement that prevailed in America. He had grown up in Europe—a relatively crowded society where resources were scarce, social mobility was uncommon, and the people lived in compact villages in which the poor and uneducated were under the supervision of their betters. But in America the relative abundance of land to population permitted most common white men to obtain substantial farms and to live remote from the oversight of magistrates and ministers. Hartwick openly longed for the more hierarchical and authoritarian society of Germany: "In Europe our churches are intertwined with the state and are supported by the state. Here in America this is not the case. Here the church is like a vineyard without a hedge, like a city without walls, like a house without door and lock." He was frustrated that after long years of study and ingratiating efforts to cultivate aristocratic patrons in Europe, he had landed on a barbaric continent where the common folk were insufficiently cowed by the wealthy and learned. To reform American society, Hartwick proposed to reorder the process of settlement by mandating compact villages strictly supervised by a minister-overlord. He modeled his communities on those "by which the German emperors have preserved their Extensive territories against the Incursions of the Barbarians, in former times." In his proposed system of New Jerusalems the laity would never dare to strike their minister and trample on his wig.[30]

To obtain lands for a pilot project, Hartwick sojourned as a preacher among the Mohawk Indians at Canajoharie. He preached in English, assisted by a translator who rendered his words into Mohawk. The language gap permitted Hartwick to nurture a cherished misconception that he could exercise an almost complete control over the minds and souls of his Indian audience. Hartwick prepared a document that he persuaded six Mohawk sachems to sign. In it, they begged Hartwick to become their minister and "help to destroy the Tyranny of the Devil which he hitherto hath exercised upon us." They promised "all the Respect, Subjection & obedience by the word of God injoyned to be due by a Christian Congregation to their true & faithful Pastor and to Contribute to his maintenance & ease all what

Shall lie in our Power." The document described the sort of dominance that Hartwick had sought for in vain among the parishes of the American colonies. Given that the Indians were even more dispersed and independent than their white neighbors, it is unlikely that the sachems understood what they signed and certain that they disappointed Hartwick's expectations. Indeed, his mission at Canajoharie was as short-lived as his tenure in his many parishes among the colonists.[31]

During his mission, Hartwick did succeed in acquiring an Indian title to a substantial tract of land. In 1754, assisted by Sir William Johnson, the influential superintendent of Indian affairs, Hartwick persuaded several Mohawk sachems to sign a deed relinquishing a tract of land on the Susquehanna just below Lake Otsego; Hartwick's survey of the tract included about 21,500 acres. In return, Hartwick promised to pay the Mohawks £100.[32]

To complete his legal title to the land, Hartwick needed an official patent from the royal governor of New York. But the patent fees amounted to £514.4.0—far beyond Hartwick's penurious means. He turned to the accommodating Goldsborough Banyar, who as New York's provincial secretary was a key figure in the official allocation of wilderness lands. Over the years Banyar accumulated an impressive portfolio of frontier lands received as kickbacks from the speculators he assisted. He agreed to facilitate Hartwick's application for a patent and to advance the balance of the money Hartwick needed for the fees. In return, Hartwick reserved one-eleventh of the land to Banyar, paid him £59.4.0 and promised to pay an additional £127.3.0, secured by a mortgage on the entire tract. The fees paid, on April 22, 1761, Hartwick received the patent for his cherished tract— thereafter known as the "Hartwick Patent."[33]

In 1766 he briefly occupied a small clearing at the foot of Otsego Lake, making him the first white man known to attempt a settlement of Cooperstown's site. Apparently, he simply seized upon the clearing recently abandoned by Moses the Mohawk and his students. But Hartwick soon had to abandon the spot upon learning that the bounds of his patent did not extend that far north. Thereafter, he neglected his lands and his impatient creditors. In 1769 the Mohawks tried to sue him for their money, but the minister could not be found and he probably never paid them for the land.[34]

During the Revolutionary War, Hartwick sought potential settlers and parishioners among the German mercenaries in the British service who had been captured by the Americans. At last the British king had, unwittingly, transported to America the German colonists that Hartwick desired for his "New Jerusalem." In December of 1777 he boarded a prison ship in Boston harbor to preach to some Germans recently taken prisoner at the battles of Bennington and Saratoga. In contrast to his previous denunciations of

American autonomy and his plans for authoritarian villages, in 1777 Hartwick discovered a new and convenient love for liberty. Addressing the prisoners, he "spoke a great deal about American freedom and Germany['s] slavery," and offered to "lead them to the promised land, Philadelphia." Together they would "establish a village" where Hartwick "would be their preacher." But his captive audience preferred remaining on their prison ship to enlisting in his New Jerusalem; and Hartwick decided he had best flee when one officer violently "pushed over the barrel on which his books were lying and warned him that unless he left the ship immediately, he would throw him into the water."[35]

With neither home nor family, and ordinarily without work as a minister, Hartwick continued to descend upon his friends to live with them at their expense for months at a time. Aware that Hartwick owned but neglected a large and potentially lucrative tract of land in New York, Reverend Muhlenberg became exasperated with his persistent guest: "He is badly off, with no home and no clothes, but he is still accustomed to be treated like a *Gentleman*. . . . he is unwilling to be tied down and prefers to be free and eat his bread without working." At last, in October 1781 Muhlenberg refused Hartwick any further support and pointedly told him to go live "with his clients whom he lured into his lands." In fact, Hartwick had not yet lured any paying settlers onto his land. In 1784 and 1785 a few Yankee squatters moved onto the land just before William Cooper looked out from Mount Vision. Moreover, by the end of the decade Cooper's plans for a commercial village at the foot of the lake would threaten Hartwick's very different vision of a New Jerusalem on the adjoining downstream tract.[36]

CROGHAN'S FOREST

In *A Guide in the Wilderness*, William Cooper implied that Otsego was no one's private property before 1785—that it was a wild, primeval common. In fact, from Mount Vision, William Cooper looked upon a terrain crosshatched with private property lines. Most of those lines had been established in the years 1768–1770 as a consequence of purchases made by land speculators from the Iroquois. On the ground colonial surveyors had marked the lines with blazes cut into trees and with piles of stones. Surveyors described their lines and the quality of the land in detailed field books submitted to their employers. At the Tryon County courthouse patent deeds from the royal governor were officially recorded, affording legal sanction to the survey lines. And maps hung on the walls of the provincial secretary's office and of the landlords' homes to show visitors that Otsego was no longer Indian territory but instead the private property of certain individuals or companies. It made a profound difference that the Otsego country had become the exclusive property of wealthy gentlemen supported by an elaborate apparatus of laws, courts, and sheriffs. No one else could safely occupy or develop land within their particular, bounded parcels without buying their permission (known as title); trespassers and squatters could be evicted and sued for damages. In a few years Cooper would learn the dangers of misreading the landscape and missing the boundaries laid out by the surveyors who had preceded him. His society rewarded those who effaced the signs of Indian occupation, but its courts penalized those who ignored the new marks of ownership sold by governors and blazed, mapped, sketched, and described by surveyors.[37]

In 1785 Cooper looked out over a forest containing many trees marked "GC CY 1768"—the initials of Col. George Croghan and his surveyor Christopher Yates and the year Yates surveyed a boundary for 100,000 acres claimed by the Colonel. Croghan was the most avid, indeed manic, land speculator in colonial North America. An ambitious immigrant from Ireland, he came to America to make his fortune in the dangerous and unpredictable Indian trade. In the 1740s and 1750s he became Pennsylvania's foremost fur trader and negotiator with Indians, and the favorite of some of Philadelphia's wealthiest merchants. He had a winning personality: convivial, generous, witty, and adaptable. His easy good humor endeared him to British army officers, Indian sachems, and Pennsylvania assemblymen alike. Best of all, he became the close friend and principal deputy of Sir William Johnson, who, as the British crown's Northern Superintendent of Indian Affairs, was the most powerful man on the colonial frontier. Like Johnson, Croghan was equally at home in a Georgian mansion and at an Indian council fire. His influence with the native peoples made Croghan valuable to the men who ran the British empire in North America. A quick study, he mastered several Indian languages and the intricate nuances of the tribal politics and diplomacy. Many Indians cherished him above all other whites because he was so fearless and enterprising, so free from prejudice, so eager and adept at living among them, and so generous in doling out presents (from his own pocket as well as the public's). He took on a series of Indian mistresses and called at least one his wife.[38]

Croghan embodied a type of capitalist that Thomas Doerflinger has dubbed "the opulent adventurer," the never-say-die gambler who lives in a high style and concocts ever more grandiose schemes as his debts mount to an inevitable catastrophe: "Gambling was in the blood of these men, and when luck ran against them, they were tempted to play double-or-nothing in order to mend their fortunes with a single spectacular deal." Croghan was a man of lavish hospitality and voracious appetites—for food, fine clothing, drink, women, and, especially, land. He paid for his excesses with severely painful gout, intermittent venereal diseases, and a reputation for feckless unreliability. He cheated his partners in trade, lied to his superiors, and gulled his friends among the Indians into giving him thousands of acres of their land. He lived far beyond his means and went spectacularly bankrupt, compelling Croghan to remain for several years among the Indians to avoid the arrest for debt that awaited him if he reappeared in Philadelphia. He plowed into land speculation the money that should have gone to his creditors. Characteristically, he recklessly speculated in vast, distant tracts of land where contested jurisdictions cast doubt on the validity of all titles. Croghan was so adept at evading arrest for debt that John Baynton, one of his partners and creditors, dubbed him "Abracadabra." Nonetheless, Croghan's charm was so infectious that many of his greatest creditors remained indulgent admirers. Baynton hoped that Croghan would, after paying his debts, retain enough property "to enable him to live according to the elegance of his desires and the nobleness of his disposition."[39]

At Sir William Johnson's urging, in 1767 Croghan turned his attention and ambitions northward to the New York frontier. For the moment, his vast land speculations in western Pennsylvania had been stymied by the claims of his creditors. He hoped to lift his burden of debt and rescue his Pennsylvania land claims not by retrenching but by launching yet another immense speculation on a new front. Johnson pointed Croghan to the extensive unpatented and unsettled lands around Otsego Lake. Johnson's sponsorship assured the success of Croghan's application, first to the Iroquois and then to New York's royal governor, Sir Henry Moore. The governor was ever willing to forget the royal restrictions on such large land grants if doing so would earn him substantial patent fees and accommodate the wealthy and influential Sir William Johnson.[40]

Croghan obtained the Indian half of his title in deeds secured from Iroquois sachems attending a grand council at Fort Stanwix on the upper Mohawk in October 1768. Under the terms of the public treaty, the Iroquois surrendered their lands in New York that lay east of the Unadilla River—including all of the country around Otsego Lake. Then, in private meetings with leading Iroquois sachems, Johnson, Croghan, and their friends (including Gov. William Franklin of New Jersey) bought the Indian title to almost all the land acquired within New York, thereby cheating the Crown that they were supposed to serve. Governor Franklin and his partners, a cartel of wealthy Quaker merchants from Burlington, New Jersey, obtained 69,000 acres in the Otego valley, southwest of Otsego Lake. Johnson acquired 54,000 acres of prime bottomland along the Charlotte and Susquehanna rivers. Croghan was the big winner, securing a tract of 100,000 acres known as the "Otsego Patent," and an additional 145,000 acres divided into four patents named Belvedere, Butler, McKee, and Skinner (see Map 2). For about £2,500.0.0 promised to the Indians and £6,009.10.0 in patent fees owed to the royal governor and other provincial officials, Croghan obtained 245,000 acres. For less than one shilling per acre, he received nearly half of what would later become Otsego County.[41]

In securing the land, Croghan paid almost nothing down for the very good reason that he had no money but plenty of connections. He paid for the Indian deeds primarily in promissory notes secured by bonds; never honored by the colonel, these proved worthless, and the natives received nothing from their bargain with Croghan (just as they never received anything from Hartwick for his tract). Nor did Croghan pay the provincial of-

MAP 2

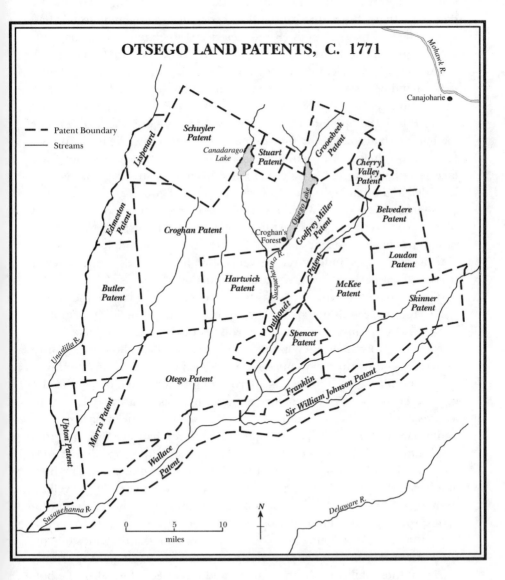

ficials in cash; instead he gave them bonds secured by mortgages on the land. Governor Cadwallader Colden, Attorney General John Tabor Kempe, Provincial Secretary Goldsborough Banyar, and Surveyor General Alexander Colden joined the swelling ranks of Croghan's creditors.[42]

Croghan had already begun the work of establishing his new home at the foot of Otsego Lake, where the Susquehanna began its long run to the sea. Croghan wanted to establish a landed estate that would perpetuate his name and provide a rich inheritance for his daughter, Susannah, and her husband, Lt. Augustine Prevost, Jr. In 1768 he persuaded them to settle beside a cove at the head of the lake on a tract of six thousand acres that he deeded to them. Born in Switzerland and educated in England, Prevost had served in the British Sixtieth (Royal American) Regiment in America during the French and Indian War (1754–1760). At the head of Otsego Lake, Prevost's workmen cleared eighteen acres and built a cluster of log buildings, including a sawmill. Teamsters and hired hands herded livestock and carted food, tools, and supplies from the Mohawk River over the watershed to the Prevost compound, where they were driven along the lakeshore or loaded into bateaux for the nine-mile journey down the lake to the outlet. In honor of the towering white pines and hemlocks that spread along the lake's southern shore, the Colonel named his new estate Croghan's Forest. Hobbled and often bedridden by his severe case of gout, Croghan did little of the immense physical work to fell the trees, erect fences, sow grass seed, plant corn and wheat, construct five log sheds and barns, and two homes, or to tend the cows, oxen, sheep, and swine. Instead, he employed an overseer, a slave, eight indentured servants, five hired hands, a gardener, a mason, at least two domestic servants, and his wife.[43]

The site delighted visitors. "His situation commands a view of the Whole Lake," Richard Smith noted. Traversing the length of the Susquehanna in 1784, Griffith Evans saw no more impressive spot than Otsego Lake on the morning of November 2: "What romantic beauties here; how does nature flourish and outstrip every conception. A morning equal to any in May; a most superb range of mountains approaching by a gradual descent to the water; a beautiful large lake below, as transparent as crystal and as smooth as a sea of glass." The lake was long (nine miles) and relatively narrow (one and a half miles). It lay 1,197 feet above sea level, had been gouged to a maximum depth of 168 feet by an Ice Age glacier, and was walled by hills covered with a heavy mixed timber of white pine, hemlock, oaks, maples, and beech. The forest's varying shades of green in summer, or bright yellow, orange, red, and brown in fall, contrasted beautifully with the lake's translucent spring-fed water. From a distance the water appeared slightly greenish, a tint that came from calcium carbonate dissolved out of the limestone on the bottom. Those who paddled along its surface marveled at the water's clarity, at their ability to see through 30 and more feet of water to the bottom's rounded gray stones "with here and there the wreck of a dead tree." Otsego Lake abounded with life, including the fish that delighted human taste: lake trout, bass, landlocked salmon, and, above all, a renowned variant of whitefish misnamed the Otsego bass.[44]

Croghan's new home was a hybrid of polished gentility and frontier improvisation—a mixture so characteristic of the man and of his time and place. Although constructed of logs, the house boasted glass windows, stone chimneys, and an interior filled with the possessions of gentility. Fashionable wallpaper festooned the walls. Superfine damask cloths covered the tables. Ivory-handled knives and forks lay at each place setting. Six fireplaces provided heat. Guests could sit on thirty chairs. Imported barrels of sugar, oysters, tobacco, sherry, and raisins, and boxes of coffee, tea, and chocolate ensured that guests enjoyed the best that the Atlantic market offered. They also tasted the abundant fish and game of the local lake and forest. Croghan's diverse guests further attested that he faced both directions at the frontier juncture; the visiting gentlemen Richard Smith reported that Indians gathered wherever the generous Croghan lingered: "At Night a drunken Indian came and kissed Col. Croghan and me very joyously. Here are natives of different Nations almost continually. They visit the deputy Superintendant as Dogs to the Bone, for what they can get."[45]

Unfortunately for the Indians and Croghan, his Otsego estate proved as ephemeral as the rest of his properties. In 1770 it became apparent that most, if not all, of his Otsego lands would fall prey to his impatient horde of creditors. That spring Croghan abruptly departed for Pittsburgh, leaving Croghan's Forest and his workmen to Augustine Prevost's supervision. Croghan never returned to Otsego. Within a year the workmen mutinied and decamped, probably for want of pay or food. Desperate for a steady income and frustrated by his father-in-law's continuing difficulties and absence, Augustine Prevost left Otsego in 1772 to reenter the British army.[46]

Once again Croghan shifted his short attention and prodigious energies to a new front, where he could construct a still more far-fetched and gargantuan land speculation intended to redeem all of his encumbered and imperiled properties scattered through Pennsylvania and New York. With every financial setback, every overdue debt, he ratcheted his ambitions up another notch. In Pittsburgh he provoked a frontier rebellion meant to transfer the surrounding region out of Pennsylvania's jurisdiction and into Virginia's. He sought to ingratiate himself with Virginia's royal governor, Lord Dunmore, in the hope that he would support Croghan's suspect claims to over 200,000 acres of lands bought from some Indians but discredited by Pennsylvania's leaders. This operation paled beside Croghan's consummate scheme—"the Grand Ohio Company"—a joint stock company with Philadelphia's richest merchants to press the imperial bureaucracy for a grant of 20 million acres in the Ohio valley with distinct status as a new royal colony known as Vandalia. Confident of imperial approval, Croghan reassured one of his leading creditors, William Franklin: "I am certain [that] in three months after the new governor makes his appearance here I shall take as much cash as will pay all I owe in the world." In fact the imperial bureaucracy stalled the scheme until 1775, when the American Revolution killed it.[47]

While Croghan schemed in Pittsburgh, his Otsego empire dissolved. Because he had never paid for the land, he never truly owned it. Indeed, no sooner had he received his New York patents than he had to sell or mortgage and remortgage the lands to mollify his creditors in Philadelphia, Albany, and New York City. New York's provincial officials received Otsego land rather than hard cash for their fees. In effect, Croghan's brief and incomplete tenure as Otsego's landlord served only to transfer the lands from his Indian friends to the array of officials and merchants who were his creditors. By the end of 1773 Croghan retained only 29,350 acres—an eighth of his original holdings in the Otsego country. That residue consisted of the lands he cherished most: the western and southern shores of Otsego Lake, including Croghan's Forest.[48]

Even the 29,350 acres did not truly belong to Croghan, for he burdened them with two mortgages and a legal judgment on one of his bonds. Croghan created the first and most important encumbrance before he had even received his Otsego patent. In December 1768 the colonel borrowed £3,000, ostensibly from Governor Franklin of New Jersey; the money actually came from a cartel of eight wealthy Quakers from Burlington and Philadelphia. Most of these investors were also Franklin's partners in the Otego Patent (located southwest of the Otsego Patent). Quite wisely, they were willing to extend credit to their royal governor and Burlington neighbor but not directly to a notorious and elusive bankrupt like George Croghan. Franklin gave the cartel, known as the Burlington Company, his bonds to repay within three years with interest or forfeit £6,000—twice the principal. Franklin tendered the money to Croghan and received his bonds to pay within three years subject to the same interest and double indemnity. As further security Croghan gave Franklin mortgage deeds covering his Philadelphia lands and mansion and 40,000 acres of his Otsego Patent. Franklin concluded the deal by assigning Croghan's bonds and mortgages to the Burlington Company. One of Croghan's friends, William Trent, assured the Burlington Company that everything "shall be done in such a manner as to prevent any future trouble." Naturally, nothing went according to plan, and everyone reaped trouble.[49]

Croghan failed to pay his debt to Franklin and the Burlington Company when it fell due in December 1771. The Quaker investors then discovered that their securities offered little hope of recouping their money. They were reluctant to sue Franklin on his bonds because he did not have enough

money to pay, and a legal judgment that ruined him was not in their interest as his partners and political allies. The alternative of suing Croghan on
his mortgage had become severely complicated because of two additional
encumbrances on the Otsego land. In March of 1770, Croghan secured a
£2,000 debt owed to Thomas Wharton, a Philadelphia merchant, and his
partners (who included one Dr. John Morgan) by giving him a mortgage
deed for 20,000 acres within the tract already mortgaged to the Burlington
Company. Apparently Croghan persuaded Wharton that the Otsego lands
were sufficiently valuable to pay off both mortgages. In October 1770 another creditor, a New York City merchant named John Morton, sued on his
long overdue bond from Croghan for £10,500 and obtained legal judgment
from the New York Supreme Judicial Court. Morton's best option was to levy
execution on the Otsego tract, Croghan's only substantial asset in the
province. In October 1773 Franklin secured his own court judgment in
New York against Croghan. In sum, three different sets of creditors—
Thomas Wharton, John Morton, and William Franklin and the Burlington
Company—had legal instruments to recoup their money from the same
parcel of land.[50]

All three parties eyed one another suspiciously, fearful that one might
strike first, obtain a legal execution to auction the Otsego tract, and gain
payment in full to the detriment of the others. A sudden forced sale of the
entire tract at public auction would yield relatively little, probably not
enough to satisfy all the debts, perhaps not even any one. Much more could
be realized by retailing the lands to actual settlers. But that would require
time and patience, for most settlers were cash-poor men who could pay virtually nothing down and would need a credit of about ten years to pay off
the principal. Moreover, settlers had proved leery of Croghan's lands, probably because they feared that his financial entanglements would render his
title worthless, imperiling the property of anyone who settled on his tract.[51]

In 1774 the creditors and Croghan's Philadelphia agent, Barnard Gratz,
agreed to divide the Otsego tract into 1,000-acre lots, each to be auctioned
to the highest bidder. Croghan assured Gratz, "I main to sell the Ottsago
Tract & gett don with that part of the Country." But Prevost urged Gratz to
reserve Croghan's Forest from the auction, writing, "as I am bent upon
doing my utmost to retain it, as it will certainly be a place worth much more
than the Paltry Sum it would now be sold for." But neither Prevost nor
Croghan had the money to redeem Croghan's Forest.[52]

From the auction proceeds Franklin was to be satisfied first, because his
December 1768 mortgage from Croghan was the oldest encumbrance.
Once paid, Franklin could at last satisfy the Burlington Company, liberating
his bonds in their possession. If the auction yielded any additional monies,
Thomas Wharton was next, owing to his March 1770 mortgage. Third in
line, John Morton would only be recompensed for his October 1770 court

judgment if the sales exceeded the full value of Franklin's and Wharton's mortgages. But Gratz never conducted the auction because the Revolutionary War erupted in the spring of 1775. Thereafter any auction would have yielded little or nothing as the value of frontier lands plunged for fear of Indian raids.[53]

A decade later, at the end of the long Revolutionary War, William Cooper ventured north to Otsego to investigate the potential of Croghan's lands and the possibility of acquiring them. He had not wandered randomly into a wilderness but sought a specific property that he hoped to acquire by untangling its complicated legal encumberances.

SETTLERS 🔥

In addition to effacing Indians and landlords from Otsego's past, William Cooper's account in *A Guide in the Wilderness* slighted the settlers who, by 1785, had already pushed into the land. On the summit of Mount Vision, Cooper was a lot closer to the clearings and buildings of white men than he implied in his book. It did not fit his purpose to mention that he found Mount Vision not in the midst of a trackless forest but on the edge of the existing settlements at Cherry Valley, Newtown Martin, and Springfield. His wilderness view came by looking south and west to the foot of Otsego Lake and beyond. When he turned around to look north and east, he saw lands that were already partially settled, some for over forty years.

Scotch-Irish settlers had begun the Cherry Valley settlement in the early 1740s on land patented by the royal governor in 1738—the very first patent in the Otsego country. Until the danger of French and Indian raids lifted with the British conquest of Canada in 1760, the settlement grew slowly. Thereafter, a steady stream of new settlers flowed into Cherry Valley until the American Revolutionary War. Some were Dutch or Palatinate Germans from the Mohawk valley to the north or the Schoharie valley to the east, but most were Scotch-Irish (and a few Yankees) who came via New England. In 1769 Richard Smith found a thriving settlement of fifty homes, a Presbyterian meetinghouse, three gristmills, a sawmill, a potashery, a gunsmith, a blacksmith, "and divers Carpenters and other Tradesmen." Sixteen years before Cooper's visit, society already verged on Mount Vision.[54]

Farther south and west, new settlements developed during the early 1770s along both banks of the Susquehanna and the lower reaches of its tributary streams: the Charlotte River on the east, the Unadilla River on the west, and the Butternuts, Otego, Cherry Valley, and Schenevus creeks in between. Strings of dispersed homesteads located on the most fertile bottomlands, these settlements appeared as scars on the larger forest, as pockets of stumps, and girdled or fire-blackened trees, of log cabins and brush fences.

By 1775 Otsego was the home for about 900 white settlers, about a third of whom lived in Cherry Valley. Although the Revolutionary War drove almost all of Otsego's settlers from their homes, many returned, and many more joined them, after the return of peace in 1783 and before Cooper ascended Mount Vision in 1785.[55]

One of the newcomers who preceded Cooper's visit was a squatter named David Shipman, who later served as a model for the hunter Natty Bumppo in *The Pioneers*. In his *Chronicles of Cooperstown* (1838), James Fenimore Cooper remarked, "Shipman, the Leatherstocking of the region, could at almost any time, furnish the table with a saddle of venison." This observation confirmed local sentiment in Cooperstown that David Shipman had inspired Cooper's most celebrated character. But Cooper became prickly over any suggestion that one of his characters—especially his most famous—was not primarily the product of his own imagination. Consequently, he denied that any one person had inspired Natty Bumppo. In her account of her father's life, Susan Fenimore Cooper restored a measure of Shipman to the Leatherstocking: "A vague recollection of Shipman seems to have lingered in the mind of the writer, and to have suggested the idea of the principal character in *The Pioneers*." She explained that during the 1790s the "old hunter by the name of Shipman" had frequently come down from his home "in the Otsego hills . . . to offer his game at Judge Cooper's door." His "rude equipment, dogs, and rifle had much attraction for the lads of the house." The son of an old Otsego settler similarly described his childhood memory of Shipman: "He dressed in tanned deerskin, and with his dogs roamed the forest, hunting deer, bears, and foxes."[56]

Born about 1730 in Connecticut, David Shipman moved to Hoosick, New York, in 1772. Located along the border with western Massachusetts, Hoosick quickly filled up with Yankees and became the source for many families who emigrated west to the Otsego country during the 1780s and 1790s. In 1787 Shipman still had property in Hoosick, but he had probably begun to sojourn around Otsego Lake, for a map indicates two settler cabins in the Otsego Patent (both of them beside Oaks Creek) at the time Cooper first surveyed his land; one of them bears the name "Shipman." Just as Marmaduke Temple had found Natty Bumppo already settled on the land, William Cooper discovered that David Shipman had preceded him to Otsego. A check of the recorded deeds in Otsego County reveals that he never held title to his land. Like Natty Bumppo, Shipman was a squatter.[57]

Natty Bumppo's partial origin in the historical figure David Shipman is especially intriguing because in 1792 William Cooper probably evicted the squatter from his possession on the point of land where Oaks Creek flowed into the Susquehanna. In January, as the land agent for Rev. John Christopher Hartwick, Cooper was empowered to take control of the land "on which was or now is a forced possession of one Shipman." The squatter

clung to his possession for at least another eight months. In August
Hartwick pointedly reminded Cooper, "I want one Shipman, a wicked In-
truder to be ejected from the usurped Place in the corner of Land between
the confluence of the Oaks & Susquehanna, and the Revd. Mr. Newman to
take Possession for me & in my Name, til further Orders." Shipman soon
left, for the point passed into Hartwick's control by the end of the year.
David Shipman moved north, up Oaks Creek, to settle on the farm belonging to his son Samuel in Otsego Township. Unlike Natty Bumppo, Shipman
did not escape to the West; instead the old hunter died on his son's farm in
1813. Apparently, the fictional conflict in *The Pioneer* between Judge Marmaduke Temple and Natty Bumppo derived from a real confrontation between William Cooper and the squatter David Shipman.[58]

GHOSTS

In *The Pioneers,* James Fenimore Cooper recomplicated his father's simpler
and briefer narrative by reintroducing an Indian, a squatter, and another
proprietor to press their own claims to the Otsego wilderness. The novelist
acknowledged that his father's possession began in a controversial tangle of
conflicting property rights rather than in the state of nature. However, the
son explored the claims of his father's competitors only to neutralize them
in the novel's conclusion. Although compelled by his own misfortunes to
consider the flawed foundation of his family's fortune, James Fenimore
Cooper ultimately reassured himself and readers that his father was the
land's inevitable and equitable owner.[59]

By including Chingachgook, the younger Cooper restored an Indian to
a landscape stripped of them by his father's description. Once a great
hunter, warrior, and sachem, Chingachgook has lost all his kin and become
an aged, pathetic, half-Christianized basket maker known to the settlers as
Indian John. In times of drunken release and at the moment of his death,
he regains his heroic identity and laments his dispossession and degradation. But he can do nothing to reverse the course of history. Although Chingachgook reminds readers that the conquest had its victims, Cooper
ultimately insisted that there was never any alternative to the Indians' destruction. An inscrutable but just Providence dictates that there is no place
for Chingachgook in the Otsego conquered and improved by Judge Temple and his settlers. Old and childless, the Mohican can condemn past in-
justices, but he cannot lay any claim to the land's future. Chingachgook is
merely a living ghost finally laid to rest by the novel's climactic forest fire.
He is the author's (and the reader's) sentimental indulgence rather than a
viable claimant to Otsego.[60]

In the character Natty Bumppo, the novelist restored the squatter presence effaced in his father's text. In Cooper's retelling, Marmaduke Temple descends from Mount Vision, pauses by the lakeshore, and spies, on the mountainside, a column of chimney smoke drifting up, in his words, from "a rough cabin of logs, the hut of Natty Bumppo who I met for the first time." Initially friendly and generous with his hut and venison, Natty grows cold upon hearing that Temple has come to survey the land and sell it to farmers. Not yet the unique and larger-than-life hero of the later Leather-Stocking tales, Natty represents a common frontier type in *The Pioneers*. Marmaduke Temple observes, "I knew him only as a man of the woods, and one who lived by hunting. Such men are too common to excite surprise."[61]

As the oldest settler on the land, Natty initially enjoys the Judge's toleration. As a solitary old man without influence, the squatter offers no threat to the new regime. Indeed, Natty is useful to the Judge's efforts to restrain the increasingly assertive and fractious new settlers who have filled the town. By acting as Natty's protector, the Judge serves notice to the newcomers that their power is limited, that they cannot exercise their prejudices to hound Natty from his cabin. The Judge thunders, "If the idlers in the village take it into their heads to annoy him, as they sometimes do reputed rogues, they shall find him protected by the strong arm of the law." Longing to drive Natty from the county, Sheriff Richard Jones scoffs at Temple's efforts to cultivate the Leather-Stocking's loyalty: "A very pretty confederacy, indeed! Judge Temple the landlord and owner of a township, with Nathaniel Bumppo, a lawless squatter, and professed deer-killer." However, it rankles Bumppo that Temple regards him as an anachronism, a dependent, a client, and a beneficiary of his magnanimous indulgence.[62]

Eventually the hunter and the landlord come into conflict as the Judge enforces a new game law to arrest, try, convict, and severely sentence Natty. At the novel's end the aged hunter flees Otsego, heading west in pursuit of the rapidly receding frontier, seeking a land with abundant game and without a land speculator and his settlers. The novelist allowed Natty, like Chingachgook, to lament his decaying circumstances as Temple and his settlers fill and change the land. But, like Chingachgook, Natty is a childless old man who cannot alter his inevitable dispossession and displacement.[63]

In *The Pioneers* James Fenimore Cooper also restored to the landscape a representative of the colonial gentlemen who had claimed Otsego before the revolution. Judge Temple is not the first landlord to own Otsego, and rumors insist that he may not be the rightful owner. Natty's mysterious companion Oliver casts aspersions on Judge Temple's character and on the validity of his title to Otsego. The penultimate chapter reveals that Oliver is the grandson of Major Effingham, "a man of the first consideration in his native colony," who had obtained an Indian title to the Otsego lands before the Revolution. As a former Indian agent and a British officer in the Sixtieth Regiment, Major Effingham is the novelist's acknowledgment of both

George Croghan and Augustine Prevost, Jr. Unlike Chingachgook, Effingham can levy a continuing claim because he has an heir. However, by an
elaborate and mechanical plot twist, the novelist patched up the seemingly
irreconcilable conflict between the Effinghams and Judge Temple, who, it
turns out, was holding half of his interest in trust for the eventual return of
the Major's heir. Oliver's subsequent marriage to the Judge's daughter and
sole heir vests the Otsego estate entirely in the couple, uniting the property
claims of the two families and legitimating the enterprise of Marmaduke
Temple.[64]

James Fenimore Cooper understood that, in 1785 from the summit of
Mount Vision, William Cooper did not look out on a primeval nature unaffected by human history. Instead, he examined a land that had, over the
preceding twenty years, been wrenched from the Iroquois, claimed and surveyed by land speculators, and partially settled by colonists. William
Cooper's vision succeeded those of Moses the Mohawk, John Christopher
Hartwick, George Croghan, and David Shipman. Cooper's town developed
where his predecessors had projected an Indian school, the New Jerusalem,
an aristocratic estate, and a squatter's haven. Otsego's history did not begin
with William Cooper. Instead, he entered an ongoing story involving other
peoples with alternative visions. Cooper's life and work take on their fuller
meaning if his story is reset in the midst, rather than at the beginning, of
the process of conquest and settlement. After 1785 he became the central
figure in that story by obtaining legal possession of the land he examined
from the crest of Mount Vision. He became Otsego's landlord by exploiting
the turmoil and opportunities of the American Revolution to supplant the
historic counterparts of Chingachgook, Natty Bumppo, and the Effinghams.

CHAPTER THREE

REVOLUTION

I T WAS WILLIAM COOPER'S GOOD FOR- tune that, beginning in 1775, the Ameri- can Revolution violently disordered society and property, creating opportuni- ties for new men to accumulate fortunes and to claim authority in a new republic. The Revolution disrupted conventional means of acquiring property and tradi- tional ways of securing prestige. The war devastated trade routes and credit sources dominated by entrenched mercantile firms and, at least for its duration, closed down the political insiders' access to spec- ulative land grants and hampered their re- liance on the courts to collect debts and
evict squatters. Conversely, the war created unprecedented opportunities for aspiring men to experiment in new trade routes and new manufactures, to supply armies, to engage in privateering, to speculate in public securities and lands, and to exploit the rapidly inflating paper currency to pay back debts at a fraction of their original value. The Revolution tended to under- cut men of established gentility while creating a nouveau riche set of would- be gentlemen. The new men sought social status and political power commensurate with their wealth, jostling and infuriating the men of older estates and prestige.[1]

"Thou wast then young, my child, but must remember when I left thee and thy mother, to take my first survey of these uninhabited mountains," said Mar- maduke. "But thou dost not feel all the secret motives that can urge a man to endure privations in order to accumu- late wealth. In my case they have not been trifling, and God has been pleased to smile on my efforts. If I have en- countered pain, famine, and disease, in accomplishing the settlement of this rough territory, I have not the misery of failure to add to the grievances."

—James Fenimore Cooper, The Pioneers, 232

Although Cooper did not assist the Revolution, serving in neither mili- tary nor civil capacity, he was one of its greatest beneficiaries. He seized an opportunity created when the war blasted the fortunes and prospects (and, in some cases, the lives) of the prominent colonists who claimed some title to Otsego. Then he benefited from both the unprecedented surge of new settlers unleashed into central New York after the war and from the new le- gitimacy afforded by the Revolution to the ambitions of middling men. Al- though he neither sought nor promoted the Revolution, he shrewdly

exploited its economic, social, and political fissures to make himself a great
man in the new republic.[2]

UPHEAVAL ❧

In 1775 Otsego belonged to Tryon County, where the leading revolutionaries were men of middling means and status opposed by the entire upper
hierarchy of wealth and power dominated by the heirs of Sir William Johnson (who had died in 1774). His nephew Col. Guy Johnson presided over
the county courts. The assistant judges were Sir John Johnson and Col.
Daniel Claus, the son and son-in-law of Sir William. The same three men
commanded the county's three militia regiments. They determined who
would be Tryon County's candidates for the assembly, favoring themselves
or a dependent like Hendrick Frey, an Indian department contractor, a justice of the peace, and the lieutenant colonel of Claus's regiment. The
county sheriff, county clerk, and county jailer were all Johnson's appointees
and tenants.[3]

The Johnson clan represented the ideal of the British empire: a hierarchy of wealth and power in which the men ensconced at the top offered patronage and protection to those on the lower rungs. Loyalists insisted that
hierarchy protected society from relapsing into anarchy while providing sufficient opportunity for aspiring and meritorious men to advance through
the patronage of their betters. The Johnsons and their dependents perceived the Revolutionary movement as a conspiracy of cunning, irresponsible, ignorant, and presumptuous upstarts tearing apart the subordination
that preserved society from anarchy. Many common people, including most
of the Johnsons' many tenants, were comfortable with the promise of a secure place in a stable social order supervised by their betters. However, on
the eve of the Revolution, the ideological promises of hierarchy were wearing thin in most of the colonies. Beneath the pose of benevolent patronage
and disinterested public service, the champions of colonial hierarchy exploited their connections to look after their own interests and those of their
friends. There was more self-interest than benevolence in the machinations
of Sir William Johnson and George Croghan to accumulate land, clients,
and influence. Tryon's Whig and Loyalist camps galvanized in relationship
to the Johnsons. Men who felt that they benefited from the patronage of the
Johnson family supported the king against those in Tryon who longed to
smash the Johnson interest. A third of Tryon's inhabitants were Loyalists—
about twice the percentage for the state as a whole.[4]

The American Whigs attacked that system of ranks and privilege that the
Loyalists defended. The Whigs insisted that common men could make it on
their own and that their supposed patrons were, in fact, self-serving para-

sites. As social revolutionaries, the Whigs promised to dissolve the hierarchical interests clustered around patrons who were attached to the empire—men like Sir John Johnson, Col. Guy Johnson, and Col. Daniel Claus. As cultural revolutionaries, the rebels disdained the aristocratic ideal of genteel leisure and instead celebrated the hard work and social mobility of middling men. As political revolutionaries, they intended to make merit, rather than connections, the prerequisite for office. As economic revolutionaries, they promised that equal and open competition would allocate property equitably. The Whigs did not insist upon achieving equality of condition, but they assumed that a competitive society of equal opportunity and possessive individualism would produce a more equitable distribution of property. They reasoned that in the British empire artificial privileges propped up the wealth and power of indolent and profligate grandees while depressing the prospects of obscure but hardworking men. Discarding the empire and substituting an independent American republic was the means to achieve the new liberal utopia of the Whigs. As with the paternalism promised by hierarchical ideology, liberalism described an elusive ideal compromised by the behavior of its champions. Interests and connections remained powerful in the new republic, privileging some in the competition for property and power, but they had to operate more subtly, more covertly than before the Revolution.[5]

The American Revolution came to the countryside relatively late. Resistance to British taxation and commercial regulations had begun in 1765 but remained largely confined to the major seaports until 1774. That spring Americans learned of the Coercive Acts passed by parliament to punish Boston and Massachusetts for resisting the imperial tax on tea. The acts closed the port of Boston, stripped the province of its traditional liberties, and imposed a military governor. Fearing that this precedent would lead to the suppression of the rights and privileges in the other colonies, the American Whigs expanded their resistance by organizing committees of safety in counties and townships throughout the countryside. In August of 1774 the Whigs formed such a committee in New York's Tryon County, which consisted of the Mohawk valley and the Otsego country. The Whig committees shared information, coordinated activities, rallied support for the Continental Congress of delegates from thirteen North American colonies, enforced a boycott of British goods, and identified and intimidated those Loyalists who would not cooperate. The goal was not yet independence, but, in effect, the local committees, the provincial congresses in each colony, and the Continental Congress in Philadelphia were an alternative political framework that systematically undermined and replaced the officials who answered, through the royal governors, to Parliament and the king's ministers. In June 1775 New York's royalist lieutenant governor, Cadwallader Colden, expressed astonishment that the congresses and committees were "acting with all the confidence and authority of a legal Government." The committees and congresses constituted a revolutionary political structure before the formal declaration of independence in July 1776.[6]

In the summer of 1775 the Whigs' Committee of Safety seized control of the Tryon County government. Acting as police, prosecutor, judges, jury, and jailers, the committee investigated, arrested, interrogated, prosecuted, convicted, and imprisoned suspected Loyalists. The Tryon committee reorganized the local militia into companies and regiments led by elected officers, undercutting the power and authority of the loyal officers commissioned by the royal governor and substituting popular for royal sovereignty. During the summer of 1775 the Whigs militia drove Col. Guy Johnson, Col. Daniel Claus, and the county sheriff from Tryon into refuge in Canada. In January 1776 the Whigs seized Johnson Hall, obliging Sir John Johnson to flee to British-held Canada. The Whigs confiscated the lands and chattels of the Loyalist refugees. Over a third of the Loyalist properties confiscated in New York State were in Tryon county. Suspected Loyalists who lingered were disarmed and obliged to take oaths of allegiance to the rebel authorities.[7]

After fending off the British invasion of the upper Hudson and Mohawk valleys in 1777, the Whigs were in control of Tryon County but subject to increasingly destructive raids by Iroquois and Loyalist rangers operating out of the British forts and Indian villages to the north and west. Before peace returned to the Mohawk valley in 1783, frontier raiders destroyed most of the settlements in Tryon County, made refugees of at least two-thirds of the inhabitants, widowed 380 women, and left about 2,000 children without fathers. The destruction was most thorough on the county's western fringes—including Otsego, which was virtually depopulated by war's end. Brutal and bloody, divisive and destructive, the war wreaked a havoc underestimated by historians who describe the American Revolution as orderly and consensual.[8]

In the Otsego country, the node of Whig power was the Presbyterian Scotch-Irish population of Cherry Valley and Harpersfield. Their leading men assumed important positions among the Tryon County Whigs: Col. Samuel Campbell commanded a militia regiment; Samuel Clyde chaired the county committee; William Harper represented the county in New York's provincial congress; and Capt. Alexander Harper led a ranger company. Throughout the colonies the Scotch-Irish tended to be especially zealous Whigs. They possessed a powerful tribal identity and memory that associated their current struggle against the British empire with their long heritage of Protestant resistance to religious and aristocratic hierarchies in Scotland and Ireland.[9]

Loyalism prevailed in the western half of the Otsego country where the Scotch-Irish presence thinned out, the number of settlers from the middle colonies or England increased, and their greater vulnerability to the adjoining Indians trumped all other considerations. They hoped to preserve their exposed lives and property by remaining neutral or by covertly assisting the Indian and Loyalist rangers. Further southwest, down the Susquehanna River, most of the Indians at Onoquaga remained loyal to Britain, primarily through the influence of Joseph Brant (or Thayendanegea), the charismatic brother of Sir William Johnson's Mohawk mistress. Identifying Indian survival and autonomy with British rule, Brant told the Onoquagans "to defend their Lands & Liberty against the Rebels, who in a great measure begin this Rebellion to be sole Masters of this Continent." Indian and white Loyalists perceived Britain as their protector against the aggressive, violent, and oppressive Whig committees and militias.[10]

In 1776 and 1777 the zealous partisans on both sides actively pressured the Otsego settlers in the middle to take sides. Whig militiamen and Continental Army soldiers from Cherry Valley and the Mohawk valley periodically descended upon the Otsego country to arrest suspected Loyalists, seize their firearms and livestock, and burn their cabins. At the same time, from his base at Onoquaga, Joseph Brant led Loyalist rangers up the Susquehanna and Unadilla rivers to attack the settlements at Springfield and in the Mohawk valley. The conflicting pressures forced increasing numbers of settlers to forsake the middle ground at Otsego. To the northeast Cherry Valley filled with Whig refugees, while to the southwest Onoquaga received Loyalists.[11]

In the fall of 1778 each side attacked the other's base located on Otsego's two margins. The Whigs struck first. In early October their soldiers descended the Susquehanna and destroyed the village and crops at Onoquaga. Eleven years later Samuel Preston, a Quaker and a surveyor, mourned over the impressive ruins he found at Onoquaga: "I have many times, when traveling in [the] back country, seen the signs of Indian settlements and remains of their old towns, but none where they appeared to have been so formidable and numerous as at this place called Ononquaga." The villagers "not only had several large apple orchards, but many thousand acres of land cleared and well cultivated." In 1778 American soldiers had "plundered, and burnt their houses, drove away and killed their cattle, mowed their corn, and cut down [the] chief of their orchards." One of the men accompanying Preston on his survey was Benjamin Dixon, who had helped destroy Onoquaga. Recalling the raid, Dixon told Preston that "when they were mowing the corn they found several small children hid there." Dixon "boasted very much, what cruel deaths they put them to, by running them through with bayonets and holding them up to see how they would twist and turn."[12]

At dawn on November 11 the Loyalists obtained their revenge for the destruction of Onoquaga. A force of 550 men, mostly Iroquois, partly white,

surprised the sleeping garrison and villagers at Cherry Valley. The fort managed to hold out, but the incompetent commander, Col. Ichabod Alden,
was tomahawked in his bed in a home outside the walls; fifteen other soldiers and thirty-two civilians died in the massacre. The victors burned the
outlying farms and marched away with seventy prisoners and a herd of cattle and horses. Thereafter, a Continental Army garrison persisted at the
Cherry Valley fort, but the surviving settlers fled east for the duration of the
war, leaving the Otsego country virtually uninhabited. In the summer of
1779 the 1,500 soldiers in Gen. James Clinton's Continental Army brigade
descended the Susquehanna bound west to join Gen. John Sullivan's expedition against the Iroquois villages. Passing through Otsego, Clinton's soldiers found a land of abandoned, plundered, and ruined homesteads.[13]

In 1782 the British government accepted defeat in America, opened
peace negotiations, and suspended military operations. In the peace treaty
concluded a year later, the British ceded all of North America south of the
Great Lakes, thereby abandoning their Iroquois allies to the tender mercies
of their enemies. Although furious at this betrayal, the Iroquois Loyalists
had no choice but to accept the harsh terms dictated to them by the American negotiators at the October 1784 Treaty of Fort Stanwix. In additional
treaties concluded in 1785 and 1788, New York's governor, George Clinton, compelled the Iroquois tribes to sell almost all their homeland, including Onoquaga's ruins. The treaties pushed the Indian boundary far to
the west of Otsego and served notice to cautious whites that it was safe to settle in central New York. In the spring and summer of 1783, Whig settlers
began to filter back to the Otsego country, reoccupying their ruined farms.
Most Tryon County Loyalists remained refugees in Canada because they did
not dare to face the victors' wrath. It was especially unwise for Indian Loyalists to return because they were doubly damned—for their race as well as
their politics. The refugees from Onoquaga followed Joseph Brant into
exile and resettled on the Grand River in Upper Canada (now Ontario).[14]

Otsego's postwar settlers benefited from the clearings and caches left behind by the Loyalists who did not return. In 1784 the Beach family, poorly
clad Yankees from Connecticut, had the good fortune to discover hidden in
a thicket a large chest containing three spinning wheels left behind by
refugees. In a burned-out cabin at Unadilla, they also found the skeleton of
a man killed by Indians during the war. On his way to Otsego in 1783,
Richard Smith stopped on the upper Delaware at Cookhouse, where the
prewar Indian village had passed into the possession of "very poor" whites
who were "not equal [to] the Indians." At Onoquaga Samuel Preston
learned that the new settlers "ploughed and found considerable quantities
of pewter, iron and brass, and perhaps there is some buried that never will
be found."[15]

In November 1784 Griffith Evans traveled south through the Otsego country, finding a promising land rapidly recovering from the war. Although Brant's raiders had "entirely demolished" Springfield's "handsome farms," many settlers had returned to rebuild in 1783 and 1784. Descending Otsego Lake, Evans found Croghan's Forest a burned-out ruin, but war had not destroyed "its natural beauties in full view of the finest land on one side, [and] the most beautiful lake on the other, diversified with mountains, vales, and levels." Proceeding down the Susquehanna, Evans noted the fertile flats ("rich and groaning for cultivation") and new cabins along the way.[16]

After the war new settlers flowed into the Otsego country in unprecedented numbers. Most of the newcomers were Yankees drawn from relatively crowded and infertile New England to New York by the glowing reports borne home by returning veterans. They came as never before because the war had broken Iroquois power, lifting the inhibiting potential of frontier raids; because the eight years of war had held back settlers, creating a pent-up demand for new farms that found sudden release with the return of peace; and because the war had introduced so many young soldiers to the agricultural potential of central New York.[17]

DOWNFALL 🔥

The eight years of revolutionary warfare had been a prolonged nightmare for New York's frontier landlords; they could neither lease nor sell land so long as partisans ravaged the settlements. But the return of peace and the accelerating resettlement and new settlement of central New York enhanced land values and promised riches to the men who owned title to large tracts of land in the settlers' path. From Albany in September of 1783 a visiting surveyor reported, "The rage for Land here exceeds all conception, and the influx of people from the East is so great that this kind of Speculation is the object of every person who has the means to embark in it." However, in 1783 it remained uncertain whether any landlord would benefit from the new settlers appearing within the bounds of the Otsego Patent, because the war had further clouded its contested title.[18]

The American Revolution devastated George Croghan and his heirs. Distrusted by both Whigs and Loyalists, Croghan spent the last years of the war and his life in retirement, poverty, sickness, and the suburbs of Philadelphia. He died in 1782, his fortune, reputation, and hopes all blasted by his own folly and by a revolution that destroyed the last vestiges of his network of interest and connections. His heirs—daughter Susannah and her husband, Major Augustine Prevost—hoped to rescue something from the wreckage of the Croghan estate, but they were hamstrung by their own heavy debts.[19]

The war also scattered and ruined Croghan's leading creditors: Gov. William Franklin, Abel James, Joseph and Thomas Wharton, John Morton, and Dr. John Morgan. Governor Franklin was a defiant Loyalist who suffered arrest, expulsion, and dispossession by New Jersey's Whigs. His exile in England, and the loss of his legal papers to a wartime fire in New York City, crippled his subsequent efforts to reclaim the Otsego lands.[20]

Next to Franklin, the principal shareholder in the Burlington Company was Abel James, a Philadelphia Quaker merchant. He suffered several months under house arrest for his opposition to the Revolution while the disruption of trade to Britain destroyed his mercantile firm. In 1784 James became a bankrupt and suffered a mental breakdown that clouded his memory and impaired his concentration. His friend and former partner Henry Drinker sadly wrote that James's "case calls for the commiseration of all who once knew his ample fortune & the rank he has maintained in life." In 1789 James lamented the "Afflicted State of my Mind for several years past," especially his inability to remember the details of his "many complicated Accounts and Transactions."[21]

The war also bankrupted the brothers Joseph and Thomas Wharton, two weighty Philadelphia Friends who held their own mortgage on the Otsego Patent. The Whigs arrested Thomas Wharton and confiscated his Pennsylvania properties; a broken man, he died in early 1782 at the age of fifty-one. His younger brother was an accomplished scholar of classical literature, a respected merchant, and a leading citizen until ruined by the war's disruption of overseas commerce. Left in genteel poverty, he nurtured desperate hopes of recovering the Otsego Patent.[22]

Among Otsego's leading claimants, only John Morton and Dr. John Morgan were active Whigs. Despite choosing the winning side, Morton and Morgan also suffered severely from the war's destruction of property and reputations. In 1776 Morton and his family lost their home when they fled from the British occupation of New York City. He died of apoplexy in 1782, a week after armed robbers had plundered his new house in New Jersey. Dr. Morgan was born into a wealthy Philadelphia Quaker family. He converted to Anglicanism, studied medicine at the finest universities in Europe, and became the leading doctor and professor of medicine in the colonies. During the war he served as director-general of hospitals in the Continental Army until 1777, when Congress sacked him, charging incompetence and cruelty. Morgan was demoralized by the dismissal, and financially ruined when British troops burned his home with its fine library and his legal records and business papers.[23]

Before the Revolution George Croghan, Augustine Prevost, Jr., William Franklin, Abel James, Thomas Wharton, Joseph Wharton, Jr., John Morton, and Dr. John Morgan had been wealthy, powerful, well connected, and prestigious men. By the end of the war, they had all been ruined. Three were dead, leaving behind depleted estates, one was in exile, another had gone both mad and broke, and three others were bankrupt or the next thing to it. Their collective travails attest to the damage that the Revolution inflicted upon the fortunes and prospects of so many established gentlemen. But while they were on their way down the social ladder, young William Cooper was on his way up to lay claim to the prize that had eluded them for so long.

DESIGNS

As a member of Burlington's Library Company, William Cooper was familiar with the members of the Burlington Company, holders of George Croghan's bond and mortgage secured by thousands of acres of increasingly valuable land on the New York frontier. Cooper shrewdly calculated that he would become a wealthy and powerful man if he could obtain possession of the Otsego Patent. Because navigating through the legal obstacles promised to be expensive, Cooper took on a partner to share the costs, the risks, and, therefore, the potential profits. He recruited Andrew Craig, a prosperous Burlington merchant and a Quaker in good standing with the Monthly Meeting. In learning, prestige, and wealth, Craig ranked above Cooper but below the town's weightiest Friends, such as Richard Smith. In their bid to acquire the Otsego Patent, Cooper contributed almost all of the entrepreneurial energy, while Craig provided half of the capital.[24]

Cooper and Craig moved rapidly and aggressively in early 1785 to buy up the five outstanding shares in the Burlington Company from James Verree, George Fox, and Abel James (William Franklin owned the other five shares). Despairing of ever collecting on their clouded title to the Otsego Patent, the elderly members of the Burlington Company were eager to sell out to the younger, more vigorous Cooper and Craig. By purchasing the shares, they obtained possession of the various bonds and mortgages that secured Croghan's original debt of £3,000 (along with the additional accumulated interest). Cooper and Craig gambled that they could make the Croghan estate pay far more than they had invested to buy the five shares. Two days after securing the shares, they informed Alexander Hamilton, the New York lawyer who had been engaged by James, that "the whole Property is now legally vested in Us."[25]

But what about the other five shares in the Burlington Company that belonged to William Franklin? In 1770 he had obtained them by paying off three of the original shareholders: Richard Wells, Henry Hill, and Samuel Preston Moore. They had given him receipts written onto the original bond, but by 1785 Abel James had detached the receipts, eliminating the evidence that Franklin had obtained half of the Burlington Company. Any other written proof vanished in the wartime fire that destroyed his papers. Franklin may have been entitled to half of whatever the Burlington Company could collect from the Croghan estate, but he could not prove it. And Cooper and Craig were not about to concede that they had purchased only half a loaf. Perhaps they knew that they were defrauding Franklin, but it is equally possible that James was to blame; either his increasingly erratic mind or his desperate need for money may have led him to detach and misplace the receipts from the bond in order to get a higher price from Cooper and Craig.[26]

Unwilling to wait on the other Otsego claimants or to share the proceeds of an auction sale, Cooper and Craig wanted to get control of the land as rapidly as possible. On May 9 they pressed Hamilton to have "the Otsego Patent sold by the Sheriff with all possible Dispatch in such part of the Patent as W. Cooper has already described to thy Clerk." After all, they had obtained the Burlington Company shares on credit, which meant that they faced large payments to James, Verree, and Fox during the next two years. Before the war, William Franklin, Thomas Wharton, John Morton, and George Croghan had cooperated in arranging for an auction sale and for the division of the anticipated proceeds. But the Revolution had postponed that sale, and Cooper and Craig had no intention of reviving the agreement with Franklin or with the heirs of the deceased Wharton, Morton, and Croghan. Instead, Cooper and Craig were determined to strike first, gain legal possession of the land, and then negotiate with the other claimants from a position of strength. A more scrupulous conduct would only prolong and complicate recovery, something they could ill afford. Their aggressive haste was in contrast to the deliberate approach of Abel James, who had delayed in hopes of accommodating his "old Friend" Governor Franklin. But in 1785 James had sold his interest to two men who were not going to treat Franklin like an old friend.[27]

Cooper and Craig must have known that Otsego's other claimants were making their own preparations to claim the prize. In December of 1781 Joseph Wharton had secured an agent in New York to record his deeds from Croghan and to prevent any auction sought by a rival claimant. Wharton wanted "to keep the Otsego tract to a future day, and a far more beneficial Price." From exile in England, William Franklin had engaged, in 1784, a New York City agent (the merchant John Taylor) and lawyer (Thomas Smith) to secure him the Otsego Patent. The lawyer was to arrange the long-postponed auction by reviving the judgment Franklin had obtained against Croghan from the New York Supreme Judicial Court in 1774. Franklin wanted the money that a sale would generate rather than to own the land himself. On November 30, 1784, Smith reported the bad news that he could not revive the judgment because the court clerk had been unable to find the original in the war-disordered records. Augustine Prevost also engaged a lawyer: Aaron Burr, who was fast becoming Hamilton's great rival in the law and politics. In July of 1782 Burr had married Theodosia Bartow Prevost, the young widow of Major Prevost's uncle.[28]

Cooper and Craig had the best lawyer, as Hamilton won the race to obtain the legal authority to auction the Otsego Patent. First, he succeeded where Thomas Smith had failed in finding the original judgment roll for Franklin's prewar lawsuit against Croghan. Second, in the spring of 1785 Hamilton somehow persuaded the court that he had the authority to revive the judgment in William Franklin's name. Where was Smith, Franklin's real attorney, when Hamilton achieved this coup? The court revived the judgment, formulaically declaring that William Franklin had appeared before the court "in his proper person." At the time Franklin was in England. The judges meant that they recognized the Burlington Company as Franklin's substitute, Cooper and Craig as that company's assignees, and Hamilton as their attorney. In the eyes of the court, Alexander Hamilton had become William Franklin "in his proper person." Six months later, on November 3, 1785, the chief justice signed the roll and issued a writ directed to the sheriff of Montgomery County (as Tryon County had been renamed in 1784), authorizing the long-awaited auction to satisfy the prewar judgment for £3,839.8.0 (£3,000.0.0 in principal and £839.8.0 in accumulated interest).[29]

While awaiting the writ, William Cooper went to Philadelphia on a scouting mission to test the resolve and means of his rivals. In late August or early September, Cooper appeared at the store of Barnard Gratz, one of Croghan's executors and the man named as the defendant in the judgment Hamilton had secured. No notice had ever been served on Gratz, who remained ignorant of the legal proceedings in New York. During his visit Cooper carefully concealed news of the judgment and the impending writ. He simply introduced himself as the new co-owner of the mortgage that Croghan had given to Franklin in 1768 for 40,000 Otsego acres. Gratz recalled that Cooper "appeared a very loquacious, forward man for a stranger"—an appearance belying his true secretiveness. Gratz warned Cooper that if he damaged Joseph Wharton's interest in the Otsego Patent "it would appear wicked and cruel in the eyes of the world." According to Gratz, Cooper retorted, " 'Let the world think as it pleased, he was determined, and that as he was young in trade, £3,000 and upwards would do him and Mr. Craig a great deal of good.' " Cooper offered to relinquish his mortgage only if Wharton paid him in full by November 1—an impossibility for the bankrupt Wharton. Several months later, upon learning the secret kept by the talkative young man, Gratz ruefully concluded, "Messrs. Cooper and Craig supposed that the greater the silence and obscurity in which they have covered the whole of this transaction, the more likely they were to escape notice, and perpetrate their deep-laid designs in darkness."[30]

THE AUCTION 🦢

Once the writ had been secured, Hamilton promptly arranged for an auction in Montgomery County. In December Sheriff Samuel Clyde placed an official advertisement in the *Albany Gazette,* setting the morning of January 13, 1786, as the time and Albert Mabie's tavern in Canajoharie as the place for auctioning the Otsego Patent. The winning bidder would receive the sheriff's deed but payment had to be in full in cash on the spot. Croghan's heirs and creditors lived in New York City and Philadelphia, far from the Albany newspaper that alone carried the sheriff's advertisement, and farther still from the frontier hamlet where the auction would be held. By the time they learned of the sheriff's notice, Croghan's heirs and creditors had less than a month to raise the cash and send representatives to bid at the auction. Getting someone to a frontier tavern in the distant Mohawk valley in the dead of winter would not be easy—which was just as Cooper and Craig wanted it. As they had informed Hamilton in May, Cooper and Craig intended to buy the Otsego Patent at the auction. They proceeded hastily to sell the land in circumstances that would deter other bidders, and thereby hold down what Cooper and Craig had to pay for the Otsego Patent. They could maximize their profits by buying all of the tract cheaply at auction for resale at an enhanced price, either to actual settlers or to their rivals.[31]

Belatedly learning of the writ, Croghan's heirs and creditors tried to block the auction. As the attorney for the Prevosts, Aaron Burr petitioned New York's Chancery Court for an injunction. His petition protested that shadowy conspirators, operating under the fraudulent cover of William Franklin's name, had "secretly and clandestinely" revived his judgment without giving notice to George Croghan's heirs, executors, and creditors. By scheduling a hasty auction in a remote corner, the conspirators sought to obtain the Otsego Patent at "a price far below its value," thereby defrauding the rival claimants.[32]

On January 4, 1786, the chancellor issued an injunction strictly forbidding the sheriff from proceeding with the sale at the risk of a £10,000 fine. Burr entrusted the injunction to his law clerk, William Ireson, whom he dispatched to call on Sheriff Clyde at his home in Cherry Valley. Ireson traveled north with Dr. John Morgan, who represented Croghan's Philadelphia creditors. On January 11 the two reached Cherry Valley, where Ireson showed the injunction to Clyde and left him a copy.[33]

Two days later Sheriff Clyde held the vendue as scheduled, in defiance of the injunction. Upon reaching Mabie's Tavern in Canajoharie, Ireson and Morgan first learned that their rivals were William Cooper and Andrew Craig, who had arrived to bid for the patent. Angry words erupted as Ireson and Morgan pressed the sheriff to honor the injunction, threatening him with the penalty for contempt. Cooper "was very active in urging on the sales," threatening to sue the sheriff if he did not proceed. Cooper also promised to bear the responsibility and any legal penalty for conducting the auction. By so promising, Cooper risked losing £10,000—far more than he was then worth. Clyde consulted the only attorney present, Christopher P. Yates, who urged the sheriff to proceed. His advice was predictable, given that he was also serving as the lawyer for Cooper and Craig. Clyde also knew that he would receive no fee that day if he failed to conduct the auction.[34]

Ignoring protests from Morgan and Ireson, Clyde opened the bidding. Dr. Morgan found himself obliged to participate in an auction that he had come to prevent. He and Cooper were the only bidders (Craig remained in the background throughout the day's contention). The sums and the tension grew. At £3,600 Cooper made his last bid, apparently exhausting his available cash. Morgan offered £3,625, and the prize was his at a little after two o'clock in the afternoon. Cooper and Craig must have been bitterly chagrined to see the prize slip from their grasp. The rivals uneasily shared the tavern room as the keeper served a midafternoon dinner while Sheriff Clyde retired to another room to prepare the deed. When he returned to the barroom, Morgan was missing. Where was Dr. Morgan, Clyde asked? "Gone to hell," Cooper replied, insisting that his rival had fled from town "as hard as he could drive and would never return."[35]

The two sides disagreed about what happened next. Ten of Cooper's supporters (including Yates) insisted that the sheriff made "public outcry that he, John Morgan, should come and appear, receive his deed, and pay the money, but no John Morgan could be found." Believing that Morgan had abandoned the town and his bid, the sheriff reopened the bidding and "cried off" the Otsego Patent to Cooper for £2,700 (£900 less than his previous bid and £925 less than Morgan's offer). Shortly thereafter, Morgan reappeared in the tavern, allegedly having "secreted himself" in a small blockhouse half a mile away "during the time he was wanted." Willing to set aside the second sale, the sheriff tendered Morgan a deed that the doctor refused to accept, whereupon Cooper received the property.[36]

Morgan and Ireson told a different story. The doctor briefly stepped out to get away from the smoke and din of the crowded tavern (and, no doubt, to be free from William Cooper's company). Taking in the fresh air, Morgan strolled along the riverbank but remained within the reach of the "voice of an ordinary cryer." He never heard any "public outcry" for his return because the sheriff confined his call to "within doors" and "paid more obedience" to William Cooper "than to the Chancellor's writ or his own duty." In Morgan's absence Clyde hastily reopened the sale and collusively awarded the property to Cooper, despite Ireson's protests that the doctor was nearby and would soon return. Reentering the tavern and learning what had hap-

pened, Morgan angrily confronted Cooper and the sheriff, who belatedly
tendered the first deed to the doctor. Prepared by Cooper's lawyer, Yates,
the deed was "a botched and defective performance, replete with mis-
nomers and other errors." Rejecting the deed, Morgan proposed repairing
with the sheriff to Albany to have another lawyer prepare a proper conveyance. The sheriff retired to another room to consult with Cooper and
Craig. Clyde reemerged to tell Morgan that he must accept the original
deed and pay his money. When Morgan refused Clyde delivered the property to Cooper and received his payment of £2,700. (The next day Cooper
and Craig paid Clyde a fee of £35—not bad for a day's work in 1786.)[37]

It was, at the very least, a highly irregular auction. Clyde showed clear favoritism to Cooper and Craig by ignoring the injunction to hold the first
bidding, by reopening the auction in the afternoon without sending someone out in search of Morgan, and by refusing to go to Albany with the doctor. And Cooper certainly behaved with his characteristic aggression and
determination. But Morgan was probably not the innocent victim that he
claimed to be. Counting on the injunction, Morgan had not planned to become a bidder. After all, neither he nor those he represented were financially solvent. When, to his surprise, the sheriff ignored the injunction,
Morgan had to improvise, had to pose as a serious bidder. After he won the
bidding his behavior suggests that he did not have the money to pay for his
bid. By disappearing at a critical juncture, by refusing the deed offered him,
and by insisting on adjourning to Albany, Morgan did all he could to prolong, complicate, and frustrate the auction. In effect, Morgan and Cooper
each came away with what he wanted. Cooper obtained the sheriff's deed to
the Otsego Patent, while Morgan provoked and witnessed irregularities that
might discredit the sale with the chancellor, the public, and the New York
State legislature.[38]

SALES

In the spring both sides exploited their particular advantages won from the
contentious auction at Mabie's Tavern. Capitalizing on the irregularities,
Morgan, Jacob Morton, and the Prevosts brought suit in New York's Court
of Chancery to set aside the auction and to prosecute Clyde for contempt of
the injunction. They also pressed a petition to the New York State legislature, seeking the appointment of commissioners to conduct a new sale and
distribute the proceeds among all the parties. Making the most of their
deed, Cooper and Craig planned and advertised for retail sales of Otsego
lands to actual settlers; they promised that William Cooper would be at the
foot of Otsego Lake in the spring of 1786 to accommodate purchasers with
deeds. Cooper and Craig wanted to quickly subdivide and sell the land be-

fore their rivals could set aside the January vendue. By swapping their shaky land titles for bonds and mortgages from settlers, they meant quickly to cash in on their sheriff's deed and make it virtually impossible for their competitors to stage a second auction. Sales of most of the land to actual settlers would make the January purchase a fait accompli that could not be readily undone by the chancellor or the state legislature.[39]

In May, Cooper proceeded north to Albany and on to Lake Otsego to retail lands in the patent, while Morgan counterattacked in the newspapers and in handbills sent to Albany and Montgomery County for free circulation. Morgan warned prospective buyers not "to be taken in by the volubility, versatility and industry of William Cooper." Calling attention to the irregularities of the vendue and to the pending litigation in New York's Chancery Court, Morgan denounced as worthless the title that Cooper and Craig offered to sell. Purchasers risked "a Law-Suit in Chancery in place of a Bargain of Lands." In response Cooper and Craig promised to warrant the titles they sold: to become legally liable should anyone else prevail in court and oust settlers or compel them to purchase anew, "so that those who incline to possess rich lands at a trifling expence need not fear trouble or difficulty from any quarter." If Croghan's heirs and creditors won in the courts, the two Burlington merchants would have to bear their settlers' legal costs and compensate their damages; if so, Cooper and Craig would be ruined by their warrantees. As with their pledge to indemnify Sheriff Clyde, Cooper and Craig gambled more than they were worth to raise the stakes and keep the pressure on their rivals.[40]

Despite the controversy, Cooper rapidly retailed the Otsego Patent to settlers eager to obtain land at a bargain rate. On May 19, 1786, Cooper reported, "I have Got to work on the Lands formerly the Property of George Crohan and am Lying it out in Lots. The Land Apeares to be, take it alltogether, Prety good, but will not Sell for Cash, tho at Ever So Low A Price, but I have Plenty of Aplications, but they have no mony nor Provisions." Encamped beside the ruins of Croghan's Forest at the foot of Otsego Lake, Cooper entertained potential buyers, and he supervised a team of surveyors running lines through the forest to demarcate lots for retail sale. In *A Guide in the Wilderness*, Cooper recalled: "In May 1786 I opened the sales of 40,000 acres, which, in sixteen days, were all taken up by the poorest order of men." A fuller story emerges from the fifty-four mortgages that Cooper received from seventy-four individual settlers. In fact, the sales began on May 23 and continued for six weeks, concluding on July 7.[41]

Determined to convert his suspect new title into bonds and mortgages from actual settlers, William Cooper meant to sell as much land as rapidly as possible by offering good land in large lots at unusually low prices on especially generous credit terms. He asked for only eight shillings (New York currency, the equivalent of one dollar) per acre: half the price demanded by other New York speculators for comparable lands. Moreover, Cooper expected no down payment, accepting a bond and a mortgage from the purchaser to secure yearly payment of the annual interest (7 percent) on the purchase sum and the payment of the principal within ten years. In New York many other landlords declined to sell their lands, preferring to lease them, and few would sell more than 200 acres to a common settler—for fear that they would default or engage in their own petty speculation. In stark contrast, Cooper urged settlers to buy his freehold title to large tracts. Indeed, he promised a free village lot (approximately 35 by 150 feet) in the town he planned at the foot of the lake to anyone who bought at least 250 acres and paid in full by 1796.[42]

Come from a region of small farms on rocky hills, Yankee settlers eagerly snapped up Cooper's land in large parcels, quickly outpacing the surveyors at work running lines to demarcate the retail lots. Consequently, he increasingly sold very large tracts to groups of men in the understanding that they would subsequently subdivide their purchases into separate farms. For example, on July 6 Cooper deeded 5,702 acres to six men from Bennington County, Vermont; a day later, he sold 3,493 acres to five men from Albany County, New York. In sum, the fifty-four sales allotted land to seventy-four individuals; only one man obtained fewer than 100 acres, while thirty-two men bought at least 500 acres (up to a maximum of 1,702); the average purchaser obtained 478 acres—about five times the acreage of a standard farm in New England. Because they paid nothing down and so little per acre, most purchasers concluded that they had nothing to lose by taking on such large tracts.[43]

Indeed, many resold large portions at a profit to others before they had to pay anything to Cooper and Craig. In 1790 most of Otsego's settlers were later comers who bought their lands from an original purchaser, rather than directly from Cooper. Consequently, he collected his payments primarily from secondary, rather than from primary, purchasers. About half of the 1786 purchasers were petty speculators who returned home to sell their Otsego acquisitions to their neighbors who wanted to buy frontier lands. For example, in 1786 Samuel Tubbs, a millwright from Bennington County, bought 1,565 acres from Cooper. During the subsequent five years he sold 1,139 acres to nine other settlers who assumed the payments due to Cooper for their particular shares in the acreage. Retaining 426 acres, Tubbs established a farm and built a sawmill.[44]

By offering such generous terms in 1786, William Cooper enlisted the settler-purchasers as allies in consolidating his title to the Otsego Patent. His special circumstances as the new owner of a flawed title meant that he had to woo and befriend settlers to a degree unusual for a landlord on the New York frontier. The purchasers of 1786 had good reason to thank William Cooper for their bargains, but he had equally good cause to thank them for imparting real value to his patent. Cooper opened the sales with a title under siege in the Court of Chancery and the state legislature. He closed the sales clutching fifty-four pairs of bonds and mortgages to secure interest payments totaling £994.0.0 every year and eventual payment of a principle worth £14,204.8.0—over three times the value of Franklin's 1774 judgment and over five times the amount of the winning bid at the January vendue. Cooper and Craig could retain those bonds and mortgages to collect annual payments, or they could sell them to pay their own creditors. Cooper's sales to settlers had generated securities that had market value, and the sales rendered it virtually impossible for his competitors to regain possession of Otsego.[45]

In 1786 and 1787 Cooper intermittently conducted desultory negotiations with his rivals, Jacob Morton and Dr. John Morgan. Cooper offered to consign the Otsego Patent to the Croghan creditors if they paid him the full value of his judgment (£3,839.8.0) plus the unspecified costs that he and Craig had incurred. Cooper was probably disingenuous, dangling an offer that he knew they could not accept for utter want of the necessary funds. That Cooper had begun to lay out a village bearing his name at the foot of Otsego Lake indicates that he meant to keep and develop his new patent. In July 1787 he informed friends that he would eventually move his family and residence to Cooperstown.[46]

After the retail sales of 1786, the resistance by Croghan's heirs and creditors steadily dissipated into ineffectuality. Because New York's state legislators favored rapid frontier development and avoided legal controversies, they were not about to imperil the titles of Otsego's new settlers. The legislators also heeded the powerful political influence that Alexander Hamilton exercised on behalf of his clients. In the fall of 1786 the Chancery Court quietly dropped the legal proceedings against Sheriff Clyde for contempt and the court did nothing to overturn the auction. Apparently the Croghan heirs and creditors lacked the wherewithal to sustain a protracted lawsuit in chancery. Cooper and Craig further weakened the opposition by mollifying their two rivals with the strongest legal standing. On December 8, 1786, they bought out Joseph Wharton's competing title to the land for £800— less than half of what he had paid for it in 1780. On November 12, 1787, Cooper and Craig gave 1,500 acres (valued at £500) to Susannah Croghan Prevost and her husband, Major Augustine Prevost, to quiet their claims. In 1790 the Prevosts conveyed the land to Aaron Burr in payment for his legal services. Cooper and Craig did nothing to satisfy the claims of the other creditors, including Jacob Morton, William Franklin, and Dr. Morgan.[47]

While fending off their rivals, Cooper and Craig pressed ahead with their plans to develop the Otsego Patent in order to facilitate regular annual payments from their many settler-debtors. While Craig looked after the partnership's affairs in Burlington, Cooper managed their distant lands in central New York. Indeed, Craig never played an active role in Otsego. The two men equally divided the bonds, mortgages, and unsold lands, but Cooper exclusively supervised their frontier operations, occasionally forwarding to Craig the payments collected from settlers on his particular properties. Because Craig rarely, if ever, visited Otsego, the settlers regarded Cooper as their sole landlord. During the late 1780s Cooper's family remained in Burlington, but he repaired to Otsego every spring to spend the warm months promoting the settlements. In the fall, he returned home to pass the winters in New Jersey's comparative comfort.[48]

In 1786 he began Cooperstown virtually from scratch. The wartime vandals had destroyed all the buildings in Croghan's compound save one—a hewn-log blockhouse, fifteen feet square, that had lodged the colonel's Indian visitors. The other vestiges of Croghan's Forest were a few scattered and rotting fences surrounding a "clearing" filled with brush and stumps. A few apple trees, first laid out either by the colonel or by his Indian predecessors, also marked the site. In 1786 a family headed by Mary Johnson, a widow, lived in the new town's only other building, a recently built log cabin. Cooper's land deeds from June and July indicate that he had already laid out a rough grid of at least four streets. One of the deeds specifies the name "Cooper Town" for the projected village—testimony that, from the beginning, Cooper regarded the Otsego venture as his personal monument. During the summers of 1786 and 1787, several dozen settlers came to the foot of the lake to seek nearby land and begin clearings; a few chose to settle in the village, building log cabins. Beside the Susquehanna and a new bridge, William Ellison established a two-story frame inn, the first in the village. In 1788 a surveyor employed by Cooper laid out a more ambitious grid of streets and lots for the village. Where Croghan had established a private estate, Cooper substituted a commercial village—a telling symbol for the social consequences of the American Revolution.[49]

In 1788 William Cooper also began to build his own home sited atop the ruins of Croghan's estate—a spatial claim to having supplanted and succeeded the original landlord. That summer and the next Cooper supervised the construction of a two-story clapboard and frame house, lying broadside to the street, braced on each side by one-story wings. He laid out a garden on the east side and barns and stables across the street. The main structure assumed the name Manor House, in honor of Cooper's local predominance and his pretensions to gentility. In the fall of 1790 Cooper's family moved from Burlington into the still incomplete Manor House in Cooperstown. The procession north via Albany consisted of Cooper, his wife, Elizabeth, two slaves, five other servants, seven children (Richard Fenimore, Hannah, Isaac, Ann, William, Jr., Samuel, and James), and several wagons bearing their household possessions. The Coopers had to wait for their household goods to catch up as four weeks of autumn rain turned the frontier roads into impassable mud holes. The move ensured that Cooper's new-born son, James, would grow up on the New York frontier.[50]

FLAWS

During the late 1780s Cooper discovered severe flaws in his original surveys and sales of the Otsego Patent. The large, rapid, and cheap land sales of 1786 had achieved their immediate purpose of frustrating his rivals but at the expense of considerable subsequent cost and trouble. In his aggressive haste to secure the patent, Cooper had sowed two sources of future confusion and discontent: he had sold lands without accurate surveys and in excessively large tracts on credit to men who could not afford their payments. At the same time that he reaped a national reputation as the consummate developer, Cooper quietly struggled with disputes and defaults in Otsego that stemmed from the flaws in his original sales.

Most of the original purchasers discovered that they had taken on far more than they could either pay for or sell to others. Very few of the 1786 sales endured without passing into other hands or reverting to William Cooper before the 1796 deadline for final payment. Because the largest purchasers were least likely either to pay for or to settle their lands, the acreage that reverted to Cooper and Craig amounted to almost half of that sold in 1786 (16,992 of 35,358 = 48 percent). But because settlers continued to flock into Otsego during the 1790s, there was no shortage of new customers to repurchase the lands that Cooper and Craig had repossessed. It mattered little to Cooper whether payment came from an original buyer or a newcomer, so long as he was eventually paid.[51]

Cooper also reaped trouble from the rushed surveys of 1786. Because he had erroneously believed that the Otsego Patent included 40,000 acres, Cooper had sold 35,358 acres to settlers in 1786. In fact, only 29,350 acres of the Otsego Patent had not been previously alienated by Croghan, which meant that Cooper had sold 6,000 acres that he did not have. Once the settlers recognized the shortfall they feared prolonged and contentious boundary disputes with one another. Shifting the blame, in 1792 Cooper complained, "[I] Have got a Great Deal of Perplexity on my hands here by Some Eroneous Lines Run by an unskilful Surveyor. I Every Day find that it is impossible to be too Carefull in the beginning." In 1790–1792 he arranged for new, more precise surveys of the individual lots and agreed to reduce the payments in proportion to the shortfalls in acreage.[52]

The rapid turnover of settlers, the defaults by most of the largest 1786 buyers, and the diminished size of the original lots combined to disorder Cooper's records, necessitating a virtually complete redeeding of the Otsego Patent, beginning in 1789 and running through 1793. He resold

27,196 acres (virtually the entire Otsego Patent) to 183 buyers. Almost all were newcomers; only 13 were original purchasers from 1786. The average lot obtained by a new buyer was 149 acres—less than a third of the 478 acres obtained on average in 1786. Rather than exploit the greatly enhanced local land values, in the new deeds Cooper charged only the original price of $1.00 (8 shillings) plus the arrears in annual interest. At 7 percent interest, the rearranged sales promised Cooper and Craig an annual revenue of $2,682 and the eventual payment of principal worth $38,313. At considerable additional trouble and cost, the 1789–1793 resurveys and resales corrected the mistakes of 1786, at last putting the Otsego Patent on a sound footing.[53]

But the most serious consequence of the 1786 mistakes lingered and threatened to undermine Cooper's wealth and reputation: his original surveys and sales had trespassed onto the adjoining Hartwick Patent. Pressed by Cooper's impatience, misinformed by his optimism, and afflicted by their own incompetence, the surveyors hastily ran sloppy lines that pressed too far south to include 3,000 acres from the northern tier of the Hartwick Patent. The trespass was potentially fatal to Cooper's fortune because he had warranted the deeds he issued to settlers; they could sue him for damages if ejected from their new lands by an adverse claimant. By hook or by crook, Cooper had to obtain control of the Hartwick Patent before anyone else learned of the encroachment.[54]

In the late 1780s the Hartwick Patent remained densely forested and sparsely settled by a few Yankee squatters. Most prospective settlers stayed away, resenting the unusually stringent terms demanded by Rev. John Christopher Hartwick, who meant to rule as Christ's surrogate in a New Jerusalem. In contrast to Cooper, who tailored his terms to please and attract Yankee settlers, Hartwick offered only leases, refusing to sell freehold title. His leases forbade the tenants to erect mills or to sell the timber and ordered them to lay out apple orchards. Hartwick also reserved "full power to search for, dig and turn up the ground," either to build his own mills or to establish mines. And he retained "full liberty of ingress, egress and regress through the said premises with his or their cattle, carriages and servants, and to carry off or to manufacture the ore within the above granted premises." Given that he had no capital to mine the ores—which, fortuitously, did not exist—these reservations deterred settlers to no good end. Most of the potential settlers circulating in Otsego were Yankees determined to obtain freehold title and averse to domineering landlords. Any treasures or ores they meant to keep.[55]

More than orchards and mining rights, Hartwick wanted control over the souls and morals of his tenants. Hartwick meant his lands as bait to secure the captive, deferential congregation that had eluded him during his long years of restless travel through the American colonies. His leases demanded that the tenant acknowledge Hartwick "for his Pastor, Teacher, and Spiritual Counsellor" and "to attend regularly, decently, attentively, and devoutly Divine Service and instruction performed and given, by the said John Christopher Hartwick, or his substitute." None of this appealed to Yankee settlers who were Baptists, Congregationalists, or freethinkers; they did not mean to accept a dictatorial German Lutheran as their spiritual overlord. Committing their souls to Hartwick was even more alarming than subjecting their farms to his prospective mining operations.[56]

As Cooper saw it Hartwick was an erratic and negligent neighbor whose unreasonable vision rendered his tract a detriment, rather than an asset, to the development of the surrounding settlements. Such a large tract of virtually unsettled land was a refuge for wolves and bears, who preyed on the livestock and crops of the settlers in the adjoining Otsego Patent. A neglected tract also accumulated squatters, who set an example that Cooper and other landlords did not wish to see their own settlers follow. On the other hand, settlement of the Hartwick Patent would increase the business that flowed through Cooperstown. Recognizing that the lands in the Hartwick Patent were more fertile than his own, Cooper anticipated that they would rapidly rise in demand and price once in the possession of a pragmatic landlord. By securing ownership of the Hartwick Patent, Cooper could convert his boundary problem into another lucrative speculation. In 1789 he promised one prospective business partner: "I know I could Sell it in One month after it is Procured for Dubble, if not trible, the first cost and a Good Deal of ready money Could be Procured from the Sales."[57]

Cooper pressured Hartwick to sell. The minister recalled, "He declared before a Number of Workmen eating at Dinner with him that I was not welcome at Coopers-Town as a Domine [i.e., a minister of the Gospel] and desired me to sell my Land to him, offering to pay for it in hard Dollars." Desiring payment in souls rather than dollars, Hartwick refused to sell. But Cooper was a determined and resourceful man. He learned of the mortgage deed Hartwick had given to Goldsborough Banyar in 1761 to secure the money needed to survey and patent the tract. For want of any payment of either principal or interest for thirty years, Hartwick's initial debt of £127.3.0 had mushroomed to £524.4.7 by 1791. Cooper approached Banyar and bought the mortgage by paying its full cash value. To Hartwick's dismay, his mortgage now belonged to the covetous and hard-driving William Cooper rather than the long-indulgent Goldsborough Banyar. The threat of impending foreclosure obliged Hartwick to generate an immediate income from his tract to redeem the mortgage.[58]

Making the best of his bad situation, Hartwick reluctantly struck a deal with Cooper, entrusting him with management of the patent. In May 1791 Hartwick gave Cooper power of attorney "to settle, lease and improve" the tract by leasing lots for ten years at an annual rent of 1 shilling per acre. Apparently at Cooper's insistence, the leases also gave the tenant the option to buy freehold title by paying an additional 14 shillings per acre, at the conclusion of the ten years. If the tenant failed to exercise that option, the lands were to revert to Hartwick. Because of the option these were leases in name only, but apparently Hartwick clung to the distinction and failed to see that he was about to swap ownership for money. In return for a commission of 5 percent of the value of the principal, Cooper was to bear the costs to survey and convey the lands. He was to collect the annual rents, retaining all of the income until he was paid his commission and refunded for the £524.4.7 that he had paid Banyar (plus a £20 loan advanced by Cooper to the impecunious Hartwick). Thereafter Hartwick would receive all additional proceeds from the "leases."[59]

Misunderstanding Cooper's intentions and the true nature of the leases, Hartwick expected to regain possession of the leased lands at the expiration of the ten years. Indeed, he naively instructed Cooper to lay out the tract in "small Lotts for a Close and easy Setlement, for I intend to Form my Setlement into a Congregation." Ignoring Hartwick's wishes, Cooper hastily leased almost all the patent before the minister could revoke his power of attorney. To transfer as much land as possible as quickly as possible from Hartwick to tenants, Cooper leased very large parcels, in direct violation of his informal instructions. During a ten-day period that began on June 11, he issued thirty-two leases to fifty-four individuals (many of the leases went to partnerships) for a total of 13,133 acres—over three-quarters of the 16,000 acres entrusted to his agency by Hartwick. The average lease was for 410 acres and almost every one was far in excess of a standard farm of 100 acres. In further defiance of Hartwick's wishes, Cooper indiscriminately leased the land to transients and petty speculators, as well as to real settlers.[60]

To minimize his own costs and accelerate the sales, Cooper issued the leases without first surveying their bounds. This was recklessly irresponsible behavior for a land agent but exactly what he had done in 1786 with his own patent. At the same time that Cooper was rectifying his previous mistakes on the Otsego Patent, he repeated them on the Hartwick Patent. Cooper understood that his rapid and extensive sales in 1786 had served his prime purpose: to preclude rivals from repossessing the Otsego Patent. Similarly determined permanently to alienate Hartwick's lands, Cooper repeated the practice in 1791. In time he would deal with the inevitable disputes and defaults.[61]

Hartwick was understandably upset at the unexpected alienation in large tracts of almost all the lands he had intended for compact settlement as the New Jerusalem. As soon as he realized what Cooper was up to (June 20), Hartwick revoked the power-of-attorney. He empowered a new agent, his friend Jeremiah Van Rensselaer of Albany, with specific instructions that he was to lease no lot larger than 100 acres; no purchaser was to have more than one lot; only actual settlers could purchase; and they were "to build their Houses in one Straight Row." But the damage to Hartwick's project had been done; there was not enough land left for his agent to shape a settlement that could be a New Jerusalem, and for at least ten years nothing could be done to reclaim the leased lands. Indeed, Cooper was at work accumulating possession of the lands he had leased.[62]

In 1793 Jeremiah Van Rensselaer ordered a comprehensive resurvey of the Hartwick Patent because he suspected that Cooper had overestimated the land included in the leases. Van Rensselaer's surveyor, William Ellison, discovered the fact that the lots were systematically "crooked & erronious" because Cooper's surveyor had "taken off every lot as much as will make up for what he Infringed on the Patent." Instead of the 13,133 estimated acres of 1791, the leased lots amounted to 11,527 acres. The average lot was an actual 371 acres rather than the estimated 410 acres. Every lot was smaller than Cooper had estimated, precisely because his original encroachment of 1786 had shrunk the lands remaining in the Hartwick Patent by about 3,000 acres. Ellison declared, "In the first place, it was a Premeditated Deception, and secondly, an Ignorant performance." Noting Cooper's refusal to cooperate with the resurvey, Ellison remarked, "He does not know what to do with himself for such bare-faced Proceedings."[63]

It became apparent that Cooper's eagerness to buy the Hartwick Patent, his purchase of the Banyar mortgage, his reckless leases in 1791, the lot shrinkage in 1792, and his attempts to discourage Ellison's resurvey in 1793 all stemmed from his determination to conceal his original encroachment of 1786. Jeremiah Van Rensselaer concluded,

> If Mr. Cooper had only part of the Candor of a Judge he would say that "I have made an Error, [at] first I suppose for the want of Better Information. I have under the original title of Croghan lapped on Hartwick's Patent & when the mistake was discovered, I obtained the agency of Mr. Hartwick to divide his patent and that, in order to Cover the Error, I deducted a proportion from Each of the Shares so as to Save the Error which I at first Committed, . . . and this deception lay Undiscovered for near 2 Years and that Complaints being made to J.V.R. he had a Resurvey made of the patent agreable to the partition deed & thereby discovered that I had in my possession, or others under my title, 3000 Acres of Land the Just Property of Mr. Hartwick's share and that, in order to Cover this Error (the best name to be put on it), I have . . . made Leases for the premises aforesaid to such persons which by previous Agreements would relinquish the same to me."[64]

Ellison's discoveries alarmed the tenants, who feared that they would have to pay for more land than they had, in fact, received and that they would endure uncertain titles and chronic boundary disputes. To ease their discontents Cooper convened a meeting of the settlers at his Manor House in early November. After assuring them that no man would be overcharged, Cooper pointedly asked, "Who would give their voice to live under him or Mr. Hartwick?" Put that way, almost all of the settlers decided that they preferred Cooper as their landlord. He persuaded all the tenants, save three, that the surest way to protect their titles and fix their boundaries was to assign Cooper their old leases and to take new subleases from him. As with his redeeding of the Otsego Patent in 1789–1793, Cooper rearranged the Hartwick Patent into smaller, more manageable lots: some 104 men received an average of 115 acres each. They would pay Cooper only for the actual acreage of their lots at the original rate of 1 shilling per acre annually and 14 shillings per acre by June 1801 to secure the permanent title. Cooper assumed responsibility for paying Hartwick the entire amount due from all the lands leased in 1791. With the reassignments Cooper obtained effective control of most of Hartwick's lands, so long as he made the payments to Hartwick on schedule.[65]

Hartwick was infuriated that the resourceful Cooper had exploited Ellison's disagreeable discoveries, and the consequent settler unease, to complete his effort to become the leaseholder for almost all the patent. Hartwick insisted that Cooper had told the assembled settlers, "that now he had at last got from the old Rascal what he had been so long after, the Right of my Patent." But there was nothing Hartwick could do to unravel Cooper's coup. Jeremiah Van Rensselaer warned him that it was wiser to accept Cooper's payments than to endure the "vexations and perplexity . . . owing to the Errors and mistakes committed by him. Whether it is done designedly by him or not is not now the question. *It is done.*" In August of 1794 Hartwick reluctantly accepted Van Rensselaer's advice and Cooper's money. Hartwick's capitulation meant that his patent would develop as a rural satellite of the commercial village of Cooperstown rather than as a New Jerusalem isolated from a materialistic world.[66]

Convinced that Hartwick was a hopeless incompetent, Cooper believed that he had done everyone a good turn by taking control of the patent and transferring possession so rapidly to settlers. At last the Hartwick Patent would develop to the benefit of Cooperstown and the surrounding county. At last settlers could obtain freehold title to farms in the Hartwick Patent. At last William Cooper was safe from the consequences of his mistaken encroachment of 1786. And at last John Christopher Hartwick had a large and steady annual income. In 1794 Cooper bluntly informed Hartwick:

> And now, Sir, having stated Precisely the truth of Our buisiness which is fair, honest, and honorably right on my Part, I have to remind you that your Situation was a deplorable one untill I rescued your Property from a Mortgage that had lain on it near thirty years at a time when money was hard to obtain. From

not haveing things Comfortable, you [now] have, by my Exertions, near [£]1,000 a year. Then you had not a friend but myself and Mr. Van Rensselaer. Those who now will Serve you for money, you then Could not Command. For me to Seeke an advantage of you would be base, but for you to give me unjust troble is the worst of Ingratitude.

Surely, Cooper reasoned, Hartwick was far better off with money than with the land that had lain idle and unproductive in his hands for thirty years.[67]

Financially, Cooper had provided Hartwick with a very good deal. In addition to rescuing his patent from Banyar's mortgage, Cooper had generated an additional £675.10.8 in revenue out of the first three years of the leaseholds. Thereafter, Cooper's arrangement provided an annual revenue from rents of at least £576.7.0 for seven more years. Moreover, Cooper was committed to pay Hartwick a further sum of £8,068.18.0 by July 1801 to secure full title to the land. In America during the 1790s, land abounded, cash was scarce, and settlers were notoriously unreliable debtors. Having the wealthy William Cooper for a debtor was a far more attractive prospect than relying on payments from several dozen settlers of limited means. Almost any other frontier landlord would have leapt at the opportunity to reap 24 shillings per acre in cash within ten years. This price compares very favorably with Cooper's purchase in 1796 of a similar tract of Otsego County land—the 16,000-acre Hillington Patent—for 20 shillings per acre.[68]

But Hartwick had not sought personal wealth. In 1795 and 1796 he refused to touch the additional revenue that Cooper collected and deposited in an Albany bank on his account. Hartwick devoted his life to the pursuit of an elusive New Jerusalem: a compact community that would sustain a harmonious and deferential congregation committed to his stewardship. Hartwick's dream collapsed when that philistine William Cooper converted his precious land into so much mammon. As Hartwick saw it, Cooper arranged the Hartwick Patent into a typical American landscape of over-large and dispersed farms where common folk could lead unsupervised lives of disorder and immorality. Aware that his time on earth was ebbing, Hartwick invested his hopes in drafting and redrafting his last will and testament. He appointed "*for my Heirs,* Jesus Christ, the son of God and man" and directed his executors to establish a "regular town, close built, to be called New Jerusalem" and to feature a seminary for training missionaries among the Indians. Hartwick counted on his executors somehow to reclaim the land and fulfill the uncompleted mission.[69]

On July 17, 1796, Hartwick died at Clermont Manor, where he had stopped on his journey up the Hudson River from New York City bound for Albany. He died but a few miles from the church where he had begun his American ministry in 1746 and where he had been assaulted and humiliated by his congregation in 1750. At his death all he owned, beyond the funds due from Cooper on the leases, were the clothes on his back, 600 books ("mostly in the dead Languages"), and the last will and testament describing his plan for the New Jerusalem.[70]

USURPER ౭

Cooper worked his way up the social ladder at the expense of the decaying estates of George Croghan, Joseph Wharton, Dr. John Morgan, Gov. William Franklin, and John Christopher Hartwick. In acquiring the Otsego and Hartwick patents, William Cooper acted within the letter of the law but violated the niceties of genteel conduct, infuriating his rivals. By wresting land away from older, more deliberate men who had been slow to protect and develop their claims, Cooper acted as a new man of the Revolutionary generation rather than with the restraint expected of the ideal colonial gentleman. Men of old prestige but diminished means, the rivals interpreted Cooper's aggressive ambition and upward mobility as perfect proof that the Revolution had disordered society and perverted justice. Regarding him as a presumptuous upstart, they considered Cooper's success as the crowning indignity in their own slide from wealth and power.

William Franklin was incredulous when he belatedly learned that the Otsego Patent had been auctioned in his name but without his permission to a former wheelwright and shopkeeper. From exile in London, he asked,

> Whether, after I had paid off half the Claimants for the Sum lent, and entered up Croghan's Judgment Bond and foreclosed the Equity of Redemption on his Mortgage, in my name, with the consent of the remaining half of the [Burlington] Company, to enable me to discharge the whole of the Debt, they could without any previous demand or Notice given me, assign the Bond and Mortgage to others, and those others proceed in my name without my consent to Execution and Sale of the Lands Mortgaged.

He fumed in impotent rage an ocean away from the intrigues and maneuvers that had stripped him of his last remaining asset in America.[71]

Unable to best Cooper in the struggle for property, the defeated gentlemen sought consolation in their self-righteous sense of class superiority. Morgan bitterly attacked Cooper and Craig as mere "shopkeepers" and as "men who place self-interest the first in the list of moral virtues and [regard] justice to their neighbors, as an obsolete command." Morgan characterized them as "men void of Principle & Veracity & full of low Cunning & Deceit." In defeat, Morgan became a poor and embittered recluse who blamed his lost fortune and declining status on the Revolution's weakening of deference by the common toward the genteel. On October 15, 1789, his friend

Benjamin Rush reported, "This afternoon I was called to visit Dr. Morgan, but found him dead in a small hovel, surrounded with books and papers, and on a light dirty bed. . . . What a change from his former rank and prospects in Life! The man who once filled half the world with his name, had now scarcely friends enough left to bury him."[72]

Mired in genteel poverty, Joseph Wharton bitterly resented losing the Otsego Patent to "Cooper, the hated Land Jobber." Wharton blamed him for "the sufferings of a virtuous family for many years by his subterfuges and contrivances—whereby we have sustained not only the loss of a great fortune, but met miseries of body and mind—in every shape unequalled and undeserved—and by which, he hath grown rich and great." In 1797 Wharton sarcastically wrote to Cooper:

> *Is there (and I apply to your own* interested knowledge*) a more unhappy Man, than I am, and have been*—principally by your virtuous Purchase of Property, which ought to have been sacredly left unbought for the benefit of the Widow, Fatherless and Oppressed? *But God! will yet do Justice; and Riches thus unmercifully and uncharitably obtained, have made themselves Wings and flown away; and hence though the sufferers in New York and Pennsylvania have been deprived of their Rights, by your unworthy and unexpected interference, they trust that they and their Children will not want Bread to eat, while you and yours, for a while, may riot in luxury and dissipation on the Spoils of their unhappy condition.*

His warning seemed to prophesy the ultimate collapse of the Cooper estate.[73]

In *The Pioneers* James Fenimore Cooper aptly represented his father's victory as rooted in a bourgeois revolutionary upheaval that permitted ambitious middling men to prey upon the property and positions of colonial gentlemen. The novelist contrasted the bourgeois character of Marmaduke Temple with the aristocratic hauteur of the Effinghams. They dedicated themselves to pursuits of military and civic honor, because they considered it "a degradation . . . to descend to the pursuits of commerce." In contrast, "Marmaduke was uniformly equable, penetrating, and full of activity and enterprise." Recognizing Temple's social inferiority as well as his entrepreneurial talents, Major Effingham's son secretly employed the young Quaker to manage a mercantile firm in Pennsylvania before the Revolution. Temple's "prudence and sagacity" quickly won "rich returns" on their capital.[74]

Then the Revolution toppled the Effinghams by promoting the upward mobility of Marmaduke Temple. Loyalists, the Effinghams fled the country while Temple profited from choosing the winning side: "Marmaduke never seemed to lose sight of his own interests; for, when the estates of the adherents of the crown fell under the hammer, by the acts of confiscation, he appeared in New-York and became the purchaser of extensive possessions, at comparatively, low prices." His acquisitions included the Otsego lands of the Effinghams. As a consequence, "His property increased in a ten-fold ratio, and he was already ranked among the most wealthy and important of his countrymen." By "purchasing estates that had been wrested by violence from others," Temple provoked "dark hints concerning the sudden prosperity of the unportioned Quaker." Just as Morgan, Wharton, and Franklin had assailed William Cooper's ascent as unmerited and unjust, the Effingham heir denounces Temple as an unscrupulous usurper: "The wolf of the forest is not more rapacious for his prey, than that man is greedy of gold; and yet his glidings into wealth are subtle as the movements of a serpent." Virtually repeating Joseph Wharton's curse, young Effingham seethes, "Let [Temple] and his daughter riot in their wealth—a day of retribution will come."[75]

In the end, by sleight of plot, the novelist dissolved all criticism of Temple's character and title, revealing that the Effinghams had misunderstood his true motives and measures: to preserve and enhance their property until they could return from exile to America. Cooper reduces Temple to a mere caretaker of aristocratic property, the proper role for bourgeois talents according to the novelist. Born to privilege, James Fenimore Cooper preferred men of inherited wealth and position and distrusted aggressive and ingenious strivers who sought and made their own fortunes—as his father had done. Although the novelist recognized the bourgeois origins and implications of the American Revolution, he was quick to insist that its rupture in social hierarchy and private property rights was only temporary. In the novel's conclusion, Cooper calls a halt to the Revolution in Otsego, by retiring Marmaduke Temple and restoring Oliver Effingham to possession of the Otsego Patent.[76]

Before this tortured resolution, James Fenimore Cooper conveyed the essential meaning of his father's ascent. By disrupting the interests of the colonial gentry, the Revolution enabled the upstart William Cooper to grab property and influence that had been far beyond his reach under the colonial regime. He exploited the revolutionary upheaval to wrest property from gentlemen scattered and weakened by the war. By aggressively accumulating property at the expense of more genteel and ineffectual rivals, William Cooper had also reaped a reputation for cunning ambition and flexible scruples. By promoting Cooper's vision of commercial settlement, the Revolution obliterated Croghan's vision of an aristocratic estate, Moses the Mohawk's vision of Indian persistence, and Hartwick's vision of a religious utopian community.

The novelist understood that William Cooper did not do full justice to himself when, in *A Guide in the Wilderness*, he cast his accomplishment at Otsego as bringing about the triumph of society over nature, of civilization over savagery. At Otsego William Cooper's primary challenge came not from nature, but from the legal and political tangles generated by his own society. Those legal and political complications encumbered the land and slowed its colonial settlement. Abetted by a Revolution he had not supported, Cooper overcame a welter of debts and mortgages that had frustrated and ruined an array of wealthier, better-connected, and more genteel men.

Chapter Four

SETTLEMENT

I N *The Pioneers* JAMES FENIMORE COOPER celebrated the transformation of Otsego into a landscape of farms, but he rued the wasteful rapidity with which the settlers conquered the forest. He detected an irrational, emotional impulse at work in the slaughter of game, fish, and trees: a mass

"No, Bess," cried the Judge, . . . "he wh hears of the settlement of a country knows but little of the toil and sufferin, by which it is accomplished."

—James Fenimore Cooper,
The Pioneers, 235

killing beyond all considerations of economic need and interest. Emigrating from districts already deforested and depleted of wildlife, settlers felt giddy with their new power to kill and consume nature on an unprecedented scale. In the novel only Natty Bumppo and Chingachgook limit their demands on nature; they alone seek an equilibrium with the forest and its creatures. The two old hunters despair at the invasion of Yankee settlers dedicated to destroying the trees and wildlife and determined to make a sport, a carnival of their carnage. Billy Kirby represents the aggressive newcomers waging spirited warfare on the forest. Gregarious, boisterous, boastful, and strong, Kirby delights in the destructive power he exercises over trees: "Chopping comes quite nateral to me, and I wish no other emplyment. . . . To my eyes, they are a sore sight at any time, unless I'm privileged to work my will on them; in which case, I can't say but they are more to my liking."[1]

The other settlers follow Kirby's example in assailing nature with a mixture of vengeance and delight. Templeton erupts with excited activity on a spring morning when a vast flock of pigeons darkens the sky: "If the heavens were alive with pigeons, the whole village seemed equally in motion, with men, women, and children." Armed with shotguns, pistols, bows and arrows, makeshift crossbows, long poles, and even a small cannon, the settlers rush to the slope of Mount Vision to indulge in an orgy of mindless, joyous, wasteful killing: "None pretended to collect the game, which lay scattered over the fields in such profusion, as to cover the very ground with the fluttering victims." Excerpting the scene from the novel, a Cooperstown newspaper editor effused in 1823 that the pigeon hunt was "painted to the life, as we can vouch, having ourselves witnessed similar sport upon the same favoured spot."[2]

One June night Templeton's settlers again achieve a sense of communitas by gathering to slaughter Otsego bass pulled from the lake. Because "the slow, though certain adventures with hook and line were ill-suited to the profusion and impatience of the settlers," they build a great bonfire to attract the fish to the beach and employ a boat to lay a seine net "fifty or sixty fathoms in length" into the dark water. Then the settlers haul on ropes to pull ashore the seine heavy with the fishes "entangled in the meshes of the net." "Inflamed beyond the bounds of discretion" at "the sight of the immense piles of fish, that were slowly rolling over on the gravelly beach," the villagers deposit "the whole shoal of victims . . . in a hollow of the bank, where they were left to flutter away their brief existence." The night and their energies spent, the villagers leave most of the fish to rot. "I call it sinful and wasty to catch more than can be eat," Natty Bumppo declaims in futile disgust.[3]

Judge Marmaduke Temple tries to persuade Natty that they share a common unease with the wasteful slaughter of the pigeons and the bass: "Like all the other treasures of the wilderness, they already begin to disappear before the wasteful extravagance of man." The judge insists that he can save a measure of nature, or at least slow its destruction, by enforcing new laws designed to restrict the settlers. But at both the pigeon hunt and the fish seining, he utterly fails to persuade his companions to limit their killing. Ineffectual, Temple forgets his qualms, succumbs to the excitement, and joins in the festive slaughter, manifesting his inability, ultimately, to rise above the emotional mass of common men.[4]

Recognizing the shallowness of Judge Temple's laments, Natty rejects his overtures. Natty realizes that Temple profits from the settler invasion; and he understands, as the judge does not, that no law can restrain the carnage wreaked on nature by the settlers. Natty Bumppo pleads, "Put an ind, Judge, to your clearings. An't the woods his work as well as the pigeons? Use, but don't waste. Wasn't the woods made for the beasts and birds to harbour in?" He later adds, "No, no: we are not much of one mind, Judge, or you'd never turn good hunting grounds into stumpy pastures." Natty gives voice to James Fenimore Cooper's understanding that his father's profits and prospects as a frontier developer depended on the changes in the land effected by the settlers. By facilitating Otsego's commercial integration into the international market, William Cooper accelerated the changes that Natty laments in the novel.[5]

SETTLERS 🔥

During the late 1780s and early 1790s William Cooper aggressively and shrewdly accumulated thousands of acres in the Otsego country. But to avert financial ruin Cooper and Andrew Craig needed to reap a steady revenue in time to meet their own pressing debts to the men who had sold them Croghan's securities. For, in selling land to cash-poor farmers, Cooper and Craig had to forgo down payments and look to the future when the settlers could pay out of the produce they generated by clearing and cultivating the land. Cooper's sales and maneuvers would all come to naught if the buyers did not stay to improve and pay for their lands, if instead they forsook their Otsego lots to try again elsewhere. On the other hand, if his first settlers persisted, prospered, and paid, word of their success would draw additional settlers, sustaining and accelerating development. The first decade of settlement would make or break Cooper's new settlement and his heavily leveraged estate.[6]

In the late 1780s it was far from certain that William Cooper was up to the complicated challenge of managing the settlement of thousands of acres in a distant forest. An outsider and a novice who had never before speculated in frontier land, he was not yet the self-assured expert in speculation and settlement who appears in the pages of *A Guide in the Wilderness* written in 1807, after he had succeeded. Before 1786 he had speculated in a few town lots and old farms in the tamed land of New Jersey, but he had never before taken on 29,350 acres of frontier land. He knew very little about either central New York or the techniques of settlement. Because he had ventured more than he was worth in buying the Otsego Patent, in indemnifying Sheriff Clyde, and in offering warrantee deeds, William Cooper faced ruin if his new settlement failed. Moreover, George Croghan and the Burlington Company were discouraging precedents. They had accrued heavy debts instead of revenue from their expensive efforts to attract paying settlers to the Otsego country before the war. Neither as wealthy nor as well connected politically as their predecessors, Cooper and Craig seemed doomed to fail.[7]

Croghan and the Burlington Company had attracted so few settlers because the Otsego hills presented an especially daunting challenge to settlement. On the one hand, Otsego was all too richly endowed with the wild life that settlers needed to subdue; a heavy, thick forest of hardwood and hemlock trees covered the hills and sheltered large populations of carnivorous mammals: bears, panthers, and wolves. On the other hand, Otsego was relatively unpromising for the grains cultivated by settlers. Owing to its elevation, 1,000 to 2,000 feet above sea level, Otsego had a growing season of only 100 to 150 days compared to 150 to 180 days in the lower, warmer Hudson and Mohawk valleys. Moreover, as a hilly country, Otsego had relatively few alluvial flats annually replenished with humus by spring floods. Consequently, settlers steadily depleted the nutrients of the Otsego soil as they stripped off the forest cover to plow and harvest for grains. Because Otsego's upland soils did not bear up well under sustained grain cropping, settlers regularly had to clear new fields for cultivation—a laborious process with oxen and axes.[8]

The longer-resident Dutch and German settlers of upstate New York disdained the uplands and clung close to the Mohawk, Hudson, and Schoharie rivers, farming the fertile alluvial flats. Subject to annual floods, the flats were rich in topsoil and annual plants but relatively free from large, thick trees. A surveyor noted, "The Flats in general are easily Cleared; in many Places a Man might Clear an Acre in a Day," in contrast to the heavily timbered hills, where it took about two weeks to clear an acre. To the Dutch and Germans, clearing the uplands hardly seemed worthwhile, given that the relatively thin topsoils of the hills began to wear out after a few years of grain cropping. Nahum Jones, a Yankee sojourning in the Mohawk valley, observed, "The Dutch People seldom attempt new settlements. They stick to the old Hive. A half dozen sons with their families will settle and continue upon the old farm with their father, though it contains no more than 200 acres. Before the [New] English came among them, they thought the upland of no worth."[9]

Unlike the old-stock Yorkers, the postwar Yankee newcomers readily settled in the hills that resembled their New England homeland. Adept at clearing a heavily timbered land and reconciled to a hilly terrain, the Yankees were the perfect settlers for Otsego. Indeed, most Yankee settlers preferred to avoid the bottomlands as unhealthy and too expensive (and too crowded with the Dutch and Germans). Yankees were hill people; Yorkers were valley people. In defying New York's authorities on behalf of Vermont's independence, the rebellious Yankee Ethan Allen had boasted, "The Gods of the hills are not the Gods of the valley." Mutual prejudice and animosity also worked to keep the two populations apart, concentrated in their different environmental niches. Fortunately for William Cooper, during the later eighteenth century circumstances impelled a swelling migration westward into New York by the very people best suited to settle his Otsego holdings.[10]

In the mid and late eighteenth century, population growth in the long-settled parts of New England set Yankees in motion northward and westward in search of the freehold land that grew increasingly expensive at home. By 1775 the typical southern New England farm of fifty acres was barely adequate to feed, house, heat, and clothe a family. New England's shrinking farms also suffered increasingly from crop pests and from a soil exhaustion wrought by overcropping and overgrazing. Firewood had also grown scarce in southern New England as the Yankees cleared away most of the region's forest. "The scarcity of fuel in the old settlements of New-England is becoming a very serious matter to the inland villages and towns. . . . Land is there much too dear and scant to raise wood upon, and as *men* and *women* are raised with less *labor* than *oaks* the disproportion in supplies of fuel, will not only continue, but must encrease," observed Elihu Phinney, who emigrated to Cooperstown. Yet Yankees continued to reproduce; the average couple reared six to seven children, only one of whom could obtain the home farm.[11]

To escape looming poverty, thousands of young Yankees sought their own substantial freehold farms by emigrating to the frontier. The Yankees of Connecticut and western Massachusetts headed northward up the Connecticut and Housatonic valleys into the Berkshires and the Green Mountains. Some in this stream spilled over to the west, across the border into New York. That spillage became the main current after 1783 as the Yankee torrent flowed westward through Albany or Catskill into central, northern, and western New York. Almost all of William Cooper's first buyers were hill Yankees from the border country where western Massachusetts and Vermont bounded on eastern New York. At least fifty-four of the seventy-four buyers came from three then contiguous counties—Berkshire in Massachusetts, Bennington in Vermont, and Albany in New York. Two especially large clusters of buyers came from the towns of Great Barrington (twenty-three) in Berkshire County and Hoosick (twelve) in Albany County.[12]

In addition to the push of population growth and land depletion at home, the Yankee migrants felt the pull of superior new opportunities in upstate New York. In particular, New York offered better lands and transportation for settlers keen to exploit the improving export market for American wheat. During the late 1780s and early 1790s the European demand for imported wheat surged as a consequence of bad harvests and devastating warfare on that continent. The swelling exports to Europe translated into enhanced prices and profits for the merchants and farmers dwelling in the Middle Atlantic states, then the great American breadbasket region. Lands previously marginal for wheat cultivation, by dint of relative infertility or distance from seaport market, assumed increased value during the 1790s. At 1772 price levels, farmers within 64 miles of a seaport could bear the cost to transport their wheat to market and still turn a profit; the enhanced prices of 1800 more than doubled that range, to 143 miles. Because Otsego lay about 80 to 100 miles from Albany, that doubling moved the region within the orbit of the wheat market. The unusually favorable market conditions more than compensated for Otsego's relative agricultural liabilities.[13]

No state received a greater boost from the expanded wheat trade than New York, which possessed both an extensive hinterland of unsettled land *and* the Hudson-Mohawk system of navigable rivers that made it relatively easy and cheap for upstate farmers to get their produce to market. Near the juncture of the Mohawk with the Hudson, Albany became the great linchpin of the wheat trade in upstate New York. Employing heavy sleighs in winter and boats or wagons in summer and fall, farmer-teamsters brought wheat to Albany in loads of about 20 to 25 bushels at a time. Levi Beardsley recalled the two-and-a-half-day journey from Otsego to Albany on a sleigh laden with wheat: "It was a curious sight to observe the immense number of sleighs, on approaching the city; a string a mile long was no uncommon occurrence." Albany's merchants bought the wheat for loading onto sloops bound down the Hudson to New York City. Sold or consigned to the city's wholesale merchants, the wheat was reloaded onto larger oceangoing ships for export to Europe. The ships returned with manufactured goods, especially cloth and metal tools, which then passed upriver in the sloops to Albany for dispersal among the farmer-customers in payment for their wheat.[14]

The wheat boom stimulated the Yankee emigration out of relatively infertile and inaccessible rural New England to the more fertile and market-accessible counties of upstate New York. Although not durable, the upland soils offered an initial bonus of virgin humus. Newly cultivated lands offered superior yields during the first few years of cropping: 20 to 25 bushels of wheat per acre, compared to the 12 to 16 that was the standard on older, long-tilled, upland fields. New lands also offered a temporary escape from wheat's debilitating parasites—especially a fungus known as the blast (black stem rust) and an insect known as the Hessian Fly. Both parasites had followed the colonists from Europe to devastate the wheat crops in much of New England and eastern New York. Both would continue to follow westward, but, by racing ahead, the frontier settler obtained a few years' dispensation. In 1795 the Cooperstown newspaper exulted, "Never Since America was first discovered did the American Farmers realize so much prosperity as in the present day." The writer urged the settlers "to exert all your efforts to improve every inch of ground, and every hand that can be put to agriculture, in multiplying provisions of every kind with uncommon industry and perseverance; for you may not for ages to come, have such another opportunity." Similarly, in *The Pioneers* Marmaduke Temple assures Billy Kirby, a Yankee settler, "So long as the old world is to be convulsed with wars, so long will the harvest of America continue." The pace of Yankee settlement was sensitive to the ebb and flow of transatlantic political and economic forces.[15]

In sum, during the 1780s and 1790s Cooper enjoyed far better circumstances for settlement than Croghan and the Burlington Company had known during the 1760s and 1770s. He acquired and began to develop his Otsego settlement at an unusually auspicious moment. Cooper and Craig obtained the Otsego Patent in the mid-1780s at a bargain price because the recent war and economic hard times had depressed the value of frontier land. Then Cooper had the good fortune to develop his new property during the late 1780s and early 1790s, when land values surged on the New York frontier as thousands of Yankee settlers migrated westward and as the demand for and price of wheat surged. At the same time, most Yankees avoided the lands farther west along the Great Lakes and in the Ohio Valley, regarding them as too distant and dangerous so long as the Indians there remained formidable and hostile. During the 1780s and 1790s the Yankee emigrants were pushed out of New England, drawn into central New York, but deterred from proceeding on to the more fertile lands and more temperate climes farther west. Never before and never again was Otsego so attractive to so many new settlers as the moment when William Cooper became a developer.[16]

To hasten Otsego's development, Cooper confronted a dual challenge. First, he had to learn how to work with his Yankee settlers. Although they were an industrious people skilled at turning marginal lands into farms, the Yankees also had a reputation with most New York landlords as cunning cheats and congenital troublemakers. Second, Cooper had to improve his settlers' access to external markets, thereby enhancing and accelerating their ability to pay him for their lands.

YANKEES

After the war Yankee migrants flocked to upstate New York in numbers that overwhelmed the old stock inhabitants, the diverse medley of Dutch, German, Scotch, English, and Huguenot French collectively called Yorkers. Compared with the diverse Yorkers, the Yankees were a homogeneous people. Almost all had descended from seventeenth-century Puritans who had fled from England to colonize Massachusetts, Connecticut, Rhode Island, and southern New Hampshire. A demanding region of long winters, stony hills, thin topsoil, and heavy forests, New England reinforced the Puritan impulses to frugality, industry, ingenuity, enterprise, and covetousness. In turn, those characteristics enabled the New Englanders to derive sustenance—sometimes prosperity, but rarely wealth—from the grudging land. Compared to other Americans, Yankees were a relatively equal and egalitarian people in the distribution of learning, property, and status. There were some wealthy and some dirt-poor Yankees, but most were literate and independent farmers, artisans, and traders of modest means but great pride. Preserving much of their Puritan heritage, the Yankees continued to think of themselves as God's favored people and resorted to scriptural analogies to describe their actions and purpose. "Emigrants are swarming into these fertile regions in shoals, like the ancient Israelites seeking the land of promise," observed Elkanah Watson, a Yankee migrant and Albany promoter. They worked so diligently, moved in such numbers, over long distances, and cleaved so tightly to one another against other ethnic groups that observers likened the Yankees to bees. "It is equally necessary that

Yankees swarm as it is for bees," one New York land speculator explained.[17]

Their relative equality had a paradoxical effect on Yankee character. On the one hand, Yankees were remarkably competitive, always seeking to win some small measure or token of superior learning, piety, property, or cunning. They prided themselves on every little triumph—in town politics, tavern argument, scriptural disputation, barnyard bargain, or common law litigation—especially if their victory turned on a small ploy of deception. On the other hand, their relative equality and homogeneity also encouraged the Yankees to cooperate in community institutions meant to achieve collective goals. The communal aspect of Yankee culture provided a limiting context for their contestatory behavior as individuals. More than any other people in eighteenth-century America, the Yankees entrusted their town governments with significant powers to sustain schools and churches and to regulate farms and transactions.[18]

The exodus of Yankees into New York brought them into conflict with the old-stock inhabitants, especially those of Dutch and German descent. Yankees could reconcile the paradox between their competition and their cohesion by uniting to contend with their new neighbors in New York. Utterly confident of their own superiority, the Yankees considered the Dutch to be stolid, slovenly, illiterate, immoral, and unambitious dullards. After declaiming against "the hateful & insipid & stupid race of the Dutch," James Kent effused, "The *Yankees* are a glorious People. They at least have good & quick Sense & polished manners & Hospitality & a disposition to oblige & soothe the stranger & the Traveller & their women are amiable & sprightly & tender." New Englanders liked to say that the way to make a Dutchman was to take a Yankee, "break his jaw, and knock his brains out."[19]

Yorkers responded to the Yankee insults in kind. Because the Yankees pursued property and salvation simultaneously and with such unrelenting zeal, Yorkers regarded them as pushy hypocrites. Anne Grant, a landlord's daughter, described the New English as "conceited, litigious, and selfish beyond measure," as "people who acknowledged no superior, who had a thorough knowledge of law and scripture, ready to wrest to every selfish purpose." In his 1760 will, the Westchester County landlord Lewis Morris, Jr., stipulated that his son Gouverneur was never to attend college in Connecticut, "lest he should imbibe in his youth that low craft and cunning so incident to the people of that country . . . though many of them, under the sanctified garb of religion, have endeavored to impose themselves on the world as honest men."[20]

Sharing this contempt for the newcomers, in *The Pioneers* James Fenimore Cooper represented the Yankee settler as Jotham Riddel: "He was of a thin, shapeless figure, with a discontented expression of countenance, and with something extremely shiftless in his whole air." Judge Temple denounces Riddel as "that dissatisfied, shiftless, lazy, speculating fellow! he who changes his county every three years, his farm every six months, and his occupation every season! an agriculturist yesterday, a shoemaker to-day, and a schoolmaster to-morrow! that epitome of all the unsteady and profitless propensities of the settlers." The classic border Yankee, Riddel sells his partly cleared Otsego farm to a "forehanded" newcomer and again moves west to repeat his life of clearing, building, and petty land speculating.[21]

Yorker landlords and Yankee settlers had especially good reasons to distrust each other. New York's colonial governors had sold frontier lands in vast tracts to their wealthy and powerful friends and allies. Determined to live on the annual rents paid by hundreds of tenants, they preferred to lease rather than to sell land. Unlike the Yorkers, who usually accepted—and sometimes prospered under—tenancy, Yankees hated and resisted it. Timothy Dwight of Connecticut found, "In the Yeomanry of this country such a rivited habitual dislike to dependence and controul" that only the most desperate were "willing to live upon rent." The Yankees who settled in the New York border counties often took up arms to defy the landlords who demanded rents or attempted evictions. During the 1770s, the Yankee settlers in the Green Mountains rebelled against their Yorker landlords, seceded from New York, and formed the independent republic of Vermont (which became a state in the American union in 1791). With great difficulty New York's authorities and landlords suppressed the similar resistance that flared intermittently after 1751 (and most seriously in 1766, 1777, and 1791) in the long, hilly strip of land lying between the Hudson and the formal boundary with the New England states. After the Revolution, growing numbers of Yankee migrants pressed on beyond the Hudson and into the newly conquered hills of central New York. There they hoped to find landlords who would sell freehold title to the land. One of those waiting landlords was William Cooper.[22]

As a New York landlord of Pennsylvania and Quaker origins, Cooper initially shared the prejudice against Yankee settlers. As a landlord, he had to be wary of their tricks and resistance. As a Pennsylvanian, he initially misunderstood and disdained the peculiar system of clearing and cultivating land that the Yankees had developed in New England. As a Quaker, he grew up in a culture that regarded the Yankees as violent, arbitrary, callous, and deceitful oppressors. Middle Atlantic Quakers resented the harrassment and persecution their New England brethren and sisters had suffered during the seventeenth century and again during the recent Revolutionary War.[23]

However, frontier experience gradually taught Cooper to admire the Yankees as the very best settlers for his hilly and heavily forested lands. In 1791 Cooper insisted: "What would frighten a Pennsylvinnia farmer is the support of an Easternite. I mean the heavy timber. The Pensylvanyman would look Round and say 'I shall starve before I can Clear me a farm in this kind of land,' but the easternite will say, 'here is a fine chance. I can get immediate Relief from the ashes and whilst I am waiting for the return of my first Crop, the [Maple] Sugar trees will afford me a very seasonable assistance.' " He praised the Yankees as "civil, well-informed, and very sagacious; so that a wise stranger would be much apter to conform at once to their usages than to begin by teaching them better." He reconciled his need for Yankees with his Quaker distrust of their religion by rationalizing that the settlers were victims fleeing from their oppressive Calvinist clergy. In 1789 he announced, "This Valuable Contry is to be Setteled it apeares to me by the heretofore Priest-Riden and Opresd People of New England." They would, he assured himself, find in him a tolerant and benevolent patron.[24]

By working with the newcomers William Cooper ensured that Cooperstown would develop as a Yankee village surrounded by Yankee farms. His success and reputation as a landlord grew in symbiosis with the Yankee exodus into the Otsego country. Among the speculators of Albany, New York City, Philadelphia, and Burlington, Cooper became known as the preeminent developer of upcountry lands precisely because he knew better than anyone else how to attract and work with the Yankees who caused other landlords so much trouble. But, in the late 1780s, Cooper's Otsego venture hung in the balance because too many poor Yankees migrated to his settlements at the wrong moment.

HUNGER

During the late 1780s the severe hardships of frontier life imperiled Cooper's vulnerable new settlements around Lake Otsego. During their first two years on the land, few settlers could clear and cultivate enough land to feed themselves. Thereafter they remained vulnerable to famine when crop diseases or early frosts cut short the harvest in their small clearings. Early settlers also had to fight an often losing battle to defend their orchards, poultry, and livestock from marauding bears and wolves, and to protect their grain and garden plants from pigeons, squirrels, and grasshoppers. In *A Guide in the Wilderness*, William Cooper recalled the early, difficult years of his Otsego settlements:

> But the greatest discouragement was in the extreme poverty of the people, none of whom had the means of clearing more than a small spot in the midst of the thick and lofty woods, so that their grain grew chiefly in the shade; their maize did not ripen; their wheat was blasted, and the little they did gather they had no mill to grind within twenty miles distance; not one in twenty had a horse, and the way lay through rapid streams, across swamps, or over bogs. They had neither provisions to take with them, nor money to purchase them; nor if they had, were any to be found on their way. If the father of a family went abroad to

labour for bread, it cost him three times its value before he could bring it home,
and all the business on his farm stood still till his return.

Even when the settlers could raise sufficient crops, they suffered for the lack
of bridges and roads to carry their produce to market and for their distance
from gristmills to grind their grain into flour. Such settlers had to pound
their corn by hand into meal with a pestle and mortar—long, tedious, back-
numbing labor.[25]

Hunger was especially severe and widespread during the late spring and
early summer, after the previous harvest had been consumed and before
the next ripened. The worst spring for the greatest number was in 1789,
when famine prevailed, threatening Cooperstown and Cooper with ruin. In
April he reported:

> *There remained not one pound of salt meat nor a single biscuit. Many were re-*
> *duced to such distress, as to live upon the roots of wild leeks; some more fortu-*
> *nate lived upon milk, whilst others supported nature by drinking a syrup made*
> *of maple sugar and water. The quantity of [wild] leeks they eat had such an ef-*
> *fect upon their breath, that they could be smelled at many paces distance, and*
> *when they came together, it was like cattle that had pastured in a garlic field. A*
> *man of the name of Beets mistaking some poisonous herb for a leek, eat it, and*
> *died in consequence. Judge of my feelings at this epoch, with two hundred fam-*
> *ilies about me, and not a morsel of bread.*

In *The Pioneers,* James Fenimore Cooper imagined his father's feelings and
assigned them to Marmaduke Temple: "I had hundreds at that dreadful
time, daily looking up to me for bread. The sufferings of their families, and
the gloomy prospect before them, had paralysed the enterprise and efforts
of my settlers; hunger drove them to the woods for food, but despair sent
them, at night, enfeebled and wan, to a sleepless pillow."[26]

Nonetheless, poor families kept arriving from New England, seeking
land and food. In May, Cooper explained to his friend (and fellow land
speculator) Henry Drinker, "The Vast Multitudes of People that Come
Dayly to this Country have Causd a Scarcity of Provitions allmost to Famine.
. . . Henry, I have had 30 in a Day Seaking Lands of me but [who] Could not
Look out much in the woods for want of Something to Subsist upon." Ironically, William Cooper had been all too successful at drawing large numbers
of new settlers to the Otsego frontier.[27]

Divine providence combined with government aid and William Cooper's
ingenuity to save Otsego from the famine. Schools of herrings ascended the
Susquehanna, filling Otsego Lake: an unusual visitation. Under Cooper's
direction, the settlers wove twigs into a crude seine net to drag through the
river and lake, capturing thousands of fish. Then he supervised the salting
and distribution of the fish to all the starving families. Noting the hunger
prevailing all along the frontier, Gov. George Clinton urged the New York

legislature to act on June 4. In mid-July the legislature appropriated funds for distribution to four counties. The supervisors of Montgomery County received £170, which they allocated among the county's nine townships on July 28. Otsego Township received the largest single appropriation (£30) despite ranking seventh in population: evidence that it was the hungriest community in the county.[28]

The famine lifted as the settlers harvested a good crop in September of 1789 and a still better one in 1790. In July of 1790 Cooper expressed relief: "The Crops here away are much Better than hath been Ever known. My Settelment will have thousands of Bushells." That summer it became clear that the settlement would survive and prosper. Confident that famine would not return, Cooper moved his family to Cooperstown that fall. As the famine receded, settlers flocked to Otsego in growing numbers. In September of 1791 Cooper marvelled, "The intollorable thorofare of People that Dayly beset me here, not in Serch, but Demanding Lands, Renders it impossible for me to Leave Cooperstown on Any Buisiness what Ever." After 1789 particular families and small neighborhoods occasionally suffered for want of food, but there was not another general famine in the Otsego country.[29]

POLICY ☙

William Cooper learned that the key to a successful development was to hasten a settlement through its difficult early stage by drawing onto the land a concentrated population able to assist one another in building an economic and social infrastructure. He explained,

> The reason is plain; the first difficulties are the greatest, and it is only by combination and cooperation that they can be surmounted. The more the settlers are in number, the more hands can be brought to effect those works which cannot be executed by a few; such are the making of roads and bridges . . . which are impossible to individuals, but which numbers render practicable and easy.

Settlers who came to farm could not afford to be unsocial individualists; they came as families, and they succeeded in overcoming their hardships by establishing social bonds with their neighbors. Cooper explained, "He who comes to better his condition, by embarking in such an enterprize, would find it no relief from his present poverty, to be doomed to a life of savage solitude; he will still desire the society of his species, and the ordinary comforts of life; he will look for some religious institution, some school for his children. There must be mechanics to build houses, and erect mills." Every newly cleared and planted acre benefited not merely one family but everyone in the neighborhood. Every expansion of fields and herds increased the local supply of food while subtracting from the forest that harbored the wild predators that afflicted their livestock and crops. Settlers usually worked as distinct family groups on their own property, but because all the families labored in the same way to the same ends, they advanced a common cause. Cooper observed, "Each man prospers in proportion as he contributes to the advantage of his neighbor."[30]

Depending on how well they fared, the first few settlers to a locale would either set in motion or curtail a chain of migration by relatives and kin. Cooper explained: "Such a one may have friends and connexions, who may want courage to face the first difficulties, or venture on untried ways, but whom he hopes to draw after him by example. It is of great importance to promote the success of such a person, and he will be justly entitled to kindness and support. His task will be to smooth the way for others." The successful first settler benefited the developer by drawing along behind a widening network of friends and relatives. The unsuccessful settler moved elsewhere, taking away his potential cluster of followers.[31]

Once a critical mass of settlers had been drawn to the land, they would overwhelm the forest and terminate the initial critical stage of hardships. Then William Cooper could readily attract a steady stream of more cautious and prosperous families by advertising, "Mills, roads, bridges, schools and other conveniences, are already established, in all the different quarters of the county; so that all the most obvious objections and difficulties attending a new settlement are surmounted. Provisions are plenty and cheap." Thereafter, development would become easy and self-sustaining. But to bring on that happy day, the landlord first had to receive and encourage families who could endure life without that infrastructure, who could build it from scratch. Only the sustained exercise of hard labor by a growing population could pull a settlement through to prosperity.[32]

The frontier developer confronted a paradox: the early hardships could only be overcome by the labor of growing numbers of settlers, but those hardships deterred the prosperous farm folk who preferred to wait until a settlement became more comfortable. Landlords longed to attract wealthy investors or prosperous farmers who could pay cash for wilderness land, but few such men ventured to new settlements. Cooper insisted that the solution to the paradox was to make the most of the poor men who were willing to take on the hardships of early settlement: "We must not despise the offer of the poor man. He can never be insignificant, who is willing to add his labour to the common stock: for the interest of every individual, from the richest landholder to the poorest settler, conspires and contributes to the great primary object, to cause the Wilderness to bloom and fructify." By laboring, enduring, and growing in number, the first settlers rendered a neighborhood safer and more attractive to later comers with more money and respectability.[33]

Cooper shrewdly encouraged an enthusiasm and optimism calculated to spur and sustain the exertions of the early settlers:

So, in rural phrase, may we compare the poor settler to the creature of draft. Unsustained, over-loaded, and oppressed, he yields no profit; well treated, in good heart, and gently driven, his labour is lighter, and his profit more. It is no[t] otherwise with man. He can bear so much, and no more; if forced beyond that, his spirits will finally sink under oppression; whereas, by timely aids, encouraging words from a landlord, who has his confidence, and whom he feels to be his friend, he will perform wonders, and exceed his own hopes.

Cooper identified four keys to attracting and inspiring the critical mass of early settlers: freehold title, credit sales at a modest price, opening all lands to settlement, and, above all, the active presence of an encouraging but vigilant landlord. "A moderate price, long credit, a deed in fee, and a friendly landlord are infallible inducements to a numerous settlement," he wrote.[34]

First, Cooper realized that a hill country landlord who sought rapid settlement by Yankees had to sell them freehold title. His advertisements promised, "The industrious farmer need never fear a haughty or griping landlord, since upon the premises here . . . he is the happy master of his own soil." Cooper's need rapidly to sell and settle Otsego converged with the Yankee desire for freehold farms. Cooper disagreed with the many other landlords who would sell freeholds only to the most prosperous settlers, restricting the poor majority to leaseholds for fear that they could never pay the value of the principal. He explained,

The poor man, and his class is the most numerous, will generally undertake about one hundred acres. The best mode of dealing with him, is to grant him the fee simple by deed, and secure the purchase money by a mortgage on the land conveyed to him. He then feels himself, if I may use the phrase, as a man upon record. His views extend themselves to his posterity, and he contemplates with pleasure their settlement on the estate he has created; a sentiment ever grateful to the heart of man. His spirit is enlivened; his industry is quickened; every new object he attains brings a new ray of hope and courage: he builds himself a barn and a better habitation; plants his fruit-trees, and lays out his garden. . . . He no longer feels the weight of debt, for having the fee, he can sell at an improved value, nor is he bound to remain against his will.

By selling freeholds, Cooper energized the Yankee skills at clearing the forest and making new farms.[35]

In contrast, leaseholds kept men poor and disagreeable, to the detriment of their landlord. "Gloomy apprehensions . . . seize upon [the tenant's] mind; the bright view of independence is clouded; his habits of thought become sullen and cheerless, and he is unable to soar above the idea of perpetual poverty," Cooper remarked. Because the tenant usually maximized his exactions from the land and minimized his improvements, most tenant farms in New York were notorious for their ramshackle buildings, slovenly fields, impoverished soil, and mounting arrears in rent. In 1804 William Cooper assured his friend Gouverneur Morris that settlers prospered where they could buy freehold title but stagnated where tenancy prevailed. "If you would Honor Us with a visit in Otsego, you would see the diference between two Extensive Pattents settled on the two Plans. One is a nest of Beggars and Thieves—the other [has] Every Mark of Welth about it. You will say my Plan is best for the Landlord, [the farmer], and the State."[36]

Second, Cooper sold land at a modest price on a relatively long credit: ten years, versus the three to five years preferred by many other landlords. In 1789 he exhorted a partner in land speculation, "Let this be the wach word: Strike wile the iron is hot: take Settelers while we Can git them for be Assured there is more Land than People—and he that Sells his Land for 10 [shillings per acre] and gits it improved is better off than he that talks of 20 [shillings] and Leaves it unimproved." Because it took about five years for a settler to derive an agricultural surplus from a new farm, a high price or a short credit would only discourage and depress his efforts. The settler would seek mere subsistence and eventually flee if he could not improve the value of his lands faster than the 7 percent annual interest accumulating on his principal. Cooper warned other speculators: "I have seen some that will take Lands on any termes and in the End Doe nothing for themselves, or the Proprietor but spend their time in Guning, Fishing &c and for a small Consideration sell their Possestion and Away for a new Place. Those the Better Sort Call *Squatters.*" The squatters minimized the labor they invested in the land while maximizing what they extracted; they meant to move on once they had exhausted the soil and timber and before the landlord could collect any payment.[37]

Third, Cooper argued that the truly canny landlord offered all of his land, even the best lots, for sale on credit at a standard price to the first comers. Naturally, the first settlers snatched up the prime lots at the modest price. But in time, as the settlement matured, later comers and the maturing sons of the first settlers would pay enhanced prices for the rougher lands. Cooper condemned the landlords who reserved valuable tracts from settlement for appreciation and future sale. Every empty lot without a settler was a deadweight on the settlement, a debit from the pool of labor needed to break the forest, and a source of resentment.[38]

A reassuring, resident landlord was Cooper's fourth and consummate key to maximizing the settlers' improving labor. Active and enthusiastic at visiting and encouraging his settlers, Cooper nurtured "that confidence which alone could animate and invigorate a difficult enterprise." In 1789 he insisted that the successful developer was "Continually among the People" acting "as a Soul to the Settelments to incorrage, Contrive, Salve over Littel matters and in short Oppose Every thing that Opposes the Progress of the Settelment. This is what hath Put my Settelment forward so rappidly."[39]

A landlord's work was not done once settlers contracted to buy land. He could not simply and safely sit back, waiting for the payments to roll in on schedule. The passive speculator received little or nothing as settlers kept their money or paid their more attentive and insistent creditors, especially storekeepers. The vigilant and diligent landlord applied varying but regular doses of encouragement, suggestion, and pressure to induce payments. In Otsego, Cooper succeeded by living on his patent and by taking pains to visit his settlers and to know their circumstances. He remarked, "As to the perplexity of recovering moneys from new Settlements is to me well known as well by Experiance as common reason—nothing but time and a residence among the Settelers will make them tollorably Productive."[40]

The canny developer guided the process by which frontier farms changed hands from the first penurious settlers to the more prosperous latecomers. Operating within a constant flux of local properties, Cooper had to be attentive for opportunities to collect his debts. He also had to be watchful lest a cunning settler skip town before paying but after stripping his land of its value in timber and topsoil. Many early settlers entered land contracts with a speculator simply to gain legal possession of land that they did not intend to pay for in full. Instead, their strategy was to build up sweat equity by improving the land with buildings, fences, and clearings in order eventually to sell out at an advance to a more prosperous latecomer who would also assume responsibility for paying the landlord. Settlers routinely sent Cooper notes directing him to deed their farms to a certain newcomer "upon such terms as you would have conveyed it to me had I not have sold it to him." Upon selling out, the farm builder moved on to repeat his work elsewhere on the frontier. Although the original farm-makers rarely paid either on schedule or in full, they served the developer's long-term interest, so long as they were hard at work adding value to the land.[41]

In selling land Cooper facilitated with encouragement, rather than complicated with restrictions, the natural process of settlement. Cooper insisted that he succeeded by avoiding the egregious errors of more meddlesome and restrictive landlords who inadvertently prolonged the difficult early stage of settlement. In contrast to many other landlords, he imposed no special covenants or restrictions on his deeds. Cooper played the limited but important role of encouraging, rather than hindering, the latent enterprise of the settlers. By "the simple measure of letting things take their own course, I find my interest and that of the whole community promoted."[42]

CIRCULATION &

In *The Pioneers* Judge Marmaduke Temple insists that economic interest drives human behavior. He characteristically reacts to conflict and responds to
problems by trying to create a market. In the novel's opening scene, he disputes with Natty Bumppo and Oliver Edwards over who owns the freshly
killed deer lying in the snow at their feet. Determined to obtain the carcass
as a trophy, Temple tries to mollify Natty and Oliver with cash: "Shall we toss
up this dollar for the honour, and you keep the silver if you lose—what say
you friend? . . . But you'll sell me the venison; and the deuce is in it, but I
make a good story about its death." Natty defiantly rejects the offer, for he
knows that the intrusion of the market into the forest is the source of his
troubles rather than their solution. Belatedly discovering that his shot had,
in fact, wounded Oliver, Temple immediately improves his offer: "All shall
be done at my expence, and thou shalt live with me until thy wound is
healed. . . . But I buy your deer—here, this bill will pay thee, both for thy
shot and my own." In a subsequent scene, when Temple feels distressed by
thousands of wounded pigeons left on the ground by his mindless settlers,
he creates a market for their mercy killing by offering a price of "sixpence
per hundred for the pigeons' heads only." The "expedient produced the
desired effect, for every urchin on the ground went industriously to work to
wring the necks of the wounded birds."[43]

Like William Cooper in history, Judge Temple in *The Pioneers* anticipates
a future landscape thick with people and their structures and busy with
their commercial activity. It pains him to see potential value laid waste for
want of a market. Temple concludes that the "wastefulness of the settlers,
with the noble trees of this country, is shocking," because they let rot logs
that "would have sold in the Philadelphia market for twenty dollars."
Richard Jones retorts, "How is the poor devil to get his logs to the Philadelphia market, pray?" This was precisely the question that Cooper wrestled
with as a frontier landlord. By integrating his settlements into the transatlantic market he meant to maximize the value of every labor and every natural resource in Otsego. Like Temple, Cooper sought to turn nature into
commodities.[44]

Persuading settlers to sign purchase agreements for land was but the first
and easiest challenge confronting William Cooper as a speculator. Next and
far more difficult was to collect annual payments of the 7 percent interest
and, within ten years, the value of the principal. Cooper's prospects depended on his ability to draw money from the settlers. "I have often compared the dealer in land to a ship," he remarked, "Money is the element he
swims in; without money, he is aground." To keep Cooper afloat, his settlers

needed to produce a marketable surplus from their land, not merely subsist on it. They had to cull from the forest and their fields some products in demand elsewhere, commodities that could be converted into money at some external market where cash could be had. Cooperstown had to become a successful market center surrounded by farms that produced commodities as well as family subsistence. "Where there is much people there will be trade; and where there is trade there will be money; and where there is money the landlord will succeed; but he should be ever in the midst of the settlers, aiding and promoting every beneficial enterprize," he explained. If in selling land Cooper pursued a laissez-faire policy, he was far more active in drawing his settlements into the transatlantic economy.[45]

Commerce did not come to a settlement after subsistence had been achieved. On the contrary, it took a few years of intense labor for new settlers to approximate household sufficiency from their new homesteads. Consequently, at first they had to depend on the market for some of their provisions, obtained by selling commodities that could be immediately culled from the forest: lumber, ginseng, animal skins, and potash. In the course of a few years, new settlers exhausted the wilderness bounty and developed the capacity of their farms to produce both a family subsistence and a surplus in grains and livestock for sale beyond the region. Instead of passing from a subsistence to a commercial economy, frontier inhabitants gradually shifted their production from one set of commodities culled from the forest to another set derived from the new fields and pastures that steadily replaced the wilderness. From the start a new settlement needed market connections.[46]

Most settlers migrated to the frontier to better their position in a market society, not to drop out of it. Cooper's advertisements reassured potential settlers that they could raise large crops and profitably transport them to an accessible market. He stressed that his patent lay within 90 miles of Albany's market; that potash alone would pay the cost to clear their land; that an Otsego acre routinely yielded 25 bushels of wheat, which sold for 7 shillings apiece—a yield of £ 8.15.0 per acre. In *The Pioneers* James Fenimore Cooper remembered, "The numberless sleighs that passed through the village, loaded with wheat and barrels of pot-ashes . . . hastening to the common market at Albany, that served as so many snares, to induce migrants to enter those wild mountains in search of competence and happiness." The pursuit of market opportunity and a family competence were reciprocal (rather than antithetical) so long as the settlers were independent producers rather than dependents obliged to sell their labor for wages or to rent land as tenants. No escape from a commercialized culture, the frontier settlement was the cutting edge of a market society.[47]

Cooper understood that enhanced commerce was the key to the settlers' immediate subsistence, as well as to their (and his) long-term prosperity. In

A Guide in the Wilderness, he explained his commercial strategy for relieving the poverty and hunger of his settlers during the late 1780s:

> *I resided among them, and saw too clearly how bad their condition was. I erected a storehouse, and during each winter filled it with large quantities of grain, purchased in distant places. I procured from my friend Henry Drinker a credit for a large quantity of [maple] sugar kettles; he also lent me some pot ash kettles, which we conveyed as we best could; sometimes by partial roads on sleighs, and sometimes over the ice. By this means, I established pot ash works among the settlers, and made them debtor for their bread and labouring utensils. I also gave them credit for their maple sugar and pot ash, at a price that would bear transportation, and the first year after the adoption of this plan I collected in one mass forty-three hogsheads of [maple] sugar, and three hundred barrels of pot and pearl ash, worth about nine thousand dollars. This kept the people together and at home, and the country soon assumed a new face.*

The potash and maple sugar paid for the provisions brought to Otsego by Cooper to relieve his hungry settlers. By easing frontier hardships and assuring newcomers of store goods and food, commerce accelerated the settlement of upstate New York.[48]

Subscribing to an analogy commonplace in late-eighteenth-century America, Cooper likened human society to a body of diverse but interdependent parts, in which commerce was the circulating lifeblood that sustained the whole. No settlement could survive without the invigorating circulation of commerce. Envisioning Otsego as a body with commerce as its bloodstream, Cooper thought of commodities as the blood cells, of roads and rivers as arteries, and of Cooperstown as the heart, pumping out produce and pumping back cash and consumer goods. "The labour of two or three hundred industrious men concentrated, is like money collected into a bank; when scattered in distant quarters its effects amount to little; when brought together it resembles the heart, from, and to which circulation flows, whilst it gives life and health to the remotest parts." By drawing artisans, storekeepers, and professionals together, a village provided a market, encouraging the settler-farmers in the surrounding countryside. Cooper explained, "There should be a mutual dependence between the farmer and the villager; the farmer relying upon the villager for the purchase of his produce, and the villager upon the farmer for the sale of the articles of his trade." Above all, the landlord would benefit. Pumped by the village, commercial growth promised to facilitate land payments from the old settlers and to inflate the land prices that Cooper could charge newcomers. Informed by this analogy, Cooper encouraged the local production of commodities that could be sold externally, improved the transportation corridors for the commodities bound to external market, and developed a store in Cooperstown to serve as a local market for Otsego's hinterland and as a conduit for trade with the wider world.[49]

Rare mineral ores, particularly gold and silver, were the ideal frontier commodities, because they required little skill to harvest and had an especially high value per weight and volume. Consequently, Cooper took a special interest in rumored ores and mines, an interest greatly disproportionate to the actual prospects of finding rare minerals in upstate New York. That fascination with hidden minerals and treasures shines in his rhetoric rife with graphic images of jewels, diamonds, and mines. Because Cooper had recently struggled up from poverty, his imagination was rich with pictures of tangible but secreted wealth, just within reach. Driven by wishful thinking, he recurrently collected speciments of purported ores—copper, iron, and silver—for eager dispatch to experts in the cities. Alas, all of Cooper's samples proved of little or no value.[50]

Recalling his father, James Fenimore Cooper invested Marmaduke Temple with an inordinate fascination for purported mines. Ordinarily cautious and levelheaded, Temple becomes animated and credulous upon hearing rumors of valuable ores ("one of his infirmities," the novelist remarks). Richard Jones captures Temple's eager attention by reminding him, "You know there are mines in these mountains; I have often heard you say that you believed in their existence . . . and have seen specimens of the ore, sir." Then Jones accuses Natty Bumppo and Oliver Edwards of covertly working a secret silver mine on Temple's land: "They are smelting, 'duke, they are smelting, and as they grow rich you grow poor." Nothing could have more alarmed Marmaduke Temple (or William Cooper), who knew what it was to be poor.[51]

For want of any mines, cattle constituted the best early commodity for the new settlements in the Otsego hills. Hardy beasts, they could endure the cold and find sustenance in the forests during the years before settlers could build substantial barns and clear enough land to provide summer pastures. Compared with pigs or sheep, cattle were better able to defend themselves against the wolves, bears, and panthers lurking in the forest. Able to fend and forage for themselves in the warm months, cattle required little attention, an important consideration where labor was so scarce and under such strain in the rigorous regimen of initial settlement. Best of all, when driven by a few men, cattle could walk themselves long distances over rough, mirey roads to get to market.[52]

Beginning in 1788, William Cooper organized annual autumn cattle drives. Taking the cattle on consignment from the settlers, he had the animals driven south to public auction in Burlington, New Jersey. After deducting his costs, Cooper credited each settler with the value his cattle obtained at the auction; that value reduced the settler's debt, either for land or for merchandise from Cooper's store. Cooper brought down eighty-three oxen in 1789 and over a hundred a year later. His success enthused Tench Coxe, who was planning the sale and development of his own similarly situated lands in the hills of northern Pennsylvania. "Your eighty-three head of black Cattle are really a pretty collection of rents and interest, and are very encouraging to our labors in the North." During the seven-year period from 1788 to 1794, cattle made up three-fifths of the value that William Cooper collected from settlers in payment for land.[53]

To render more of Otsego's resources profitable as commodities in external markets, Cooper meant to improve one or both of the region's two potential transportation corridors. The first passed north over the hills to the Mohawk River and east to Albany, a total distance of about 80 miles from Cooperstown. The second corridor proceeded south down the Susquehanna River approximately 375 miles, either to the Pennsylvania trading towns of Harrisburg, Lancaster, Middleburg, and Columbia (all with good road connections to Philadelphia) or all the way to Chesapeake Bay near Baltimore. In the late 1780s Otsego's economic orientation—either east or south—hinged upon which corridor could be improved to become preeminent. Although within the political jurisdiction of New York, Otsego might, by virtue of the Susquehanna, develop as an economic satellite of Pennsylvania.[54]

As a newcomer to New York with older and better connections to the merchants of Philadelphia and Burlington, Cooper initially looked southward for capital and for markets. Because he initially thought of the Susquehanna as Otsego's chief outlet to market, he laid out Cooperstown on a north-south axis beside the river. To improve transport in the shallow river, Cooper proposed constructing at Cooperstown a dam to build up a head of water for periodic release in surges to render the upper river navigable for boats during the low-water summer months. In March 1789 Cooper and Craig obtained needed capital by recruiting three leading Philadelphia merchants—Henry Drinker, Tench Francis, and Tench Coxe—as partners in their projected "Water Works." In addition to anticipating profits from the tolls charged on each boat benefiting from a surge, the Philadelphians hoped to draw commerce to their city from a new and promising quarter. However, the New York state legislators refused to pass the necessary enabling legislation for fear of assisting Philadelphia and Baltimore in their commercial rivalry with Albany and New York City for the hinterland produce.[55]

Although frustrated in his Susquehanna plan, Cooper found that the New York state legislature favored his secondary scheme: to improve the northern road linking Cooperstown with the Mohawk valley and Albany. For, as Gov. George Clinton explained, it was New York State's interest and policy "to facilitate the means of communication" with frontier settlements "as well to strengthen the bands of society, as to prevent the produce of those fertile districts from being diverted to other markets." Despite his own close ties to Philadelphia, Cooper readily warned Albany's merchants and New York's state legislators that they must counteract "the manuvers of the merchants of Philadelphia who have been active to secure the trade of this Western Country to their city." He sought a better northern road by appealing to the jealousy in New York of Pennsylvania, which had stymied his Susquehanna scheme. Enlisting support from Albany's leading merchants, in March 1790 Cooper secured a £400 appropriation from the state legislature to construct an improved road from Canajoharie, on the Mohawk, over the hills to Cooperstown. In June the state government awarded the construction contract to William Cooper and two partners, who subcontracted to settlers the actual work of felling trees, removing stumps, bridging the streams, and "Causwaying where Wet Land appeareth" at the rate of £20.0.0 per mile. Upon completing his assigned section, a settler received payment in cash or in credit from Cooper's store. At the end of the year the road was complete, "passable for loaded carriages," and "much travelled."[56]

STORE

To bring commerce closer to the settlers, Cooper constructed a store and a warehouse in Cooperstown in the summer and fall of 1789. He boasted that the new store was "thirty by Seventeen [feet] with Proper Shelves on three sides, Counters, Desk, Counting house, &c." Opening for business in late January, the store was the first established in the Otsego country. The store's diverse array of West Indian produce and British-made cloth, clothing, housewares, and tools displayed the complexity of the transatlantic economy and its capacity to penetrate deep into the North American forest in rapid pursuit of new settlers. Cooper could launch a store, well stocked with an array of consumer goods, because he enjoyed a generous line of credit with at least thirteen wholesale mercantile firms: six based in New York City, four in Albany, and three in Philadelphia. In 1790 and 1791 these thirteen suppliers provided Cooper's store with goods worth £6,509. Such a substantial credit manifests both the ambitious scope of Cooper's store and the confidence of leading merchants in his capacity and prospects.[57]

Busy with his extensive land speculations, Cooper entrusted most of the day-to-day management of the new store to a partner, Richard R. Smith, who received a third of its profits. He was the son of Richard Smith, a weighty Friend in Burlington who had formerly led the Burlington Company and who owned thousands of acres in his own right in the Otego valley. In the summer of 1789, Richard R. Smith was a bright and well-educated young man who had yet to marry or settle on a career four years after graduating from Princeton. Cooper liked Smith's genial, worldly personality and the idea of patronizing a young member of the preeminent family in Burlington; impressing the Smiths was Cooper's early standard of success. On February 11, Cooper informed Henry Drinker, "Nothing Could have ben so hapy with me in buisiness as my taking Richard [R.] Smith with me. He Sutes me Exactly and Pleases the People." At the end of the year, Cooper increased Smith's share in the profits to one-half.[58]

The new store proved extraordinarily popular, attracting a throng of customers in the winter of 1790. On February 11, a tired but exhilarated William Cooper wrote a letter at the end of a typically long and busy day in his new store: "The trade of this Place is Great. . . . The Store (tho Larg) is full of Customers Every Day and many of them Come from 40 to 100 Miles to trade, and go away Pleased with Our prices." Consequently, he could "Seldom eate Dinner for Want of Time." Cooper understood that his new store was a powerful selling point for attracting settlers to buy his lands. Access to a store with a generous credit policy was especially important to poor families without the means to provide their own year-round subsistence. His newspaper advertisements reassured "Poor Men" that he had established a store in Cooperstown "for the reception of country produce" to "obviate the difficulties of settling a new country."[59]

Cooper and Smith generously extended credit to local settlers. It is a striking measure of the store's inclusiveness that 315 settlers had accounts in 1790, more than the total number of households in Otsego (302). Linking the names in the store book with the heads of households named on the 1790 Federal Census return for Otsego Township and adjoining Canajoharie Township indicates that nearly two-thirds of the heads of households who dwelled within a dozen miles of the store had credit accounts, as well as half of those dwelling on the margins of the township. According to the 1788 tax list for Otsego (then called Old England District), the creditworthy were men of ordinary means. In fact, the average assessment of the account customers (30 pence) was slightly less than that of those residents without store credit (35 pence).[60]

Although modest means did not bar credit, the female gender did. Almost all of the credit customers were men. Only 4 of the 315 store accounts belonged to women—a bit more than 1 percent. Women rarely appeared in the store book because its chief purpose was for legal documentation to prod lagging debtors. By law only heads of households were liable for debts and men headed almost all of the households in Otsego Township (298 of 302, according to the 1790 census). Because a married woman could not be sued, her husband was liable for her debts. Therefore, when a woman did come to the store, Cooper and Smith usually recorded her debit or credit to the name of her husband or father, thereby obscuring women's economic activities as producers and consumers.[61]

Cooper's store promoted and assisted the local enterprises of the most entrepreneurial settlers, especially their production of potash: the potassium salts refined by boiling and baking wood ashes. Used to manufacture soap, saltpeter, dyes, bleach, glass, and some drugs, potash was in great and growing demand in Great Britain's expanding factories. By turning abundant but bulky hardwood trees into a compact and valuable commodity, potash manufacture was ideal for New York's frontier conditions: the settlers produced bushels of ashes as they cut down and burned off the forest to make pastures, meadows, and grain fields. Indeed, by offering good prices for ashes, storekeepers invited settlers to accelerate their clearing and burning. James Wadsworth, a land speculator in western New York, explained:

> *Many times when a new settler was under the necessity of raising money, or stood in need of store trade, he would go into the forest, chop down maple and elm trees, roll them together, and burn them, for the ashes alone, without reference to clearing. The proceeds of ashes have supplied many a log cabin in this region with the common necessaries of life, in the absence of which there would have been destitution.*

An acre of hardwood land ordinarily yielded 60 to 100 bushels of ashes; in 1790 each bushel was worth 6 pence at William Cooper's store; therefore, a settler could earn at least £1.6.0 and as much as £2.10.0 per acre ($3.25 to $6.25) from potash—a considerable subsidy toward the $7.50 cost to have an acre cleared by hired labor. A settler's son recalled that *"ashes were silver and gold to the young or poor farmer."*[62]

Cooper's store played a pivotal role in the rapid expansion of potash production in Otsego. Obtaining potash kettles on credit from Henry Drinker's Atsion Ironworks in New Jersey, Cooper entrusted them on credit to settlers who promised to pay in potash. He also honored the receipts issued by the local potash makers to the settlers who supplied them with ashes. For example, on February 9, 1790, Darius Warren of the Pierstown settlement came into Cooper's store with a receipt issued by Solomon Pier for 40 bushels of ashes. Cooper accepted the receipt and allowed Warren a credit of 6 pence per bushel (£1.0.0 for his 40 bushels) toward store goods. Cooper simultaneously debited Pier that amount. In effect, Cooper loaned Pier the store goods necessary to buy Warren's ashes. In 1790 Cooper granted store credit to 133 settlers for delivering ashes to twelve local potasheries. A potash maker needed to procure from Cooper and Smith an entry like this of December 7, 1791: "This Day agreed with Israel Foster & Joell Coe to Carrey on A Perle ash work on the Otego Creek for Us and to Draw Orders on Our Store." The system enabled Otsego's poorly capitalized potasheries to buy ashes from the settlers. And it permitted the cash-poor settlers to obtain consumer goods. Because the receipts could change hands to settle other debts or make other bargains before ending up in Cooper's strongbox, they also functioned as a badly needed medium of exchange in the cash-short settlements. Cooper accumulated a growing pile of receipts and recorded mounting debits beside the names of Otsego's potash makers. To cancel the debts and earn a profit, he counted on eventual payment in potash from the makers.[63]

Cooper shipped the potash to market in Albany and New York City. Sale there started the reverse flow of credit upstream through Albany toward Cooper and the Otsego potash makers. The Albany and New York City merchants credited Cooper on their books, permitting him to draw more store goods from their warehouses and even to obtain some cash. Cooper could then credit each maker with any surplus over and above his debits for ashes, barrels, transportation, and official inspection. After the annual balancing of accounts, the makers with a surplus had the option of receiving cash or banking it as store credit toward future purchases.[64]

Through Cooper's road and store, the Otsego frontier was tied to, rather than disconnected from, the transatlantic market. Britain's industrial revolution, the rapid commercialization and urbanization of Albany and New York City, and the extensive development of the New York frontier were all interdependent, all linked through the potash and wheat trades. Otsego's trees fell and burned in ever greater numbers to provide the potash demanded by Britain's growing factories. The settlers also killed the trees to make grain fields whose wheat fed European factory workers as well as the local farmers. And, from Cooper's store, the settlers obtained an array of English manufactures and West Indian produce. Instead of escaping from commerce, settlers extended it. William Cooper succeeded as a landlord by promoting Otsego's integration into the world market.

SUCCESS ♨

From his Manor House on Cooperstown's main street, Cooper could see and hear the growing numbers, increasing commerce, and rising buildings brought to Otsego by improved access to external markets. From a single family in early 1786, Cooperstown had grown by 1790 into a village of thirty-five inhabitants (two of them enslaved Blacks), comprising eight households dwelling in seven houses. A third of the inhabitants belonged to one household: William Cooper's. The Manor House was crowded with his wife, children, servants, and a lodger: his store partner Richard R. Smith. In 1791 the new store, the improved road to Albany, and the legislative formation of Otsego County with Cooperstown as its shire town combined to accelerate development. New tradesmen and professionals arrived from New England and eastern New York, hoping to make a profitable niche by tapping the expanding commerce of a promising frontier village. William Cooper's ledger book for 1791 identifies sixteen tradesmen resident in or near the village: three carpenters, three masons, two tailors, two tanners, and one innkeeper, blacksmith, hatter, miller, cooper, and potter. The first lawyer, Abraham C. Ten Broeck, and first doctor, Charles Powers, also arrived that year.[65]

New buildings sprouted among the stumps, especially around the juncture of Second and West Streets, a block west of the Manor House. Frame houses and stores steadily replaced log cabins, which were usually moved back from the streets and converted to sheds and stables. In September 1791 Cooper boasted, "Cooperstown grows fast. Scarce a week [passes] without a Raising of a House, Some very Large and Spacious, say 40 feet Square, 2 Storys high, &c." During the day the village was alive with shouting men, clattering hammers, creaking wheels, and droning saws. "Thirty carpenters are imployed every day in building houses in this town which together with the great Number of teems hauling brick, stone, lime, sand, timber, &c. and the trade, travelers, and Boats makes a Constant din or Noise," Cooper explained, in celebration rather than complaint. A sawmill, a gristmill, and two fulling mills were in operation, powered by falls in Oaks Creek and the Susquehanna River. A bridge of hewn timber spanned the sixty-foot-wide river near its beginning as the outlet for Lake Otsego. Cooper even anticipated establishing linen, wool, and rope manufactories. Delighted by the progress, he assured his friend Henry Drinker that Cooperstown was

> on a full Carier to be a very considerable Manufacturing and trading place, to the accomplishing of which I am so deeply interested that thee must excuse my so frequently unlading my mind to thee. How supremely pleasing it is to see this Country, that in the year 1787 was uninhabited, now Plentifully peopled [with] Roads, Bridges, Mills, Stores, Schools, in short Every Convenience that reasonable men could wish for, at hand.

By April 1795 the village had fifty houses, of which a quarter were "respectable two-story" dwellings. Thirty more buildings went up during the ensuing six months. In addition to the occupations present in 1791, by mid-decade Cooperstown had added a clock maker, brick maker, druggist, painter, brewer, baker, and saddler. The professionals consisted of five lawyers, three doctors, a schoolmaster, and a newspaper and book publisher. By 1796 Cooperstown boasted four stores and three inns where there had been only one of each in 1791.[66]

In the late 1780s and early 1790s, William Cooper's success in so rapidly selling and settling Otsego made him a national, even an international, celebrity. Virtually uninhabited at the end of the war, the Otsego country surged in population to about 2,700 by 1790 and to 21,343 by 1800. The newcomers dramatically remade the landscape, pocking the forest with clearings, barns, houses, fences, roads, and bridges. It seemed that Cooper had mastered the art of developing new settlements—highly valued knowledge at a time when so many capitalists had plunged into land speculation and competed for settlers. Curious travelers and aspiring land speculators, both European and American, ventured to bustling Cooperstown to consult Cooper and learn his methods. Flattered by the attention, he was a genial and expansive host. In 1791 Jan Lincklaen, an agent for Dutch investors, obtained a letter of introduction from Alexander Hamilton that he might meet the famed William Cooper. Traveling to Cooperstown, Lincklaen and a companion "brushed off the mud" and "went to see Mr. Cooper." Lincklaen reported, "We found him both frank & sincere, a man of attainments & of a very sound judgment." In 1793 Simon Desjardins, the representative of a French land company, made a similar pilgrimage to Cooperstown to find inspiration for his own plans. He recounted:

> The location of this city and environs, in a circumference of ten miles, was in 1786, all covered with woods. If Coopers-town, built within this period, and which owes its origin to only one man (Cooper), is already famous for its commerce and manufactures, what ought we not to expect from the cities founded by a company whose means and interests are much more powerful than those of a private individual?

In 1786 Cooper had begun with little capital and no prior experience upon lands that had defied the prior efforts of wealthier and more powerful speculators. Five years later he was celebrated far and wide as the preeminent expert in the sale and settlement of frontier land.[67]

As his fame spread Cooper was in great and growing demand as a land agent employed by wealthy and prestigious speculators who owned tracts in central New York but resided in New York City, Albany, Burlington, Philadelphia, or London. Surely, they reasoned and he confirmed, William Cooper could sell, settle, and collect money from their lands faster than anyone else. It was "rare," Cooper boasted, "that a Stage arives from New York without one or more Applycations to me to Undertake the Sail and Settelment of Lands." In return for supervising surveys, sales, and collections of annual interest, Cooper charged a 5 percent commission on the value of the principal. His agencies within Otsego County included most of the 69,000-acre Otego Patent; the 14,000-acre Colden Patent; and a 14,200-acre tract within the Morris Patent. Cooper represented such prominent men as Antoine Rene Charles M. de la Forest, the consul general of France posted in New York City; James Donatien Le Ray de Chaumont, a wealthy French émigré, financier, and speculator; and the eminent New York lawyers Cadwallader David Colden and Josiah Ogden Hoffman. Cooper must have been especially delighted to receive the agency for the lands south of the Susquehanna (now in Delaware County) belonging to William Temple Franklin, the prestigious but alienated son of William Franklin. By employing Cooper, William Temple Franklin further antagonized his father, who continued to seethe at having lost the Otsego Patent to Cooper and Craig in 1786.[68]

Cooper also aggressively expanded his own portfolio of frontier lands, usually in partnerships that brought both needed capital and prestigious contacts. His new holdings stretched beyond Otsego into the counties farther north, west, and south. Over the course of the 1790s, Cooper and various partners acquired the Arthurborough Patent, 41,000 acres located north of the Mohawk River in the Adirondacks; 27,345 acres in Clinton County, near Lake Champlain; 9,442 acres within the Otego Patent south of Cooperstown; 10,200 acres in the Military Tract of the Finger Lakes Region to the west; 27,000 acres in Tioga County; and the Hillington Patent— 16,000 acres located beside Butternuts Creek in southwestern Otsego County. During the 1790s no other New Yorker had his hand in more frontier land speculations within that state than did William Cooper.[69]

Cooper's increasingly complicated and extended partnerships were driven as much by his longing to enmesh his interest with those of prestigious and powerful men as by his desire for new profits. William Cooper's partners and patrons included the preeminent lawyers in New York City: Josiah Ogden Hoffman, Richard Harison, and Col. Robert Troup. Cooper also found partners among the merchant princes of Albany and New York City: Leonard Gansevoort, Stephen Lush, Philip S. Van Rensselaer, Gerret Van Schaick, and Abraham Van Peters. Many of Cooper's deals involved Goldsborough Banyar—Albany's oldest and canniest speculator—or Stephen Van Rensselaer, the wealthiest and most prestigious landlord in the state. Cooper's partners in the Hillington purchase were Miers, Samuel, and Thomas Fisher, brothers and wealthy Philadelphia Quakers. The partnerships afforded Cooper cherished opportunities to dazzle gentlemen with his expertise at speculation and settlement. He offered his inside knowledge of land and settlers to urban investors with superior capital and political connections but without frontier experience.[70]

As Cooper spun ever wider webs of partnership and accumulated acreage (and mounting debts), he lusted for yet more. He could not conceal his envy when, in the summer of 1791, he learned of the vast tracts of New York frontier land recently obtained by two other ambitious speculators: Alexander Macomb of New York City and Robert Morris of Philadelphia. Macomb and his partners had purchased 3,635,000 acres in northern New York from the state government for a mere eight pence per acre. For the same price, Robert Morris had acquired 1,000,000 acres in the Genesee country of western New York from two Massachusetts speculators. It bothered Cooper that others had acquired, and might develop, more frontier land than he had. "McComb and R. Morris has Skipped over Us all and in fact Done too much for any one American family. . . . This is Doing Buisiness at such [a] Monstrous rate that the Very thoughts of it flashes Over the mind Like Extravigant ideas," Cooper marveled. Determined to be the state's leading speculator and developer, Cooper offered to buy Macomb's entire tract. Predicting an implausible profit of £1,500,000 in ten years, he cast about for fifty partners with the necessary capital. Although Macomb and his partners declined to sell, the proposal reveals the colossal growth in Cooper's ambitions. Just six years after having acquired his first lands in New York, Cooper was angling to become the preeminent landlord in the state and the favored partner of its wealthiest capitalists.[71]

To be sought after and flattered by wealthy men from prominent families was a heady experience for Cooper. Recalling that he had been a mere storekeeper ten years before and a penurious wheelwright when the Revolutionary War began, Cooper reveled in his new friends and associates. His conversation and correspondence effused an expansive self-assurance, manifesting the importance he placed on the approval won from the great men of the seaport centers. In 1790 Dr. Benjamin Rush, a leading man in Philadelphia, observed, "William Cooper dined with me this day. His conversation is full of enterprise and amusing anecdotes of the first Settlers in our New Country." Cooper delighted in calling the great men "my Friends."[72]

It especially pleased Cooper to receive a letter from Isaac Smith, a man of old prestige but slipping fortunes back home in New Jersey. Smith begged his "good Friend" to take in and patronize his son Charles. "I commit him to your Friendship and Direction with Pleasure and Confidence, and beg you to teach him the Way to gain Property, for you know how;—I do not, either by Precept or Example." Cooper could consider himself a success when the old gentry had to concede his superior wealth and expertise, and were even willing to entrust their sons to his management. Beating the odds and confounding his rivals, Cooper had won fame and fortune as one of the new republic's premier frontier speculators and developers.[73]

Chapter Five

JEWELS OF THE FOREST

W ILLIAM COOPER WAS PROUDEST of his new association with Philadelphia's weightiest Friend, the wealthy, prestigious, and philanthropic Henry Drinker (1734–1809). The longtime business partner of the ill-fated Abel James, Drinker had been the leading merchant in prerevolutionary Philadelphia and a leader in that city's Yearly Meeting, the preeminent Quaker body in North America. Arrested by Pennsylvania's Whigs in 1777 for opposing the American Revolution, Drinker spent eight months in internal exile in rural Virginia. Upon release he returned to Philadelphia and shifted his capital out of overseas shipping and into his Atsion Ironworks in the piney woods of southern New Jersey. He also speculated in urban rental properties and in thousands of frontier acres in northeastern Pennsylvania. As a land speculator, Drinker was intrigued by Cooper's evident success in settling industrious Yankees on a hilly upcountry.[1]

[A] cheerful fire, of the hard or sugar-maple, was burning on the hearth. The latter was the first object that struck the attention of the Judge, who, on beholding it, exclaimed, rather angrily, to Richard—

"How often have I forbidden the use of the sugar-maple, in my dwelling. The sight of that sap, as it exudes with the heat, is painful to me, Richard. Really, it behooves the owner of woods, so extensive as mine, to be cautious what example he sets his people, who are already felling the forests, as if no end could be found to their treasures, nor any limits to their extent. If we go on in this way, twenty years hence, we shall want fuel."

—*James Fenimore Cooper,*
The Pioneers, *105*

A paragon of the weighty Friend, Drinker shrewdly and persistently accumulated wealth that he might play a leading role in his religious meeting and public charities. In her diary Elizabeth Sandwith Drinker celebrated her husband: "He is perpetually and almost ever employed; the affairs of Society and the public . . . I believe takes up ten-twelfths of his time. If benevolence and beneficence will take a man to Heaven . . . H.D. stands as good, indeed a better, chance than any I know of." Benjamin Rush paid tribute to his old friend as "a man of uncommon understanding, and great suavity and correctness of manners" who "possessed talents and judgment in business" and who "was universally esteemed and beloved" by Friends. A pious man of austere speech, manners, and morals, Drinker nonetheless possessed an immense brick house on the west side of Front Street, near his riverside wharf. If Drinker's greatest pleasure came from serving others, a close second was criticizing their faults, especially any want of the rigid self-discipline that he had so perfected. In 1792 he exhorted Samuel Preston, his land agent at Stockport on the upper Delaware River,

> *Every piece of information relative to a reformation of manners amongst the people your way I shall be pleased to hear—a more contemptible set of Beings are hardly to be found than many of those who make their appearance in Spring and Fall with Boats and Rafts from your parts. If they can be brought off from their habits of Drunkenness and Profanity it will be a good work, to which I wish much success. Some books shall be thought of.*[2]

Because Henry Drinker was the consummate weighty Friend but no easy man to please, Cooper was especially keen to cultivate his goodwill and patronage. Invited to sell and settle Drinker's frontier lands, Cooper delighted in the opportunity to ingratiate himself. He assured Drinker, "The whole depends on the contrivance and industry of H.D. and W.C. Some will talke and others write, but we must be Doing in fact." Entrusted with a generous credit from Drinker's Atsion Ironworks in 1789, Cooper gratefully observed, "I fully believe thee hath Gon Greater Lengths to serve me than I have Ever before Experienced."[3]

Drinker introduced Cooper to other eminent Philadelphians, especially Tench Coxe (1755–1824), then the assistant secretary of the treasury, and Benjamin Rush (1745–1818), the preminent physician in the nation. Although non-Quakers, Coxe (an Anglican) and Rush (a Presbyterian) were closely associated in politics, business, and philanthropy with Philadelphia's weightiest Friends. They joined with Drinker in land speculations and in benevolent schemes that promised social and moral reform. Avid publicists, Coxe and Rush filled pamphlets and newspaper columns with their calculations and enthusiasms. In a letter to Coxe, Rush effused their love of social betterment through economic innovation:

> *Let it be our pride & pleasure to open new sources of wealth & happiness to our country—to lessen human misery by inviting the distressed of all nations to partake in our ample & easy means of existence—to contend with vice & ignorance in every shape—to protect the innocent—to wipe away the tears of widows & orphans—and to do every other good thing that reason, patriotism & religion shall dictate to us.*

They shared with Drinker and Cooper the pleasing notions that all good things could be readily achieved by the simple discovery and application of new knowledge and that private profit and public service were reciprocal.[4]

In association with Drinker, Coxe, and Rush, in 1789 William Cooper launched two daring and ambitious new ventures intended to prove his worth to an elite audience in Philadelphia, the nation's premier city. First, on behalf of his new friends, Cooper assumed responsibility for developing the Beech Woods, an especially rough and daunting tract of land nestled in the northeastern corner of Pennsylvania. Mountainous, remote, stony, and heavily timbered, the Beech Woods had deterred potential settlers and frustrated the previous efforts of land speculators and their agents. By selling and settling the area, Cooper would demonstrate the genius and universal power of his program for developing frontier lands. He spoke of his "Method of forceing a Setelment," as if his sheer will and persistence would fill the Beech Woods with settlers and clearings. Cooper insisted that he could settle the very worst lands because "all difficulties will be surmounted by spiritedly rushing upon them with a number of people and continuing them until they become familiar." He exhorted his employers to keep pace: "Take the Immigrants in their flight, for they are Now on the wing and when this Flight is over we may wait a Long time for another and that Valluable Country {will] Lay Neglected as heretofore."[5]

Second, Cooper enlisted Philadelphia's leading men into his enlightened, perhaps utopian, scheme to mass-produce maple sugar as a marketable commodity. By developing a new market for maple sugar, Cooper meant simultaneously to promote Otsego's commerce, advance his own fortune, and garner renown as the benevolent patron of forest and settlers. Maple sugar would bring cash to the settlers so that they could more readily pay their debts for land, and it would bring William Cooper to the attention of the Republic's preeminent gentlemen.

THE BEECH WOODS

The Beech Woods was named for its heavy forest of tall, thick maple, oak, hemlock, and—especially—beech trees. The dense canopy cast a deep shade, rendering the forest floor a dark, mossy, damp morass "full of roots & mire holes" and "rotten heaps" of dead and decaying wood—no appealing sight to prospective settlers. In spring and summer predatory insects delighted in the moist gloom of the dense Beech Woods. In 1807 the visiting botanist Frederick Pursh complained, "I don't think any place can be more infested with muscidoes & gnats . . . as this country is. The people are obliged to make fires before their doors to keep them out of the houses, & them who milk cowes are obliged to kindle fire & make a smoke to be able to stand milking, in the evening and morning." Pennsylvania and New Jersey farmers preferred to head west to the Ohio valley, bypassing the nearby Beech Woods with their voracious bugs, heavy stones, and thick trees.[6]

Used to rolling hills, a stony soil, and heavy timber, Yankees seemed to be the only people who could settle the Beech Woods. In January of 1789 Drinker and Richard Wells approached Cooper because, as they told him,

they had "a favorable opinion of thy experience & judgement in such improvements & also of thy influence with a Class of People in New England,
who are said to be sober & respectable & may probably on thy representation be engaged to become purchasers & to sit down on the Lands."[7]

Cooper agreed to manage their lands but insisted upon a free hand
to apply his particular "Method of Setteling those Wooden Countrys": offering warrantee deeds for no money down, annual interest payments, and
a ten-year credit to pay the principal—all secured by the settler's mortgage
and bond. Cooper would receive his usual 5 percent commission. Self-
confident, he promised to "Settel a many thousand acres of Land in the
Course of the insuing Summer," filling their tract with "Many industrous
Poor Men Setelled upon Principals of Justice and Eaqually advantagous to
both the buyer and seller." Drinker and Wells assented, entrusting Cooper
with 16,000 acres to sell in lots of 200 to 300 acres for 10 shillings per acre
but only "to such as immediately sit down on the premises & proceed to improvements." Then Drinker persuaded some of his friends and fellow land
speculators—Miers Fisher, Thomas Clifford, Samuel Meredith, and Robert
Morris—to engage Cooper to sell and settle their lands in the Beech Woods,
raising his assignment to approximately 30,000 acres.[8]

In the late winter and spring of 1789, Cooper threw himself into the
Beech Woods promotion with his usual zeal and vigor. Drawn by Cooper's
newspaper advertisements and his reputation as the settler's friend, dozens
of prospective buyers came west from New England to Cooperstown in April
or early May to join his progress downriver to the Beech Woods. One man
explained that "it was the report of William Cooper selling such good land
so very cheap had brought him out."[9]

In June 1789 Cooper reported dramatic success: he had sold almost all
the lands entrusted to his management: "This is not a fictional and Nominal Sale, but Grounded on the Broad Basis of Sollid Contracts made with
men of Carrector." The buyers were, he promised, improvers, not petty
speculators: "Some are now at work on thy Land and will have Severall acres
of wheat in this Fall." Cooper insisted, "This Sale and Setelment . . . will
Breake the Nets of All the Dificultys of Setelment of this Country." Pennsyl-
vanians dwelling on the edge of the Beech Woods were astonished by
Cooper's success. They thought it "very strange that [Yankees] should come
so far and give such a price for land, which they would not have as a gift, because it was so full of hemlock and hard to clear." In July, Cooper returned
to Philadelphia in triumph bearing the mortgages and bonds given by approximately seventy settlers to secure their purchases. In less than a month
he had sold at least 24,626 acres worth £12,313 in principal, earning him
about £615 in commissions.[10]

The Philadelphia landlords were ecstatic that at last their lands in the
Beech Woods would develop and yield an increasing annual revenue.

Robert Morris applauded: "It appears to me that Mr. Cooper has done this Business like a master workman and that he understands well the thing which he has undertaken." Morris promptly engaged Cooper to manage an additional 45,000 acres on the upper Susquehanna in Tioga County, New York. That summer and fall twenty-three other Philadelphians committed to Cooper's care new tracts in the Beech Woods, totaling at least 90,000 acres. His new patrons included such preeminent men as Tench Francis, Col. Isaac Melcher, Samuel Pleasants, Tench Coxe, Benjamin Rush, and Rev. William White. Cooper boasted that he would readily sell "the whole of those Enormous Tracts now before me, in the Peopling of wich I take a Supreem Pleasure." In June of 1790 Cooper returned to the Beech Woods and sold twice as much land as the preceding year. He retailed at least 51,556 acres for commitments worth £25,778 to the landlords, netting him another £1,289 in commissions. It seemed that the Beech Woods promotion had perfectly fulfilled Cooper's ambitions to win the plaudits of (and commissions from) leading gentlemen as well as the gratitude of common settlers.[11]

MAPLE SUGAR 🍁

At the same time that Drinker recruited Cooper to sell and settle the Beech Woods, Cooper drew Drinker into the promotion of maple sugar production. In June of 1789 Cooper assured Drinker that promoting maple sugar would accelerate the sale and settlement of the Beech Woods; settlers would flock to Drinker's lands if they could obtain cash or store goods by making maple sugar. As the owner of Atsion Ironworks, Drinker had yet another incentive for supporting an enterprise that would demand hundreds of iron kettles. It also pleased Drinker, a Quaker abolitionist, that he could profit from a promotion that promised to strike a blow against slavery. Appealing to a medley of motives that he shared, Cooper assured Drinker, "*Land will Likewise Sell for Cash . . .* and wee shall have the Satisfaction of Seeing that we have interrested ourselves in a Good Work." Doing good while earning cash pay was the sweetest promise of maple sugar to William Cooper and Henry Drinker.[12]

Abundant in the hills of New England, New York, and northern Pennsylvania, the sugar maple *(Acer saccharum)* was a majestic hardwood tree that grew 120 feet tall and 3 feet thick. Yankee settlers had learned from the Indians how to tap each tree with a V-shaped cut of the ax; to insert a hollow spout made of the thin, supple bark of alder or sumac to drain the dripping sap into hardwood troughs; to collect the sap in pails; to boil the juice in iron kettles set over fires to produce a molasses; and to strain and dry the syrup in wooden molds to render a crude, brown sugar. The more thorough settlers built log houses to shelter their kettles from the wind and rain, and they cleared away the underbrush and rival trees in a surrounding grove of sugar maples to create "a Sugar Bush." Sugaring was the work of men and boys during a three- to six-week period at the end of winter and beginning of spring (March and April), when warm days alternate with frosty nights to keep the sap in circulation. A settler's son recalled: "The tapping of the trees, the regular rounds made to empty the vessels, the filling of the kettles, the keeping up of the fire, the watching of the process as the transparent sap first changed into syrup, and then into sugar; and all this in the woods, fast budding into life and beauty, formed an annual festival scene whose coming we anticipated with joy."[13]

Initially, Otsego's Yankee families produced maple sugar in modest quantities strictly for household consumption. It seemed that maple sugar could not compete in urban and foreign markets with the whiter, purer sugar produced from canes grown on slave plantations in the West Indies. But William Cooper became convinced that maple sugar could be refined and mass-produced to compete in both quality and quantity with cane sugar.[14]

Cooper considered maple sugar the ideal commodity for new settlers because its production required little labor and less capital. Simply by tapping existing trees, settlers could produce maple sugar immediately, without clearing the old forest to cultivate new plants. Properly done, tapping neither damaged nor killed a tree, permitting a sustained harvest year after year. Because March was a slack season for farming, the increased production of maple sugar mobilized underemployed labor instead of sacrificing some other enterprise. Because the capital necessary was limited to a kettle, a ladle, a few pails, troughs, and molds, the production could be decentralized among many farm families drawing upon their own labor working their own land. Boys "old enough to carry a pail . . . or to feed a fire with light fuel" could do most of the work.[15]

Cooper concluded that maple sugar was the key commodity that would unlock the full economic potential of the northern upcountry to the benefit of consumers, settlers, landlords—and even West Indian slaves. He set out to persuade his countrymen that, if properly promoted and produced, maple sugar could drive imported cane sugar from the American market, that New York and northern Pennsylvania had more than enough sugar maples to satisfy the entire national demand, and that American maple sugar could be exported profitably to Europe. By substituting for the most valuable agricultural commodity imported into the United States, maple sugar would alleviate the new nation's balance of payments deficit, striking a blow for economic independence. Deprived of their markets for cane sugar, West Indian planters would have to shut down their plantations and liberate their slaves. Produced by free families "without exercising the lash of cruelty on our fellow creatures," American sugar would advance the day "when the minds of men are become so liberal as to view liberty in its true light—when slavery shall be done away." The money that was flowing into the coffers of importers and West Indian planters would instead pass into the pockets of American farmers, enhancing their standard of living. Become prosperous, farmers could readily pay their debts to landlords. Eager to share in that new prosperity, migrants would flock west to settle in the New York hills, paying increased prices for lands covered with sugar maples.[16]

But there was no time to waste, for settlers were "wantonly and foolishly destroying" the sugar maples by the thousands as they cleared the forest. Because maple trees were especially valuable for firewood or potash, they quickly attracted the interest and axes of new settlers. Cooper hoped "to rescue from destruction these trees; these diamonds of America; these gifts of Heaven, which never created any thing in vain. Thousands of them are daily destroyed. . . . I stand alone for their protection, and plainly perceive that our country will soon be deprived of them; but knowing their value, I now plead their cause." In *The Pioneers* James Fenimore Cooper paraphrased his father's rhetoric, placed in the mouth of Judge Marmaduke Temple, who condemns the "practice, which devotes these jewels of the forest, these precious gifts of nature, these mines of comfort and wealth, to the common use of a fireplace." Temple calls the maple trees "jewels" as Cooper called them "diamonds": both evocations of the longing to find hidden treasures lurking in their lands.[17]

Cooper sought to conserve the sugar maples not out of any romantic aesthetic or any ecological sensibility but from a conviction that their long-term value as sugar producers vastly outweighed their immediate value as potash or firewood. He did not mean to stop all deforestation, merely to preserve the groves where sugar maples were most numerous: "There is land enough where they stand thin, for the purpose of plowing, sowing, mowing, and pasture." Cooper was very much like Marmaduke Temple, who explains, "It is not as ornaments that I value the noble trees of this country; it is for their usefulness."[18]

Cooper faced a hard sell to change both consumers' tastes and producers' habits. First, he had to overcome consumers' entrenched preference for the whiter, purer cane sugar, widely considered a token of good and fashionable taste. Second, he had to persuade the common farmer to invest the additional time, effort, and equipment to make surplus sugar for the market. Third, he had to induce that farmer to produce a finer sugar that met the expectations of urban consumers. By taking greater pains to keep falling water, blowing dirt, and thirsty cattle out of their troughs, pails, kettles, and molds, the settlers could render their sugar "a Suitable Artical among those of a Delicate Taste." Fourth, he had to establish a distribution network to link the sugar producers in the hills of New York to the seaport markets. "I know that the idea has an extravagant appearance, and will be thought by most people an enthusiastic, fanciful and visionary plan; but let reason usurp the throne of prejudice," Cooper pleaded.[19]

To prove maple sugar's commercial potential, Cooper proposed to run and publicize a pilot program on his patent. Otsego offered the perfect combination of industrious but needy Yankees and maple-abundant land. Cooper assured Henry Drinker, "I therefore find much Depends on my Exertions" on the Otsego Patent, "a New thick seteled Country full of interprising People whose wants of Many articals of Life together with . . . my influance (Excuse me Henry for Saying it for I think I can speak to thee of facts without Blushing) will Procure a great quantity of well made Sugar wich I shall bring Every Pound to your City." Because men would only believe what they could see, Cooper meant to evangelize for maple sugar by "the repeated testimony of occular demonstration . . . laid before the eye of the public."[20]

In June of 1789 Cooper reached an understanding with Drinker to produce maple sugar in Otsego for the Philadelphia market. Drinker agreed to make, ship, and consign to Cooper on credit 300 iron sugar kettles, each with handles and a capacity of 15 gallons, at a price of 18 shillings apiece. Cooper went to work touring Otsego and the other Montgomery County settlements, proselytizing for men to take the kettles on credit and produce sugar in payment. He also constructed a store and a warehouse in Cooperstown to dole out the kettles and take in the sugar. That summer and fall he wrote numerous letters and newspaper blurbs "to Spread the flame and be Politically advantageous; and indeed too many truths cannot be Said on this Subject in order to make it more *Popular*" and thereby "set this Valluable Tree in that Conspicuous Point of View as to Prevent the Divestation that are Dayly taking Place among them." In October, Cooper gleefully reported to Drinker that "the number of kettles talked of by us [is] far short of the Applications made to me by the inhabitants of the Country." In mid-November, Drinker shipped the kettles, and they reached Albany onboard the sloop *Nancy*. From Albany teamsters hauled the kettles on sleighs over the snow, westward up the Mohawk and across the hills to Otsego Lake and Cooperstown.[21]

While Cooper planned production in Otsego, Drinker drummed up support in Philadelphia. Tench Coxe and Benjamin Rush helped by publishing pamphlets and newspaper blurbs extolling the delights, benefits, and prospects of maple sugar. Dr. Rush portrayed sugar, especially maple sugar, as an elixir and dismissed critics: "It has been said, that sugar injures the teeth, but this opinion now has so few advocates, that it does not deserve a serious refutation." Drinker, Coxe, and Rush prepared a guaranteed market and price in Philadelphia for maple sugar by enlisting other leading

Philadelphians into a subscription. They promised to pay 7 pence per pound for the maple sugar that Cooper would, they promised, deliver in the spring. Interest and idealism combined to draw in the subscribers, described by Coxe as "the friends of the Slaves & of Manufactures, Landholders and public spirit people." A dozen were land speculators who had hired William Cooper as their agent for tracts in the Beech Woods. The subscribers also included the Quaker leaders of the Pennsylvania Society for the Abolition of Negro Slavery. But the promoters failed to move the unsentimental merchant Robert Morris, who replied to Drinker's solicitation: "I wish the Plan of using maple Sugar in the City may take, but the success will depend upon the quality and Price. Agreements & subscriptions don't hold long unless supported by convenience or interest." His caveat prophesied the difficulties that would soon follow. As completed on September 3, 1789, the list named seventy-four men who subscribed for a total of 15,800 pounds. Henry Drinker led the way, promising to buy 2,000 pounds, but most subscribers pledged to take only 100 or 200 pounds.[22]

In Cooperstown on January 21, 1790, Cooper began to sell sugar kettles on credit for £1.12.0 each. The settlers could pay for their kettles with sugar in the spring. At the price of 6 pence per pound, 64 pounds of maple sugar would pay for a kettle. By mid-March he had sold all the kettles supplied by Drinker. The 166 individuals who bought kettles in 1790 represented over half his store's customers (166 of 315 = 53 percent). Matching names in the store book with the heads of household on the 1790 federal census reveals that at least a third of the settlers within Otsego Township—and over half of those dwelling on Cooper's patent, nearest the store—obtained a sugar kettle. Cooper entrusted sugar kettles on credit to almost anyone who applied, no matter how poor. In the maple sugar promotion, as in his 1786 land sales, Cooper was the common settler's friend.[23]

In February the extraordinary demand for sugar kettles fed Cooper's boundless optimism. Throughout Otsego he detected "a Spirit of Preparation for the Sugar Buisiness—so much so that not a Doubt is Left with me of the amount being Prodigious." He projected a harvest of 50 tons. Nothing, it seemed, could go wrong: "The Common invention of man Leaves many Crises that Oposing winds Blow through, whereas the Present Plan (Let me Say it with thankfulness) Seemes to Stand in the Clear Sunshine."[24]

However, the weather failed to cooperate with Cooper's plans, as an unusually frigid March and early April delayed the season. By the end of the truncated season in early May, Cooper had received, weighed, and packed into hogshead barrels about 20,000 pounds of sugar—a fifth of the amount that he had predicted in February. Only about two-fifths of the settlers (64 of 166) delivered enough sugar to pay for their kettles in full. Indeed, almost a third of the kettle buyers (49 of 166) produced no marketable sugar whatsoever. On average, each producer brought in 80 pounds of sugar: far below the 500-pound target set by Cooper in October. In late May, Cooper informed Drinker: "The Season for Sugar hath ben the Poorest that hath ben known for this 20 yeares. People that made 1000 lb Last year, has not this with Double the exertions and Convenancys made 300."[25]

None of the sugar collected would benefit Cooper and his associates unless he could get it to Philadelphia over bad roads and rough rivers. In July he packed the sugar into hogshead casks, which, when filled, averaged 535 pounds. Teamsters loaded the hogsheads onto ox-drawn carts bound northward over the hills to the Mohawk and then eastward to Albany: "a great work attended with much Expence and Loss by raines" that clogged the roads with mud and drenched the hogsheads. Ominously, Cooper informed Drinker that the rain had penetrated at least eight hogsheads, perhaps damaging the sugar within.[26]

Prospects brightened once the hogsheads reached the Hudson and their progress became a triumphal procession well publicized in the newspapers. "The Sight makes Albany stare," Cooper boasted. He scored a public relations coup by persuading Albany's preeminent grandee, the manor lord Stephen Van Rensselaer, to host a maple sugar and tea party at his Manor House for "a large company of ladies and gentlemen." Understanding the importance of creating an aura of celebrity and fashion, Cooper published their statement that his maple sugar was "superior in flavor to the best muscavado sugar." On August 14 a sloop laden with the maple sugar set sail down the Hudson for New York City and Philadelphia to the applause of newspaper editors primed by Cooper's letters.[27]

Traveling overland from New York City via Burlington, Cooper reached Philadelphia in time to greet the sloop, which arrived on September 8 to the acclaim of the subscribers. Ecstatic, Henry Drinker predicted that his frontier lands would soon quintuple in value. William Cooper was the toast of Philadelphia. As with his opening campaign to settle the Beech Woods, Cooper's first season as maple sugar's champion seemed a coup that won him a national reputation for enterprise, ingenuity, and benevolence.[28]

In the wake of his triumphant progress to Philadelphia, William Cooper became a celebrity among the gentlemen of the urban Northeast—who were fascinated with the commercial prospects and benevolent implications of maple sugar. In 1791 the New York Society for the Promotion of Agriculture, Arts, and Manufactures invited Cooper to deliver an address at City Hall in New York. Presided over by the great manor lord (and chancellor of New York's court of equity) Robert R. Livingston, Jr., the society was a conclave of the state's leaders. After the speech Cooper boasted that he had addressed "a full meeting at the City Hall in [New] York," that the society had published his remarks, and that they had elected him a member—three reassuring proofs that he had been accepted by the gentility who governed the Republic. He assured Benjamin Rush that the speech had been "so

Clear, yea had I not ben Prepairing it my self I should not hesitate to say it must force Convincement into every mind. . . . and I have no Pride in inclosing it to thee but as their may be something worthy of attending to in it." Cooper basked in the attention of renowned men like Livingston and Rush. Because of maple sugar he could play to the audience whose approval he so earnestly wanted and needed to validate his recent ascent from poverty and obscurity. Whatever its failure as a marketable commodity, maple sugar opened important doors for William Cooper.[29]

Through surrogates Cooper even reached the attention of the preeminent American gentleman: President George Washington. In the spring of 1791, Cooper sent his associate Arthur Noble to Philadelphia bearing samples of maple rum and maple sugar. Benjamin Rush arranged for Noble to meet his friend Thomas Jefferson, the secretary of state. The Anglophobic Jefferson took a keen interest in the experiment as potentially liberating the United States from its reliance on the British West Indies for sugar and molasses. "He is as Sanguine as you or I about the Maple Sugar. He thinks in a few years we shall be able to supply half the World," Noble assured Cooper. Jefferson even planted a few sugar maples at his Monticello estate in Virginia. Before departing Philadelphia, Noble left his samples with Rush for formal delivery to the president in August. Washington accepted, wrote a gracious reply, and emulated his secretary of state by planting a few maple trees at Mount Vernon. Newspaper publication of Washington's reply served to promote maple sugar and to link Cooper's name with the president.[30]

Cooper's fame even extended across the Atlantic as maple sugar became a sensation in the circles of enlightened gentlemen committed to linking scientific progress with social reform. Drinker sent promotional pamphlets and samples of Cooper's sugar to prominent English Quakers and abolition-minded members of Parliament, including William Wilberforce. Jacques Pierre Brissot de Warville, president of the French society for emancipating slaves, also took an avid interest in the activities of Drinker and Cooper. Such was the European demand for samples that, in May 1791, Drinker begged Cooper for 500 pounds "of the very best quality thy Stock will afford. If any Man in America or indeed elsewhere, has a right to a preference in this matter, surely it is H[enry] D[rinker]." The best market for maple sugar was as samples sent to curious and benevolent foreigners; maple sugar was most valuable as a fashionable curio associated with enlightened reform. The samples served as so many calling cards, introducing William Cooper's name to the gentlemen of London, Paris, and Amsterdam.[31]

A highly personal crusade, the maple sugar promotion united and harmonized William Cooper's diverse ambitions: to become at once rich, respected, and beloved. He sought to enjoy private wealth, the accepting approval of great men, and the loving gratitude of common folk. By creating the maple sugar market, Cooper hoped to complete his ascent, becoming the father of his settlers, the benefactor of West Indian slaves, the peer of New York's gentry, a favorite of the eminent Philadelphians, and the champion of enlightened Europeans. In long, chatty letters Cooper took pains to impress and flatter his patrons. He informed Drinker that teaching the settlers to produce sugar of marketable quality "was a Dificulty that few besides W[illiam] C[ooper] whould have attemted. The People are now Passified with the alteration and bring it in Rapidly. Only think what a Pleasure it is to me to give thee this information." Eager to please, he informed Drinker, "We never weigh off a Parcel of Sugar but we Speak of thee, Dr. Rush, T[ench] Coxe and other friends to our Experiment." He plotted flamboyant promotions and dramatic presentations that would, in the service of maple sugar, bring and keep his name before the public eye. In particular, Cooper carefully planned his triumphal appearance in Philadelphia with a sloop load of maple sugar to receive the applause of his illustrious patrons. He intended "once more [to] see my friends in Philadelphia with Boldness, having the Evidence of my former Declarations with me to Produce." Cooper envisioned the success of maple sugar as a personal triumph; those "who are now opposed to the business, will look around and reflect on the havock universally made, and say, I now join in opinion with WILLIAM COOPER." However, that raw, aggressive personalism—as well as the flamboyant misspellings, malapropisms, and mixed metaphors of his speech and his writing—only marked Cooper's social awkwardness, for a polished gentleman more carefully masked his ego and his insecurities.[32]

DISENCHANTMENT

However, in Philadelphia the public euphoria gradually gave way to private disenchantment as Edward Pennington, a sugar refiner engaged by Henry Drinker, opened the celebrated hogsheads and discovered the damage inflicted by the summer rains. Water had penetrated all the hogsheads, rendering most of the maple sugar too dark and moist to have any market value: "It may do to look at and afterwards be applied to some use in thy Family." At great expense and trouble, Drinker had bought a very bulky novelty. None of the Philadelphia refiners would accept the maple sugar he had obtained from Cooper.[33]

At about the same time, Drinker and his fellow land speculators discovered that Cooper's dramatic early success in the Beech Woods was also too good to be true. Contrary to their specific instructions and Cooper's repeated promises, he had sold most of their land in large parcels to petty speculators rather than to occupying improvers. Cooper had sold so much

land so quickly by demanding no down payment and offering virtually un-
limited acreage to almost anyone, even to men who had already defaulted
on their large purchases in the Otsego Patent. Very few of the Beech Woods
purchasers paid anything or settled on the land or sold to families who
would settle and pay. The lands remained largely unsettled and a dead loss
to their landlords. In sum, Cooper had repeated and compounded in the
Beech Woods the mistakes that he had made in first retailing the Otsego
Patent: hasty sales without accurate surveys of large tracts to common men
without the means to pay for so much land. He should have known better;
at the same time that he sold the Beech Woods he was resurveying and redeeding the Otsego Patent in an expensive and arduous attempt to correct
his original mistakes. Less fertile and more rugged than Otsego, the Beech
Woods were not good enough lands to compensate for Cooper's mistakes.[34]

On the other hand, the few men who had actually settled in the Beech
Woods also felt misled and cheated. In some cases Cooper had not even
seen the lands he sold. For want of accurate, prior surveys, settlers often discovered that their assigned lots overlapped or that they were inarable
parcels of ledge, mountaintop, or hemlock swamp. These discoveries were
especially unpleasant because Cooper's newspaper advertisements had
promised that the lands were free from hemlocks, mountains, and stones.
Many began to curse Cooper and his patrons. Eager to tell everyone what
they most wanted to hear, Cooper had overpraised the settlers to the landlords—and the land to the settlers—setting up both groups for disillusion
and recrimination. He had oversold his capacity to settle any tract of land,
no matter how rugged and remote.[35]

Cooper had spread himself too thin by taking on far too much. Hungry
for the approval of distinguished men, he seemed unable to turn down any
of their patronage. He accepted more and still more responsibilities, virtually guaranteeing that he would fail at most. At the same time that he tried
to settle much of northeastern Pennsylvania, he was opening a store in
Cooperstown, supervising his own extensive settlements in the Otsego
Patent, managing for other speculators an array of New York lands scattered
in Otsego, Tioga, and Herkimer counties, and launching the ambitious
maple sugar promotion. All these complicated enterprises suffered from his
divided attention. Cooper recklessly overestimated the sheer power of his
will and the magical effect of his policies. He grossly underestimated the
time and energy necessary to make his Beech Woods sales and settlements
endure and develop. Drinker reproved Cooper, from "a real regard for thy
good name & reputation," for his reckless haste: "Beware of doing too
much, as more dangerous in some cases than doing too little. The great
matter is to move safely either for immediate pay, or if a credit is granted,
that it be to such as may be relied on for safety & punctuality."[36]

Because Cooper had treated the Beech Woods as a personal crusade to validate his ascent and prove his worth, he felt wounded by the mounting criticism: "I have Surmounted many Such Kicks and must Expect a many more." Employing a revealing metaphor, he added that it would have been "Strange if I should run Such a Long Gantlet and Receive no Stripes." Alone, he ran through a gauntlet of difficulties hurled by those certain that he must fail. Despite his earlier insistence that he had sold only to improvers, in March 1790 Cooper mounted a belated and labored defense of his sales to petty speculators. He assured Benjamin Rush,

> *I know very well that Fears will arise with Some of my Employers that Sales will be made to some persons that are not only poor, but speculating, and will have no care whether they settle or not. Very well, we will suppose among many, some such may appear, yet those are all in our way — For, in the first place, we must raise a Party, by way of breaking the Ice where there is difficulty and, in the second place, they always settle themselves or sell to others that do, generally answering the purpose expected.*

Cooper became prickly and defensive: "Those that believe in the Observations of others more than in my Conduct had better imploy them." He depicted as troublesome the lands he had so recently extolled: "I could wish those fearfull Ones to Remember that we have a Very Dificult Country to settel remote from Mills, Settelments, or Markets, [and] having the People Predjudiced against it."[37]

Demanding more autonomy from his employers, Cooper implied that the Beech Woods were really *his* promotion—that he cared more for their progress than their Philadelphia owners did, and that he alone could assure eventual success. He confided to Rush, "It seems as though the whole of the advancement of that Country [is] lieing on my Shoulders." Equally chagrined and defiant, Cooper vowed to Drinker, "Henry, I now Declare Hartily that if Providence spares me with helth and Strength that I will Continue to Perseveer Untill the Settlement of all that Country is Accomplished. Little Did I Ever think when I first Undertook to sell for thee and R[ichard] W[ells] that I should ever feel myself halfe so restless for the Advancement of So Large a Space of Country as I now Doe." He promised, "[I] Shall never be Easey Untill I see your Country in as flourishing Condition as those heretofore Setteled by me in the state of New York, wich hath gon forward to the great Suprise of all thinking People, for in Less than four years they have Surmounted Dificultys and now Experience Conveniancys."[38]

Convinced that problems reared only in his absence, Cooper insisted that he would readily set everything straight simply by visiting the settlers in the Beech Woods: "I should have ben with them, for they were too Young to be by themselves. They wanted incorragment and their minds Braced against many frightfull Objects that Apear to strangers in a new Place wich generally Vannish as they become more Acquainted." Likening the complaining settlers to overmatched children, Cooper claimed that his paternal presence would restore their happiness. In May 1790 he returned to the Beech Woods to restore settler morale with a heavy dose of his genial, gregarious, encouraging persona. "After much Paines and troble, I have Salved over the wounds of my Last Summer's Settlers. Some got Frightened at the Rocks and Mountains," he reported.[39]

Despite all of Cooper's promises, the Beech Woods promotion remained an utter failure. In 1794 Samuel Stanton, another land agent for Drinker, reported, "None of those persons who purchased thy lands of William Cooper in the summer of 1789 are now on those lands." The few buyers who could be traced were impecunious speculators living near Cooperstown or in western New York. Some had sold their claims to actual settlers— who were few, only eighty-two families, and all too poor to "make any present pay." In 1800 Drinker had yet to receive a penny of either interest or principal from Cooper's contracts, ostensibly worth about £10,000 when made, ten years earlier.[40]

Very few of Cooper's Beech Woods sales produced any revenue, because most of the original buyers were petty speculators who could not sell the land and would not settle there themselves. In 1795 the petty speculator Daniel Johnson complained to Cooper that the confused surveys and mountainous terrain hindered his attempts to retail farms within his 5,000-acre purchase. He lamented, "I have got little or nothing for all the trouble I have had with that land." The petty speculators could not unload their holdings because the potential settlers quickly recognized that most of the land in the Beech Woods was unsuitable for sustained agriculture. The extraordinary labor to clear the land of its massive trees yielded a large initial crop thanks to the rich, virgin humus, but thereafter cropping quickly exhausted the topsoil, revealing a relatively sterile and acidic base. Contrary to Yankee belief, large trees did not guarantee a durable soil. Upon exhausting the humus, most settlers abandoned their lands and their contracts, moving on, usually to the Finger Lakes region of western New York. Those who remained eked out a living by combining scratch farming with logging, hunting, and keeping a few cattle on the common range provided by the unsettled mountains. Unable to pay for their lands, they blighted the landlords' prospects of deriving a revenue from their speculation. Upon visiting the Beech Woods in 1802, one Philadelphian described the settlers as "a set of lawless depredators" who "only purchase for the privilege of cutting timber and getting all the value from the first working of the soil, & leave it a barren waste, not able to fulfill their engagements."[41]

Instead of ensuring settlement, Cooper's sales had encumbered the Beech Woods with a tangle of conflicting deeds and a set of uncooperative settlers. In 1794 Samuel Stanton explained, "Many who purchased have never come to see the land or made any improvements which has helped

encrease the difficulties of those who did." The deeds Cooper issued in
1789 and 1790 were worse than useless because they prevented the landlords from reselling the lots to others who might settle and pay. Tracking
down and suing the footloose and impecunious buyers was a thankless, expensive, and often impossible task. In 1793–94 the disgusted Philadelphians gave up on Cooper and his program. They pressed him to seek out the
purchasers and persuade them to relinquish their deeds in return for their
worthless bonds and mortgages. Although unable to pay, several buyers
clung to their deeds, necessitating costly lawsuits. In 1802 Drinker observed
that after "very heavy expenditures in paying an attorney, sheriff & court
fees," he had at last been "reinstated in the situation I was in 12 or 14 years
since." Instead of yielding annual interest payments, Cooper's sales had cost
Drinker "many hundred pounds by the experiment made."[42]

The Beech Woods had defied Cooper's confidence in the genius of his
program for settling the roughest lands. He had exaggerated the power a
developer could exercise over the largely autonomous and natural process
of migration and settlement. No amount of planning, goodwill, and encouragement could compensate for poor quality land and an isolated location (relative to external markets). Settlers sought and improved fertile
land well located for market opportunities, whether or not proprietors were
there to beat the promotional drum. On the other hand, few settlers would
come to, or linger in, a marginal district no matter how famous and encouraging the promoter. The Beech Woods simply could not compete in
quality with the more fertile, less expensive, and more accessible lands available to settlers in nearby upstate New York.

Cooper's trademark policies made worse the bad situation in the Beech
Woods. His partiality for selling lands to petty speculators was at odds with
the orthodoxy among other landlords and land agents. His stubborn persistence in that policy, despite repeated failures and against conventional
wisdom, suggests that he identified with the petty speculators. Risen from
poverty through luck, persistence, and pluck, Cooper could not resist the
temptation to assist those ambitious poor men in whom he saw himself.[43]

ABANDONMENT

During the winter and spring of 1790–1791, Cooper renewed his maple
sugar promotion in the hope that a second season would provide better
weather and a chance to correct his mistakes in production and packing.
Despite Cooper's large overdue debt for the previous year's ironware,
Drinker shipped 653 more sugar kettles to Cooperstown in the late fall of
1790. To enhance settler demand, Cooper lowered his retail price for a kettle by 2 shillings to £1.10.0. In 1791 Cooper retailed more kettles to more

customers than the year before (385 kettles, a 28 percent increase over 1790, dispensed to 224 customers, up 35 percent). In 1790 a third of the households in Otsego Township had procured sugar kettles from Cooper. The additional sales of 1791 raised that proportion to over one half.[44]

Cooper also constructed his own elaborate "Sugar Works" on a maple-rich tract just south of Cooperstown within the Hartwick Patent. He intended this personal works as a showplace to inspire and teach the settlers to produce more and better sugar. He contracted with settlers to make 2,000 wooden troughs to catch sap flowing from as many trees. If each maple made good Cooper's estimate of 10 pounds, his trees would yield 20,000 pounds (in addition to all the sugar independently produced by the settler-debtors entrusted with kettles). Cooper's hired workmen constructed a wooden sugarhouse with a brick foundation and chimneys. Within he installed "Large Pine Cisterns . . . hooped with iron" to receive the sap and sixteen kettles to render the molasses and sugar. He hired twenty men "to tap all the trees that are within one mile." Rather than entrust raw sugar a second time to Philadelphia's fussy refiners, Cooper was determined to refine his own sugar, relying upon printed instructions. He meant to ship a finished sugar packed tightly into boxes (each 3 feet by 1.5 feet), rather than employ leaky hogsheads a second time.[45]

Once again the weather did not cooperate with Cooper's ambitious plans, as a long, cold, snowy winter postponed sugaring until early April. Although the settlers made a little more sugar than in 1790, their production again lagged far behind Cooper's targets (see Table 4). And his own sugar works was a disappointment. "The Extrem failure of Performing at the Sugar house, almost makes me ashamed to render an account of the Present year's Produce at that Place," he confided to Drinker.[46]

The second successive disappointing season and the continued failure of his moldy sugar from the previous year to sell in Philadelphia soured Cooper's mood. "Not so bad a Season for Sugar as Last year, but what signifys makeing it if it will not sell?" he pointedly asked Drinker. Indeed, Cooper began to snipe at the weighty Friend whom he had, a year before, most wanted to impress. He was especially upset at the failure of Drinker and the other Philadelphia subscribers either to buy all his sugar or to help pay for his new sugar works as they had promised to do that winter during a meeting held at Carpenters Hall. Their defaults had confirmed Robert Morris's skepticism about subscriptions. Disgusted with Philadelphia's subscribers, refiners, and consumers, Cooper fumed that the "bosted Spunk" and "Patriotism of Philadelphia" had "Evapurate[d] in air at Carpenters Hall." Having invested his self-worth into the promotion, he took every slight and disappointment as a personal affront. Cooper seemed irritated with the enterprise that he had launched with such energy and high hopes two years earlier.[47]

Maple sugar had added to Cooper's fame and influence, but it threatened to make him poor once again. The value of his production lagged far behind his ballooning debt to Drinker for ironwork, shipping costs, and interest on the arrears. On August 6, 1791, Cooper's debt to Drinker stood at a staggering £1,756.16.3. He decided to cut his losses. After April 1791 Cooper obtained no more sugar kettles from Drinker and invested diminishing energy in promoting maple sugar. During his third season as maple sugar's promoter, Cooper seemed merely to go through the motions. In 1792 he sold only 140 kettles (all unsold inventory from the previous year), down from 385 in 1791. Only eighty-six men bought kettles, about a third of the number who had obtained them the year before. For a third straight year the weather was poor for maple sugaring in March and early April. Indeed, 1792 was far worse than the preceding two seasons. As measured by store book credits, maple sugar production plummeted to just 1,862 pounds: one-seventh the total in 1791. The store credited only 42 producers (down from 152) and each averaged only 44 pounds—half the level of a year before. Nearly three-quarters of that year's kettle buyers produced no marketable sugar. "*No Sugar this Season*—of Course no remittance in that artical," Cooper bluntly informed Drinker in late April. Twelve days later he added, "The Sugar Season has ben Dredfull."[48]

Cooper was done as an active participant in the promotion that he had launched so vigorously in 1789. He informed Drinker on May 3, 1792: "I think I shall quit [the] trade this fall. Of Course [I] shall not want any Sugar kettels—yet any servises that I can now or Ever heareafter Render thee or Any of thy family or any other Person thee may desire me to accomodate will be cheerfully gone into by thy assurd Friend, William Cooper." He had already broken up his own sugar works, selling off the kettles and the building in late April. Thereafter Otsego's settlers continued to produce maple sugar, but only for household use or local barter.[49]

After Cooper's withdrawal the other friends of maple sugar persevered for an additional three years. Keeping the faith, Henry Drinker sought to replace Cooper's sugar works by organizing, in September 1792, the Union Sugar Company, a joint stock company capitalized at £1,462. The stockholders included Philadelphia's leading land speculators and many longtime friends of maple sugar: Drinker, Benjamin Rush, Tench Coxe, Samuel Meredith, James Wilson, John Nicholson, Samuel Pleasants, Samuel Hodgdon, and Timothy Pickering. Even Robert Morris subscribed. On Little Equinunck Creek in the Beech Woods, the society established a sugar works known as the Union Farm. Harsh winters, late springs, and inexperienced laborers exhausted the capital while producing very little sugar. On November 1795 the Union Company folded, bringing to a close the maple sugar promotion begun six years earlier with such high hopes.[50]

Maple sugar had failed as a marketable commodity for two reasons. First, the sugaring season was too short and volatile to provide the reliable supply sought by seaport merchants. Second, the many small, ill-trained producers could not achieve the high, standardized quality demanded by urban consumers.

As his enthusiasm for maple sugar waned, Cooper increased his involvement in the potash trade that burned up the trees he had previously tried to protect. In 1791 he curtailed his sugar kettle purchases but dramatically increased his orders for potash kettles, acquiring thirty-six for sale on credit to settler producers. In a November 1791 letter to Drinker, Cooper identified potash as Otsego's most valuable commodity and ranked maple sugar a distant sixth (behind wheat, beef, cheese, and butter, as well as potash). As the value of maple sugar diminished on Cooper's store books, the value of ashes and potash grew. In the first five months of 1792, the potash passing through the store was thirteen times as valuable as the maple sugar credited there (see Table 5). Cooper replaced his sugarhouse with an elaborate and innovative furnace designed to produce the highest grade of potash, known as pearl ash. At his invitation the inventor, a Philadelphia Quaker named Samuel Hopkins, spent the spring in Cooperstown, supervising the construction and initial operation of the furnace. In June of 1792 Cooper extolled potash as "an immediate relief to the new beginer, and a great affair to the Continent"—the same praise he had once bestowed on maple sugar. Unable to sell enough maple sugar to pay for his sugar kettles, Cooper had to send Drinker the growing proceeds of his potash sales. In effect, the maple sugar promotion had generated a debt that Cooper could only pay by encouraging and facilitating the burning of maples and other hardwoods. Only by turning more trees to potash could Cooper pay for his failed attempt to save them.[51]

Cooper's shift was environmentally destructive because making potash was detrimental to the land's long-term fertility. By transforming trees into minerals with a cash value, settlers interrupted the circulation of energy and nutrients on their land. In a natural cycle the trees would die, fall, and rot to enrich the topsoil with the humus that nourishes living plants. By killing and burning the trees, settlers wasted much of the biomass degraded into the heat and smoke of the fires. Those settlers who kept the ashes to spread over the fields retained some of the organic nutrients to benefit their new crops of domesticated plants. Indeed, they obtained a short-term windfall, because the phosphorus and potassium in the ashes counteracted the natural acidity of the Otsego soil, enhancing crop growth for the first few years (but at a cost to the soil's durability). However, when settlers carted away their ashes for sale to make potash, they entirely sacrificed the fertilizing potential of their trees and forsook a supply of future fencing, firewood, lumber, and tools.[52]

By forsaking maple sugar in favor of potash, Cooper also turned from an egalitarian to a more hierarchical enterprise. Because potash kettles were larger, thicker, and heavier than sugar kettles, they were seven to ten times as expensive. As fewer men could afford potash kettles and their apparatus, potash production was more specialized and more lucrative. During the first five months of 1792 Cooper and Smith's store dealt with only four potash makers (who obtained raw ashes from ninety-two settlers), compared with forty-two sugar makers. The average potasher produced £149.11.0, compared with the £1.2.2 mean for the sugar makers (see Table 6).[53]

By turning from maple sugar to potash, Cooper forsook much of the enlightened enthusiasm that had characterized his early schemes as a developer. He abandoned his effort to create a new market in favor of fitting into an existing one. He forsook the conservationism and egalitarianism of maple sugar production in favor of the more destructive and hierarchical manufacture of potash. He had little choice, for he would go bankrupt and return to obscurity if he failed to produce an annual revenue in excess of the inexorably mounting annual interest on his debts. That relentless interest expressed capitalism's demand for sustained growth; a capital imploded if it did not appreciate faster than the 7 percent annual interest. To remain a capitalist Cooper had to abandon his more utopian visions and become a more conventional developer.

CONTRADICTIONS

William Cooper was guilty of the inconsistency attributed to Marmaduke Temple in *The Pioneers*. As the proponent of both maple sugar and potash, Cooper displayed the same contradiction that Temple manifests by decrying but joining the settlers' slaughter of wild pigeons and fish. Although Judge Temple does not fling off his coat to join Billy Kirby in attacking the trees, his commitment to preserving the sugar maples proves as rhetorical as his defense of the passenger pigeons and Otsego bass. Some scholars have interpreted Marmaduke Temple's concern for the sugar maples in *The Pioneers* as homage to the enlightened environmentalism of William Cooper. I would suggest instead that James Fenimore Cooper meant to undercut his father's claims to social and environmental authority by casting doubt on the depth of his commitment and the effectiveness of his leadership. Ultimately, the settlers' unchecked assault on the forest exposes Temple's inability to exercise the genteel authority he covets. The novelist remembered his father as an ineffectual protector of sugar maples who also (and increasingly) promoted their burning to make potash.[54]

In a dialogue among the Judge, his daughter Elizabeth, and Richard Jones, the novelist discredited his father's leadership in the maple sugar promotion. Ridiculing the quantity and quality of Temple's sugar, Jones remarks, "It is a pity, Judge, that you do not introduce a little more science into the manufacture of sugar, among your tenants." Jones advises building "a sugar-house in the village" and inviting "learned men to an investigation of the subject . . . men who unite theory with practice." He envisions a manufactory that will make loaves of sugar "as big as a hay-cock." In effect, Jones speaks for Drinker, Rush, and Coxe, who faulted Cooper for not hiring a professional sugar refiner and for giving up before scientific experimentation and mass production had been given a fair chance. Elizabeth jumps to her father's defense: "Really, sir, the world is of opinion that Judge Temple has tried the experiment fairly, though he did not cause his loaves to be cast in moulds of the magnitude that would suit your magnificent conceptions."[55]

In the novel Elizabeth usually has the last word, as the voice closest to the author's, and Jones is almost always the consummate fool and braggart. But on this occasion James Fenimore Cooper invites Temple to convict himself with a nonsensical addition: "I hope to live to see the day, when farms and plantations shall be devoted to this branch of business. Little is known concerning the properties of the tree itself, the source of all this wealth; how much it may be improved by cultivation, by the use of the hoe and plough." For once, Jones can trounce his rival's reasoning: " 'Hoe and plough!' roared the Sheriff;—"would you set a man hoeing round the root of a maple like this, . . . Hoeing trees! are you mad, [Marma]duke?" It is a bad turn, indeed, when a character comes off as more foolish than Richard Jones. The novelist unmasks Temple as a presumptuous upstart, embarrassing himself by pretending to a learning and expertise beyond his ken. James Fenimore Cooper implied either that the maple sugar promotion was thoroughly ludicrous and doomed from the start or that his father was the wrong man to lead it.[56]

Lacking the learning and dignity to impress the settlers, Temple cannot correct their sloppy production of maple sugar. Late in March, Judge Marmaduke Temple visits and closely examines the "Sugar Bush" of Billy Kirby. The consequent debate between the two characters represents James Fenimore Cooper's understanding of the resistance by settler traditionalists to his father's drive for a more systematic and higher-volume production. Although "one of the best sugar-boilers in the county," Kirby conducts an "extremely wasteful and inartificial arrangement." Temple faults Kirby for operating on too small a scale, with but two kettles, for lacking any rational system, and for damaging the trees. Unable to command, Temple must "earnestly beg" Kirby to mend his ways. Far from being cowed by his landlord, Kirby laughs off the criticisms, reiterating his preference for limited production, his reliance on tradition and intuition rather than instruction and experiment, and his delight in killing trees. Kirby does not share the

Judge's vision of sustained, efficient production. His Sugar Bush is a temporary operation that he will drive to exhaustion, then relocate.[57]

The problem is not that Kirby ignores the lures of the market. Indeed, he drives a hard bargain with the storekeeper who accompanies Temple to the Sugar Bush. But Kirby resists any challenge to his independence as a small producer. When he (mistakenly) decides that the storekeeper has mocked him, Kirby plays a cruel trick that curtails the bargaining despite the generous price offered (10 pence a pound). He cherishes money so long as it reiterates, rather than inhibits, his boasted independence. Temple and his party ride away, leaving Kirby to persist, unmoved by the visit. Their parting glance at Kirby tending his fires and kettles in the midst of the forest presents "no unreal picture of human life in its first stages of civilization"—rather than the rationalized manufacture sought, in vain, by the ineffectual Judge.[58]

Judge Temple is a superficially formidable figure who is not truly the master of his own home, much less the surrounding settlement. Entering his Manor House, Temple sees that Richard Jones has built "a cheerful fire" of sugar maple logs. The Judge flies into a rage. Dismissing the complaint, Jones successfully changes the subject, leaving the fire to turn the logs into ashes: a hint of the potash trade that betrayed William Cooper's defense of the sugar maples. James Fenimore Cooper reiterates that hint when Temple visits Kirby's Sugar Bush. Criticized for damaging the trees, Kirby quickly turns the subject to potash, asking the Judge, "What's the best news, Judge, concarning ashes? do pots hold so that a man can live by them still?" Taking the bait, Judge Temple enthusiastically predicts a strong and enduring European demand for potash, the commodity that takes a far greater toll on the sugar maples than Kirby's careless tapping. Temple is all too easily distracted—unable to control a conversation, much less persevere in a complex and difficult enterprise such as the maple sugar promotion. Although well-meaning he fails the test of genteel authority set by James Fenimore Cooper: to govern the destructive energies of the common settlers.[59]

In 1794 the English traveler William Strickland posed the same test to New York's gentry and found them sadly wanting. Unlike their English counterparts, New York's gentlemen preferred to dwell in dusty towns such as Albany rather than out in the countryside, where they could supervise their estates and control their tenants: "A lamentable loss to any country, but to this in its present unfortunate circumstances of being inhabited by the most destructive race that ever disfigured and destroyed a beautiful and luxuriant country, most deeply to be regretted." He blamed their inattention on their "little petty trafficking, landjobbing spirit." Strickland equated a powerful aristocracy with the conservation of natural resources and with a stable, civilized social order. In his opinion England's great landlords perpetuated their class and served their nation by controlling access to nature's bounty, by preserving the forests from the shortsighted predation he considered innate to the common people. In his eyes America was a barbarous land precisely because the gentry were unable or unwilling to check the massive destruction wrought by the common settlers taking ax and fire to the forest. Hopelessly bourgeois, the American gentry were incapable of governing their aggressive and greedy countrymen.[60]

Strickland detected the contradiction of American gentlemen who sought the power, and copied the manners, of English aristocrats but who depended upon commercial ventures for their income (and upon popular support for their political offices). A former wheelwright enriched and sustained by "landjobbing," William Cooper lived this contradiction as he strove for genteel standing. In maple sugar he had sought a commodity with a magical capacity to reconcile his genteel aspirations with his bourgeois ventures—a means to derive cash from trees while protecting them. Although noble, his effort failed.

RECRIMINATION

Disappointed by the linked and failed Beech Woods and maple sugar promotions, Cooper turned away from his past and his old patrons. After 1792 he avoided and neglected the Philadelphians he had previously tried so hard to please. Once numerous, long, detailed, chatty, and revealing, his letters to Drinker, Rush, and Coxe became rare and terse after 1792. Formerly a frequent and gregarious visitor, Cooper avoided their homes during his sojourns in Philadelphia after 1792. In July 1794 Drinker complained to Cooper, "Thy Letters & thyself have been rare & scarce here for a considerable time." When he did call, Cooper's stay was brief and his departure abrupt. On December 20, 1795, Elizabeth Drinker (Henry's wife) acidly noted, "William Cooper called this evening, stay'd a short time and took a French leave." In 1798 Henry Drinker sarcastically observed that he had belatedly learned of Cooper's recent appearance in Philadelphia "upon some grand scheme—small ones not being often an Object with William Cooper. Since then I have heard of thy being in or near this City, but was not favour'd with a visit from thee & when we are to have thy company here again is to me unknown." Preferring to forget his failures as quickly as possible, Cooper treated his Philadelphia friends as so many bad memories.[61]

His neglect was especially frustrating for Henry Drinker, who in June 1792 still needed £1,070.0.11 to balance his books for all the sugar kettles, potash kettles, stoves, pans, and other ironware shipped to Cooper on credit beginning in 1789. "It is with reluctance, I censure the conduct of my friend

William Cooper, for whom I entertain a real regard, but I cannot think that he has paid a proper attention to the state of my account," Drinker complained. All too ready to forget a debt associated with losing ventures, Cooper procrastinated. In July 1793 he advised Drinker to apply for payment to Richard R. Smith, Cooper's former storekeeping partner. When Smith did not reply to his letters, Drinker exploded:

> *I think myself extremely ill & ungratefully used. You have not acted with that punctuality & delicacy which becomes Persons who really value their credit & wish to be ranked among honorable Traders. This is the last letter I intend to trouble thee with on this business—it is William Cooper that is accountable to me & if he continues, while abounding in wealth, to keep me out of my just due, I shall sett him down a less clever Fellow than I once deem'd him to be.*

The outburst prompted Cooper to make some partial payments, and to confess that he had plowed into new land speculations the monies that ought to have paid Drinker. Nonetheless, Cooper expressed hurt at Drinker's dunning letters, "and more so, as until then I had a Supreem Pleasure in writing about such things as offered to, as I soposed, my best Friend."[62]

Cooper's debt to Drinker lingered into the next decade, steadily draining away their friendship. Unable to obtain cash from Cooper, Drinker had to accept lands in payment. When Drinker learned that some of the lands lay in the cold and mountainous Adirondacks—an even less promising region than the worst lands in the Beech Woods—he fumed: "William Cooper has too much character at stake & sets too much value on his honour and reputation to leave room or give cause to charge him with a deception so gross & dishonourable." Defending the quality of the tract and denying any intent to defraud Drinker, Cooper angrily replied that he had no "right to Reflect on William Cooper." It was his last letter to the man he had once tried so hard to impress.[63]

As Cooper turned away from his Philadelphia friends, he cultivated new patrons among the great men in Albany and New York City. He increasingly shared their interest in state and national politics, in part because he recognized the power of the state government to promote or hamper his frontier investments by funding or withholding internal improvements. In a letter to Henry Drinker in the spring of 1792, Cooper simultaneously announced his withdrawal from the maple sugar promotion and his new preoccupation with New York state politics: "We have a fair Prospect of being governd by John Jay, but this is [a] Dry buisiness to thee, but not so with me who is so much interrested in a State that wants a Liberal government, whose welth is Such as to Enable them to do many Usefull and Liberal Acts." Cooper expressed a new engagement with politics that was at odds with the apolitical Quaker heritage he had once shared with Henry Drinker.[64]

Part II

POWER

Chapter Six

FATHER OF THE PEOPLE

WILLIAM COOPER PURSUED wealth not merely as an end in it-self for private consumption but that he might achieve social respectability and public authority. His ambitions were those of an eighteenth-century gentle-man: to acquire wealth *and* to spend it in ways that built influence and reputation. His ideal was a secularized version of the weighty Friend—the trustee for the well-being of his humbler neighbors. By accumulating wealth Cooper sought the means to do good and to reap the gratitude of his community. He meant to transmute mere lucre into the ultimate payment he most desired: high social standing as a gentleman and public deference from common men.[1]

The order was obeyed promptly, though not servilely; the members of the crowd nodding familiarly to the members of the procession, as it passed. A party of constables with their staves followed the Sheriff, preceding Marmaduke and four plain, grave-looking yeomen, who were his associates on the bench. . . . The rear was brought up by another posse of constables, and the mob followed the whole into the room where the court held its sittings.

—*James Fenimore Cooper,* The Pioneers, *359*

Cooper aspired to become the beloved and respected patriarch of his large, extended "Family of Setelers." He claimed responsibility and took credit for their well-being. In 1789 Cooper reported, "Many men and Some with their Wifes are Gon in quest Down the River for Mr. Cooper's Lands as they call them. The Poor Creatures think all is Safe if they setell on Land under my care." Cooper regarded them as *his* settlers, dependent upon his protection: "I find my Self in a Very Humble Situation seing so much is Expected from me and . . . such a number of People and the many Dificultys they will have to Labour Under on my account has frequently caused me to solisit their welfair with teares."[2]

Cooper often helped the settlers by calling into play his contacts with powerful gentlemen dwelling in the external centers of wealth and power. During the famine of 1789 he coodinated relief efforts in Otsego and lobbied the state government for emergency food aid. Drawing upon a generous line of credit with Henry Drinker's Atsion Ironworks, Cooper subsequently promoted the maple sugar and potash manufactures so that the settlers could produce an immediate cash crop to purchase desperately

needed supplies. During the early 1790s he wrote letters recommending
Otsego storekeepers to urban wholesalers for credit, and he drafted petitions for settlers seeking redress from the state legislature. Cooper also exercised his influence in the state government to reward his favorite settlers
with political offices. Appointed a justice of the peace, James Aplin told his
wife, "My dear, last night you slept with James Aplin; to-night with James
Aplin, Esquire. God bless my good friend Judge Cooper." Drawing upon his
friendship with Tench Coxe, the assistant secretary of state, Cooper sought
a patent for an especially ingenious settler; Abraham Mudge traveled from
Otsego to Philadelphia bearing Cooper's letter and "a Mill in Miniature
about which he hath spent much time and study." Cooper assured Coxe,
"What ever attention you may shew him in the business will be considered
as a compliment paid to your Real Friend, William Cooper." When the ten-
year-old daughter of a Mr. Jones of Cooperstown became "Seized with
an acute Pain at Exactly 7 Minutes after Six Every day in her Left Leg, . . .
and always Screemes Violently untill she faints," Cooper wrote to Dr. Benjamin Rush of Philadelphia, seeking a diagnosis. He explained, "As the
father of the child is [a] laborious, useful, Honest Man, I have become interested in his Fealings." Cooper nurtured the well-being of the ingenious
and laborious people that he deemed valuable to the work of developing his
settlements.[3]

William Cooper reaped public recognition as the benevolent patriarch
primarily responsible for the well-being of Otsego's settlers. Paying tribute
to him, Dr. Joseph White effused that "under the guardianship of a MAN of
happy genius, sent by Heaven to civilize this country," Otsego had passed
from "a dismal wilderness: a habitation for the wolf, the bear and the panther" to "a state of high cultivation—producing all the necessaries and many
of the luxuries of life." Ebenezer Averill lauded Cooper as "A friend to the
Poor & Needy & to Mankind at Large." Another Yankee settler, Jedediah
Peck, extolled Cooper as "the poor man's benefactor and the widow's support—the Father of his County." No praise would have been sweeter to
Cooper's ear. In an equally telling tribute to Cooper, in 1787 the settler Bill
Jarvis named his new son William Cooper Jarvis.[4]

As the father of his county, William Cooper mediated between his common neighbors and the state's elite gathered in Albany and New York City.
His standing depended upon a mix of local popularity and social acceptance by the informal statewide brotherhood of gentlemen. To gather
power at the center, Cooper had to deliver the votes and land payments of
his people to his patrons. At the same time he had to demonstrate to his
neighbors clout with the state's powerful men—a capacity to deliver legislative redress and patronage appointments, patents for inventions and treat-
ments for disease. The two sides of the equation could work in tandem:
Cooper's influence at home won him friends in high places who, in turn,

delivered favors that increased his prestige and popularity among the settlers. However, during the late 1780s, as a newly risen landlord with rough manners, Cooper was more secure in his local popularity than in his social acceptance among the gentlemen of Albany and New York City. To gain their respect he needed to develop a genteel style.[5]

GENTILITY

As Cooper achieved wealth, celebrity, and influence, he tried to reinvent himself as a gentleman. He sought to prove to himself and onlookers that he was a natural aristocrat innately deserving of the rewards he had seized. In eighteenth-century England and America, gentility was a conspicuous and self-conscious style meant to define a sharp boundary between those included as polite and refined and those excluded as rude and common. Claiming superior morals, taste, and talents, gentlemen looked down upon the common farmers and artisans as obtuse and mean. Committed to ideals of harmony, grace, delicacy, and refinement, gentility required considerable self-discipline, self-control. Only men and women with both substantial property and some leisure could afford the money and time to obtain the proper possessions and to practice the appropriate affectations needed to win acceptance into polite dinners, teas, and balls. The genteel performed constantly for one another, ever watching and ever watched for the proper manners, conversation, dress, furnishings, and home. Every action, every statement, every object was on display and subject to applause or censure. The well-trained eye and ear heeded every detail of self-presentation for the proper nuances of fashion. A faulty performance damned the unfortunate as an impostor, as ridiculous as a rustic clown.[6]

In America maintaining gentility's boundary was such a chronic and demanding preoccupation precisely because there was sufficient social mobility both to produce a steady stream of the nouveau riche *and* to threaten the old elite with genteel poverty. Americans of means pursued gentility with a special anxiety and zeal because their fortunes were often so new and usually so insecure—dependent on the volatile fluctuations of international trade and speculative land values. Genteel manners promised distinction above all the common strivers in commercialized America. Its practitioners sought some secure and lasting preeminence, transcending the social and economic flux of American life.[7]

When mixing with the common people, a gentleman was supposed to display "condescension"—a word with a more positive connotation in the eighteenth century than in our own time. A condescending gentleman graciously and conspicuously displayed a certain affability carefully modulated between reserve and familiarity. Visiting John Jay at his country estate in

Westchester, James Fenimore Cooper admired the way the former New York governor and chief justice of the United States received local farmers. He performed "little acts of bland courtesy, which while they elevated others, in no respect subtra d from his own glory." Jay's condescension expressed a superior self-assurance unthreatened by contact with the common folk.[8]

Determined to pass for a gentleman, William Cooper set out to demonstrate that he could not only make money but also consume it in a genteel fashion. He bought objects meant to display his new mastery over both money and the landscape. In 1788 he erected his substantial Manor House in the midst of Cooperstown and atop the site of Croghan's Forest, as a symbolic claim to have supplanted his predecessor. Cooper's surveyor radiated the streets of Cooperstown outward from the Manor House—which the landlord intended as the center of attention, business, and power for the village and, by extension, for all of Otsego. Garnering another trophy of gentility and succession, Cooper stocked his mansion's library with books that he purchased from the confiscated estate of Sir William Johnson, formerly the kingpin of the New York frontier. He also brought to Cooperstown a light carriage—a symbol of genteel wealth and the first such in Otsego. By subsuming the old foundations and displaying symbols of old wealth, Cooper insisted that he was the natural successor to the colonial elite.[9]

Because owning other people was an especially coveted symbol of superior wealth and status, Cooper purchased indentured servants and slaves. In 1791 he boasted to Henry Drinker:

> *This [letter] is Coppyd by an Irish boy that I Purchesd from on bord the Ship Salley on my way home from Philadelphia Last Summer. He turnes out trusty and handy. I also Purchesd an Elderly woman from on bord the Same Ship. She is a Very Religious Minded body and has Once ben in repute amongst her Neibours. . . . I mention those Irish Persons as Prodigys — that two should be Obtaind of Such Excelent qualitys. The woman is worth a Jew's Eye in my family.*

The passage expresses Cooper's ethnic prejudices, as well as his pride in owning unusually respectable servants and his eagerness to impress leading men such as Drinker.[10]

Cooper pursued gentility with the same aggressive enthusiasm that had driven his ascent to wealth. Unfortunately, that energy utterly contradicted the conspicuous self-control and disciplined restraint essential to a truly genteel style. Clumsy, bombastic, and zealous, his assertions of gentility only highlighted that he was in over his depth, unable to transcend his humble origins and belated education. Despite his ambitious reading and extensive correspondence, his letters remained colorful potpourris of misspellings, grammatical errors, colloquialisms, and mixed metaphors that collectively betrayed his rough origins to every correspondent. In 1789 he apologized to Henry Drinker, "P.S. Thee will at all times be Pleasd to excuse bad Spelling as I was Never Larnt to write nor Cypher but have taking [them] up my Selfe."[11]

Cooper's untrained taste and the rigors of a frontier settlement imparted a jury-rigged quality to his genteel possessions. Although a substantial two-story house with one-story wings on each side, his Manor House was built without ornamentation and of wood, rather than of the brick or stone that characterized the best houses in eastern towns. His mansion sat among log cabins and sheds and beside a dirt street, rather than set back amidst ornamental gardens as a truly genteel house would have been. In siting his home, Cooper commercialized Croghan's Forest, producing a hybrid of the bourgeois and the aristocratic that typified his ventures; he staked out a position of dominance but allowed tradesmen and storekeepers and street traffic to press close around his home. Consequently, its name, Manor House, at once honored and mocked Cooper's pretensions to gentility. Recalling the structure as "*low* and *straggling,* stretching between sixty and seventy feet on the highway," James Fenimore Cooper regarded the Manor House as testimony that his father had more ambition than taste. So too with the carriage: whenever Cooper ventured out of Cooperstown into the surrounding hills, hired men had to walk along beside, steadying the vehicle as it jolted over the rocky, rooty, miry roads. The Irish servant boy also gave ironic testimony to Cooper's gentility, for he had far better handwriting than his ostensible superior. The boy's genteel script was superior to the colloquial expressions that he copied for his master. And the lad was probably not as trustworthy as Cooper boasted, for no subsequent letter survives in his hand, suggesting a sudden escape from the judge's possession.[12]

Unlike landlords born to wealth and educated to think themselves of a superior class, Cooper mixed with his settlers, sharing their pastimes and a measure of their hardships. At a crude frontier inn Cooper found graffiti written over the fireplace by a recent visitor, the young and elitist Washington Irving:

> *Here Sovereign Dirt erects her sable throne,*
> *The house, the host, the hostess all her own.*

Cooper composed and scrawled a retort:

> *Learn hence, young man, and teach it to your sons,*
> *The wisest way's to take it as it comes.*

Gregarious and earthy, Cooper relished his banter with the settlers, as he visited their farms or they came into Cooperstown to trade. Levi Beardsley vividly remembered the day that Judge Cooper came out to the family farm to perform a marriage ceremony:

The judge was in his long riding boots, covered with mud up to his knees, his horse was fed, that he might be off when the ceremony was over; the parties presented themselves, and were soon made man and wife as his "Honor" officially announced. He then gave the bride a good hearty kiss, or rather smack, remarking that he always claimed that as his fee; took a drink of rum, drank health, prosperity and long life to those married, ate a cake or two, declined staying even for supper, said he must be on his way home, and should go to the foot of the lake that night, refused any other fee for his services, mounted his horse and was off.

Beardsley's memory conveys the energy, enthusiasm, haste, and accessibility that so impressed Cooper's settlers. He often forgot the dignity expected of a gentleman; in September 1791, shortly after becoming the presiding judge in Otsego County, Cooper wrote a letter dispensing experienced and graphic advice on how to slaughter cattle—not something that John Jay could or would have done.[13]

At ease with hardworking men, Cooper was ever ready to throw off his coat and plunge into their wrestling matches. "I have often heard you say that you were not afraid to wrestle with any man of your size," a friend reminded Cooper. A brawny former wheelwright, he was as proud of his strength as of his new prominence as a landlord. In the ring wrestle a circle of cheering, betting, clamoring men surrounded two opponents trying to hurl each other to the ground. Once a contestant prevailed, a new challenger came forward from the ring. Levi Beardsley recalled one episode in the spring of 1794 when his father went to Cooperstown to attend the courts. After the court adjourned Cooper doffed his judicial robes to join the wrestling matches in front of Joseph Griffin's Red Lion Tavern, in the muddy main street of Cooperstown. The judge boasted that he could throw any man in the county. Timothy Morse, a strapping settler who had been a Continental Army soldier, put his hand to Cooper's shoulder and announced, "Cooper, I believe I can lay you on your back." Cooper replied, "If you can I will give you one hundred acres." Morse could and did, receiving a receipt good for his debt on 100 acres. It is hard to imagine John Jay or Henry Drinker wrestling with a settler in a muddy street before a public tavern.[14]

Although a rich and powerful landlord and merchant, Cooper was not yet a polished gentleman. Instead, he was remarkably like his son's depiction of Judge Marmaduke Temple: a well-meaning man who consistently falls just short of gentility's self-mastery. In *The Pioneers* opportunism or exuberant enthusiasm frequently overcome Judge Temple's tenuous restraint, taste, and judgment. By denouncing the settlers' excessive slaughter of passenger pigeons and Otsego bass, Temple claims an aristocratic superiority that he quickly undercuts by joining in the hunt and the fishing. Unable to resist the excitement, he reaffirms his common indiscipline.[15]

BROTHERS AND SISTERS 🦂

Cooper's efforts to remake himself as a gentleman also suffered from the continuing—and often inconvenient—presence in his life of needy brothers and sisters. During the 1790s at least six of his seven siblings were reduced to seeking financial rescue from their wealthy brother. Restless, roaming, and indebted, they were more typical of most common men and women than was their remarkably successful brother. To William Cooper's unease their plain manners and impoverished circumstances reminded onlookers that his origins were anything but genteel.[16]

Letitia Cooper Woodruff was his most embarrassing sibling, because she was the poorest and the most conspicuous to the elite families Cooper so wanted to impress. She usually lived in Philadelphia, sharing the streets with the congressmen, weighty Friends, and prominent capitalists who knew her brother William. In 1791 she was a widow unable to support her several young children, who were put out by the city as apprentices to tradesmen. She began calling at the door of Henry Drinker's mansion, begging for money in the expectation that he could dun her brother (and his partner in maple sugar and land speculations). Chagrined by her begging, Cooper notified Drinker on July 29: "Please to inform *my Sister* that thee hath no money of *William Cooper* in thy hands. I expect to Put her in Some Way when next in Philadelphia." But Letitia needed immediate help, and she continued to call upon Drinker monthly, usually receiving £1.0.0 or £1.10.0. The sums steadily accumulated in Drinker's accounts, as Cooper was slow to compensate. Exasperated, on June 13, 1793, Drinker wrote Cooper a pointed letter:

> I remember thou formerly desired me to tell thy Sister Letitia that I had none of thy money in my hands. . . . Nevertheless, she has been at times for many months past in such deep distress and extreme want that I could not avoid handing her out some aid, or she must undoubtedly with her two Children become an expence to the Parish, which I conclude would hardly tell well, when one Circumstance became known, that she was the Sister of rich Judge Cooper. . . . If thou sayst she and her children must not look to thee for assistance and may be left to the Parish, I will tell her so, and if the few pounds I have been constrain'd to furnish her with is objected to, I will bear the Loss.

Drinker knew that nothing could have so alarmed Cooper as the prospect that his inattention and his poor sister would become the subjects of shocked gossip in Philadelphia. Drinker was also exasperated with Cooper for his prolonged delays in paying large debts incurred for ironware advanced him during the maple sugar promotion of 1789–1792. Affording charity to Letitia was, for Drinker, a small but cherished opportunity to embarrass her procrastinating brother. And she must have recognized that by calling on Henry Drinker she maximized the social pressure on her brother to be generous.[17]

As Woodruff and Drinker anticipated, their tacit collusion sorely wounded Cooper's pride. He replied, "I feel a Littel hurt that thee should Sopose that I would not refund what thee hath advanced to my Poor, Unhappy Sister. I have Sent an Order to have her Brought up hear where I meane to Set her on a Farme Near me." He built "a convenient house for her" in Cooperstown, and he extended the invitation to his other widowed and impoverished sister in Philadelphia: Ann Cooper Kelley (1759–1818). In Cooperstown he could better care for them, and they would be far from the watching eyes and wagging tongues of prominent Philadelphians. Reluctant to leave behind their children and friends, Letitia and Ann delayed their move to Cooperstown until late 1795 or early 1796.[18]

Ann remarried and remained in Otsego Township as the wife of the settler Jabez Hubbell, but Letitia drifted back to Philadelphia—to her brother's dismay. There she married again, to a Joseph Ashton, but he was dead or absconded by September 1806, when Letitia Cooper Woodruff Ashton renewed her pleas for charity: "Dear Brother, I do not want to Court thee with any fond Expressions. I have often thought of thee Since my absence from your Country and have wisht to feel thee Near to me in the Best things, Tho' thee has Slighted me and don't wish to own me as a sister, tho' it is publickly Known here in this City that I am thy sister." Once again she knew where to pressure William Cooper: at his concern for public appearances and, especially, for the good opinion of leading Philadelphians. In a further attempt to shame her brother, she invoked their Quaker legacy: "It is not being poor that makes folks miserable, but it is them that is without the good Spirit that makes them miserable." As for her two sons, now grown and working as tradesmen, "If they give now and then a meal's victuals, they think that is as much as they can spare." She never reappeared in either Cooperstown or William Cooper's surviving papers, and it is unlikely that her brother supported her so long as she refused to return.[19]

In early 1796, shortly after relocating his sisters Letitia and Ann to Cooperstown, William Cooper tried to find a third sister, Susannah Cooper Breese. Heeding rumors that she and her family had moved to Loudon County, Virginia, Cooper wrote to the local congressman, Col. Leven Powell. In February Powell reported his success at locating the Breeses: "They are really poor, owing, she says, to the frowns of fortune." A "poor but an industrious little shoemaker," John Breese was "an honest man & not an Idle one, but rather deficient in management." They lived as sharecroppers "on a poor farm," paying a third of the produce in annual rent, leaving "a very scanty subsistence for a family of nine Children." Susannah was delighted at her brother's offer of a free farm if she would move to Otsego: "She desires to be kindly remembered to you & that I would inform you [that] she had seen hard times since she had seen you." But the Breeses could not leave the county for want of the money to pay their vigilant, suspicious, and impatient local creditors. In late 1796 Cooper agreed to compensate Powell for advancing to the Breeses the money to pay their debts and to finance their travel north. He provided them with a 100-acre farm in the town of Otego. Distrusting their management, he leased them the farm for a token rent ("one fat hen," paid every Christmas Day) but refused them title—for fear they would lose it to satisfy new debts. The Otego tax list for 1800 pegged their farm and livestock as worth $666: a below-average property for that fertile town.[20]

Apparently, Cooper intended to draw all of his siblings to Otsego, where they could best benefit from his largesse and least embarrass his reputation in the wider, cosmopolitan world. In the spring of 1796 he also subsidized the removal to Cooperstown by his older brother James (1753–1849) and family. A Continental Army veteran, James was scraping by as a small farmer in Bucks County, Pennsylvania. As it had for the Breeses, William's money paid his brother James's debts and his moving expenses from Pennsylvania to Cooperstown. James Cooper was a plainspoken and rough-hewn man who worked as a teamster and logger and as a foreman in the sawmills and gristmills along the Susquehanna on the southern edge of Cooperstown. According to the 1800 tax list for Otsego Township, he possessed property worth $356—about 1 percent of his brother's net worth in that town alone ($33,260).[21]

In the mid-1790s William Cooper drew four siblings to Otsego, but a fifth got away: younger brother Levi. In 1789 he had moved to Otsego from Bucks County, Pennsylvania, buying 269 uncleared acres from his brother and running up a large debt at his Cooperstown store. Unable to pay for his land, Levi relinquished the title back to his brother and moved northeast to buy on credit a new farm in the Mohawk valley. Again lagging in his payments, Levi begged William in early 1796 for the money to avert impending foreclosure proceedings.[22]

In December of 1796 William received a similar plea from his youngest brother, Benjamin, who owned a small but debt-encumbered farm outside Philadelphia. He desperately needed $136: "Had I a friend on Earth that could or would suply me with it, and Oh! was that friend to be my brother, I should esteem a favour far beyond my humble claim of Merit." William was in Philadelphia attending Congress when he received this note. Sensitive to their "inequality of Rank and Fortune," Benjamin conceded that "prudence whispers I must not be too familiar in a publick manner." Indeed, Benjamin had decided to write after a fleeting attempt to call at his brother's lodgings in a fashionable part of the city. Upon reaching the door Benjamin had frozen, as he wrote, "unable, from reasons I know not how to describe, to call and make myself known." Instead of knocking, Benjamin returned home to draft his abashed letter. There is no more telling testimony to the social distance that William Cooper had traveled than the image of his brother standing in front of a fine Philadelphia home, unable to knock on the door.[23]

WIFE 🕯

William Cooper's claims to gentility also suffered because his wife, Elizabeth Fenimore Cooper, proved unable or unwilling to play the role of a polished, elite hostess. Her patrimony had been essential to Cooper's early ascent in Burlington as a storekeeper and petty speculator, but she became a burden or afterthought as he sought to make himself into a gentleman.

Elizabeth remains an elusive figure, seen fleetingly and incompletely through brief and often cryptic observations in the letters of others. The voluminous Cooper papers contain no letters written by Elizabeth—apparently because she could not write, not even a signature. When obliged to co-sign a land deed or lease, she made an X as her mark. When away from home William had to obtain news of his family from friends and neighbors who could write. In Cooperstown in early 1790, Cooper urged his friend Henry Drinker: "Be sure to find out how my Family is as my Burlington Friends Neglects me on that head." That she could not write does not mean that Elizabeth could not read. Indeed, letters from family and friends refer to her delight in reading, especially novels. In the late eighteenth century it was common for families to teach their daughters to read but not to write. Her silence in the documents leaves the biographer with great latitude to reconstruct Elizabeth's personality and story. James Franklin Beard insists, "Mrs. Cooper was a patrician who detested the frontier. With her books, her music, her flowers, and her hospitality to all respectable company, she insisted on the primacy of civilized values." Henry W. Boynton reaches a harsher conclusion: Elizabeth Cooper was "an imperious personage, less friendly to all the world than her genial mate." A fuller and fairer reading of the evidence suggests that Elizabeth was neither a patrician nor a harpy but a plain Quaker woman who became, over the years, ever more withdrawn and sickly. She was often ill in body and spirit, apparently in reaction to what Boynton calls her husband's geniality: his boisterous engagement with outsiders to the neglect of his own household.[24]

Preoccupied with his complicated, diverse, far-flung, and extensive enterprises both speculative and political, William Cooper was often away from home and family. In June of 1790 he departed for the Beech Woods of northeastern Pennsylvania, leaving Elizabeth behind in Burlington with seven children, including the nine-month-old infant James. In the Beech

Woods on June 7, Cooper wrote a long letter to Henry Drinker, adding as an afterthought, "Be kind Enuff to send word to my Family that thee hath heard from me that I am well & hope to see them in a few months, say August, as I am so Pinch'd for time that I cannot write." Yet he did have the time to write frequent, detailed, and solicitous letters to Drinker, a recent acquaintance but a wealthy and prominent merchant whom Cooper wanted to cultivate. Cooper's references to Elizabeth in his letters to others were as infrequent as his correspondence home. James Hibbs corrected his nephew: "Thou gave account of self, children, brothers, sisters, &c. but nothing of thy wife, who I should have been glad to hear from."[25]

The family's removal from Burlington to Cooperstown in the fall of 1790 must have been traumatic for Elizabeth. At least in Burlington she had the emotional and physical support of relatives and friends, as well as the comforts of an old and thriving town well supplied with stores, a library, and a Quaker meeting. If married to a chronically absent husband, far better be in Burlington than in a frontier hamlet like Cooperstown. A family tradition plausibly maintains that, just as the Coopers were about to embark in their wagons for the trip north, Elizabeth rebelled, planting herself in a wooden armchair, refusing to budge. Losing patience, the brawny William Cooper picked up the chair and placed it and her in the waiting wagon. Significantly, the tradition identifies the armchair as a legacy from her recently deceased father; in vain Elizabeth clung to her memories and kin in Burlington. In November of 1790 Cooper reported that their journey was long and arduous as four weeks of daily rain produced a "Horridness of the Roads." Indeed, for the time being the family had had to leave in Albany much of their furniture—no doubt including the fabled armchair.[26]

In combination with the deaths of four of her children during the preceding decade, the removal to the frontier profoundly demoralized Elizabeth Cooper. During the 1790s family correspondents almost invariably discussed Elizabeth exclusively in terms of her health, physical and mental. The letters usually describe a sickly, uneasy, withdrawn, and apparently depressed woman. "My wife is very unwell and hath been for some Months. I scarcely expect she will recover her usual Health," William Cooper wrote in 1792. Four years later Hendrick Frey reported to an absent Cooper that Elizabeth was on the mend. Frey expressed more sympathy for William than for Elizabeth: "She must have been Afflicted with the common Disorder attending Women who do not give over Breeding, Viz. Hysterics." It was a pleasant surprise for a correspondent to report that Elizabeth was feeling well. In 1800 Frey heard from Richard Fenimore Cooper that "he Never saw his Mother so healthy as she has been this Winter, that she Reads Novels till 12 at Night. Even tempered & Every thing that could be wished to make the life of a family under the Auspices of an Empress happy and Agreeable." Implicit in Frey's marveling tone is that too often the Cooper household was less than happy and agreeable, because the "Empress" was so rarely healthy and even-tempered.[27]

Her illnesses and discontent peaked during—or in immediate anticipation of—her husband's absences. In the summer of 1792 Cooper had to cancel a planned trip to New York City because, he explained with some disappointment, "The situation of my wife is Such that I cannot Leave her at Present." It seems that sickness not only expressed her distress but was Elizabeth's one means to keep her peripatetic husband at home.[28]

She had a particularly severe illness and depression in the late winter and early spring of 1796, when William was away attending Congress in Philadelphia. Elizabeth was especially lonely because her husband had taken along their son Isaac and daughter Ann (also known as Nancy). Hearing in March that his wife again had fallen ill, Cooper wrote to Elihu Phinney, the editor of the village newspaper, seeking his "honest" assessment. On April 7, the editor breezily replied, "Mrs. Cooper is recruited very fast. An hour ago I met her walking very spruce along with Mrs. Woodworth [sic], your sister; you need not give yourself any concern on account of her health, in my 'honest' opinion." However, that same day Moss Kent, Jr., a lodger in the Manor House, described a profoundly discontented Elizabeth Cooper in his letter to William Cooper:

> Mrs. Cooper is gradually gaining Strength. She has rode out in the Carriage for several Mornings past & means to continue riding when the weather will permit. Mrs. C[ooper] has enjoined it upon me to inform you that she lives very unhappy & is very impatient for your return & wishes you to bring Isaac & Nancy with you. She is also desirous that you should engage a House at Burlington before your return as it is her determination never to spend another winter in this Country. I could have wished that [your eldest son] Richard had wrote you on this business, but Mrs. Cooper enjoined it on me, & my duty & politeness to her induced me to be obedient to her request.

This letter was especially difficult for Kent to write and for Cooper to receive, because the two men were political rivals at bitter odds over the impending April election. By engaging Kent, rather than her son Richard, to write, Elizabeth maximized her husband's embarrassment. When William continued to linger in Philadelphia, she obliged Kent to write a sequel on April 21:

> Mrs. Cooper still continues weakly & very low-spirited. She is very anxious that you should return soon & not wait till Congress adjourns. She blames me much for having written some time since that I thought she was getting hearty again, as she expects it will prevent your returning so soon as you otherwise would. I do not think Mrs. C[ooper] so well as a fortnight ago. She is very thin, has but little appetite to eat & thinks she has a fever every afternoon.

Eight days later Kent added that Elizabeth remained "very low spirited & very impatient to have you return." Declining to cut short his attendance on Congress, Cooper did not return home until mid-June. His triumphant greeting in the streets and taverns of Cooperstown was probably not matched when he repaired, at last, to the Manor House.[29]

Elizabeth conveyed her profound unhappiness to her husband so persuasively that he agreed to bring her south to winter in Burlington with the children when he returned to Congress in November of 1796. She seems to have remained in Burlington through the summer of 1798, although her husband had left Congress and returned to Cooperstown in the spring of 1797. Apparently Elizabeth had resolved never again to live in Cooperstown. Making the best of the situation, in March of 1798 Cooper entrusted the Manor House, outbuildings, gardens, and livestock to innkeeper Samuel Huntington for use as extra lodging, stables, and supplies for guests. Cooper and "such of the family of the said William as may Reside in the Mansion house" retained the right to board there. In September of 1798 William bought Elizabeth a house in Burlington (but put the title in the name of daughter Hannah). A month later Elizabeth suddenly changed her mind and agreed to return to Otsego. William wrote from Burlington to Richard Fenimore Cooper at Cooperstown: "Your mother hath alleved her mind [and] is comeing home. Have the Bed Down stairs by the 21st. We shall be home by that day. Have good fires. If you could have the Room white-washed, so much the better." Decades later James Fenimore Cooper explained his mother's change of mind: "So great was the grief of my brother and myself at giving up our lake and haunts [in Otsego] that she abandoned her own wishes to ours, and consented to return." Another factor may have been the fifth death of a Cooper child; born in Cooperstown in late 1792, Henry Frey Cooper died as a child in Burlington at an unknown date, probably during his mother's sojourn there in 1798.[30]

Word that Otsego Hall, the family's new mansion in Cooperstown, was nearing completion probably eased Elizabeth's decision to return. She had never liked the Manor House, and Cooper may well have designed the grand new mansion with such extensive grounds in part to make Cooperstown more palatable to his wife. The decision to build came in the fall of 1796, in the wake of her crisis that spring. The extensive gardens were especially meant to appease Elizabeth, who delighted in flowers. In June of 1799 the family moved into Otsego Hall. Thereafter the mansion was Elizabeth's cherished refuge as she became increasingly reclusive. Clinging to the Quaker identity and piety that her husband had forsaken, Elizabeth disliked the raucous, worldly, and Yankee village beyond the Cooper grounds. Pleasantly surprised by a visiting Quaker preacher from Byberry, Pennsylvania, she made him welcome and helped arrange a religious meeting. The preacher later informed Cooper that Elizabeth had confessed "her Discouragement on account of the Dissipation of some poor Creatures in your place."[31]

AUTHORITY

As an ambitious man of great wealth but flawed gentility, Cooper became caught up in the great contest of postrevolutionary politics: whether power should belong to traditional gentlemen who styled themselves "Fathers of the People" or to cruder democrats who acted out the new role as "Friends of the People." He plunged into political life during the 1790s—a peculiarly confusing time to pursue power, because the recent Revolution had clouded the nature of legitimate authority. Many New Yorkers, especially but not exclusively among the old elite, still subscribed to the traditional presumption that economic, cultural, social, and political authority should be united in an order of gentlemen distinguished from the common farmers, artisans, laborers, and sailors who had to work with their hands. Claiming superior talents, morals, and motives, gentlemen insisted that they alone could rule as wise and benevolent fathers over the common people. However, by asserting the equal rights of, and promising equal opportunities for, all white men, the Revolution questioned the gentility's claim to be a superior class, uniquely qualified to rule. The Revolution emboldened growing numbers of politicians to seek power by posing as Friends of the People—equals rather than superiors. Postrevolutionary New York's acrimonious politics pivoted on whether deference or democracy should determine leadership in the new republic.[32]

During the Revolution New York's Whigs had transformed their colony's political structures to approximate the republican ideal of a government dependent on the popular will (of adult males who owned property). Under the new state constitution adopted in 1777, elections became more frequent, more important, and more accessible to a larger electorate. Before the Revolution some counties had but one polling place; by permitting polls in every township, the new order made it far easier for rural men to cast their votes. Written ballots replaced the oral voting that had subjected common men to overt political intimidation by their landlords and creditors. Because the colonial governor had been a royal appointee—who in turn had named the members of the upper house, with the consent of the assembly—the colonial voter had been able to vote only for township officers and for representatives to the assembly. After the Revolution a New York citizen could also vote for governor, lieutenant governor, state senators, and federal congressmen. The colonial system had allocated but two assembly seats for every county—no matter how large or small—but reserved special seats for the largest manorial estates. The new state constitution mandated a more proportional system by abolishing the special seats, allocating from two to ten assembly seats per county depending on relative population, and mandating the regular addition and redistribution of county seats as population grew and shifted. Whereas colonial assembly elections were called by the royal governor and could be as infrequent as once in seven years, New York's postrevolutionary voters chose assemblymen every year, their congressman biennially, their governor and lieutenant governor at triennial intervals, and their state senators every fourth year. Finally, the new order widened the electorate for the assembly and U.S. Congress by allowing the vote for those offices to all adult males who resided within their counties for six months, paid taxes, and owned freehold property worth £20 ($50) clear of debts or who paid an annual rent in excess of £2 ($5). The historian Alfred F. Young has shown that in 1790 about three-fifths of the adult males were eligible to vote for assemblymen and congressmen.[33]

However, the gentlemen who wrote the new state constitution also included conservative features meant to restrain the democratic elements. To render the governor, lieutenant governor, and state senators more solicitous of property than popularity, the constitution confined their electorate to those men who owned freehold property worth at least £100 ($250)— less than a third of the adult men in 1790. Recognizing that wealthy and prestigious men stood the best chance of winning election from relatively large districts, the framers also stipulated that state senators would be elected by four multicounty districts designated the southern, northern, eastern, and western. Moreover, the conservatives secured a powerful state judiciary insulated by life appointments from popular influence. To preclude agrarian agitation for a redistribution of New York's great manorial estates and vast speculative tracts on the frontier, the constitution explicitly protected all land titles previously bestowed by the royal governors. In sum, although it dramatically expanded the influence of common white men, the state constitution tried to protect great property by excluding the poor and rootless from political rights and by giving the gentry disproportionate political influence.[34]

Unlike their Loyalist cousins who had fled the state, the Whig gentry were pragmatic conservatives who supported the Revolution in hopes of moderating and channeling its democratic energy. Insisting that every society had a natural aristocracy, the Whig gentry hoped that independence from Britain would allow the meritorious to rise gradually and gracefully to their proper honors. But their republican meritocracy meant no abolition of hierarchical ranks with a distinct and unitary elite at the pinnacle. Those who acquired new property in the Republic were supposed to take further pains to polish themselves into cultured and cosmopolitan gentlemen and to await social acceptance by the genteel before they sought political office and authority from the people.[35]

The Whig gentry drew a sharp distinction between a republic, which they supported, and a democracy, which they dreaded. According to their nightmare scenario, in a democracy unscrupulous demagogues would promote the forcible confiscation of great property, provoking violent anarchy and culminating in a draconian reaction as the survivors sought order in the rule of a tyrant. The conservatives insisted that only a proper republic guided by the gentry could defend property and liberty from the false allure and menacing abyss of democracy. In their republic the male electorate could choose their rulers but should elect only those gentlemen distinguished by birth, education, property, and connections; and between elections the voters should quietly defer to their rulers, who would govern according to their superior judgment and information, free from popular agitation and pressure. Robert R. Livingston, Jr., insisted that "the better sort" alone should govern because "the learned, the wise, the virtuous . . . are all aristocrats." Gouverneur Morris agreed: "There never was, and never will be a civilized Society without an Aristocracy."[36]

However, to the gentry's disgust, the New York state constitution proved far more democratic in operation than its conservative authors had intended. During the Revolution ambitious men of modest origins pushed their way into political offices as justices of the peace, state legislators, county sheriffs, and militia officers. Emboldened by the Revolution's liberal vision of equal rights and opportunities, they garnered political offices that had been dominated by old-school gentlemen in the colonial era. In the early 1780s three-quarters of New York's assemblymen and a majority of the state senators were middling men, rather than the gentry who had dominated the much smaller colonial legislature. The manor lord and chancellor Robert R. Livingston, Jr., described the new assemblymen as "unimproved by education and unrefined by honor." Another manor lord, Gen. Philip Schuyler of Albany, denounced the new magistrates as "wretches that would disgrace the most despicable of all governments." Although not truly poor, the new officeholders usually lacked the genteel "tone" required to set them apart and above their modest origins and common constituents. The new men had accumulated property and offices without acquiring gentility. Because political office traditionally certified high status in eighteenth-century America, the gentry regarded the advent of the new politicians as a degradation of all social distinctions.[37]

The old gentry were especially troubled when George Clinton won New York's first gubernatorial election in 1777, defeating the wealthier and more prestigious Schuyler. The son of a prosperous surveyor, farmer, and judge in Ulster County, Clinton was a man of middling, rather than either poor or genteel, origins. Before the Revolution, Clinton had begun to rise as a successful lawyer and an influential assembly representative. The Revolution accelerated his ascent as he became a brigadier general of militia and, in 1777, governor of the state. Through canny speculations in public lands, he quietly accumulated a substantial estate. Yet rather than cultivate a genteel style, he preserved the plain manners, blunt speech, and easy accessibility of a commoner. The astutest politician in revolutionary New York, Clinton understood the power of symbolism and the new popularity of a plain style—especially when practiced by a man with the means and accomplishments to set himself above the common people. Most common voters appreciated that Clinton symbolically affirmed their way of life instead of embracing the traditional elitism within his grasp.[38]

Clinton recognized that the Revolution had created new opportunities for ambitious men to achieve and sustain power by seeking popular support. He shrewdly and persuasively posed as the principled, egalitarian, and uncompromising patriot zealously defending the liberties of the common farmers and artisans from the greedy ambition of aristocrats determined to subvert the new Republic. He was the champion of middling men who owned their modest farms or shops—not of laborers without property, for they could not vote for governor and Clinton sought no reform of the state's electoral system, which served him so well. Despite his own power and wealth, Clinton's public persona endeared him to the commonality while aggravating most of the gentility, especially the manor lords of the Hudson valley. Although his actual policies did little to hurt the estates of the gentry, it rankled them that he posed as a counterweight to their influence, that he helped create and legitimate a path to power that circumvented their approval.[39]

In the eyes of the conservative gentry, a common governor and legislators disgraced and discredited their republic, beginning an ominous slide toward anarchy. Lewis Morris assured his son Jacob that "a man of Mr. Jay's dignity and superior understanding would give respect to the government," but his Clintonian opponent Robert Yates was "a man of *Grog* and had rather smoke his pipe and deal out his knowledge to skippers, than associate with gentlemen." By contrast, the common accessibility that demeaned Yates in Federalist eyes recommended him to Clintonians. In an electoral appeal, they celebrated: "His sentiments are republican, his manners plain, his integrity unquestionable, and his ability adequate." To Clintonians the common touch was more important than exalted talents in a republican leader.[40]

During the 1780s Clinton won every gubernatorial election while his supporters captured and held most of the legislative seats, but the conservatives remained electorally competitive because many common people still deferred to the gentry. In 1788 a Clintonian asked, "Will anyone say that there does not exist in this country the pride of family, of wealth, of talents, and that they do not command respect among the common people?" After 1788 New York's conservatives got a boost by supporting the new and increasingly popular federal constitution that Clinton had opposed (because it clipped the power of state governors and legislators by creating a superior national government). Identifying themselves with the new constitution, Clinton's critics adopted the name Federalist and invidiously labeled their foes Antifederalists. In reaction, Clinton's friends called themselves Republicans and insisted that the Federalists were aristocrats or their dupes united in enmity to popular government.[41]

Clinton's principal foe was Gen. Philip Schuyler (1733–1804) of Albany, a manor lord born into a family of old wealth and entrenched power. In stark contrast to Clinton, Schuyler had more than perfected the genteel style of austere formality and haughty superiority that demanded deference from the common people. Defeated in the 1777 gubernatorial race, Schuyler complained that Clinton's "family and connections do not entitle him to so distinguished an eminence." Schuyler had no such doubts about his own entitlement, boasting that although the voters "may chuse who they will" for their state legislators, "I will command them all." Because Schuyler's arrogance was too perfect for most voters, a political friend lamented, "It is Schuyler's misfortune to be very generally disliked, & I am afraid will ever remain so; I have long predicted that no party can flourish under his direction." He lacked the talent for condescension that a gentleman needed to garner popularity.[42]

Marriage and kinship united the elite families of eighteenth-century New York. Two of Schuyler's sons-in-law helped him lead the conservative opposition to Clinton's ascendancy. In 1783 Margaret Schuyler married Stephen Van Rensselaer (1764–1839), heir to the largest manorial landholding, the greatest fortune, and the most prestigious name in New York. He was often known as the Patroon because his manor of approximately 700,000 acres dated to the seventeenth-century New Netherlands colony, when such an immense tract was called a patroonship. More affable and condescending than his imperious father-in-law, Stephen Van Rensselaer enjoyed greater success in electoral politics. Whereas Schuyler seemed to demand deference, Van Rensselaer coaxed it from the common people.[43]

A second son-in-law was Col. Alexander Hamilton (1755–1804), the brilliant, mercurial, and acerbic lawyer and politician who served George Washington in war as an aide-de-camp and in peace as the new nation's first secretary of the treasury. Born illegitimate and raised in poverty in the West Indies, Hamilton had exploited the Revolution to rise even further and faster than Clinton had. But, unlike the governor, Hamilton had taken pains to cultivate the style, learning, and friendships of the old families, perfecting an elitism disdainful of the common mass that he had risen from. Hungry for assimilation into the elite, Hamilton succeeded by marrying Elizabeth Schuyler in 1780 and by constructing the Grange, an ornate mansion in New York City. His acceptance into the Schuyler–Van Rensselaer connection attested that the old elite welcomed new talent—provided they affirmed their loyalty to genteel ways and attitudes.[44]

Having exploited the revolutionary moment to clamber to the pinnacle of the social pyramid, Hamilton and other Federalist arrivistes wanted to grasp the social distinctions traditionally enjoyed by the colonial gentry. The Federalist gentry, cooperative newcomers and old elite alike, meant to consolidate the Revolution and stabilize America's social flux before it elevated over their heads still newer, cruder men. It appalled the Federalists that their opponents were ready to change the rules by developing the democratic shortcut to political authority, circumventing approval from the old elite. Angry at the prospect of losing out to men seeking an easier path to wealth and power, the Federalists identified themselves with social order and characterized their challengers as unscrupulous and ambitious demagogues out to substitute anarchy for society. They insistently preached the necessity of a hierarchical and stable social order, guided by precedent: the sort of society that America had approximated before the Revolution, the sort of society that would have obstructed the rise of Alexander Hamilton—or of his client in 1786, William Cooper.[45]

THE RIVAL

Cooper faced a fundamental decision as he ventured into New York's contentious politics. Would he affiliate with the governor and the revolutionary politics of democratic assertion? Or would he endorse the traditional elitism championed by Schuyler, Van Rensselaer, and Hamilton? Would he challenge or embrace gentility as a prerequisite for power? Would he be a Father or a Friend of the People? Brawny, ill educated, blunt spoken, and newly enriched, Cooper had more in common with George Clinton than with his aristocratic rivals. For a rough-hewn, new man like Cooper, the democratic politics practiced by Clinton certainly offered an easier path to power. Yet, like Hamilton, Cooper wanted to escape his origins by winning acceptance into the genteel social circles where Clinton was anathema. To an ambitious but insecure new man such as William Cooper, the approval of Stephen Van Rensselaer or Philip Schuyler was far more precious, because more demanding, than the favor of George Clinton. Cooper's origins pulled him in one political direction, his longing in another.

The choice obliged Cooper to confront his own contradictions—his impulses both to challenge and to impress the old elite. On his way up he had attacked the vulnerable estates of faltering gentry—George Croghan's heirs and creditors—while currying favor with more secure gentlemen, principally the weighty Friends of Burlington and Philadelphia. During the early 1790s Cooper's expanding land speculations in New York had introduced him to new partners and friends among the Albany or New York City gen-

try. Many of these associates—including Goldsborough Banyar, Cadwallader D. Colden, Josiah O. Hoffman, and Hendrick Frey—had opposed the
Revolution. As former Loyalists they allied as Federalists with the conservative Whigs, who favored postwar reconciliation—in contrast to the Clintonians, who sustained the Revolution's fervor and antipathies. As an
erstwhile Quaker who had remained passive during the Revolution, Cooper
was more comfortable in the company of Loyalists than with the zealous
Whigs who clustered around Clinton. Although Cooper owed his new fortune and standing to the revolutionary upheaval, during the late 1780s he
entered a social and business orbit dominated by men who meant to tame
the Revolution. Consequently, in 1789 Cooper made "great exertions" in
Otsego for the Federalist gubernatorial candidate unsuccessfully pitted
against George Clinton.[46]

Nonetheless, Cooper's political identity and allegiances remained
volatile. In 1790 he suddenly changed course, casting his lot with the Clintonians. At that moment he needed to curry the governor's favor because his
petition for establishing a new Otsego county was pending in the legislature.
By turning to the Clintonians, Cooper also hoped to frustrate a formidable
rival for preeminence in Otsego: a fellow frontier landlord named Jacob
Morris (1755–1844). Wellborn, well educated, and well connected, Morris
had the better claim to gentility and traditional authority. He was the son of
Lewis Morris, a Hudson valley manor lord and a Continental congressman.
An officer in the Continental Army, Jacob Morris had served as an aide to
Generals Charles Lee and Nathanael Greene. After failing as a merchant in
postwar New York City, Morris removed westward to take charge of his family's frontier estate, a 30,000-acre tract beside Butternuts Creek in Otsego's
southwest corner. With the help of a few slaves and many hired hands, Morris established a mansion and sawmill, and he began to retail farm-size lots to
new settlers. He expected to become the social and political patriarch of the
Butternuts—just as William Cooper meant to do at the foot of Otsego Lake.
The difference was that Morris was reprising on the frontier the aristocratic
role his family had played for generations on their Hudson valley estate,
Morrisania, while Cooper was trying to master a difficult new part.[47]

At first Cooper effusively welcomed Morris's arrival as a boost to Otsego's
reputation and development. He expressed delight "that I shall have so Advantagous a Neibour for my Self and femely to Associate with—I hope
Often." Cooper invited himself into Morris's social circle, anticipating that
their two families would commence and lead the gentility of their developing region. For want of Morris's reply, it is uncertain what he thought of the
prospect, but the rampant misspellings in Cooper's letter could not have
been reassuring. Relations between the two men cooled as it became apparent that Morris expected to represent Montgomery County in the state
legislature—an ambition at odds with Cooper's desires for that seat.[48]

In 1790 the emerging polarity between the two men helped push Cooper into the Clintonian camp, for Morris claimed, as a sort of birthright, the political patronage of Albany's Federalist elite. Because Morris seized the Philip Schuyler role, Cooper was obliged to play George Clinton in Otsego. That spring, in his first bid for electoral office in New York, Cooper ran as a Clintonian against Morris for one of Montgomery County's seats in the state assembly. Cooper's handler was Maj. Christopher P. Yates, a leading Mohawk valley Clintonian who in 1786 had been Cooper's lawyer at the Mabie's Tavern vendue that secured the Otsego Patent. Fanning the rivalry between the two frontier landlords, Yates wrote to Cooper: "You can form a judgment how far Morris' machinations have gone & how far it becomes us to counteract his Schemes. I do sincerely think him a dangerous man & can't help thinking you must be of my opinion as his views of aggrandizement must be evident to you." In the April 1790 election both Cooper and Morris lost, lagging behind other candidates who won the six seats allotted to Montgomery County. But Cooper had won a larger prize: sufficient trust among Clinton's friends to help secure a new county named Otsego.[49]

OTSEGO COUNTY

As an aspiring gentleman Cooper sought the honors and validation of high political office that a new county would pull within reach. The shortage of significant offices threw the ambitious Cooper and Morris into rancorous competition for the political crumbs that Montgomery County permitted Otsego Township. By creating a slate of county magistrates, a new county would ease the contention between the two landlords and provide patronage to bestow upon ambitious middling men among the settlers.[50]

A new county would also advance Cooper's program of commercial development, especially if his village became the seat of county government. As the host for the courthouse, jail, surrogate's office (registry of probate), registry of deeds, and gallows, Cooperstown would quickly attract the lion's share of the county's lawyers and civil officers—judges, treasurer, surrogate, clerk, and sheriff. Men of superior learning, status, and property, the new county officers and lawyers would bring valued capital and would lend a social and intellectual élan to the village. They would further stimulate the village economy by spending in local shops, stores, and taverns the income from their fees. The periodic court sessions would bring surges of country folk, drawn into the village as plaintiffs, defendants, witnesses, jurors, deputies, and spectators. Before and after the court sessions, they would patronize the village businesses.[51]

As the leading landholder and creditor in the vicinity, Cooper stood to profit from any measure that brought more people and trade into his village. The enhanced prosperity would facilitate settlers' land payments and would push up land values. A new county, with a courthouse and clerk's office within walking distance of his Manor House (rather than sixty miles away in Johnstown, the seat of Montgomery County), would also facilitate Cooper's voluminous and complicated legal business as a landlord, agent, and store owner. He had dozens of mortgages to record at the Registry of Deeds, and when debtors lagged in their payments for land or store goods, Cooper had to resort to a court of common pleas to foreclose mortgages or to secure judgments on notes, bonds, or store accounts.[52]

Because of the economic and political benefits, the leading communities in a prospective frontier county vied heatedly in the state legislature to become the shire town. In 1790 Cooperstown's chief rival was Cherry Valley, a dozen miles to the northeast. On the merits Cherry Valley had the edge: forty years older, nearly five times as populous, and blessed with a substantial infrastructure of framed buildings, including a Presbyterian church. Newer, less populous (only thirty-five villagers in 1790), and cruder, Cooperstown was at an initial disadvantage.[53]

Cherry Valley also enjoyed support from its offshoot: Harpersfield, the third center of settlement in the proposed county. In the early 1770s John Harper and his five formidable sons—Alexander, James, John Jr., Joseph, and William—had emigrated from Cherry Valley to found Harpersfield on the southeastern bank of the Susquehanna (in what is now Delaware County). A hard-driving, hard-drinking, hard-fighting, Scotch-Irish clan, the Harpers had prospered as Indian traders, sawmill owners, and land speculators. As vigorous supporters of the Revolution and staunch opponents of the federal constitution, they had suffered from Loyalist raids but benefited from George Clinton's political patronage.[54]

History, topography, and ethnicity drew Cherry Valley and Harpersfield together in opposition to Cooperstown and its environs. Unlike the new Yankee settlements in the Otsego hills, Cherry Valley and Harpersfield were older, bottomland communities naturally allied by ties of Scotch-Irish kinship and by memories of shared services and sufferings in the recent war. Because they had enjoyed more significant offices and influence in Montgomery County than had Cooperstown, the leaders of Cherry Valley and Harpersfield were less anxious for a break. Troubled by the growing numbers of postwar Yankee settlers, the leading men of the old settlements feared domination in a new county. The residents of Cherry Valley also bitterly resented William Cooper for bypassing their village when locating the state-funded road from the Mohawk to Cooperstown in 1790.[55]

To counteract Cherry Valley's advantages, Cooper counted on the superior political interest he could bring to bear in the state legislature on behalf of Cooperstown. Beginning in early 1790 he aggressively lobbied the politically powerful friends he had made in Albany and New York City during his extensive travels and transactions as a land speculator, maple sugar promoter, and frontier merchant. Cooper especially benefited from the friendship of the two state senators who represented the western district: Stephen Van Rensselaer had befriended Cooper's maple sugar promotion, and Leonard Gansevoort, a leading merchant in Albany, bought most of his potash. Cooper secured their support for the proposed bounds of a county designed to marginalize Cherry Valley geographically on the northeastern outskirts while creating a relatively central location for Cooperstown. This artificial centrality justified making Cooperstown the shire town despite its raw underdevelopment. Established by legislative act (and gubernatorial approval) on February 16, 1791, the new county extended south and west to the Unadilla River and consisted of three large townships: Harpersfield to the south, Cherry Valley on the east, and Otsego Township (including the village of Cooperstown) to the north and west (see Map 3). "My County is set off by Law and Cooperstown [is] the County town and Every other thing has gon to my wish," Cooper exclaimed proudly and possessively in a letter written on February 17. Otsego was *his* county.[56]

The "other thing" that had gone Cooper's way was the appointment of civil officers for the new county. On February 17 the state's Council of Appointment—Gov. George Clinton and four state senators—approved, without amendment, a civil list for Otsego proposed by Cooper and endorsed by Gansevoort and Van Rensselaer. Cooper's slate triumphed over a rival civil list, proposed by Col. John Harper, Jr., that was weighted in favor of Cherry Valley and Harpersfield. Cooper's victorious slate awarded a disproportionate share of the premier posts to the settlers of Otsego Township. William Cooper became the first judge, while his friend and storekeeping partner Richard R. Smith became the county sheriff. Already the principal landlords and creditors in the region, Cooper and Smith garnered the new county's two most powerful positions. As first judge and county sheriff, they became primarily responsible for the regulation of property rights, the preservation of order, and the conduct of elections. Untrained in the law, Cooper was qualified for first judge only on political grounds. Three associate justices joined him on the county bench: Platt Townsend of Harpersfield, Jedediah Peck of Otsego Township, and Edward Griswold of Cherry Valley. Jacob Morris was mollified with the post of county clerk. Four days later Clinton compensated the Harpersfield–Cherry Valley interest with the lion's share of the appointments as officers in the Otsego County militia, including Alexander Harper (John's brother) as the lieutenant colonel in command. The two sets of appointments divided the new county's most ambitious men: Cooper's friends dominated the magistracy while his foes controlled the military.[57]

As zealous Whigs, fellow Antifederalists, and avid Clintonians, the Harpers had a stronger claim to the governor's patronage than did Coo-

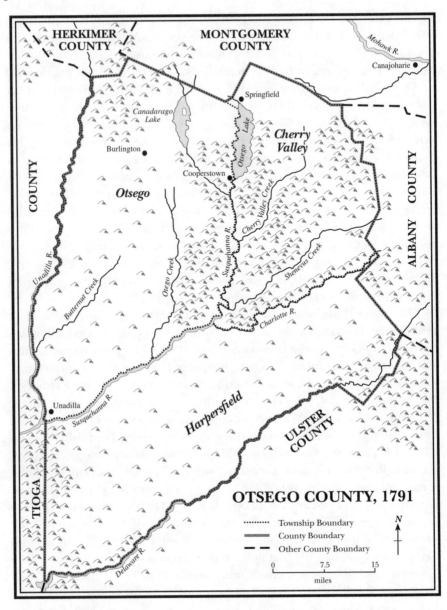

MAP 3

per—a newcomer from New Jersey with friends among the governor's political enemies and without any service to the Revolution. Why, then, did
Clinton's Council of Appointment favor Cooper's civil slate? Apparently,
Clinton concluded that he had more to gain by cultivating Cooper, a rising
power, than by rewarding old but slipping allies. An adroit and cunning
politician, Clinton was ever alert to opportunities for wooing new friends by
offering a taste of his goodwill. Because Cooper had cooperated with the

governor's party in the spring election of 1790, Clinton had reason to be-lieve that he could clinch Cooper's political friendship in early 1791. Prop-erly rewarded, Cooper might help the governor's reelection bid in 1792.[58]

William Cooper took pride in the new county and his new office as per-sonal monuments, attesting both to his success as a developer and to his in-fluence among the gentlemen who governed New York State. Writing to Dr. Benjamin Rush, Cooper celebrated his dual triumph:

> *In Reward for my industry in this Late wilderness Part of the state, the Legis-lature has, at my request, Set off a County for the most Part setteled by my Self, Containing about 8 or ten thousand inhabitants. The Prison and Court house [are] to be Built at Cooperstown this summer. By this thou wilt Perceive, Dear Dockter, that fortune Continues to smile on my Labours and why not, Seeing that I have not Onely Delt fairly but also Honnestly, Exerted my self and that without Ceasing to facilitate those whome I have Planted in Every Way that apeard to me advantageous and [I] have for my Pay the answer of a good Con-science together with the sanction of the Publick.*

Political honor certified Cooper's standing as Otsego's great landlord and benevolent patriarch.[59]

To entrench Cooperstown as the shire town for his new county, Cooper immediately donated a village lot and quickly erected a combination court-house and jail before the leaders of rival Cherry Valley could reopen the issue in the state legislature. Like Cooper's preemptive land sales of 1786, the sudden new building successfully frustrated rival claims. Thirty feet square, the two-story structure featured a log-walled jail on the ground floor with a yellow-painted clapboard and frame courtroom on the second. Cooper's haste dictated wooden construction instead of a more attractive, se-cure, and durable structure of brick or stone. Consequently, jailbreaks were alarmingly easy and frequent. In June 1795 the building was less than four years old, yet the county grand jury declared that the "Gaol has been for a Considerable time past and is at present in a very poor, weak, miserable Con-dition, unfit for the Reception of Criminals or even Debtors." Very much like Cooper's sloppy land surveys and sales of 1786, which had so quickly re-quired expensive resurveys and new deeds, the hastily constructed court-house and jail rapidly fell into a disrepair that demanded costly correction.[60]

BETRAYALS

Cooper owed his new county and judgeship to patrons in both political or-bits—to the Federalist state senators Gansevoort and Van Rensselaer as well as to their foe, Gov. George Clinton. In return, both camps expected Cooper's assistance in the spring election of 1791, obliging the new judge to choose. In January 1791 Clinton induced the state legislature to remove

Philip Schuyler from the U.S. Senate, replacing him with Aaron Burr, then the state attorney general and allied, for the time being, with the governor. Schuyler sought vindication by running for a state senate seat in the district that included the western counties as well as his native Albany. On April 14, 1791, in Cooperstown a public meeting chaired by Sheriff Richard R. Smith unanimously denounced Schuyler's removal from Congress and endorsed his candidacy for the state senate. The unanimity and Smith's chairmanship both signaled Cooper's covert commitment to Schuyler. In the polling later that month, Otsego's strong turnout was critical to Schuyler's victory, a blow to Clinton's prestige in upstate New York and an ill omen for his reelection bid looming in 1792. By putting Smith up front and keeping his own profile low in the election of 1791, Cooper may have thought that he could avoid the governor's wrath, may have hoped to continue to work back and forth across the political divide as he had done in 1789 and 1790. If so, Cooper underestimated George Clinton, who was as quick to detect and punish his enemies as he was to identify and reward potential friends. The governor concluded that the newly appointed judge of Otsego was an ingrate.[61]

Clinton conveyed his displeasure in the summer of 1791, when Cooper sought a share in the immense public land sales conducted by the commissioners of the New York State Land Office. Between May and September they sold 5,547,170 acres—most of the state's public domain—for an average of about 1 shilling per acre. Chaired and controlled by the governor, the commission bestowed most of the acreage on his political favorites, including Alexander Macomb of New York City, who headed a cartel that bought 3,635,000 acres in northern New York for a mere 8 pence per acre. Envious of Macomb's coup, Cooper pressed the commissioners to sell him thousands of acres of public lands near Arthurborough in the Adirondacks for about 1 shilling per acre. Forgetting his recent debacle in the Beech Woods, Cooper played up his success in settling Otsego so quickly: "I flatter myselfe that Lands sold to me at the same Price is better sold than to most others because *I settel all* amediately—wich in a Politicall Point of View is not the most trifeling Consideration." In seeking landed patronage from the governor's commission, Cooper also conveniently forgot that he had betrayed Clinton in the spring election. In August the commissioners rejected his application, ostensibly because the bid was too low. Given that Cooper offered a higher price than Macomb paid for lands of comparable quality, the rejection was transparently political—a rebuke for having supported Schuyler.[62]

Now it was Cooper's turn to feel betrayed and dishonored. Blaming the governor, Cooper tied himself more tightly to Albany's Federalist gentry. Indeed, he quickly became proverbial as New York State's most partisan Federalist. He even began to favor Federalists and slight Republicans in selling land and awarding credit. For example, in his memorandum book Cooper recorded that the settler Ebenezer Averill was "a very valuable, honest Man and ought to be encouraged—that he is a very firm Federalist." Determined to please his Federalist friends and to punish the governor, Cooper avidly endorsed and preached Philip Schuyler's accusation that the land sales of 1791 were a corrupt giveaway meant to enrich Clinton and perpetuate his power. With remarkable speed and vociferous venom, Cooper turned on the man who had honored him as Otsego's first judge earlier in the year.[63]

Cooper also had good reason to believe that the Federalists would triumph in the approaching gubernatorial election. In 1789 Clinton had narrowly won reelection, and his support seemed weaker still in 1792, especially after the state senate election of 1791 revealed the new Federalist strength in the frontier counties. Having served five terms, the governor had wearied many old voters and had yet to win much support among the Yankee newcomers, who were the fastest growing segment of the electorate, especially in upstate New York. Ambitious men among the Yankees were impatient for a larger share in the state patronage and for increased state expenditures on roads and canals to serve their new settlements—rewards they expected from a change in administrations. As an aspiring politician Cooper naturally wanted to be on the winning side, to share the spoils that the victors could dispense. At the same moment that Clinton's strength seemed spent, the Federalists ran their strongest ticket: John Jay for governor and Stephen Van Rensselaer for lieutenant governor.[64]

The Federalists and the Clintonians both posed as the true champions of a republic imperiled by an insidious threat. The electoral rhetoric pivoted on what sort of leader best protected—or most threatened—the liberty and autonomy of the white male citizenry. Were they best served by a gentleman of superior birth, education, and social standing or by someone of common origins? The Clintonians celebrated the governor's modest origins, stingy financial acumen, and plain style as proof that he would protect the people's rights from aristocrats dangerously arrogant with inherited wealth and privilege. In an appeal to the anxieties of the middling majority, the Clintonians slyly spread—and the Federalists angrily denied—a rumor that Jay had declared "that there ought to be but two sorts of people in America, the one very rich and the other very poor." In sharp contrast, the Federalists defended the traditional argument for political elitism: that inherited wealth and liberal education endowed Jay and Van Rensselaer with the honor, talents, and connections necessary to protect the common good and the public treasury. Conversely, the Federalists depicted Clinton as proof positive that a man of common origins and morals could not resist the temptation to enrich and empower himself at the public's expense. They charged that Clinton had perpetuated himself in office by prostituting state patronage to partisan ends and that he had grown rich by lining his pockets with the proceeds of corrupt public land sales to political favorites. "Which is generally the most assuming, overbearing, and proud," the Federalists demanded, "he who was born in tolerable circumstances, or he, who, in his profession or office has in a few years become rich?"[65]

It seems ironic that William Cooper—an aggressive, newly risen, self-made man—would enlist in the Federalist crusade to rescue New York from the arriviste George Clinton. However, the Federalists extended an invitation alluring to Cooper and many other new men eager to transcend suspicion of their recent ascent. In the electioneering of 1792 the Federalist gentry lowered their standards, inviting into their confidence, and promising patronage to, new men with the clout to deliver votes in their towns and counties. By enlisting in the coalition against Clinton, Cooper meant to cleanse away the stain of his humble origins and sudden fortune. By turning upon Clinton, Cooper claimed his place in the trust, correspondence, and homes of Philip Schuyler, Stephen Van Rensselaer, Leonard Gansevoort, and John Jay. As a Federalist, Cooper affirmed what he wanted to become by denying where he had come from.[66]

Aware that the Federalist gentry were watching his performance, Cooper treated the gubernatorial election of 1792 as an audition for their approval and respect, as a chance to win some of their prestige and power. During the campaign he wrote Van Rensselaer and Schuyler long, chatty letters filled with detailed news of his prodigious exertions and boundless optimism. He tried to conform his writing to genteel standards, dropping his old Quaker diction ("thee" and "thou" and "hath") and his Quaker style of dating (which did not name the months). In his new letters his old Quakerish closing—"Thy Real Friend, William Cooper"—gave way to a much more florid and genteel flourish. He ended a letter to Stephen Van Rensselaer: "Adieu my Dear friend, Adieu with all Possible Cordiallity and friendship. Once more Adieu, William Cooper." Although the style differed, his electioneering letters resembled in purpose his correspondence with Henry Drinker, Benjamin Rush, and Tench Coxe during the maple sugar and Beech Woods promotions of 1789–1791. Cooper had found a new cause and new patrons, but the impulse was the same: to impress prestigious men. He anticipated that those who mobilized the most voters for Jay could expect the greatest influence in, and patronage from, a Federalist administration. In particular Cooper wanted to win support from the Albany grandees for his ambition to run for Congress in the federal election later in the year.[67]

Cooper also won a key concession from the Albany gentry: precedence over Jacob Morris as their political viceroy in Otsego. By obliging Morris to run for the assembly, rather than for the more prestigious state senate seat that he coveted, the Albany gentry subordinated his formidable ambitions to those of the judge. Swallowing his resentments for the time being, Morris joined Cooper in vigorously campaigning for the Federalist ticket. After the election of 1792 Cooper boasted to Van Rensselaer, "Morris is a true trout. He went the Rounds with me and Rendered good Service. . . . Pay attention to him Next Winter as I send him to Represent us in the assembly as per my former Promis." Cooper claimed Morris as his protégé, owing election to his promise, and deserving the Albany gentry's patronage as a favor to the judge—rather than in his own right—claims that must have infuriated Morris.[68]

Despite his faulty gentility, Cooper won entree into the homes, correspondence, and confidence of New York's preeminent gentlemen. In part they forgave his flaws in appreciation of his boisterous and infectious good humor. Indeed, many developed a special fondness for Cooper's visits and letters. Few New Yorkers were better connected and more polished than the lawyer Josiah O. Hoffman, who, referring to his wife, Beulah, assured Cooper: "The woman continues to love you, but neither Man nor Woman loves you more, than your affectionate friend, Josiah Ogden Hoffman." During one session of the state legislature, Cooper and Van Rensselaer roomed together at Mary Daubeny's boardinghouse on Wall Street in New York City; delighted by Cooper's good spirits, Van Rensselaer thereafter rued a different roommate at a subsequent session: "[he] ill supplies the place of the Chief Judge of Otsego."[69]

The gentry were also inclined to overlook Cooper's foibles because they found him useful. They relied on his expert assistance to their own frontier land speculations. Better than they, he knew how to mix with and manage common settlers, knew how to endure discomfort and hardship while seeking out promising lands. Although lacking in gentility, Cooper partially compensated by his expertise in the common and utilitarian knowledge that gentlemen preferred to hire rather than master. Dr. Alexander Coventry observed, "Judge Cooper appears a man of strong mind and great experience in the common concerns of life." The gentry also cherished the votes that he could rally in Otsego on behalf of their candidates. Schuyler lauded Cooper's success in mobilizing Otsego's voters in support of John Jay: "Report says that you was very civil to the young and handsome of the [female] Sex, that you flattered the Old & Ugly, and even Embraced the toothless & decrepit in order to obtain votes. When will you write a treatise in Electioneering? Whenever you do, afford only a few copies to your friends." Amused, Schuyler could celebrate Cooper's possession of popular arts that he would have found frightening either in the opposition or in himself.[70]

Chapter Seven

TRIALS

I N EARLY 1792 COOPER REGARDED THE approaching gubernatorial election as a referendum on his benevolence as a landlord, as a measure of his worthiness as a Father of the People, as a critical test of his influence in Otsego. He also considered the election as a test for his settlers: if virtuous and perceptive they would unite in support of John Jay and Stephen Van Rensselaer, deferentially affirming the commitments made by their landlord and patron, William Cooper.

"And a mighty big error ye would mak
of it, Mister Todd," cried the landlad
"should ye be putting the matter int
the law at all, with Joodge Temple, wh
has a purse as long as one of the
pines on the hill, and who is an a
man to dale wid, if yees but mind th
humour of him. He's a good man
Joodge Temple, and a kind one, an
one who will be no the likelier to do th
pratty thing, bekaase ye would wish
tarrify him wid the law. . . . I hope
Lather-stocking, ye'll no be foolish, an
putting the boy up to try the law in th
matter; for 'twill be an evil day to
both."

— James Fenimore Cooper,
The Pioneers, 153–54

UNITY

Taking dissent personally, Cooper felt hurt and betrayed by any settler who supported Clinton instead of Jay. Although the Clintonians were few in Otsego Township, nothing less than unanimity would satisfy Cooper. A Clintonian named Joseph Whitford recalled entering Judge Cooper's office, next to the Manor House, shortly before the election; Cooper said, "I am sorry you are against us. There are but three men in our town who are against us, that is yourself, James Butterfield, and Joseph Tunnecliff. As you are all men of sense, I expect you will turn."[1]

Depicting himself as the head of a virtually united community, Cooper wrote two letters rebuking Capt. James Butterfield for supporting the governor. "For god sake, don't be against the settlement. What is the reason you so frequently pull against us? Joine the virtuous and oblige William Cooper." He added:

I fear you are so obstinate and determined to remain so. Why will you not be advised? Can you think that George Clinton or any of his friends will go such lengths to serve you as William Cooper would? Or can you think that his election is more deare to you than the friend who has never advis'd you against your

interest[?] I wish you to give your vote free, but I wish you to give it on the in-
formation of your friends, as it is impossible you should know the existing faults
of the present administration. You attend to your farme. Others are acquainted
with the affairs of the government, and . . . let me tell you that determining on
this matter as you have is a mark of weakness that I suposed you cleare of, altho
I have seen some thing of it before. Believe me James, your friend, William
Cooper.

Because Butterfield had prospered as one of Cooper's earliest settlers, the judge could not comprehend his refusal to defer.[2]

In soliciting deference to his judgment, Cooper claimed inside knowledge as a man in high office and as a confidant of the Albany gentry. However, in his boisterous enthusiasm for the Federalist ticket, he recklessly dispensed misinformation, abusing his position as an intermediary between Otsego and external realms of power and information. In his zeal to recruit every possible voter, Cooper erroneously maintained that the state legislature had recently rescinded the property requirement to vote, permitting any white man, however poor, the franchise. Cooper also insisted that the state legislature had exhaustively investigated and decisively censured Clinton's conduct of the public land sales. In fact, the legislature had not yet taken any action, and when it did, on April 10, the assembly exonerated Clinton and the other land commissioners in voting along strict party lines.[3]

As the campaign intensified, Cooper gained increasing notoriety as the governor's most vociferous and irresponsible critic. In a stump speech given March 21, 1792, Cooper asserted, "[Clinton] has robbed the State of five millions of money and put it into his own pocket." Cooper was engaged in more than his usual hyperbole, for the total land sales had amounted to only a little over $1 million, and there is no evidence that Clinton profited financially from the sales. On April 12 in Cooperstown, Cooper confronted Clinton's local supporters, charging, "Governor Clinton is a robber, for he has robbed the State of some millions of money in the Sales of the Lands belonging to this State and he was as great a traitor as [Benedict] Arnold, for had Arnold carried his point in selling West Point he could not have done more injury to the Country than the Governor had done, and this is the kind of man you hold up for Governor." Only fourteen months after Clinton had named him Otsego's presiding judge, Cooper publicly equated the governor, a proud war hero, with the Revolution's most notorious traitor—an insult the grim and vengeful Clinton was unlikely to overlook. It was especially unseemly for Cooper, who had done nothing for the Revolution, to cast aspersions on the governor's patriotism. On April 15 in Cooperstown, the judge charged that Clinton's land sales were part of a treasonous plot hatched in collaboration with the British authorities in Canada. Working himself into a rhetorical frenzy, Cooper added a day later that the governor was "a rogue" who had "robbed the State of more money than the whole continental war cost and if I do hear any person speaking in favor of Governor Clinton, I will take a firebrand and put his barn on fire."[4]

Cooper's alleged threat to burn barns sounds like one of his jokes gone awry through careless repetition around the settlements. After the election, and under oath, Joseph Whitford recalled the words as joking: "Judge Cooper turned to me again in a laughing manner, and said, if you hear any man speak in favour of Governor Clinton, tuck a fire brand in his barn. I replied, that will not do, Judge. He then said, knock him right down then. Strike him right here, pointing to my forehead. There were some jokes passed between us afterwards, and we parted." Gregarious, talkative, and indiscreet, Cooper loved to play with words, to banter and argue, without fully considering how others would subsequently interpret his meaning. Words tumbled from his mouth with little forethought to their implications or consequences.[5]

Cooper's popular persona of bonhomie could suddenly give way to resentment and anger toward those who rejected his paternal authority. At the polling in Cooperstown in late April, he pressed a gubernatorial ballot bearing John Jay's name into the hands of James Moore, a young settler who later testified:

> I opened it, and looked at the name that was in it and made answer in a laughing manner, "Judge Cooper, I can not vote so, for if I do vote for Governor, I would wish to vote clearly from my own inclination, as I did not mean to be dictated to by any person at that time." Judge Cooper appeared in a joking manner, and in good humour until that time. He then took the ballot out of my hand; which he had given to me, and appeared to be in a passion. Judge Cooper then said to me, "What, then young man, you will not vote as I would have you. You are a fool, young man, for you cannot know how to vote as well as I can direct you, for I am a man in public office." He then walked away, and seemed to be in a passion.

The judge saw Moore as a stubborn and ignorant young man who ill understood how much Cooper had staked—psychologically as well as politically—on producing a large and virtually unanimous turnout for Jay.[6]

Nor could Cooper leave well enough alone. Stewing over the young man's resistance, Cooper resumed and escalated the confrontation later in the day, when Moore cast his ballot for assembly representative. Accosting Moore, Cooper demanded payment of a £20 debt. Incredulous, Moore retorted that he "never owed him a shilling" and had "not come there to be treated in such a manner." According to Moore, "Judge Cooper then gave me very abusive language, and made the matter worse, instead of better. I was trying to defend myself as well as I could. Judge Cooper told me that if I used any bad language, he would fine me. I told him I thought I had enough by me to pay for all the oaths I had sworn there that day. Judge

Cooper told me that would not excuse me, he would take better care of me, by imprisonment." These explosions unmasked Cooper as a former wheelwright trying too hard to be a gentleman and protesting far too much ("for I am a man in public office"). A polished and dignified gentleman would have been insulated from such a frustrating encounter with an unusually independent voter. Philip Schuyler could count on his prestige to awe commoners and on his underlings to press ballots into the hands of voters.[7]

Cooper's sudden, angry outbursts during the election revealed the emotional stakes he had wagered in the crusade to defeat Clinton. After the poll closed Cooper sought out Joseph Tunnecliff, a Clintonian, at Butterfield's tavern. The judge pulled from his pocket, and read aloud to the people in the barroom, a published attack on Clinton's land sale to Macomb. Tunnecliff reported, "Then Judge Cooper turned round in a rage, and said *'What an infernal damned rascal Governor Clinton was'*; and he turned to me, and pointed with his finger, and said, 'you see *what an infernal rascal you have voted for*, I know you are sorry for it.' " Any vote for Clinton severely agitated Cooper, who could not bring himself to desist, even after a man had cast his ballot. Cooper reacted to independent settlers as if they were the aggressors, as if their stubborness was a personal assault on his character.[8]

A medley of four pressures drove Cooper's increasingly angry and even irrational rhetoric and actions. First, because he had invested his self-worth into the campaign for virtual unanimity in Otsego, Cooper could not stand to leave anything unsaid that might win another vote for Jay. Second, the weakness of Cooper's gentility left his standing with the state elite overly dependent on his ability to deliver the votes of his neighbors. Cooper knew that if he failed to manage his settlers, he would lose his welcome among the gentry. Third, having irremediably crossed the governor, Cooper felt vulnerable so long as Clinton remained in power. It fed Cooper's unease that, on the eve of the election, Clinton used his power over the Council of Appointment to pack Otsego's magistracy with his supporters: Cherry Valley or Harpersfield residents who, as Clinton intended, worked zealously for his reelection. To regain mastery over Otsego's government, Cooper would have to help oust Clinton from state power. Finally, the judge was exorcising his own past, attempting to prove to himself and onlookers that he was *not* a Clintonian, that he had transcended his common origins to become a Federalist gentleman. Indeed, Cooper cast Clinton as the very inversion of his own ideal self-image: "[Clinton] has in his politics oppressed the soldier, the widow, and the fatherless; he has violently opposed the Constitution. . . . He has shewn himself to be a man of pashion, party, and intirely void of commercial knowledge." In sum, Clinton was not a benevolent landlord, guardian of widows and orphans, supporter of the Federal Constitution, proponent of community unity, and personification of mercantile wisdom. Of course, Cooper's excessive efforts to prove his gentility were self-subverting; they only manifested his lack of that emotional self-control and rhetorical restraint expected of a true gentleman.[9]

CHALLENGES 🖎

Cooper's efforts culminated in the five days of polling that commenced on April 24 at the new courthouse in Cooperstown. Thereafter, to facilitate voting throughout the far-flung township, the inspectors of election and the judge relocated the ballot box every day to a new settlement, concluding on April 28 at John Sleeper's tavern on Otego Creek. Taking no chances on voters prone to misspelling, the Federalist state committee in Albany produced and forwarded to their allies, including Cooper, standardized ballots bearing the names of John Jay and Stephen Van Rensselaer. As the committee expected, Cooper zealously pressed these ballots upon voters as they approached the polling place. He exhorted and even tugged at voters to approach the polling table and watched as each presented his ballot to the inspector. John Hargrove, Jr., complained that Cooper gave him a ticket "and took hold of his arm and led him up to the window, where the Ballot was given to the inspectors (against his will) and would not give him time to read the ballot, but obliged him to give it in." Joseph Tunnecliff saw Cooper "give ballots to several men, taking them by the arm, and dragging them to the poll." In particular, Cooper pressed a ballot upon "George Johnston, and laying hold of his arm, dragged him about half way across the room— Johnston told Judge Cooper, that he was not ready, and would not go to the poll before he took another drink. Then Judge Cooper took him by the arm, and led him up to the poll, and there he voted."[10]

Otsego's Clintonians also charged that Cooper abused his formidable power as a landlord and store owner to coerce his many debtors. Cooper allegedly boasted "that he had been round to the people, and told them [that] they owed him, and that unless they voted for Mr. Jay, he would ruin them." Refuting that charge, Cooper's defenders insisted that they had heard him loudly declare during the polling "that should any man vote for Mr. Jay on account of his being in debt, he would ever consider such a man as a poor, pitiful wretch." Whether by intent or inadvertence, such a public declaration would, in fact, subtly remind voters of their dependence rather than set their minds at ease. Indeed, a New York landlord or storekeeper had to walk a fine line in playing upon the dependence of his tenants or customers. Although indebted, settlers proudly clung to their self-image of masculine autonomy; therefore the shrewd landlord or storekeeper was well-advised to practice the indirect reminder rather than resort to overt threats.[11]

Whether by hook or by crook, Cooper was spectacularly successful at mobilizing Otsego's vote for Jay. By the end of the polling, at least 600 men had voted in the township, a tenfold increase over the 63 votes cast in Otsego in the previous gubernatorial election in 1789. The region's rapid population growth accounted for most of that increase, but Cooper's activity turned out virtually every male eligible to vote—and many who were not. Because Otsego was a frontier county where poor newcomers predominated, few settlers had yet improved their new farms up to the £100 value (over and above the mortgage debt) required to vote for governor. According to James Butterfield, the township's tax collector for the preceding year, Otsego had only 522 taxpayers, of whom a mere 27 owned property worth £100. Joseph Mayall, a tax assessor for the town, calculated that only a quarter of the men he saw vote were legally qualified. Several laborers and new settlers disqualified by some combination of youth, poverty, or lack of legal residency later testified that they were not only permitted but cajoled to vote by Cooper. During the campaign he had attacked Clinton for "usurping" his original gubernatorial election in 1777 by packing the polls with "the common soldiers contrary to the Constitution," but the judge did much the same thing with transient laborers and poor settlers in Otsego in 1792. In service to the elitist John Jay, Cooper mobilized poor men who had been intentionally disenfranchised by the state constitution Jay had written.[12]

During the polling it became apparent that the inspectors of election in Otsego Township were Federalists who would not challenge any of the voters presenting Jayite ballots. However, according to New York's election law any citizen could challenge any voter, obliging the inspectors to demand an oath. If the challenged voter took the oath that he was a legally qualified voter in the township and had not previously voted, the inspector had to accept the ballot; but a false oath would expose the voter to prosecution for perjury (and imperil his immortal soul), so it was not uncommon for challenged men to withdraw.[13]

To counteract Cooper's efforts, a few daring Clintonians attended the polls in Otsego Township, determined to challenge voters of uncertain property and residence. But Cooper and Jacob Morris intimidated the Clintonian poll-watchers into quiescence. For example, on the morning of April 24, Andrew Cannan, a Scotch-Irish resident of Cherry Valley, rode into Cooperstown vowing to "make the damned Yankees all swear." Entering the village, Cannan found an unruly crowd led by Judge Cooper, who angrily assured Cannan "that there would [be] no body come to support George Clinton for Governor, but such rascals as he was." Cooper threatened to incarcerate Cannan for thirty days if he challenged any voters. Frightened, Cannan backed down, watching the polling in sullen silence.[14]

Cooper's powerful, controlling presence at the polling both derived from and contributed to the overwhelming consensus for Jay among Otsego's settlers. Surrounded and emboldened by a strong majority, Cooper and his lieutenants brazenly confronted the leading Clintonians, who, sensing their own vulnerability, quickly backed down. Jay's overwhelming success at Otsego's polls manifested the weakness of the local Clintonians as well as Cooper's strength. Because Cooper acted so quickly and forcefully, he precluded the development of any alternative cluster of authority around which wavering voters might rally.

When the polls closed Cooper was confident of local victory and suspiciously precise about its dimensions, for he and his partisans had carefully watched and tallied as voters cast the externally distinctive ballots the judge had distributed. Cooper was ecstatic as he calculated Otsego's overwhelming vote for the Federalist ticket. He gleefully reported the results to Van Rensselaer: "After some work and much Expence, I can inform you that . . . My Settlment gave 585 Sollid Licks for Jay and would have Raisd 800 had it not ben for a Child that was Lost in the woods that took all the inhabitants of . . . the West End of my Settlement to Serch for it and of Course, Could not Vote." Cooper estimated that in Otsego Township, Jay received at least seven times as many votes as Clinton.[15]

The judge eagerly awaited word that the Federalists had triumphed in the state as a whole: "I am Preparing to Illuminate as well the town as the Lake on wich We shall Raise Bonfires on Platforms, Cannonading, Musick, Hornes & Conkes Shels, turn out all the wine in my Celler & on Jay's Election, Huza for Our Side at Last, but if Clinton Suckeeds, I must hang up my fiddle." Having conceived of the election as a crusade to unite Otsego under his leadership, Cooper meant to culminate it with a communal festival. He would reward deference with generous largesse, restarting the cycle by creating new obligations among his settlers. His promises of festivity had probably loomed at least as large in mobilizing voters as any veiled threats.[16]

Throughout the state, Federalist leaders shared Cooper's assurance that Jay and Van Rensselaer had won, ousting the hated George Clinton from power. Van Rensselaer prepared a triumphal procession of Albany's militia units to greet the new governor-elect. "We have no doubt of success," he explained to Cooper. The Federalists crowed when the Clintonians refused to accept further bets on the results of the election because they were so "lowspirited." Philip Schuyler offered three-to-one odds that Jay had prevailed, but still found no takers. However, the Federalists would soon have to cancel their victory celebrations as it became clear that the Clintonians were determined to steal the election. And into the bargain they meant to ruin William Cooper.[17]

CANVASSERS

In May 1792 the Federalists celebrated electoral victory prematurely, for the state board of canvassers—six state senators and six assembly representatives specially chosen by their peers—had yet to count the ballots and certify the results. The canvassers were empowered to reject the ballots from any township or county where the boxes arrived in any fashion deemed irregular. In the 1786 gubernatorial election the canvassers had thrown out more than half the ballots owing to irregularities in their transmission. To Cooper's chagrin, at the gubernatorial election of 1789, the board of canvassers had rejected Otsego's ballots because neither the clerk nor the inspector had signed the attached poll list, as required by law. Sensitive to criticism of that fiasco, Cooper was determined to avoid a repeat by exercising more personal oversight over the ballot boxes in 1792. In early May, when pointedly asked if Otsego would again lose its votes, Cooper allegedly replied that "he would be damned if they could, for that he had put them up with his own hands." If Cooper said so, he was very indiscreet for, by law, only the county's sheriff was authorized to seal and forward a county's ballots to Albany.[18]

Ebenezer Foote, a Federalist assemblyman from Ulster County, understood better than his colleagues that the Federalist celebrations of electoral victory in early May were premature. They blithely underestimated a Clintonian gambit that had won them control of the canvassers on the eve of the election. In early April, in a bipartisan compromise, the state senate chose three Federalists and three Clintonians as canvassers. In the assembly the Federalists thought they had struck a similar deal with the Clintonians for an equal division of their house's six canvassers, but on April 3 Foote reported,

> The Clintonian Party in the assembly have by a damned Maneuvre got the better of us in appointing Canvassers for the next Election. We, as honest men, agreed to vote for a part of their List, and they agreed to vote for half of ours. We kept our word and they, as usual, disregarded theirs. In Consequence of which, they have Got every one of the Committee on their Side. Thus you see, we are Duped & fooled every way and shall Continue so to be as Long as we act honestly and Candidly in anything which concerns them.

Consequently, nine Clintonians and only three Federalists sat on the board of canvassers that would count the ballots.[19]

Anticipating defeat if their canvassers counted all the returns, in May the leading Clintonians cast about for grounds to reject the votes from Otsego County. They focused on Otsego precisely because they knew that Cooper had engineered the most lopsided Federalist vote in the state. Indeed, Cooper had won a national notoriety as, in the words of Thomas Jefferson, "the Bashaw of Otsego and furious partisan of Jay." Clintonian newspaper essayists denounced "the shameful arts which were practised in Otsego county, and which a certain party are so lost to decency as to make a public boast of." By doing too much too conspicuously, Cooper invited the special attention of men determined to win in the canvassing the election they had lost in the polling.[20]

The Clintonians quickly detected two problems with the box of Otsego ballots sitting in the secretary of state's office in Albany. First, a political schism in Cherry Valley had induced Sheriff Richard R. Smith to package some of that township's votes in an unorthodox fashion. Determined to control Cherry Valley's supervisor, who would chair the township's inspectors of election, the contending political parties had held rival town meetings and had chosen rival town supervisors: the Federalist Eli Parsons and the Clintonian Benjamin Griffin. After conducting separate polls, Parsons and Griffin delivered competing returns to Smith. On May 1, Cooper and his fellow judges ruled that Parsons was the legitimate supervisor, implying that his poll alone was legal for Cherry Valley. Consequently, Smith only included Parsons's poll within the box he sealed on May 3. But rather than take the legal risk of discarding the Griffin poll, Smith attached it to the outside, leaving the ultimate decision to the canvassers.[21]

The second, and ultimately more serious, problem involved whether the box of ballots had been handled exclusively by the appropriate officer—the county sheriff. Acting as sheriff, Smith had received the votes from the county's three townships—Cherry Valley, Harpersfield, and Otsego—and had bundled them into a box entrusted to a deputy for delivery to Albany. However, Smith's legal authority to receive, package, and forward the ballots was dubious: he had tendered his resignation as sheriff on January 13; the state's Council of Appointment had received that letter on February 4; his commission as sheriff had expired on February 18; he had been replaced by the Council of Appointment on March 30; and he had been elected to another office—supervisor of Otsego Township—on April 3 (by law a sheriff could hold no other office). However, his successor, Benjamin Gilbert, did not receive word of his commission until May 9 and did not assume office until May 11, eight days after Smith had forwarded the ballots.[22]

During late April and early May, Smith had alternated between the legally incompatible offices of town supervisor and county sheriff, depending on the needs of the Federalist cause. During the polling (April 24 through 28) he had exercised the powers of a town supervisor: announcing the daily opening and closing of the poll and ruling on challenges to voters. In the most absurd touch, at the end of the polling Smith, acting as supervisor, sealed the Otsego Township ballot box for transfer to the county sheriff; becoming sheriff, he received that ballot box from himself. His flipping back and forth continued on May 1 at the meeting of the county board of supervisors. As Otsego Township's supervisor, he cast the vote critical to the ruling in favor of Parsons and the votes from his poll in Cherry Valley. When the Clintonian supervisor for Harpersfield protested that Smith could not vote because he was still the county sheriff, he countered that he had resigned as sheriff and been replaced. Nonetheless, two days later Smith acted as sheriff to forward the ballots to the secretary of state's office in Albany.[23]

It added to the bad odor that for the five days between when the polls closed and when he forwarded the ballots, they lay in the strongbox of his store co-owned by William Cooper. Had Cooper exploited his access to rummage through the ballots? It also did not look right that the deputy entrusted with delivering the box did not reside in Otsego: Leonard Goes lived in Kinderhook (in the Hudson valley) and was an emissary for Stephen Van Rensselaer, who had sent him to Otsego with political instructions for Cooper and Smith. What was the messenger of a candidate for lieutenant governor doing handling the official box of ballots that would probably determine the election? Smith won no points for plausibility when he later insisted that Goes's relationship to Van Rensselaer was "a matter of perfect indifference, either to the public or myself." It is very unlikely that Cooper, Smith, or Goes tampered with the ballots, given their confidence that Otsego had produced near unanimity for Jay. They had simply taken excessive precautions to safeguard the precious ballots that would, they anticipated, carry the election. Ironically, those excesses doomed the ballots.[24]

Who was to blame for the six-week delay in empowering Gilbert as Smith's replacement? Anticipating removal for his Federalist partnership, Smith had written a letter of resignation that Cooper sent to Van Rensselaer for submission to his fellow members of the Council of Appointment (he was the token Federalist member) on February 4. Clinton vetoed the successor recommended by Smith and proposed by Van Rensselaer, but the governor procrastinated naming his own candidate, delaying the new appointment until March 30. Considered a political neutral, Benjamin Gilbert was a compromise candidate, agreeable to both Clinton and Van Rensselaer. Clinton had delayed the appointment for nearly two months, apparently to complicate the transfer until the onset of the April mud season that would hinder the delivery of anything to Otsego. Thereafter, Van Rensselaer added his own delay. On April 13 he took responsibility for conveying the new commission to Gilbert in Otsego. But Van Rensselaer hung on to that commission until April 30—two days after the polls had closed—and then sent it to Cooper rather than directly to Gilbert. Van Rensselaer explained to Cooper:

> *I delayed sending Sheriff Gilbert's commission till after the Election lest by some irregularity your Poll, which in all probability will turn the Election should be rejected. I trust my friend R. Smith will excuse this Liberty. I will make every acknowledgment to him when I have the Honor of his acquaintance, which I covet very much. Pray detain the Commission untill Smith has deputed some faithful person to deliver the box [of ballots] to the Secretary [of State].*

Cooper received the letter on May 2, but retained the commission for another week before informing Gilbert of his appointment.[25]

Cooper and Van Rensselaer fell prey to the delusion that they were more clever than the governor; they tried to turn the lateness of the new appointment to advantage by further delays meant to keep the partisan Smith as sheriff through the election and delivery of the ballots. However, this gambit backfired when the Clintonians seized upon Smith's dual role to discredit Otsego's ballots. Consequently, Van Rensselaer's miscalculation was primarily responsible for the pretext that cost him his election as the lieutenant governor. If so, George Clinton surely enjoyed the irony.

The canvassers began their deliberations on May 29. As it became clear that Clinton had only a bare majority in the other counties, his friends sought to discredit the Otsego ballots which were certain to elect Jay and Van Rensselaer. Seeking legal cover, the canvassers solicited opinions from the state's two United States senators. True to their respective political alliances, the senators split. The Federalist Rufus King insisted that Smith was the legal sheriff and that Otsego's ballots should be counted; the Republican Aaron Burr disagreed. As at the Otsego vendue of 1786, Burr was again pitted in legal combat against William Cooper. Meanwhile, the Federalists pressured the canvassers by holding raucous public celebrations of Jay's election as governor.[26]

On June 12, their final legal deadline for a decision, the canvassers announced their verdict. By a seven-to-four vote largely along party lines (one Clintonian canvasser abstained and a second strayed; the three Federalists hung together), they rejected Otsego's ballots. In a vain attempt to seem consistent, principled, and nonpartisan, they also rejected the votes from two other counties—Clinton and Tioga—thought to have provided small majorities for the governor. Those ballots had been forwarded by unauthorized deputies. But everyone well understood that the purpose of the rejections was to discard the Federalist majority of at least 400 votes in Otsego. The canvassers declared Clinton the victor by a bare 108-vote margin: 8,440 to 8,332. To prevent any recount, the leading canvasser, Thomas Tillotson, hurled the rejected ballots into a flaming fireplace, incinerating the fruits of Cooper's prodigious labors.[27]

PROTEST 🔥

The canvassers' ruling and burning shocked and outraged Federalist partisans, who felt cheated of the election they had worked so hard to win. On June 12 in New York City, Sarah Livingston Jay sadly informed her husband, John: "There is such a ferment in the City that it is difficult to say what will be the consequences. . . . People are running in continually to vent their vexation. Poor Jacob Morris looks quite disconsolate." Indulging in that medley of classicism and hyperbole so dear to Federalists, Josiah Ogden Hoffman raged, "A more daring attack on the Rights of a free People Caesar himself never attempted." His victory celebration canceled, Cooper was apoplectic and hinted at armed rebellion: "I am Alarmd, Provokd and Mortified. The People are hardly Restraind from Desperate Determinations. We must and we will have Redress. All Laws Passed and Decissions made Contrary to Common Justice and National Right is void in themselves, and a Face of Flint ought to be set against the insult." Angry Federalists spoke of reclaiming their victory with armed, revolutionary force. On June 27 Ebenezer Foote warned, "In fact Sir, the die is cast, Clinton must quit the Chair, or blood must and will be shed,—and if no innocent blood was to flow, I would not care how soon it began to run."[28]

In some locales the rhetorical violence became manifest. In Kingston, on the Hudson, defiant Federalists gathered to toast Jay, fire a fourteen-gun salute, wave flags, hear a band, parade through the streets, and drink heavily. The local Clintonians poured out of a rival tavern to confront the Federalist procession. A Jayite reported: "[The Clintonians] offered an Insult to some of our friends by holding a black flag before their faces. It was resented and a general and promiscuous Club Battel ensued—both severe & bloody. Judges and Justices, Law and Gospel were neither heard nor attended to." A similar brawl between Federalists and Clintonians roiled the streets of Albany. In a New York City tavern, Marinus Willett (a Clintonian partisan) and William Willcocks (a Jayite provocateur) swapped insults that culminated in a formal exchange of pistol shots; both men missed.[29]

As gentlemen committed to ideals of self-restraint and public deference, the leading Federalists were uncomfortable with their own anger and with their efforts to rouse public outrage. According to Federalist rhetoric, it was the Clintonians who were supposed to be consumed by self and passion and recklessly quick to foment popular disorder. Regarding themselves as the true defenders of social order from anarchic demagogues, the Federalists hated to see the Clintonians posing as the friends of social order defending the constituted governor from violence and sedition. "Must we sink in passive obedience, or assume a manly Resistance; a choice of difficulties!" Peter Van Schaack lamented. Rufus King worried to Alexander Hamilton that, if Clinton refused to resign, "and the sword be drawn, he must go to the wall—but this, my dear Sir, is a dreadful alternative." Away in Philadelphia as secretary of the treasury, Hamilton urged restraint upon his Federalist colleagues back home: "A ferment may be raised which may not be allayed when you wish it. Tis not to be forgotten that the opposers of Clinton are the real friends to order & good Government; and that it will ill become them to give an example of the contrary." He advised keeping "alive within proper bounds the public indignation. But beware of extremes." Hamilton

wanted Clinton politically embarrassed without the sort of social upheaval
that Federalists were ill suited to manage. Distrusting extreme emotions,
the Federalists struggled to regain their self-mastery. John Jay assured his
wife that it was "of more importance to me to have governed *myself* than to
have governed the *State*."[30]

However, the angry and insulted William Cooper continued to press for
a larger and more provocative protest: a mass march by hundreds of his aggrieved settlers from Otsego to New York City to demand satisfaction from
the state legislature. Mere report of Cooper's proposal was an embarrassment, because it seemed to confirm the Clintonian charges that the Federalists intended sedition and violence. Such a march would have triggered
the bloodshed that the Federalist leaders were backing away from. At
Kinderhook a Clintonian militia vowed to resist the "vulgar threats of a western braggadocio judge." To preclude trouble, Stephen Van Rensselaer
scotched Cooper's plans for a march, in favor of sending a few delegates
from each county to the state capitol.[31]

Van Rensselaer was responsible for alternately energizing and restrain-
ing Cooper's boisterous enthusiasms. The patroon had to buck up the
judge whenever other Federalist leaders treated him dismissively. After
Cooper left one meeting with hurt feelings, Van Rensselaer wrote,

> *I regret that you left us at the moment you did as I have since had opportuni-
> ties of lashing those cold inanimate beings. That friends should be indifferent
> towards one in difficulty is not uncommon, but I flattered myself [that] your
> services & zeal in the good cause would have exempted you from the general
> Lot. One friend you can resort to at all times & who is willing & ready to stand
> or fall with you. Do not be discouraged.*

Revered by Cooper as the beau ideal of wealth, prestige, gentility, and
power, the Patroon was the best man for managing the judge. But sometimes even Van Rensselaer became impatient with Cooper's appeals for approval and friendship. In one pointed reply, Van Rensselaer snapped,
"Professions of friendship I shall not make, leaving that to Boys & love-sick
Girls. Mine you know, or if you do not, I hope you will experience it."[32]

Entanglement with William Cooper nearly cost Van Rensselaer his life.
During a visit to Cooperstown, he became involved "at the Table of William
Cooper" after dinner in "a Heated Conversation" about Dr. Thomas Tillotson, the leading canvasser. Feeling the influence of his host's tasty Madeira
and reckless rhetoric, Van Rensselaer forsook his usual discretion to denounce Tillotson as "a Raskle." Fighting words to an honor-sensitive gentleman, they filtered back to Tillotson, who challenged Van Rensselaer to a
duel. Armed with pistols, the two men met outside Albany on the morning
of November 10, but Van Rensselaer averted damage to his fine clothes and
young body by offering a last-minute apology—which Tillotson accepted.[33]

CONTEMPT 🔥

After the canvassers' ruling, the Federalists and Clintonians competed to persuade the citizenry to accept their diverging versions of a common story: that an arrogant, deceitful, and overblown tyrant was conspiring to deprive the citizens of their masculine pride, economic autonomy, and political freedom by stealing control of the state government. Both political camps posed as the selfless defenders of the people, by revealing the insidious machinations of the tyrant. Of course, the two sides cast their narratives with different villains and champions. According to the Federalists, the tyrant was Governor Clinton operating through his tools, especially the canvassers. Conversely, the Clintonians tried to recast the controversy around Judge William Cooper's conduct of the election in Otsego. In their version, Clinton and the canvassers had saved the republic of New York from an election corrupted by a domineering landlord. Naturally, each party regarded the other's story as a gross deception that had to be exposed to save the people from tyranny. Through the media of tavern talk, mass meetings, newspaper essays, and circulating petitions, the Federalists and Clintonians competed to define themselves and their opponents.[34]

While promoting the Federalist offensive to recover the stolen election, Cooper also had to defend himself from Clintonian counterattacks. On June 16 the Clintonians published in the *New-York Journal* thirteen affidavits documenting William Cooper's electioneering excesses. They had been gathered a month before in Otsego by Christopher P. Yates, a leading Clintonian who had formerly been Cooper's lawyer and political confidant. The affidavits collectively depicted Cooper as an overbearing landlord and unscrupulous judge bullying his settlers with his formidable combination of economic and judicial power, packing the polls with unqualified voters, and intimidating Clintonian pollwatchers. Cooper also damned himself in two electioneering letters, dated April 6 and 8, that he had sent to James Butterfield, that Butterfield turned over to Yates, and that the *New-York Journal* gleefully published to confirm the affidavits. Clintonian writers followed with newspaper essays viciously assailing Cooper's character and conduct as depraved.[35]

Appealing to Yorker prejudices, the Clintonian essayists expanded their attacks to savage Otsego's Yankee settlers as lawless and violent refugees who had fled from New England to escape prosecution for participating in Shays's Rebellion (or, as the participants preferred to call it, the New England Regulation): an uprising in rural Massachusetts during the winter of 1786–87 by common farmers angry at the high taxes, scarce money, demanding creditors, frequent lawsuits, arrogant lawyers, and callous state government. Dispersed by an army loyal to the Federalist governor of Massachusetts, hundreds of defeated Regulators sought refuge in the new settlements of northern Pennsylvania and central New York. In 1792 the Clintonians recognized that the principal source for Otsego's settlers was the Yankee borderland of western Massachusetts, southern Vermont, and eastern New York: the hotbed of the Regulation. The Clintonians were especially delighted to discover that Eli Parsons, one of Cooper's principal political lieutenants, had been a Regulator commander in Berkshire County, Massachusetts. On July 14, 1792, a Clintonian denounced "C[oope]r, and his *Shaysite* clan at Cooper's town, despicable wretches, fearful that the vengeance of the law will light upon their guilty heads, menace rebellions and insurrections and a *procession* from Otsego."[36]

It seems paradoxical that former Regulators such as Parsons would emerge in frontier New York as partisans of the conservative Federalist party. After all, Federalists had taken the lead in suppressing the Regulation in New England. They had also drafted and ratified in 1787–88 a new national constitution meant, in part, to discourage further agrarian uprisings. The answer to the paradox can be found in another: despite his public persona as the yeoman's friend and the aristocrat's nemesis, George Clinton had acted forcefully to repress Yankee agrarians active along New York's eastern border with New England. During the 1780s he had tried repeatedly and vigorously, but in vain, to suppress the secession movement in Vermont by Yankee farmers determined to achieve independence from New York's landlords and courts. In 1787 he had broken the New England Regulation by scattering the armed refugees massed along his state's eastern border. In 1791 Clinton had even helped Philip Schuyler subdue a renewed outbreak of antirent resistance by the Yankee tenants on his lands in New York's eastern borderland. When push came to shove, Clinton brooked no disorder in his state, especially from Yankee interlopers. Consequently, the former Regulators who had settled in central New York were not inclined to regard George Clinton as their friend. Moreover, because the essence of the Regulation was a defiant localism, the former Regulators thought parochially rather than nationally in their politics. Consequently, they did not equate New York's Federalist state leaders with the Federalists who had harried them from Massachusetts. In New York their foe was George Clinton, and the Federalist enemies of their enemy were their new friends. Ambitious men such as Parsons also saw in the Federalist crusade of 1792 a vehicle to cleanse themselves of their checkered past—just as did William Cooper.[37]

Responding to the Clintonian attacks, Cooper mustered for publication his own set of affidavits sworn before a justice of the peace. Four inspectors of election for Otsego Township insisted that the judge had exerted no undue pressure on anyone during the election. Better still, two of his critics—John Hargrove, Jr., and Joseph Whitford—issued new affidavits recanting their originals as deceitfully obtained and worded by manipulative Clintonians. Apparently a pliant man, Whitford recanted his recantation a month later, assuring Otsego's Clintonians that, upon further reflection, he stood by his original charges against Cooper.[38]

During the summer Cooper and his supporters also stigmatized the Otsego Clintonians as moral reprobates self-placed beyond the pale of decent society by their sexual and alcoholic transgressions. Primarily militia officers of Scotch-Irish ancestry, the leading Clintonians probably were harder-drinking men than Cooper's Yankee friends. He assailed the affidavits as given "in the moment of intoxication" by "a few weak-minded men," of whom three had "fled the state for fear of prosecutions for perjury." Richard R. Smith published a letter attacking Judge Alexander Harper:

> *I despise the drunken fool who made the affidavit . . . and however dignified his station in the county may be, I am not afraid to contrast my reputation with his. I am seldom seen staggering about—neither am I in possession of those talents for cringing and servile flattery, by which he is so eminently distinguished—which mark him as the qualified tool of party, and fit him for any dirty work his masters chuse to set him at.*

Flourishing his classical education, Jacob Morris derided the Otsego Clintonians as "the factious sons of Bacchus." In a petition to the Council of Appointment, Cooper and six supporters demanded the removal of John Cully, another hostile affidavit giver, from his post as a justice of the peace. They accused him "of the most scandalous Fornication by taking another without Marriage into his Bed, in less than a few Days of his Wife's Decease and is generally suspected of false swearing, to say nothing of his poorness of circumstances & total want of Respectability." On June 30 in Cooperstown a public meeting of 119 settlers denounced the hostile affidavits as the work of "vagrant persons and unprincipled wretches" out to destroy "a valuable inhabitant among us, the Father of our County." In effect, the Cooperites drew a circle of reason and virtue; placed themselves within; and read out the Clintonians as slaves to their vicious and irrational passions.[39]

The Otsego County grand jury joined the enterprise of discrediting and threatening Cooper's enemies. On June 21 the grand jury indicted two leading Clintonians who had given hostile affidavits published five days earlier. The grand jurors charged Joseph Whitford with keeping a "common, ill-governed and disorderly house" frequented by "evil and ill-disposed Persons as well men as women of dishonest conversation . . . drinking, tipling, whoring & misbehaving themselves." The grand jurors also indicted Andrew Cannan for allegedly attempting to rape Jenny Young. As presiding judge, William Cooper continued both cases, which had the effect of keeping Whitford and Cannan under bond and in suspense until the court re-

convened in January. On July 28 a second Otsego grand jury indicted and
jailed two more leading Clintonians on charges of forgery: Alexander
Harper and William McFarland. Once released on bond, Harper apparently vented his rage against Cooper by seizing and twisting his nose—a
painful indignity known as a snouting. All four indictments were more political than legal; in January 1793 the court had to drop the cases against
Whitford and Cannan for want of evidence; in June 1793 a trial jury found
Harper not guilty, and the attorney general promptly dropped the prosecution of McFarland.[40]

While smiting Cooper's enemies the Otsego settlers also rallied to his defense. In June and again in July, Otsego County grand juries investigated
and dismissed the charges against Cooper as amounting "only to mere trifling imprudences, and not to the most distant appearance of bribery, imposition, fraud, menace or violence." His triumphant supporters then
erected a liberty pole, fifty feet tall, in front of the courthouse, "without,"
they stressed, "the least tumult or noise." The Cooperstown liberty pole recalled those erected throughout the colonies during the 1770s by the Whigs
as rallying points for American resistance to British rule; in effect, the Cooperstown pole equated Clinton with tyranny and called for his overthrow. In
September Cooper staged an informal, special election to choose three delegates to journey to New York City and "Solicit of the Legislature reliefe for
the Outrage Comitted on the Right of Sufferage." He was one of the delegates elected. The turnout was also gratifying: at least 600 men voted; 530
of them also subscribed to a petition attesting that they had voted for Jay
and Van Rensselaer in April. In a published letter Cooper exulted over his
local support:

> Although my exertions have tended to populate a wilderness, and by offering
> beneficial terms, I have induced some 1000 to 1500 families to settle near me;
> yet they are as far above the sway of an undue influence, as they are remark-
> able for their industry and honesty. . . . With such men have I endured all the
> toils and hardships incident to a new settlement—with the future prosperity
> and happiness of such, I feel my own intimately connected, with them then will
> I stand or fall.

He felt relieved and touched by their public affirmation of his social benevolence and political patriarchy.[41]

Most of the settlers in Otsego Township regarded the charges against the
judge as impugning their own integrity and independence as substantial
freeholders beholden to no one. Citizenship, personal autonomy, property
holding, manhood, and patriarchy were inextricably intertwined in the
minds of white men in the early American Republic. Consequently, the settlers considered the Clintonian charges of their poverty and docility as
provocative challenges to their freedom and masculinity. At their June 30

meeting in Cooperstown, the settlers insisted, "We resent the insinuations promulgated by vile defamers, of our being compelled to vote through fear—and, that we are not in possession of property enough to entitle us to vote for governor." Vowing to seek redress "with manly firmness," they resolved, "We will, as one man, quietly march down to New-York, and sollicit of the Legislature our dearest and highly prized rights, as a testimony to our children that they may see that their fathers did not quietly submit to a precedent operating in favor of tyranny." By resisting and marching, they would reassert their title to manhood and paternity. Cooper explained that his settlers would "shew them by Occular Demonstration that they are not Nominal but Real men."[42]

While Otsego Township—the largest in the county—rallied around Cooper, the Clintonians mustered in Harpersfield and, to a lesser degree, Cherry Valley. At public meetings held in Cherry Valley on August 31 and in Harpersfield on September 22, they charged Judge Cooper with corrupting the election and inciting an insurrection against the state constitution and legitimate government of George Clinton. The older and predominately Scotch-Irish towns of Cherry Valley and Harpersfield resented their recent political subordination to the more numerous Yankee newcomers settled in Otsego Township and led by a judge and a sheriff newly arrived (in 1790) from New Jersey. The Harpersfield Clintonians accused: "The distracted partyism in this county is owing to a very few self-conceited, self-interested, and sedicious seeds of a luciferian growth, that have lately been, by an unfriendly gale, wafted from neighbouring states & have, by deep laid, mischievous, and unwarrantable measures, endeavored to become monarchical in this county." Just as the Cooperites in Otsego Township tried to marginalize the Clintonians as drunks and sexual deviants, the Clintonians in Harpersfield and Cherry Valley strove to restore their local preeminence by defining their rivals as seditious interlopers.[43]

In the struggle of 1792–93, the Scotch-Irish leaders of the older settlements defended their American Revolution. By bleeding and enduring they had won the Otsego country from their Loyalist enemies only to see it politically usurped in the early 1790s by undeserving newcomers. Unlike Cooper and Smith, who had sat out the Revolution in New Jersey, most of Otsego County's leading Clintonians—Ephraim Hudson, the Cullys, Cannans, and Harpers—were old settlers and zealous Whigs who had suffered the wartime destruction of their frontier farms. An exception was the Loyalist Joseph Tunnecliff, but at least he shared an old residency and wartime suffering with the other local Clintonian leaders. Like their governor, the Otsego Clintonians perpetuated in politics a memory of the revolutionary struggle. In contrast, the Federalists insisted that the Revolution was over and deemed its internal divisions no longer relevant to politics.[44]

DEPENDENCE &

In Otsego County the political crisis of 1792–93 generated affidavits, meeting proceedings (published in newspapers), and petitions that identify the political affiliation of 363 men: 189 aligned with Cooper and 174 against. Linking their names with other sources (the 1790 Federal Census, a 1788 tax list, registered land deeds, and William Cooper's store books) reveals the distinctions between Cooper's local friends and foes. Most of his supporters were Yankee newcomers clustered around Cooperstown, indebted to Cooper, and grateful for the judge's restraint and patience as a creditor. His opponents tended to be longer-resident settlers of Yorker (especially Scotch-Irish) ethnicity who dwelled on the county's margins, resented the newcomers, and feared Cooper's power (see Table 6).[45]

The political equivalent of gravity, Cooper had the most powerful hold over those living nearby, in Cooperstown and the adjoining Otsego and Hartwick patents, which the judge owned or managed. There Cooper enjoyed almost unanimous support: 94 percent. Beyond his lands in the rest of Otsego Township, his majority slipped to 56 percent. Moving still further away, his friends were few in Cherry Valley (24 percent) and Harpersfield (12 percent) on the county's eastern and southern margins (see Table 6). In the political culture of eighteenth-century America, community unity was an ideal and partisan division was disreputable. Consequently, townships tended to unite in politics, often in polarized reaction to the allegiance assumed by some nearby rival community, especially if the two were ethnically different. Reacting against one another, Otsego Township overwhelmingly rallied to Jay while Harpersfield and Cherry Valley defiantly clung to Clinton. In 1793 George Metcalf observed, "In Otsego [Township], from the very strong opposition made to Cooper by the Cherry Valley people, many determined to vote for Cooper." Within each township the dissident few who resisted the majority were marginalized as malcontents.[46]

Because ethnic groups tended to settle in clusters, ethnicity was closely associated with residence in explaining men's political affiliations. Relying on surnames as a proxy for ethnicity suggests that three-quarters of the Yankees supported Cooper, versus only a quarter of the Germans and Dutch and only a fifth of the Scotch and Scotch-Irish. Yankees accounted for 80 percent of Cooper's support but for only 29 percent of his opponents'. Conversely, men with Scotch-Irish surnames were 14 percent of his friends but a full 55 percent of his opponents (see Table 7).

Business dealings with Cooper for land or store credit also distinguished his supporters from his opponents. Among the partisans, almost all who had bought their land directly from Cooper stuck by him politically: 95 of

98 (97 percent). When Cooper's store customers took sides, they also clung to their creditor: 87 of 118 (74 percent). At least 80 percent (152 of 189) of Cooper's known political friends had either bought land from him or had done business with his store, compared with only 29 percent (50 of 174) of his foes. Cooper's support did not extend far beyond the reach of his credit. That association of apparent dependence and conspicuous loyalty to Cooper was precisely what so alarmed those living just beyond his reach in Cherry Valley and Harpersfield. They regarded Cooper's almost universal support in Otsego as unnatural and dangerous, a machine of imposed dependency that threatened to spread and overwhelm them.[47]

Historians usually rely on the vivid—but partisan—testimony of the Clintonians to characterize William Cooper as an overbearing landlord and political tyrant. Dixon Ryan Fox describes the "sinister" purposes, "ugly" politics, and "well-supported threats" of "a testy and choleric gentleman easily wrought into passion." According to John Kaminski, Otsego County "was run with an iron hand by Judge William Cooper." Even more flamboyantly, David Hackett Fischer characterizes Cooper's politics as "an unholy combination of persuasion, flattery, force, fraud, bribery, favoritism, imposition, intimidation, demagoguery, arm-twisting and elbow-bending, which went on the whole year round." These historians depict Cooper as a dark genius in firm control of his county.[48]

Naturally, Otsego Township's settlers preferred another explanation for their loyalty: that they clung to Cooper because they best knew his benevolence. In 1794 a public meeting at Joseph Griffin's tavern in Cooperstown resolved: "*We are well acquainted with Judge Cooper—that his dealings have been very extensive amongst us*—and *we freely declare that he has been honest, punctual and humane.*—And *further*, that he hath, in every *public trust*, amongst us, acted with *firmness* and *decision*; not to mention his almost unparreled usefulness in settling and forcing into respectability and good order, an almost entire wilderness." Contrary to distant detractors, they understood that Cooper was the magnanimous Father of Otsego County.[49]

Indeed, dependence alone cannot explain Cooper's hold over the settlers in Otsego Township, for three reasons. First, Otsego's settlers were Yankees, a people universally renowned, or detested, for their difficult independence and their cunning devotion to self-interest. There was a fundamental inconsistency in the Clintonian attacks on the Otsego settlers as both Cooper's intimidated tools *and* rebellious, anarchic Shaysites. Defiant, agrarian rebels were unlikely to settle tamely on the lands of an arbitrary tyrant. In July 1792 the Otsego grand jury aptly expressed their incredulity that settlers "from the Eastern states—the very bulwark of liberty and republicanism—where the greatest independence and propriety are very strictly observed at elections" could be charged with dependence, "unless their emigrants here are strangely transformed indeed."[50]

Second, Cooper had done much to win settler gratitude and little to abuse his power. Unlike other New York landlords, he had sold freehold title to lands in generous quantities, at a modest price, and on a long credit. Thereafter, he had been remarkably patient with debtors, provided they were settled upon and laboriously improving their lands. Similarly, as a store owner, Cooper encouraged, organized, and financed local enterprises and exchanges, often without charging any fees. And he showed a similar patience with store debtors, bringing no lawsuit before the 1792 election. Finally, as a politician he spent lavishly that settlers could have a festival at the pollings and subsequent victory celebrations. In sum, Cooper sacrificed much of his immediate, pecuniary self-interest to enjoy the luxury of playing a Father of the People. Settler deference did not come cheap. As Otsego's landlord, Cooper sought wealth and power that he might perform the coveted role of political patriarch—not the reverse, as the depiction of tyrant insists.[51]

Third, truly cowed men would not have exercised the initiative evident in the support given Cooper in Otsego Township. Something more than intimidation spawned the numerous, widespread, and crowded meetings and pollings, the well-subscribed petitions, the support of two grand juries, the boisterous liberty pole raising, and the pervasive sense of shared outrage at the attacks on *their* Judge. Intimidation might prevent men from opposing the judge, but fear could not generate their energetic determination to defend Cooper from his powerful enemies. The psychology at work among Otsego's settlers was more subtle and complicated than simple fear of an overpowering tyrant. Aware of Cooper's very real power, the settlers felt sincere gratitude at his restraint. It was the looming but suspended possibility of their dependence that generated so much energy on Cooper's behalf. In the early 1790s the settlers were as eager to see Cooper as their benevolent Father as he was keen to play that part. It was in their interest to encourage Cooper in a patriarchal role that postponed payments, averted lawsuits, secured favors, and provided election festivity. The settlers gained more than they lost in pretending to be Cooper's political children.

In *The Pioneers* James Fenimore Cooper captured the provisional nature of deference. During the religious service held at the academy, Judge Temple's party occupies "the high place of the tabernacle"—the front benches closest to the pulpit—while the common settlers sit in the rear. However, "This distinction was rather a gratuitous concession, made by the poorer and less polished part of the population, than a right claimed by the favoured few." Like his alter ego Judge Temple, William Cooper was less powerful and more vulnerable than most historians have depicted. His occasional angry explosions manifested his weakness as a leading man, not his mastery. In 1792–93 he was a flawed gentleman under new pressures from ostensible friends as well as bitter enemies.[52]

IMPEACHMENT 🔥

During the fall Cooper delighted in plans to gather protest delegations and petitions to confront the Clintonian-dominated state legislature meeting in New York City. After a conspicuous tour down the Hudson in a sloop, the delegates would "Enter New York with Pompous Parade, for the whole of our Prospect is to make the will of the People manifest. . . . Remember Littel *Stroakes* fell great *Oakes* and by hacking in the Right Places, the Corrupt Junto will be brought Low." However, by November, when the legislature reconvened, Federalist enthusiasm for the legislative appeal was waning. Despairing of redress, only a few other counties joined Otsego in sending delegates to New York City. "I regret that the true spirit of Otsego does not pervade the State to the degree that I wish or expected," Van Rensselaer lamented. Undaunted, Cooper led the small body of protest delegates to the city hall where they formally presented their petitions to the legislature. However, after a desultory investigation, on January 10, 1793, the Clintonian majority predictably passed a resolution vindicating the canvassers and declaring their decision final. All of the Federalists' effort, organization, and outrage over the preceding year had come to naught. George Clinton remained the governor of New York.[53]

Then the Clintonians turned remorselessly to the counterattack. In early January affidavits and petitions from Cooper's foes in Otsego had accumulated on the assembly docket. One petition charged that his "*depraved or vitiated mind*" had sowed "the seeds of discontent and animosity among those who might otherwise live in mutual habits of friendship." In particular, Cooper had exploited his "great number of dependents" to subvert the elections in Otsego County. On January 18 the Clintonian majority launched impeachment proceedings against Judge William Cooper for "mal and corrupt conduct." The Federalist assemblyman James Kent worried, "I expect it will detain us till April and I expect they will ruin Cooper."[54]

Leading Federalists worried that Cooper was not up to the challenge, that he would fail to organize his own defense, thereby discrediting and dragging down his political friends as well. Jacob Morris exhorted Cooper:

> For God's sake, for your own sake, and for the sake of your friends, and above all my sake, let me entreat you not to let the sanguine persuasion of your innocence prevent your exerting every nerve to obtain a glorious triumph over the corrupt party so enemical to the true interest of this state and so hostile to the fame of a man who I believe upon the present occasion has committed no political sin.

The judge was in a sad fix indeed when he needed advice and exhortation from his old rival (who rather gratuitously inserted the qualifier "upon the present occasion," hinting at their past difficulties). Morris concluded his letter with congratulations "upon the increase of your family": on December 29, 1792, in the midst of political turmoil, Elizabeth Cooper gave birth to a son named Henry Frey Cooper, the Coopers' twelfth birth.[55]

Stephen Van Rensselaer also dreaded that Cooper would succumb to a paralyzing depression. Three months earlier the patroon had balked at reciprocating Cooper's effusions of friendship, but in January 1793 Van Rensselaer took unusual pains to bolster his imperiled friend, writing: "I love you. I respect you. While I have life, I will never forsake you. While I have a voice, I will ever speak in your favor." In a time of personal despair and uncertainty, Cooper won what he most cherished: affirmation of the patroon's affection and respect.[56]

The prompt and determined response of his many friends in Otsego was also gratifying. Breaking his political neutrality, Sheriff Benjamin Gilbert promised to rouse "all the friends to truth and Justice. I shall get on Horseback early tomorrow morning and make every possible exertion during the Day and Night following." Staging public meetings in Cooperstown and at least five other settlements, his friends generated an impressive array of nineteen petitions, extolling the judge and damning his local enemies.[57]

Meanwhile, the testimony before the state legislature did not go as well as the Clintonians had expected. Between February 19 and 23, their witnesses persuasively testified that Cooper had aggressively pressed ballots into the hands of voters and had pulled them up to the poll or had cursed those who resisted his embrace. But, although unseemly, Cooper's behavior was neither illegal nor unusual, given the low standards of electioneering that prevailed in New York. The Federalists were quick to point out that the Clintonians had practiced the same techniques in their townships. On February 23 Cooper's witnesses began their testimony. The county clerk (Morris) and sheriff (Gilbert), another judge (Jedediah Peck), the Otsego Township inspectors of election, and a grand jury foreman all vigorously vindicated Cooper's conduct. By the end of the month, the Clintonians rued their substantial investment in an investigation that was going nowhere. John Addison, a Federalist representative, chortled, "Not the least spark of Criminality has appeared. . . . This Inquiry is of immense advantage to Cooper. They have established his reputation instead of injuring it." In early March, James Kent substituted exultation for his January despair: "The inquiry respecting Cooper has been highly to his Honor and the Honor of Otsego. Never was a Party so deceived and mortified in a Project as our Majority have been. They do not attempt even a Resolution of censure or disapprobation."[58]

Instead the Clintonians sacked Sheriff Benjamin Gilbert for abandoning the political neutrality that had won him appointment in the spring of 1792. The Clintonians in Cherry Valley and Harpersfield complained: "Instead of taking care of the County and labour[ing] to keep the peace and good order thereof, he has Joined with the refracktory party of that County who has been making parties and Raising liberty poles to inflame the minds of the uninformed, and has been a Chairman at one or more of their unconstitutional meetings." On March 11, 1793, Clinton's Council of Appointment replaced Gilbert with Samuel Dickson, a Clintonian partisan from Cherry Valley.[59]

On the same day, the Clintonian legislators suspended their investigation of Cooper for resumption at the next session. They ordered newspaper publication of the testimony in the misapprehension that it would damage the Federalists in the approaching legislative elections. In effect, the Clintonians tried to make Cooper the central campaign issue. However, in the late April polling the Federalists completely triumphed, capturing both houses by impressive margins. On February 12, 1794, the new, Federalist-dominated assembly passed a resolution clearing Cooper and dismissing the charges against him "as frivolous and vexatious."[60]

VINDICATION

By winning control of the state legislature, the Federalists also secured the great prize and instrument of power in New York State: the Council of Appointment. Consisting of the governor and four state senators chosen by the assembly, the council appointed the state's executive officers and filled all of the county judicial and military positions from first judge and Brigadier General all the way down to coroner and coronet. Because every New Yorker with any ambition had to solicit the patronage dispensed through the Council of Appointment, it was a powerful mechanism to build or to destroy political coalitions. Taught by Clinton's cunning example, the triumphant Federalists cherished their own opportunity to run that wonderful "Machine for creating influences" (despite their previous, pious declamations of Clinton's partisan appointments). In January 1794 the legislature named four new councillors: three Federalists and a token Republican. As governor, Clinton remained the chairman, but he and the other Republican were routinely overruled and outvoted by the three Federalists. Led by Philip Schuyler, the Federalist councillors not only rejected Clinton's nominees but named their own, over his bitter protests that constitutionally only the governor could nominate. John Addison, a Federalist assemblyman, exulted, "The present Council of Appointment is properly disposed to grant any thing and every thing to our Friends."[61]

One of those friends with a long wish list was William Cooper. In early 1794 he waited impatiently for word from Albany that the Council had removed his enemies and substituted his friends as Otsego's magistrates. After two months passed without apparent action, he exploded on March 9, writing a letter of resignation:

> *The Almost Constant intoxication, Extreem ignorance, and total want of respectabillity of a Majority of the Judges and Assistant Justices with whome I have to associate in the Courts of Justice for the County of Otsego renders it Absolutely necessary that I should resign the office of first Judge of the County aforesaid as well [as] to bear a testimony against Such Undignified Carrecters.*

The letter was never delivered because, shortly after drafting it, Cooper learned that the council had already rammed through his slate over Clinton's objections on March 7.[62]

Although vindicated in the legislature and triumphant with the Council of Appointment, Cooper remained embattled in the courts. During 1793–95 he fought a variety of libel suits generated by the vicious slanders he had exchanged with his enemies during the heated election of 1792 and its bitter aftermath. On November 15, 1793, Cooper lost the first and most significant of the suits: George Clinton's prosecution of the judge for his electioneering diatribes denouncing the governor as an embezzler and traitor. The evidence included the two damning letters Cooper had indiscreetly written to James Butterfield in April 1792. The judge's reckless words cost him dearly. After deliberating for less than two hours, the jury awarded Clinton £400.0.0 in damages—an unusually large amount intended to impress upon Cooper the irresponsibility of his public statements. He also had to pay Clinton's legal costs of £101.7.9. Thereafter, Alexander Harper and William Cooper battled to a draw, each winning his prosecution of the other. In October 1794 one trial jury convicted Cooper of slandering Harper as a murderer and awarded the Colonel £150.0.0 in damages (plus court-assessed costs of £52.12.0). A year later another jury priced Harper's slander of Cooper as a forger at £141.0.0 (but he got only a token 6 pence in assessed costs, an apparent snub). This last victory induced Cooper's three remaining opponents—James Cannan, Jacob G. Fonda, and Ephraim Hudson—to capitulate. Loyal to Cooper, the Cooperstown newspaper reported: "They all humbled themselves, paid costs and were generously forgiven. . . . The judge has completely foiled his enemies." In fact, Cooper's courtroom record was mixed: his two big losses cost him much more than he won in his four modest victories.[63]

In late 1792 and early 1793 Cooper also pursued vindication at the polls, by running for the congressional seat representing all five counties in western and central New York: Montgomery, Herkimer, Ontario, and Tioga, as well as Otsego. It was bold, even brazen for Cooper to seek a political promotion with impeachment proceedings and libel suits still pending against him. An incredulous Clintonian from Otsego County reacted, "I would advise him to retrieve his character (if possible) rather than expose his weakness, or does he yet think that he and his sycophants and tools can do as they please. I blush for so vile a wretch."[64]

Cooper faced two opponents. The Clintonians ran John Winn (1746–1809), the sheriff of Montgomery County. A Yorker of Dutch ancestry and common origins, Winn had been, during the Revolution, a radical Whig who served on the Tryon County Committee of Safety and commanded a ranger company that had raided the Otsego country to arrest and plunder Loyalists. A quintessential Clintonian, Winn appealed to the old settlers of the Mohawk valley and of Harpersfield and Cherry Valley, but he made little headway with the district's new Yankee majority. Unfortunately, Cooper faced a second rival from within his own party: Silas Talbot (1751–1813), a Yankee emigrant from Rhode Island with a distinguished Revolutionary War record as an officer in both the Continental Army and Navy. As a Federalist, war hero, and New Englander, Talbot was especially appealing to the Yankee majority and especially damaging to Cooper's prospects. In the polling held during the last week in January 1793, Cooper finished a respectable second (961 votes), behind Talbot (1,209) but ahead of Winn (838). Almost all of Cooper's support came from his home county, where he captured 78 percent of the votes, despite losing all 95 votes cast in hostile Harpersfield. He lost the seat for want of support in the district's other counties. Cooper was a controversial, polarizing figure—immensely popular close to Cooperstown but distrusted in the rest of upstate New York.[65]

In 1794 Cooper again sought the seat, encouraged by Talbot's retirement from politics to accept a commission in the revived U.S. Navy. Once again the campaign pivoted on the judge's character and, especially, his behavior during the gubernatorial election of 1792. A Clintonian essayist exhorted the voters: "Let not the vile breath of the *Slanderer* ever diffuse its malignant poison within the sacred walls of the *House of the People.*" In response, a Cooperstown meeting denounced the Clintonians for their "train of calumny, against a man, whose rising character they envied." Cooper again faced John Winn and a rival Federalist (the lawyer James Cochran, this time). On his second try Cooper benefited from his vindication by the state legislature in February and the triumph of his Otsego civil slate in March, as well as from Talbot's absence, Winn's weakness, and Cochran's late start in the campaign. In the polling held in December, Cooper won by a gratifying margin: 2,535 votes (56 percent) to Winn's 1,426 (32 percent) and Cochran's 535 (12 percent). Cooper not only increased his proportion of Otsego County's vote—up from 78 percent in 1793 to 85 percent in 1794—but he also captured majorities in every county save Montgomery, the home of both Winn and Cochran.[66]

While Cooper's political star was ascending, the power and prospects of George Clinton continued to ebb. By capturing the state legislature in April

1793 and the Council of Appointment in early 1794, the Federalists rendered Clinton a lame duck deprived of the tools to practice his masterful
politics of patronage. Aware that he risked further repudiation, Clinton
chose not to seek reelection to a seventh term. In the 1795 election John
Jay and Stephen Van Rensselaer won handily, defeating the Clintonians
Robert Yates and William Floyd. At last, Cooper could hold his victory festival for Governor Jay. After ringing the village's bell and firing its cannon,
the celebrants drank fifteen toasts at Griffin's Red Lion Tavern. "On this occasion the citizens of Cooperstown, as by an electric attraction, were instantly assembled—every countenance beamed pleasure," reported the
Federalist editor of the village newspaper.[67]

CONGRESS

Cooper's election to Congress completed his three-year struggle to win the
respect of New York's Federalists and to weather the assaults of George Clinton's partisans. Cooper had endured difficult voters, doubts among the Federalists, withering scorn in the Clintonian newspapers, sworn enemies
among the county magistrates, impeachment proceedings in the state legislature, slander suits in the courts—and at least one snouting—to win the
sweet vindication of a congressional seat. Raised in a poor, rustic Quaker
family in the outskirts of Philadelphia, he returned to that city (then the national capitol) in 1795 as a wealthy and influential judge and congressman.
President George Washington invited Cooper to dine at least twice—a considerable honor for a former wheelwright. His ascent into the national elite
of wealth and power seemed complete.[68]

As a congressman Cooper earned notoriety as an especially partisan
Federalist dedicated to defending Washington's administration. He denounced the Republican opposition as "hot-headed Lawyers, Bankrupts,
mortified Politicians of our own Country mixed with the unfortunate
Refugees & soured Sons of Europe." Exercising and mixing his metaphors,
Cooper concluded that the Republicans had "formed into a kind of
whirlpool Skum to go down when the subject of their Cabal is brought to a
focus, rising again in many Bubbles on the surfice to be brought together &
sent down again on some other occasion, operating as way marks to teach
us the value of constitutions, Treaties & other useful Institutions in Government." Alexander Hamilton and Stephen Van Rensselaer sometimes
had to urge restraint on the new congressman.[69]

Cooper distinguished himself by vigorously championing the controversial treaty that John Jay had negotiated with Great Britain on behalf of the
Washington administration. Although the Federalist senate was responsible

for ratification there was a danger that the Republican house would deny the necessary appropriations. In support of the treaty, Cooper delivered several speeches and presented to congress a petition signed by 5,365 men from his district. He dreaded the alternative of a war that might again destroy Otsego's settlements, blighting his prospects. "My whole fortune, which I have obtained by the dint of industry depends [on Peace]," Cooper explained. Remembering his Quaker principles, Cooper exhorted Senator Rufus King: "Preserve the Peace of America if you can—for we have *All to Lose* and *Nothing to Win* by War. Remember that *Peace* makes *Plenty*—*War* makes *Poverty*." Cooper also shared the Federalist conviction that the Republicans meant to foment a social upheaval by the discontented poor in the urban seaports. Indeed, Cooper feared that congressional defeat of the treaty would imperil the fragile new American union. On April 13, 1796, Cooper worried: "Things look gloomy as to the American nation—[the next] two weeks will unfold our fate."[70]

Cooper's zeal on behalf of the treaty bolstered his standing among the Federalist gentry. Stephen Van Rensselaer congratulated his friend: "As you are not a vain man I will inform you that on Saturday last at Club your speech was read by Judge Laurance in the presence of Hamilton & others. It was pronounced a sensible & proper *talk* & as such did you great honor, not that it was unexpected for we all know your talents." Of course, Cooper was delighted by the approving attention of such prestigious and powerful men as Alexander Hamilton, John Laurance, and Stephen Van Rensselaer. Cooper also won applause from his Federalist friends by composing and distributing a song that celebrated Washington's administration and Jay's Treaty.[71]

Nonetheless, Cooper remained too voluble, gregarious, and passionate to speak consistently as a gentleman. In one characteristic speech on behalf of Jay's treaty, Cooper rambled, "Mr. Chairman, for my part I don't want to cram the treaty down the throats of the gentlemen opposed to me. I want to cram it down their understanding, but they have no understanding; so I can't do it." Unlike other congressmen who made a great show of their extensive learning, Cooper cited the common maxims of mercantile trade and the homely metaphors of rural life. Unimpressed by Cooper's speeches, songs, and sayings, Republican congressmen treated the judge with ill-concealed contempt. On April 13, when Cooper tried to speak in Congress, Edward Livingston, a Republican colleague from New York, cut in, sarcastically observing that if the judge "delivered his sentiments with that ability, politeness, and delicacy of manner . . . in which he sometimes delivered himself, he might as well be silent." Cooper retorted angrily and the assembled congressmen bickered "in great heat."[72]

Clumsy as a gentleman, Cooper constantly struggled to defend his dignity and standing against the slings and arrows of scoffing foes. Despite his considerable accomplishments as landlord and politician, and despite the Federalists' eventual success in ratifying Jay's Treaty, Cooper continued to feel embattled and in danger of toppling from his new and slippery eminence.

Chapter Eight

THE VILLAGE

I N *The Pioneers,* JAMES FENIMORE COOPER recalled the village of his youth as a jarring intrusion on a recently wild land, a place where aspirations exceeded taste and means, where pretentious but awkward structures sprouted among the lingering ruins of a formidable forest. Grandiose streets of urban dimensions and regularity ran amidst stumps and "huge heaps of logs that were daily increasing rather than diminishing in size, notwithstanding the enormous fires that might be seen through every window." An "incongruous group of dwellings" rose among the "unsightly remnants of trees that had been partly destroyed by fire . . . rearing their black, glistening columns twenty or thirty feet above the pure white of the snow." The village consisted of about fifty wooden houses, few of them painted. Those usually bore a cheap and dingy red or brown rather than the more prestigious and expensive white. Several "economical but ambitious owners" painted their housefronts white and the three less conspicuous sides red. A few lawyers, merchants, and doctors dwelled in the most "pretending" style: two stories tall, clapboards over a frame, painted white on all sides, with green shutters around glass windows. In an ironic touch, these houses usually lay behind a few forlorn ornamental willow or Lombardy poplar trees newly imported from the East and freshly planted beside the street so recently cleared of native trees.[1]

Soon after the village had been formally laid out, in the streets and blocks that resembled a city, a meeting of its inhabitants had been convened, to take into consideration the propriety of establishing an Academy. . . . To [their] flourishing resolutions, which briefly recounted the general utility of education, the political and geographical rights of the village of Templeton, . . . the salubrity of the air, and wholesomeness of the water, together with the cheapness of food, and the superior state of morals in the neighbourhood, were uniformly annexed, in large Roman capitals, the names of Marmaduke Temple, as chairman, and Richard Jones, as secretary.

—*James Fenimore Cooper,* The Pioneers, 99

Despite its ragged appearance Cooperstown had a commercial potential that Judge Cooper meant to develop and maximize. Designated the county seat and located at the foot of Otsego Lake and beside the source of the Susquehanna, Cooperstown was well positioned politically and geographically to become the marketing center for Otsego County. By capturing the

trade of Otsego's farmers, Cooperstown would grow more populous, prosperous, and cosmopolitan than the many agricultural towns of the county
hinterland. Moreover, Cooper intended his village to prevail in a competition with other upstate villages for the people, capital, and institutions that
distinguished a preeminent market town. At the very least Cooperstown had
to best Cherry Valley for primacy within Otsego County. And Cooper hoped
for still more: for Cooperstown to become the largest and most prosperous
trading center in all of western and central New York. To accelerate Cooperstown's development, Cooper imposed a spatial design upon his village,
supervised the villagers' conduct, and established community institutions
meant to cultivate an ethos of harmonious and genteel cooperation. But the
judge had his work cut out for him because a frontier village with commercial and political potential tended to attract especially ambitious, competitive, and contentious men.

MAP 🌿

William Cooper designed Cooperstown as an especially dense and compact
village. In 1788 he hired a professional surveyor, Daniel Smith of Burlington, to survey, arrange, and map the village around the handful of buildings and through the surrounding tangle of trees, brush, and stumps.
Following Cooper's instructions Smith created an unusually detailed and
ambitious plan for such a raw, new village. Cooper and Smith shaped the
village as a rectangular plot of 112 acres located on the west bank of the
Susquehanna River and at the foot of Lake Otsego. The mapped village had
six short but broad cross streets running east-west and, at right angles, three
longer north-south streets. Front was the name of the northernmost cross
street along the shores of the lake, "and the others parallel to it were numbered from Second up to Sixth street." Cooper called the easternmost
street, next to the river, Water Street and that at the opposite end West
Street. (See Map 4.) In *The Pioneers*, when Elizabeth Temple protests the
folly of projecting a rigorous grid of streets upon a rough terrain, Richard
Jones retorts, "We must run our streets by the compass, coz, and disregard
trees, hills, ponds, stumps, or, in fact, any thing but posterity. Such is the
will of your father."[2]

At Cooper's insistence the surveyor subdivided Cooperstown's blocks
into 197 small, rectangular lots (in addition to several larger, unnumbered
lots retained by Cooper or his old partner Andrew Craig). Most lots had
only 25 to 50 feet in street frontage and ran back 150 feet. By design these
were unusually small and narrow lots for a new village on the New York frontier. Ordinarily inclined to let men pursue their own desires and interests
without intrusion or restriction, Cooper asserted that "the only point in

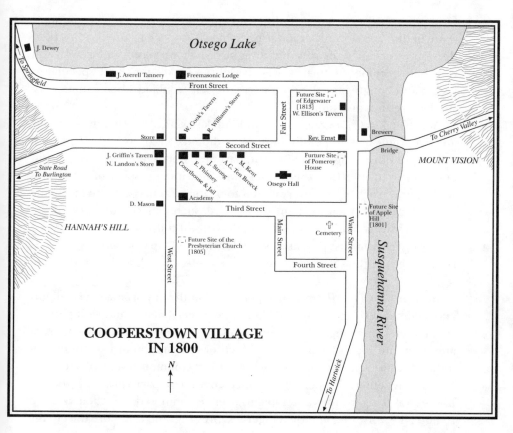

Otsego Lake

J. Dewey

To Springfield

J. Averell Tannery   Freemasonic Lodge

Front Street

W. Cook's Tavern

R. Williams's Store

Fair Street

Future Site of Edgewater [1813]

W. Ellison's Tavern

Store

Rev. Ernst   Brewery

To Cherry Valley

Second Street

Bridge

MOUNT VISION

J. Griffin's Tavern   J. Strong   M. Kent   Future Site of Pomeroy House

N. Landon's Store   E. Phinney   A.C. Ten Broeck

Courthouse & Jail   Otsego Hall

State Road To Burlington

D. Mason   Academy

Third Street

HANNAH'S HILL

Future Site of Apple Hill [1801]

Main Street

Cemetery

Water Street

Future Site of the Presbyterian Church [1805]

West Street

Fourth Street

Susquehanna River

COOPERSTOWN VILLAGE IN 1800

N

To Harwick

MAP 4

which I would thwart the wishes of the settler, whether merchant or mechanic, would be in the desire which most entertain of possessing a large [village] lot." Willing to sell unusually extensive tracts of countryside, Cooper insisted on restricting village lots to especially small dimensions. He insisted that village and country, villager and farmer, had to be starkly dichotomized for the benefit of both.[3]

Cooper believed that a compact, dense village of many small lots would develop more rapidly and stimulate more commercial activity because its inhabitants would have to specialize in a craft or trade, eschewing farming on the side—"for if he be half tradesmen and half farmer he will neither prosper as one nor as the other." It vexed Cooper when

> the barber, instead of being in the way to shave his customers, will be found weeding his onions; the shoe-maker hoeing his potatoes; the watch-maker, who has neglected to repair the farmer's watch, will think it an excuse that his orchard required his immediate care; the blacksmith who has been tilling the ground when he should have been providing himself with coal, will be unable to shoe the traveller's horse, or mend the carrier's waggon.

Only where villagers were confined to small lots was there "no awkward waste of time, no slovenly or loitering habits." Cooper's insistence on a rigid division of occupations is ironic in light of his own past as a farmer's son who had become, in turn, a wheelwright, storekeeper, land speculator, judge, and congressman. Nonetheless, he felt troubled when others were similarly restless and mobile.[4]

According to Cooper, a village could make or break its vicinity—morally and economically—depending upon the dimensions of its lots. He insisted that a sprawling village of inefficient, part-time tradesmen was a drag on an entire district, infecting the farmers with a crippling spirit of waste and sloth. Conversely, "where every man is to be found at his post, the mechanic in his work-shop, the merchant in his store, such a place will carry off the prize of industry, and become the rendezvous of traffic and prosperity." By requiring industrious specialists, small lots would help Cooperstown best its rival villages in the struggle to absorb the trade, capital, and people of up-state New York.[5]

In *A Guide in the Wilderness,* Cooper dwelt on the importance of small lots and a compact village at unusual length, in special detail, and with particularly forceful, even angry, language. No other subject receives such extensive attention and intensive argument. Much of that argument is counterintuitive, as in his insistence that disputes are less common where villagers live crowded together. Cooper even denied that a compact village of wooden houses was dangerously vulnerable to fire; he countered that "help is more remote, the sense of common danger less pressing, and therefore the energy in surmounting the evil less excited" in the dispersed village.[6]

The better to oversee the villagers, Cooper placed his Manor House and grounds at the very center of Cooperstown as mapped by Daniel Smith: on the south side of Second Street, interrupting the middle long street—which bore the name Main to the south and Fair to the north of the Cooper compound. By radiating the streets around his compound, Cooper meant for the Manor House to be the focus for the village's life—the center of power, activity, and attention.[7]

In addition to mandating small lots, Cooper shrank the village, in an existential sense, by supervising *his* villagers and their enterprises. Acting as a paternalistic monitor, he meant to harmonize and unify the selfish interests of the individual villagers. Walking the village streets, he poked into every store, shop, and tavern—bantering, inquiring, and cajoling to take the measure of the villagers' opinions, circumstances, and prospects. Considering himself the moral and economic overseer of his village, Cooper readily advised and cautioned those he deemed wayward. He worried that excessive drinking, gambling, or conspicuous consumption could bring on a cycle of unpaid debts, lawsuits, curtailed credit, foreclosure, and insolvency that would deprive the village of a valued shop or store. In 1796, during

Cooper's absence to attend Congress, the blacksmith Samuel Huntington sold his shop and bought the village's principal tavern, the Red Lion, from Joseph Griffin. Learning of the transactions, Cooper disapproved for three interrelated reasons: he valued Huntington as a blacksmith; he doubted his means and ability to manage a tavern of special importance to the village; and he feared the loss of the popular Griffin from Cooperstown. Alarmed by Cooper's displeasure, Huntington quickly and anxiously wrote to defend his actions, adding, "[I] Do Earnestly wish for your approbation in the affair as I Ever did, so I still do wish to act consistently with your opinyon." Cooper's concerns were well founded: in 1797 Huntington defaulted on his payments, declared bankruptcy, and, to the judge's relief, the tavern reverted to Griffin.[8]

Because the withdrawal of Cooper's patronage would imperil an enterprise, village tradesmen and merchants were solicitous of his goodwill and anxious at intimations of his displeasure. In late 1795 Cooper warned Elihu Phinney, Cooperstown's newly arrived newspaper publisher, to avoid gambling at cards. The printer quickly replied,

I have spent but two evenings at loo since you left town and these were so spent out of respect to our good friend, the Sheriff, who has been in town at two different times. Your caution, on that point, is a proof of your disinterested friendship for me, as well as your ardent wishes for the prosperity of this delightful place; and as such will be cherished by me with scrupulous regard to your advice.

However, Cooper could be more indulgent with unskilled laborers, because for want of credit or capital to lose, their moral lapses were less threatening to the local economy. In March 1794 Cooper negotiated an understanding with his hired hand Luke Flint, who would earn £30 a year plus room and board for himself and wife in return for working "every day in the year for the Said Cooper unless it be on the Last Saturday in Every month which the said Luke reserves to himselfe for the purpose of being Drunk."[9]

Obsessed with achieving a dense village, bearing his name, clustered around his own Manor House, and under his watchful eye, Cooper evidently regarded commerce with private anxiety as well as public celebration. Without the proper blueprint and close supervision, commerce's energy could become negative, manifest in selfish contention, waste, indolence, and insubordination. Cooper felt that his close supervision was necessary to preserve village harmony from the anarchic energies bubbling just beyond his oversight. The village of Cooperstown was at once the repository of his most utopian dreams and of his deepest anxieties.

Cooper had good reason to worry about the order and harmony of his village. The early American Republic was increasingly a land of new communities created on the frontier at a moment when the rhetoric of a recent revolution urged men aggressively to seek and exploit new opportunities. The settlers left behind communities where old families monopolized prestige and power; they reached settlements where the institutions of authority—schools, churches, governments, courts, and jails—were rudimentary or nonexistent. By no means did most newcomers seek to live without those institutions or without any social hierarchy, but most emigrated in hopes of exploiting their new circumstances to stake claims to higher status and greater property than they could have commanded at home. The Yankee migrants to upstate New York wanted to replicate New England, but with themselves in more exalted circumstances. Inevitably, their enhanced ambitions brought men into competition and friction. In nearby Herkimer County, Jonas Platt complained, "This part of the state is under the curse of browbeating influence—Men's characters are not known, and the State of Society is not properly graduated."[10]

In Cooperstown one of the losers was the village's first doctor, Charles Powers. Apparently unimpressive, he did not enjoy credit at Cooper's store, and on June 9, 1791, the visitor Alexander Coventry recorded, "Saw a Dr. Powers: seemingly a clever man, but no wit." Some slight—perhaps exclusion from the party—induced Powers to slip a powerful emetic into the punch served to a group of women and men who had gathered to hold a ball on the evening of October 4, 1791, probably at the Red Lion Tavern. The emetic must have produced considerable distress and embarrassment among the company. Most of the victims were tradesmen and their friends; evidently Powers meant the emetic to mock their pretensions to hold a genteel assembly. They had exercised their power to exclude him; he responded with his power to make them miserable and ludicrous. But Powers's perverse triumph proved short-lived and led to his complete downfall as an aspirant to local prestige.[11]

Suspected and apprehended, Powers drafted and read a public confession, supervised by Judge Cooper and addressed to the victims:

Worthy & much Injured Gentlemen & Ladies. From the Bottom of my Heart, I sincerely Regret my Presumtuous, Unhappy & Ungreatfull Conduct towards you on the Evening of the 4th Instant October. Gentlemen & Ladies, you will do me the honour to believe me when I say that the Tart Emetic I put into your Liquor was owing partly to Intoxication & partly to the Insinuation of the Adversary of Men; it was not done from any Pique or Prejudice I had against the Company, for I acknowledge you are a Company of very Modest, Respectable young Gentlemen & Ladies. I declare before God & his holy Angels that what I did was done to have a little Sport & from no other Motive. I Declare as solemnly, that I had no Intention of Injuring the Health of any Person, for had I wanted that, I could have put in the Sollution of Corrosive Sublimate which is the strongest preparation of Mercury which would have acted as a slow, but certain Poison. Or I might have put in Liquid Laudanum, a Preparation of

> *Opium, to such a Quantity that it would have thrown you all into a profound Sleep, from which tis not probable all of you would have awaked; both of which medecines are much cheaper than the Tart Emetic. It is needless Gentlemen & Ladies for me to be more particular. I now humbly ask the forgiveness of God, Angels & Men for my foolish Conduct & hope & pray I may never be left to Conduct in such a Manner again.*

By abasing himself and exalting the gentility of his victims, Powers inverted the humiliation that he had inflicted with the emetic. After suffering the further shame of a few hours in the public stocks set before the courthouse, Powers left the county never to return. Given his evident knowledge of how to kill with poison, his departure must have evoked considerable relief. In this episode Cooper acted as the arbiter of respectability, awarding it to the injured tradesmen and their women, denying it to Charles Powers.[12]

ASSOCIATION

In addition to designing the village and supervising the villagers, Cooper tried to refine Cooperstown, and uplift the hinterland, by creating a web of social associations sustained by new institutions. During the 1790s he established or patronized a courthouse, brewery, library, academy, and Freemasonic lodge. Cooper suspected that frontier distances and isolation bred a selfish and narrow-minded parochialism that could only be cured by increasing the social contact and commercial circulation of the inhabitants. He believed that the compact, institution-rich village was more harmonious, cosmopolitan, and enlightened: "There is a quicker circulation of sentiment and mutual convenience; each follows his own art without deviation, and becomes more perfect in it; there is more emulation; a kind of city pride arises, and acts advantageously upon the manners and modes of life; better houses are built, more comforts introduced, and there is more civility and civilization." He meant for Cooperstown to provide the county with the institutions, occasions, and buildings for the gatherings that would construct their mutuality and harmony. Cooper and his fellow village promoters also hoped to attract aspiring men, bearing needed capital and better manners. In 1795 the *Otsego Herald* urged the importance of recruiting "respectable people . . . whereby our manners might receive a polish, and the rising generation be still further improved." Otherwise, genteel emigrants would bypass Cooperstown for rival villages like Whitestown—or, worse still, nearby Cherry Valley.[13]

In the business of village improvement, Cooper's most important recruit was an ambitious Yankee publisher named Elihu Phinney. Connecticut-born in 1755, Phinney had fought in the Continental Army, enduring "undescribable hardships." After the war he settled in Canaan, New York—a

Yankee town along the New England border—where he married, founded
a newspaper, and joined the local Freemasonic lodge. Encouraged and subsidized by Judge Cooper, in early 1795 Phinney relocated his press and family in Cooperstown. He set up his press, a book bindery, and a book and
stationery shop near the village's central intersection. In addition to al-
manacs, books, and pamphlets, on April 3, 1795, he began to issue the
weekly *Otsego Herald*, the first newspaper in Otsego County. Phinney was
willing to publish almost any book that might sell; his advertisements offered *Mrs. Wollstonecraft's Memoirs* as well as *A Copy of a Letter, Written by our
Blessed Lord and Savior, JESUS CHRIST, and Found Under a Great Stone, Sixty-
Five Years After his Crucifixion.*[14]

During the 1790s Phinney hewed to the Federalist politics professed by
William Cooper and joined him in boosting the village's social institutions.
In reward for his services and attentions, Phinney reaped a steady income
by publishing Cooper's electioneering pieces, land advertisements, and
foreclosure notices. He also enjoyed the judge's political patronage, securing appointments in 1796 as the county treasurer and as an assistant justice.
Two years later he won promotion to a seat next to Cooper as an associate
justice on the county bench.[15]

Late in life Phinney aptly described himself in a letter to his hero, former
President John Adams: "My turn of mind is rather serious, occasionally facetious, fond of knowledge (where is it?) and true Wit, even in an enemy, [I]
began 'the world' $20 in debt, am now worth Thousands of dollars, gained
by my own industry and attention to business. You, sir, have now a sketch of
my character." He measured his own character in dollars. Phinney confidently anticipated meeting Adams "in paradise" because "Hell was not ordained for Elihu Phinney, nor the great and good John Adams." Phinney's
wit manifested the Yankee delight in clever sallies meant to belittle a com-
petitor. When Dr. Nathaniel Gott tried to best Phinney in a rhyming contest
at a village tavern, Phinney quickly and savagely retorted with a mock epitaph for his rival:

> *Beneath this turf doth stink and rot,*
> *The body of old Dr. Gott;*
> *Now earth is eased and hell is pleased,*
> *Since Satan hath his carcass seized.*

Shamed by the tavern laughter, Gott stormed out and never forgave Phinney. Shrewd, witty, entrepreneurial, eclectic, and opportunistic, Phinney was
a tireless champion of favorite politicians, village improvements, and his own
self-interest. He was the quintessential Yankee and village editor, a type that
James Fenimore Cooper came to loathe in life and to blacken in novels.[16]

The chief instrument of village improvement was the voluntary subscription, rather than the public appropriation of tax revenues. In the early

American Republic, such subscriptions were the characteristic means to mobilize leadership, enthusiasm, and money for a new community venture. They reveal the ligaments and contradictions of that society, at once competitive and cooperative, culturally egalitarian and socially unequal, fluid and in search of stability. In Cooperstown during the 1790s the subscribers were exclusively men, for they claimed a monopoly on the public activity of households. The subscription was a voluntary, private association of like-minded men promoting a public good, a subsection rather than the whole community. Only those who promised money could participate, but within those bounds the subscription operated as a little republic. For example, on June 5, 1795, the *Otsego Herald* invited the subscribers for an academy to gather at the courthouse "to choose three directors for the work, and one collector and a treasurer." Mere money was necessary but not sufficient to purchase social respect in the early Republic; money had to be transmuted, through the alchemy of the subscription, into proof of a benevolent dedication to the common good. For a price the subscription list permitted men to reconcile and combine two otherwise conflicting claims: that they were richer than many others but that they honored the public good above the mere self-interest that counseled parsimony.[17]

A public subscription served not only to fund improvements but also to negotiate a hierarchy of status among the diverse newcomers in the many new, frontier communities. The subscription list enabled men to peg their own worth—within limits. The names and sums on a subscription list were public knowledge within the village; by the amount pledged a subscriber testified to his relative prosperity and asserted his proper standing in the community. By donating the largest sum (£50 and a village lot) as well as by launching and leading the subscription for the academy, William Cooper reiterated his preeminence in Cooperstown. By pledging £10 to £17, the next tier of academy subscribers claimed a status in the village second only to that of the landlord. These men included the farmer-brickmaker William Abbott; the innkeepers Samuel Huntington, Joseph Griffin, William Cook, and Benjamin Griffin; printer Elihu Phinney; and lawyer Moss Kent. The bottom tier (those giving something less than £10) at least distinguished themselves from those who gave nothing. Claiming inclusion among the respectable and enlightened, the small givers obtained participation in the little republic of village benevolence. However, there was only a certain range within which the astute could comfortably bid. In pledging, men could stretch upward but not overleap the existing rough consensus of their worth. The man of modest or humble means who subscribed too much risked ridicule as presumptuous and foolish. It would have been counterproductive—because ludicrous—for the printer Elihu Phinney to have matched Cooper's pledge or for the carpenter James White (£6) to have subscribed as much as Phinney (£16).[18]

Cooper, Phinney, and their fellow promoters grandly imagined that Cooperstown could become, within a few years, the preeminent city in up-state New York, perhaps even the seat of state government—provided it evaded a catastrophic fire. Proud anticipation mingled with increasing anx-iety as the small lots in the village center (at the juncture of Second and West streets) filled with wooden buildings vulnerable to a contagious fire. Ironically, William Cooper's stubborn insistence on a tightly built village wrought a growing danger that a massive fire driven by the wind would race from one wooden house to the next, consuming most of his cherished Cooperstown. In 1796 Elihu Phinney published a mock news story dated four years in the future:

> With extreme grief we announce that, on Thursday evening last, the beautiful and flourishing City of Cooperstown fell a prey to the devouring element of FIRE. This intelligence we received from a gentleman, who on Friday morning passed through the smoking ruins—out of 600 buildings he counted only 23 which remained. What heightens the melancholy of the scene is, that a number of persons perished in the flames, through their eagerness to save their friends and property. The Legislature of this state, which adjourned to sit in Coopers-town, in January next, will be necessitated to meet in some other place. Four years since, when the population was three-fourths less than when destroyed, a subscription was set on foot for purchasing a Fire Engine; but, by a fatal apa-thy in the citizens the laudable attempt failed. . . . One Fire Engine would have prevented this fatal catastrophe. The loss cannot be estimated at less than £250,000.

Unmoved by Phinney's alarmist prediction, the villagers ignored his zealous promotion of a subscription to procure a fire engine. Instead, they contin-ued to count on bucket brigades to deal with fires. On December 22, 1797, a blaze erupted in Phinney's printing office, but the villagers' "spirited ex-ertions in turning out in the extreme cold" to douse the flames narrowly averted "a general conflagration." William Cooper and ten other leading villagers did respond to the growing fire danger (and the increasing house-hold demand for water) by establishing the Company of the Water Works in Cooperstown. They laid a system of wooden pipes (hollowed-out logs) that bore water into the village from a spring in the side of a hill to the west.[19]

An even more significant proof of Cooperstown's advancing civilization was that beer, as well as water, flowed in the village by early 1796. As in the maple sugar promotion, William Cooper encouraged a brewery as an act of both social benevolence and economic service. During the 1790s many en-lightened gentlemen promoted the drinking of beer and ale as antidotes to Americans' swelling consumption of the more ardent distilled liquors asso-ciated with alcoholism, poverty, and violence. In New York City, Cooper met and recruited Walter Morgan and George Mulcock, English immigrants and brewers who removed to Cooperstown in the spring of 1795. Extolling the projected brewery as a "patriotic and philosophic manufactory," Phinney's newspaper asked and exhorted the locals: "What shall we do? Drink beer, till we are merry." During the summer and fall of 1795, Morgan and Mulcock constructed a substantial, two-story brewery, 83 feet long by 25 feet wide, located on the west bank of the Susquehanna between the lake and the bridge, just around the corner from the Manor House. William Cooper advanced them £273.15.10 to procure construction materials and to pay workmen—proof of his devotion to the new brewery. In January the brewers began producing, and one merry customer, the blacksmith Samuel Huntington, assured Cooper that the beer was "excellent." Even stronger testimony to its popularity came in early December, when a fire erupted in the brewery and the villagers rushed out to subdue the flames, minimizing the damage.[20]

During the 1790s Cooper and his allies also worked to improve the village by establishing three institutions for promoting genteel association: a social library, an academy, and a Freemasonic lodge. Led by Cooper, in 1794 forty-five subscribers organized a social library modeled on the Library Company of Burlington. Each signer agreed to pay £4 to fund the purchase of "entertaining and instructive writings" that were "too expensive for any of us to hold in severalty." On March 16, 1797, the subscribers began to draw upon the collection, kept in a room at the house of their librarian, Capt. Timothy Barns, the village clockmaker.[21]

In 1795 William Cooper concluded that Cooperstown also needed an academy—a school where boys could learn some classical language and literature as a means to gentility and, perhaps, admission to a college. Although he had not enjoyed any classical learning, Cooper desired it for his own sons, and he deemed an academy necessary for the continued growth and polish of his village. In 1795 no means of education beyond a country grammar school existed in Otsego County. News that Cherry Valley was preparing an academy spurred Cooperstown's boosters into action. It would not do for their rival to have the county's first and only academy. Once again Cooper led the way by opening a subscription on April 5, pledging £50.0.0, and allocating a free village lot for the building. "The Honorable William Cooper has, with his usual magnanimity, subscribed a noble sum," Elihu Phinney trumpeted in the *Otsego Herald*. Indeed, as construction costs mounted, Cooper added donations that raised his overall contribution to more than two-thirds of the £1,502.16.2 cost to erect *his* academy. Like Judge Temple in *The Pioneers,* Judge Cooper "concluded to bestow the necessary land, and to erect the required edifice at his own expense."[22]

The academy subscription was strong in the village but weak in the hinterland. According to the *Otsego Herald,* the country folk "talked a good deal, at first, about what fools we was to give five or six pounds apiece to make Cooperstown shine, and that the folks there was quite proud enough now, and if they got a Caddemy they would be as proud agin." In response, Phinney created a rural Yankee character who retorted

> that Cooperstown was the greatest place in the county & what a dreadful good thing 'twould be to have it like a city, for then we shou'd all get a mazing high price for our wheat, and grain, and barley, and shugar and fresh meat, and fish, and work; and that they was a going to build above twenty famous houses there this summer, and they wasn't half so proud as some imagined . . . and they was the friends of the farmers, and try'd to help them all they cou'd, and if we didn't help build up Cooperstown, the rich gentlemen that keep coming with an aboundation of money from France, and Old England and New England, wou'dn't come any more, cause they want a fine place to go to visiting—and if we could make a city there 'twas better than to try to hurt it, for then we cou'd go there with our friends that come a great ways to see us, and shou'dn't be ashamed of our county town.

Here was the creed of the village booster: Cooperstown would benefit everyone by generating a larger local market by becoming a bustling city attractive to gentleman-capitalists. But here also was evidence that the country folk were growing resentful of the village as an alien and arrogant place. Ironically, as the boosters succeeded in distinguishing Cooperstown from its hinterland, they generated a new wariness among the farmers.[23]

At last, in the summer of 1797, the Cooperstown trustees completed their academy building and hired a teacher to conduct an English school for about fifty students. The largest building in the village, the academy was 66 feet long by 40 feet wide, two stories tall, and topped by a belfry that rose 70 feet above the ground, overlooking the village and the lake. The academy had two rooms on the first floor and a single large meeting room on the second. Although large, it was wooden, poorly constructed, and ungainly—just like the nearby courthouse. In September 1797 the trustees of the Cherry Valley Academy sneered that their rivals' building in Cooperstown was "constructed in so slight a manner that it is already out of shape & consequently must soon be in ruins." James Fenimore Cooper, one of the first students, remembered, "It was one of those tasteless buildings that afflict all new countries." Although "a very comfortless, open place, through which the daylight shone with natural facility," the academy became "the boast of the village, the study of young aspirants for architectural fame, and the admiration of every settler on the [Otsego] Patent."[24]

At the same time that leading villagers established the social library and the academy, many of the same men founded a third institution dedicated to social benevolence and genteel association. Led by Elihu Phinney, thirteen Freemasons gathered at his house on March 1, 1796, to organize Otsego Lodge, to elect Phinney their master, and to nominate seven of their friends for membership. The new lodge grew rapidly, adding 66 members during 1796 and another 38 during 1797, raising the total to 117. The Otsego Freemasons hoped to draw into their lodge the leading men from every town in the county. Although Cooperstown (23) and the rest of Otsego Township (21) provided the largest contingents, by the end of 1797 a majority of the members came from the hinterland, some from as far away as Butternuts, Unadilla, and Harpersfield. In June of 1797 the Freemasons laid the cornerstone for their new meeting hall in Cooperstown on a Front Street lot given to them by Judge Cooper. Six months later they dedicated their hall, a substantial, two-story frame and clapboard building.[25]

The brethren met about twice a month to nominate and initiate new members, to elevate old members to higher degrees, to parade around their room, and to drink (not necessarily in that order). The initiation fee of £4.16.0 from every new member built up a considerable treasury to procure liquors, buy regalia, and finance their hall. That large fee also affirmed that only men with substantial property would become brethren. The great majority of the Otsego Freemasons were substantial farmers and successful artisans or shopkeepers, rather than born gentlemen. They joined Otsego Lodge seeking practice in the ways of gentility. These aspiring men participated in what Richard Bushman calls "vernacular gentility"—the pursuit of respectability by the middle classes after the Revolution. Some of the most prominent gentlemen in the county did join, including Dr. Joseph White of Cherry Valley and Jacob Morris of Butternuts, but other Otsego gentlemen held back, including the county's preeminent landlord, William Cooper. He probably regarded membership in a select and secret society as incompatible with his ambition to serve as the patriarch to all the people settled in Otsego. Cooper was, however, a generous patron because he shared their desire to polish and harmonize Otsego's aspiring men.[26]

Few in colonial America, Freemasonic lodges rapidly proliferated after the Revolution. Before 1780 New York State had only eight lodges, all in the Hudson valley; eleven more appeared during the 1780s and sixty-eight during the 1790s, mostly in the new towns of western, central, and northern New York. The Revolution and its legacy of frontier expansion combined to promote the explosive growth of Freemasonry in the early American Republic. Both the Revolution and the accelerated internal migration undercut traditional claims to authority based on inherited wealth, status, and residence. Freemasonry tried to fill that vacuum, especially in the new villages, by promising to fulfill the liberal promise of the American Revolution: to create a new translocal network of leading men distinguished by merit and public service rather than by inherited privilege. Like a public subscription, a Freemasonic lodge served as a mediating institution that enabled aspiring men to translate their new property and influence into a certification of superior merit and prestige.[27]

Lodges were rare in agricultural hamlets but ubiquitous in the larger and more commercial villages, where ambitious strangers from diverse origins competed for property, status, and power. Ambitious men turned to Freemasonry to fulfill their conflicting desires for both an advantage in, and a refuge from, that competition. Freemasonry appealed to both the aggressive individualism and the longing for mutuality that formed the central tension in postrevolutionary America. On the one hand, Freemasonry promised to distinguish aspiring men from the common mass, certifying that they belonged to a natural elite of talent, sensibility, liberality, and virtue. A New York Freemason explained that the purpose of the society was "to unite all men of sense, knowledge, and worthy qualities." On the other hand, Freemasonry also served their longing for sincere friendship, harmony, cooperation, and community. In 1796 John Camp instructed the Freemasons in Cooperstown that their purpose was to "combat with and overcome all disorderly passions . . . to inspire a sense of honor, fidelity, friendship and Brotherly Love." At the ceremony to lay a cornerstone for their new hall, the Otsego Freemasons sang a song written by Elihu Phinney for the occasion:

> Let your hearts be blythe and gay,
> Joy and mirth let all display,
> No dull care
> Shall enter here,
> For this is Masons' holiday.
> Social Pleasures here invite,
> To fill the soul with sweet delight,
> While hand in hand,
> Our friendly band,
> In love and harmony unite.

Their insistent, public repetition of the words *peace, harmony, unity, love, decorum, decency,* and *joy* attests that these values were especially fragile (and longed for) in the new village.[28]

Practicing moral oversight to investigate and expel the wayward, a lodge functioned as a secular church. In the older communities of the East, church membership had served to certify a man's honesty. In the newer villages of the frontier, churches were slow to organize, and growing numbers of men sought the same function from the Freemasonic lodge. Despite their extravagant professions of reverence for Christianity, lodges attracted men who were either Episcopalians (like Jacob Morris) or irreligious and irreverent freethinkers (Richard Edwards, Elihu Phinney, and Dr. Joseph White). Elihu Phinney routinely wrote and published essays that mocked evangelical religion as vulgar superstition and denounced ministerial influence as "spiritual oppression and intolerance." During the years 1796–1809 at least 252 men joined Otsego Lodge, but only 2 of them were among the 44 men who belonged to the local Presbyterian church (the only church in the village before 1810). Most devout people suspected Freemasons of covert deism, scandalous blasphemy, "nightly Revels and unseasonable Hours," and "days of Pomp with expensive Ceremonies and costly dresses."[29]

CHURCH ☙

Institutionalized religion lagged in Cooperstown behind the development of more worldly associations and the construction of their buildings. Dominated by profane rather than pious men, the village developed a courthouse, jail, stores, taverns, newspaper, waterworks, brewery, library, academy, and lodge years before the villagers attracted a permanent, resident minister or erected a church building. Indeed, many of the worldly institutions rendered more difficult the prospects of establishing a church. The stores retailed alcohol by the gallon and encouraged the villagers to spend their money on the conspicuous consumption of imported cloth and clothing. Neither the brewery nor the Freemasonic lodge encourage public sobriety or a quiet Sabbath. And the raucous, drinking crowds that gathered in Cooperstown for elections and court sessions discouraged religious contemplation. Moreover, the village's irreligious freethinkers found haven and mutual encouragement in the taverns, social library, and lodge.

Although tame by Kentucky standards, Cooperstown was a rowdy place compared with the settlers' sedate New England towns of origin. In *A Guide in the Wilderness,* William Cooper recalled, "The settlement of Cooperstown . . . was made by the poorest order of men; they laboured hard all the week, but on Sunday they either went a hunting or fishing, or else collected in taverns, and loitered away the day, careless of their dress or actions. The sons caught the manners of the fathers, and for the first ten years before any religious establishment was formed, the want of it was manifest." In New England's old towns magistrates and ministers discouraged public drunkenness and enforced a Sabbath, forbidding work and amusements to encourage people to spend the day in religious worship and contemplation. Breaking temporarily free from religious institutions, a majority of the early settlers made Cooperstown notorious for heavy drinking, public altercations, and boisterous electioneering. In 1791 the Methodist circuit riders in Otsego complained that "the people were poor, wicked and restless. . . . Freed from the restrictions of the Puritanic code, they, as a general thing, broke loose from all moral restraints, and were a Sabbath-breaking, irreligious race, some of them almost as wild and savage as the wolves and bears which often invaded their inclosures." In 1795 less than a quarter of the county's adults formally belonged to a church. Although Otsego County had a population in 1795 of 2,276 families dwelling in five townships (Burlington, Cherry Valley, Otsego, Richfield, and Unadilla), there was only one church building: that belonging to the Presbyterians in Cherry Valley. In the other towns the devout met in log cabins and barns, or in open fields, when weather permitted and an unusual crowd demanded.[30]

Although Cooper eventually lamented the irreligion of his early village, he was partly to blame for the delay in establishing a church with a settled minister. In general, Cooper was skeptical of religion and—as an erstwhile Quaker—especially hostile to the Calvinist churches (Baptist, Presbyterian, and Congregationalist) preferred by the devout minority among his Yankee settlers. If the judge had shown the same initiative and generosity for founding a church that he lavished on the waterworks, brewery, library, academy, and Freemasonic lodge, Cooperstown would not have gone so long without a settled ministry.[31]

In 1795 the devout residents of Otsego Township organized the United Ecclesiastical Society, dedicated to funding a minister and building a church. The members raised a generous subscription but, because they espoused diverse Protestant denominations, they bickered over which ministers should receive invitations and money to preach in Cooperstown at the academy. In 1797 the society received an unexpected but welcome boost when William Cooper suddenly manifested a vigorous desire for settling a minister in Cooperstown. His belated interest derived from a new scheme to capture the earthly funds left behind by the recently deceased Rev. John Christopher Hartwick, the proprietor of the Hartwick Patent, who had lived long enough to regret entrusting his properties to the judge's management. When Hartwick died on July 17, 1796, he willed his estate—principally his annual income from the Hartwick Patent—to Jesus Christ. Responsibility for managing Christ's new property and for realizing Hartwick's dream of a New Jerusalem on the frontier passed to three executors: Jeremiah Van Rensselaer of Albany, Frederick A. C. Muhlenberg of Philadelphia, and the Lutheran Rev. John C. Kunze of New York City. The executors wanted to approximate Hartwick's intent by founding a seminary to train Lutheran ministers, hoping that some would become missionaries among the Indians. Ever alert to finding some better purpose for Hartwick's property, Cooper approached the executors with a proposal: they should merge their projected seminary with his new academy in Cooperstown. In return for funding the hybrid institution, the executors could name the principal who would double as the village's settled minister, drawing additional support from the United Ecclesiastical Society. This proposal almost certainly disturbed Hartwick's repose in his still fresh grave, for Cooperstown was no New Jerusalem and his old enemy William Cooper would not have passed as an acceptable surrogate for Jesus Christ.[32]

In September 1797 the executors had named Rev. John Frederick Ernst to launch their seminary, preferably on the Hartwick Patent as Reverend

Hartwick had intended. Ernst and Hartwick were old friends who had lodged together in 1780 in New Hanover, Pennsylvania, where Ernst had been the schoolmaster. In July 1796 Ernst was the Lutheran minister in Lunenburgh and Claverack when Hartwick fell fatally ill at nearby Clermont Manor. Ernst tended to Hartwick during his last days and pronounced his funeral sermon.[33]

Ernst had risen from humble circumstances as an indentured servant who emigrated from Germany to America in 1765. He plied his trade as a tailor in Philadelphia in the early 1770s until a patron, Rev. John C. Kunze, discovered his piety and intelligence. Tutored in Latin, English, and Lutheran theology by Kunze, Ernst became a schoolmaster in 1775 and a pastor in 1780. Overcompensating for his humble origins, Ernst developed a stubborn, arrogant, and confrontational personality much like Hartwick's. Although the Reverend Henry M. Muhlenberg admired Ernst's talents (as he had admired Hartwick's), he sadly concluded, "Mr. Ernst was too proud."[34]

Like Hartwick, Ernst had difficulty keeping a parish. Between 1780 and 1791 he took on and rapidly lost posts at New Hanover, Easton, Dryland, Greenwich, Moore, and Maxatawny townships, all in Pennsylvania. In 1791 he moved to New York State, taking charge of the parishes at Claverack and Lunenburgh in the Hudson valley. But the parishioners there quickly began to abandon his preaching and their paying upon discovering his new and fervent engagement with Freemasonry. In December 1796 the dedication ceremonies for the new Freemasonic hall in the town of Hudson featured prayers and anthems specially written for the occasion by Brother Ernst. His Freemasonry alienated his German parishioners, who imagined "that Masons stand immediately connected with the Devil, who discovers all Secrets to them." Freemasonry was his school to replace the wearisome Germanness of his boorish parishioners with the polished manners and pleasing information of Anglo-American gentility: "I joined the Society from a Desire of Knowledge & removing Ignorance. . . . I've broken in my Boat the Ice of Prejudice, as no other German Minister in this Country is initiated to my knowledge." He wrote and published a pamphlet extolling Freemasonry as "truly Christian," but he exhorted a bookseller, "Don't let it come to the hands of unlearned or prejudiced Germans & others who would deal with it, as Swines with Pearls. Neither let any peruse it before they have bought it."[35]

His audience dwindling and his income exhausted, Ernst was available in 1797 for the invitation from Hartwick's executors to establish a seminary in Otsego County. He benefited from the patronage of Reverend Kunze, who had joined the board of executors and had formal direction of the seminary but no intention of leaving his comfortable parish in New York City. Like so many other clergymen down on their luck or on the run from trouble, Ernst sought a fresh start in a frontier village. In November he headed west to visit Otsego and assess his opportunities.[36]

Ernst found an eager reception in both the Hartwick Patent and adjoining Cooperstown from rival groups keen to retain his services that they might capture the Hartwick estate's funds. It did not seem to matter to either Ernst or the rival groups that none of the settlers, in either the Hartwick Patent or Cooperstown, were Lutheran. All the parties discovered in their financial desires a convenient new ecumenicalism. Indeed, the villagers kept straight faces as they assured Ernst that they cherished an "entirely neutral" Lutheran minister as uniquely able to cope with their bitter religious divisions.[37]

The Hartwick Patent settlers invited Ernst to become their "minister, teacher, overseer, and Curate of Souls" and to build his seminary in their midst. But William Cooper proposed merging that seminary with his new academy, welcoming Ernst to Cooperstown as both the schoolmaster and the village's settled minister. In that dual role Ernst could top off his $250 salary from the Hartwick estate with the $302 annually subscribed by the United Ecclesiastical Society for preaching in the village (led by Cooper's $50). According to the judge, everyone (except the Hartwick Patent settlers) would benefit: the Hartwick estate would be spared the cost of constructing a building; the academy would gain a desperately needed endowment and master; the village would, at last, obtain a settled minister; and Ernst would enjoy a substantial income. Cooperstown's boosters also saw to it that Ernst especially enjoyed his November visit. Gathered at Joseph Griffin's Red Lion Inn, they resolved to pay Ernst's tavern bill. Cooper recalled, "I instantly gave two dollars. Others gave to the amount of nine or ten dollars—of this Mr. Earnst was Ignorant untill he found his bill Paid."[38]

Ernst enthusiastically embraced the Cooperstown offer because, in contrast to the rustic Hartwick Patent, the village offered much better pay and a more genteel society, including a Freemasonic lodge. As a sop to the disappointed settlers on the Hartwick Patent, he proposed establishing there a 1,500-acre farm-school "for teaching the Indians the blesing of a civil life." Resettling a group of Indians within the Hartwick Patent was hardly an attractive prospect for the settlers, much less any consolation for losing the seminary. Moreover, there was no parcel of 1,500 acres left unsold within the patent—which was just as well because there were no prospective Indian students for Ernst's disingenuous proposal. Humiliated by Cooperstown's victory, the Hartwick settlers angrily complained that the villagers had begun "to mock us, and well they may, when we have and must forever hereafter be Shaking the Tree and them gathering the Fruits."[39]

In the late 1780s Cooper had repelled Hartwick's desire to become the local minister; a decade later, lusting after money for his new academy, the judge welcomed as Cooperstown's pastor the demanding legatee of the difficult Hartwick. In June of 1798 Ernst and Jeremiah Van Rensselaer visited Cooperstown to finalize the merger. "Judge Cooper, whom we met on our Road thither going to Albany, was kind enough to return—lodged us in his house and shewed us considerable civility," Ernst reported. He planned to move to Cooperstown with his family and furniture at the first of the new year. However, during his June visit Ernst detected a new opposition spreading within the village, encouraged by John McDonald, a defrocked Presbyterian minister held as a debtor in the county jail.[40]

SCANDAL ☙

Although an immigrant like Ernst, Rev. John McDonald came from a higher station in European society. In 1785 he arrived in America not only free but with a degree from Edinburgh University, a further five years of theological study, and a license from the Church of Scotland to preach as a Presbyterian. Recognizing McDonald's distinguished family, education, and credentials, Princeton College granted him an honorary degree within a year of his arrival in America. He quickly secured a prestigious and comfortable post as pastor of Albany's First Presbyterian Church, that denomination's most important parish north of New York City. The congregants could hardly believe their good fortune, for such highly qualified clergymen were rare in America and so many other immigrant ministers came driven by some scandal at home.[41]

Combining deep learning with religious zeal in his pastoral activities and a passionate, spellbinding eloquence in the pulpit, McDonald became the most popular and effective clergyman in upstate New York during his first decade in Albany. Charming and charismatic, he had a "great tenderness and affection in his manner" and "a peculiar gift of attaching to him warm personal friends." In addition to expanding and invigorating membership in his Albany church, he periodically made missionary tours to the poor, new settlements to the north and west—including those in Otsego County. In 1790 the Presbyterian ministers in upstate New York organized an association—the Presbytery of Albany—and chose McDonald as their moderator. Indeed, no other Presbyterian in the state could match the time, energy, and ability that McDonald invested to strengthen and expand that denomination.[42]

The prime purpose for the new presbytery was to preserve the reputation and discipline of their church amidst the peculiar challenges of a rapidly expanding frontier society. New settlements attracted a disproportionate number of disorderly preachers: uneducated, self-appointed itinerants, moral exiles from regular churches, and outright impostors. Determined to

reclaim the settlers for religious orthodoxy, the Presbytery of Albany examined and licensed authentic ministers and purged their ranks when clergymen committed moral lapses. Disdaining most of his American colleagues
as ill-educated slackers and bunglers, McDonald took the lead in constructing Presbyterian order on the New York frontier. He rankled several colleagues who envied his superior gifts and extraordinary popularity and
resented his officious arrogance in correcting their mistakes. However, Mc-
Donald's commitment to Christ did not preclude his becoming a Freemason. Indeed, McDonald knew Reverend Ernst as his brother in the Royal
Arch Chapter of the Freemasonic lodge in Hudson, New York.[43]

The one possible flaw in his public persona of Christian perfection was
the irregular state of his family. McDonald came to America with a young
daughter, Eliza, and a still younger son, George, but without his wife. Re-
portedly an invalid incapable of a transatlantic voyage, she remained in
Scotland. In 1794 McDonald wrote to his daughter, then away at the Mora-
vian boarding school for girls in Bethlehem, Pennsylvania. After exhorting
her to remember Christ's "tormenting death" and "to crucify for his sake
every sinful desire & every unhallowed temper," he reported, "Your mother
continues very poorly when I heard last from her. Forget her not." A letter
from Eliza to her mother would "make the tear of parental joy start from her
eyes which pain bedews." Cynics wondered why McDonald had abandoned
his sickly wife to pursue an American career. Did his great show of selfless
dedication to Christ in fact mask a more selfish nature? One critic later observed, "The strange and mysterious separation of Mr. McDonald from his
wife, through such a series of years, may be considered as the foundation of
all his misfortunes."[44]

McDonald toppled from his pinnacle of honor, influence, and celebrity
in 1795, when a member of his congregation, Margaret Yates, gave birth to
his child. According to common report, a year earlier her dying mother
had "called Mr. McDonald to her bedside &, with unbounded confidence
in him, committed her children to his care & requested him to act the part
of a father to them." Still, the scandal might have been hushed up had
Margaret been some obscure servant girl. Instead, she was the eldest
daughter of Peter W. Yates: an eminent lawyer, Albany's mayor, and the
city's second wealthiest taxpayer (trailing only Gen. Philip Schuyler). Yates
probably nurtured a special sense of betrayal because, as the senior grand
warden of the lodges in Columbia County, he was McDonald's superior in
Freemasonry. After all, Freemasonry was supposed to certify moral conduct, protect the virtue of women, promote trust between brethren, and
command deference to superiors. In September 1795 Yates publicly denounced Reverend McDonald for seducing and impregnating his daughter. For the ruin of Margaret's virtue, Yates meant to destroy McDonald's
reputation.[45]

The scandal embarrassed McDonald's fellow ministers in the Albany Presbytery. They needed to protect their collective reputation from the ridicule of sinners and the contempt of rival denominations. On September 24, the presbytery convened a special session, where McDonald abjectly confessed to

> *criminal conversation with Margaret Yates, a young unmarried Woman of my Congregation. This Crime ought not so much as to be named among Christians—in a Minister of the Gospel it is still more odious & by it he justly forfeits his ministerial Office. . . . Against God, against his People, & against my own Soul I have sinned, sinned exceedingly. I hear with horror the Blasphemy of the wicked, the Scoff of the Scorner, & the tales of the Slanderer which my conduct has excited.*

A day later the presbytery deposed McDonald as a minister, expelling their most able, famous, and popular member. They further ordered McDonald to make a public confession during a Sabbath service before his former congregation in Albany.[46]

Nothing if not proud, McDonald balked at a public confession before his long-adoring congregation. Visiting McDonald in Albany, Rev. John Blair Smith was troubled by his breezy attitude: "In general, his countenance exhibited an air of greater indifference than I expected to find, & he mixed in company with that smiling familiarity for which he has usually been remarkable." Accustomed to being the indispensable minister, McDonald seems to have anticipated applause, followed by a quick restoration, for his eloquent performance as the penitent. Determined to manage his own repentance and stage his own rehabilitation, McDonald was angry and incredulous that the presbytery would not follow his cues, as they had done in the past. Indeed, McDonald believed that they took vindictive pleasure in humbling the man who had, for so long, pointed out their defects.[47]

Impervious to McDonald's attempted directions, the presbytery clung to its sentence. Conceding temporary defeat, McDonald made his public confession before his congregation on the last Sabbath in December. Reverend Smith presided and later reported,

> *He appeared deeply affected, as well as many of his friends. His floods of tears almost prevented utterance sometimes whilst he was making his confession. It was indeed a pitable, an affecting sight to see the man who had been esteemed a Saint of the first magnitude standing as a criminal & degraded from his honourable office which he had filled with such credit. The scene was almost too much for me to act in with firmness. I was obliged to shed tears & sometimes pause for a moment to recover the tone of my voice.*

Once again McDonald had risen to the occasion with an emotional and affecting performance.[48]

However, his written version of that confession reveals more shrewd calculation than spontaneous sincerity. McDonald exercised his mastery over words to frame an eloquent but self-serving narrative in which he fell victim to his own excesses of humane sympathy and religious zeal. Addressing Rev. Ashbel Green of Philadelphia, McDonald began with the promise "to unveil the whole business & unbosom my self without disguise." The daughter of irreligious parents, Margaret had found "religious conviction" by attending his sermons. With her parents' consent, she importuned a reluctant McDonald to take her on as a student:

> Her progress exceeded my most sanguine expectations. I believed her, (I wish still to believe her) a sincere convert. The frequent relation of the sufferings which she underwent from her family, from her former young companions & from the world on account of her religious conduct endeared her to my heart & gradually procured my esteem. A more tender & interesting passion succeeded. Alas! It was reciprocal. I beheld her affectionate respect & suffering for my Master through the medium of my own regard & affection. I struggled to conceal an attachment which religion & reason did not permit. The attempt, I fear, displayed instead of smothering the flame. My views as far as I knew myself were innocent. I resolved to avoid her company as much as possible & to await a period when to declare what I felt might be without danger & without offence. But an unguarded moment met with an unshielded heart. Without premeditation the deed was committed whose stain cannot blot out & whose arrows death alone can fully extract. The fruit of this unlawful commerce soon ripened to the confusion & shame of the guilty parties, to the grief of the pious & the Blasphemy & rebuke of the prophane. My Friend! My God! I shudder at the recollection!

Her father demanded that McDonald marry Margaret—regardless of his wife in Scotland. McDonald recounted, "The proposal filled me with horror. I rejected it with abhorrence." In his narration he became the principal victim, betrayed by a collusion among his tender passion, a weak and complicit woman, and her vicious and avaricious father ("without principle & skilled in the evasion of human laws"). Contrary to her insistence that their relationship had lasted for weeks, McDonald implied that he was guilty of but one brief lapse, for which he suffered the inordinate, lifelong punishment of public shame and blasphemous insult, as he waited stoically and reverently for death to relieve his pain.[49]

By early February, Reverend Smith had come to distrust the confession that had moved him to tears in December, as McDonald hinted that his public repentance merited immediate restoration to the ministry. In 1796 and 1797, encouraged by McDonald, most of his former congregants repeatedly petitioned the Presbytery of Albany and its supervisory body, the Synod of New York, to restore their cherished minister. However, the presbytery and the synod refused to reinstate McDonald so long as he "continued to live in a state of separation from his wife." Indignant, McDonald raged against "their defect in charity & their obvious malignity."[50]

In the meantime McDonald pursued a new career by opening a bookstore and launching a newspaper, the *Albany Chronicle,* in September 1796. But disaster struck on the night of November 2, when a spark from a candle in his hand "communicated the flame to some dry paper on a line." Raging out of control, the fire consumed his home, office, press, books, stationery, binding tools, and furniture in less than thirty minutes. He estimated his loss at £2,000. McDonald procured a new press and resumed publishing in January 1797, but he fell deeper and deeper into arrears with his impatient creditors. In January 1798 he fled from Albany to escape a writ for his arrest as a defaulting debtor, leaving his newspaper and bookshop to the management of a new partner. Overtaken by a deputy in Otsego County, he was incarcerated as a debtor in the Cooperstown jail. His fall from grace and influence seemed complete.[51]

Resilient and resourceful, McDonald discerned in his troubles a divine demand for his earthly redemption as a minister. From the confines of the Cooperstown jail, he could see that the destructive fire was a divine message from an angry God impatient for McDonald to forsake worldly business and return to his proper calling. It did not escape McDonald's attention that, because Reverend Ernst had yet to relocate, Cooperstown still did not have a settled minister. McDonald also noted that, as a thriving and rapidly growing village, Cooperstown promised a decent living to a popular minister. He began his self-rehabilitation with his jail mates: "On the morning of my confinement, I proposed to my fellow prisoners the propriety of commencing and closing every day with religious exercises. To this they cheerfully assented and appointed me to lead our devotions." A success with his fellow captives, McDonald hinted that he was willing to carry his preaching into the village. Unlike the jail's criminals, the debtors were permitted by law to leave their cells during the day, provided they remained within a portion of the village specified as "the gaol liberties." This portion consisted primarily of artisans' workshops, where debtors could, by hiring out, make some money to satisfy their creditors—and thereby win their freedom. At sundown the debtors had to return to their cells for the night.[52]

The Otsego United Ecclesiastical Society enthusiastically embraced the opportunity to employ McDonald's extraordinary talents. The occasional Baptist itinerants and Congregational or Presbyterian missionaries who passed through town could not match his combination of extensive learning, fine manners, and powerful eloquence. To many it seemed a stroke of divine providence that a man of McDonald's rare gifts should land in Otsego's jail. Albany's loss could be Cooperstown's gain. In their desire to enjoy his ministry, the local devout were willing to overlook his scandalous past and his current imprisonment. Still a frontier village, Cooperstown could not have recruited a man of McDonald's credentials and accomplishments but for that taint which denied him employment in a larger,

richer, older, and more comfortable town. The popular enthusiasm for Mc-
Donald, despite his devalued status, attested both to the villagers' provin-
ciality and to their genteel aspirations. Like their uneducated judge,
ungainly academy, fractious Freemasonic lodge, wide but muddy streets,
rectangular but stumpy lots, erratic brewery, grandiose but rotting courthouse, and pretentious yet plain Manor House, the villagers' enthusiasm for
a minister who was learned but jailed, persuasive but tainted, was one more
evidence of Cooperstown's flawed gentility. The United Ecclesiastical Society invited McDonald to preach every Sabbath in the courthouse, upstairs
from his debtor's cell on the ground floor.

To defuse any lingering suspicions, McDonald opened his renewed public ministry in Cooperstown with "a full Account of the causes of my humiliating condition." Thereafter he preached every Sabbath to growing numbers
drawn by the spreading report of his religious genius and animated eloquence. His new admirers included the lawyer Moss Kent, Jr., who had previously shown scant interest in God. Kent observed, "[McDonald] has
conducted himself with so much propriety that he has gained the very general Esteem & Goodwill of the People of this Place. He preaches to us every
Sabbath & has a very crowded Audience. I regularly attend & am highly entertained with him." McDonald was just as pleased with his performances:

> The effects of our Meeting and of our discourses were soon sensibly felt. Infidels
> and profligates found themselves censured and checked. This procured their
> odium, their opposition, their persecution. The Sabbath, hitherto shamefully
> profaned, began to be observed. Multitudes gave a strict and solemn attention.
> Many men & women formerly thoughtless and profane espoused openly the
> cause of the Cross.

According to McDonald, sin was embattled and in remission in its longtime
stronghold, the village of Cooperstown. But he had become what he had
fought against earlier in his career: an irregular, self-appointed preacher
exploiting the lax standards, and filling the religious need, of a frontier
village.[53]

McDonald encouraged the locals to believe that he would linger on as
their minister when released from jail. Hoping to retain the most talented
minister in upstate New York, growing numbers of settlers in Cooperstown
and the rest of Otsego Township decided that they no longer wanted the services of Ernst, a Lutheran with a thick German accent. Raised in the Calvinist religious culture of New England, almost all of the devout settlers
preferred McDonald's Presbyterianism to Ernst's more alien Lutheranism.[54]

In Hudson preparing for his move to Cooperstown, Ernst was enraged by
reports that his support in Otsego was flowing into McDonald's camp. He
both envied and detested the persuasive power of McDonald's fluent
tongue: "By smooth speech, flattery, &c. [he] has insinuated or ingratiated

himself with the wicked, the ignorant & the weak, and particularly the WOMEN, with whom he endeavours to excite their compassion & to make them believe, not that he seduced Miss Yates, but that she, as a wicked, designing woman, seduced him." According to Ernst, such was McDonald's spell that his blind addicts swore "that they would prefer him, should he even be the father of an hundred Bastards, and have committed fornication between his prayer & his Sermon." McDonald's opposition was especially offensive to Ernst because the two men were Freemasonic brethren, belonging to the same lodge in Hudson, New York. Like their Christian calling, shared Freemasonry was supposed to induce trust and harmony between brethren, but instead they engaged in a bitter, divisive competition for religious authority in Cooperstown.[55]

CONFLICT

Defying the growing opposition, Ernst removed with his wife and children from Hudson to Cooperstown, arriving in January 1799. No sooner had Ernst reached Cooperstown than the villagers began to wish him away. They had accepted Ernst as their minister in the expectation that he would also direct and teach in their academy and that he would induce the Hartwick executors to provide a steady flow of funds. However, the executors made no further investment in the academy beyond the $250 salary paid Ernst (on top of the $302 subscribed in Cooperstown), because they had developed qualms about the merger. Nor did the Cooperstowners get a schoolmaster for their own money, because the newly arrived Ernst announced that he was primarily a minister not a teacher; he would only visit the academy once a week to catechize the children. Deprived of the endowment and schoolmaster they had sought, the villagers were stuck with a preacher whose strong accent, stubborn personality, and Lutheran doctrines irritated them. Although he had been too acculturated for his German parishioners in the Hudson valley, Ernst proved too foreign for his new Yankee congregants. They grumbled that his "hard german dialect" was "too uncouth for tender juvenile ears." They complained that he arrived tainted by a long history of contentions with his previous parishes. In 1799 the villagers suddenly became troubled by the flaws that they had so eagerly overlooked a year before when his advent promised to fund and staff their ailing academy.[56]

Most of the inhabitants boycotted Ernst's services at the academy, preferring McDonald's sermons at the courthouse. And they failed to deliver the firewood and monies promised to Ernst by their subscription. When pressed to explain their delays, the villagers insisted that nothing could be done for him while William Cooper was away for the winter on business. The minister sarcastically observed,

The continual & unanimous cry during the Absence of the Honorable Senior
Trustee (without whose approbation nothing may be carried on with success)
was: WE'LL WAIT, 'TILL THE JUDGE COMES HOME! This awaiting his
return, with the hopes of hearing some animating news respecting the appro-
priation of the Hartwick revenues—and the intricate as well as more neces-
sary business *of electioneering, have been sufficient reasons to me, for the*
neglect of this less important business *of Church and School matters.*

Such was Cooper's influence, enthusiasm, and wealth, that his absence par-
alyzed village benevolence and boosterism, just as his presence was so energizing. All the effort to bring Ernst to Cooperstown dissipated while the
judge was away and the villagers became enamored of McDonald.[57]

Returning home in late March, Cooper found his neighbors up in arms
over Ernst. The judge took charge of the village opposition, for he too expected to get what he had paid for: a schoolmaster and an endowment. According to Ernst, Cooper assured the villagers that "if *he* brings a man into
a Scrape, he'll help him out again, thereby alluding to his driving them
largely to subscribe to me last year." Ernst complained, "Since the return of
the Judge, matters here have taken a different Aspect. Faces have suddenly
become more sullen & surly. Behaviour has been sensibly altered, not only
by himself, but also by the people. Tho' attention on divine service was before but indifferently paid—it is now entirely slighted." Only five or six villagers continued to attend Ernst's Sunday services in the academy, while
McDonald preached to crowds a block away. Apparently some villagers
menaced Ernst, for an ally exhorted, "Let us not be intimidated at the angry
threats of the Sons of Violence."[58]

On April 25, 1799—at the peak of the confrontation—McDonald delivered two Fast Day sermons that implicitly rebuked Ernst and curried
Cooper's favor. In a not-so-subtle dig at the reluctant teacher, McDonald insisted, "A faithful Schoolmaster is the most useful member in society, and
claims corresponding respect and reward." By implication the negligent
master warranted disrespect and no support. McDonald also reminded his
audience of their disappointment with the Hartwick estate by insisting that
"Public Seminaries . . . should be constantly collecting treasures, and sending their streams to enrich the surrounding country." Embracing Cooper's
Federalist opinions, McDonald promoted a war with France's revolutionary
regime. With unconscious irony McDonald warned of an impending French
invasion that would expose Americans' "fields, their flocks, their wives and
their daughters, to be insulted and polluted by the dregs of human depravity." Also speaking from unacknowledged experience, he lamented that the
prevailing economic depression had led unscrupulous debtors "to desperate remedies, or fraudulent concealments." He declared, "Our prisons are
crouded, beyond example, with unjust, or with unfortunate Debtors."[59]

While McDonald stiffened the United Ecclesiastical Society against

Ernst, the latter rallied some local support by calling upon his brethren in Otsego Lodge. Because the Freemasonic hall lay outside the jail liberties, Brother McDonald could not attend the meetings. In contrast, Ernst played a prominent role in the lodge. During his December 1797 visit he delivered the prayers and sermon at the dedication ceremonies for the new Masonic Hall. In September 1798 Elihu Phinney—the master of Otsego Lodge as well as the publisher of the *Otsego Herald*—implicitly assisted Ernst by printing on the front page a detailed account of a recent lawsuit against a Methodist minister who "under the cloak of religion" had seduced, impregnated, and ruined a young parishioner. Phinney subtly but surely meant to remind the villagers of McDonald's scandal, meant to puncture their infatuation. In May 1799, at Ernst's solicitation, the lodge suspended Brother Timothy Barns for his vociferous public criticism of the Lutheran minister, deemed "unmasonic and immoral conduct" that "endangered the character of the Lodge." Throughout the controversy the moralistic Ernst was in the ironic position of mobilizing support among the irreligious Freemasons to counter the conspicuously devout members of the United Ecclesiastical Society who favored a defrocked and jailed minister. Inversions prevailed in Cooperstown in 1799.[60]

Support from the Freemasonic lodge was not enough to stem the growing antipathy of the village majority. Characteristically, Ernst made matters worse by responding to his opponents with a tactless and patronizing counterattack. He likened their opposition to the behavior of "a Bumble-bee in a chamber, dashing & sousing with incessant soaring from one corner into another, only hunting and catching at Flies." Instead of reneging on their commitments, they ought to reform their rampant immorality: "Profaning the Lord's day with walking the streets . . . together with brawling are no symptoms of regularity, order, good-breeding, civil conduct or benevolence."[61]

Embarrassed and offended by the unseemly spectacle in Cooperstown, the Hartwick executors voted on June 11, 1799, to give up the merger and to terminate Ernst's salary as soon as he could depart the village. After prolonged and acrimonious negotiations, Ernst reached a compromise with the Otsego subscribers, who in December 1803 agreed to pay him $250 to drop his claims. In the meantime (1802), Ernst had left Cooperstown to take a new post as the Lutheran minister in Manheim, Lancaster County, Pennsylvania. Back among his fellow Germans, he had to promise to forsake his beloved Freemasonry. On October 24, 1805, he died in Manheim at the age of fifty-seven.[62]

It probably consoled Ernst that, in the end, McDonald could not claim the prize he had helped wrest from his Lutheran rival. In late 1798 news of McDonald's irregular ministry had alarmed the Presbytery of Albany, who demanded an explanation. Preaching without formal authority from a presbytery was, they charged, an especially dangerous precedent "in a New Coun-

try where Churches are already too much dispos'd to be irregular, as it is calculated to encourage ill-designing men to enter in and rend the flock of
Christ." His return from scandal to preaching would also "give occasion for
the enemies of Religion to scoff." McDonald replied that he obeyed a higher
authority than the Presbytery of Albany. With adept sophistry, he added that,
although he preached, exhorted, and led prayers, he carefully refrained
from conducting the sacraments—baptism and communion—that properly
defined the role of a minister. Therefore, he acted only as a lay exhorter and
was still in technical obedience to the presbytery's deposition.[63]

In late 1799, after nearly two years as a jailed debtor, McDonald won his
freedom, probably because his creditor tired of paying his board bills at the
jail, as the law required. However, to his surprise and chagrin, the United
Ecclesiastical Society declined to retain McDonald as their settled minister.
Apparently, the denunciations by the Presbytery of Albany had gradually
sobered the leading villagers. In late 1799 they concluded that a less controversial minister would better advance their longing for genteel respectability in the eyes of the wider and more cosmopolitan world.[64]

For a few months McDonald lingered in Cooperstown, studying law with
Moss Kent, Jr., tutoring students, and occasionally preaching in the vicinity.
In March 1800 he suddenly decamped for Albany, determined to regain his
ministry there. In August the presbytery once again rejected McDonald's
application after a heated hearing. Defiant, McDonald sought and obtained
admission to the irregular Presbytery of Montreal, which had never before
meddled in New York State. In October 1800 he formed his own Albany
congregation of dissident Presbyterians, chiefly drawn from his former
parishioners. A spokesman for the Presbytery of Albany, the Reverend Jonas
Coe, denounced McDonald in the columns of an Albany newspaper:

> What a strange and inscrutable mixture of wisdom and folly—of order and
> confusion—of truth and error—and of irreligion and zeal, appear to constitute
> the character of the man! Once a popular preacher of the gospel; but now a pub-
> lic defamer of its ministers. Once a rigid observer of order; but now acting in
> wild disorder. Once building up and cementing the church; but now pulling
> down and dividing her.

McDonald published an angry counterattack that did nothing to promote
the cause of Christianity. His arrogance intact, he dismissed his Presbyterian opponents as social inferiors and mental midgets: "unsuccessful candidates, in the *arts* of the *awl*, the *needle* and the *chopping axe* . . . whose minds
fair science only shot a few oblique reflected rays during their rapid passage
thro' her suburbs." In subsequent years McDonald preserved his new
church in Albany but endured a continuing ostracism by other Presbyterians. He never recovered his former preeminence. In 1819 infirmity compelled his retirement, and death claimed him shortly thereafter.[65]

By checking each other Ernst and McDonald ensured that neither would prevail as Cooperstown's minister. Instead, the prize fell to a younger, less contentious newcomer with impeccable credentials: the Reverend Isaac Lewis. He had the advantage of sharing with the Yankee settlers of Otsego a Connecticut ancestry and upbringing. The son of a Congregational clergyman, Lewis attended Yale, graduating in 1794. Thereafter he lingered in New Haven, studying theology, first with Ezra Stiles and then with his successor as president of Yale, the formidable Timothy Dwight. Ordained in 1798, Lewis headed west as a missionary, probing for an opportunity in a promising new village. In the spring of 1800, shortly after McDonald's departure, Lewis preached in Cooperstown as a candidate on probation. In April an enthusiastic Hannah Cooper wrote to her brother Isaac, "I have just returned from hearing a new minister who is offered a situation here. His name is Lewis—from New England. His discourse was very agreeable. Would we get him, we shall have no occasion to lament Mr. McDonald's absence." Tired of their recent contentions and taken with Lewis, the United Ecclesiastical Society invited him to persist as their permanent minister. At his instigation the society formally reorganized as a Presbyterian church and applied for and received admission to the Presbytery of Albany. In October the Cooperstown Presbyterian Church formally installed Lewis—to the immense relief of the beleaguered presbytery. Fourteen years after its settlement began, Cooperstown had its first permanent clergyman. But they did not erect a church building until 1805–6, continuing to meet in the academy or courthouse in the interim.[66]

The Cooperstown Presbyterian Church derived support from both genders but in different forms: lacking their own property, women committed their souls, while most men advanced only money for want of sufficient piety. Ten of the thirteen charter members were men, but thereafter most of the new members were women as the Cooperstown church grew steadily. Over the decade 1800–1809 women amounted to 55 percent of the members and men only 45 percent. For admission to membership an applicant had to confess to the church his or her religious experience and undergo searching questions from the laity. More women than men were willing to expose their souls to this public scrutiny. Unlike women, men were trained by their competitions and contentions to shelter and fortify their most personal thoughts and experiences. Although only 44 men became members, at least 241 subscribed money for the church during that decade (only one woman did so). Apparently, many men of limited piety supported the church financially as a community service. Forsaking his early detestation of Yankee religion, William Cooper contributed generously to the Presbyterian church and occasionally attended services without becoming a member. Although only two Freemasons joined the church, forty-one others, including Elihu Phinney, subscribed money. Whatever the Freemasons' intent, their contributions had the welcome effect of stilling criticism from the devout of the infidelity lurking in the lodge.[67]

Although the Presbyterian church was relatively late to take root in Cooperstown, it thrived and endured, while the village's earlier, secular institutions all stagnated or died. As the Presbyterian church waxed, the Freemasonic lodge waned, declining from a peak of membership and influence in 1800. During the 1790s the Otsego Lodge nearly achieved its members' ambition to unite the leading men from every county town, but after 1800 the lodge became a more parochial institution, as the distant members dropped out and the new initiates rarely dwelled beyond Otsego and Middlefield townships. From a peak of thirty-five members per monthly stated meeting in 1800, average attendance fell steadily to eighteen in 1805. The lodge's influence declined as the post-1800 initiates were far less prosperous and prestigious than their predecessors. According to the 1803 tax list for Otsego Township, the new members averaged $666 in property, compared with $1,421 for the old (the mean for all taxpayers in town was $701). The brewery was a financial loser that closed in June of 1800. The premises and the debts reverted to Cooper, while the villagers rededicated themselves to drinking whiskey. In 1804 a fire consumed the former brewery. The private waterworks proved an expensive disappointment that led the *Otsego Herald* in 1807 to editorialize for a new village government that could establish a municipal water supply. The academy also withered. Sobered by the Ernst debacle, Cooper and the other trustees forsook their ambition to make a classical academy and settled for a country English school conducted by a succession of short-term teachers. Ambitious men seeking a classical education for their sons sent them away to eastern academies. Although William Cooper had spent over £1,000 for the Otsego Academy, he had to dispatch his sons to boarding schools in Schenectady, Albany, and Burlington. In 1809 fire destroyed the Cooperstown Academy, and the villagers declined to rebuild it. In sum, the village institutions that Cooper cared most about faltered while the church that he had been relatively slow to support prospered.[68]

Contrary to Cooper's expectations, during the 1790s the village's growth brought greater diversity rather than homogeneity, increased dissension rather than harmony. Indeed, his insistence on village unity contributed to the tensions as individuals and factions competed to own that elusive ideal. The institutions that were supposed to foster harmony became the cockpits of bitter competition. And his imposition of small lots in the village meant that rivals and enemies came into daily contact and friction—and suffered from increasingly destructive fires. Cooper's failure to mandate harmony in his cherished village was an ill omen for his political authority throughout Otsego County.

Chapter Nine

THE POLITICAL WARS

T he Pioneers OFFERS AN APPARENTLY thorough depiction of frontier society in Otsego through thc seasonal cyclc of a year in the early 1790s. James Fenimore Cooper describes sleighing, deer hunting, a church service, tavern drinking, a turkey shoot, maple sugaring, a pigeon slaughter, fish seining, a trial, a jailbreak, a forest fire, a militia expedition, and even treasure seeking. But the novel avoids any reference to the political elections that so preoccupied men every spring and alternate falls in the Otsego of history. The omission is jarring because

The inspectors were assembled in a quiet room of the inn, with the ballot-boxes placed before them, on a table. The voters entered at their leisure, and delivered their different ballots to the officers, who, holding them up as lottery numbers are usually exhibited, called the name of the voter aloud, and then deposited the ballot in its proper box. . . . Nothing could be more quiet and orderly than this meeting.

—James Fenimore Cooper, Notions of the Americans, vol. 1, 262

political partisanship characterized the early Republic, especially during the 1790s; because New York was nationally notorious as the state most devoted to political passions and intrigue; and because New York's elections so frequently pivoted on controversies in Otsego County. The exclusion of an election scene is also striking because electioneering so consumed the author's father during the 1790s. The greatest gap between the history told in *The Pioneers* and that revealed by William Cooper's surviving correspondence is the son's excision of the elections that preoccupied the father. Writing to please himself, the son preferred to remember Otsego shorn of the politics that had initially sustained but eventually destroyed his father's public authority. He imagined an Otsego where Judge Temple enjoyed power by influencing the notables of state government, without any apparent dependence on a common electorate. A detailed reconstruction of the political culture in upstate New York during the 1790s reveals why an election scene was not a pleasant memory for the son of William Cooper.[1]

During the 1790s the political culture in New York was an unstable hybrid as leading men tried to adjust colonial electioneering practices to the republican rhetoric and institutions of a new age. Elections manifested a fundamental clash between two divergent ways of conducting politics. One

was overtly republican, legitimated by the Revolution, and preoccupied
with minimizing any interference in the spontaneous generation of leadership from the sovereign people. The other way was rooted in colonial electoral practices and was devoted to constructing a hierarchical network of
influence known as "an interest." During the 1790s candidates and their
friends considered politics to be, in their recurrent phrase, the business of
"making interest" or, as William Cooper put it, "the art of Hook & Snivey."
They meant the use of intrigue, trickery, and favors to build coalitions of
local notables who could deliver the votes of their common neighbors.[2]

That the republican ideals were so compromised in electoral practice did
not diminish their appeal to the public. Voters were of two minds about
electioneering: they took an avid interest in the competitive sport, the high
spirits, the intriguing reports of scandal, and the dramatic scenes at the poll,
but they also nurtured a prickly unease that could be aroused by any suggestion that they were dependent on the will of another. Precisely because
the republican ideal was so powerful *and* because it was so consistently violated, every New York election became a bitter contest to claim possession
of the elusive ideal. The challenge facing the friends of a candidate was to
exploit voter enthusiasm while projecting voter unease onto the rival campaign. If convinced that the opposition alone bore the sins of electioneering, a candidate's voters could feel virtuous while surrendering to the
pleasures of the election season. Every competing faction sought legitimacy
by investing itself with the trappings of republicanism, by masking its devia-
tions from the ideal, and by exposing the unrepublican machinations of the
opposition. This behavior was not entirely cynical because everyone believed that he resorted to electioneering only to counter the greater and
previous efforts by his rivals. Interests were involved in a paradoxical game
where victory came to that faction best able to appear to be the passive instrument of the common interest; creating that image required a good deal
of management.[3]

In the hybrid political culture of the 1790s, elections served two contra-
dictory purposes: to determine the proper gentlemen fit to rule *and* to preserve the Republic from aristocratic plots. On the one hand, election to
public office was the capstone of social ascent, the definitive certification by
a deferential electorate that a gentleman had acquired the right combination of property, learning, manners, and connections. On the other hand,
the Revolution had empowered the people with ballots to prevent aristocrats from gaining and exploiting power to corrupt and destroy the fragile
new Republic. The victor in an election could simultaneously claim the people's recognition as a superior gentleman *and* as the best friend to their liberty. However, there was a tension between the two roles because lofty
gentlemen made the most plausible villains for the electioneering stories
warning that aristocrats were plotting against the liberties of common men.

Already George Clinton had recognized the contradiction and summoned the voters to resent conspicuous gentlemen and to prefer the common style practiced by the "Friends of the People." As the internal contradictions of the political culture became increasingly manifest over the course of the decade, the democratic potential of the Revolution was gradually realized in New York's politics. In 1799–1800 that realization would doom William Cooper's authority as a Father of the People.[4]

During the mid-1790s Cooper became caught in a cross fire of challenges from aggressive rivals determined to exploit his flaws as a gentleman and to discredit his brazen pursuit of political interest. To his right three ambitious and arch-Federalist lawyers from Cooperstown sought increased prestige and power by undermining the judge's influence. The leading lawyer was Moss Kent, Jr., a dashing but arrogant young man who had enjoyed but ultimately betrayed the judge's patronage. Although the lawyers largely shared Cooper's political principles, they disdained him as a vulgar upstart unworthy of honor and office. Their rupture of the political consensus in Otsego invited a challenge from the other political flank as Jedediah Peck began to craft a democratic alternative to the rule of either the Father of the People or the Cooperstown lawyers. Expanding from his base in the rural town of Burlington, Peck played to the resentments felt in the hinterland toward the arrogance and power of the Cooperstown and Cherry Valley villagers. Caught in the middle, Cooper faced a new dilemma: could he reunite the county leaders, or would he have to cast his lot unambiguously with one of the new factions—the village lawyers or the hinterland populists, with Moss Kent or Jedediah Peck? Two more different bodies and personalities could hardly be found among Otsego's men: whereas Kent was tall, handsome, young, genteel, erudite, conservative, and conceited, Peck was short, homely, older, common, uneducated, populist, and shrewd.

INTERESTS

According to the republican thought of revolutionary America, candidates for public office were supposed to emerge freely and spontaneously from "the people"—a phrase that, in political life, meant only free white men with enough property to support themselves. In New York State during the 1790s, it was very bad form for an aspirant to announce his candidacy and openly to seek votes. A fitting candidate kept a low profile, leaving all the exertions of a campaign to his "friends." Self-promotion branded the aspirant as a dangerous demagogue or a deluded fool and, in either case, as entirely lacking in the dignity that came to the man who seemed to wait for the unsolicited nomination and acclamation of the citizens. One rare and daring

self-promoter was Sheriff John Winn of Montgomery County, who ran for
Congress in 1792 and 1794. A hostile observer remarked, "Winn's personal
exertions were great & such as to make every honest man despise him." Another critic denounced "the ambition of self-nominated candidates" and
preferred a candidate "who will not condescend personally to solicit our
votes, but who will receive them with becoming gratitude, as an honorable
testimony of our approbation of his conduct." Winn lost both of his campaigns by wide margins, garnering less than a third of the vote in each race.[5]

According to republican precepts, the proper candidate emerged from
a public nominating meeting, ordinarily held for a township or a county
and convened about a month before the election. Mandated neither by
New York's state constitution of 1777 nor by any subsequent statute, nomination meetings were informal institutions that rapidly developed during
the 1780s to fit the new principle of popular sovereignty. Open to all adult
male residents of the township or county, a nominating meeting was supposed to be devoid of partisan or factional identity. Once gathered, "the
people" were to choose a moderator to conduct their discussions, a secretary to record their resolutions, and a committee of correspondence to
communicate the results to those unable to attend. It was appropriate for
certain local notables to be "spoken of" informally as deserving candidates
before a meeting, but it was most improper for anyone to organize any effort to influence the meeting. A potential candidate demonstrated a proper
sense of humility by staying away from the meeting. The proper meeting
freely and spontaneously discussed deserving gentlemen, in search of a consensus candidate who could emerge with unanimous or near-unanimous
support. In 1795 the *Albany Gazette* insisted, "The true will of the people
must approach to a unanimity" because "the interests of the people are uniform. It will avail nothing to say that the will of the people is determined by
the voice of a majority."[6]

However, no actual nominating meeting held in upstate New York ever
fulfilled the ideal. Republicanism presupposed a society of free and equal
men acting for the common good, but society in rural New York was fractured into many unstable and hierarchical interests clustered around
wealthy men. Those interests competed for power by manipulating the
nomination and election of political officeholders. Contrary to republican
assumptions, the elections held in New York during the 1790s demonstrated that some men were more equal than others in their ability to sway
and mobilize votes.[7]

Interests were more powerful than parties in New York politics before
1800. People frequently spoke of "parties" in postrevolutionary New York,
especially in referring to the enduring split that pitted the supporters of
George Clinton against his critics among New York's old families of prestige
and wealth. In 1788 the anti-Clintonians endorsed the new national consti-

tution and adopted the name Federalists. In reaction, during the early
1790s almost all of Clinton's friends began calling themselves Republicans.
Before 1800, however, New York's parties were names that candidates
claimed rather than organizations capable of disciplining subordinates.
Both parties were loose and shifting alliances of multiple competing interests sensitive to new opportunities. From western Massachusetts in 1802,
Theodore Sedgwick looked over the border and observed that the "line of
division" between political parties "was more obscurely marked" in New
York than in other states because the voters "were more under the domination of personal influence." Similarly, Oliver Wolcott of Connecticut
lamented, "After living a dozen years in New York, I don't pretend to comprehend their politics. It is a labyrinth of wheels within wheels, and it is understood only by the managers."[8]

An interest coalesced around a gentleman with the wealth and power to
influence others and reward his supporters. The lesser partners reaped
small favors from the more powerful in recognition of their support—a support that bolstered the authority of the man at the top. A great man's interest reached down through intermediaries, with their own local interests,
to the common voters. Candidates and their friends presumed a hierarchical and deferential political culture where common voters took their cues
from local notables. In 1793 Cooper anxiously waited for Michael Myers, a
state senator from German Flats, to enter his interest: "A number of his nei-
bours has told me [that] if he urgd them in my favour, they would all voat
so, but as yet he had not wrote them, onely to suspend their Opinion untill
they heard further from him."[9]

Building an interest required outlays of money that only the wealthy
could afford. Candidates usually paid most of the bills, but often they received financial support from their friends, who entered into a subscription
to pay the electioneering expenses at the conclusion of the polling. One
subscription for a campaign in Ulster County in 1794 totaled £108.0.0. In
1793 two of Silas Talbot's friends in Montgomery County submitted accounts for £16.5.0 and £27.9.9, respectively. The money went to pay riders,
to hire sleighs and drivers, to engage poll attendants, and above all to ply
voters with alcohol. George Metcalf, an especially systematic friend of Talbot, estimated that an outlay of £5 "may produce about 100 votes." Another
political operative remarked, "Money is the deity to whom *all* pay adoration.
It is a truth, though I would not promulgate the sentiment, but it is a solemn
truth, that there can be no reliance on the *virtue* of the people when assailed
by this mighty conqueror." The costs of campaigning determined that gentlemen played the roles of candidate and their friends while voters received
their favors and flattery.[10]

In eighteenth-century America a gentleman's business and his office
were routinely intertwined, each equally private and public. A leading

man's interest consisted of his mix of political and economic power. Wealth and influence were different sides of the same coin—"an interest." Indeed, it did not seem that one sort of power could be distinguished from the other, much less exist for long without the other. On the one hand, holding office could help a gentleman accrue more property. On the other hand, it was common practice for the politically ambitious gentleman to employ his property "to interest" local notables in his campaigns.[11]

In the course of his races for Congress, William Cooper made important friends by selling them large parcels of land within the Military Tract (in Onondaga County) at below market value. Neither Cooper nor his correspondents were slow to link his private patronage to their political friendship. In August 1794 Peter Smith offered his support in return for some of Cooper's land at a price "one or two shillings less than you have done to any Body else." Cooper sold him 3,200 acres, and Smith actively promoted Cooper's political interest that fall and again two years later. Similarly, in 1794 Thomas R. Gold informed Cooper of his electioneering efforts and concluded, "P.S. I should be glad by & by to make a snug purchase in new land. If it should offer, please to inform me." Cooper took Gold into his military tract investment and he redoubled his efforts for the judge's reelection bid in 1796. A foe insisted that Cooper built his interest "thro the medium of powerful connections of bonds and mortgages." Another critic assured his friend Silas Talbot, "Judge M[yers] pledg'd himself to JVR [Jeremiah Van Rensselaer] to support you—to Peter Yates to support Winn & after all by some *greasing* from Cooper he supported him. Thus, my friend, you see what an abominable world we live in."[12]

The local notable who agreed to make interest with a candidate became known as his "friend." Seeking Cooper's "friendship" for a political appointment, Josiah Ogden Hoffman explained, "When I say friendship I mean not a dead, inactive exertion, but a lively and anxious interest in my behalf." *Friend* conveyed an important fiction by implying that the support came from disinterested affection and loyalty rather than from a calculation of the benefits of making interest with the candidate. The term masked the inequality of the patron-client relationships that composed an interest. The mask slipped halfway off when Joshua Dewey, a Cooperstown schoolteacher, saluted William Cooper as "my worthy Friend and Patron." Calling political support "friendship" also served to create a bond of honor between men, a bond that was not supposed to be broken by any shift in the fortunes of interest.[13]

Rivals sought to unmask the fiction by insisting that the opposition's friends were, in fact, "tools": men without wills of their own and subject to the dictate of their candidate. In 1796 Jonas Platt (a friend of James Cochran) assailed Thomas R. Gold (a supporter of William Cooper): "A slave to your own ambition; a tool to that of others; a friend to no man, and

without a friend on earth—you enjoy unenvied the fruits of your own mean-
ness." The epithet *tool* grievously wounded gentlemen. Proud and sensitive
to any challenge to their independence, they insisted that they were the candidate's friends, for a friend made a free gift of his support. After exerting
himself on Cooper's behalf in the congressional election of 1794, Moss
Kent felt obliged to assure his brother, the jurist James Kent, "You are too
well acquainted with the firmness & independency of my Character to infer
from my riding so much in behalf of the judge that I am becoming what in
the Language of Party is called a *Tool*. No, you will impute it to the proper
cause, to the goodness of my Heart & to the warm & animated concern
which I always take in the interest & happiness of my friends."[14]

But candidates were all too aware that friendship was fickle. Two years
after protesting his devoted friendship to the judge, Moss Kent became notorious for his unstinting efforts to destroy Cooper's political career. "I always treat my Friends with warmth and Sincerity and am mostly deceived,"
Cooper lamented. Because political friends were so unreliable, an interest
was volatile and required constant maintenance. A leading man had to work
to retain support and to build alliances with other, potentially useful, interests. An interest decayed the moment it could no longer command a majority of votes in its territory, bestow favors on adherents, or punish those
who strayed. A gentleman measured the strength of his own, of allied, and
of competing interests in seasons of election. With annual state and bien-
nial congressional elections, public life in New York featured a steady succession of political campaigns, as leading men tested their interests and
honor every April and every other December or January. Never entirely secure in his power, Cooper faced repeated challenges within his congressional district and home county during the 1790s.[15]

CHALLENGERS

By 1795 three lawyers had moved to Cooperstown, drawn by the increasing
litigation of Otsego's growing population. First came Abraham C. Ten
Broeck, a Dutchman from New Jersey, followed by two Yankees: Joseph
Strong from Long Island and Moss Kent, Jr., from Dutchess County. They
were aggressive, ambitious young men blessed by genteel origins, classical
educations, and reactionary mentors. During the late 1780s they obtained
their legal and political elitism by clerking for three of the most conservative ideologues in New York: Ten Broeck for his cousin Abraham Van
Vechten of Albany, Moss Kent, Jr., with his brother James, and Strong with
Alexander Hamilton in New York City. From their teachers, the three
lawyers developed a distaste for the democratic impetus of the recent Revolution. In early 1787, on the eve of the constitutional convention, Strong

helped covertly disseminate, as an anonymous trial balloon, Hamilton's counterrevolutionary proposal to abandon republican government in favor of a British-style monarchy and aristocracy.[16]

Cooper had welcomed the lawyers as essential to Otsego's progress toward prosperity and respectability. In his opening address to the Otsego grand jury in 1791, he praised "well reade lawyers" while urging the suppression of their cheap competitors—uneducated and unlicensed "pettifoggers" (such as John Bull of Cherry Valley, who worked sporadically as shoemaker, schoolteacher, and pettifogger, occasionally attracting grand jury indictments for perjury). The Otsego courts promptly adopted rules restricting the local practice of law to men who had clerked for at least three years with a licensed lawyer and who could pass an oral examination before the bench.[17]

Cooper lavished his private and public patronage upon Strong, Ten Broeck, and especially Kent. They conducted his lawsuits and reaped favorable opportunities to invest in the judge's land speculations. Cooper also secured lucrative political appointments for Kent, as county surrogate (registrar of probate), and for Strong, as Cooperstown's federal postmaster. In the spring of 1794 Cooper spent £50 to build for Kent an office in Cooperstown with a view of Otsego Lake. The judge even welcomed Kent into the Manor House as a rent-free lodger and as his agent, responsible for managing monies and records during the judge's frequent absences. "I do live most agreeably at Judge Cooper's. He shews me a great deal of esteem & respect & Mrs. Cooper tells me that I am becoming her favourite," Kent boasted.[18]

In late 1794 and early 1795, Cooper and Kent seemed perfectly satisfied with each other, as patron and protégé, as almost father and son. During the congressional campaign of 1794, Kent "felt warmly engaged in favor of my friend the judge," riding extensively in Otsego and Herkimer counties to rally voters. In early 1795 Kent marveled, "I never lived more agreeably in my Life. Mrs. C[ooper] I think is a very fine woman & both she & the judge treat me with almost *parental* attention." Self-absorbed, Kent reported the Coopers' attentions primarily as fitting tributes to his worth, rather than as proofs of their special generosity. Referring to the Coopers' youngest sons (William, Jr., Samuel, and James), Kent reported: "They have three little Boys from 5 to 9 who are as sweet & lovely little fellows as ever born of a woman & they are extremely fond of me." After years of financial, professional, and emotional struggle, Kent enjoyed bright prospects, thanks to the paternal patronage of Judge Cooper and the affection of his family. In February, Kent calculated, "Should the friendship & good understanding between me & the judge prove permanent, & I can see no reason why it should not, I believe, to speak within bounds, that the business of his office will be worth £100 a year, besides saving my board." However, that friendship began to fray just two months later when Kent cast his lot with Ten Broeck and Strong to challenge Cooper's political and judicial power.[19]

During the mid-1790s the Otsego courts assumed increasing importance as the volume and complexity of their caseload grew apace with the county's exploding population of contentious, litigious Yankees. During the county's first three years (1791–93) Otsego's two criminal courts, the Court of General Sessions of the Peace and the Court of Oyer and Terminer, convicted only five men. During the subsequent three years (1794–96) these courts sentenced twenty men. The caseload of the county's civil court, the Court of Common Pleas, mushroomed from just 15 resolved lawsuits during its first three years to 173 during the next three.[20]

In 1795 the local lawyers concluded that the Otsego judges lacked the learning and dignity to cope with the increasing and demanding caseload in their courts. Untrained in the law, presiding Judge William Cooper and his associate judges, Jedediah Peck and Dr. Joseph White, had risen from obscure origins by applying their sharp wits to frontier opportunities. As the county's greatest landlord Cooper led the way and then secured judicial appointments for Peck and White, in order to attach their influence to his political interest.[21]

Judges Peck, White, and Cooper frequently dispensed with formal precedents and statutes to rely on their intuitive (and highly patriarchal) sense of justice. In 1791 the first criminal trial held in Otsego County revealed the loose standards of justice in William Cooper's frontier court. A jury convicted Benjamin Batchelor and two friends of kidnapping his estranged wife Esther. In his first sentence as a judge, Cooper merely fined Benjamin Batchelor £2.10.0—a surprisingly small sum for his crime. The accomplices avoided punishment by escaping, "the Justices winking at it," according to a spectator at the trial.[22]

The judges expressed themselves in a rough mix of the colloquial and the legal. David Jewitt had spread the vicious rumor that Sarah Brigham had committed an adultery that had infected her husband, Josiah N. Brigham, with syphilis, which apparently accounted for the sores disfiguring his face. Outraged by the slander, Judge Cooper charged the jury:

Their cannot be a more cruel thing in a new Country than that of Distroying the Peace of a family by Circulating reports that are worse than deth founded on weeknesses to which human nature is at all times liable. Here, as I said before, where our farmers are Exposed to heats and Colds, to Labour Straines, and [to] but indiferent norreshment to brace up the Sistom—you must Expect gentelmen that some of those cases will occur where men will be afflicted with inocent [disorders] that are more afflicting than the Venereal Disorder, tho no scandal is attachd to it because the disorder hath no Poisoning nor can it be spread. The one is a weekness in our Sistom—the other an illegal act of our own. Then Gentelmen if a poor man is Liable to this Misfortune how cruel it is

to turn it into the Ruin of their Reputation for Ever. Therefore the Court think
you must find the defendant guilty and in what sum you are the judges.

Agreeing with Cooper, the jury convicted Jewitt, and awarded $118.33 in
damages to Josiah N. Brigham. In his charge Cooper was preoccupied with
protecting the husband's, rather than the wife's, reputation. As in his light
sentence for Benjamin Batchelor, Cooper was at pains to bolster the patriarchal authority of his settlers. The idiosyncratic logic and fractured
rhetoric of his paternalism baffled and annoyed the local lawyers who
sought to gain wealth and power by capitalizing on their learning.[23]

In addition to origins and education, age and property also set the Otsego lawyers and judges apart. In 1795 the three Cooperstown lawyers were
aged twenty-eight to twenty-nine years, in contrast to the judges who were
thirty-one (White), forty (Cooper), and forty-seven (Peck). Whereas the
lawyers were young, restless, and mobile men on the make, the judges were
more mature men already in possession of substantial farms or, in Cooper's
case, of vast, speculative landholdings. Two years later, after the lawyers
openly broke with Cooper, he dismissed them as "young men [who] can put
all they are worth in their saddle baggs and leave the county in a few hours."
The judges were more traditional patriarchs who expected that real estate
and greater age should command respect and deference from the younger
and less substantial lawyers.[24]

The judges' rough manners, crude speech, and shallow training cheapened the prestige of gentility and learning—the foundations for the
lawyers' claims to social supremacy. In a series of essays published in the *Otsego Herald,* Abraham C. Ten Broeck denounced the Otsego bench for "arbitrary practice," "intriguing insinuations," and "browbeating threats and
declarations." He was shocked that the judges readily mixed with the locals
in the Cooperstown taverns, openly discussing and debating ongoing cases,
instead of cultivating a dignified reserve and a conscientious silence on
pending business. He urged the state legislature to "secure better abilities
on the bench" by replacing the incumbents with law-learned men who
would appreciate and second the expertise of the Cooperstown lawyers.[25]

Especially aggressive and grasping, Joseph Strong provoked an open rift
between the lawyers and the judges in early 1795. He antagonized the
judges by presenting inflated accounts for his fees and by demanding that
the courts increase the fines levied on convicted criminals. Alluding to
Strong's delight in playing cards, Judge Peck charged that the lawyer was furious "because the fines were not high enough to please his holiness, so as
to replenish his gaming Table." At a meeting of county supervisors, Judge
Cooper publicly upbraided Strong, "for being a villain, making false erroneous accounts." Cooper insisted that Strong "should have had the severity
of the law before now" except that the bench felt sympathy for his "virtuous

wife and innocent children." Insulted by these rebukes, Strong sought revenge by conspiring against Cooper's interest.[26]

In the electioneering of April 1795, the three lawyers declared their independence from Judge Cooper, their defiance of his fellow judges, and their determination to control Otsego's politics and jurisprudence. To discredit Cooper, the lawyers turned against his friend and fellow judge Dr. Joseph White, who was running for Otsego's seat in the state assembly. They promoted the rival candidacy of Jacob Morris. Ever resentful of Cooper's preeminence, Morris was all too happy to cooperate with the lawyers against the judges. To Cooper's chagrin, Morris prevailed at the polling despite the judge's reiterated, but belated, support for White.[27]

In both the April election and Ten Broeck's essays, the lawyers aggressively exploited the *Otsego Herald,* newly established in Cooperstown by Elihu Phinney. Their characteristic weapon was sarcastic ridicule. In November, Ten Broeck derided a public address given by Dr. White as a "harrangue" and a "mere school-boyish declamation and a jumble of words without meaning." Disdaining doctors as a lesser class defined by manual labor, Ten Broeck urged White to stick to "cutting and healing," leaving "writing and speaking" to the lawyers. Although Phinney repeatedly protested his devout preference for social harmony, he readily published vicious polemics whenever the author paid for the printing. After all, Phinney had bills to pay and his fortune still to make. The *Otsego Herald* rapidly and widely circulated character assaults that in the past had depended on the slow, partial, and irregular operation of oral gossip. Post riders carried into every corner of the county news that had once been confined to particular neighborhoods. In 1795 Phinney printed 800 copies of his newspaper every week and probably reached at least ten readers or listeners per copy, as subscribers shared with, and read to, family members and neighbors. In addition to increasing the extent and velocity of news, print reduced variation as, unlike gossip, every copy was virtually identical and unchanged in its handling between producer and consumers. Consequently, the newspaper had a semiofficial status as the purveyor of truth. The lawyers recognized that it provided a vehicle for ambitious men to make their case to a broad and largely anonymous public, circumventing the traditional local leading men, such as William Cooper, who had previously mediated the flow of information into, through, and beyond Otsego. As the newspaper broadcast acrimony, fomented divisions, and dominated county communication, Cooper must have wondered at his decision to bring Phinney's press and the three lawyers to Cooperstown.[28]

In early 1796 Cooper believed that he had brokered a political truce between Morris and White, thereby neutralizing the dissident lawyers. In response to Otsego's dramatic population growth, the state legislature increased the county's representation from a single seat in the assembly to

five assemblymen and two state senators. Cooper and the Albany gentry reasoned that White and Morris could split the two Otsego state senate seats,
restoring the political harmony that the judge so cherished.[29]

But Cooper underestimated the capacity of Morris and the Cooperstown
lawyers to undermine any agreement. Heady with their recent electoral triumph over White, they smelled blood and longed to complete the downfall
of Cooper's interest. Joseph Strong seized control of the county nominating
meeting held in Cooperstown on March 17, 1796, taking advantage of
sparse attendance (owing to a severe snowstorm) and of Cooper's absence
(in Philadelphia attending Congress). The lawyers rammed through Ten
Broeck's nomination for an assembly seat and Kent's for the state senate. By
nominating Kent as Morris's running mate for the state senate, the lawyers
sacrificed White, upsetting Judge Cooper's arrangement.[30]

Despite his obligations to Cooper's hospitality and patronage, Kent eagerly accepted the nomination, heeding his hungry ambition and his sol-
idarity with fellow lawyers. In his April letters to Cooper in Philadelphia,
Kent reported family and business news in detail but carefully said nothing
about politics. Kent's betrayal was especially embarrassing because he was
living in Cooper's house and managing his properties. If Cooper could not
command Kent, his surrogate son, who could he control?[31]

White and his political friends appealed to Cooper for decisive intervention. Benjamin Gilbert wrote,

> I call on you ([as] father and chief of this County) to take a very active part
> in this business. . . . One leading, influencial man in each County, who is a
> firm friend to good government, and whose preponderating influence will dis-
> troy the equilibrium of parties, and give a sanction to all legall measures, I hope
> will always be found. That you have been that man in this County I admit—
> that you may so continue I wish, altho' the leaders of Mr. Morris's party last
> year, did then and now, declare they had done you over, that your influence in
> this County was no longer of any amount, . . . and I do believe the alteration
> in the Senate ticket was made for that purpose.

Gilbert and White made clear that Cooper's standing as Otsego's political
father was at stake.[32]

Responding to the challenge, Cooper urged Kent to abandon the race
and then assured his political friends in Albany, Otsego, and the rest of the
Western District that Kent would withdraw. Prompted by Cooper's letters,
the Albany gentry—Stephen Van Rensselaer, Leonard Gansevoort, and
Philip Schuyler—dispatched their own electioneering letters westward on
April 9, reaffirming their support for White. Judge Cooper also wrote an appeal to the Otsego electors, which he sent to Phinney for publication in the
Otsego Herald. However, as Cooperstown's postmaster, Strong intercepted
and secreted Cooper's letter to Phinney for a couple of weeks, delaying its
publication until April 21. Despite Cooper's exertions, Kent defiantly re-

mained in the race and impulsively published a blistering attack on the judge and the Albany gentry as aristocrats conniving to manipulate the election and dominate the settlers.[33]

THE PLOUGH-JOGGER

Cooper's political troubles in Otsego were not confined to his resentful lodger and Cooperstown's conniving postmaster, as a surprising fourth candidate suddenly emerged in early April: Judge Jedediah Peck. By exploiting the division wrought by the lawyers, Peck hoped to steal into the state senate. In their attempt to bring down Judges White and Cooper, the lawyers reaped the countercampaign and growing popularity of the judge they hated most: Jedediah Peck.

Born in Lyme, Connecticut, in 1748, Peck was one of thirteen children raised by an obscure farmer. Lacking the means for any formal education beyond a country grammar school, Peck taught himself by reading, rereading, and memorizing the Bible. Prayer and the Bible had helped him cope with a morbid depression that gripped his mind in 1771 after the early deaths, in rapid succession, of his parents, three brothers, and a sister. For the rest of his life Peck carefully preserved in a secret drawer in his desk the journal that he wrote in late 1771, when he returned from a sea voyage to learn about the spate of family deaths. In it, he longed for the "Days and times past when my father and Mother and all my bretherin and Sisters were about me in helth and prosperity but alas! trubel and Sorow hath Sorounded me and I am a poor Disconsolate Cretur. There is no place that Seemes to be home to me." Seeking "a hope of Ever Lasting Salvation," Peck developed an evangelical faith that later set him apart from the rest of the legal elite in Otsego County, lawyers as well as judges. But that faith bound him to the great majority of the rural settlers, who disliked the religious skepticism found among the leading villagers.[34]

Peck obtained his political education in popular republicanism by serving as an enlisted man in the Continental Army during the Revolutionary War. As a common soldier he experienced "the horrors of war and . . . long and tedious marches, summer heat, and winter's frost, perils, hunger, thirst, and nakedness." Shared with fellow soldiers, those sufferings deepened Peck's lifelong commitment to the new American Republic and heightened his zeal to detect and defeat would-be aristocrats.[35]

After the war Peck migrated westward to settle in Burlington, a dozen miles west of Cooperstown. There he prospered, won Judge Cooper's patronage, and secured appointment to the county judiciary in 1791. A frontier jack-of-all-trades, Peck was an evangelical preacher as well as a farmer, surveyor, carpenter, millwright, politician, and judge. Untrained in theology and unaffiliated with any denomination, Peck preached as an independent itinerant paid by contributions. A friend remembered:

> *Judge Peck, although a clear-headed, sensible man, was an uneducated emigrant from Connecticut. His appearance was diminutive and almost disgusting. In religion he was fanatical, but in his political views, he was sincere, persevering and bold; and although meek and humble in his demeanor, he was by no means destitute of personal ambition. . . . He would survey your farm in the day time, exhort and pray in your family at night, and talk on politics the rest part of the time. Perhaps on Sunday, or some evening in the week, he would preach a sermon in your school house.*

His nimble mind and keen political instincts compensated for his unappealing appearance: short, heavy, and slightly hunched. Peck personified the stereotypical Yankee: resourceful, versatile, shrewd, pious, and opportunistic.[36]

Peck combined political populism with his evangelical faith, regularly extolling the democratic energy, divine origin, and global mission of the American Revolution. He preached, "Monarchical Government is the literal kingdom of Satan, and the antichrist or the image of the beast. Representative government is the literal and peaceable kingdom of the Messiah. . . . So Representative Government shall chase, break and destroy Monarchical Government and spread itself over the earth and become peaceable." Eclectic in his inspirations, Peck celebrated the democratic writings of Thomas Paine, despite Paine's notoriety as a religious skeptic. Although ostensibly a Federalist, Peck applauded the radical French Revolution that convulsed Europe beginning in 1789. In a newspaper essay published in 1793, Peck exhorted his countrymen to contribute money and wheat to assist France, then embattled by counterrevolution and by neighboring monarchs. Indeed, he preached world revolution: "May the fire of liberty, that is now burning in France spread over Europe, Asia, and Africa, and destroy tyranny and despotism."[37]

Judge Peck infuriated the lawyers by boldly asserting the superiority of his common sense to their legal learning. He railed, "Now by the influence of these lawyers, the British common law is established in this State, by which means they have the advantage of all the intrigue, wit, and cunning of their ancestors from the days of King Alfred to this day, to interweave and entangle the laws and to hide the truth behind the curtain, where they work their Hocus Pocuses." A later lawyer (Levi Beardsley) recounted with amusement a case of criminal conversation (adultery) in which the defense conceded the act but presented testimony that "proved the wife . . . of infamous reputation." Contravening law, Peck ruled that, far from mitigating the crime, the woman's notoriety was actually "a gross aggravation, which ought to enhance the damages against the defendant for having anything to do with the dirty slut." In this episode Peck championed the traditional New England folk concern with using law to maintain community morality. Peck insisted that an adulterer who would associate with a notorious woman *especially* needed punishment, in order to protect a moral community of patriarchal households. In contrast, the lawyers were utilitarian men who wanted to peg the appropriate monetary value of the wife's virtue because they considered law to be a commercial science meant to regulate property, contracts, and transactions. Peck's populism was a blend of traditional morality and patriarchy with revolutionary egalitarianism. Conversely, the lawyers were political reactionaries but legal and moral modernists.[38]

In the election of 1796 the other candidates and county notables did not take Peck seriously, for he lacked the genteel tone and pretensions that they deemed essential in a legislator. White derisively referred to "Granny Peck," mocking his age and small stature and assigning him the female gender: the consummate insult in the masculine world of electoral politics. But Peck quickly emerged as the most tireless, cunning, resourceful, and innovative politician in the county, repeatedly outwitting and outmaneuvering his overconfident rivals.[39]

Wanting gentility and wealth, Peck could not practice the traditional politics of making interest. Instead, he defied convention by promoting his own candidacy while itinerating through the county as a preacher. A friend recalled, "He always had his saddle bags with him, filled with political papers and scraps, that he distributed whenever he went from home, and then at night and frequently on Sundays, would hold meeting and preach." Making aggressive use of the local newspaper, Peck published numerous essays. Unlike his lawyer rivals, who preferred classical pseudonyms, Peck published under either his own name or his well-known nickname of "the Plough-Jogger." It conveyed his identification with the common farmers in contrast to his rivals who were at pains to display their superior gentility and learning. Instead of writing in their obscure, wordy, and pretentious style, Peck mastered a colloquial voice, rich in vivid metaphor, rural humor, and Yankee sagacity.[40]

Morris and the lawyers preferred to operate behind the scenes, writing private electioneering letters, manipulating nomination meetings, penning anonymous essays, and secretly distributing prepared ballots. Determined to discredit their traditional style of politics, Peck used the newspaper to expose his foes to publicity. He challenged Jacob Morris to defend his policies, not in a private letter, but "through the channel of the public Newspapers," addressing "the public mind." When Joseph Strong privately urged Peck to withdraw from the race, Peck published an outraged reply that obliged Strong to come forward in print. Then Peck boasted that he had meant "to draw this viper out of his hole; and now I think he is in plain view of the electors of this county." Peck was constructing public opinion—a mass of anonymous readers paying sustained and critical attention to political men and measures.[41]

Whereas interests avoided issues and, instead, flaunted their power and largesse, Peck sought influence through persuasion. Although he compounded Otsego's electoral divisions, Peck posed as the defender of county harmony and unity, as well as the champion of popular sovereignty, moral families, and mixed metaphors:

> *Let us all shout with one voice the sovereignty of the people; long live the Law which is king, Liberty and Equality; . . . and dash this party spirit with a flying stroke and stamp and grind it to powder as fine as the summer's thrashing-floor, so that the wind of the gentle south gales of charity may blow it into the Susquehanna River, and Cherry-Valley Creek, . . . to sink in oblivion. . . . Then we will disband, and each of us walk peaceably home, and set our houses in order.*

Making a virtue of his commonality, Peck cast himself as the farmers' candidate, as the populist champion of the hinterland towns rebelling against the county domination exercised by the proud and propertied villagers of Cherry Valley and Cooperstown—especially the lawyers: "These lawyers are an intriguing set, it is they that have woolled up the practice of the law, in such a heap of formality, on purpose so that we cannot see through their entanglement, to oblige us to employ them, to untangle them, and if we go to them for advice they will not say a word without five dollars." Making an issue of the lawyers' notoriety for impiety, cardplaying, and drinking, Peck also posed as the candidate devoted to "good family government, which is the basis of civil [government]." More cunning than consistent, he carefully exempted Moss Kent, Jr., dubbing him the county's one "honest lawyer." Peck recognized that the public excluded the handsome and dashing Kent from their generalized dislike of tricky lawyers.[42]

Although still calling himself a Federalist, Peck vigorously championed the democracy that his party strove to contain. He challenged the elitist notion of the legislator as a superior gentleman who ought to act free from public opinion. He exhorted the common people to assert their sovereign power over their legislators: "In Representative governments, the people are master, all their officers from the highest to the lowest are servants to the people." Peck insisted that only tireless and suspicious vigilance by common people could preserve the Republic: "Fellow-citizens, you are the only guardians and pilots of your ship LIBERTY, and if you do not watch her course, by small degrees she will depart from the small hemisphere of republicanism, and find herself involved in the frozen ocean of monarchy, bound down with the icy bars of despotism."[43]

In particular, Peck urged the people to scrutinize the conduct of assemblyman, and would-be state senator, Jacob Morris. The county's most conspicuous and choleric elitist, Morris made an easy target for Peck's populist assault. In newspaper essays, he assailed Morris for opposing the emancipation of New York's slaves and for attempting to strengthen the governor's control over the Council of Appointment. According to Peck, both stands demonstrated that Morris was an aristocrat hostile to the liberties and well-being of common people. Peck proposed a radically democratic and decentralized alternative: replacing the governor on the council with an additional state senator and obliging the council to act upon nominations forwarded from town meetings.[44]

Morris, Strong, and Ten Broeck thought that they could intimidate and discredit Peck with erudite and elitist displays of their contempt and ridicule. And they defended the traditional, elitist notion of the proper legislator as a polished and learned gentleman. Strong insisted, "He ought to be a man well acquainted with the common law, and laws of his Country, a perfect scholar." Morris dismissed Peck as "this wou'd be Senator, wou'd be Colonel of Militia, and wou'd be every thing else, if he were able to cajole the people to believe him as clever a fellow as he vainly supposes himself to be." Ten Broeck likened Peck to a frog, an "insignificant animal that just so vainly imagined its little self swelled, or about to be, to the size of an ox." Morris and the lawyers wrote as if they could humiliate Peck into silence, treating him as they would a dirty tradesman seeking entree into a genteel ball.[45]

In fact, the increasingly intemperate attacks by Morris, Ten Broeck, and Strong proved Peck's case and built his popularity. The settlers appreciated Peck as the best of their sort: a commoner of uncommon self-assurance and intelligence who persisted in speaking and thinking within the colloquial idiom. They insisted that "there was not a more clever, honest man in the county." In the *Otsego Herald* David Goff, a Peck supporter, forcefully rebuked his elitist foes:

> Now a word to the Great, the Wise, the Learned, and boasted friends to Cooperstown and the County, accept this sweet and salutary admonition . . . not to mispend any more of your valuable time in censuring, ridiculing, criticizing, and carping at almost every thing but your own egregious, supercilious, opinionative performances, fixing upon at the epithets of ignorant, insignificant, and ungrammatical. It is true, we do not pretend to be critics, or polished grammarians nurtured with you at the seminary of erudition—but what of that, must we not say a word in [our] own just defence, when imposed upon by those petty-upstart Gentry for fear of their sneers or observations. . . . We are sensible by your lampooning that you wish to awe us from publishing.

Championing Peck's plain and accessible discourse, Goff reminded the lawyers that at least nine-tenths of the county inhabitants were "steady, industrious Farmers who know but little about *twistification, ambiguity*, etc., in comparison to you, who are well versed in the most intricate *figures, tropes* etc." He advised the lawyers "not to be so haughty, neither wise in your own conceits. Consider that your whole dependence is upon those Farmers, whom you look upon with so much disdain."[46]

Peck won popular applause as a common man who could provoke and outwit the lawyers in a medium that they had previously dominated—the newspaper essay. With every exchange, he grew more self-assured and sharp-witted. When Morris publicly denounced Peck as an "ambitious, mean, and grovelling demagogue," Peck serenely replied: "Where did you learn these compliments you have returned to me for my polite letter, in the college or assembly?" Nothing could have more infuriated the aristocratic Morris than to appear less composed in public than a Yankee so common as Jedediah Peck.[47]

Peck was especially fortunate in making a foil of Abraham C. Ten Broeck, the most pompous and dull-witted of the three lawyers. Notorious for his wordy and convoluted style (replete with parenthetical asides), Ten Broeck repeatedly satirized himself and his profession in attempting to parry Peck's vivid and folksy thrusts. Offended by Peck's insinuation that Kent was the only honest lawyer in Cooperstown, Ten Broeck huffed,

> Should it be answered that you have sufficiently insinuated that (which you have very plainly) and that as a Judge you are to be believed; give me leave to tell you that I have known some Judges (I profess too much politeness to say I here intend you as one) devoid of all honor and principle (I mean in their private capacity); next I say that where they are otherwise than I take you to be— they can justly do nothing nor support any charge without evidence, and you, assassin of private reputation as you are, and all the world, are challenged to produce any thing against the morals of Mr. Ten Broeck.

Better still, Ten Broeck foolishly jumped on Peck's insistence that republican government best suited a large country like America. Displaying his superior learning, Ten Broeck cited a French political writer utterly alien to Otsego's farmers: "Montesquieu and the others, of his class, tell us that of all kinds of government, the despotic or absolute is best calculated to preserve itself in a large extensive territory."[48]

Quick to spring the trap that the lawyer had made for himself, Peck charged that Ten Broeck evidently favored a "despotic government" for America. Peck gleefully declared that Ten Broeck was "a Monarchite, under the garb of Federalism; and one of those obsolete book readers." Peck mocked, "It is dangerous keeping too close to your old books; in so doing, you become a mere machine and are wrought upon by your authors, as a clock is by the gravitation of its weights." Peck claimed a superior source of wisdom: "but as I was not favored with many books, I gained what I call my principles, chiefly from the study of nature." Triumphant in these exchanges, Peck wrested from Morris and the lawyers primacy in the *Otsego Herald,* previously their vehicle to belittle and discredit the unlettered.[49]

The contentious election culminated with the polling during the last week of April. Abraham C. Ten Broeck barely weathered Peck's newspaper attacks, capturing the county's final assembly seat by finishing fifth in a pool of nine candidates. In the balloting for state senators in Otsego County, Moss Kent, Jr., was the big winner, garnering 925 votes, despite Judge Cooper's opposition. Jacob Morris finished a distant second at 546. Despite his late start and unorthodox style, Jedediah Peck finished a surprisingly strong third at 473, outpolling his judicial colleague, Joseph White, who ran a weak fourth at 352. Nonetheless, White joined Morris in the state senate because they overwhelmed Peck and Kent in the polling in the other counties within the Western District. By persuading outsiders that Kent would garner few votes in Otsego, Cooper ensured that the lawyer lost in every other county.[50]

In June, William Cooper returned from Congress to find his home county still roiled by the recent election. The especially rancorous election left most of the participants—even the victors—in a sour, sullen mood. Morris was furious with Peck for daring to criticize his conduct as a legislator. White remained enraged at Strong, assuring Cooper: "It is impossible to calculate or even conceive of the wickedness of that rascal. . . . Except you come forward and bear the most pointed testimony against that vile man, all is gone. He is determined to destroy all order in the county." Kent bitterly resented Cooper for intervening to ruin his campaign: "I failed my election by reason of the base Imposition of William Cooper & one Sheriff Gilbert on the People of Albany. William Cooper has always professed a warm friendship for me, but his Heart is as base as his Tongue is trifling." Angry over a newspaper attack, Sheriff Benjamin Gilbert publicly challenged Ten Broeck to a duel, but the lawyer wisely demurred.[51]

Nor could the judge find any satisfaction in an election that so divided his county and so weakened his prestige. By offering an array of new electoral opportunities, the April 1796 election was supposed to bring peace, harmony, and unity to Otsego. Instead, a subordinate judge and Cooperstown's three lawyers (including his agent and lodger) had all defied his interest. Kent especially embarrassed his patron by polling so well in Otsego despite Cooper's intervention and prediction. Neither the conspicuous insubordination nor the embarrassing returns boded well for Cooper's impending campaign for reelection to Congress.[52]

Only Jedediah Peck took apparent delight in the outcome. Although he had lost his race, Peck understood the April 1796 election as a first, and surprisingly successful, step in his long-term crusade to promulgate democratic ideas and build a base for future campaigns. Running a permanent campaign, he kept up the public fight in the newspapers through the spring and summer of 1796, to the growing fury of his antagonists—Abraham C. Ten Broeck, Joseph Strong, and, especially, Jacob Morris. Delighting in the open debate that so unhinged his rivals, Peck floated a subscription in late May to finance the publication of a book entitled *The Political Wars of Otsego: Or, Downfall of Jacobinism and Despotism.* Published in the fall, it was a compilation of Peck's newspaper essays combined with his opponents' intemperate but ineffectual responses.[53]

The list of 205 subscribers for *The Political Wars of Otsego* reveals Peck's political base: the small and middling farmers living in Otsego County's northwestern quarter. Nearly half of the subscribers (93 of 205) resided in Burlington, Peck's hometown, and most of the rest lived in the adjoining towns of Richfield (31) and Otsego (54). In the April election, Peck had garnered almost all of his votes from those same three towns. Only 2 subscribers came from Cooperstown and very few were Freemasons—the cosmopolites of Otsego County (only 14 of 205 = 7 percent). According to tax assessment lists for Otsego County, the subscribers were men of modest means, averaging $809 in net worth—just about the $778 mean for the town of Burlington. Most were significantly poorer than the book's main targets: Abraham Ten Broeck ($984); Joseph Strong ($2,211); Joseph White ($4,687); and, especially, Jacob Morris ($16,444). In sum, Peck built his democratic challenge among the poor and middling farmers of the hinterland by focusing their resentments upon the county's leading gentlemen, especially those who dwelled in Cooperstown.[54]

Publication of *The Political Wars of Otsego* further enraged Jacob Morris. On October 5 during a court session in Cooperstown, Morris confronted Peck, seizing and twisting his nose. Peck's foes rushed a triumphant notice into the next day's newspaper: "The great Political Plough of this County is rendered unfit for service, having by the phrenzy of its owner encountered a sound stump by which it had its nose twisted."[55]

Peck quickly recovered, first in the courtroom and, a week later, in the newspaper. On the day of the assault, the county grand jury rallied to Peck, indicting Morris for assault. He pled guilty but, in an appeal to the bench to mitigate his fine, Morris read aloud and submitted one of Peck's essays, deeming it provocatively "false & scandalous." Rejecting Morris's defense, Judge Cooper and his associates levied a heavy fine of £7.10.0 meant to reiterate the proper dignity and immunity of their bench from public attack. In another triumph for Peck, the grand jury also acted upon his accusation to indict Joseph Strong for forgery. Postponing trial to a future session, the court demanded bond from Strong (a year later the attorney general dropped the prosecution without explanation). In a newspaper essay, Peck celebrated by refuting with sharp humor the ill-considered gibe hastily published by his foes: "It is true [that] the nose of the Plough at first twisted a little, but by a sudden jerk of the Plough-jogger and the elastic nature of the nose, it vibrated with double force, and threw the stumps slap against the Grand Jury, from whence they were reverberated with violence against the judges' bench." No matter what his foes did or wrote, Peck had the last word, winning the battle for public opinion.[56]

PRETENDED FATHER

Meanwhile, during June and July, Kent and Cooper tried to pretend that their relationship remained unaffected by the bitter election that April. On July 8 Kent insisted, "I still continue in [Cooper's] family & live on habits of apparent Friendship with him. Not a syllable has passed between me & him on the election since his return. . . . I am treated attentively by all his family." But both men were too emotionally volatile to suppress their simmering resentments indefinitely. Something happened during the following four days to break down their mutual denial. On July 12 Kent wrote a pointed note to the judge:

> *I have concluded to remove my quarters. I do it from a perfect conviction that it is no longer your desire that I should attend to the business of your office & that it is your wish that I should remove. . . . I know that I have conducted myself towards you with perfect propriety & have shewed you every deference not in-compatible with a Spirit of Independence & with that becoming Respect which every Man ought to entertain for himself.*

Kent vigorously, if implausibly, denied his dependence upon, or obligations to, Cooper's patronage: "The expectation that I might be servicable in your business without any Injury to myself, and not any pecuniary Emolument that I might receive, was the sole motive that induced me at first to accept your Invitation." Despite his obsessive, private preocupation with accumulating money, Kent posed as the ideal gentleman contemptuous of mere commerce and committed to disinterested friendship. The abrupt note hints at a recent and explosive argument, in which the judge vented his sense of betrayal by an ungrateful surrogate son.[57]

If Kent ever left the Manor House, he quickly returned. Cooper needed him to manage his land and legal business when the judge left home to attend Congress in the fall, and Kent needed the income and place to board while he furnished his newly bought house in Cooperstown village on a lot adjoining the Manor House grounds.[58]

Nonetheless, there was a strain within the Manor House as the fall congressional campaign loomed and James Cochran, an attorney from Montgomery County, announced his challenge to the judge's reelection. Although a fellow Federalist, Cochran aspired to Cooper's office and was contemptuous of his abilities. Strong, Ten Broeck, and Kent rallied to the campaign of their fellow lawyer and cherished friend. In September, Kent reported, "I am decidedly in favor of Cochran & do not hesitate to declare it, notwithstanding I still live at the judge's Table & there is an apparent good understanding between us." That superficial amity quickly collapsed after Cooper tried to "mortify" Kent by boastfully displaying around town a strictly confidential letter from the lieutenant governor, Stephen Van Rensselaer, praising the judge's candidacy. When Van Rensselaer learned of, and bristled at, the broken confidence, Cooper promptly but disingenuously blamed the leak on his agent Kent, who raged, "in order to apologize to the Lieutenant Governor for his own folly & imprudence, he has had the wickedness to charge me with it."[59]

After Cooper departed for Philadelphia in October, Kent remained in the Manor House, dutifully managing the office and regularly corresponding with the judge about business and family matters. At the same time Kent vigorously campaigned for Cochran and against Cooper, using the Manor House as his base. In his newspaper essays Kent took particular pains to deny Cooper's claims to be Otsego's father. By attacking Cooper as a "pretended Father," Kent also declared a very personal defiance of the judge's attempts to claim him as a son. Embittered by his spring defeat, rankled by the judge's presumptuous paternity, and frustrated by his own persistent economic dependence, Kent anticipated relief and pleasure in proportion to the disappointment and unease he could inflict through politics on William Cooper. In early December Kent confided to his brother: "Should Cooper fail, it will be a most mortifying disappointment to him."[60]

Despite the assistance from the Cooperstown lawyers, Cochran faced an uphill battle in the congressional election of 1796. Over the preceding decade, the judge had assembled the components of a powerful interest: the possession of great property and the friendship of great men, especially Philip Schuyler and Stephen Van Rensselaer. Although Cochran was a well-born, well-connected, well-educated, and wealthy lawyer, he posed as the modest and accessible friend of the people. By championing the republican purity of elections, Cochran set out to transform Cooper's advantage at making interest into a menace (and to turn his own relative weakness at traditional electioneering into a virtue). Cochran's friends meant to reveal and discredit their opponents' instruments of interest by holding them to the republican standards of public rhetoric. "True liberality is an amiable virtue," a Cochranite piously insisted, "but the shewing it, chiefly on the eve of elections, or for election purposes, as often happens, should excite our alarms and horror—as intended indirectly to purchase our votes." Cochran's friends urged voters to feel insulted, rather than impressed, by the pro-Cooper electioneering letters sent westward by the Albany gentry. Sarcastically thanking them for attempting "to enlighten and controul the ignorant and uncivilized electors of the western counties," a Cochranite hoped that the Albany grandees would continue to "use every art of domineering intrigue to ensure [Cooper's] election."[61]

To work their alchemy the Cochranites exploited the four newspapers recently established in the Western District. The genre of the newspaper essay favored the writing talents of Cochran's lawyer friends, and it bypassed the more traditional leading men who favored Judge Cooper. His friends were fellow large landholders, mill owners, storekeepers, and justices. Wealthy but lacking college educations, they were adept at treating voters but beyond their depth when writing for publication. The simultaneous proliferation of newspapers and lawyers came together in electioneering essays to expand their mutual influence in society. In Cochran's 1796 campaign we see lawyers and printers taking political command, as they did throughout the early Republic.[62]

With more zeal than consistency, Cochran's friends worked both sides of the electoral tension between the conflicting ideals of genteel superiority and republican equality. They lauded Cochran as both a learned young gentleman with polished manners and an allegedly modest and accessible friend of the people. Conversely, they depicted Cooper as both an unworthy pretender to gentility and an overbearing tyrant. They dwelled upon his lack of the learning, self-restraint, public decorum, and rigid honor expected of a gentleman, as well as upon his absurd pretensions to aristocratic power. The Cochranites took particular pains to assail his rambling and colloquial speeches as unworthy of a congressman. James Kent remarked, "Judge Cooper will talk very much at random to find his purpose or to apologize for himself & perhaps after all, nothing he may have said is worthy any attention." Cooper's clumsy and excessive attempts to display gentility only invited further ridicule. A Cochranite mocked his use of a carriage on frontier roads: "His *Electioneering* Chariot thunders over the rocks, or plunges through the mire of the district to secure recruits for the coming campaign." According to the Cochranites, Cooper was a monstrosity both absurd and menacing—at once too vulgar and too tyrannical.[63]

With malicious glee the Cochranites distorted the reception accorded Cooper in Cooperstown upon his return from Congress in June. The pro-Cooper *Otsego Herald* had reported, "When his carriage had passed the bridge, he was welcomed by a double row of citizens, who testified their joy on his arrival by three cheers. Never was a character received with a more cordial welcome; all ranks of people united in manifesting their approbation of his conduct, thro' a long, an arduous, and an important session." That evening Cooper "very obligingly attended his fellow citizens, convened at Huntington's Inn, and in a concise and comprehensive manner recited the most important events of the session" (a description akin to Judge Temple's mingling with the men gathered at the Bold Dragoon Tavern in *The Pi-*

oneers). Meant to impress voters with the deference Cooper had earned at home in Otsego, this report became, in Cochranite treatment, evidence of a dehumanizing tyranny. In the Cochranites' imaginative retelling, the inhabitants of Cooperstown had unhitched Cooper's horses to draw his carriage through the streets by themselves like so many "cattle." A Cochran friend regarded the episode as proof that "the malign influence of overgrown property" had reduced the Cooperstowners to "conscious dependence."[64]

Cooper's friends responded in traditional terms, defending him as a benevolent patriarch deserving grateful deference from his political children, the settlers of upstate New York. Offended by the attacks on the Cooperstown reception, Elihu Phinney sarcastically retorted, "The *Merchant* must not greet the author of his *fortune*—the *Mechanic* his constant benefactor, nor the *Farmer* his tried friend and father!" Thomas R. Gold extolled Cooper as "the *Farmer's Patron and the Poor Man's Friend*" because, "by a conduct particularly benevolent and paternal towards settlers," the judge had "converted that *wilderness* into *smiling cornfields*." Reacting against the Cooperstown lawyers, Jedediah Peck lept to Cooper's defense, honoring him as "the *poor man's benefactor,* and the *widow's support,* the Father of his County." However, by reiterating their candidate's patriarchal claims, the Cooperites unwittingly reinforced the Cochranite charge that the judge exercised an unnatural control over his settlers.[65]

Because the congressional election of 1796 was so close and so heated in the Western District, the polling was particularly tense and the attending gentlemen especially prickly. "It has been the most contested Election I ever knew: every vote in this County has been solicited by both parties warmly," Joab Griswold observed in Herkimer County. With every vote of import, the stakes were high as rival friends competed to press ballots upon the electors and to challenge dubious voters. Fights broke out. Dr. Joseph White, a Cooperite, slyly observed, "In Cherry Valley it is said that Dr. White gave the famous Sheriff Dickson a severe wound over the right Eye." In Whitestown, Thomas R. Gold, a Cooper friend, exchanged "some little horsewhipping" with Arthur Breese, a Cochranite: "Breeze struck Gold with a loaded whip which brot him to the Ground & in his turn Gold brot Breeze to the Ground." Elsewhere in Herkimer County, Joab Griswold reported, "Mr. Clark and myself have had a bloody contest." In Montgomery County, Hendrick Frey and Philip Van Alstyne exchanged blows with loaded whips. Two weeks later, the recuperating Frey reported to Cooper, "This Election has been a Serious one, indeed the Best of Friends have Separated in so much that they Never will be United. Bloody Noses and Broken Heads have been the Result." Frey insisted that his wounds were "just wearing off and [I] shall, if I live, stand Ready to face the Next [Election] with undaunted Resolution."[66]

The heated rhetoric and close competition of the 1796 election brought a turnout at the polls unprecedented for a congressional contest in the sprawling district. When the polls closed Cooper's friends assured him that he would be reelected by a margin of at least 300, and as many as 1,000 votes. Even Cochran's friends despaired and refused further bets on the election. However, in late January, the state's board of canvassers reported that Cochran had scored a major upset, by the bare margin of 18 votes out of a total of 5,968 cast for the two major candidates.[67]

The returns demonstrated that Cooper was a polarizing figure, extraordinarily popular at home but alarming beyond Otsego. He captured 91 percent of the votes in Otsego County—even better than the 86 percent of his 1794 race. In the township of Otsego (including Cooperstown village) Cooper got a full 97 percent of the ballots. Although Cooperstown's lawyers worked zealously for Cochran, they could muster only 15 in Otsego Township. But Cochran prevailed in the district's other five counties. Outside Otsego, two-thirds of the voters accepted his invitation to a moral crusade against the sins of electioneering, all of which were borne by William Cooper and his friends. By making Cooper's interest the central issue, Cochran had masked his own.[68]

The judge blamed his defeat on the Cooperstown lawyers, especially Moss Kent, Jr. They had long exploited Cooper's generous patronage only to betray him. Elihu Phinney assured the judge, "You have been fostering a sett of vipers in your bosom. Hell has mustered all its forces against you in the shape of a sett [of] restless and ungrateful lawyers." In a letter to Governor Jay, Cooper confessed that he was "Mortifyed" by the defeat primarily because it had been effected "by those who have ben brought forward by my Owne Exertions." Six months later he sought a new lawyer, explaining, "Those we have here became ambitious and quit the interest that hath suported them." Cooper recruited David Mason, who moved to Cooperstown and assumed management of the judge's extensive and lucrative legal business.[69]

Kent savored Cooper's surprising defeat. Sitting in a Canajoharie tavern on March 21, 1797, he looked out the window to see Cooper riding by, heading home to Otsego. Taking up a pen, Kent reported to his brother: "[I] did not speak to him. I suppose that he & myself shall be pretty distant towards each other for the future, as he will undoubtedly impute the Loss of his election to my exertions against him & I believe he can do it with truth, & it is a matter of Triumph to me to think so. He is a base Scoundrel & has used me most basely." Even in victory Kent insisted upon thinking himself the aggrieved victim, although he had been lifted from bankruptcy to prosperity by the judge's indulgent generosity.[70]

Cooper's friends felt deeply shamed by the defeat of their patron and the triumph of their foes. "Cochran's friends in this and Montgomery County exult in an unpardonable degree. . . . I have been so Chagrined [that] I could hardly speak with temper even to my friends," Benjamin Gilbert lamented. In the political culture of eighteenth-century America, a man's pride and honor were staked to *his* candidate and invested in disgracing his opponents. There was a certain shame in becoming identified with a losing candidate and a delicious pleasure in dishonoring local enemies by defeating their champion. Electioneering lost most of its meaning and energy when there was no one to compete with, no one to intimidate, no one to shame. Issues and principles played minor roles in the politics of making interest. Instead, politics expressed a masculine ethos of competition and self-assertion conducted in camaraderie with like-minded men and in defiance of rivals. Designating officers and deciding issues were by-products in contests primarily conducted by leading men to test their influence and joined by common voters to share vicariously in the power of the victors.[71]

COMEBACK

After the acrimonious spring and fall elections of 1796, the judge repeatedly tried, but failed, to reclaim his resentful protégé, Moss Kent, Jr. Taken with Kent's superior education, gentility, and élan, Cooper longed to win his affection as a surrogate son. By accepting Cooper's symbolic paternity, Kent could help validate the judge's worthiness as a gentleman. But the association sought by Cooper was repellent to Kent. Apparently terrified that other gentlemen would set him down as the mere tool of the rich but boorish Cooper, Kent was at pains to deride the judge's rough manners and speech. Hating his financial dependence on Cooper's favor, Kent seized upon elections as cherished opportunities conspicuously to assert his defiant autonomy. Because Cooper so persistently sought reconciliation, Kent could enjoy the luxury of repeatedly betraying his patron. Daniel Hale warned his friend Cooper against trying to reconcile with a man so "capable of wantonly and maliciously insulting and attempting to Villify the Character of a man of honor, particularly when that man has been his warm friend and patron." But Hale's warnings were in vain, for as Kent reiterated his resistance, Cooper's unrequited longing grew keener.[72]

Kent and Cooper renewed their rivalry in the spring of 1797 as the state election season commenced. In March, upon Cooper's return home from Congress, Kent had moved out of the Manor House. Contemptuous of Cooper's renewed overtures, Kent yearned to complete the judge's political downfall by defeating his friends running that spring for seats in the state senate. "Should we succeed, it will be a glorious Victory over Corruption & Intrigue," Kent confided to his brother. In the April polling Otsego's voters preferred Cooper's slate by a three-to-one margin, but most of Kent's candidates prevailed in the Western District as a whole. Once again the lawyer prided himself on a victory that humiliated the judge.[73]

Despite this setback, Cooper meant to reclaim his congressional seat in the election of 1798. He benefited from a redistricting that set off Otsego into a new district, along with the newer and more sparsely settled counties of Chenango, Onondaga, Ontario, Steuben, and Tioga. The new congressional district excluded Montgomery and Herkimer, populous counties where Cooper had lost in 1796. He had an early chance to test his new district, because the legislature also rescheduled the congressional election in New York to coincide with the state election in April 1798, just fifteen months after his loss to Cochran.[74]

Despite the new, more favorable district and the short lead time, Cooper faced the most formidable possible opponent, a popular figure who might split Otsego's votes: Moss Kent, Jr. In the past, Cooper and Kent had competed through surrogates. In 1798, for the first time, they faced off for the same office. At the late April polling, the voters narrowly returned Cooper to Congress with 52 percent of the vote. The geographic pattern was familiar: Cooper won big at home in Otsego County (76 percent) and especially in Otsego Township (95 percent), but he lost badly in the other four counties, where Kent received 67 percent of the votes. Reclaiming his cherished seat in Congress, Cooper felt vindicated and took renewed confidence in his influence, at least within Otsego. He seemed at last to have safely piloted his embattled interest through the succession of political wars that had roiled Otsego since 1795.[75]

Chapter Ten

FRIENDS OF THE PEOPLE

B Y MAKING HIMSELF OVER INTO A Federalist elitist (if not a true gentleman), William Cooper underestimated the democratic possibilities of the American Revolution. Indeed, like the other Federalists, Cooper set himself up for a fall by attempting, during the 1790s, to bring the Revolution to a premature close. He succumbed to a mirage that had prevailed at the moment when he achieved wealth and power: the Federalists' illusion that they could restore the late colonial era's unity of economic, social, political, and cultural authority in an order of gentlemen. The Federalist gentry failed to recognize the enduring potential of the revolutionary legacy to legitimate upstarts unwilling or unable to achieve or to endure genteel authority. Cooper did not see that, in the wake of the Revolution, political authority and social status would become disconnected as voters increasingly distrusted gentlemen as their rulers.

The lawyer rose from his chair, and turning his back to the fire, and facing the company, he continued . . . .

"This is a country of laws; and should like to see it fairly tried, whether a man who owns, or says he owns, hundred thousand acres of land, had any more right to shoot a body, than another. . . . The law, gentlemen, is no respecter of persons, in a free country. It is one of the great blessings that has been handed down to us from our ancestors, that all men are equal in the eye of the law, as they are by nater. Though some may get property, no one knows how, yet they are not privileged to trangress the laws, any more than the poorest citizen in the state." . . .

A subject so momentous, as that of suing Judge Temple, was not very palatable to the present company, in so public a place; and a short silence ensued.

—James Fenimore Cooper,
The Pioneers, *151–53*

He did not anticipate that by trying to impress an elitist social circle, he would lose his popularity with the common settlers.[1]

The mirage dissolved in 1799–1801 when the Federalists confronted Republican challengers who, following George Clinton's lead, spoke of themselves as "Friends of the People"—equals rather than superiors. Republicans recognized the obstacle to their further ascent posed by the Federalist efforts to consolidate power and regulate social mobility. They saw their opportunity in promoting more explicitly democratic politics, by inviting the common people to reject the politics of paternalism. Primarily ambitious men of middling origins, the New York Republicans promoted a

liberal vision of society where an impartial, minimal government would secure equal opportunity for all by refusing to countenance superior privileges for the elite. They promised voters that equal rights and equal
opportunity would free the market to reward the industrious poor rather
than perpetuate the idle rich, gradually eliminating all vestiges of hierarchy
from American politics, society, and culture. In Otsego the Republicans rallied around Jedediah Peck, the renegade Federalist who had long supported Judge Cooper and long enjoyed his patronage.[2]

Instead of opposing Peck, Cooper should have joined with him in support of social mobility and public equality: the professed values of a new liberal social order. Ill-educated, rough-hewn, and self-made, Cooper could
have been a Republican—had his timing been better, his perception
keener, and his politics more agile. Indeed, in 1797 some Federalists found
plausible a rumor that Cooper was about to bolt their ranks and endorse a
Republican candidate for governor. After all, he felt betrayed by the Federalist lawyers of Cooperstown in his failed bid for reelection to Congress in
1796. Moreover, despite prodigious efforts to cultivate gentility, Cooper remained, in his boisterous manners and colloquial speech, more like the
common Peck than the genteel Kent. But Cooper remained fixated on what
he wanted to become, unwilling to accept his enduring commonality. He
quixotically persisted in seeking the approval of Federalist gentlemen who,
as often as not, treated his pretensions with ill-concealed contempt. It was
Cooper's public tragedy that he missed his opportunity as a popular leader
by clutching after a genteel persona and elite acceptance that were both just
beyond his grasp.[3]

The years 1799 to 1801 corroded William Cooper's prestige and authority in Otsego, an individual crisis entangled with the downfall of the
Federalist party in New York and the nation. Self-deceived by a brief political comeback in 1798, he overestimated his power as a Father of the People
and tried to suppress his local critics. This miscalculation initiated the rapid
collapse of his political authority and contributed mightily to the downfall
of his party in Otsego County, New York State, and ultimately in the United
States.

Preoccupied with national celebrities, historians ordinarily describe the
Republican movement of the 1790s as the top-down creation of the Vir-
ginians Thomas Jefferson and James Madison. But in New York, as in the
other northern states, the Republican insurgency owed precious little to Jefferson and Madison. Northern Republicanism is better seen as a popular
movement, as the aggregation of many local challenges to Federalist gentlemen by ambitious democrats. In national politics northern Republicans
cooperated with Jefferson and Madison but they rarely relied upon their
writings. By mobilizing common voters, local insurgents like Jedediah Peck
built the popular constituency that the national leaders attached themselves

to. Only by transcending the current fixation with Jefferson and Madison can historians recover the social significance and national scope of the Republican movement.[4]

DISTANCE

As William Cooper accumulated wealth and powerful friends, he and the Otsego settlers gradually became more distant. As the settlers became more numerous and prosperous, they no longer depended on the judge's capital and contacts to market their produce and to obtain consumer goods. In 1792 Cooper withdrew from storekeeping, potash making, and maple sugar production—enterprises that had made him familiar to, and influential among, the county's settlers. His withdrawal opened opportunities for new entrepreneurs to garner and subdivide the information, transactions, and power that he had once monopolized. In 1790 Cooperstown had only one store (Cooper's) and one tavern (Ellison's); by 1799 the village featured at least five stores and three taverns. Because men gathered and loitered at stores and taverns, discussing candidates as well as business, their proliferation factionalized local politics. For example, Rensselaer Williams's new store became a rallying point for the disruptive campaigns run by the village lawyers. The new academy, newspaper, brewery, and masonic lodge further multiplied the forums for villagers and visiting farmers to obtain and debate political information, to the further detriment of William Cooper's predominance. Similarly, the judge's success in politics literally increased his distance, as he spent the winter and spring of both 1795–96 and 1796–97 attending Congress in Philadelphia. In his absence rivals wreaked havoc with Cooper's political arrangements and with his social vision of a unified and harmonious county.[5]

Incrementally but inexorably, Cooper and most Otsego settlers became strangers to each other. In 1790, when Otsego had been a more homogeneous and intimate set of small settlements, William Cooper knew the names, faces, and circumstances of most of the settlers. At least two-thirds of the men dwelling within a dozen miles of Cooperstown had accounts at Cooper's store. During the subsequent decade newcomers flocked in, while about a third of the early settlers sold out to move on, usually heading for a still newer settlement further west. Consequently, the early settlers, those best known to Cooper, became a dwindling minority in the growing county population. In 1800 the town of Otsego had 743 households; only 74 (10 percent) of the heads of household had resided as adults in the county a decade earlier. By 1799 the great majority of the county inhabitants knew of the early hardships and Cooper's prodigious efforts in the 1780s only as stories. The influx transformed Otsego from a single, far-flung, and sparsely settled township with a population of 1,702 into a county of fourteen towns and 21,343 inhabitants (see Map 5). As Otsego County became more crowded and diverse, every town developed a cluster of ambitious and propertied men who contended for the honors of political office, often in defiance of the judge's wishes.[6]

The gradual disengagement of the settlers and the judge from each other could be read in the Cooperstown landscape. In the late 1780s Cooper had planned and mapped a compact village of small lots clustered

MAP 5

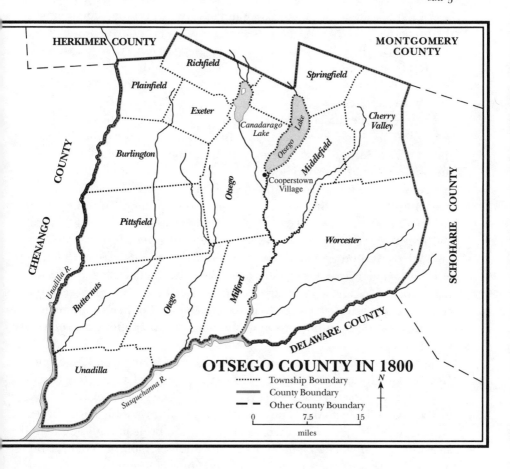

HERKIMER COUNTY

MONTGOMERY COUNTY

Richfield

Springfield

Plainfield

Exeter

Canadarago Lake

Cherry Valley

Burlington

Otsego Lake

Middlefield

COUNTY

Cooperstown Village

Otsego

SCHOHARIE COUNTY

Pittsfield

Worcester

CHENANGO

Unadilla R.

Butternuts

Otego

Milford

DELAWARE COUNTY

Unadilla

Susquehanna R.

OTSEGO COUNTY IN 1800

N

·········· Township Boundary
▬▬▬▬ County Boundary
▬ ▬ ▬ Other County Boundary

0   7.5   15

miles

around his own Manor House and oriented north-south along the Susquehanna River. By so arranging the villagers spatially, Cooper meant to exercise a close supervision that would secure the village's prosperity, harmony, unity, and enlightenment. But over the course of the 1790s, village development deviated from Cooper's map and vision. First, except for along the village's two main streets (Second and West), most of the small lots vanished into larger as the inhabitants bought and consolidated the parcels. Second, new construction steadily reoriented the village onto an east-west axis defined by the increasingly important state road passing through the village bound from Albany for Chenango County. The reorientation reflected both disappointment in the Susquehanna as a transportation corridor and the increasing number of travelers, emigrants, and produce flowing along the state road. That flow accelerated in 1798–99, when the state extended the road ninety miles west through the village and across Otsego and Chenango counties to reach the newer settlements around the Finger Lakes in western New York.[7]

Because Cooper had intended West Street as the village's western boundary, in 1791 he had allowed Joseph Griffin to build his tavern, the Red Lion Inn, out into Second Street, to serve as its terminus. Consequently, when the new state road appropriated Second Street for its passage through the village, it had to bend around the tavern on its progress westward. As the courthouse, jail, another tavern, a store, and Phinney's printing press sprouted around the Red Lion, the village's social, business, and political activities became concentrated there at the intersection of West and Second. What was supposed to be the edge of town became its center. That shift left the Manor House marginalized on the eastern edge of town. That a newspaper office and a set of taverns had replaced the Manor House as the village pivot perfectly symbolized the erosion of Cooper's paternalistic dream and the substitution of a more contentious, competitive, and diverse social order.[8]

At the same time that the villagers withdrew spatially from the Manor House, Cooper detached his family from the village by constructing a new, grander, and more secluded mansion named Otsego Hall. Cooper had grown dissatisfied with the Manor House as the village had filled with newer and bigger buildings. When erected in 1788 it had been an imposing frame structure for a small, new hamlet of one-story houses, most built of logs. But by 1796 there was little to distinguish the Manor House from the substantial new homes of Cooperstown's lawyers, merchants, and doctors. Moreover, its setting grew unpleasant as Second Street became part of the state road and the swelling traffic increased the intrusion of dust, noise, odors, and stares. At the same time that the world pressed in at their door and windows, the Cooper family had come to desire more privacy as essential to their gentility. They responded to a new fashion established in eastern villages and cities by prominent families who carved out green oases by setting their houses back from the street and by surrounding them with ornamental trees and gardens as a buffer. Sensitive to genteel fashion, the Coopers wished to retreat from the busy street with its noisy and nosy commoners.[9]

In 1796 Judge Cooper decided that a newer, larger, and more fashionable house would reaffirm his family's local superiority and manifest their new premium on privacy. Construction of the house, outbuildings, fences, orchards, and gardens began in the spring of 1797 and concluded two years later. The new complex occupied a three-acre lot immediately behind the Manor House, which was hauled away by oxen to clear a view down Fair Street toward the lake. A picket fence surrounded the grounds, demarcating the private domain of the Coopers from the village of Cooperstown.[10]

Although set back from the street, the finished house was a more powerful presence than the rather pedestrian Manor House had been. Otsego Hall was the first brick structure in the county. Lest anyone miss the bricks from their remove beyond the picket fence, Cooper had them painted a vivid red with the mortar between lined in bright white. To further catch the eye, he had the roof shingles painted red, and he fronted the pediment with a light wooden railing painted white. Seventy-feet long by fifty-two feet wide, and two full stories between a cellar and an attic, Otsego Hall was the largest private house in New York west of Albany. In dimensions and internal layout, the house copied Stephen Van Rensselaer's grand Albany mansion, which had impressed Cooper during frequent visits. By building a copy Cooper claimed equivalence to the wealthiest landholder and preeminent gentleman in the state. The new mansion shocked a visiting Quaker, who admonished Cooper for his "want of good Philosophy in Laying out Money to adorn thy House, which I thought Looked more Like [that of] the Lofty Spaniard, attached to popish Immegary, than the wise and prudent American." But Cooper was willing to shock the piously plain in order to impress the worldly genteel. A visiting James Kent exclaimed, "The House of Judge Cooper with his yard, gardens & view of the Lake is, taken altogether, the most splendid establishment in the western country."[11]

The house simultaneously claimed enhanced privacy and asserted greater grandeur. Cooper meant Otsego Hall both to command attention and to tell the onlookers to keep their distance. The spatial remove and the increased scale combined to further the family's alienation from the common settlers and villagers. Unwittingly, Cooper sacrificed the accessibility and common rapport so essential to his early success as a landlord and political father. By fulfilling his genteel longings in brick, Cooper ironically contributed to the collapse in 1799 of his popularity. The Coopers' move into the house that June coincided with the onset of a crisis when Cooper needed more, not less, contact with the common settlers.

At the same time Cooper began to lose his vaunted patience as a land-

lord. He had long subordinated his self-interest as a speculator to his paternalistic ambitions as a judge and congressman. Until the late 1790s Cooper
was reluctant to sue or foreclose on his many laggard debtors, for fear of
puncturing his image as the settlers' patron. But even a landlord as wealthy
as William Cooper could ignore the bottom line for only so long. Under
pressure from his own creditors, Cooper began to sue his debtors in 1799,
straining his tacit understanding with the voters. In 1799 he won lawsuits
against thirteen men for $5,115 (compared with only two suits for a total of
$1,699 during the three preceding years).[12]

By attending to his self-interest as a landlord, Cooper undercut his public persona as a political father who was supposed to be above concern with
profit and loss. Facing a newly demanding landlord, the settlers found less
reason to honor him with deference and office. Once Cooper became another griping landlord, it was no longer in their interest to keep him as their
political father.

The house and the lawsuits symbolized changes in William Cooper's social attitudes. Over the course of the 1790s, he gradually abandoned the
utopian optimism that had characterized his early years, when he had imagined Otsego as a refuge for common strivers fleeing from exploitative ministers and manor lords. Instead, Cooper began to perceive common people
as innately anarchic and in need of close supervision from their betters. Although a former wheelwright risen from poverty and obscurity to wealth
and power, William Cooper came to fear the ambitions of common people
as menacing to social order. His growing elitism showed the wearying effect
of advancing age and accumulated experience, and it manifested his acquisition of wealth, status, and power. Become the close associate of the Albany
grandees, he gradually adopted their views. But while Cooper became more
reactionary, the republic's political culture evolved toward the democratic
assertion of popular control over political gentlemen. That contradiction
brought William Cooper into conflict with Jedediah Peck.

IMPENDING WAR 🔥

In the spring of 1797, Jedediah Peck renewed his populist crusade by form-
ing a rival slate to compete with the regular Federalist ticket for Otsego's
four seats in the assembly (the county had lost one seat with the detachment
of the southern towns, including Harpersfield, to form Delaware County
earlier in the year). Peck detected a new threat to liberty in the Freemasonry
shared by all four candidates on the regular slate. Labeling his rivals the
"Masonic Nomination," Peck presented his slate as the "Freeman's Ticket":

> *By voting for the latter ticket, you will shew that you are determined to govern
> for yourselfs, independent of that society, or any other self-created and assum-*

*ing body of men, who, by their nominations would wish to rule over you — Look
arround you, judge for yourselves, regard your own honor, and respectability
more than the bargains, nominations or jealousy of other greater men — light up
your lamps and be vigilant.*

Once again Peck appealed to the pervasive anxiety among common men
that someone powerful was plotting to dishonor and subordinate them. He
insisted that their votes could defend their imperiled liberty and prosperity
from crypto-aristocrats. An avid crafter of populist themes, Peck anticipated
by a generation the Anti-Masonry that would sweep through upstate New
York during the 1820s. But Anti-Masonry did not work for Peck in 1797. In
the late April polling, his dissident slate garnered less than a third of the
votes won by the regular ticket. Indeed, Peck had lost ground, polling fewer
votes than the year before, when he had been a new candidate, running for
a higher office (state senate) against more formidable opponents (Jacob
Morris and Joseph White).[13]

Peck rebounded in 1798, apparently with William Cooper's help. Although Peck had yet to break through to county leadership, he remained
the most popular and influential figure in his populous hometown of
Burlington. In 1798 Cooper faced a tough race in his electoral bid for a return to Congress. Needing every possible vote, he welcomed Peck's endorsement and assistance. In return the judge quietly supported Peck's
renewed bid for an assembly seat. As a result Peck was the most popular assembly candidate in the county, garnering 1,129 votes—more than three
times what he had received the year before. After three years of struggle
Peck had won the legislative seat that he had so long coveted.[14]

The rupture between Peck and Cooper began in the following summer,
when the nation stood on the brink of foreign and, perhaps, civil war. In
1798 a diplomatic crisis with France emboldened the Federalists to suppress their domestic critics. In the early 1790s almost all Americans had welcomed the French Revolution that overthrew France's monarchy and
aristocracy, substituting a republic. At first it seemed that the French and
American revolutions and republics were closely related and that their interests and prospects were interdependent. However, in the mid-1790s
growing numbers of Americans, especially Federalists, lost their enthusiasm
as the radical Jacobin party seized control of the French Revolution and
executed thousands of their opponents. More Americans turned against
the French as they invaded, conquered, and occupied their Dutch, Swiss,
and Italian neighbors, and threatened to do the same to Great Britain. In
late 1796 Dr. Joseph White confessed to Cooper, "I have always ben amaz-
ing partial to [France], or rather to the principles of their revolution, but
I am getting out of all patience with their insolence." At the same time
the French government was exasperated with the United States for ratify-

ing John Jay's Treaty because it favored their enemy, Great Britain. The French retaliated by attacking American merchant ships on the high seas. In 1797 the new American president, the Federalist John Adams, hoped to avert war by sending a delegation to Paris for negotiations. However, in the spring of 1798 Adams reported to Congress that the negotiations had broken down when the French foreign minister demanded bribes and tribute. Most Americans regarded the demands as an insult to their national honor and as the familiar first step in the French pattern of bullying, subverting, invading, and conquering weaker countries. The federal government prepared for war, levying new taxes, building additional warships, and organizing an army. To suppress domestic opposition, Congress passed a Sedition Act, virtually outlawing public criticism of the federal government.[15]

Despite the surge of popular support for Federalism, there were a few staunch clusters of Republican opposition to the war fever and, especially, to the new taxes levied by the Federal government. The new Stamp Tax on legal documents was especially provocative because it was so reminiscent of the hated tax levied in 1765 on the colonies by the British empire. To protest the new taxes and war preparations, New York Republicans erected liberty poles in locales where they prevailed. Recalling their counterparts erected by the American Whigs to protest British rule, the new liberty poles symbolized a sense of the Revolution betrayed and of the Republic imperiled by Federalist rule. In early April 1798 some Republicans erected a liberty pole within Otsego County at Butternuts—a brazen act in so Federal a county. At the raising ceremony a Republican orator expressed the class resentment that was a common feature of resistance to the Federalist tax and war policies. Referring to the sharp symbolic distinction between the fine ruffled shirts worn by gentlemen and the hardy work clothes of farmers and mechanics, the orator insisted "that it was time to leave behind all these ruffle men and to send to Congress or our Legislature only leather apron men." The pole was an affront to the principal ruffled shirt in Butternuts, Gen. Jacob Morris, who was unused to any public challenge within his settlement. He staged a countermeeting that adopted resolutions for publication in the *Otsego Herald:* "We believe that living under a government of our own, Liberty poles and tumultuous meetings, cannot be but standards of idleness, which begets poverty; that they must have a bad effect on our youth, and are calculated to spread distrust and divisions amongst friends and neighbors."[16]

The Butternuts liberty pole was exceptional (and probably short-lived) in a Yankee county committed to the Federalist war effort. In a conspicuous show of county unity, Otsego's leading men gathered at the Cooperstown courthouse on May 19. They chose William Cooper to chair their meeting and General Morris as the secretary—a rare display of harmony by the longtime rivals, which conveyed to the public their unusual and urgent sense that a national crisis required unity and deference within Otsego. The meeting vigorously endorsed the war preparations and taxes, leading Elihu Phinney to boast that Otsego would turn out "thousands of its hardy and industrious inhabitants against the foe; who will find another sort of soldiers to contend with, than the effeminate spawn of Italy." The Otsego Federalists were also prepared to suppress local dissidents. At Cooperstown's Fourth of July celebration, the villagers toasted "Confusion to French partizans, . . . arrayed in a garb of tar and feathers—May they be suspended on Liberty Poles, until their souls are purified from the venomous contagion of French politics."[17]

Leading Federalists fomented popular outrage against both the French regime and the Republicans in America who still hoped that diplomacy could avert war. The Federalist press and orators demonized the Republican opposition as subversive anarchists and French tools. Refusing to concede to them the popular name of Republicans, the Federalists insistently called their political opponents Democrats or, worse still, Jacobins. With war impending most Federalists regarded political dissent as akin to treason rather than a tolerable difference of opinion. Placing Republican dissidents beyond the pale of decent society, the Federalists characterized them as turbulent, discontented, unscrupulous, and irrational strivers. Unwilling to accept their proper, subordinate position in society, the Republicans were malcontents who violently opposed every mark of superior virtue and merit.[18]

In the politics of the early Republic, men tended to project pessimistically into the future, tended to perceive in small, immediate events the beginnings of some accelerating process that would destroy liberty and order. Both the Republicans and the Federalists indulged in and fomented these grim anticipations, warning the citizens to beware of internal enemies. Denouncing the Republicans as closet Jacobins, a Federalist insisted,

> It is through little revolutions that they march to greater; it is by small associations that they invade and weaken the general association, and break the charm of public union. It is by the powers of local combination—it is by numerous particular strokes, in every part and place, given in exact concert, and incessantly repeated, that factious men now hope to beat and break down the grand machine of government.

Men of both political coalitions were so edgy because the American Republic was so new, so tenuous, so risky, and its proper powers still so undefined and subject to acrimonious debate. Moreover, with the perversion of the French Revolution into militarism and dictatorship, the United States was the only republic in a world dominated by monarchies and empires hostile to popular government. Federalists and Republicans alike knew that, in history, all previous republics had been unstable and short-lived. Consequently, both parties saw their cherished republic as threatened by powerful and insidious enemies from within as well as without.[19]

Although they subscribed to a common habit of escalating dread, the Republicans and Federalists told fundamentally different stories about the American Revolution. The Republicans insisted that the Revolution had been a social upheaval and transformation that had won equal rights, liberties, and opportunities for common men by defying domestic aristocrats as well as British rule. They argued that the revolutionary legacy remained chronically imperiled by internal enemies: the Federalists, who were latter-day Loyalists longing to replicate the British system of monarchy and aristocracy. By enlarging and centralizing power, funded by increased taxes, the Federalists meant to impoverish and subdue the common people, subverting their republic. The Republicans detected an ongoing "war of principles":

> *a war between equal and unequal rights, between Republicanism and Monarchy, between Liberty and Tyranny. It is our boast, it is our glory, that the strife began in America, and that Liberty first triumphed in our Country. We hold, that the contest is still going on; and that although the British fleets and armies have left our shores, yet that they have left their mantle behind, and that in the bosom of our Country, there are many, very many, who have long been aiming at unequal privileges, and who have but too well succeeded. This they have done by arrogating to themselves the right to be considered, as the only friends of the constitution, the guardians of order and religion.*

For the Republic to survive, the Revolution had to be permanent, as a properly vigilant people continuously detected and cast out the eternal enemies to equal rights and popular sovereignty.[20]

Conversely, the Federalists delimited the Revolution as a brief, orderly, consensual affair that was over and done with once national independence had been secured and the federal constitution ratified. Indeed, a Federalist writer insisted that the war for national independence "was but one stage in a great national progress; it was not a revolution." He warned the citizens:

> *The demagogues, who infest you, know not how to trace the history of your liberties: they confound it with the history of your independence; they rest at the period of your revolution. . . . The truth is . . . your revolution was undertaken not to acquire, but to maintain liberty, not to settle and determine your rights, but to repel an attack upon them. It resulted in independence and a separation; . . . but the interior of your social system, the spirit of your institutions, and the body of your rights and liberties suffered no modification. They derived their birth from the seeds planted in the formation of society.*

By defining the Revolution as conservative, the Federalists insisted that the people should fear attacks on order rather than inroads on their liberties. Once the state and national constitutions secured the election of rulers, they warranted obedience, rather than suspicion, from the people. The true danger came from insidious malcontents eager to replicate the French Revolution. In contrast to the Republican efforts to arouse the people, the Federalists appealed to "every man who is desirous of a settled order of things, and averse from continual innovation and revolution." They depicted the ideal polity and society as at rest, in stable and harmonious equilibrium as men of diverse wealth, ranks, and capacities kept each to his proper place, united in deference to the gentlemen they had elected to higher office. In sum, in 1798–1801 the Federalists and Republicans competed to determine the meaning of the American Revolution.[21]

CONVERSION

The Federalist war fever put Jedediah Peck in a bind. On the one hand, although ostensibly a Federalist, he had constructed his political rhetoric and influence by defying Otsego's leading Federalists, especially Gen. Jacob Morris. Now those Federalist gentlemen were leading the local war effort against the French Revolution that Peck had celebrated so effusively in the past. On the other hand, Peck considered himself the servant of the people—and in early 1798 the great majority of his constituents were enraged at France and ready for war. Swimming with the popular current, Peck embraced the Federalist mobilization: "Let us throw by all petty disputes, while our country is in danger; . . . it is high time to arise, as one man—join heart and hand, in the defence of your own government and country." But Peck carefully preserved his political independence and high profile. Rather than participate in a subordinate capacity at the regular county meeting in Cooperstown, he staged and chaired his own meeting in Burlington, publishing the proceedings in the newspaper. The Burlington settlers resolved "to gird on our warlike weapons as in the year '75, and defend our independence, and Support the honor and dignity of the United States, to the last drop of blood and cent of property. We will take one pull for it, and let them know [that] we are Freemen of America, and not Slaves to despots." In Peck's latest version of his populist appeal, the French regime temporarily displaced lawyers, gentlemen, and Freemasons as the gravest threat to the self-respect and autonomy of America's common men.[22]

To the dismay of his Federalist colleagues, Peck sustained his independence as a state legislator. During the special August session called to prepare New York for war, he frequently broke party ranks to vote with the Republican assemblymen, led by Aaron Burr. Peck's unpredictability infuriated his Federalist colleagues from Otsego: state senators Jacob Morris and Joseph White and assemblymen Joshua Dewey, Benjamin Gilbert, and Francis Henry. In private letters written to their friends in Otsego, they angrily denounced Peck as a dangerous trimmer who had joined "the French party." Returning home in early September, Peck characteristically challenged his critics to a public debate in his favorite forum, the *Otsego Herald*. Taking the bait, Dewey, Gilbert, and Henry assured the readers that the "ignorant or wavering" Peck had become "an Antifederalist, and one highly tinctured with Jacobinical principles." Joining the fray, Elihu Phinney denounced Peck as an "apostle of Sedition" and a "noisy Drumhead," striving "to advance his station, by scribbling libels, and foul defamation."[23]

Peck's foes attributed his insubordination to a dangerous combination of mental instability, compulsive ambition, religious hypocrisy, and inadequate gentility. The Federalists regarded him as further proof that common men should not be entrusted with high office. "No minds are more susceptible of envy than those whose birth, education & merit are beneath the dignity of their station," one Federalist insisted. They concluded that it was high time for Peck to return to his manual trades of raising crops, surveying farms, and repairing mills.[24]

The Federalist leaders repeated their mistake made in 1796: assuming that ridicule and class contempt would discredit Peck in the eyes of the rural public. In fact, common voters took personally the abuse heaped on a man they identified with. Indeed, Phinney foolishly extended his contempt to Peck's rural supporters by mocking the errors of grammar and spelling in their letters and resolves sent to the newspaper. Consequently, Phinney soon faced a profit-sapping rebellion as about half of his country readers cancelled their subscriptions. Many of the readers who abandoned the *Otsego Herald* turned to the *Albany Register*, a Republican paper that, in early 1799, became the new vehicle for Peck's essays. As copies of the *Register* proliferated in Otsego, Republican ideas became widely available in the county for the first time—with corrosive consequences for the local Federalist consensus.[25]

Having lured his foes into the press, Peck relentlessly counterattacked, at first in the *Otsego Herald* and later in the *Albany Register*. Empowering the reading public to determine his worthiness as their legislator, Peck invited the common men to overrule their Federalist leaders. Attacking his foes on moral and cultural grounds, he assailed their genteel affectations, so at odds with the plain style and folk Christianity of their country constituents. Peck revived charges that Dr. White was a deist who had denied biblical revelation and pronounced Jesus a bastard. He denounced Dewey and Henry for keeping late hours to gamble at cards and quaff multiple bottles of wine and brandy. He charged that White and Henry had even opposed a proposal to permit imprisoned debtors to attend the religious services held at the Cooperstown Academy.[26]

Peck stressed that he had vigorously opposed a bill supported by his Otsego colleagues to increase the pay of state legislators. He knew that his country constituents begrudged the legislators any more money and, instead, favored Peck's proposed alternative: to spend the money on public schooling in rural towns. In a public letter addressed to his foes, Peck accused them of seeking a legislative pay raise to subsidize their high living, "till you have eat up our school money, which causes a cry to be heard from the poor in all parts of our county." He inverted the jeers of his genteel foes:

> *You say I was rendered the ridicule of the Legislature; who ridiculed me, Mr. Henry? All the* honorable *gentlemen who played cards, made a by-word of you around their gambling tables, while they were drinking their bumpers of wine and brandy. What did they say? There is old Peck, an old fashioned thing, he'll not play cards like a* gentleman, *for fear he'll have a bottle of wine to pay for; yes, yes, Mr. Henry, the County is disgraced by old Peck; for after he had been spouting some of his silly talk against the* honourable *Mr. Dewey's bill to raise the wages of the Legislators, old Mr. Burling, another old fashioned member, went to him and told him [that] he believed he came from a country, where the people knew nothing but pure honesty!*

Peck's populism was simultaneously economic and cultural: a defense of small farmers' property as well as of their morals and manners.[27]

His accusations delineated the divide, of both class and culture, that separated the leading villagers from the hinterland farmers. His five critics were all men of genteel pretensions who delighted in a convivial life characterized by drinking, exchanging witty sallies, playing cards and billiards, and reading secular and often irreverent texts. All lived in the villages of Cherry Valley or Cooperstown except Gilbert who resided in the intervening town of Middlefield. All five were Freemasons belonging to Cooperstown's Otsego Lodge, but none was in communion with any church. Henry ran a Cooperstown tavern and Dewey was a Yale graduate who conducted the village school in the academy building. Peck's critics regarded a stint in Albany as a cultural promotion, a move closer to the metropolitan sources of the fashions, manners, morals, and ideas that they emulated. But for Peck, to sojourn in Cooperstown, much less in Albany, was to pass from a moral countryside into a troubling den of sensual materialism at odds with both his evangelical faith and his republican virtue.[28]

Peck's conspicuous, acrimonious, and divisive insubordination profoundly embarrassed Judge Cooper who had helped secure his election to the legislature. His Federalist friends in Otsego and his gentry mentors in Albany pressured Cooper to prove his claims to be the political Father of Otsego, able to subdue dissidence. In January 1799 Daniel Hale, the New York secretary of state, wrote to Cooper about his Peck problem: "This man appears to me and to many who know him, to be a strange, inconsistant, turbulent and I believe unprincipled Character. He appears to be neither federal, antifederal, or any thing else." Hale encouraged Cooper's plan to suppress Peck: "I agree with you that it would be best for himself and for Society in general that he was reinstated in his original obscurity. This I believe will be *compleatly* the case before long and I am happy to find that you are disposed to further the business." Cooper needed to reaffirm his authority over Otsego in order to sustain his claim to be a natural aristocrat belonging in the Federalist inner circle.[29]

The Federalists thought that summarily sacking Peck from his judicial post would disgrace and discredit him, ensuring his quick demise in electoral politics. In a petition to the Council of Appointment, the Otsego Federalists charged that Peck had become too "old & superanuated" to perform his duties as a judge and that he was "of a restless, turbulent disposition, and frequently excites quarrels and discontents among the good and peaceable inhabitants of the Said County." On March 9 the council, chaired by Governor Jay, revoked Peck's commission as a judge. In defiant response, Peck vowed to seek vindication from the Otsego voters in the April election.[30]

In Otsego the assembly election became a referendum on Jedediah Peck. Confident that judicial removal had conclusively disgraced him, the Federalists continued to ridicule Peck as an unworthy bumpkin. They denounced his speeches as "unintelligible jargon and puerile arguments" and mocked his rural Yankee diction, never considering that country voters might resent attacks on a man for thinking and speaking as they did. Indeed, the rural folk longed to avenge the many slights they had felt from the arrogant gentlemen of Cooperstown and Cherry Valley. Skillfully exploiting the Federalists' miscalculation, the *Albany Register* pointedly asked voters: "Are those men who despise Plough-Joggers fit to rule in a Republican state? . . . How then will the enlightened yeomanry of Otsego relish the Aristocratical notion that the profession of a plough-jogger is beneath the *dignity* of a Judge?" Republican exaltation combined with Federalist ridicule to make a folk hero of Jedediah Peck.[31]

In the assembly, as in the pages of the *Albany Register,* the Republicans welcomed and lionized Peck, accepting the gift presented to them by his Federalist ostracism. They saw him as their wedge to split the rural Yankee constituency that had been so staunchly Federalist since 1792. With Peck's help the Republicans could expand their popular base beyond the Hudson and lower Mohawk valleys into the hilly and Yankee counties of western and central New York. To that end in February 1799 the Republican legislators conspicuously adopted Peck's two pet proposals for decentralizing and democratizing New York's political structures. First, he proposed subdividing the large, multicounty, and multimember senatorial districts into individual county districts. Second, he suggested that the state's presidential electors should be popularly elected, rather than chosen by the state legislature (as had been done at all previous presidential elections in New York). Anticipating a Federalist state legislature in 1800, the Republicans preferred to take their chances with a popular vote for electors. By adopting Peck's program they made a Republican of him during the winter of 1798–1799. On February 16, Peck marked his conversion by voting with Burr and the other Republicans to denounce the Federal Sedition Act as "contrary to the dearest interests of Freemen." His Otsego Federalist colleagues voted with the majority to endorse the Sedition Act.[32]

DIVISION

In early 1799 Peck's increasing daring, prominence, republicanism, and popularity alarmed and infuriated the Otsego Federalists. He personified their ultimate nightmare: the unscrupulous demagogue bent on overturning social hierarchy and moral order by stirring up popular discontent. In early 1799 Timothy Morse, a Burlington Federalist, intercepted one of Peck's circular letters and reported, "He is striving to alarm the common People by crying Monarchy, a domestic Master, &c., &c. In my oppinion, he is the most dareing and dangerous wretch that ever this County was Cursed with."[33]

William Cooper dreaded that Peck would benefit from the clashing ambitions and petty rivalries that continued to divide the county's Federalists. Hoping to reconstruct Federalist unity in Otsego, Cooper announced a countywide political meeting to gather at the courthouse in Cooperstown on March 27. He explained, "At a time too when French Emissaries are in pay amongst us, this attempt will appear neither assuming nor ostentatious, but the result of a sincere wish to establish harmony in a county, the welfare of which must be always near the heart of WILLIAM COOPER." A month later, on the eve of the election, Cooper became more explicit, publishing a warning: "Every man who circulates two seditous printed Papers, disseminated by Jedediah Peck, through this County, is liable to two years imprisonment, and a fine of two thousand dollars, at the discretion of the Court." Invoking the Sedition Act, Cooper was threatening prosecution in the federal courts. He meant to regain control of his county by defining the populism promoted by Peck as criminal sedition.[34]

With these two public notices Cooper staked his prestige and interest on halting Peck's political momentum. Although Cooper was not running for office in the spring election, he made himself Peck's leading opponent in the public eye. The Republicans delighted in this turn of events, welcoming the chance to contrast the common democrat Jedediah Peck with the great landlord and notorious Federalist William Cooper. In the *Albany Register* an Otsego Republican boldly predicted electoral victory, "notwithstanding C[ooper]'s scare-crow Circular, and malicious denunciations; the ignoramus supposes [that] we must believe all he says, whether true or false, but you will shortly be able to determine whether he directs the people, or they think and act for themselves."[35]

As if Cooper did not have enough to cope with, he also faced a resurgence of Moss Kent's hyperactive ambition. Oblivious to the manifest importance of Federalist unity, Kent decided again to challenge Dr. Joseph White, who was seeking reelection to the state senate. Kent's unexpected loss to White in 1796 still rankled his formidable pride. Federalist state leaders begged Kent instead to run for a seat in the assembly, and thereby help defeat Peck. Even James Kent—never before one to dampen his brother's ambition—assured him: "You are more wanted & therefore would do more good by your Influence in the assembly. The present is a very weak House & the spirit of Jacobinism increases. I think you would be able to influence & controul all your associates, at least from Otsego." But not even flattery from his cherished brother could deter Kent from seeking a higher office and settling his old grudge with White. Once again, Kent and Peck put their starkly different styles into play in the same election, severely complicating Cooper's efforts to hold the middle for Federalism.[36]

Political affairs in Otsego quickly spun out of Cooper's control as a consequence of the county political meeting that met at the courthouse in Cooperstown on March 27. He had called the meeting to restore county unity and Federalist hegemony in the face of Peck's gathering challenge. But Kent's friends had damned the unity effort by seizing control of the meeting to ram through his nomination for the state senate. The maneuver was doubly embarrassing to Cooper because Kent's friends had shrewdly implicated the judge by choosing his new lawyer, David Mason, as the meeting's secretary. Newspaper readers of its proceedings would assume that the judge had betrayed White. Apparently following Cooper's advice, Mason delayed sending the proceedings to the press. Growing impatient with the delay, Kent's friends sent Dr. John Russell, the Cooperstown pharmacist, to demand from Mason his certified copy of the meeting proceedings. Rebuffed, Russell framed his own set of proceedings for publication in the *Albany Gazette* on April 5. To Cooper's further chagrin, Mason and Russell proceeded to abuse each other in an exchange of newspaper polemics.[37]

But there was still worse to come: an attempted political assassination in Cooperstown on April 12. Obscured in public sources, the full story emerges only from the personal docket book kept by William Cooper. Kent's friends were furious at Mason for publicly disavowing the published proceedings of their nomination meeting. On April 11 a Kentite delegation confronted Mason with their copy of the meeting resolves, demanding that he certify their accuracy in writing. When Mason refused, Abraham C. Ten Broeck plotted a more pointed effort at persuasion. On April 12 Ten Broeck invited Mason into his office, where they could talk in private. As

soon as Mason entered Ten Broeck shut and locked the office door, pock-
eting the key. Presenting the certificate, he demanded that Mason sign. He
refused. According to Mason's vivid testimony:

> *The said Abraham then said he would make him and immediately took from the
> head of his bed a Cane from which he drew a dagger and approached towards
> the said David, who laid hold of a piece of planed pine to defend himself—and
> that the said Abraham then with the said drawn dagger did make a full thrust
> with it at the body of him the said David and with such force as that the said
> dagger would have Passed through the Body of him the said David if he had
> not turned its Point with his arm—that the said Abraham then struck at his
> head but hit his shoulder.*

Passing by in the street outside, Thomas Wattels heard "a greate noise" from
Ten Broeck's office "and saw the glass fly out of one of the windows." Hearing Mason call out, "for God sake, take the Sword from him," Wattels forced
open the window and "with difficulty" helped wrench the dagger from Ten
Broeck.[38]

Then Mason and Wattels hustled the struggling Ten Broeck to the
Manor House for an immediate hearing before an astonished Judge
Cooper. For years Otsego's contentious politicos had frustrated Cooper's
cherished vision of county harmony and unanimity, but now he confronted
the very nadir: the attempted murder of his lawyer by a rival over the resolves from a nominating meeting. Ever anxious for the tenuous dignity of
his county bench, Cooper lamented that Ten Broeck had acted "in View of
the Magistrates of the County, which if [they] let Pass would bring disgrace
on our Courts." Abetted by his colleague Judge Elihu Phinney, Cooper committed Ten Broeck to the county jail to await trial in June for attempted
murder. A day later his friends Rensselaer Williams and Moss Kent posted
$500 in bail to release Ten Broeck from his jail cell.[39]

Political strife in New York was often rough, but attempted murder was
virtually unknown. It was symptomatic of Otsego's peculiar political mania
in 1799 that such a violent frenzy could so consume the ordinarily cautious,
dull, and pedantic Abraham C. Ten Broeck. A less likely murderer could
scarcely be found in all of Otsego. Ten Broeck's act shocked the bickering
villagers into a temporary truce brokered by Cooper and Kent. On April 13
David Mason and John Russell met "together with a number of gentlemen"
to reconcile their differences. Two days later they subscribed to a joint statement regretting their "intemperate and indelicate language." Representing
the village's two rival Federalist factions, Cooper and Kent formally attested
to the statement as its two witnesses. However, newspaper publication of the
statement came too late in the campaign to repair the severe damage already done to Federalist unity and credibility.[40]

At the end of April the polling was doubly damning to Cooper's pretensions as the political father of Otsego. First, in the state senate race, Kent triumphed over White by a margin of almost two to one in the Western District as a whole and by over four to one in Otsego County. Second, Peck won reelection to the assembly, garnering the second largest cache of votes in the county (the top four candidates won seats). Despite, or perhaps because of, Cooper's forthright denunciations of Peck, Otsego's voters had rallied to his democratic insurgency. Cooper's review of recent events was sobering: Peck's rebellion and reelection; Kent's continued fractiousness; the angry feud between Mason and Russell; and Ten Broeck's murderous outburst. Moreover, March and April of 1799 had also featured the bitter public controversy between the village's rival ministers, John F. Ernst and John McDonald—similarly marked by angry meetings, bitter ultimatums, and threatened violence. In a further symptom of Cooper's declining influence, on June 13 a trial jury acquitted Ten Broeck of attempted murder, convicting him only on the lesser charge of assault and battery; the bench assessed a $50 fine.[41]

CONFRONTATIONS

In aggressive pursuit of their individual ambitions, the leading villagers had perverted Cooper's vision of Cooperstown as a harmonious settlement united in deference to his paternal authority. Cooper associated his decaying local influence with the national spread of the American Jacobinism so luridly described in the Federalist press. He took seriously the Federalist essays urging magistrates to save the nation by detecting and suppressing local Jacobins. In the summer of 1799 an Albany newspaper exhorted Federalists "to root out those poisonous weeds that grow up and flourish in our own Soil" and thereby "save the people from anarchy and confusion." Cooper concluded that he could help rescue the Republic by acting forcibly to restore his own power in Otsego. In June he moved simultaneously to silence the two principal sources of local disputes: the democratic insurgent Jedediah Peck and the reactionary conspirator Joseph Strong. Although starkly different personalities and old adversaries, Peck and Strong became yoked together as the twin target of Cooper's desperate bid for renewed control.[42]

Cooper's critical actions against both men occurred during the three days June 25 through 27. The heavens marked this period with a sensational, prolonged thunderstorm that electrified and drenched Otsego during the night of June 26: "a Spectacle surpassing every thing of the kind . . . in this country since it has been penetrated by civilized beings." Almost incessant flashes of lightning and peals of thunder accompanied a torrential downpour that raised Otsego Lake nearly three feet overnight—something unprecedented in the settlers' memories. A boy later recalled, "The vault above was illuminated; the world seemed to roll in an ocean of flame, and trembled, as if in agony, under incessant peals of deafening thunder. . . . The terrors of an angry God and the awful judgment day were continually in my mind." In Otsego County the lightning burned several houses, killed many cattle, and did "vast damage . . . by the destruction of the crops, bridges, mills, mill dams, and tan works." Prone to detect divine warning in sudden and severe weather, the settlers regarded the devastating storm as anticipating some ominous, impending crisis in their public affairs. June was also a momentous month for the Coopers because they then moved into their grand, new mansion: Otsego Hall.[43]

Cooper's climactic confrontation with Strong began one day in early June, when the farmer Ebenezer Sherman "came hallowing and swearing into town." This was hardly unusual behavior in a village so notorious for raucous drinking and street scuffles; but Sherman arrived at a moment when Cooper had newly resolved to tighten morality and order in Cooperstown. Arraigning Sherman, Cooper levied a severe fine and committed the enraged farmer to the county jail pending payment. Visiting the jail, Joseph Strong urged Sherman to sue Cooper for false arrest, observing "that he would teach Cooper better than to conduct in such a manner." Strong was ever keen for legal business, especially something that would embarrass and cost the judge. But to solicit litigation was "barratry," a technical violation of Strong's oath as a lawyer. Twice before, in 1796 and 1798, Otsego grand juries had indicted Strong for corrupt practice as a lawyer, but on both occasions he had escaped conviction (the state's attorney dropped the first case, and a trial jury acquitted him of the second charge). Determined to get Strong this time, Cooper bypassed the intermediaries of state's attorneys and trial juries. Supported by his subordinate judges, Phinney and White, Cooper took testimony and issued judgment against Strong on June 27, the day after the great thunderstorm. The judges announced, "The Court have reprimanded the said Joseph Strong at almost every Term for several years for his ungovernable Conduct and Extravagant Bills of Cost [and] are at length worn out with his improprieties." Pronouncing him guilty of soliciting Sherman's lawsuit, the justices suspended Strong from practicing law in Otsego for six months. They added a rebuke to Strong's advocate, Moss Kent, Jr., who had denounced the court's proceedings without a prior grand jury indictment as "arbitrary, tyrannical, illegal, and oppressive." Informing Mr. Kent that he misunderstood the law, the judges sniffed that "he had better in future inform himself by Books"—a dig at Kent's excessive pride in his superior reading. At last it seemed that Cooper had secured the judiciary's preeminence over the lawyers in Otsego.[44]

At the same time, Cooper also moved against Jedediah Peck for publicly denouncing the Sedition Act and its Federalist authors. During the spring and summer Peck vigorously circulated printed copies of a Republican pe-

tition demanding congressional repeal. The petition's text described the
Sedition Act as part of a Federalist plot to destroy the Republic and substitute an aristocracy and monarchy. One day Cooper caught Peck "in the act,"
confiscated his parcel of petitions, and sent them to Richard Harison, the
federal attorney for New York. Deeming the petition seditious, Harison authorized Cooper to collect affidavits as further evidence against Peck. On
June 25 and 27, bracing the great thunderstorm, Cooper and Phinney took
affidavits and forwarded them to Harison in New York City. The judge
feared the worst if Peck remained at large: "Dissatisfaction [will] grow
among the people untill it is too late for the Civil System."[45]

In early September Harison presented the affidavits to a federal grand
jury in New York City, which promptly indicted Peck for sedition. A federal
judge issued a warrant for his arrest. Still Cooper worried: "There is a want
of Energy to silence those wretches. Mercy is a cardinal Virtue, but the Public tranquility is a Consideration not to be neglected." In late September
Cooper at last arranged Peck's arrest in Burlington. Handcuffed and
guarded, Peck made a five-day journey to New York City, where he was ar-
raigned for trial there in April. After posting bail he returned home to Otsego for the interim. Determined to compound his woes, Cooper also
brought civil suit against Peck for his unpaid and overdue land debt, winning a $220 judgment from the Otsego County Court of Common Pleas on
October 17. Forgetting all past friendship and alliance, Cooper pursued
Peck with a grim determination.[46]

In early October Cooper also suppressed a gang of counterfeiters based
in Burlington. Mixing pewter, lead, tin, arsenic, beech bark, and aqua fortis, they counterfeited Spanish silver dollars. Because nothing was more sacred to Cooper than the free flow of commerce and a mutual trust in
transactions, he was appalled to find a ring of counterfeiters at work in his
county. They threatened the fundamental basis of his estate and authority:
the stability of property. It seemed more than mere coincidence that coun-
terfeiting erupted in Jedediah Peck's hometown, for in Cooper's mind
democracy and debased coinage were variants of a common degeneracy
and deception. Issuing warrants on October 3, Cooper secured the arrest of
at least four of the seven suspects, and he persuaded one to turn state's evidence against his partners in crime. By acting so decisively, Cooper seemed
to have suppressed the economic, as well as the political, strain of Jacobinism in Otsego.[47]

Close on the heels of these seeming victories over Strong, Peck, and the
counterfeiters, Cooper unexpectedly won a windfall fourth triumph over an
old adversary. On October 16, 1799, James Cochran rode into Cooperstown to confront the judge. In part, Cochran probably sought to avenge the
humiliation recently dealt out to his dear friend Joseph Strong. In part,
Cochran wanted satisfaction for a story Cooper had been telling detrimen-

tal to Cochran's genteel dignity. Noting Cochran's reputation as a fiddler, Cooper had joked that, by playing for country dances, the lawyer "had fiddled himself into office." In effect, Cooper insisted that Cochran had won their contest in 1796 by engaging in undignified electioneering, by pandering to the people in his lust for office. By recasting Cochran as the vulgar demagogue, Cooper reclaimed the role of dignified gentleman that had been denied him by defeat in the congressional campaign of 1796.[48]

Confronting the judge as he strode out of the courthouse onto the main street, Cochran cut Cooper with a whip. The two men grappled, "clinging and beating one another." The stronger and more experienced wrestler, Cooper compelled Cochran to beg for release "in a submissive manner." The lawyer pleaded, "I acknowledge [that] you are too much of a buffer for me." Inordinately proud of his triumph in their "bruising match," Cooper gathered depositions, describing Cochran's defeat and submission, for public circulation in published handbills. Across the top of a personal copy, Cooper happily scrawled, "Oath, how I whipped Cochran." Three years after his electoral defeat, Cooper had obtained a sweet measure of revenge from Cochran. By taking such pride in a public brawl that embarrassed his Federalist colleagues, Cooper betrayed the superficiality of his self-made gentility.[49]

DOWNFALL

Cooper's buoyant mood quickly dissolved at the end of the month as his apparent victories turned into disastrous defeats. His suppression of Joseph Strong exploded in late October, when the State Supreme Court of Judicature heard the lawyer's appeal. On the 25th the justices ruled that Strong's dismissal was illegal, and they ordered his immediate reinstatement to the Otsego bar—a stunning and humiliating blow to Cooper's prestige and authority. Although Strong's vindication was more immediately embarassing, Peck's arrest caused more enduring and widespread damage to Cooper's standing. Far from discrediting Peck and stemming Republicanism in Otsego, arrest made him a hero and confirmed his warnings that the Sedition Act imperiled freedom in America. An aging veteran of the Revolutionary War and a man of slight and hunched stature, Peck evoked popular sympathy and outrage as he passed in irons through the countryside to New York City in late September. Republican papers in New York and Connecticut lionized him as a democratic martyr, and public opinion followed suit. Jabez D. Hammond recalled, "A hundred missionaries in the cause of democracy stationed between New-York and Cooperstown, could not have done so much for the republican cause as this journey of Judge Peck, as a prisoner, from Otsego to the capital of the state." Moreover, the arrest came to naught as Richard Harison suspended his prosecution of Peck in April of 1800 for want of any witnesses willing and able to travel the two hundred miles from Otsego to New York City during mud season. Federal authorities also belatedly recognized that a trial would only compound the debacle in public relations created by Peck's arrest.[50]

His credibility and popularity reeling from the double blow, Cooper recognized that he had become an embarrassing liability to the Federalist cause in Otsego. Indeed, Strong had abandoned Federalism to make common cause with Peck and the Otsego Republicans. Setting aside ideology, Strong found common political ground with Peck in their mutual determination to bring down Judge Cooper. On October 25 (the same day that the supreme court ruled in Strong's favor), Cooper submitted his resignation as Otsego's presiding judge to Gov. John Jay. Five days later Cooper publicly announced that he would retire from Congress upon completing his term. The judge hoped that his withdrawal would permit Otsego voters to rally around less controversial Federalists in the approaching spring election.[51]

Cooper understood his resignation and retirement as his ultimate acts of paternalism, as he sadly explained to Governor Jay:

> The Great Violence of Party amongst us, makes it necessary to strive for a Cure and my withdrawing from all offices will not only make way for Others, but also in some degree show that to give way and to forgive is the Onely Balsom that can heal animosities of the kind Existing among us and it will Come from no Person in the first instance better than from William Cooper, who had rather the child should be Nursed by a stranger, than that it should be hewn in pieces.

In resignation, Cooper still thought of himself as Otsego's father, as the one man willing to sacrifice his interest to spare his child from further political conflict. In January, the Governor and his Council of Appointment accepted Cooper's resignation, and disciplined his subordinate judges by admonishing Joseph White and sacking Elihu Phinney (who was restored to office in October).[52]

Even Cooper's apparent triumph over the Burlington counterfeiters turned into an utter failure. Three of the seven counterfeiters eluded arrest. Two of the four imprisoned suspects escaped on the night of January 2, 1800, assisted by five accomplices, who broke open Cooperstown's log jail with axes, saws, and screw augers. Their escape with outside assistance was further testimony to the widespread contempt for the legal magistrates in Otsego County. One of the two suspects remaining in custody avoided punishment by turning state's evidence against the other, but his testimony proved worthless, failing to persuade the jury that acquitted the only member of the gang ever brought to trial.[53]

Instead of learning moderation from his defeats, Cooper remained a rigid and partisan Federalist upon returning to Congress for the winter ses-

Painted by the most fashionable and expensive American artist of the 1790s, this portrait represents William Cooper's ascent to wealth and his aspirations to gentility. Significantly, he holds a map of Cooperstown, the foundation for his elevated status and fortune. *Judge William Cooper,* c. 1794, by Gilbert Stuart (1755–1828). Courtesy of the New York State Historical Association, Cooperstown.

Burlington, New Jersey, served as William Cooper's model in planning his new settlement at the foot of Otsego Lake. He was especially fond of Burlington's orderly street grid, narrow lots, and tight cluster of brick houses. *A Plan of the Island of Burlington and a View of the City from the River Delaware,* 1797, by William Birch. Courtesy of the Library of Congress.

Otsego Lake stretches northward in this photograph taken from the foot of the lake and the beginning of the Susquehanna River, with Mount Vision looming to the right. A 1988 photograph by Milo Stewart. Courtesy of the New York State Historical Association, Cooperstown.

In 1774 George Croghan and his creditors had made a new survey and map of his holdings south and west of Otsego Lake. Their anticipated auction of its lots never occurred because the Revolutionary War erupted in 1775. The inset represents Croghan's Forest, his estate at the foot of the lake on the present site of Cooperstown. *George Croghan's Patent,* 1774, by Robert Picken. Courtesy of the Hartwick College Archives, Oneonta, New York.

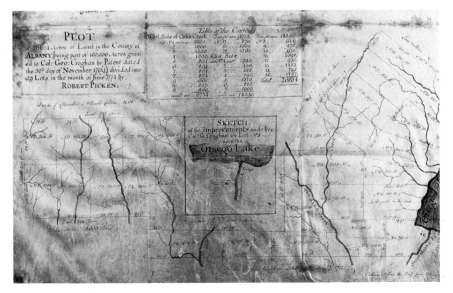

During the 1790s William Cooper's political pa-
-on was the manor lord Stephen Van Rensselaer,
he wealthiest gentleman in New York State.
*tephen Van Rensselaer, 1819, by Ezra Ames (1768–
836). Courtesy of the New York State Historical
ssociation, Cooperstown.

During the 1790s Moss Kent, Jr., began as William
Cooper's protégé, became his foremost political
enemy, and ended the decade as the suitor of his
daughter Hannah. *Moss Kent, Jr.,* 1823, by Samuel F. B. Morse (1791–1872). Courtesy of the New
York State Historical Association, Cooperstown.

n 1789–1791 William Cooper tried to develop maple sugaring as a
ommercial enterprise. The open kettles, hand tools, and wooden troughs
ndicate the crude techniques that helped frustrate his venture. *Women
isiting a Maple-Sugar Camp in the Woods,* by Alexander Anderson. Cour-
esy of the Print Collection, Miriam and Ira D. Wallach Division of Art,
rints and Photographs, The New York Public Library, Astor, Lenox, and
ilden Foundations.

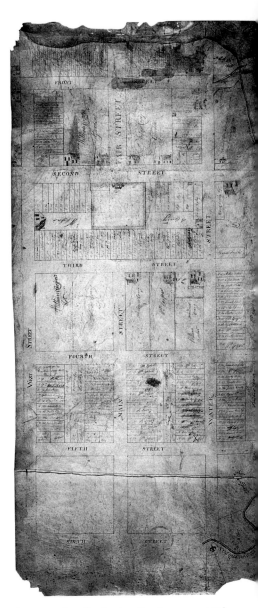

In 1795–1796 Elihu Phinney founded Cooperstown's first newspaper and Freemasonic Lodge. He
prospered from William Cooper's patronage during the mid-1790s but shared in his political downfall in 1799. Phinney turned against his patron and
became a bitter political enemy in 1807. *Elihu Phinney, 1799,* attributed to Ezra Ames (1768–1836).
Courtesy of the New York State Historical Association, Cooperstown.

On the south side of Second Street, the 1788 map
represents several of the small one-story wooden
buildings typical of the early village. Across the
street stands the Manor House; although much
larger in fact, here it appears smaller than the other
structures. Detail from *Map of Cooperstown, 1788,* by
Daniel Smith. Courtesy of Hartwick College
Archives, Oneonta, New York.

A surveyor from Burlington, New Jersey, prepared
this map of Cooperstown to William Cooper's
specifications. His Manor House appears at the
center of the village, on the north side of Second
Street. Elaborate, systematic, and symmetrical,
the map represents Cooper's intentions rather
than the actual village of 1788. Most of the more
than 200 lots remained unoccupied, and no development occurred on Fourth, Fifth, or Sixth
Street during Cooper's lifetime. *Map of Cooperstown, 1788,* by Daniel Smith. Courtesy of Hartwick College Archives, Oneonta, New York.

Based on the 1788 map, this sketch represents the Manor House built by William Cooper. His family, including the infant James, moved into this house in 1790. Courtesy of the New York State Historical Association, Cooperstown.

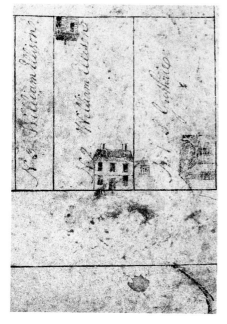

William Ellison's tavern, the oldest in Cooperstown, appears on the west side of the Susquehanna River in this detail from Daniel Smith's 1788 map. Courtesy of Hartwick College Archives, Oneonta, New York.

Apparently William Cooper continued to update Smith's 1788 map, for this detail represents the brewery built beside the bridge on the west bank of the Susquehanna in 1795. The brewery failed in 1800 and a fire destroyed it four years later. Courtesy of Hartwick College Archives, Oneonta, New York.

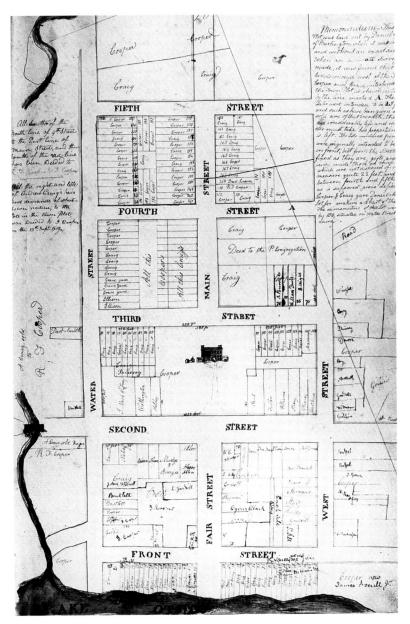

This 1804 map updates and corrects Smith's 1788 map of Cooperstown. In this map, north is at the bottom and south at the top. At the center, the Manor House has been removed and replaced by Otsego Hall, set back from Second Street. On the northwest corner of West Street, Joseph Griffin's tavern lot juts out into Second Street. The academy sits at the southeast corner of West and Third Streets, and the courthouse lies on the northeast corner of West and Second, across from Griffin's tavern. The lakeside tannery of James Averell, Jr., occupies the map's southwestern corner. Most of the many long, thin lots of the 1788 survey and map have been consolidated into fewer, larger lots, contrary to Cooper's intent. *Map of Cooperstown*, c. 1804. Courtesy of the Hartwick College Archives, Oneonta, New York.

This detail from the 1804 map represents Otsego Hall with its outbuildings, four chimneys, and grand entrance. Replacing the Manor House, this grand mansion was built of brick in 1796–1799 to Judge William Cooper's design. Courtesy of the Hartwick College Archives, Oneonta, New York.

Based on the 1804 map, this sketch depicts Otsego Hall. In 1834–1835 James Fenimore Cooper remodeled the mansion in the Gothic Revival style. It burned to the ground in 1853, two years after his death. Courtesy of the New York State Historical Association, Cooperstown.

William Cooper shows his advancing age in this portrait, probably made in his fifty-second year. In contrast to his 1794 portrait, he wears shorter hair and a smaller cravat, in keeping with changing fashion. *Judge William Cooper,* c. 1806, by Ezra Ames (1768–1836). Courtesy of Henry S. F. Cooper, Jr.

Led by William Cooper, the mourning admirers of Hannah Cooper erected this marble monument beside the road where she died, thrown by her horse. *Hannah Cooper's Monument,* 1988 photograph by Milo Stewart. Courtesy of the New York State Historical Association, Cooperstown.

Ezra Ames also made this portrait—similar to the one opposite—of the judge's eldest son, Richard Fenimore Cooper, who appears heavy and older than his thirty-one years. *Richard Fenimore Cooper,* c. 1806, by Ezra Ames (1768–1836). Courtesy of Henry S. F. Cooper, Jr.

A year before her death, the novelist's mother appears in the central hall of "Otsego Hall," with plant boxes and her butler, Joseph Stewart, in the background. *Elizabeth Fenimore Cooper,* 1816, by George Freeman (1789–1868). Courtesy of the New York State Historical Association, Cooperstown.

From the vantage point of Apple Hill, the former estate of the late Richard
Fenimore Cooper, this 1829 painting depicts the Susquehanna River,
with the Cooperstown bridge; village buildings and fences lie in the middle ground; Otsego Lake stretches northward into the distance. Mount
Vision appears to the right; the ascending column of smoke probably
hints at Natty Bumppo's cabin in *The Pioneers*. The elegant women in the
foreground and the carriage on the bridge convey that the landscape
has been domesticated, rendered orderly and genteel. The artist was a
close friend of James Fenimore Cooper. *View from Apple Hill*, c. 1829, by
Samuel F. B. Morse (1781–1872). Courtesy of the New York State Historical Association, Cooperstown.

Above left: Beautiful, vivacious, reckless, and headstrong, Ann Low Cary Cooper helped ruin her husband Richard Fenimore Cooper. Shortly after his death in 1813 she married his friend and her lover, George Hyde Clarke, an English-born gentleman with vast landed estates in New York State. *Mrs. George Hyde Clarke,* 1838, by Charles C. Ingham (1796–1863). Courtesy of the New York State Historical Association, Cooperstown.

Above right: By embracing Republican politics, this handsome young lawyer succeeded where Moss Kent, Jr., had ultimately failed, becoming the dominant lawyer and politician in Coopers-town during the late 1810s and early 1820s. Ambrose Jordan sparred with James Fenimore Cooper in a street fight in 1815 and in the courts during the 1830s and 1840s, defending clients against the novelist's libel suits. *Ambrose Latting Jordan,* by Ezra Ames (1768–1836). Courtesy of Jane Forbes Clark and the New York State Historical Association, Cooperstown.

Left: During the early 1820s this young lawyer and land speculator made himself rich by win-ning legal control of the ruined Cooper estate. *William Holt Averell,* c. 1825, artist unidentified. Courtesy of the New York State Historical Associ-ation, Cooperstown.

The plot of *The Pioneers* opens with Judge Temple's shock at discovering that his bullet has wounded the mysterious young Oliver Edwards instead of killing a disputed deer. Elizabeth Temple occupies the sleigh in the background while a disgruntled Natty Bumppo stands to the side with one of his hunting dogs. Edwards's steely gaze and finely coiffed hair convey his inner gentility, hidden beneath the rags of his coat. By contrast the Judge lacks a genteel demeanor to complement his fur-trimmed coat. *Edwards Showing His Wound to Judge Temple*, drawn for *The Port Folio* (August 1823) by Henry Inman and engraved by Francis Kearney. Courtesy of the American Antiquarian Society, Worcester, Massachusetts.

This 1822 portrait captures James Cooper's commanding self-assurance; that year he wrote *The Pioneers*, upon the heels of his triumph with *The Spy*. *James Fenimore Cooper*, 1822, by John Wesley Jarvis (1780–1840). Courtesy of the New York State Historical Association, Cooperstown.

In a subsequent scene from *The Pioneers*, an amused Billy Kirby watches as the Leatherstocking drives off a terrified Hiram Doolittle, who has come to search the cabin. The painting apparently pleased the Cooper family, for it came into the possession of Susan Fenimore Cooper, probably through the agency of her father, the novelist. *Leatherstocking Meets the Law*, 1832, by John Quidor (1801–1881). Courtesy of the New York State Historical Association, Cooperstown.

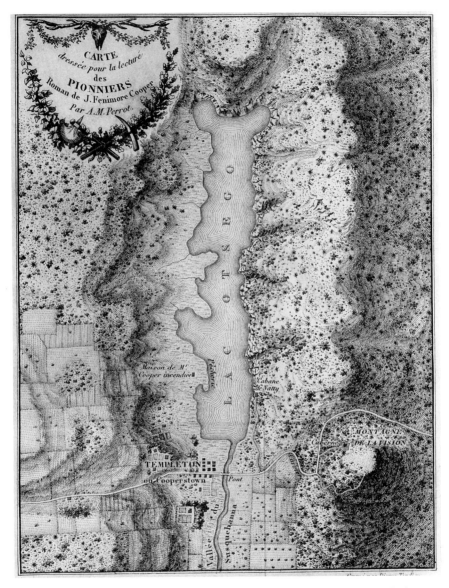

Corrected and approved by James Fenimore Cooper before publication, this map merges the fictional Templeton with the historic Cooperstown. To the east the map represents Mount Vision, including Natty Bumppo's cavern and cabin. To the west the map identifies the site of the novelist's mansion, recently destroyed by fire. *Map Showing the Setting for* The Pioneers, by A. M. Perrot for Volume 18 of *Oeuvres Complètes de J. Fenimore Cooper* (Paris, 1828). Courtesy of the American Antiquarian Society, Worcester, Massachusetts.

This mid-nineteenth-century landscape depicts
Cooperstown and Otsego Lake, looking northward from a vantage point on the western shore.
No longer a wilderness but still not a city, Cooperstown has settled into the quiet prosperity
of the middle landscape that prevailed in the
rural northeast. In the foreground a county
judge, bound on a fishing excursion, strolls
along the dirt road beside a field of hops
and past a tall hemlock that represents the ves-
tigial wild. *Cooperstown from Three Mile Point,* by
Louis Remy Mignot (1831–1870). Courtesy of
the New York State Historical Association,
Cooperstown.

No portrait of Jedediah Peck survives, but this painting represents his legacy: the ascendancy to political power and judicial dignity by middling farmers and artisans. Doubling as a justice, the shoemaker has set aside his tools, but remains attired in his leather work apron as he hears a case, assisted by a jury of fellow commoners and harangued by two finely dressed country lawyers. The justice's posture conveys his informality, but his expression reveals concentration and acuity. The court meets in a tavern that doubles as the local post office; mailboxes can be seen at far left. The man with the bandaged head is evidently the plaintiff in a suit for assault and battery. The subdued man on the far left appears to be the defendant. The artist grew up in Peck's hometown of Burlington, New York. *Justice's Court in the Backwoods,* 1852, by Tompkins Harrison Matteson (1813–1884). Courtesy of the New York State Historical Association, Cooperstown.

sion. Indeed, on January 23, 1800, he voted with a narrow majority to retain the Sedition Act, as he remained blind to the severe damage done to his standing and to his party's fortunes by that ill-conceived law. He also pressed the federal government to secure a supply of the copper needed to sheath the hulls of warships. In April Congress passed his pet bill to send an agent west to seek out, and buy from the Indians, a rumored copper bed on the southern shores of Lake Superior. At Congressman Cooper's request President Adams appointed Richard Fenimore Cooper, the judge's eldest son, as the agent. The scheme united four of Cooper's leading passions: to promote western commercial development, to seek out hidden mines of valuable ores, to sustain the federal military establishment, and to advance the interest of his progeny.[54]

Back home in Otsego Cooper's resignation from the bench and announced retirement from Congress failed to heal the bitter divisions wrought by the Peck and Strong controversies. Indeed, his published notice of retirement provoked an angry retort from an embittered Otsego Federalist—someone close to Joseph Strong, probably Moss Kent, Jr. The author denounced Cooper for imperiling Federalism with his reckless, bombastic, and heavy-handed suppression of critics:

> *Suppose a man in the possession of two very respectable stations, rides through the country as the champion of a political cause, and says to this man, who may not accord with him in opinion, "you are a rascal and a villain"—to that man, "if you do not come into my measures, I will prosecute you"—and to another who proves a little more refractory, "I will put you into the stocks or in jail." Suppose he actually puts these threats into execution . . . what is to become of that cause? Unless these wicked efforts be counteracted by weight of talents and integrity, it must perish.*

The writer assured Cooper, "You can hardly have the vanity and arrogance to believe that any recommendation of yours will be received with any other sentiment than that of the profoundest contempt." The lingering divisions did not bode well for the Federalists in the approaching April 1800 election. Abraham Van Vechten worried, "In the Western District every thing appears at Loose Ends. The Devils Imps are at work, and I dread the result."[55]

THE REPUBLICAN REVOLUTION

Indeed, in April the New York Republicans won a stunning electoral victory, capturing a twenty-seven-seat majority in the assembly and most of the open seats in the state senate (the Federalists retained control of that body because they held most of the seats that were not subject to that election). The two keys to the Republicans' victory were their unprecedented success in New York City and in most of the Western District, both hitherto Federalist

strongholds. In New York City, they benefited from Aaron Burr's resourceful, tireless, and cunning management. In the Western District, the Republicans benefited from the popular backlash against Cooper's arrest of
Jedediah Peck.[56]

By their vicious infighting over patronage and precedence, the New York
Federalists abetted the Republican victory. The feuds in Otsego were all too
typical of Federalist divisions throughout the state. Their jealous bickering
and perverse intrigues belied their claims to be the defenders of stability,
morality, and order. Paradoxically, the Republicans were purposeful, disciplined, and united as they promoted the cause of democratic sovereignty
and decentralized government. On the eve of the Republican victory, a Federalist grimly noted the paradox: "Unfortunately the system of disunion, discord, and disorganization appears to be conducted upon principles of
undeviating perseverance, harmony, and unanimity, while that of peace,
order, and good government is conducted on too many occasions, with neglect, discord, and disorganization." The same paradox characterized the
national struggle as the Republicans hung together while Alexander Hamilton and his fellow hard-liners intrigued to dump the more moderate John
Adams as the Federalists' presidential candidate.[57]

In Otsego the Republicans won a state senate seat and captured three of
the four seats in the assembly. Running for reelection, Jedediah Peck was
the county's leading vote getter. Anticipating defeat, Jacob Morris had declined reelection to the state senate, joining William Cooper and Dr. Joseph
White in forced political retirement. Writing to Cooper, Stephen Van Rensselaer mourned, "Otsego is become Anti-[Federalist]. . . . How the times are
changed since you & I were leaders."[58]

In Otsego the Republican base was a rural hinterland resentful of the
older, larger, wealthier, and more cosmopolitan towns at the county core
around Otsego Lake. The Federalists commanded all four of the core
towns—Middlefield, Cherry Valley, Springfield, and Otsego (which included the village of Cooperstown)—as well as two outposts on the southern periphery, Unadilla and Butternuts, in the vicinity of Jacob Morris. The
Republicans prevailed in eight towns, all on the county's rural fringe:
Burlington, Exeter, Otego, Pittsfield, Plainfield, Richfield, Suffrage (now
Milford), and Worcester. On average the Federalist town was 25 percent
more populous (1,712 versus 1,372) and a bit wealthier ($144 per capita
compared with $128). A tax aggregation for the county indicates the num-
ber of residents per township who owned a gold watch—a mark of wealth
and gentility. The Federalist town averaged seventeen gold watches to eight
for the typical Republican town.[59]

The Republican triumph in New York State had national consequences.
By winning control of the assembly that would dominate the smaller state
senate in jointly choosing the state's twelve presidential electors in the fall,

the New York Republicans provided the critical margin of victory for Thomas Jefferson over the incumbent John Adams. To clinch New York's Republican electoral votes, Jefferson accepted Aaron Burr as his vice presidential candidate. Belatedly the New York Federalists wished they had accepted the Republicans' preelection proposal that New York's voters should choose their presidential electors by district. But Governor Jay rejected Alexander Hamilton's provocative proposal to call the old Federalist state legislature back into session to reopen the issue. Unlike George Clinton in 1792, Governor Jay so cherished his genteel self-control that he could not stoop to stealing an election, no matter how momentous.[60]

When the U.S. Congress reconvened in early 1801, the Federalists had a second, unanticipated opportunity to deny Jefferson the presidency. Because all of the Republican electors cast one vote for Jefferson and one for Burr, the two men finished with an identical number: seventy-three (to Adams's sixty-five). Although the Republican electors intended Jefferson to become president and Burr to become vice president, the United States Constitution did not then permit that distinction in the electoral college voting: the top vote getter was to become president and the second man was to become vice president. According to the Constitution, the tie vote threw the election into the House of Representatives, where the next president had to capture majorities from nine of the then sixteen states. Consequently, the congressional Federalists could determine which of the two Republicans would become president. Detesting his old rival Burr even more than he distrusted Jefferson, Alexander Hamilton urged his fellow Federalists to support the Virginian. But most New York Federalists preferred the devil they knew: Aaron Burr. His new Federalist friends included the lame-duck Congressman William Cooper—who had to set aside a long history of conflicts with Burr, including his attempts in 1786 to prevent the Otsego vendue; his support for the destruction of Otsego's ballots in 1792; and his political seduction of Jedediah Peck in 1798. The politics of 1801 made strange new bedfellows; in 1786, as Cooper's lawyer, Hamilton had opposed Burr, the lawyer for the Croghan heirs; in 1801 Cooper ignored Hamilton to push Burr for the presidency.[61]

Burr played a clever game, lying low at home, neither overtly rejecting nor openly soliciting election as president, but apparently ready to claim the prize if it fell his way. For seven days in mid-February, the House deadlocked. "The suspense is awful," remarked New York congressman Jonas Platt. On February 17, on the thirty-sixth ballot, Jefferson prevailed as a few moderate Federalists gave up the fight and abstained. On March 4, 1801, Jefferson was inaugurated as president. With painful reluctance, the Federalists surrendered the national government, which they had created, to a party that they detested.[62]

The incoming Republican administration was committed to reducing government expenditures and taxes by dismantling most of the civil and military establishments constructed by the Federalist regime. The shrinkage had the fringe benefit of driving hundreds of Federalists from office, depriving them of salaries. One of the first acts of the new administration was to cancel William Cooper's pet project: the western expedition in search of the great copper bed on Lake Superior. The assistant secretary of state recalled Richard Fenimore Cooper just as he was about to embark from Schenectady for the west.[63]

In April 1801 the New York Republicans consolidated their ascent by capturing the governorship. Recognizing his dwindling popularity, Governor Jay declined to stand for reelection, and the Federalists instead ran Stephen Van Rensselaer. The Republicans countered with their old warhorse, George Clinton, who came out of political retirement for the contest. The Federalists mounted a last-ditch struggle on behalf of traditional leadership exercised by a gentleman who united superior education, wealth, manners, connections, and power. The Republicans replied that Clinton's achieved prosperity was a better qualification for office than Van Rensselaer's inherited wealth. The Federalists presented themselves as defending "the peace and order of society" against "the spirit of disorganization" championed by Jacobins. The Republicans countered that the Federalists were aristocratic Loyalists out to betray the Revolution and subvert the Republic by accumulating power and by heaping heavy taxes on the common people. An Otsego Republican, perhaps Jedediah Peck, assured rural voters: "Our *seaport nobility* still cherish the hope, that they shall yet be seated on the backs of their fellow-citizens of the country, . . . and that the free, happy proprietor will become the degraded, wretched *peasant.*"At the polls a large majority rallied to the Republican crusade to cast out the Federalist aristocrats, as Clinton garnered 24,808 votes (54 percent) to Van Rensselaer's 20,843 (46 percent).[64]

Otsego was among the counties with a majority for Clinton—quite a change from 1792, when he had been anathema there. The Republicans won handily by mobilizing as voters an unprecedented proportion of Otsego's white men: 51 percent cast gubernatorial ballots, and 58 percent voted for assemblymen—up from 30 and 42 percent the year before. As in 1800, the Federalists retained majorities in the core towns surrounding Otsego Lake—Otsego (including Cooperstown village), Springfield, Cherry Valley, and Middlefield—while the Republicans captured eight towns, all on the rural periphery, including Burlington, Peck's base. The two exceptions to the pattern were the Federalist and hinterland towns of Butternuts (where Jacob Morris still predominated) and Plainfield (see Map 6). In addition to helping Clinton's victory, the Otsego Republicans captured all four assembly seats, with Jedediah Peck once again leading the pack. That

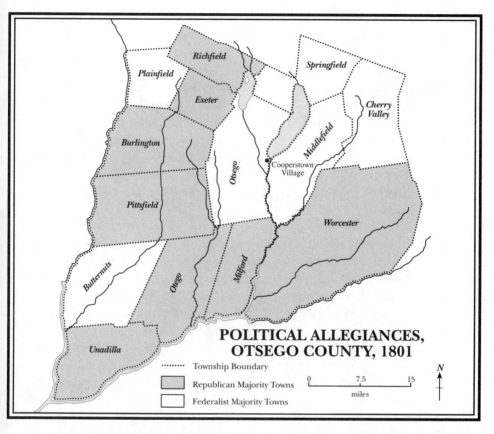

POLITICAL ALLEGIANCES,
OTSEGO COUNTY, 1801

········ Township Boundary

▨ Republican Majority Towns

☐ Federalist Majority Towns

0   7.5   15
miles

N

MAP 6

the Republicans scored even larger majorities in the assembly races than in the gubernatorial voting indicates their special appeal to poor men: to the tenants and marginal freeholders (possessing farms worth less than \$250) who could vote for assemblymen but not for governor. Four-fifths of the Otsego men who voted for the assembly, but not for governor, cast Republican ballots. In Otsego County, Republicanism was primarily a movement of relatively poor, small farmers living in the hinterland.[65]

Having won possession of both houses of the legislature and of the governorship, the Republicans seized control of the Council of Appointment, the great machine for building or destroying political coalitions in New York state. Beginning in August 1801, the council systematically purged Federalist officeholders, from county as well as state posts, installing Republican replacements in reward for their electioneering efforts. One Federalist angrily predicted that the removals would inevitably lead to "confiscation of property, banishment, and loss of life; the period to this state of things is fast approaching." Their excessive dread of impending anarchy, class war, and despotism conveyed their sincere shock at being displaced by men they disdained and dreaded as undeserving and menacing inferiors.[66]

In Otsego County, the council replaced 69 percent of all the civil officeholders (38 of 55), including ten of the eleven major positions: sheriff, county clerk, surrogate, four judges, and four assistant justices. The sacked Federalists included Jacob Morris, Benjamin Gilbert, Elihu Phinney, Joseph White, Joshua Dewey, Francis Henry, and Richard Fenimore Cooper. The county surrogate, Moss Kent, Jr., was the only Otsego Federalist to retain a major office, probably because he had cooperated with Peck to bring down Judge Cooper in 1799–1800. After the purge, 10 of the top 12 officers were Republicans.[67]

Comparing the 36 new appointees with the 38 ousted men reveals the significant transformation wrought in Otsego by the Republican electoral revolution. Otsego's Republican appointees were not a propertyless rabble, but most were small farmers markedly poorer and less cosmopolitan than the Federalists they displaced. Predominant under the Federalist regime, Freemasons lost office under the new. Twenty-one of the 38 purged officers (55 percent) belonged to Cooperstown's Freemasonic Lodge, compared with only 3 of the new men (8 percent). Four-fifths of the new officers (at least 30 of the 36) were farmers, whereas the ousted included many more merchants, landlords, doctors, and lawyers (15 of 38 = 39 percent). According to township tax lists, the average new officer possessed only half as much property as his ousted counterpart: a mean of $1,143 for the new compared with $2,262 for the displaced. Where 31 of the 38 purged officeholders owned property worth at least $1,000, only 13 of the 36 new men did (82 versus 36 percent). Indeed, two of the new Republican justices were landless and penurious, possessed of only $30 and $92 in personal property; such men would never have been appointed under the Federalist regime. Shocked by the fundamental turnover of the county magistracy, Elihu Phinney's *Otsego Herald* mocked the new justices as virtual illiterates.[68]

In Otsego County Freemasonry, superior property, and a commercial occupation were mutually reinforcing in making Federalist leaders. Conversely, a hinterland residence, modest property, and a shared suspicion of villagers, Freemasons, and Federalists combined to draw common but ambitious men to Republicanism. Electoral victory then invested some of them with the honor, income, and influence of county offices previously reserved to men of greater property and wider connections.

Worst of all in Federalist eyes, the Council of Appointment restored Jedediah Peck to the Otsego bench and promoted him to first judge. Worth a modest $1,325 according to Burlington's tax list, Peck owned less than a third of the property enjoyed by his immediate predecessor, Dr. White ($4,687), and a mere hundredth of the riches possessed by Otsego's original first judge, William Cooper ($131,720). Elevation to the county's pre-eminent post of honor was a sweet triumph for a common man summarily dismissed by his Federalist enemies just two years earlier. Where William Cooper had presided, there now sat Jedediah Peck. The Father of the People had given way to the Friend of the People.[69]

In April 1804 Peck successfully tested his ascent by running for the state senate and defeating the most popular Federalist in the county: Moss Kent, Jr. Peck captured majorities in eleven of the fifteen towns, garnering 1,399 votes (61 percent) to Kent's 891 (39 percent). No one, not even Kent could match Peck's popularity in Otsego County. In reward for this victory the Republican legislators placed Peck on the Council of Appointment, the great instrument of power in the state. Peck promptly exploited his new position to remove his old enemy Jacob Morris as the brigadier general in command of the Otsego militia.[70]

As first judge, state senator, and councillor of appointment, Jedediah Peck had become the most influential man in Otsego County. "For many years he controlled the politics of the county, put up and put down who he pleased," Levi Beardsley recalled. Federalists could neither comprehend nor bear the elevation of Peck and his like. One incredulous Federalist complained, "There is a Senator from the County of Otsego who can scarcely write a line without misspelling a word. . . . And yet this man is one of the judges of the County Court."[71]

Many Republican leaders proved to be mere opportunists and office-seekers, but Jedediah Peck remained a committed and consistent democrat, both honest and tireless in his dedication to the common people. In the legislature Peck pressed vigorously for measures meant to enhance the economic prosperity and to protect the political sovereignty of ordinary farmers and artisans. He urged the popular election of presidential electors, the subdivision of the vast state senatorial districts, the abolition of imprisonment for debt, the emancipation of slaves in New York, and protection for the settlers in the Military Tract from eviction by land speculators with suspect titles. He also pressed his concern for public morality by proposing legislation to require daily Bible readings in schools and to stiffen the criminal penalties for adultery and dueling. Unfortunately, most other Republican politicians showed increasing concern for their incomes and a dwindling dedication to the common interest. In 1805 Peck defiantly resisted the bribes proffered by the lobbyist for a Federalist bank seeking legislative incorporation; but many of his more venal Republican colleagues eagerly accepted the offers and passed the bill.[72]

Peck's greatest and most enduring cause was to secure state funding for common schools. His dedication to public education for common people derived from his own experience, from the self-confidence and upward mobility that he had acquired by reading. Public education would, he promised, "bring improvement within the reach and power of the humblest citizen." He regarded widespread, free access to education as essential for the Republic to endure. Peck reasoned that European monarchs and aristocrats dominated and exploited their common people by keeping them poor and ignorant. "In all countries, where education is confined to a few people, we always find arbitrary governments and abject slavery." Therefore, only an educated people would protect and sustain the republican government that alone could preserve their prosperity and liberty. While pushing for common school funding, Peck resisted Federalist counterproposals to increase instead the state subsidies paid to academies and colleges, small private institutions that primarily benefited the sons of gentlemen. No doubt thinking of the Cooperstown lawyers, Peck lamented that so many college graduates became "greedy speculators and miserable tools of ambition, the greatest enemies to industry and peace, which this or any other country ever produced." Almost every year, Peck sponsored bills to increase state subsidies for common schools, finally obtaining in 1812 a comprehensive program for public financing based on his report.[73]

In 1824 the state's geographer, Horatio Gates Spafford, paid tribute to his late friend, Jedediah Peck, as the paragon of popular republicanism:

> *Judge Peck was a man of humble pretensions to talents, and still more humble learning; but of principles as firm and incorruptible, uniformly, through a long life, as ever any man possessed, in any country or in any age. There was a pure principle of honest patriotism about him, that made him quite obnoxious to certain dictators; and the youth of this republic should be reminded of the sneers of a class of politicians, anxious to put him out of their way, who vainly strove to fix all sorts of imputations and odium on [his] character. . . . Youth of the Republic! He enjoyed a complete triumph, lived to see it, and his memory lives in honor, committed to your safe keeping, an instructive lesson for your remembrance.*[74]

In 1800–1801 New Yorkers experienced the transfer of power from Federalists to Republicans as a profound social and political watershed. An Albany resident remembered, "So great was the change, and so sudden the turn of the executive wheel, that the event was felt through all the ramifications of society, and the period became as memorable as that of the birth of the nation." In particular, the Republicans effected two momentous transformations: the creation of a political party and the construction of a new democratic political culture.[75]

First, the Republican upstarts developed a political party united by ideological commitment to democratic sovereignty and ready to oust those who put individual ambition ahead of party unity. The Federalists had never developed a true political party because they perpetuated the traditional, elitist politics of making interest characterized by the volatile alliances of leading men unable to build mutual confidence. Because Republicans lacked the private wealth essential to constructing a traditional interest, they had to innovate by creating a party framework of committees and conventions that transcended county lines to determine candidates and to turn out the vote. The political party enabled men of common means, like Jedediah Peck, to compete and win in the multicounty state senate districts. Indeed, the Republicans were so successful at statewide coordination that they quietly dropped Peck's call for subdividing of the great senatorial districts.[76]

Second, the Republican triumph transformed the standards for public honor and office. During the 1790s the Federalists had convinced most of the voters that elections were primarily meant to confirm the accomplishments and acquisitions of gentility. The people were supposed to choose between gentlemen and then defer to their superior judgment in office. In 1800–1801 the Republicans triumphed by persuading the majority that professed friendship for the people was the proper and fundamental basis for authority. All other considerations—of wealth, birth, connections, manners, even education—were either irrelevant or actually menacing to the republic of common men. Men of private gentility could still win office, but only by publicly downplaying their fine manners, only by flaunting their public comfort with the company of common men. Elections almost invariably turned on who could best depict the opposition as crypto-aristocrats out to corrupt the Republic. The social order did not become more equal in the early nineteenth century, and that inequality remained a persistent source of popular unease. The most skilled political managers periodically mobilized, exercised, and channeled the unease, projecting the blame for persistent social distinctions onto plausible villains. In the process the new political rhetoric perpetuated republican ideals without affecting the social inequality that compromised them.[77]

The democratization of American politics transformed beyond recognition the imperatives that had induced William Cooper and James Cochran to pummel one another in a Cooperstown street in 1799. In the 1840s Benson J. Lossing visited upstate New York, gathering information for his history of the American Revolution and the early Republic. He called upon an aged and ailing James Cochran to inquire after his political career. In reply Cochran boasted that he had "fiddled himself into Congress" in 1796. The same words that had so insulted his gentility in 1799 had become, by the 1840s, his badge of democratic honor. In memory Cochran reinvented himself as just the sort of democrat he had fought against in the 1790s. The fighting words of 1799 were now his own boast as he entertained a visitor from a new century seeking information about a dying generation.[78]

DENIAL &

In *The Pioneers* James Fenimore Cooper remembered, encoded, and modi-
fied the painful events of 1799–1801 that undercut his father's prestige and
authority. As in so much of the novel, Cooper felt impelled both to recall
the alarming and to reshape it into a more reassuring form. The novelist
mourned that he had been deprived of his proper inheritance: social, economic, cultural, and political authority combined in the hands of genteel
families. What his father had lost in the Otsego of 1799–1801, James Fenimore Cooper meant to revive in the Templeton of fiction.[79]

The action in the novel ostensibly begins in December 1793 and continues into October of the next year, but the novelist constructed Templeton
from his memories of people, buildings, and events in Cooperstown from
throughout the 1790s. Templeton includes the newspaper and academy
that Cooperstown acquired in 1795 and 1797, and the novelist's depiction
of the Mansion House interior actually describes the Otsego Hall of 1799.
Moreover, the Templeton villagers display a growing insubordination that
derives from the Otsego of 1799 rather than from that of 1793–94, when
William Cooper's popularity and power were at their pinnacle. James Fenimore Cooper signals the association of the novel's plot with the political
troubles of 1799 by including the arrest and incarceration of a gang of hinterland counterfeiters, as happened outside Cooperstown in October of
1799. The historic counterfeiters' escape by cutting through the jail's log
walls with outside assistance also informs Natty's similar escape in the novel.
As part of his memory management, the novelist transposed in fiction the
unchecked discontents of 1799 back to an earlier, more tractable place in
time—the Cooperstown of 1793–94—when the historic judge could have
restored order as the fictional judge eventually does in *The Pioneers*.[80]

The principal characters in Otsego's political drama of 1799 have close
counterparts in *The Pioneers*. Dirck Van Der School derives closely from
Abraham C. Ten Broeck, the dull, pedantic, and hypercautious lawyer of
Dutch ancestry. Van Der School replicates Ten Broeck down to their common tic, in writing and speech, of piling qualification upon qualification by
nesting parentheses within parentheses. As the sly and insinuating Yankee
lawyer, Chester Lippett represents Joseph Strong. Lippett agitates in the tavern, trying to foment a lawsuit against Judge Temple—just as Strong solicited Ebenezer Sherman to sue Judge Cooper in 1799, instigating the
confrontation that culminated in Cooper's downfall.[81]

Of course, Judge Marmaduke Temple is but the thinnest of veils thrown
over the author's memory of Judge William Cooper. Like Judge Cooper,
Judge Temple steadily loses power to subordinates who abuse his patronage

and indulgence. Temple recognizes that the law has been cheapened in Otsego by the indiscriminate and excessive lawsuits promoted by litigious settlers, corrupt lawyers, and greedy justices. Judge Cooper's disgust with Joseph Strong's barratry appears when Temple declares, "Nothing gives me more pain, than to see my settlers wasting their time and substance in the unprofitable struggles of the law." Similarly, in *A Guide in the Wilderness* William Cooper denounced "a spirit of litigation" as "mischievous" and "shameful" because "time and money are spent, which if well employed would have added to the comfort of the family, and increased the stock of the farm."[82]

In *The Pioneers* Moss Kent, Jr., appears as Oliver Edwards—both handsome and high-strung young gentlemen quick to detect and resent an insult to their honor. Edwards enters Judge Temple's mansion and office as his guest and agent, just as Kent took up residence in the Manor House as Cooper's protégé in 1794. Eventually, Edwards storms out after a tiff with Judge Temple very much like the falling-out between Cooper and Kent in July of 1796. And Edwards becomes enamored of Judge Temple's cherished daughter Elizabeth, just as Kent aspired to marry Judge Cooper's beloved daughter Hannah. Although Edwards strikes most contemporary readers as insufferably arrogant, he represents Cooper's ideal of the young gentleman utterly contemptuous of bourgeois equivocation. The chief difference between Edwards and Kent is that Edwards is not specifically a lawyer. An idealized gentleman, he is so perfectly above all truck with commerce that he has no occupation, no particular profession. In crafting Edwards, the novelist paid homage to Kent's conceit that he disdained mere money.[83]

A resident in the Cooper household for nearly three years, Kent was idolized by the impressionable young James Cooper, who was four years old when the dashing lawyer arrived, in 1794, and seven in early 1797, when he moved out. Young Cooper began calling himself "James Kent Cooper" (he did not then have any legal middle name). Indeed, the earliest surviving piece of Cooper's writing is a letter to his father composed on March 3, 1800, and signed James K. Cooper. By identifying with William Cooper's rival, the then ten-year-old boy seems to have been declaring psychological independence from his real father. In *The Pioneers* Cooper reaffirmed his identification with Kent and his ambivalence toward his father by subtly favoring Edwards in his struggle with Temple for possession of Otsego.[84]

In *The Pioneers* Hiram Doolittle plays the Jedediah Peck role (as understood by James Fenimore Cooper): the frontier jack-of-all-trades, long on Yankee cunning but short on legal principle. The novelist inverted Peck's appearance to craft Doolittle as tall and gaunt with sharp features, but both men, the fictional and the historic, had faces "that expressed formal propriety, mingled with low cunning." Cooper recalled Peck in Federalist terms as an impertinent upstart promoted to offices beyond his limited abilities and low character.[85]

In his representation of Doolittle, the novelist elliptically remembered Jedediah Peck's challenge to William Cooper's authority in 1799. Adept at manipulating men of slower wits and greater morality—men who cannot anticipate his intrigues—Doolittle slyly maneuvers the ponderous Judge Temple into issuing a warrant for Natty Bumppo's arrest. With equal cunning Doolittle recruits Billy Kirby as a deputy, before revealing that his duty will be to arrest his friend, the Leather-Stocking. By flattering and treating Kirby "as if he were an equal," Doolittle secures his uninformed consent. These two manipulations—of Temple and Kirby—symbolically convey the novelist's understanding of what happened in Otsego, and indeed the nation, in 1799–1801. James Fenimore Cooper suggested that his father was too slow to counteract the insidious ambitions and intrigues of his supposed ally, Jedediah Peck. Too late William Cooper realized the abilities of domestic demagogues to acquire power by flattering and deceiving a gullible public (Kirby). The novelist fundamentally misunderstood his father's downfall: in fact, William Cooper lost because he tried vigorously to suppress Peck not because the judge was too indulgent for too long. The novelist's reworked memory inverts the conflict between Cooper and Peck by making Doolittle the instigator, instead of the victim, of legal persecution.[86]

The novel betrays the rage that the novelist felt toward Peck and his ilk for undermining the public authority of gentility, in general, and of the Coopers, in particular. In three scenes, the novelist took vicarious revenge by inflicting brutal beatings on Hiram Doolittle. Cooper narrates all three in an odd mélange of gruesome detail and happy-go-lucky celebration. First, when Doolittle tries to force his way into Natty's cabin, the Leather-Stocking seizes the justice, hurling him twenty feet in the air and over an embankment. Later, in front of a crowd at the courthouse, Benjamin Pump pummels the justice, working "away with great industry and a good deal of skill, at his occupation using one hand to raise up his antagonist, while he knocked him over with the other. . . . By this considerate arrangement, he had found means to hammer the visage of Hiram out of all shape." Third, when the village militia besieges Natty's cave, the Leather-Stocking shoots Doolittle in his hindquarters, inflicting both pain and humiliation—which Cooper again described in a jocular manner. In addition to venting the novelist's animus, these fictional assaults may recall that Peck was "abused in the Execution of his office as magistrate" in 1795 and had his nose twisted by Jacob Morris in 1796.[87]

In the body of the novel, James Fenimore Cooper unleashed the common malcontents to wreak havoc, but ultimately he indulged in historical denial and wish fulfillment. At the end, a bruised and battered Doolittle must flee in defeat upon discovering "that neither his architecture, nor his law, was quite suitable to the growing wealth and intelligence of the settlement." He proceeds farther west to some newer, poorer, and more ignorant settlement still vulnerable to his legal and architectural follies. Instead of overthrowing the judge and democratizing public culture as Peck did in the historical Otsego, Doolittle abandons Otsego to the aristocratic rule of Oliver and Elizabeth—the happiest of fictional endings for James Fenimore Cooper.[88]

Part III

LEGACIES

Chapter Eleven

HANNAH

ALTHOUGH POLITICALLY DEFEATED and publicly dishonored, Cooper was still a very wealthy man after 1799, collecting the annual revenues from hundreds of settlers living on thousands of acres that he had sold or rented. According to tax assessments, in 1800 his property within Otsego Township alone amounted to $33,260—more than six times as much property as the next richest man in town. Adding Cooper's extensive real estate in Butternuts ($68,000), Burlington ($10,710), Milford ($1,085), Otego ($13,750), and Pittsfield ($4,915) raises his total wealth within Otsego County to $131,720. According to his own records, Cooper possessed an additional $77,429 in real estate elsewhere in New York and Pennsylvania, as well as bonds and mortgages from settlers to secure $162,312 in principal. Although politically disgraced, William Cooper could still dress in fine silk clothes, ride in a carriage, drink imported wines, and dwell in the grandest house in New York west of Albany. Contrary to the Federalists' paranoia, the advent of white male democracy did not bring about any leveling of property, any dispossession of the wealthy, any redistribution of land. Cooper exemplified the overt separation of public authority from private wealth that was the great transformation wrought in the northern states by the Republicans' "Revolution of 1800." He remained wealthy, but political honor passed to upstarts such as Jedediah Peck: a new breed of professional politicians, full-time Friends of the People.[1]

Painful experience gradually taught Cooper that the cultivation of personal gentility required at least two generations. After his political debacle, Cooper increasingly looked to his seven children to complete the social ascent that he had begun but could not finish. In 1800 his offspring were two daughters, Hannah (b. 1777) and Ann (b. 1784), and five sons: Richard

> *"Then, sir," said Elizabeth, with an air that was slightly affected, as if submitting to her father's orders in opposition to her own will, "it is your pleasure that [Oliver] be a gentleman."*
>
> *"Certainly; he is to fill the station of one; let him receive the treatment that is due to his place, until we find him unworthy of it."*
>
> *"Well, well, 'duke," cried the Sheriff, "you will find it no easy matter to make a gentleman of him. The old proverb says, 'that it takes three generations to make a gentleman.'"*
>
> —*James Fenimore Cooper,* The Pioneers, *205*

Fenimore (b. 1775), Isaac (b. 1781), William Jr. (b. 1786), Samuel (b. 1787), and James (b. 1789). The judge would provide the money, education, and contacts while they were to acquire the proper social style and acceptance that still eluded him. They began with the advantages that Cooper had to accumulate through economic struggle. By investing his wealth in their education, Cooper hoped to repurchase for his lineage the public authority and prestige that he had lost so suddenly in 1799. He expected his children to redeem his dream of uniting all forms of power—social, economic, political, and cultural—as Otsego's reigning family. "Nothing can be more interesting to me than to make you Happy," William Cooper assured his son Isaac in 1804.[2]

However, by training his children in gentility Judge Cooper unwittingly produced a cultural distance between the generations. They made their way into genteel circles that regarded William Cooper with condescension or suspicion. As Cooper's children mastered refined mores and manners, they began to see their father as a bumptious upstart, as well-meaning but lamentably common. The patronizing portrayal of Marmaduke Temple in *The Pioneers* was the fruit of William Cooper's investment in the genteel education of his son James. The novelist longed to assert his superior gentility by demonstrating that he recognized the moral and cultural flaws of his arriviste father. Marmaduke Temple appears well-intentioned, but inconsistent and ineffectual; and his estate appears suspect until entrusted, at the conclusion, to the next generation who more truly deserve to be rich and influential.[3]

The novelist described the interior of Temple's thoroughly bourgeois mansion as manifesting wealth without taste. Determined to impress, without knowing the importance of restraint, Temple overstuffs the rooms with garish ornaments and clumsy furniture characterized by "diversity of taste and imperfection of executions." His ill-trained servants overset the dining table so that "there was scarcely a spot where the rich damask could be seen, so crowded were the dishes, with their associated bottles, plates and saucers. The object seemed to be profusion, and it was obtained entirely at the expense of order and elegance." Closely derived from memory of Otsego Hall, the novelist's description of Temple's household passed derisive judgment on William Cooper's faulty gentility.[4]

In his depiction of Judge Temple, James Fenimore Cooper expressed ambivalence and condescension, rather than anger, toward his father. As William Cooper's heir, the novelist felt torn. On the one hand, he needed to reaffirm the legitimacy of his father's enterprise and acquisitions as the basis for his own inheritance and status. On the other hand, he had to cope with the dilemma of the wealthy scion—that he could never match his father's achievements. Born into riches, James Fenimore Cooper could never rise from rags. Rather than accept that implicit inferiority to his father, the novelist cultivated an aristocratic contempt for the bourgeois striving that had made the judge rich.[5]

EXPECTATIONS

William Cooper wanted his children to master the elitist political principles that he had adopted during the 1790s. Determined to preserve his sons from democratic notions, in 1802 Judge Cooper took offense at something said or done by Oliver Corey, the village schoolteacher (at that time Samuel Cooper was probably studying with Corey). Recognizing his dependence on Cooper's patronage, Corey quickly apologized, adding: "[However,] as I have ever been invariably a sincere friend, and wellwisher to you, and your worthy family (admitting that I have done wrong in this instance,) I think I have a just claim to your pardon; if not to a share in your future friendship. As to my political principle, I can assure you, that I ever have been and still continue to be as true a Federalist, as is possible for a poor person to be." The Cooper papers also include a child's penmanship exercise with a political moral: "If I had a dog that had not more modesty than a Democrat, I would shoote him. There is not one of them but thinks himself fit for any Office in the United States—a devilish likely set of fellows to be sure aint they? ha! ha!! ha!!! 1801." The hand is probably that of the youngest son, and future novelist, James, then an eleven-year-old boy. Twenty-two years later James Cooper explained to a friend, "You know my antipathies, as you please to call them, to Mr. Jefferson. I was brought up in that school where his image seldom appeared, unless it was clad in red breeches, and where it was always associated with the idea of infidelity and political heresy." All five of the judge's sons became Federalists active in electioneering letters, meetings, and committees. But none ever ran for office, recognizing the lingering unpopularity of their family name in Otsego politics.[6]

Much of the children's education in gentility occurred at home, in the Manor House and Otsego Hall. The surviving evidence suggests an affectionate and playful but teasing household that took its cues from their sociable father's delight in jokes, poetry, and stories. James Fenimore Cooper fondly recalled his "noble looking, warm hearted, witty father, with his deep laugh, sweet voice and fine rich eye, as he used to lighten the way, with his anecdote and fun." Discussing the strong Yankee accent that he encountered at Yale College, James Fenimore Cooper recalled an incident characteristic of life in Otsego Hall:

> When I was a boy, I was sent from a middle state, for my education, to Connecticut. I took with me, of course, the language of my father's house. In the first year I was laughed out of a great many correct sounds, and into a great many vulgar and disagreeable substitutes. At my return home to pass a vacation, I

almost threw a sister into fits by calling one of her female friends a "virtoous an-
gel," pronouncing the first syllable of the last word like the article. It was in vain
that I supported my new reading by the authorities of the university. The whole
six weeks were passed in hot discussion between my sister and myself, amidst the
laughter and merriment of a facetious father, who had the habit of trotting me
through my Connecticut prosody by inducing me to recite Pope's Temple of
Fame, to the infinite delight of two or three waggish elder brothers, who had got
their English longs and shorts in a more southern school.

The Cooper household was usually a setting of comfort, laughter, and sociability. "To be good and happy is what we live for," daughter Hannah explained in 1799. Two years later James Kent spent a week at Otsego Hall "in
the midst of agreable company & amusement."[7]

Richard R. Smith fondly recalled his stay in the Cooper household as the
best four years of his life. In 1794 he departed the Manor House and Cooperstown for Philadelphia to pursue his interest as a merchant. Thereafter,
he rued his decision and dreamed in vain of returning. From his new home
he assured his old friend, "I believe I shall make more money by the exchange of place, but hang me if I expect more happiness. . . . I often think
of Mrs. C[ooper]'s kindness to me with gratitude and pleasure. I hope she
enjoys health." Smith especially missed the Cooper boys: "Kiss the dear little Children for me. Tell them I certainly shall remember to send them
something whenever I have an opportunity. It grieves me that I can't stop
and help you eat a Turkey or so of a Sunday. Remember me most affectionately to the Lads, tell them I often think of them and wish I could take
a Rubber or two."[8]

Determined to construct a genteel setting, Cooper accumulated refined
clothing, dishes, furniture, ornaments, books, food and drink, servants and
slaves. The family's most prized possession was a large upright mechanical
organ that Cooper bought in New York City and had transported over rivers
and hills to Cooperstown. Like a player piano, the organ piped loud, cheerful music whenever someone inserted one of its long, heavy wooden rolls
and turned the handle. The organ's arrival caused a sensation as its music
first wafted through the compact little village, which had never before
known any mechanically produced music. Oliver Corey quickly adjourned
his class at the village academy to hasten with his students to the bounds of
Otsego Hall, the better to hear the astonishing new sound. Placed in the
central hall and played almost every evening, the organ became central to
the Coopers' social activity at Otsego Hall. On July 12, 1800, Hannah wrote
to her younger brother William Jr., then away at college: "It is very late at
night, nobody in the House up save myself and Mama, who is playing upon
the Organ. This amusement engages her every night after the family have
seperated, and a very pretty effect it has being not unlike a Serenade." She
added, "Our Fourth of July passed very brilliantly away. . . . The Lads and

Lasses repaired in the evening to our House and we had quite a large party to dance," apparently to the organ's music.[9]

During the summers Judge Cooper entertained genteel friends venturing out from Philadelphia, Burlington, Albany, and New York City to see the countryside. He relished these visits as occasions to delight his friends and as opportunities to introduce his children to urbane people. Their visits usually occasioned a "lake party," a day trip in the family boats to their favorite picnic grounds: Myrtle Grove, located at Three Mile Point on the lake's western shore, where William Cooper had the underbrush cleared and a small cottage erected. There the Coopers, the guests, and their servants took in the clear air, green hills, and translucent waters; ate and drank; napped and fished; and cut their initials in a large and cherished beech tree. Writing from Philadelphia in 1802, Richard R. Smith fondly recalled his summers with the Coopers: "I sometimes fancy myself of a warm day, upon a lake excursion, partaking of the social *Sap Cyder* under the Shady Trees—But this is a kind of ranting."[10]

The labor of slaves made much of this comfort, ease, and pleasure possible for the Coopers and their guests. New York's gradual emancipation law of 1799 did not entirely free the state's slaves until July 4, 1827. Enslaved African-Americans were few in Cooperstown: only seven in 1803, approximately 2 percent of the village population; and only five of the village's sixty-two households included a slave. Despite William Cooper's origins among the Quakers, who denounced and worked against slavery, he owned enslaved Blacks: one in 1790 and three in 1803 according to village censuses. The one of 1790 was probably the "wench" Rachel, who, according to a shoemaker's bill, obtained a new pair of shoes in December of 1792. James Fenimore Cooper recalled the three of 1803 as Joseph Stewart, a butler; "Sarah, the cook; and Betty, the chambermaid." The Coopers prized their slaves as domestic servants and status symbols rather than as agricultural workers.[11]

The best known of the Coopers' Black servants was Joseph Stewart, who eventually became free but continued to serve the family for over twenty years as a butler and valet. He may have been the "negro boy Joseph" whom William Cooper rented from Abraham C. Ten Broeck for $76 to $80 a year between late 1799 and mid-1802. The Coopers called Stewart "the Governor" in mock honor of his dignified manner. A tall, slender, and well-dressed Stewart appears on the background fringe of the 1816 George Freeman portrait of Elizabeth Cooper in Otsego Hall. Paying homage to Stewart in death, the Coopers permitted his burial in their own family plot rather than in the corner reserved in the segregated village cemetery for Blacks.[12]

Apparently at least one of the slaves resented and resisted her status. In August 1799 William Cooper placed an anonymous advertisement in the *Otsego Herald:*

A YOUNG WENCH FOR SALE. *She is a good Cook, and ready at all kinds of house-work—None can exceed her if she is kept from Liquor. She is twenty-four years of age—No Husband or Children. Price two hundred dollars. Inquire of the Printer.*

Determined, like Judge Temple in *The Pioneers,* to mask his slaveholding, Cooper carefully kept his name out of the newspaper, using the printer as a broker in the sale. Only Elihu Phinney's account billing for this notice identifies the judge as the woman's owner. The surviving evidence does not reveal her name or whether and when she was sold, merely that the advertisement ceased to run after the October 3 issue. Perhaps the threat of sale served to intimidate her into docility. In January of 1800 Hannah Cooper assured her absent father that order had been restored in the household: "The servants conduct themselves with unusual propriety—we have had no squabbles since you left us."[13]

TRAINING

Servants, fine possessions, and genteel visitors were not sufficient to give the Cooper children the full social polish and knowledge they needed for elite status. Because genteel families were few in Cooperstown and because its academy had failed to become more than a country grammar school, the children had to go away for schooling in more urbane towns and cities: Burlington, Philadelphia, New York, Albany, and Schenectady. Ambitious for his children, Cooper had to sacrifice their company for several months a year, usually during the long winters, when gentility rarely visited Otsego. Not sharing her husband's social aspirations, Elizabeth Cooper was uneasy with the prolonged absences of one or more of her sons and daughters at almost any given time. Moreover, her husband often got to see the absent children during his visits to the cities for business and politics, while Elizabeth remained behind in Cooperstown.

The children left home at an early age. Hannah Cooper spent the winters of 1791–92 and 1792–93 in New York City, apparently boarding with the family of the merchant William Wade. She was fourteen going on fifteen. Isaac had just turned thirteen in late 1794, when he first went away to school in Burlington, staying with the old family friend, Andrew Craig. On the way south, escorted by Richard R. Smith, Isaac saw his sister Ann, who was wintering with friends in New York City. She was ten years old. Homesick, she wrote: "I hope my dear papa will soon write to me, for I am very anxious to hear from home."[14]

By mastering genteel manners and learning, the children were supposed to win applause from elite families of discernment, which would reflect well on their father. Diligent and endearing, the Cooper children pleased the judge by delighting their urban hosts and teachers. In 1794 ten-year-old Ann wrote home from New York City: "Dear Papa, I have begun to learn dancing, and am very much pleased with it. I hope to improve in this and every part of my education. I remain dear Papa and Mama, your dutiful daughter." After visiting Ann (who was commonly called Nancy), Richard R. Smith reported to her father: "She has grown to be a charming Girl. . . . I mean that she has improved." He added that in the city, "everybody is pleased with Nancy."[15]

Because the Cooper children went away so early for such prolonged sojourns, their teachers and hosts assumed much of their upbringing. In October 1791 Josiah Ogden Hoffman, a prominent New York City attorney, lavished praise on Hannah in a letter to his friend William Cooper:

> *We had your charming daughter to pass the day with us yesterday. My good Lady & her two sisters are greatly pleased with her. Her manners are easy, her conversations lively, and her deportment ingratiating. . . . We consider her entirely as one of the family and you would have smiled to have seen our quick intimacy. Mr. and Mrs. were soon changed into Papa and Mama. We have adopted her and she us. Take care, lest we truly supplant you. I know not what arrangements you made here, as to her supplies, cash, clothes, &c. I can only say [that] I, in this respect, proffer to you my services. I should then be in reality her second Parent.*

Nothing could have delighted Cooper more than Hannah's success at dazzling her elite host and hostesses, but there was a price: he had to share her with distant, surrogate parents who might displace him in her affections.[16]

Because the essence of gentility was the keen perception of, and sharp disdain for, the common, the Cooper children learned to see the social flaws in their father and his village. In 1795 the celebrated duc de Talleyrand, then a refugee from the French Revolution, visited Cooperstown, lodging in the Manor House. Taken with young Hannah Cooper's charm and mind, he penned a poem that exalted her as too refined for her frontier setting (the poem is also an acrostic; read down, the first letter of each line spells Anna Cooper, as Hannah often called herself):

> *Aimable philosophe au printemps de son age,*
> *Ni les temps ni les lieux n'alterent son esprit.*
> *Ne cedent qu'a ces gouts, simple et sans etalage*
> *Au milieu des deserts, Elle lit—pense—ecrit.*
> *Cultivez, Belle Anna, votre gout pour l'etude;*
> *On ne saurait ici mieux employer son temps.*
> *Otsego n'est pas gai—mais tout est habitude;*
> *Paris vous deplairait fort au premier moment.*
> *Et qui jouit de soi dans une solitude,*
> *Rentrant au monde, est sur d'en faire l'ornement.*

Absorbing this message, Hannah wrote a revealing letter to a friend in
Philadelphia in September 1799. After years of schooling and sociability in
urban centers, Hannah feared that she would be stranded for the approaching winter in remote Otsego. Her dutiful attempts to put the best
face on the prospect only convey her real unhappiness:

> I do not know when I shall again emerge from these northern forests. My sister
> sets a noble example. She is willing to remain at home through the winter pro-
> vided I will. Upon mature consideration, perhaps a more perfect knowledge of
> society is not very necessary to her happiness. By being insensible to her own de-
> ficiencies, she will be less observant of the deficiencies of those around her.

Gentility was the art of seeing the common in others and of repressing it in
yourself.[17]

SENSIBILITY

By all accounts Hannah was the most lovely, graceful, charming, accomplished, and cherished of the Cooper children. She had an ethereal quality.
"Her cheeks were usually colorless, her hair was almost *flaxen,* and her form
was the extreme of lightness and delicacy," recalled her brother James. To
virtual perfection she learned, embodied, and lived the ideals of feminine
gentility: Hannah was chaste, polite, articulate, empathetic, pious, benevolent, and well-read, yet modest. She reached the pinnacle of gentility: such
mastery of its elaborate artifices that they seemed natural and unaffected.[18]

When in New York City or Philadelphia, Hannah thoroughly charmed
her genteel hosts—men and women, young and old. After she left, they
wrote letters longing for her news and her return. Mary Daubeny of New
York City wrote to William Cooper, "How is my Dear Hannah? I hope well
and Happy for I really Love her, so do my Girls and every Body that knows
[her]." Members of the Federalist elite looked more favorably on William
Cooper because of their delight in Hannah. Cooper brought her to
Philadelphia during his congressional sessions, so that he could introduce
her to that city's elite and so that her charms could reflect well upon him.
Learning that Hannah was in New York City awaiting passage to Philadelphia, U.S. Senator Uriah Tracy of Connecticut wrote to her father: "I shall
be very glad to oblige you & her, by any attention & assistance I can give, in
her passage to Philadelphia." Hannah looms far larger than her mother or
any of her siblings in the letters received by her father.[19]

Talented and devoted, Hannah earned the devout affection of her female friends. In early 1800 Eliza McDonald (the daughter of Rev. John Mc-
Donald) learned that Hannah had begun to correspond with their mutual
friend Chloe Fuller. Eliza quickly and enthusiastically wrote to Chloe: "Your

sister tells me Miss Cooper has written to you. Fail not Chloe in answering it. Her friendship is a blessing, her correspondence an Improvement. She is, I think, a pious, sensible, amiable and accomplished woman! I admire her much. I almost envy you the privilege of her correspondence." Eliza and Chloe considered Hannah to be their "pious pattern."[20]

Hannah earned a saintly reputation for her charity and piety. She exhorted herself to humility and service, "whilst there breathes an human being whom we can assist by our advice, relieve by our alms or encourage with our approbation, to whom our pity can supply comfort and our affection pleasure." She called at the homes of the village poor, delivering donations of food and clothing, and she frequently visited the county jail to distribute religious tracts and to exhort the prisoners to adopt "the truths of morality and religion." After helping a family who had fled to Cooperstown from a yellow fever epidemic in New York City, Hannah explained, "My heart aches for them and for every unprotected person or wanderer."[21]

During the late 1790s, within the Cooper household Hannah increasingly filled the role of hostess and mother left void by Elizabeth Cooper's lack of gentility and recurrent illnesses and depression. Beloved by all and dedicated to burnishing family bonds, Hannah became pivotal to the flow of letters and purchases that sustained the household during the frequent absences of the father. In her affectionate but monitory letters to younger brothers, she was at once sisterly and maternal. In 1798 she wrote to Isaac: "Pray, how do you like Albany? What are your studies? and who your Companions? The last thing is of vast consequence—and I sincerely hope you may not become intimate or acquainted with the low, vicious Boys of which you have so many around you." She was twenty and he was sixteen. Hannah had become her father's viceroy in promoting allegiance to the genteel and disdain for the common among her younger siblings. For the rest of his life, James Fenimore Cooper remembered Hannah as a "second mother to me" and honored her "with a reverence that surpassed the love of a brother." She looms larger in his recorded memory than the sparse and spare references to his true mother. And it is telling that in *The Pioneers* he depicts Judge Temple as a widower whose daughter Elizabeth presides as the mistress of his household. In fiction, the novelist completed the disappearance of his mother and perfected her displacement by Hannah.[22]

It is more than coincidence that the virtuous Hannah Cooper seems the quintessential heroine of a sentimental novel. Like so many young women in England and America, Hannah sought to define herself by emulating the heroines found in didactic fictions. Vicariously absorbed in the travails of fictional characters, readers learned and replicated genteel modes of thinking, speaking, posing, and acting. Historian Richard Bushman remarks that readers "thought of their own lives as stories, following narrative lines like the ones they so frequently read. They intermingled literature and life." In diaries and letters young women emulated the rhetoric that they found in fictional texts. Especially systematic, Hannah kept a commonplace book in which she carefully copied, in immaculate handwriting, sentimental poetry and morally didactic stories culled from fashionable magazines and compilations, mostly of English production.[23]

Like other young women of her time, Hannah looked to literature for insights into romance and marriage. Novels and stories alerted readers to the dangers of an impulsive marriage. Because husbands had almost complete legal power over their wives, and because divorce was virtually impossible, marriage to an exploitative or abusive mate usually meant lifelong misery. Deeming "the Choice of a Husband . . . the most important of all Subjects," Hannah copied a fictional letter from an unhappily married woman warning her younger sister to avoid "Men of libertine principles . . . devoted to gambling, women and all manner of vice." Another piece warned: "In the fate of a woman marriage is the most important crisis. It fixes her in a fate of all others the most happy or the most wretched." The ostensibly female author assured Hannah: "It must never be forgotten that the only Government allowed on our side is that of Gentleness and attraction and that its power . . . must be invisible to be complete." So much rode on the marriage choice because the culture required women to accept subordination to their husbands.[24]

Many sentimental fictions were mournful tales of the tragically premature deaths of virtuous heroines victimized by cruel fate and predatory men. Especially fascinated by the morbid, Hannah diligently copied "Marie Antoinette's Lamentation in her Prison," "On the Death of an Infant Daughter," "Anna's Urn," "Maria's Grave," and Thomas Gray's "Elegy in a Country Church-Yard." At least twelve of the twenty-five entries in her commonplace book are meditations upon mortality written from the perspective of the dying or the grieving. The pieces promote a passive resignation to fate, a virtual welcoming of death. The last entry in her book is an untitled poem that seems to have been composed by Hannah. It appropriately summarizes the morbidity that she constructed in her commonplace book:

> *Why sinks my soul beneath this leaden gloom?*
> *What woe is this that steals my youth away?*
> *Why wish I for thy cold embrace, my tomb,*
> *Ere twenty suns have seen my natal day?*
> . . .
> *No foul dishonour stains my youthful fame,*
> *No secret guilt appals my conscious soul;*
> *I never ting'd my parents cheeks with shame,*
> *Nor wish'd to wander from their just controul,*
> *Why sink I thus beneath this leaden gloom?*
> *What woe is this that steals my youth away?*

> *O love! O cruel love! You write my doom,*
> *You sign my death—and I, content, obey.*

Hannah's commonplace book suggests a private despair that accompanied
her bustling public activity.[25]

Through the mediation of her commonplace book, her morbid reading
became her own speech and writing, as she was increasingly preoccupied
with preparing for death. In January of 1800 she observed, "We are all
mourning for our illustrious Washington, and all wish, though few aspire to
it, that in death as in life we may feebly imitate him." In August a New Jersey admirer, Congressman James H. Imlay, visited Hannah in Cooperstown.
She led him on a stroll through the small cemetery south of the Cooper
grounds, where she mused, "What a vapor—how insignificant compared
with that state of existance which awaits me hereafter—how important
that—of how little moment this." She told Imlay and others that she did not
expect to live long.[26]

As in her commonplace book, Hannah's resignation was closely associated with the pressure of expectations that, as she entered her twenties, she
must soon decide on a husband and subordinate her wishes and abilities to
his. Marriage and children would constrict her travel and access to friends
in New York City and Philadelphia. Never again would she be as free as in
her late teens as the unmarried daughter of a wealthy family committed to
her education and contacts. She felt obliged to please family and genteel
friends who expected that all her training was meant primarily to secure a
husband appropriate to her class. Her choice in marriage would not only
determine her life but also reflect upon her parents, siblings, and friends.
In the late 1790s Hannah did not lack suitors, but she was reluctant to
marry. In 1799 the then young and Republican William Henry Harrison
met her in Philadelphia. Dazzled, he proposed marriage, which she re-
spectfully declined. Years later his confidant recalled that in 1799 the future
American president "was dying with love for Miss Cooper." It eased her rejection of Harrison that her father could ill abide a Republican son-in-law.
But in 1800 she faced a more serious courtship from the man her father
most wanted as a son-in-law: Moss Kent, Jr.[27]

THE SUITOR

The letters of Moss Kent, Jr., reveal a prolonged struggle to find a wife up
to the exacting standards he shared with his brother James. They understood the proper marriage as critical to sustaining a genteel social standing
underwritten by a substantial estate. During the 1790s Moss Kent tried to
build the fortune that would win the proper wife, who, in turn, would cer-

tify and solidify his elite status. There were many false starts. In a 1792 letter to his brother, Moss slyly announced that he had procured as a housekeeper "a likely *young* Widdow" with "an illegitimate Child at her Breast, a circumstance that will lead you to conclude that she is *amorous* as well as young." The news alarmed James, who worried for his younger brother's reputation and interest as a gentleman. Both would suffer from a liaison with, or marriage to, a common frontier housekeeper. James replied with a warning: "If you should suppose marriage essential to your best Interests, I trust you will reflect well on the subject. In such new, simple & unpolished Society as that in which you now live, every grace & endowment is apt to be greatly overated for want of proper objects by which to compare them." He urged the importance of marrying "some Person whose Connections & Station would also contribute to your Interest & Pride." Thereafter, the amorous housekeeper disappeared from Moss Kent's letters, and probably from his household, for he quickly reassured brother James: "I expect my Choice of a Wife will perfectly coincide with your wishes."[28]

Deeming a wife "essential to my Interest & my happiness," Moss Kent announced in September 1792 that he meant to marry within a year. But marriage remained elusive despite a succession of prospects who appeared in the letters only to recede, usually without explanation. Kent seemed ever on the verge of proposing to a woman whose family and fortune would satisfy himself and his demanding brother. In 1794 Kent wooed Jerusha Kirkland, the daughter of the famous and prosperous Reverend Samuel Kirkland of Herkimer County. He wrote, "The connexion, should it take place, will be most flattering to my pride. They are a genteel, literary & very respectable Family & the old Gentleman is a man in independent Circumstances." But Jerusha politely rejected Kent's proposal. A year later Kent had a new prospect: his cousin Sally Kane, the daughter of a wealthy merchant. Kent anticipated that she would "add to my Happiness & advance my Prosperity to many *Thousand*. I shall never be contented till I make the experiment." But he subjected the choice to James Kent's decision: "Your advice dear Brother, shall be with me *conclusive*, . . . for I mean never to take any important Step in Life without first asking the advice of so affectionate & judicious a Brother." In reply, James Kent warned: "I have so little respect for most of her connections . . . that I believe your Interest would dictate against the Connection & probably your political consequence would dictate so also." Moss Kent quickly dropped Sally Kane, assuring brother James that he too held her "family connexions" in "perfect contempt & detestation." In 1796 Kent turned his attentions to Sally Kirkland, the younger sister of Jerusha. Kent appraised his prospects: "I shall make the same proposal to her that I did to her eldest Sister & have no great fear that it will not be accepted. It is one of the most agreable Families I ever knew. The old Gentleman is a man of large fortune. I believe him to be worth £2000 . . . & lives like a Prince." But in early 1797 Kent backed away, perhaps because it had become clear that Sally shared her sister's distaste.[29]

Kent did have an ardent admirer in Eliza McDonald, the lone daughter of his controversial friend, the defrocked Reverend John McDonald. In late 1798, after Eliza and John McDonald had left Cooperstown for Albany, she wrote in despair to her friend Chloe Fuller: "You would make me believe [that] Mr. K[ent] sometimes talks of me. I fear it is only when you remind him that there is such a person in existence." Hoping to spark Kent's interest, Chloe Fuller showed him one of Eliza McDonald's letters, but he responded with "indifference." After all, her father no longer had any money or much respectability: Kent's chief criteria for a wife. In June Eliza sadly concluded, "He is however a worthy character and a sincere friend of my Father's. He therefore merits my *esteem* & gratitude."[30]

Given his longing to marry wealth, Moss Kent was remarkably slow to settle on the obvious and proximate choice: the elder daughter of Judge William Cooper, the greatest landlord in Otsego County. Sharing the Manor House with the Coopers from mid-1794 to late 1797, Kent knew Hannah as she matured from age sixteen to twenty and became eligible for marriage. Ever inclined to think that parents were eager for their daughters to marry him, Kent insisted that the Coopers were especially keen: "I am not without my suspicions that I am an object of Love. I know that her Parents are desirous of a connection. The Mother has recommended her Daughter to me in the Presence of her Husband." Although self-interested, Kent's insistence is plausible given William Cooper's manifest longing to make a son of the dashing young lawyer. And what better way to subdue Kent's troublesome ambitions than to bring him into the family?[31]

Although initially attracted to Hannah, Kent backed away in mid-1795, shortly after he began to break with Cooper politically. Increasingly contemptuous of the judge as a distasteful vulgarian and political enemy, Kent did not relish becoming his son-in-law. Determined to deny the match deemed so obvious by others, Kent expressed private contempt for Hannah in a July 1795 letter to his brother: "I am *not at present* in Love notwithstanding the young Lady is at Home of whom I spoke so highly when I saw you. To the eye of my reason, unobscured by *Passion,* what little natural Grace she possesses is distorted by affectation, whatever smattering of Learning she has, is turned into disgust & Ridicule by her pedantic display of it." Wedded to his own sense of superiority, Kent refused to believe that William Cooper was capable of raising a truly genteel daughter.[32]

Kent alone detected flaws in a young woman deemed perfect by every other gentleman and lady in New York and Philadelphia. Indeed, James Kent urged his brother to reconsider, insisting: "Hannah is agreable & well informed." James shared his brother's distaste for William Cooper: "The judge, you know, is always facetious & trifling." But, dazzled by the judge's wealth if not by his manners, James insisted that Moss should not so quickly throw away his chance to acquire Cooper's money: "Such an Union would place you in a most happy Independence." Although he had, at last, found a prospect who satisfied his demanding brother, Moss rejected her, preferring to prosecute his political struggle against her father through the late 1790s.[33]

Kent rediscovered his love for Hannah in the summer of 1800, after her father had accepted his political demise and resigned as judge the previous October. Less than a year after helping Joseph Strong hound Cooper from office, Kent resolved to become his son-in-law. With the judge's public authority and prestige in ruins, Kent could, at last, enter the Cooper family on his own terms: as the county's preeminent Federalist. Returning to Cooperstown from a trip in late August 1800 Kent wrote:

> Never was a Person more affectionately welcomed than I was by the judge's family, particularly by Mrs. Cooper & Miss Nancy & Mrs. Kelley, the judge's Sister. I have spent a very considerable part of my time since my arrival with Miss [Hannah] C[ooper] & if I do not obtain her, which is the supreme desire of my Heart, it will not be owing to my diffidence, my want of perseverance & my good Generalship, but because the Fates have decreed otherwise.

Indeed, the fates decreed that Hannah would be dead within two weeks.[34]

DEATH

On Wednesday morning, September 10, 1800, Hannah set out with her brother Richard Fenimore and a few friends on a twenty-four-mile ride southwest to visit the mansion and family of Gen. Jacob Morris in Butternuts. Proud of her equestrian skills, Hannah insisted, over her brother's protests, on riding a newly acquired and especially spirited thoroughbred. The party rode along a road filled with mud holes and tree roots, passing through a hilly and heavily forested countryside interspersed with new clearings filled with blackened stumps, rail fences, and log cabins. Late in the afternoon, within two miles of their destination, Hannah's horse took fright from the racket made by men threshing buckwheat with wooden flails near the road. Just as she brought her horse under control, a barking dog rushed from the yard on the east side of the road, leaping over a fence. Her horse reared violently, throwing Hannah. Her head smashed against a stump, shattering her skull. According to Jacob Morris, the blow terminated

> her precious life as instantanious as if she had been shot through the heart with a Cannon Ball. I reached her in about 8 minutes after the fatal catastrophe. Nothing of life remained but the throbbing of the pulse. She appeared lovely even in death. I immediately had a Bier made in a few minutes, put a bed on it, lay

her decently on it, & brought her down on our shoulders [to my house] where
she was laid out [and] put into a coffin.

That night his son, Richard Morris, raced to Cooperstown, bearing to Otsego Hall the shocking news.[35]

The next day William Cooper, Moss Kent, Jr., and several family friends rode to Butternuts with a wagon to retrieve the corpse. That afternoon and evening they returned, James Kent later reported, "over Hills & thro deep woods. The moon rose an Hour before they reached Cooperstown & gave the Procession of a dozen Mourners following the Waggon an awful Solemnity." A day later an Episcopalian priest, Rev. Daniel Nash, conducted the funeral service in the central hall of "the judge's large & agonizing House." The mourners included dozens of villagers as well as her parents, her sister Ann (Nancy), and her brothers James, Samuel, and Richard Fenimore. Brothers Isaac and William Jr. were away in Philadelphia and Princeton, respectively. The service concluded, thirteen pallbearers shouldered the mahogany coffin and exited the house through the front door to a waiting hearse. A "very large concourse of weeping citizens" joined the procession around the block to the Cooper family burial plot, located behind Otsego Hall, where Hannah found her grave.[36]

Hannah's dramatic death at the peak of good health and in the midst of every comfort, universal acclaim, and brilliant prospects stunned her many friends and admirers. Her death and funeral were reported in the New York City and Philadelphia newspapers. Editors and friends paid tribute to her perfected gentility and virtue. Reporting the "Melancholy Catastrophe," Elihu Phinney credited Hannah with "every amiable quality which could endear her to society, every worldly blessing which could render her desirable, and every pious sentiment which could disarm death of its terrors." James Kent regretted his brother's loss: "This Miss *Hannah Cooper* was a most elegant, lovely & accomplished Woman & united Beauty, Taste, Learning, Virtue & Religion." Her many good works and prominent public presence left her mourned by hundreds in Otsego County. Gen. Jacob Morris lamented, "No young woman of her age, 23 years, had more highly cultivated her understanding which she had been enabled to do from the advantages of a good education and a strong mind. She was kind, benevolent, charitable & virtuous and our whole community is over whelmed with grief on account of our loss." Reading the news in a Philadelphia newspaper, Elizabeth Drinker wrote in her diary: "a very good Character. . . . Poor W[illiam] C[ooper], it will be a great blow to him." Many of the mourners referred to Hannah as a precious *possession,* an immaculate *jewel*—words with a special resonance for her father. Another Philadelphian, Catherine Wistar Bache, tried to console William Cooper: "When time has mellowed your present feelings it will be to you, Sir, I have no doubt, a source of delightful recollection that you were once in the possession of such a Child; and to me that I possess'd the friendship of such a Woman." Anne Francis assured Cooper, "She was a jewel of immense value to *you* & to her Friends." Eliza McDonald exhorted her friend Chloe Fuller, "I have hardly a fonder desire for you or for myself than that we might be and live like her, whose memory I trust we shall ever cherish." Friends in Albany and New York requested and received, as mementos, locks of Hannah's hair cut from her head by the family before sealing her coffin.[37]

Hannah's death seared William Cooper. Already reeling from his precipitous political downfall of the year before, Cooper suddenly had to deal with the loss of the person he most loved, the daughter who had been the proof of his true worth. The judge was, he said, "bowed down to the very dust." To cope with his grief, Cooper created two monuments to his daughter and her tragic death. First, he composed verses for inscription on her tombstone:

> *Adieu! thou Gentle, Pious, Spotless, Fair,*
> *Thou more than daughter of my fondest care,*
> *Farewell! Farewell! till happier ages roll*
> *And waft me Purer to thy kindred Soul.*
> *Oft shall the Orphan and the Widow'd poor*
> *Thy bounty fed, this lonely spot explore,*
> *There to relate thy seeming hapless doom,*
> *(More than the solemn record of the tomb,*
> *By tender love inscribed can e'er portray,*
> *Nor sculptured Marble, nor the Plaintiff lay,*
> *Proclaim thy Virtues thro' the vale of time)*
> *and bathe with grateful tears thy hallowed shrine.*

The verses express a unique identification with Hannah, a very personal, rather than a collective and familial sense of loss. In death as in life, William Cooper claimed Hannah as especially his daughter. In early 1801 he also designed a marble monument to mark the spot where she died. Assisted by the similarly grief-stricken James H. Imlay, Richard R. Smith, Catherine Wistar Bache, and Jacob Morris, William Cooper acquired the monument in Philadelphia for transport to Otsego and erection near Butternuts Creek, where it still stands.[38]

The Cooper family also memorialized Hannah by turning into relics those items most closely associated with her life and death. The dining table on which Hannah's coffin lay during her funeral service became an especially cherished heirloom that James Fenimore Cooper later kept in his library, ever near as he wrote. The family converted Hannah's commonplace book into a monument by appending copies of the letters of condolence and tribute received from family friends and by adding an epitaph: "the within selection of elegant Poetry and Scraps reflect honor on the hand which is now mouldering in the dust." William Cooper similarly memorialized Hannah's Bible by inscribing a poem and preserving the volume for presentation to a granddaughter who would bear her name. The poem began:

> *In years to come, when aged grown,*
> *May some sweet grandchild of my own,*
> *Bearing my Hannah's name,*
> *With female love on me attend,*
> *And be her aged Grandpa's Friend,*
> *Then he'll be blest again.*
> *With hopes like those I hail the morn,*
> *On which the lovely babe was born,*
> *The seraph place to fill,*
> *On whose dear lips sweet accents grew,*
> *More gentle than the morning dew,*
> *To comfort every ill.*

On November 15, 1808, Hannah's younger sister, Ann, gave birth to a baby named Hannah Cooper Pomeroy, who received the cherished Bible from her grandfather. William Cooper's will stipulated that, after his widow died, the surviving children were to divide the furniture in Otsego Hall with one exception: he reserved the contents of the northern bedroom on the second floor—Hannah's room—for his eldest granddaughter, named Hannah, born in 1802, the daughter of Richard Fenimore Cooper. Unable to bear the thought that Hannah was gone forever, the Cooper family preserved an almost mystical hope that a granddaughter would reembody her spirit.[39]

AFTERSHOCKS

Moss Kent, Jr., was shattered by the catastrophe, so devastating to his hopes. On September 12, 1800, he informed his brother James, "I am one of her most afflicted Mourners & long shall I bear her in melancholy remembrance." Moved by his loss, James Kent appended a note to the letter: "His attachment to her had been growing for six years past & there was every solid reason to conclude [that] she had an equal attachment to him & that they would shortly have been married." Given the frequency with which Moss Kent, Jr., had erroneously predicted his impending matrimony, perhaps we should be skeptical that they were about to marry—but it is significant that William Cooper included Kent in the party that retrieved Hannah's body. In the following months grief debilitated him with fever and ague: "I have not been perfectly in health since the Loss of my invaluable Friend. I was not sensible of the extent of my affection & esteem for her

till death had snatched her from my Society." Her sudden death seems to
have shocked Kent into an unprecedented feeling for someone other than
himself or his older brother. Permanently stunned by his loss, Kent remained a bachelor for life. In late 1804 he departed Cooperstown, emigrating north to Jefferson County in the St. Lawrence valley.[40]

Kent was not alone in his devastation: her other ardent suitor, James H.
Imlay, continued for years to mourn Hannah. He helped fund and arrange
the marble monument to her, and he referred with melancholy to her
tragedy in his every letter written to the Coopers over the next decade. Like
Kent, he never married, explaining, "I have not since the summer of 1800
felt much like getting in love."[41]

Elizabeth Cooper coped with the tragedy by turning inward. Hannah's
death deepened her disengagement from the world beyond the picket
fence surrounding the Cooper grounds. Making a cocoon of Otsego Hall,
she rarely ventured out and usually disliked letting outsiders in. She lavished care on the house and gardens but was uninterested in entertaining
her husband's many visitors, abdicating the formal role of hostess to her
daughter Ann or to a daughter-in-law. In February of 1809 Alexander
Coventry visited Otsego Hall and reported:

> The judge received me kindly. His lady appears rather odd: is an active, stir-
> ring little woman, rather plain in her manners and a little contradictory
> withal, but a notable housekeeper. A very genteel and accomplished daughter-
> in-law, formerly Miss Clason, did the honors of the table, and by her sweet ami-
> ableness, filled the place beautifully, and the mother-in-law, although seeming
> a little outre [sic] at first, improves much upon acquaintance.

A family tradition insists that the mansion once caught on fire, attracting
the village's volunteer fire company. Rather than permit them in, Elizabeth
Cooper locked the doors and repelled the firemen with boiling water while
her servants subdued the blaze. In December of 1813 her son Isaac and his
family moved into a new house around the corner from Otsego Hall; in
June of 1814 he recorded astonishment in his diary: "*Mother* actually came
to see us. First time she ever saw the House." Isaac was more surprised that
she had come at all than that it had taken her six months to travel one
block.[42]

She was most at peace when withdrawn within Otsego Hall, surrounded
by flowers, and lost in a novel. Her granddaughter Susan Fenimore Cooper
provides our most vivid and sympathetic description of Elizabeth Cooper:

> Occasionally I was taken to the Hall to see my Grandmother. I have a dim rec-
> ollection of her sitting near a little table, at the end of the long sofa seen in her
> picture, with a book on the table. She always wore sleeves to the elbow, or a lit-
> tle below, with long gloves. She took great delight in flowers, and the south end
> of the long hall was like a greenhouse in her time. She was a great reader of ro-

mances. She was a marvellous housekeeper, and beautifully nice and neat in all her arrangements.

Susan Fenimore Cooper referred to George Freeman's painting made in 1816 depicting Elizabeth Cooper in Otsego Hall. She sits in the foreground thoroughly encased by walls, floor, ceiling, and furniture, and by layers of clothing that leave only her kind but mournful face exposed to the viewer. Orange trees in boxes fill the back wall, and a flowering plant nestles at her feet, as a protective sentry.[43]

While his wife turned inward, William Cooper characteristically dealt with his grief by throwing himself into a new enterprise that pulled him away from Otsego with its tragic associations. In February 1803 Cooper plunged into an ambitious new land speculation in DeKalb, a wilderness township in the distant St. Lawrence valley near the Canadian border. Thereafter Cooper spent most of his time in DeKalb or in New York City, where he cultivated partners for his new speculation. In New York City he lodged at the fashionable boardinghouse on Wall Street kept by the widow Mary Daubeny. She and her children became Cooper's second, surrogate family. In 1803 Charlotte Daubeny closed a letter to Cooper, "I remain your affectionate daughter by adoption." In December 1805 Cooper addressed Mary Daubeny as "Dear Mother" and promised to spend the approaching winter in New York City: "I shall see you every day." Among the Daubenys, Cooper temporarily forgot the painful memories associated with his family in Otsego.[44]

ELIZABETH TEMPLE

The person longest affected by Hannah's death was her younger brother James. He sought renewed communion with Hannah by three paths: via spiritualism, through his own daughter, and by creating a fictional heroine given immortality. Intrigued by spiritualism, the novelist attended a seance in New York City in 1850, communicating with a spirit he identified as Hannah. Of his many dead friends and relatives, she was the one he most longed to reach, even fifty years after her death.[45]

In 1849 James Fenimore insisted that his daughter Susan Fenimore Cooper replicated the lost Hannah: "How I love that child! Her countenance is that of a sister I lost, by a fall from a horse, half a century since, and her character is very much the same. They were, and are, as perfect as it falls to the lot of humanity to be. I am in love with Sue, and have told her so, fifty times." Terrified of losing Hannah a second time, James Fenimore Cooper discouraged Susan's suitors and dissuaded her from marriage; she remained in his household for life—hostage to a tragedy of 1800.[46]

But Cooper's most successful strategy for reclaiming and perpetuating Hannah was as a fictional character. In *The Pioneers* he reanimated her as Elizabeth Temple, the daughter of Judge Temple and the perfection of feminine virtue and gentility. The novelist completed the transformation of Hannah into a fictional heroine, a process she had begun by emulating the virtuous but tragic characters whom she copied into her commonplace book. As in the novel's recall of Judge Cooper's political downfall, James Fenimore Cooper both exercised and exorcised his pain in remembering Hannah. In a transparent reference to Hannah's fatal accident Cooper describes Elizabeth Temple mounted on a spirited horse, riding aggressively over a rough frontier road, disdaining the caution of her worried father (as Hannah had ridden a powerful thoroughbred to the Butternuts, probably over the objections of her anxious brother). Temple warns, "If thou venturest again, as in crossing this bridge, old age will never overtake thee, but I shall be left to mourn thee, cut off in thy pride, my Elizabeth." In 1832 James Fenimore Cooper added a footnote alerting readers that this episode referred "to facts": "More than thirty years since, a very near and dear relative of the writer, an elder sister and a second mother, was killed by a fall from a horse, in a ride among the very mountains mentioned in this tale. Few of her sex and years were more extensively known, or more universally beloved, than the admirable woman who thus fell a victim to the chances of the wilderness."[47]

Obsessed with Hannah's fatal accident, James Fenimore Cooper imagined Elizabeth exposed to three deadly dangers, all set in the Otsego hills: a falling tree, a panther's attack, and a forest fire. In all three episodes the novelist credited Elizabeth with the passive resignation to death that Hannah had constructed in her commonplace book. When a rotting tree begins to fall toward Elizabeth's skull, she looks up "with an unconscious but alarmed air," rather than spurring her horse forward. Later, when a panther prepares to spring, "Miss Temple did not, or could not move. Her hands were clasped in the attitude of prayer, but her eyes were still drawn to her terrible enemy. . . . The moment seemed now to have arrived for the fatal termination, and the beautiful figure of Elizabeth was bowing meekly to the stroke." Finally, she prepares for death as a forest fire surrounds her and Oliver on the slope of Mount Vision. " 'This mountain is doomed to be fatal to me!' she whispered,—'we shall find our graves on it!' " "For me there is no hope!" She faces death with the "resigned composure" expected of "the most delicate of her sex," announcing, "We must die; yes—yes—we must die—it is the will of God, and let us endeavour to submit like his own children." The novelist simultaneously honored his sister's memory and promoted the passivity and morbidity that he deemed the proper ideals of genteel women.[48]

In all three crises Elizabeth's morbid passivity invites the saving intervention of a man. Judge Temple rescues his daughter from the falling tree by pushing her forward, yelling "God protect my child!" Natty Bumppo suddenly appears to shoot the panther dead, sparing Elizabeth and her companion Louisa Grant: "The death of her terrible enemy appeared to Elizabeth like a resurrection from her own grave." Later, when the forest fire closes in on Elizabeth and Oliver, Natty bursts through the flames and leads them through smoke, cinders, burning logs, and falling branches to safety. The pure resignation of the perfect woman brings out the best in the best of men, empowering them to act as the protectors of female vulnerability and virtue.[49]

Of course, the real savior was the novelist, who created and employed the characters who spare Elizabeth. By thrice rescuing Elizabeth at the last possible moment, James Fenimore Cooper exercised in fiction a power that he devoutly wished he had enjoyed in life. At the forest fire, Oliver speaks for the novelist to Elizabeth/Hannah: " 'Die!' the youth rather shrieked than exclaimed, 'No—no—there must yet be hope—you at least must not, shall not die.' "[50]

In *The Pioneers* the novelist's kindest service to his father is the homage paid to his grief for Hannah and to her love for him. At each escalation of the forest fire, Elizabeth thinks primarily of her father's anguish. When the fire encloses her refuge, she sobs, "My father—my poor, my distracted father!" As the fire draws nearer, she looks out from the mountain to see Judge Temple in the distant village: "This sight was still more painful than the approaching danger." " 'My father!—My father!' shrieked Elizabeth. 'Oh!—this surely might have been spared me—but I submit.' " Preparing for death, she instructs Oliver Edwards:

> "You will see my father; my poor, my bereaved father! Say to him, then Edwards, say to him, all that can appease his anguish. Tell him that I died happy and collected; that I have gone to my beloved mother; that the hours of this life are as nothing when balanced in the scales of eternity. Say how we shall meet again. And say," she continued, dropping her voice, that had risen with her feelings, as if conscious of her worldly weaknesses, "how dear, how very dear, was my love for him. That it was near, too near, to my love for God."

The angelic Elizabeth validates the judge, who for all his faults has trained her and won her enduring love.[51]

During the forest fire scene, the novelist three times calls attention to the dangerously flammable dress worn by Elizabeth: "Those flowing robes, that gave such softness and grace to her form, seemed now to be formed for the instruments of her destruction." (Of course, being a perfectly genteel and virtuous heroine, she cannot think of disrobing in front of Oliver, even to escape a burning death.) The author's preoccupation with her combustible dress almost certainly draws from another painful memory: the death in

1811 of Miss Elizabeth Cooper, his seven-year-old niece and Richard Feni-more Cooper's daughter. She died "in consequence of her clothes having accidentally taken fire from a candle."[52]

In *The Pioneers,* James Fenimore Cooper indulged himself, first with the melancholy of recall, but ultimately with the pleasure of allowing his lost sister (and a measure of his dead niece) to enjoy a better fate by surviving danger to marry and inherit the judge's estate. In life young James Cooper identified with Moss Kent, Jr., who had courted his beloved older sister and "second mother." In *The Pioneers* Cooper recalled that courtship, encoding Kent as Oliver Effingham—the personification of male, aristocratic honor. By ultimately marrying Oliver to Elizabeth, Cooper realized the unconsummated match of Moss Kent, Jr., and Hannah Cooper. Moreover, because the Effingham of fiction, like the Kent of life, represents James Cooper's self-idealization, the marriage is the novelist's vicarious opportunity to espouse his sister's memory. In his 1851 preface to *The Pioneers,* Cooper explained that he regarded Hannah "with a reverence that surpassed the love of a brother." The literary critic Stephen Railton concludes, "Oliver's . . . uncontested possession of Elizabeth and the judge's estate fulfill[s] Cooper's most heartfelt wishes. He could not have conceived of a happier ending."[53]

In *The Pioneers,* Richard Jones, Hiram Doolittle, Jotham Riddel, and Marmaduke Temple seek precious ores in the Otsego hills, but the real treasure, kept at the Mansion House, is Elizabeth. She is not only the judge's fondest possession but his sole heir who will bring to her successful suitor and husband all that her father possesses. Better still, because she is the perfection of feminine gentility, her favor will validate the man who merits her love and esteem—will prove him, above all others, the worthiest of gentlemen. Through the mediation of Oliver Effingham, James Fenimore Cooper won his sister's complete love and approval, proving himself the complete gentleman. And he secured in fiction the inheritance that was, he felt, his due.[54]

Chapter Twelve

FATHER AND SONS

DURING THE DECADE AFTER 1800, travelers marveled at the rapid development and manifest prosperity of Cooperstown and its hinterland. In 1803 the Quaker preacher John Simpson assured William Cooper: "Beholding thy Situation & how that Wilderness Land was Changed & Goodly Buildings erected, . . . it made me think of the Prophet's Expressions that the Wilderness Should Become as Eden and the Desert as the Garden of the Lord." In the summer of 1808 Miers Fisher of Philadelphia was dazzled by his first view of Cooperstown and vicinity: "We reach'd the Vale of Susquehanna at the Head of which this town is built. This View coming suddenly on me after winding down a long, steep Hill appeared like an enchanted painting thro' the magic Lantern & the whole distance within 3 Miles [was] the best & most improved farming Country I ever saw."[1]

Impressed by Otsego's prosperous appearance and Cooper's conspicuous wealth, observers concluded that the judge had perfected the arts of land speculation and development. In 1803 a rival speculator conceded to Cooper, "No man knows better than you the secret of subdueing the Wilderness & converting forests into Cultivated fields." William Sampson, a celebrated New York City attorney, was similarly impressed by Cooper's success at "reclaiming from its rude state the barren wilderness, and scattering the smiling habitations of civilized man in those dreary wastes."[2]

In 1807 Sampson induced Cooper to write his celebrated memoir, *A Guide in the Wilderness.* Cooper and Sampson were unlikely friends and collaborators: the judge was a staunch Federalist who favored good relations with the British empire and who denounced Irish immigration to America; Sampson was a prominent Irish radical and nationalist who had been arrested, jailed, and deported by British authorities. Taking refuge in New York City, he espoused Republican politics and vigorously defended the

The mind of Judge Temple . . . had received, from his peculiar occupations, a bias to look far into futurity, in his speculations on the improvements that posterity were to make in his lands. To his eye, where others saw nothing but a wilderness, towns, manufactories, bridges, canals, mines, and all the other resources of an old country were constantly presenting themselves.

—James Fenimore Cooper, The Pioneers, *321*

legal rights of Irish immigrants and striking workers. The arch-Federalist James Kent denounced Sampson's political and legal philosophy as "utopian & wild & radical." But Kent conceded that Sampson was also "gentle & amiable & had wit & Genius"—qualities especially cherished by the genial and humorous William Cooper, who apparently met the lawyer during a visit to New York City in late 1806 or early 1807. Charmed by Sampson's talent and personality, the judge was willing to overlook his politics and ethnicity.[3]

Impressed by Cooper's stories of frontier settlement, Sampson hoped to encourage increased Irish immigration to America by publishing the judge's insights. He exhorted Cooper to advise "the poor, the unfortunate, whom want and oppression drive from their native land." In response to Sampson's written queries, Cooper wrote *A Guide in the Wilderness,* apparently during the late winter and early spring of 1807. Prompted by Sampson's flattery, Cooper boasted of his unmatched prowess as a speculator and developer: "I have already settled more acres than any man in America. There are forty thousand souls now holding directly or indirectly under me." By May 12 Sampson had transcribed Cooper's brief manuscript and approached several publishers in New York City, with discouraging results. Undaunted, he sent the manuscript to Ireland where his brothers arranged publication in 1810.[4]

TENANTS

Otsego's prosperous appearance seemed to indicate a rooted population of enduring freeholders. In fact, the settlers and the landscape were in constant flux and rapid transformation. Most settlers departed within two decades, selling possession of their farms to newcomers that they might repeat the process of settlement farther north or west in some still newer county. A third of the taxpayers in Otsego Township in 1800 departed within three years; nearly half of the heads of household present in 1800 had died or departed before the federal census of 1810. Of course, many more newcomers arrived every decade to keep Otsego's population growing. The prosperous tended to stay, while relative poverty goaded others into departing in search of opportunity elsewhere. The persisting taxpayers of 1800–1803 averaged $799 in property, compared with $574 for those who departed: a difference of 29 percent. For most settler families Otsego was a way station in a migratory current carrying them from a New England or eastern New York birthplace to eventual graves farther west in New York or even Ohio and Michigan.[5]

In general, the settler treated a frontier farm as a place where his family could apply their labor to the soil and timber free from the direct supervision and exploitation of an employer. They worked both to obtain an immediate subsistence and to create an enhanced value that could be realized by selling the improved farm to a newcomer. Many early settlers entered land contracts with a speculator simply to gain legal possession of land that they did not intend to pay for in full. Instead, their strategy was to build up sweat equity by improving the land with buildings, fences, and clearings in order eventually to sell out at an advance to a more prosperous latecomer, who would also assume responsibility for paying the landlord. Settlers routinely sent Cooper notes directing him to deed their farms to a certain newcomer "upon such terms as you would have conveyed it to me had I not have sold it to him." Upon selling out, the farm builder moved on to repeat his work elsewhere on the frontier—as Jotham Riddel does in *The Pioneers*.[6]

William Cooper could not anticipate that a buyer would remain in Otsego long enough to complete the payments on his farm. Indeed, multiple and successive families often occupied and worked a frontier farm between its initial settlement and final disposition. For example, in 1795 Elisha Fullam agreed to buy 60 acres in Hartwick Patent from William Cooper, but in 1797 Fullam sold the premises to Jared Clark, who resold them to Bille Williams, who eventually completed the payments and obtained Cooper's deed. Although the original farm makers rarely paid either on schedule or in full, they served the developer's long-term interest, so long as they were hard at work adding value to the land.[7]

The canny developer guided the process by which frontier farms changed hands. Cooper explained his policy toward poor settlers who fell into arrears: "I shall raise the price but allow them another Period to sell their improvements into such as can Pay for the Soile—a Priviledge they will feel grateful for, and in some degree oile the way for my Passage to a good Sale of the farmes in question." To obtain eventual payment Cooper often brokered the turnover of farms from the first settlers to more prosperous newcomers. For example, in 1794 Cooper sold a lot of Otego Patent land at $4 per acre to the newcomer Jacob Mook but also required him to pay to the occupants "what two men Shall say the improvements are worth made by the Dutch men on the Primises."[8]

When settlers failed to fulfill their purchase contracts but wanted to retain their farms, Cooper gave them the option to remain as his tenants, paying annual rent in cash or in produce (corn, wheat, butter, or pork). Although Cooper applauded himself for selling rather than renting land, tenant farms proliferated on his Otsego domains especially after 1799 as growing numbers of settlers failed to fulfill their purchase contracts. Rather than summarily evict defaulters, Cooper preferred to issue them leases for their farms, provided they had worked hard to clear and cultivate the land. He explained: "For if a man has struggled ten years in vain, and is, at the end of that time, unable to pay, not only humanity, but self-interest dictates

another course, and some new expedient for reciprocal advantage." His
leases stipulated that the tenant could, at any point in the future, procure a
freehold title simply by paying the principal value of the farm:

> So here, the tenant instead of being driven for the principal, will not only keep
> his possession, but retain the privilege of re-acquiring the principal at a future
> day, by the very produce of the lands. He will be happy in the idea of still pre-
> serving his home, will pay his rent with cheerfulness, and the landlord has so
> much certainly added to his capital, whether the tenant re-purchases the fee or
> not.

The chief difference between the new leases and the original sales was that,
if the tenant was more than 50 days late in the annual rent payment, he
could be summarily evicted without the long, costly, and cumbersome
process of foreclosure. Although the permanent option to buy was generous, Cooper's rental rate of 28 bushels of wheat per 100 acres was higher
than normal for upstate New York (15 to 20 bushels).[9]

Tracking the fate of a particular set of purchases reveals the steady
turnover of settlers, the declining access to freehold title, and the surprising
growth of tenancy within Cooper's domain after 1800. During the five years
1794–99, Cooper sold farms in Hartwick Patent to 104 settlers. On average,
the buyer agreed to pay $254, within seven years, for a 115-acre parcel:
$2.21 per acre. All but 9 of the purchasers obtained modest farms, of less
than 200 acres. The buyers were highly transient. Barely half of them (54 of
104 = 52 percent) still resided in Hartwick or adjoining Otsego Township
in 1803, less than a decade after their purchases. Moreover, even most of
the persistent failed to complete their payments and so failed to obtain clear
titles to their farms. Only 24 of the 104 (23 percent) persevered, prospered,
and obtained a deed from William Cooper. A slightly larger number (27 of
104 = 26 percent) failed to retire their debt but remained on the land as
tenants, paying their annual rents to Cooper. Over half of the original purchasers received neither a deed nor a durable lease, usually because they
had departed from the vicinity, selling out their homestead to someone
else. By 1803 almost all of the purchasers who obtained neither deed nor
lease (43 of 53 = 81 percent) had left Hartwick and Otsego Townships.[10]

The Hartwick tenants were significantly poorer than the freeholders. According to the 1800 tax list for Otsego Township (which then included the
Hartwick Patent), the 27 tenants averaged $580 in net worth, compared
with $1,088 for the 24 freeholders. And at 89 acres the average leasehold
farm was much smaller than the typical freehold farm of 134 acres. Those
original purchasers who obtained neither deed nor durable lease were
middling men: more prosperous than the tenants but poorer than the freeholders ($836 on average). The pattern suggests that only the most pros-
perous quarter of the settlers could afford to persist and buy their farms

from Cooper. The middling half tended to sell their improvements and move on before their final payment became due. And the poorest quarter remained on the land but had to accept tenancy, apparently trapped by their relative poverty. By no means did the overall prosperity of Otsego mean the absence of tenancy or poverty from the county.[11]

Despite the celebration of freeholding and denigration of tenancy in *A Guide in the Wilderness,* Cooper abetted the steady proliferation of leaseholds in Otsego. His rent roll for 1806 identifies at least 141 tenants. In the twin towns of Hartwick and Otsego, where Cooper was the dominant landlord, one-fifth of the families were tenants in 1808, only slightly less than the average for the entire county of 25 percent. Freehold opportunity narrowed for the rural settlers of Otsego at the very moment that Cooper wrote *A Guide in the Wilderness* to celebrate his success in rescuing men from tenancy.[12]

DEKALB

Rendered overconfident by his early and unique triumph in Otsego and by the subsequent praise of his admirers, Cooper concluded that he had the magic touch, the unfailing secret to managing settlers and their settlements at any time and in all settings, no matter how infertile and remote. Beginning in 1803 William Cooper gambled his estate on an expensive new speculation in a distant and unpromising corner of the state. In February 1803, he paid $1 per acre to acquire DeKalb, a 62,800-acre township, from another land speculator. Located in the St. Lawrence River valley near the Canadian border, DeKalb was part of the massive and notorious Macomb purchase of 1791 that Cooper had so coveted during his bitter controversy with Gov. George Clinton. Unfortunately, getting a measure of what he had so long wanted would prove disastrous to Cooper's estate. Hilly, unsettled, and heavily timbered with maple, beech, ash, butternut, elm, and white pine, DeKalb was just the sort of land that Cooper specialized in as a speculator. Smitten with the St. Lawrence country, in 1804 Cooper bought an additional 34,914 acres in parts of four different townships. After his purchases of 1803–1804, William Cooper owned more land in St. Lawrence County than in Otsego. Blind to all warning signs, he insisted that St. Lawrence was "in my judgment, soil and trade considered, a county as valuable as any in the estate" [*sic,* Cooper meant *state* but his slip reveals the centrality of DeKalb to his own *estate*].[13]

The new venture was Cooper's bid to recapture his dramatic early success as a developer. With Otsego thickly settled, a landlord's work had become the mundane collection of payments and the unpleasant resort to lawsuits and foreclosures against the most laggard debtors. Cooper preferred the camaraderie, excitement, and possibility of a new settlement. Humiliated by his recent political downfall, he also felt newly driven to prove that he still had a special ability to convert the wilderness into a garden. He longed to regain the influence and honor he had enjoyed in Otsego's early days. By moving north to the frontier, he could, in effect, reverse time, stepping back into a simpler stage of development, when settlers seemed more dependent and deferential, when he could again be a Father of the People. In addition, the DeKalb speculation enabled Cooper to turn his Otsego properties over to his sons. Finally, by absorbing his time and attention, DeKalb helped William Cooper cope with Hannah's death. Seeking distraction from his grief and a second chance at political paternity, Cooper gambled his immense estate on a risky new speculation.[14]

To acquire the capital he needed to buy and develop DeKalb, Cooper sold shares amounting to over half of the acreage (35,610 of 62,800) to six friends, mostly residents of New York City. At the center of the DeKalb partnership was Mary Daubeny, a wealthy widow and the owner of a fashionable New York City boardinghouse on Wall Street that Cooper had long frequented. The other partners included her daughter Charlotte, son Lloyd, and son-in-law Henry Waddell, as well as John B. Murray, a New York City merchant, and Nathaniel Smith, a lawyer from New Haven, Connecticut. Cooper retained 27,190 acres, the largest single share in DeKalb. Rather than subdivide the DeKalb tract at once among the partners, Cooper managed the whole, promising his investors the profits in proportion to their shares in the acreage.[15]

The new set of associates was the third in Cooper's land speculating career. In the late 1780s he had worked primarily with wealthy and older men, mainly weighty Friends, from Philadelphia and Burlington. During the early 1790s, they parted ways with Cooper in mutual disappointment over the failed Beech Woods and maple sugar promotions. During the mid-1790s Cooper cultivated a new array of partners among the Albany gentry (Stephen Van Rensselaer, Leonard Gansevoort, and Goldsborough Banyar) and New York City lawyers (Richard Harison, Josiah Ogden Hoffman, and Robert Troup). At the end of the decade, they too became disgruntled with his management. Cooper then applied his considerable powers of persuasion to recruit a third set of partners for the DeKalb speculation. Better versed in his Otsego success stories than in his subsequent failures in the Beech Woods and the Military Tract, the new partners banked on the judge's mystique as the unerring developer—as had their predecessors.[16]

In May 1803 Cooper began the new settlement by leading forty men north from Otsego County the 200 miles to DeKalb. His settlers had to construct a rough new road through to DeKalb from the nearest settlement, 10 miles away. A settler recalled "the singular appearance of Judge Cooper in his two-wheeled carriage with several men on each side of it to keep it from upsetting, as he was leading by way of Lowville, a large company of pioneers through the dense forests to De Kalb." Cooper brought along in wagons a bulky cargo of consumer goods, and he immediately opened a store in a log cabin. During his first month at DeKalb, Cooper spent $1,162 for surveys, road and bridge construction, land clearing, deeds and other legal papers, and for the provisions, rum, and whiskey to feed and entertain forty men.[17]

Within a year Cooper retailed almost all the land in the township to forty-one men for the respectable price of $2.50 per acre—two and a half times what he had paid to buy the tract a year earlier. The contracts committed the buyers to pay in ten years a principal sum of $150,157.50. In the interim the purchasers were supposed to pay the annual interest of 7 percent on the value of the principal: a tidy $10,511.03 annually. In 1804 Cooper returned from DeKalb, boasting, "I have bin from home for Many Months Erecting a large and Extensive settlement on the Saint Lawrance which goes on with more Rapidity than any I have undertakin." Other speculators were amazed. Daniel Hale of Albany marveled, "Your success at De Kalb really astonishes me. If you have actually Compleated what you have described, you have done wonders and really merit all you may make by your speculation."[18]

But, as with Cooper's earlier speculations in Otsego and the Beech Woods, his apparent overnight success was deceiving. Once again his hasty surveys created erroneous property lines that later proved expensive and difficult to correct. As in the past Cooper sold so much so quickly by entrusting most of the acreage on credit to a few petty speculators. He clung to that practice despite the debilitating consequences manifested in all of his previous speculations. The six largest purchasers accounted for 48,330 acres—80 percent of the total sold (60,063 acres). The acreage entrusted to the six was far out of proportion to their ability to pay. For example, the largest single purchaser was Isaac Stacey, a Cooperstown innkeeper of substance but not wealth. Worth $3,991 in 1803, he acquired 13,641 acres in DeKalb, taking on a debt of $34,102 in principal plus $23,872 in interest over ten years—a total debt fourteen times his total assets. Of course, the petty speculators did not intend to retain and pay for their entire tracts. Instead, they planned to resell at a profit to small farmers before the principal fell due. One assured Cooper that he would return to DeKalb "with a considerable number of my friends and neighbors. I intend to survey the Land into Farms, and hope to have Settlers on it in a very short time. I expect to go their to live my Self and shall be glad of all the encouragement you can give." The many smaller, secondary purchasers were supposed to work the land and, ultimately, pay the landlord.[19]

Cooper received almost no money up front from the impecunious settler-purchasers, and getting an impressive set of bonds and mortgages was far easier than collecting cash on them. Cooper noted, "The perplexity of recovering moneys from new Settelements is to me well known. . . . Nothing but time and a residence among the Settelers will make them tollorably Productive. Indeed, it is proverbial that Landed men are not monied men." To facilitate future payments of interest and principal Cooper tried to hasten the development of market opportunities for the commodities that the settlers generated as they cleared and cultivated their new farms: potash, livestock, maple sugar, timber, shingles, boards, and grain. The more settlers could produce and the easier their access to market, the greater their cash surplus would be. From that income eventually they could pay their debt for the land to Cooper and his partners.[20]

However, in the short run, Cooper compounded his debts by building an expensive infrastructure for his new and distant tract. Within DeKalb Township, Cooper laid out a new commercial village, which he named Williamstown, once again laying personal claim to *his* settlement as monument and testament. As at Cooperstown he mandated a compact village of small lots: 50 by 150 feet. He located Williamstown on the east bank of the Oswegatchie River, beside a waterfall, where he constructed a stone dam, 16 feet high, and cut a millrace through 14 feet of ledge to provide waterpower for a gristmill and a sawmill. The latter employed the latest and most expensive technology, including a "Machine for drawing up loggs." His hired hands cleared and fenced 25 acres of pasture and cropland near the mills and erected a frame house and barn. On a nearby hill, Cooper's laborers constructed a substantial hotel, 60 feet square and three stories tall—a prodigious building for so distant and raw a settlement. Replacing the log cabin store, Cooper also built a framed structure stocked with potash kettles and sugar kettles, tools, alcohol, cloth, and other consumer goods. He valued his store and inventory at $4,067 and the dam and mills at $9,049. "The expensive buildings that William Cooper has erected in the Village he Expects to keep himself," the judge informed his partners. Ever intrigued by rumored minerals, Cooper even tried to establish an iron mine and forge at DeKalb.[21]

Entrusting his new enterprises and buildings to employees and tenants, Cooper reaped severe aggravation, as the DeKalb settlers helped themselves to his tools, furniture, and supplies, with little opposition, and much collusion, from Cooper's initial agents. His greatest difficulties were with the young brothers Alexander and Andrew McCollom, both emigrants from Otsego County. In return for half the profits, Alexander ran the DeKalb store while Andrew, a lawyer, managed the judge's legal affairs and land office. They infuriated Cooper with their public profanity, heavy drinking, open contempt for his program, haughty treatment of the settlers, and repeated pilfering from the store. Cooper blew up when he found Alexander's wife "cloathed in the most Expensive articals in the store." The judge warned, "I cannot Loose my property which I have got by the dint of industry." When the McColloms ignored his instructions, Cooper sacked them in early 1805. He empowered his brother James Cooper and Potter Goff as land agents. The judge entrusted the store and mills to Thomas B. Benedict, the son-in-law of another DeKalb partner, Nathaniel Smith.[22]

Cooper's DeKalb enterprises also suffered a succession of expensive catastrophes. He had to rebuild his costly dam and mills after a flood carried them away in the fall of 1804, drowning an employee in the process. In late 1806 Cooper lost two more men and a cargo of store goods worth $250 when his boat, bound for DeKalb, sank on Lake Ontario. The greatest blow to DeKalb came in December 1807, when President Jefferson declared an embargo on commerce with the British empire, including Canada. Distance, bad roads, and the Adirondack Mountains rendered the Albany market impractical for St. Lawrence County produce. Consequently, the north country settlers depended on transportation down the St. Lawrence River and across the border to Montreal to market their potash, pearlash, lumber, grain, and livestock. Without a market the settlers could obtain no cash to pay Cooper for their lands and their store debts. Nor would any newcomers settle and buy where they could not find a market for their produce. Without payments from the old settlers and sales to newcomers, Cooper could not repay his speculating partners and other creditors. In sum, the embargo threatened to stifle DeKalb and ruin William Cooper. As a lifelong champion of free trade, Cooper detested the embargo as the ultimate proof of Republican folly and perfidy.[23]

Unfortunately for the Jefferson administration, but fortunately for the St. Lawrence settlers, the embargo proved unenforceable along the wild and lengthy northern border. British officials and Montreal merchants eagerly colluded with American smugglers, who included Cooper and his new storekeeper. Indeed, Thomas B. Benedict promised Cooper that he could "entirely monopolize this business" between the Oswegatchie valley and Montreal. Cooper made the best of a bad situation by shipping produce and goods north from Otsego to DeKalb for smuggling across the border to Canada, where the partially effective embargo produced the shortages and higher prices that were the smugglers' boon. Suspected by Republican politicians and United States officials, Cooper disingenuously wrote to the Secretary of the Treasury, Albert Gallatin, in December 1808. Cooper claimed that his unusually large shipments of pork and flour to DeKalb were merely meant to save his settlers from "fammin." Although DeKalb had fewer than a hundred families, he assured Gallatin, "I have many hundreds [of settlers] to aid in their infant state." Ironically, while William Cooper was illicitly shipping potash and provisions to Canada, his son, Midshipman James Cooper, was posted on a naval brig in nearby Lake Ontario with orders to seek and seize smugglers' boats and cargoes.[24]

FOLLY 🔥

By erecting a costly infrastructure at his own expense and by operating his mercantile ventures through agents, Cooper violated principles that had served him so well in Otsego during the 1780s and 1790s. He also contradicted the precepts that he championed so eloquently in *A Guide in the Wilderness,* written at the same time that he developed DeKalb. In his book Cooper extolled the minimalist developer who did not get in the way of the natural process by which settlers migrated into the forest and transformed the land into farms: "[By] the simple measure of letting things take their own course, I find my interest and that of the whole community promoted." Indeed, Cooper considered it folly for "wealthy theorists" to spend a lot of their own money to build infrastructure: "When the landlord undertakes to construct buildings, bridges, and roads, and the people labour for hire, each man strives to get the most he can for the least services." He also argued that it was far wiser to sell mill seats, taking a mortgage for payments, because a purchaser "will work better and cheaper for himself than for you; you will not then be cheated, and you will have a good profit in the convenience and advantage which your settlement will derive from it." In *A Guide in the Wilderness,* Cooper boasted that at Otsego he had accomplished so much while spending so little, but in DeKalb he spent lavishly to no good end.[25]

Why did Cooper so deviate at DeKalb from the principles espoused in *A Guide in the Wilderness?* In part he was driven by his initial mistake: buying a marginal township so far from urban markets and from the main westward flow of frontier emigrants. In contrast to the Otsego Patent of 1786, which lay contiguous to old settlements and within 20 miles of the Mohawk valley—the principal travel corridor in upstate New York—DeKalb in 1803 was an isolated and unoccupied tract about 150 miles north of the Mohawk. According to the young lawyer and future writer Washington Irving, who traveled to the Oswegatchie Valley in August 1803, the road was, for its last 60 miles, "dreadfully rugged and miry," full of stumps and roots, little more than a horse path passing through a dense forest. In 1809 the St. Lawrence County settlers aptly described their situation as "on this remote margin of the nation; now in a great measure shut out from all communication with other parts of the State." Because of its northern situation St. Lawrence County also suffered from a relatively brief growing season that in the coldest years was too short for some grains, especially corn, to mature. Cooper built roads and bridges, mills, a store, and a hotel in an expensive bid to alleviate DeKalb's isolation by attracting attention, creating a local market, and diverting the channel of emigration. In effect, he threw good money after the bad spent to buy such a distant and unpromising township.[26]

Second, Cooper hoped to preserve his patriarchal authority from the diversity and dissent that had developed to ruin his public power in Otsego. By building and owning the mills, store, and hotel, he would retain his privileged position as the mediator between his settlers and external sources of capital, consumer goods, and information. In DeKalb he sought greater influence over the settlers' morality, instructing his agents: "Frown on that odious practice too manifest in the Settlement of profane Swearing; get the people to form a religious Society and Establish schools as soon as you can, and in every perplexity that arises interfere to quiet them, discourage Litigation. Have Nothing to do with the plans of settlement of other Towns, But proceed Straight forward on my plan of settleing Dekalb." In his new efforts to suppress litigation and profanity, Cooper expressed lingering resentment of his fateful confrontation with the lawyer Joseph Strong in 1799 over Ebenezer Sherman's blasphemous swearing. According to the geographer Horatio G. Spafford, Cooper got what he wanted from DeKalb: "His fatherly attention to the wants and interests of the early settlers, is remembered with gratitude." But that deference cost William Cooper dearly as his numerous agents, elaborate buildings, and costly enterprises were a constant, debilitating drain on his estate. Being a Father of the People was an expensive luxury, at odds with his interest as a land speculator.[27]

Cooper's minimalist policies of the late 1780s and early 1790s had been driven, in part, by his initial lack of capital. In *A Guide in the Wilderness,* he made a virtue of his early necessity. However, after 1800 Cooper could lavish money on his new projects—could afford to deviate from the practices that had made him so rich during the 1790s. Forty-nine years old in 1803, he felt pressured by his advancing years to act quickly, to use his new money as a substitute for the time that had been in greater abundance when his capital had been smaller. DeKalb became the penalty Cooper paid for becoming rich from his earlier, unique, and misunderstood success. At DeKalb the judge became precisely the sort of impatient, meddlesome, and spendthrift landlord that he warned against in *A Guide in the Wilderness.*

Cooper's partners grew anxious as their revenues from DeKalb lagged far behind his projections. Obliged repeatedly to calm his urban partners impatient for income, Cooper preached, "You must not Expect money soon, as the lands lay far in the wilderness and can onely be made Productive by giveing Easey termes to Poor men to Cultivate them." Nonetheless, he insisted that, in time, great profits were inevitable: "From Experiance I have found Every Season that settlements was not made a Loss to land holders." In November 1804 Cooper promised Henry Waddell that, although his investment of $12,500 would "be Paid tardily, it will be Paid certainly at last. The Settlement increases cleverly and Promises well." Cooper's glowing predictions persuaded Waddell, who replied, "With respects to my property in De Calb, I am induced to hold it fast, from the great encouragement which you give me that it will turn out profitable." In fact, after the initial burst in 1803–1804, the land sales and settlement of DeKalb stagnated; in 1810 only about 100 families dwelled there.[28]

Timing no longer favored William Cooper's speculations. In contrast to the Otsego Patent, which Cooper acquired at a bargain price in 1786 on the eve of a great boom, he bought DeKalb in 1803 at the peak of the land market and suffered from its subsequent prolonged stagnation. During the late 1780s and early 1790s, circumstances—especially the postwar surge of Yankees into central New York—had inordinately blessed Cooper's early venture as a speculator and developer. Thereafter, increasing numbers of settlers bypassed New York in favor of the warmer, more fertile, and cheaper lands in the Ohio valley opened to settlement by American victory over the Indians there in the mid-1790s. Moreover, the federal government sold midwestern lands for $2 per acre, in contrast to the $3 to $5 per acre sought by Cooper and most other New York speculators. At the same time, the embargo of 1807–1809, followed by the war of 1812–1815 with Britain, further depressed the settler demand for lands in the isolated and vulnerable St. Lawrence valley of northern New York. Consequently, after 1800, and especially after 1807, the relatively cold, infertile, and overpriced hill lands belonging to New York speculators stagnated or declined in value.[29]

In *A Guide in the Wilderness,* Cooper dwelled on his remarkable, early success in the Otsego Patent but neglected to recount his subsequent and equally spectacular failures in the Beech Woods and St. Lawrence County. Far from having been a consistent success as a developer, Cooper enjoyed one initial triumph in Otsego followed by a string of failed speculations everywhere else. Misled by William Cooper's self-promotion in *A Guide in the Wilderness,* historians often exaggerate his abilities and success as a developer. For example, Lyman H. Butterfield credits Cooper with converting "750,000 acres from forest into farms, homesteads, and villages. In magnitude there is probably nothing in our history to match this accomplishment. Other land promoters operated on a larger scale, but they failed and he succeeded." Butterfield concludes, "The more we learn about William Cooper, the greater stature he acquires." In fact, the fuller record reveals that Cooper failed more often than he succeeded.[30]

In general, recent historians of settlement overpraise the frontier land speculator as if he was essential to rapid and rational development. In fact, most New York settlers sought out good land, cut roads, built houses and barns without any financial assistance from landlords. The flow of families into the forest ordinarily occurred with or without any landlord's assistance. On the other hand, no amount of promotion or investment could draw or retain settlers to an inferior tract. Far from driving the process, landlords went along for a profitable ride. The flow of settlers onto new lands was a vast and largely autonomous process that speculators could harm more eas-

ily than they could initiate and control to advantage. In the last analysis, settlers did not need speculators nearly as much as speculators needed settlers.
Recognizing that fact in his early Otsego speculation, Cooper had flourished. Forgetting the true source of his early success, he subsequently
reaped a string of failures that undermined the estate that he would pass on
to his children.[31]

DISTRACTION

It was bad enough that the DeKalb speculation was a consistent loser that
annually depleted Cooper's capital. Worse still, DeKalb preoccupied and
distracted him to the detriment of his many other investments and responsibilities. During the five years after 1803, he delayed paying his mounting
debts, ignored his old land agencies in Otsego for other landlords, allowed
a mercantile partnership to languish and die, neglected his turnpike company launched in 1801, and wrote off his land speculation in the Military
Tract as a dead loss. In sum, his preoccupation with the St. Lawrence lands
took a heavy and increasing toll on his reputation, credit, and net worth. As
the years passed and his other ventures withered, Cooper's estate came to
depend on the risky DeKalb speculation. In 1805 Cooper confessed, "I am
so taken up with deKalb that I can attend to nothing else."[32]

Beginning in 1803 Cooper spent most of his time supervising his new settlement in the north or visiting and wooing his urban friends and partners,
leaving little time in Cooperstown for his family and old properties.
Cooper's many old creditors became ever more frustrated as the judge
lagged in his payments and ignored their letters. Returning to Otsego in August 1804, Cooper apologized for his long neglected corrrespondence, explaining that he had been away "from home almost since April 1803."
Aware that Cooper spent diminishing amounts of time in Cooperstown, one
shrewd creditor instead sought out the judge at Ballston Springs, a favorite
summer haunt of the fashionable families who invested in Cooper's speculations. The creditor explained, "I knew you had business every where & I
was in some expectation of seeing you there."[33]

After 1803 Cooper also neglected his old agencies for absentee landlords
with holdings in Otsego County. Many were weighty Friends of Burlington
who had been his earliest patrons and, at one time, the men he had been
most eager to please. Cooper not only failed to collect monies from their
settler-debtors in Otsego, but declined for months, even years, to reply to
their increasingly uneasy letters. In 1807 after four unanswered letters over
the course of nearly three years, William Allinson of Burlington complained: "Why William art thou thus silent? . . . I have often thought thou
hast not been sufficiently open with me. My enquiries respecting things

which appeared right & reasonable that I should know have often been for years past entirely neglected, & sometimes. thou has treated me, I have thought, rudely."[34]

Weary of his old and distant patrons, Cooper welcomed opportunities to withdraw from agency work. In 1805 he explained, "As I have spent twenty years in setteling new lands, with good suckcess, and by which it is Reasonable to sopose that I have Procured all the Practical information necessary for the improvement of a wilderness, I claim not to be shackeled with the thongs of others not Professors in this singular Line of business." Determined to concentrate on his own venture in the St. Lawrence valley, Cooper persuaded most of his old employers to transfer the management of their Otsego lands to his eldest son, Richard Fenimore Cooper.[35]

Unfortunately for the nonresident speculators, Richard was an inept agent. Cold, formal, unimaginative, and indolent, he lacked the gregarious charm and entrepreneurial drive critical to his father's early success. Although trained in the law and admitted to the Otsego County bar in 1797, Richard ignored his practice and in 1803 escaped from it by leasing his name as an ostensible partner to a more aggressive and ambitious newcomer, Farrand Stranahan, who did all the work. Richard received one quarter of the revenue and entrusted to their partnership his legal business as a leading landlord and land agent in the county. Instead of practicing law, Richard concentrated on his duties as the judge's principal legatee: the management of valuable mills and lands in Otsego given to him by the judge and to the coordination of Federalist electioneering in the county. Although disorganized and diffident, Richard was "a handsome man with remarkably fine manners"—precisely the gentleman that his father had wanted his eldest son to become.[36]

Impatient for an increased income from their lands, the absentees instructed their new agent to demand prompt payment from the many settler-debtors under pain of immediate suit for eviction. Lacking the resolution either to confront the settlers or to correct his patrons, Richard Fenimore Cooper simply ignored his duties for months on end. His employers became annoyed with their agent's delays, irregular records, and lapsed correspondence. In March of 1805 Robert L. Bowne sarcastically asked, "Will it be too disturbing to thy repose to oblige me with a particular and of course a long Letter in answer to this & my others and that too within 2 or 3 Weeks?" In December Bowne complained that of his many settlers "there is hardly one that has had any thing paid." Fed up, he fired Cooper as his agent in May of 1806. A month later Joseph Bloomfield exploded, "Six years has already elapsed and I have not received a Cent for the $15,000 advanced to your Father, in exchange for the lands under your direction." Richard's indifference compounded his father's distraction to tarnish the Cooper family's reputation for business.[37]

A mercantile partnership with Daniel Hale of Albany also fell victim to William Cooper's increasing preoccupation with DeKalb. Formed in the fall of 1801 with an initial capital of $8,300, the firm invested in Hale's store in Albany, established a satellite store in Cooperstown, operated a whiskey and gin distillery, and ran a regular freight wagon, dubbed the Columbus, ferrying Otsego produce to Albany and returning with store goods. The firm lost $5,408 during the next three years. The losses included deaths by four of the firm's five horses, a debit of $550. The wagon was "nearly worn out" and only "the worst horse" was left. Unable to bear the drain, in October 1804 Hale begged Cooper to settle their accounts and dissolve the firm. It especially rankled him that Cooper had plowed into DeKalb the capital that might, instead, have bolstered and rescued their flagging firm. Cooper replied, "As to finding fault, when things do not turn out as fortunate as we could wish, is of little use, and [I] hope we shall keep up the same good understanding, as though we had been enriched by the Connection." Because he remained wealthy, this sentiment was easier for Cooper than for Hale, who was virtually bankrupted by their "truly unfortunate connexion in business."[38]

Cooper's frequent and prolonged absences from home were also detrimental to the Second Great Western Turnpike Company, which he had organized and which the state had incorporated in 1801. Rather than levy taxes to construct state roads, after 1800 the New York state legislature preferred to charter private companies to build new roads at their own expense, lured by the opportunity to profit by collecting tolls at gates erected every 10 miles. The Second Great Western Turnpike Company had authority to sell shares and build a ninety-mile toll road westward from Cherry Valley through Cooperstown to Sherburne on the Chenango River. In August of 1801 the shareholders met at the Red Lion Tavern in Cooperstown to elect thirteen directors, including the leading shareholder, William Cooper, who became president. The corporation's secretary was his lawyer David Mason, and the treasurer was his longtime political ally, James Averell, Jr. Another director, the editor Elihu Phinney, boasted in his newspaper:

> *This Road will be the great funnel, through which will be carried to market, the produce of several of the richest Counties in the Western District of this State. The Farmer, who with great difficulty found a passage down the Susquehannah, or over the Catskill Mountains, to vend the produce of his fields, will now find a broad, smooth road to Albany, the great emporium of the Northern and Western parts of this State.*

In the summer of 1803 the subcontractors finished the road and William Cooper announced, "The gates are up and we shall declare a dividend February next." That dividend was modest, only 50 cents followed by another

50 cents in August—an annual return of little more than one percent on a
$25 share bought in 1801.[39]

Thereafter, the turnpike quickly displayed the problematic hallmarks of
an enterprise launched by William Cooper, as the rapid construction and
apparent early promise gave way to mounting costs and disillusionment.
Poorly designed and sloppily built, the toll road soon became a muddy
mess. In the spring of 1805, less than two years after the road opened, a
state road commissioner informed the company directors: "I have inspected
the Road and find it out of repair and I do hereby warn you to put it in such
repair as the law directs or open the gates on Said Road Without Delay."
The costly repairs meant that the company's board could announce no div-
idends in 1805. Moreover, in June 1806 the turnpike remained in such disrepair that the state prosecuted William Cooper and the other directors,
securing a guilty verdict and the considerable fine of $20 from every direc-
tor. Under the pressure of that verdict, the company secretary warned stockholders in July of 1806 that their toll road required such "extraordinary
repairs" that there would again be no annual dividend. Blaming the problems on Cooper's absences and distraction, the other directors pressed him
to appoint a vice president who would at last "put the Road in such order as
to render it permanently productive to the stock holders." His continued
neglect worsened what was already a poor investment, for very few New York
toll roads proved profitable.[40]

The judge also lost heavily on his expensive speculation in the Military
Tract located among the Finger Lakes in Onondaga County, New York. The
Military Tract was fertile but cursed with a tangled and potentially worthless
legal title. To provide bounty lands to Revolutionary War veterans, in 1788
the New York State legislature set aside approximately 1.5 million acres that
surveyors divided into twenty-five townships, each subdivided into 100 lots
of approximately 600 acres. In 1791 the state held a lottery to award specific
lots to individual veterans (or their heirs). Because so many veterans were
too poor or crippled or unmotivated to emigrate, most sold their claims for
immediate cash to speculators who accumulated thousands of acres. In
1793 Cooper and two partners—Richard Harison and Col. Robert Troup,
both prominent lawyers and politicians in New York City—had obtained
10,200 acres in thirty-one separate parcels scattered among thirteen townships. Harison and Troup entrusted Cooper with selling the land and collecting payments. Unfortunately for Cooper and his partners, many
veterans had sold their claims repeatedly to rival speculators, multiplying
the titles to every lot, and casting doubt on all. Clever forgers and intruding
squatters added to the adverse claimants, producing a legal nightmare.[41]

Cooper further entangled his Military Tract purchase by employing the
quick, large sales on credit to petty speculators that had so complicated his
patent in Otsego and utterly crippled his venture in the Beech Woods. He

sold all 10,200 acres to just seven men, none of whom became settlers and all of whom eventually defaulted on their payments. Distrusting the title offered by the petty speculators, the tract's actual settlers refused to buy their farms. Unable to retail any land, one of the large purchasers bitterly complained to Cooper in 1799, "I have been murdering 4 or 5 years to no purpose, and I may . . . murder 3 or 4 more, and then be worth nothing." He begged Cooper to take back the unsold lands and cancel his bond and mortgage.[42]

The legal tangle and balky settlers discouraged Cooper's partners, who longed to cut their losses. In 1804, Harison and Troup wearily hoped "that this tedious affair may soon be brought to a conclusion." Upon dividing up the lands, bonds, and mortgages to dissolve their partnership, Harison discovered that all of his lots had worthless titles. Soured by the dead loss, he assured Cooper in 1807, "You & I will probably never bargain [again]. You are too deep for me. You wish to put off some of your excellent Bargains and I do not feel that I have any occasion for them. So, my good Friend, the least said is soonest mended." In fact, Cooper also lost heavily on the Military Tract. Harison got it backward: it was Cooper's folly, rather than his cunning, that had ruined the Military Tract speculation. Even in utter failure the judge preserved his reputation as the consummate land speculator.[43]

PRINCETON 🔥

After Hannah's death in 1800 and especially after the DeKalb purchase of 1803, William Cooper became a distracted and distant husband and parent, assuaging his grief with frenetic activity. In his absence most of the authority over the adolescent sons—James, Samuel, and William—devolved upon the older sons, Richard Fenimore and Isaac, who married in 1801 and 1804. Because Isaac was genial, affectionate, and witty, he enjoyed far greater rapport with the rest of the family than did the austere and dull Richard Fenimore. But both were too involved with their own properties and families to devote much attention to their younger brothers. As a result, the decade following Hannah's death produced three more family crises: William Jr.'s expulsion from Princeton, James's expulsion from Yale, and the latter's flight from Cooperstown to seek a sailor's life.

William Cooper, Jr. (b. 1786), was second only to Hannah as the object of his father's hopes. Precocious but undisciplined, young William got mixed reviews from family friends. He was six years old in 1792, when a New York City merchant reported to Judge Cooper: "William behaves tolerably well. If he was not so damned proud, he would be a fine young Fellow." Convinced that young William was the brightest of his five sons, Judge Cooper made unusually early and elaborate plans for his future. William Jr. was "a

Good Griek Scholar" but only fourteen years old when his father announced: "I mean him for a lawyer." Cooper intended to send his son to Princeton College, followed by two or three years in Edinburgh or London, to pick up British gentility. The younger William would have every advantage never known by his father.[44]

Playing his elite connections for all they were worth, in early 1800 the judge persuaded the influential Dr. Benjamin Rush of Philadelphia to help get young William into Princeton and into the household of its celebrated president, the Reverend Samuel Stanhope Smith. Cooper explained, "Altho I seek with much Expence and more industry the Best Education to be had for my children, yet it is my Primary object to have such a shape gave to their Manners and Morrals as to leave a hope [that] they will turne their knowledge to a Proper use." Cooper was impressed with Smith's reputation for moral rigor and political elitism, for rigid adherence to old-school Federalism. Indeed, Smith denounced Thomas Jefferson and prayed, "May the *patricians* yet be able to save the republic when the *tribunes* shall have urged it to the brink of ruin!" Sharing these sentiments, Cooper concluded that Smith was the perfect man to give young William the proper direction in life. Lobbied by Rush, President Smith accepted William into Princeton and his own home. The judge agreed to pay $250, exclusive of tuition, for his son's boarding—twice the cost of living in the regular college housing.[45]

In July of 1800 William Cooper sent his teenage son off to Princeton with a formidable set of expectations recorded in a letter. Young William must become "the first of Schollars, knowing that your Abilities and memory are Eaqual to any of your age and you have Every thing to make you ambitious. Here is a great Country and no young man has such an opportunity as yourself of being the first man in it. On your industry depends whether you are to be the great, good, and Useful man, or nothing." As the judge saw it, there was no middle ground but only a stark choice between greatness and failure, between being first or last in the Republic. Having faltered in his own drive to become the great man, William Cooper invested his money and hopes in his son and namesake.[46]

But young William was still only fourteen—too young to go so far away with so much money. After a year in college he wrote an affectionate and homesick poem for his older brother Isaac:

> Otsego's shady banks by you are seen,
> Tis true indeed that these I oft have been,
> And pleasures there I frequently have found
> In shady groves or wandring oer the mount,
> Those times have been but now, alas!, they're gone,
> And when I wake at Princeton in the morn,
> I think myself at home prepared to walk
> With Samuel, and on politicks to talk

> . . .
> *Or with my sister Nancy to go out*
> *After (you know) she's cleaned her butterboat.*
> *Much do I long to be at Myrtle Grove,*
> *To be, to talk, to live with those I love.*

He closed by announcing with pride that at Princeton he was called "the fa-mous hopper (you must know that I can hop 28 feet in 3 hops)." Still a boy, William Jr. was obliged prematurely to become a young man far from home. In 1801 the greatness he cherished was as a hopper rather than as a lawyer.[47]

At first President Smith deemed young William "very prudent & capa-ble." In December 1800 he expressed to the judge "very sincere pleasure in the conduct of your son." Eight months later Smith confirmed, "It gives me pleasure to be able to assure you that your son promises to answer your hopes & all the expence you bestow on his education." But this letter also conveyed the first, subtle signs of warning: young William bought too many new clothes and hired "a horse & carriage in the evening more frequently than is strictly necessary for his amusement." These qualms ripened into alarm in February of 1802, when Smith warned the judge, "I have urged upon him frequently to be more moderate in his expences than he was the last year. He assures me he has. But his reliance on your fortune still makes him less sensible of the value of money than I think he ought to be."[48]

Drawing on his father's generous credit with the Princeton store owners and tavern keepers, young William became the dissipated young dandy. He bought an expensive wardrobe of gloves, coats, suspenders, silk stockings, knee buckles, linen shirts, velvet pantaloons, striped satin vests, and a "best silk, velvet cape." His bill with one tailor for just four months amounted to $110.74—more cash than an Otsego farmer saw in a year. William Jr. also spent lavishly on fine wines and brandies, procuring thirty-five quarts from just one store during the five months following September 29, 1801. This was a prodigious intake for a boy turning from fifteen to sixteen (perhaps he shared the alcohol with his friends who lacked so much credit). Appar-ently a boisterous drinker, he went through glassware almost as rapidly, buy-ing twelve tumblers, eighteen wineglasses, four pitchers, and two decanters. He also obtained twenty-five Spanish cigars. His five-month bill for these liquors, glassware, cigars, sugar, molasses, and other sundries totaled $123.17. The storekeeper cautioned young William that his father might disapprove. "To this he replied that he should do as he pleased and if he could not get the things of me, he would apply else where. Thus situated, I have let him have whatever he has demanded," the storekeeper confessed to the judge.[49]

Concerned friends told William Cooper a timeless story: His impression-able young son had fallen in with the wrong crowd, with dissipated new friends who cultivated their alienation from reputable society by drinking

with the Blacks and poor whites at the village's loosest taverns. Although almost all belonged to genteel families, these students behaved as if they were
the riotous, drunken Jacobins of their parents' lurid nightmares. Their raucous conduct belied the insistence of Federalist parents and professors that
their supervision alone could preserve America from anarchy. For all his
vigorous posturing as the last great defender of morality and subordination,
President Smith was singularly ineffectual at controlling his young lodger,
who, as the son of another great Federalist, was not supposed to run with
tavern sots and enslaved Blacks.[50]

In January of 1802 the president and faculty tried to restore moral order
in their college and village. The students' especially drunken and riotous
celebration of Christmas Day induced the faculty to suspend six from the
college. Rallying to their defense, most students boycotted classes and demanded the restoration of their friends. The defiant majority included
young William, who denounced the faculty for "the oppression of arbitrary
power." The faculty compromised by reinstating four of the suspended students, whereupon their fellows ended their strike. But the subsequent calm
did not last long.[51]

Disaster struck the college on the afternoon of March 6, 1802, as the students ate dinner. A fire erupted in the belfry of Nassau Hall and quickly
spread along the roof and down into the wooden interior, gutting the college's principal building, destroying its library and scientific collection and
much student property. By 6:00 p.m., when a rain squall quenched the
blaze, Nassau Hall was a smoking, blackened shell. A day later another suspicious fire broke out in Ferguson's tavern. Given the recent student agitation, the townspeople and college authorities were quick to blame student
arsonists for the two blazes. Ever on the alert for lurking Jacobins, President
Smith blamed students committed to "those irreligious & demoralizing
principles which are tearing the bands of society asunder." Meeting at the
president's house on March 16–17, the college trustees agreed that Nassau
Hall "was *intentionally set on fire.*"[52]

William Cooper must have been horrified to learn of this latest Jacobin
outrage, this further proof that democracy was a moral cancer spreading
through the republic. His horror deepened, when he subsequently learned
that the prime suspect held in custody was his own son and namesake.
When suspected of the fires, certain young slaves had implicated several students, including William Cooper, Jr. Although unable to prove arson, on
March 19 the college's Board of Trustees formally expelled young Cooper
and five others for participating in the various "immoralities, disorders, and
combinations which prevailed among some of the students during the late
session." The magistrates in the town of Princeton did charge young
Cooper with arson. Posting bond, he was released on bail pending his trial
in June.[53]

Joseph Bloomfield—the governor of New Jersey, president of the college trustees, and an old friend of Judge Cooper's—believed young William guilty of drunken indolence but innocent of arson. In a letter to the father, Bloomfield wrote, "I advise you *to call him home forthwith* and put him immediately into a Lawyer's office for a year at least in your town, where he may recover the laudable habits of study and lose that dissipated conduct, which from being allowed too much money, he has most unfortunately for the last six months fallen into and if not *immediately* checked will be his ruin." Taking Bloomfield's advice, Cooper summoned his son back to Cooperstown in early April. Satisfied that he was innocent of arson, the judge pressed President Smith to "exculpate" young William. Smith demurred, insisting, "The charges with all the disagreeable consequences, he must ascribe entirely to his ever suffering himself to mix with persons so far below him, & so improper for him." Indeed, Smith remained furious with young William for regaling his friends with stories that "treated the character of my oldest daughter with the greatest indecency & indelicacy."[54]

In June, the legal authorities dropped the charges against William Cooper, Jr., for want of evidence. No one was ever convicted for the Nassau Hall and Ferguson's tavern fires. It is unlikely that students would have set fire to their own dormitory and a favorite tavern. Both fires may have been accidents. Or they may have been the work of disgruntled young slaves, striking back at the whites of Princeton. Then the Blacks shifted the blame by taking advantage of the generational division among the local whites caused by the recent troubles at the college.[55]

After mounting a successful fund drive, the college rebuilt Nassau Hall and imposed a strict new set of student regulations. They promised to treat the students with "that discipline, and that only, which is suitable for children." In particular, they forbade students to enter taverns, to obtain goods on credit without parental approval, to lodge outside of Nassau Hall, or to travel more than two miles from Princeton without special permission.[56]

Although considered "wonderfully clever, quite a genius, a delightful talker, [and] very witty" by his family, William Cooper, Jr., never achieved the greatness expected of him. He did not return to Princeton and never completed a college degree. Instead, he served an apprenticeship in the law as a clerk in two successive law offices: one year with Moss Kent, Jr., in Cooperstown followed by four years in the New York City office of Richard Harison, the judge's friend, partner in land speculation, and fellow Federalist. Then, at a cost of $11,000, Judge Cooper gave his son a house on Pine Street in New York City and bought him a library of law books. If young William ever practiced law, he earned neither distinction nor much money at it. In 1808, he married Eliza Clason, the daughter of a prominent New York City merchant who was an old friend of the judge's. Her father had opposed the marriage, convinced that young William was too indolent and in-

efficient to support a family. Judge Cooper replied that he expected marriage to tame his ne'er-do-well son. But the marriage turned out badly as the
couple embarrassed or amused observers with their open bickering, and he
squandered his inheritance on investments in a variety of follies—including
a hot air balloon. In 1813, during the war with Britain, he built for the U.S.
Navy an octagonal floating platform, sixty feet long, made of hewn logs and
meant to support a battery of sixteen cannons. Alas, en route across Lake
Ontario to Sackett's Harbor, the unwieldy contraption collapsed and sank,
wiping out his $5,000 investment and adding public ridicule of "Cooper's
Ark" to his burdens. Losing confidence in himself, Cooper felt resigned to
living without purpose off his dwindling inheritance. Seeking a bank loan,
he conceded, "I am not, and probably, never shall be in any business by
which money can be made or lost, and therefore must rest my security upon
my patrimony." Instead of becoming the great man, William Cooper, Jr.,
ended up as a nothing. He was ruined by the insidious combination of too
much money too easily had with expectations far beyond his abilities to
achieve. The same fate nearly befell the judge's youngest son: James Cooper
(who did not add the "Fenimore" to his name until 1826).[57]

YALE

Because James Fenimore Cooper drew so heavily upon his memory of
William Cooper to craft Judge Marmaduke Temple, *The Pioneers* invites special attention to the relationship of father and son. Literary critics usually
detect a son struggling to cope with his painful memory of a formidable father. Charles Hansford Adams observes, "To the boy James Cooper, the
judge must have seemed like a god. But growing up with a god typically
prompts a deep and lasting psychic conflict; the father is established as the
central figure in the child's consciousness, so that whether worshipping or
abusing it, the son's identity is largely defined by the father's." Similarly,
Stephen Railton considers William Cooper "the most important influence
in the novelist's mental life."[58]

Indeed, some literary critics insist that William Cooper was a severe and
demanding father who provoked his son James to resentment and rebellion. According to Railton, William Cooper was "stern as a judge, despotic
as a patriarch, [and] violent as a man." Consequently, James Cooper's "adolescence was a sustained revolt against the figure of his father." Warren Motley argues, "In Cooper's case, the power of Judge Cooper to act within his
son's mind as the harsh arbiter of his worth survives in the severe judgment
James Fenimore Cooper levels at fictional fathers throughout his thirty-year
career."[59]

This depiction of William Cooper as tyrannical father is doubly skewed.

First, it interprets Cooper's fatherhood by extrapolating from his contentious political career. Second, the reading of that political career is highly selective, relying primarily on the charges levied by his Clintonian enemies in 1792–93. To be sure, the judge pursued politics with a boisterous vigor, but only the most strained and selective reading of family documents can suggest that he conducted his domestic relationships in the same contentious manner. As the downfall of his son at Princeton demonstrates, William Cooper's failings as a father were overindulgence combined with prolonged absences, rather than any disposition to tyranny.[60]

Gray-eyed with light brown hair, a ruddy complexion, and a strong build, James resembled his brother William, who was his closest friend in the family. Both were bright but unreliable, charming but undisciplined. As children, they delighted in roaming around the village, through the forest, over Mount Vision, and across the lake. Hannah said of her younger brothers, "They are very wild and show plainly [that] they have been bred in the woods." A plausible tradition insists that James especially loved to haunt Elihu Phinney's printing office, occasionally lending a hand with the typesetting. The novelist later remarked that Phinney's wife had "endured more noise of my making than any other woman." James's formal education began in the desultory grammar schools conducted in the Cooperstown Academy by Joshua Dewey and Oliver Corey. But, like young William, James was early destined for the law and sent away to private schools in Burlington (during the winters of 1796–97, 1797–98, and 1798–99) and Albany (1801–1802) to learn the Latin and Greek required for admission to college.[61]

In Albany, James studied and boarded with the Reverend Thomas Ellison, an English-born and Oxford-educated Episcopalian. He had a taste for high living, a delight in witty sallies, and a hatred for democracy—all of which recommended Ellison to William Cooper's friendship and esteem. The novelist later recalled that Ellison had "entertained a most profound reverence for the king and nobility; was not backward in expressing his contempt for all classes of dissenters and all ungentlemanly sects; was particularly severe on the immoralities of the French Revolution and, though eating our bread, was not especially lenient to our own." He "hated a democrat as he did the devil; cracked his jokes daily about Mr. Jefferson and Black Sal, never failing to place his libertinism in strong relief against the approved morals of George III." Nonetheless, Ellison lived a secret discovered only years later by Cooper: the Reverend had seduced and eloped with another man's wife, fleeing to Albany in America, where they could pass as lawfully married. At Ellison's, in addition to learning elitism and the classics, James Cooper made useful friendships with his fellow students, the sons of New York's most prestigious and wealthy families, including two Van Rensselaers, a Livingston, and William Jay, the youngest son of the former governor. By design Judge Cooper had posted his son in the uppermost reaches of the American gentility with instructions to master their mores and manners and to win their esteem and friendship.[62]

In early 1803, accompanied by his friend William Jay, James Cooper enrolled at Yale College in New Haven, Connecticut. Princeton was out of the question, given his brother's scandal, and Yale probably appealed to Judge Cooper because its domineering and arch-Federalist president, Timothy Dwight, had a reputation for strictly supervising his students' morals and politics. Cooper hoped that President Dwight would succeed with James where President Smith had failed with young William. In fact, despite their president, Yale students were notorious for drinking, dancing, courting, sailing, picnics, football games, and blowing up privies with gunpowder. Young William's debacle of the preceding year seems not to have taught his father the folly of sending his sons away to college so young. In early 1803 James was only thirteen, a year younger than his brother had been upon entering Princeton.[63]

Indeed, James soon replicated much of his brother's folly: spending extravagantly, neglecting his studies, indulging in pranks, and flirting with the local girls. "My misfortune was extreme youth," the novelist later confessed. Educated at better schools than most of his classmates, he was able "to play—a boy of thirteen!—all the first year." He scraped by on charm, rather than excelling through diligence. His favorite professor, the chemist Benjamin Silliman, indulgently remembered James as "a fine, sparkling, beautiful boy of alluring person & interesting manners." Despite at least $270 in cash provided by his father, James ran up an additional $500 in debts during his first two years. From a single shoemaker over the span of eleven months, he bought, on credit, seven pairs of shoes and three pairs of boots (cost: $39.45).[64]

Nonetheless, James might have slid through and graduated from Yale with neither distinction nor disgrace, but for his violent scrape with a fellow student, John P. Boyle, on May 23, 1805. Getting the better of their fight, Boyle viciously pummeled James about the face and head with his fists and a stick. "James was treated in a most savage manner by one of his fellow students, treatment more barbarous & cruel, I never was acquainted with," Nathaniel Smith of New Haven reported to William Cooper. Politics may have been involved, for Boyle was a Marylander with a reputation for zealous Republicanism—a double rarity in Yale, a bastion of Yankee Federalism. On James's behalf, Smith brought civil suit against Boyle and, in December of 1805, won $250 in damages and $36 in costs.[65]

In the meantime the college authorities had expelled both Cooper and Boyle. Eventually, the college permitted Boyle to reenroll and to graduate with the class of 1807, but Cooper never returned and never graduated. Why, if Cooper was the victim in their fight, was he treated more severely?

A family tradition offers an explanation: in apparent revenge for the fight, James used a gunpowder charge to blow off the door of Boyle's dormitory room. There is no contemporary evidence to confirm this story, but it is plausible, given the frequency with which Yale students blew up privies, and it would explain why the college treated Cooper more harshly than Boyle. Considering that Cooper's older brother was associated with the fire that had destroyed Princeton's Nassau Hall, Yale's authorities did not want to take any chances by readmitting a student who had endangered a college building with gunpowder. James felt unfairly treated, which may have initiated his powerful animus against Yankees as consummate hypocrites.[66]

In June of 1805 a second of Judge Cooper's sons returned to Cooperstown in disgrace, accused of having violently damaged his college. James's expulsion was yet another setback to the judge's hopes that his children could perfect the gentility that had eluded him and restore the family to the prestige and power that he had lost. How could William Cooper ever claim public restoration as a Father of the People if he could not even train and control his own sons?

THE SEA 🔥

James resumed his studies under the direction of the Reverend William Neill, Cooperstown's newly arrived Presbyterian minister. Neill later recalled that his most famous student "was rather wayward, cordially disliked hard study, especially of the abstract sciences; [and] was extravagantly fond of reading novels and amusing tales." Cooper also daydreamed of running away to sea.[67]

In the summer of 1806 James Cooper abruptly terminated his studies, departed Cooperstown, and embarked as a common sailor—a momentous and mysterious turn of events. His embarkation was momentous because he subsequently pioneered the American sea novel. His departure was mysterious because it was so unusual for a well-educated son of wealth and privilege to assume the hardships, drudgery, dangers, and low status of a common sailor. Why had Judge Cooper suffered his pampered son of sixteen to become a seaman?[68]

The novelist's biographers insist or imply that William Cooper arranged for his son's first voyage, although they disagree over whether the judge acted to serve James's wishes or to curb his rebelliousness. At one extreme, Stephen Railton maintains, "Tired of his repeated transgressions, William Cooper finally sent his son to sea to be tamed, but before abdicating his authority in this way he unquestionably would have tried to tame the boy himself." On the other hand, George Dekker presents Judge Cooper as an indulgent and benevolent parent who, by arranging the first voyage, got

James "started successfully in his second (and probably much wished-for) career as a naval officer."[69]

In fact, James Cooper demonstrated more initiative and seized more power over his future than traditional accounts have allowed. Two letters written by Richard R. Smith, a Philadelphia merchant and old family friend, reveal that James ran away from home determined to go to sea against the wishes of his father and older brothers. Similarly, in Cooper's *Afloat and Ashore* (1844) the autobiographical character Miles Wallingford defies his family to flee from his home in rural New York and proceed to New York City, where he embarks on a merchant vessel as a common sailor. When Miles broaches his nautical ambitions to his guardian, he dismisses "any project as visionary and useless as the hope of seeing the world in the character of a common sailor"—which hints that James first tried but failed to secure his family's consent. Like James in early September 1806, when he set sail, Miles "wanted a few days of being seventeen."[70]

Evidently Cooper's ambition had taken shape by June 16, 1806, when he observed a solar eclipse in Cooperstown and at the climactic moment, as he later recalled, daydreamed of the sea: "My fancy was busy with pictures of white-sailed schooners, and brigs, and ships, gliding like winged spirits over the darkened waters." Shortly thereafter, James fled from Cooperstown, heading first to New York City, where his beloved brother William lived. Unable to find a berth on a sailing ship at that port, James headed to Philadelphia, preceded by William's letter to Smith. From that letter, Smith concluded on July 18 that "James had left home rather in an uncommon manner" which "must have been without consent of his Friends." Anticipating James's arrival in Philadelphia, Smith sought advice by writing to Isaac Cooper in Cooperstown. Noting the apparent conflict between James Cooper's intentions and his family's desire to squelch them, Smith observed: "I would wish to serve him, and at the same time not disoblige his Family." Smith knew much more on August 8, when he wrote his second letter. James Cooper had arrived in Philadelphia and had revealed some of his intentions: he was "resolutely bent on the Navy" and "some Plan seemed fixed in his mind that he did not like to communicate to me." Already James had secretly written to the War Department, seeking a warrant to become a naval officer. To strengthen his application James sought some nautical experience by enlisting on a merchant ship.[71]

According to Smith, James especially hoped for a berth on a vessel bound "to join Miranda." A native of Venezuela, Gen. Francisco Miranda (1750–1816) was a liberal revolutionary determined to liberate his homeland from Spanish rule. Believing he had the tacit support of Thomas Jefferson's administration, Miranda acquired a ship, munitions, and about 200 men in New York City. On February 2, 1806, he sailed to Venezuela, proceeding via Santo Domingo. During the spring and summer of 1806, American newspapers carried breathless updates of Miranda's glorious (pseudo) accomplishments and prospects. In Cooperstown, James Cooper must have followed the expedition through the weekly reports in the *Otsego Herald*. The April 24 issue reported that the New York volunteers "expected to be enriched at one dash." In June the newspaper published a letter from "General" George W. Kirkland: a volunteer from Oneida County, a political friend of Judge Cooper, and the brother of Jerusha and Sally Kirkland. Proclaiming Miranda "a New Washington," Kirkland boasted, "There is not the shadow of a doubt but that new success will crown so holy an enterprise."[72]

Promising adventure, wealth, honor, and glory for the American volunteers, and republican uplift for the downtrodden of Latin America, the rhetoric in the *Otsego Herald* must have animated the ambitions of a proud young man who had suffered the public embarrassment of an expulsion from college for his want of discipline and purpose. What better way to reestablish his honor, prove his manhood, and escape the power of those who doubted him, than to run away, join the "New Washington," liberate Latin America, return an experienced sailor and soldier, and enter the American navy as an officer? Bored with his family's plan to make a lawyer of him, James Cooper bolted. It is appealing to think that James Fenimore Cooper enjoyed a moment of youth—years before he settled down as the Squire of Cooperstown, the national scold, and the public champion of New York's great landlords—a moment when he longed to be a Latin American revolutionary.

However, it was characteristic of James Cooper to hedge his bets. While running away from home and toying with romantic dreams of Latin American revolution, he sought out (and apparently stayed with) an old family friend. James also borrowed $80 by drawing on the line of credit his older brother had with Smith. Just as Henry David Thoreau sought his wilderness where he could walk home for dinner in Concord village, Cooper was careful not to discard all the advantages of his wealthy family when he ran away to become a sailor. He displayed the attitude of Miles Wallingford, who fled from his New York estate named Clawbonny and went to sea but assured himself: "I knew I was sufficiently secure of the future to be able to risk a little at the present moment. . . . If I made a false step at so early an age, I had only to return to Clawbonny, where I was certain to find [a] competence and a home."[73]

Smith and the Coopers were convinced that a merchant ship was no place for a sixteen-year-old boy who had been raised in luxury and had never been to sea. Smith tried to dissuade his "young Friend" by pointing out "the hardships he was likely to suffer." Smith insisted that "he is certainly too young to be launched into the world without protection." In 1806

America's maritime commerce was booming but exposed to violent predation by the warring powers of Europe. The British routinely seized and impressed American seamen to serve on their warships in the long and bloody war with Napoleon's France. Joining Miranda's quixotic attempt to revolutionize Latin America would have been especially dangerous. Indeed, during the month of August, while Cooper sought a vessel in Philadelphia that could take him to the Caribbean, Spanish forces routed Miranda's flotilla; ten captured volunteers were executed while others languished in a dungeon. Young Cooper's efforts to find a berth on a Philadelphia ship were as futile as Smith's efforts to dissuade him. On August 7, James left Philadelphia to seek a ship in New York City, taking the money he had drawn from Smith on his brother Isaac's account.[74]

During the undocumented interim between Smith's letter of August 8 and Cooper's embarkation from New York on September 1, James Cooper probably reached a compromise with his family that permitted him to go to sea but on a vessel and a voyage that would be relatively safe. Apparently, Jacob Barker, a wealthy Quaker merchant and a Cooper family friend, arranged for James to serve on the *Stirling*, a fine new ship (on her second voyage) commanded by a humane and competent captain and bound for England—then the safest possible destination for a transatlantic merchant ship. (On subsequent legs of the voyage, before returning home, Cooper and the *Stirling* passed through the more dangerous waters off Spain.) After enduring many of the hardships and some of the danger that his family and friends had feared, James Cooper returned to the United States in mid-September 1807. The Secretary of War issued Cooper a warrant as a midshipman on January 1, 1808, and he entered the navy in the spring. During his two years as a midshipman, Cooper served on board three small warships based either in New York City or on Lake Ontario. Serving during peacetime, he never saw battle.[75]

Although during the summer of 1806 Cooper ran away, it was not to escape from a tyrannical father. Indeed, by 1806 the older brothers Isaac and Richard Fenimore Cooper exercised more authority over the younger sons than did the judge, who, after Hannah's death, had abdicated many of his familial responsibilities. Smith corresponded with the brothers, rather than the judge, in the belief that they made the family's critical decisions. In a prickly letter written to his eldest brother on December 19, 1808, James Cooper expressed a similar sense of having confronted the collective authority of brothers and father (rather than one overbearing patriarch) in 1806. James recalled the "Family dissensions" and avowed an "ardent wish to bury them in oblivion—could it be done consistent with my own honor, and that of my family. The ebullitions of *my* youth, will I hope be forgotten." Indeed, Richard Fenimore Cooper loomed larger and more negatively in

James's late adolescence than did his jocular and often absent father. If Cooper experienced tyranny in Cooperstown, it was from his severe eldest brother rather than from his overly indulgent father. It is more plausible that James Cooper ran away to attract, rather than to evade, the attention of William Cooper.[76]

Chapter Thirteen

MURDER AND BLOODSHED

B Y REDUCING TAXES, REPEALING THE hated Sedition Act, and enjoying an economic boom based on overseas trade, the Republican administration of Thomas Jefferson grew in popularity as the Federalists sank deeper into public opprobrium. In New York the Republican state administration of George Clinton basked in the success of the new national regime. The Republicans' success seemed to confirm their story that the Federalists were corrupt aristocrats who had nearly subverted the Republic. In the annual spring elections of 1802 and 1803, the New York Republicans captured overwhelming control of both houses of the

Animated by their own noise, the men now rushed on in earnest, . . . when Judge Temple appeared on the opposite side, exclaiming—
"Silence and peace! why do I see murder and bloodshed attempted! is not the law sufficient to protect itself, that armed bands must be gathered, as in rebellion and war, to see justice performed!"
"Tis the posse comitatus," shouted the Sheriff, from a distant rock, "who"—
"Say rather a posse of demons. I command the peace."
— James Fenimore Cooper,
The Pioneers, 435

legislature. In Otsego County they won every legislative seat, and the Republican percentage of the votes rose from 57 percent in 1802 to 61 percent in 1803. Formerly staunchly Federalist, Otsego became a Republican stronghold.[1]

Otsego's leading Federalists were incredulous and sullen at their rapid and complete fall from public honor and authority. They hated the new, overtly democratic style of politics, and they despaired of returning to power until the nation had gone through the full cycle of anarchy, terror, and tyranny that they so confidently predicted. Dr. Joseph White insisted that the nation could not long endure "under our present form of Government or under any form Purely Republican." Because the people had become "the dupes of fashion . . . in Politics," he had "totally withdrawn from the tumultuous contest." Similarly, Jacob Morris complained, "I hate the name of politics which appears now only . . . in the mouth of every Ruffian in our once happy country." Embittered, he pronounced republican government "a visionary and chimerical Theory." Morris hated "the midnight assassins of democracy" and desperately clung to his gloom in the face of occasional Federalist victories: "No partial success of Federalists will, however, induce me to alter my opinion as to the certainty of the ultimate downfall of the Republic from the effects of democracy."[2]

Their rage is especially striking because Morris and White continued to prosper economically under the Republican regime they so detested. White thrived as a surgeon, medical professor, and president of the bank founded in Cherry Valley in 1818. Morris still reaped wealth from his vast landholdings in Butternuts and vicinity, built a grand new mansion in 1805, patronized the local Episcopal church, promoted agricultural reforms, and championed the colonization of freed slaves from America back to Africa. But it was precisely the detachment of political prestige from great estates that so aggrieved Morris and White. They pined for the era when political honor had accrued almost automatically to gentlemen of superior wealth, education, and connections—the era terminated by the Jedediah Pecks of America.[3]

As subsequent elections compounded their political impotence, leading Federalists indulged in self-contempt as well as rage against the common people. In 1803 Ebenezer Foote lamented, "[We] are sunk to and form a small column of *Grumblers* who appear to have no plan to execute but [are] determined to find fault with all that is done & without spirit sufficient to make any effectual opposition. . . . Our Pusilanimity renders us Contemptible."[4]

The New York Federalists reached their nadir in the gubernatorial election of 1804. When George Clinton declined reelection, the Republicans nominated Morgan Lewis, then the chief justice of the state supreme court. The Federalists conceded the futility of running one of their own and instead supported a dissident Republican: Vice President Aaron Burr. Suspected of trying to steal the presidency from Jefferson in early 1801, Burr had become unwelcome in Republican circles. Frozen out of the state and national patronage by Clinton and Jefferson, he sought a political comeback by running for governor of New York with Federalist support. One of his Federalist supporters assured Richard Fenimore Cooper, "This my friend is the last great stake of Federalism in this State and most probably in the United States." However, because most Federalists could muster little enthusiasm for Burr and because most Republicans hated his flirtation with their foes, Lewis cruised to an easy victory, capturing 58 percent of the vote. The Federalist defeat was especially great in Otsego County, where Lewis won 62 percent of the votes. It seemed that Federalism was virtually dead in New York, unable to compete for power even in alliance with a disgruntled Republican minority.[5]

While Cooper, Morris, and White persisted in Otsego and in enforced political retirement, the three ambitious young Federalist lawyers—Moss Kent, Jr., Joseph Strong, and Abraham C. Ten Broeck—left the county, hop-

ing to reconstruct their political and legal careers elsewhere. Despite his official reinstatement to the Otsego bar, Strong's law practice dwindled. In
mid-1800 he closed his Cooperstown law office, resigned as postmaster, and
removed to New York City, where he abandoned the practice of the law in
favor of running a store. But a fire destroyed his new business, ruining
Strong financially. In 1802 Ten Broeck sold his Cooperstown house, rented
his slave to Judge Cooper, and returned to his native New Brunswick, New
Jersey. Defeated in his reelection bid for the state senate (and devastated by
the death of Hannah Cooper), in November 1804 Kent resigned his office
as Otsego County surrogate. Selling his house in Cooperstown, he removed
northward to Jefferson County, located amid the new settlements of the St.
Lawrence River valley. There he practiced law, served as a land agent, and
revived his political career. Running as a Federalist, he won state assembly
seats in 1807 and 1810 and congressional races in 1812 and 1814.[6]

PUBLIC MORALITY 🔥

In the wake of Federalism's decline and his own political downfall, William
Cooper developed a greater appreciation of religious institutions. Like so
many other Federalists driven from office, he began to hope that churches
would reclaim the common people from their infatuation with democracy.
Regular religious instruction by learned ministers might restore the proper
appreciation for public order and popular subordination. In 1806 Cooper
insisted, "I have thought for two or more years back that our Political Welfare depends much on adhearing to the rules of religion." He credited the
advent in 1800 of a Presbyterian church in Cooperstown for the persistent
Federalism of the village, in contrast to the raging Republicanism of the hinterland—where religious indifference alternated with evangelical fervor.[7]

Formerly contemptuous of churches, Cooper became their ardent supporter—but for social and political purposes rather than out of any new personal piety. He occasionally attended the public worship available in
Cooperstown: sometimes Quaker, often Episcopal, but usually Presbyterian.
However, Cooper never joined a church and never expressed any personal
dedication to Christ. In 1806 he extolled the social effects of the Presbyterian church in Cooperstown: "It is manifest that a happy Union of spirits has
ben cultivated—good order advanced and a temper of Meekness more than
I Perceived before seems to give a little light to men walking in the dark." In
A Guide in the Wilderness, Cooper added that the Presbyterian church had
produced "new and better morals" in the village: "and it is now become a
matter of honest pride, and as it were, a fashion to be orderly and correct.
If any still follow the ancient practice of fishing and hunting, on a Sunday,
they no longer go openly and publicly, but privately and unseen."[8]

To help rescue the Republic from a Jacobinism that the Federalists deemed at once moral and political, Cooper encouraged and subsidized new churches in Otsego. Between 1800 and 1807 he gave five small lots of land to provide building sites for churches in Burlington, Butternuts, Hartwick, Cooperstown, and Fly Creek (a rural district in Otsego Township). Cooper was especially generous to the Cooperstown Presbyterian Church, providing a free village lot, contributing toward construction of the church, and subsidizing the salary of its minister. To his considerable gratification the village Presbyterians honored their patron by soliciting his approval of their measures. In March 1806 they asked Cooper to affirm the Reverend William Neill as their new minister: they felt "it a duty they owed both to you and themselves to take your opinion on a subject of so much importance as the settlement of [a] minister before they come to a final decision." Cooper's approval was virtually a foregone conclusion because he had recruited Neill to come to Cooperstown. Indeed, Neill lodged with the judge's daughter Ann and her husband, George Pomeroy.[9]

Cooper's religious patronage was selective, reserved for the more orthodox and conservative denominations committed to public decorum and a learned ministry: Congregationalists, Presbyterians, and Episcopalians. Conversely, he bestowed no favors on the more evangelical, emotional, and egalitarian sects active in Otsego: the Baptists, Methodists, and Christian Connection. Nor did he aid the rationalist but theologically radical Universalists. With good reason Federalists regarded the more plebeian and enthusiastic denominations as akin to political democrats in their shared dislike for genteel education and authority. As a rule the preachers for the upstart denominations avoided overt political partisanship, but their followers generally recognized that the Republicans best expressed their distaste for hierarchy and elitism.[10]

Reverend Daniel Nash, the Episcopalian missionary in Otsego County, took special pains to nurture Judge Cooper's new solicitude for community religion. Devout, dedicated, tireless, and resourceful, Nash understood the strategic importance of establishing an Episcopal church in prosperous, populous, and influential Cooperstown. Soliciting Cooper's patronage, Nash insisted that the hierarchical and genteel Episcopal Church would "counteract the Spirit of Jacobinism." Nash enjoyed important assistance from Cooper's new daughter-in-law, Mary Ann Morris Cooper, a dedicated Episcopalian who brought her husband, Isaac, into that church. Moreover, the judge felt grateful to Nash for conducting Hannah's funeral service in 1800.[11]

Contributing at least $1,600 toward erecting Christ Church in Cooperstown, Cooper financed about half of the construction costs for the building dedicated in 1810 and completed in 1815. Nash shrewdly located Christ Church directly behind Otsego Hall and beside the Cooper family burial plot, which featured Hannah's grave and tombstone. Thereby Nash ensured that most of the judge's children would regard Christ Church as their own institution and as the keeper of the grave most sacred to their memory. He cemented the Coopers' allegiance to Episcopalianism by absorbing their most cherished relic into the grounds of Christ Church.[12]

Although William Cooper could never bring himself formally to join the Episcopalians—or any other church—he delighted in becoming their patron. In 1806 he explained, "I am not of that Society, tho' I love them, and [am] led into the Measure solely from the good that is manifest since Mr. Nash has brought them together." Cooper also pleased his business and political partners in New York City and Albany who were staunch Federalists and committed Episcopalians: Robert Troup, Richard Harison, Daniel Hale, Frederick De Peyster, Rufus King, William Ogden, and Josiah Ogden Hoffman. Finally, Cooper regarded Episcopalianism as a genteel faith that would help polish the manners of his sons and enrich their cosmopolitan connections to the urban gentry.[13]

In general, the new churches had only a limited effect on public morality in Cooperstown. While many villagers cultivated greater self-discipline in pursuit of respectability, a defiant element remained fond of drinking, profanity, ballplaying, horse racing, card playing, and Sabbath breaking. Travelers were struck by the close juxtaposition of churches and taverns, prosperity and poverty, industry and indolence, piety and profanity, sobriety and intemperance, and of reputation and infamy in the compact little village. In 1809 a visitor described his impressions of Cooperstown:

> Found houses very crouded—streets narrow. . . . Saw some large houses—conclude the people must be rich—thought what a fine thing it is to have nothing to do but spend property. Found two meeting houses—conclude the people must be very religious. . . . Find good many round the tavern—appear to be very fond of whisky, rum, brandy, &c. . . . What a pity it is [that] the lake in this place was not filled with whiskey—what a happy place 'twoud be!! . . . Attended meeting—had good preaching—preacher was animated—felt and believed what he said—boys were disorderly in the gallery—preacher had to stop and talk to them—shameful—parents should teach their children better. After meeting returned to my lodgings—saw people walking the streets long before sunset—saw others carting hay—conclude [that] they are not very religious—this contrary to my former conclusion concerning meetinghouses.

The village Federalists pressed for a concerted and coercive public effort either to reform or to oust "the vile" people from Cooperstown. But the local Republican leaders regarded the village sots as a minority who were better ignored or privately admonished than used to justify yet another Federalist initiative meant to restrict individual rights. The Republicans were properly suspicious of Federalist schemes to reclaim public authority by championing religious order and moral reform. Indeed, Republicans regarded the

Federalist moralizers as hypocrites in light of their previous association with deism, Freemasonry, gambling, and tippling.[14]

FIRES 🕯

In 1807 a new split in Republican ranks offered to rescue the Federalists from political impotence and oblivion. Although elected as a Republican in 1804, Gov. Morgan Lewis was a wealthy and pompous landlord who belonged to the aristocratic Livingston clan and felt uncomfortable with democracy. Once in office Lewis quickly alienated the Republican party's dominant faction, led by George Clinton, his nephew DeWitt Clinton, and his son-in-law Ambrose Spencer. The Clintonians—who included Jedediah Peck—became incensed at Lewis for checking their power over the Council of Appointment and for supporting legislation to incorporate a bank sought by Alexander Hamilton and other New York City Federalists. Abandoned by the Clintonians, Lewis needed Federalist support to win reelection. Beginning in mid-1805 Lewis befriended leading Federalists, including William Cooper. Exchanging letters, Governor Lewis and Judge Cooper confirmed their mutual commitment to elitism. "The People cannot receive political, as divine Truths, by Inspiration; they must be illuminated by those who have Leisure and knowledge to instruct," the governor assured Cooper. They also agreed that Peck remained the chief obstacle to a conservative revival in Otsego. "Old Peck, I fear, has your County in a string and if he was himself Sprung, I believe it would be a common benefit," Lewis wrote. The governor sealed his covert alliance with Cooper and the other Otsego Federalists during a September 1806 visit to Cooperstown, ostensibly to review the local militia.[15]

The game of political realignment worked both ways, inviting disgruntled Federalists to shake that unpopular identity by announcing their new love for the orthodox, Clintonian brand of Republicanism. Needing every reinforcement in their battle with Lewis, the Clintonians welcomed Federalist deserters. By 1807 Elihu Phinney, the Federalist editor and publisher of the *Otsego Herald,* had grown uncomfortable with his dwindling circulation, profits, and influence in an increasingly Republican county. Because his primary allegiance was to the dollar, rather than to any abstract principles, Phinney suddenly forsook his old political friends to endorse the Clintonian candidate for governor, Daniel D. Tompkins. Adopting populist rhetoric, Phinney depicted the election as a crusade by Tompkins, "the son of a farmer," to frustrate "a combination of rich families," including the Coopers, who were determined to subvert the Republic. With remarkable speed and ease, Phinney turned against his longtime patron Judge Cooper.[16]

The Republican majority in the state legislature quickly rewarded Phinney for his remarkable and politically valuable conversion. The legislature was considering two rival petitions to incorporate the village at the foot of Lake Otsego. Incorporation would provide Cooperstown with a government distinct from Otsego Township. Ostensibly the rival petitions disputed the official name for the incorporated village: in one, Cooper and the village Federalists sought to retain the name Cooperstown, while the other, championed by Elihu Phinney and his new Republican friends, favored Otsego Village in order to dishonor the judge. But something more tangible and valuable was also at stake: water. Compact and wooden, Cooperstown was vulnerable to fire and needed a steady supply of water. In 1794 William Cooper and ten associates formed the Company of the Water Works in Cooperstown and laid a system of wooden pipes (hollowed out logs) that bore "pure water" to the village from a spring in the side of a hill to the west. To obtain some of that water, a villager had to buy a membership from the company (which imposed a £3 fine on any member who permitted a nonmember to draw water). In their 1807 petition Phinney's group sought to undercut that monopoly by obtaining legislative incorporation of a competing company named The Aqueduct Association in the Village of Otsego. The judge spent much of March in Albany haunting the assembly lobby to press for passage of his bill. Instead, on April 3, the day after Phinney openly endorsed Tompkins in the *Otsego Herald,* the state legislature passed a bill incorporating Otsego Village and empowering Elihu Phinney and four associates to establish their aqueduct company.[17]

Wounded by the theft of *his* village, William Cooper plunged into the campaign of 1807 with a vengeance. It became his personal mission to punish Phinney and the Clintonian Republicans by helping to defeat their candidate for governor. Enthusiastic and reckless in political battle, Cooper could not resist the temptation to stump vigorously for Lewis. However, by campaigning so vigorously and conspicuously, Cooper imperiled Lewis's reelection. Because the Federalists were such an unpopular minority in New York State, they were supposed to keep a low profile until election day, allowing Lewis's Republican supporters to present the governor as an orthodox Republican beleaguered by Clintonian heretics and ingrates. The governor needed Federalist votes, but he also had to downplay his reliance on them, for fear of alarming the Republicans who remained in his camp. Because Cooper was so notorious as an unreconstructed Federalist, his flamboyant exertions for Lewis betrayed the collusion. The Republican newspapers gleefully trumpeted the news of Cooper's activities as proof that Lewis had forsaken his party to succour the detested Federalists.[18]

Alarmed at the prospect of a Federalist revival, most voters rallied to the Clintonians. In the state as a whole, Tompkins prevailed by over 4,000 votes. In Otsego County, he garnered 1,821 votes to Lewis's 1,170. Many Otsego voters explained that they had "voted against Mr. Lewis" primarily because the "Federalists were said to vote for him." Keeping the Federalists in public disgrace and away from public office remained of paramount importance to the majority in Otsego and throughout the state. Overt association with William Cooper and his compatriots had ruined Lewis's chances. The governor had also damaged his cause during his September 1806 review of the Otsego militia. Moralistic and lofty, Lewis had declined to treat the men to the customary hogshead of rum per brigade, losing most of their votes in the subsequent election. By adopting the Federalists' program of moral reform, Lewis reaped a share in their unpopularity.[19]

Flushed with victory, Phinney and his associates aggressively moved to implement the new government for Otsego Village. The May 14 issue of the *Otsego Herald* announced Tompkins's sweeping victory *and* summoned the villagers to meet at the courthouse on Tuesday, May 19, to elect five trustees. But Phinney and Metcalf underestimated the resiliency and the anger of the Federalists, who were still a solid majority in the village, if no longer in the county at large. On the nineteenth the Federalist majority packed the courthouse and elected five trustees favored by William Cooper. Four days later the village Federalists reconvened at Maj. Joseph Griffin's Red Lion Tavern. They instructed the new trustees not to act until the legislature amended the incorporation and restored the name Cooperstown. Frustrated at the check delivered to his plans, Phinney jeered, "Oxen when accustomed to the yoke will haw or jee, as their master dictates." He disdained the Federalist opposition as "the scoff and sneers of aristocrats" and a feeble attempt "by Judge Cooper, and his few adherents, to retain a name which the easy compliance of the first settlers yielded to his vanity."[20]

Enraged by Phinney's betrayal, Cooper urged his neighbors to cancel their subscriptions to the *Otsego Herald*, and he launched an effort to bring another, solidly Federalist newspaper into the village. In late 1808 the Cooperstown Federalists established their own newspaper, misnamed *The Impartial Observer*. As editor Cooper recruited William Andrews, a recent immigrant from England whom the judge had met in New York City. Cooper advanced $500 to buy and relocate a printing press, and he provided a building on Fair Street in front of Otsego Hall. The local Federalists also subsidized Andrews by entrusting their sons to the school "for young Gentlemen" that he and his wife operated in the local academy building.[21]

In the newspaper war that ensued, the stolid Andrews was no match for the resourceful and witty Elihu Phinney. The Federalist paper's ill-chosen name and the unfortunate ethnicity of its editor were severe liabilities that Phinney relentlessly exploited with searing sarcasm. As an English immigrant, Andrews was an easy mark for Phinney's Republican attacks on the Federalists as the treasonous sycophants of English aristocrats. And Phinney nicknamed the rival paper the Imp—a word that then meant a small demon rather than a mischievous child. Enraged by Phinney's barbs, Andrews responded with mean-spirited diatribes that assailed the diminutive and hard-drinking Phinney as a "pigmy Editor, drunk one hour and insane the next."[22]

The vitriolic attacks—and Andrews's presumption in publishing some of them without Cooper's prior approval—profoundly embarrassed the judge, who so cherished the elusive ideals of unity and harmony. Recognizing that Andrews was a hopeless liability—witless, insubordinate, and English—Cooper sacked him in late March, transferring the paper to the assistant editor, John Holmes Prentiss, who was conveniently Yankee as well as staunchly Federalist. Two months later Cooper and Prentiss jettisoned the unfortunate name *Impartial Observer* in favor of the more accurate and less easily satirized *Cooperstown Federalist*. Although lacking Phinney's keen wit, Prentiss possessed a bulldog tenacity that rendered his paper a formidable and enduring rival. For the time being Cooper remained the real owner of the newspaper, but Prentiss gradually paid off the debt and eventually acquired full title.[23]

Begun in 1807 the dispute over the village name, water, and government dragged on for five years. On the one hand, the Federalist majority in the village refused to put the act of incorporation into operation until the legislature restored the name Cooperstown. On the other hand, the Republican-dominated state legislature refused to back down and alter the original act that called the place Otsego Village. Meanwhile, Cooperstown suffered severe fires for want of the fire code, company, and engine authorized by the act of incorporation but stymied by the deadlock over the village name and government.

The farcical standoff included apparent divine retribution in a pair of fires on March 30 and 31, 1809, almost two years after the act of incorporation. The first fire erupted in the bookstore belonging to Elihu Phinney's two sons, Henry and Elihu, Jr. It then spread and consumed the new and adjoining house of William Dowse, a young Federalist lawyer who had achieved notoriety for publishing vitriolic attacks on Phinney and other village Republicans. The second fire broke out in the academy building, then used as a school by William Andrews and his wife. Demonstrating the same evenhanded sense of justice as the first fire, the second spread to the adjoining house of Elihu Phinney. The academy was destroyed, but the villagers' efforts minimized the damage to Phinney's home. Because, by Cooper's design, the village center was so compact, political enemies lived cheek by jowl with daily opportunities for abrasive encounters and for exposure to the same contagious fires.[24]

Led by the magnanimous Judge Cooper, villagers of both parties joined in a subscription to compensate the victims. The *Impartial Observer* reported, "The worthy and philanthropic founder of this Village, which bears his name, as has been his uniform practice on all public occasions, gave one more proof of his elevated mind in leading a subscription for the relief of the unfortunate sufferers by a contribution of 300 dollars." In contrast, Phinney's account ignored the judge's particular generosity and blandly awarded equal credit for the subscription to all the villagers. Rather than accept any charity from Judge Cooper, the Phinneys rejected the subscription money and instead repaired and rebuilt with $1,000 borrowed from Dr. John Russell, a political ally.[25]

The political stalemate—and the consequent fires—persisted for another three years, until the Federalists briefly obtained a majority in the state legislature and, in June 1812, pushed through a bill reincorporating the village as Cooperstown. The new act made no provision for Phinney's water company. The village's Federalist majority promptly organized a government, established a fire code, recruited a fire company, and accepted a fire engine donated by the heirs of William Cooper. The first test of the engine came in late 1812, when a fire erupted in the warehouse belonging to Isaac and Richard Fenimore Cooper; the building burned down, but "the timely exertions of the citizens with the new Fire Engine" saved the rest of the village. The judge had not lived to see his name restored to the village, but his son Isaac Cooper emerged as the president of the new village board of trustees. Meanwhile, Elihu Phinney refused to accept defeat and stubbornly preserved "Otsego Village" on the masthead of his newspaper for as long as he lived. On July 17, 1813, the *Otsego Herald* bore a black border and reported the death and funeral of the paper's founder, publisher, and editor. And, for the first time in over six years, the paper's masthead was rearranged by his less politicized sons to list the place of publication as Cooperstown.[26]

THE FEDERALIST REVIVAL

In late 1807 the Republican national administration of Thomas Jefferson declared a trade war with Great Britain by imposing an embargo on American exports. Because the export of wheat and potash was critical to New York's economy, the embargo brought on a commercial depression that corroded popular support for the Republicans. For want of a foreign market, the price of wheat in Albany plummeted from $2.00 a bushel in 1807 to only 75 cents a year later. Declining farm incomes meant swelling debts and increasing lawsuits from impatient and alarmed creditors, producing widespread discontent. In 1808–1809 the debt cases tried by the Otsego County Court of Common Pleas soared to 467, more than double the number resolved in the two years, before the embargo. Thirty-four Otsego men declared bankruptcy in 1808–1809, up from twenty-one during

1806–1807. As a result of the commercial depression, property values per
Otsego taxpayer declined by 15 percent between 1805 and 1810: from
$741 in 1805 to $633 in 1810 (see Tables 8–10).[27]

When Republicanism no longer equaled prosperity, many New York voters began to have second thoughts. In the 1808 legislative elections, the
Federalists made significant gains, and they captured a majority in the assembly in 1809—a remarkable comeback for a party that had been mori-
bund two years before (the Republicans retained control of the state
senate). In Otsego County in 1808 the citizens again elected Republicans to
the state legislature, but with only 53 percent of the vote, down from the
usual 60 percent of previous elections. A year later, in an especially heated
contest, the Otsego Federalists narrowly captured all four assembly seats for
the first time in over a decade, winning 51 percent of the vote.[28]

Although the Republicans carried thirteen of the county's twenty towns,
the Federalists won the 1809 election because their communities were
more populous than the Republican towns in the more sparsely settled hinterland. The county's four most populous towns were all Federalist strongholds, while the Republicans controlled the eight smallest towns (see Table
11). On average, the Federalist town was 1.7 times larger than the typical
Republican town—2,651 versus 1,528—and 1.8 times richer in aggregate
wealth: $230,697 versus $127,866. In large part the greater population and
wealth of Federalist towns were a function of relative age; on average the
Federalist township was older, incorporated in 1795, compared with the
1800 mean for the Republican townships. In general, the county's political
geography of 1809 closely resembled the pattern of 1801: a Republican periphery around a Federalist core centered upon the villages of Cooperstown
and Cherry Valley (see Map 7). The main difference was that in 1809 the
Federalists mobilized a larger vote in their older, populous, and commercialized strongholds, which were especially hurt by the embargo.[29]

As partisanship revived in 1808–1810, the parties held annual county
conventions and competed to publish lists of their delegates, secretaries,
chairmen, and committees to prove their local strength. Lists in the newspapers from the campaigns of 1808, 1809, and 1810 identify 202 party activists: 71 Federalists and 131 Republicans. All the activists were men, and
most were Yankees, but both parties included some leaders drawn from the
German, Dutch, and Scotch-Irish minorities in the county. Formerly the
critical political divide in Otsego, ethnicity no longer distinguished the
county's parties.[30]

The key difference between the parties was the presence of a larger
county elite of landlords, merchants, and lawyers at the pinnacle of the Federalist hierarchy. Most of the leaders in both parties were farmers, but their
preponderance was greater among the Republicans than among the Federalists. I can identify the occupations for 58 of the Federalists and 78 of the

POLITICAL ALLEGIANCES,
OTSEGO COUNTY, 1809

········ Township Boundary

▨ Republican Majority Towns

☐ Federalist Majority Towns

0   7.5   15
miles

N

MAP 7

Republicans. Farmers accounted for 64 of the 78 Republicans (82 percent), compared with 32 of the 58 Federalists (55 percent). The latter party's leaders included nine merchants and four lawyers, compared with the Republicans' two merchants and three lawyers. The county's six preeminent landlords were all Federalists. As a group the Federalist leaders were far more prosperous than their Republican counterparts. The 1803 tax lists for Otsego towns reveal the assessed property values for 58 of the Federalists and 102 of the Republicans. The average Federalist partisan ($2,131) possessed more than twice as much property as his Republican equivalent ($959). Both parties honored property in allocating leadership to their most prosperous partisans, but the Federalists had a larger and wealthier stratum at the top of their party than did the Otsego Republicans.[31]

Although the two parties continued to represent different constituencies, they converged in their political structures and public styles. When opportunity knocked in 1808 and 1809, the active Federalists reinvented themselves as more professional and popular politicians. Forsaking the unpopular old pretensions of the Fathers of the People, the younger Federal-

ists posed as new-style Friends of the People. Following the Republican example, the Federalists developed a formal party mechanism with a hierarchy of town, county, district, and state committees selected by annual
conventions of delegates. Recognizing the popularity of the name Republican, they sought a share by renaming themselves Federal Republicans.[32]

Forsaking their old reputation as private cabals of lofty gentlemen, the
new-style Federalists reached out to the electorate. In 1809 a public appeal
written by an Otsego Federalist announced, "We have not called you together in a corner, nor is it our intention to consult only such as have
heretofore acted in sentiment with us. We wish to consult all and that in
open day light." Indeed, the Federalists boasted that their county convention, held at the Presbyterian church in Cooperstown on February 28, 1809,
attracted 1,000 electors. No longer harping on the superiority of gentlemen
and the ignorance of the people, their essayists often adopted a folksy voice.
In December 1808 an Otsego Federalist pretended to be a humble farmer:

> *After I had done my day's work, I set down by the fireside to shave a stick that
> I had cut for an axe handle, my Wife had put all the Children in bed and was
> turning over and contriving patches for their Clothes. . . . I finished my axe
> handle and an excellent piece of Timber it was, and I thought if we were as care-
> ful in looking for rulers as we are in choosing an axe handle we should have
> better times.*

Posing as the truest friends of the people, the reborn Federalists denounced
the Republican politicians as hypocrites and parasites who sucked offices
and salaries from taxes levied on the long-suffering people. Stealing Republican rhetoric, the Otsego Federalists exhorted: "Arouse honest Yeomanry of our Country, with you under divine providence rests the Salvation
of this Nation. If you are not now vigilant and at your posts, we are undone—we must become a Nation of Slaves. Arouse then before it is too late
and change your Rulers." One clever Otsego Federalist even proposed cutting the salaries of county clerks—all of them Republicans, of course—to
provide more funds for common schools. Thereby he aroused keen partisan alarm, exposing the Republican leaders as officeholders more interested in their incomes than in the well-being of the common people.[33]

In Otsego County the older and wealthier Federalists—principally Judge
Cooper, General Morris, and Dr. White—remained critical to party fi-
nances. But the old guard conceded most of the organizing, writing, and
canvassing to a new generation of aggressive young conservatives, primarily
printers and lawyers on the rise and on the make. Active leadership largely
passed to three new residents of Cooperstown, who arrived with little property, good educations, and active ambitions: the lawyers Robert Campbell
(1782–1847) and William Dowse (1770–1813), and the editor John
Holmes Prentiss (1784–1861). By combining their talents and versatility

with the largesse of the wealthy but archaic grandees, the young Federalists meant to revitalize their party and thereby reap offices, influence, and wealth. In effect, they were the second coming of the three Federalist lawyers—Moss Kent, Jr., Joseph Strong, and Abraham C. Ten Broeck—who had recklessly grasped for county power in the 1790s only to immolate their own careers along with the power of the local great men. But the new troika was shrewder at cultivating the old guard, who, in turn, were now ready to concede active leadership to younger men. Marriages also helped bind the young and the old Federalists of Otsego: Campbell married a sister of George Pomeroy, the husband of Ann Cooper, while Prentiss married the youngest daughter of Jacob Morris.[34]

Although the old guard and the new men needed one another, their co-operation was sometimes uneasy. On the one hand, the young Federalists had greater respect for the money than for the judgment of their seniors. In the eyes of the new, the old men seemed stubbornly wedded to the overt elitism and archaic paternalism that had been their downfall in 1799–1801. On the other hand, the party elders insisted that their deep pockets and long experience warranted control over the reckless young Federalists. Sometimes the old guard doubted that their ambitious, flexible, and often unscrupulous new allies were significantly better than their Republican rivals. Morris grumbled,

> As to politicks, and particularly electioneering, which is now confined princi-
> pally to the lowest, and vilest parts of the community, I am sick at heart of it,
> and loathe the very name. . . . Federalists will never be preferred to office untill
> the people are persuaded that there is more democracy in that party than in the
> party which has now the ascendency and God knows there is too much in both.

Become all too comfortable in their self-righteous and self-pitying gloom, the old guard wondered if electoral victory was worth the effort and the compromises.[35]

Relations occasionally became strained when the young ignored their elders to maneuver in clever ways that seemed dangerously "Jacobinical" to the old guard. In the spring of 1808 an old-style Federalist, Ebenezer Foote of Delaware County, stood for election to Congress in the district that included Otsego. Running in the traditional manner, Foote counted on the support of old friends and local grandees such as the Coopers. But he did not bargain on the interference of young Federalists contemptuous of his old-fashioned persona. During the last week of the campaign, a special committee of young Federalists from Delaware County repaired to Cooperstown to warn their Otsego counterparts that Foote was hopelessly unpopular at home. To sow dissension among the Republicans, the delegation urged jettisoning Foote in favor of a dissident Delaware County Republican named Gabriel North. Readily persuaded, the Otsego Federalist committee fol-

lowed the lead of Campbell and Dowse, publicly disavowing Foote's candidacy. Consequently, North won twice as many votes as Foote—but both men
lost to the regular Republican candidate, Erastus Root. Foote felt embarrassed and insulted by the sudden abandonment and his overwhelming defeat—especially because North was an old and bitter rival at home in
Delaware County. Misperceiving Dowse and Campbell in old-style terms as
William Cooper's pliant tools, Foote felt betrayed by the judge. In an angry
letter to Cooper, he complained in the traditional manner: "God knows I
never *did* nor ever shall solicit their suffrages for myself. But Sir, I have a
right to complain of their . . . exposing me to the Insult and abuse of *Jacobins*
and *Scoundrels*—and then abandoning me for the purpose of takeing up
one of the most bitter and uniform *Jacobins* in Delaware [County]." In his
father's absence Isaac Cooper replied, expressing chagrin at the conduct of
the young Federalists: "I must say they acted as much like Democrats as ever
I knew Federalists to do." But Isaac could no more explain his family's inability to restrain Campbell and Dowse than Foote could account for his betrayal by his county's new Federalist activists.[36]

REPUBLICAN REACTION ⚱

As a new breed of printers and lawyers reinvented the Federalist party, the
alarmed Republicans increasingly looked for leadership to their own young
lawyers. The Otsego Republicans concluded that it took a lawyer to beat
another lawyer, in a battle that increasingly revolved around convention
maneuvers and the arguments published in newspapers, pamphlets, broad-
sides, and handbills. Farmer-politicos such as Jedediah Peck and Robert
Roseboom continued to serve as the Republican candidates for Otsego's
legislative seats, but a new breed of lawyer-politicians assumed management
of the party's county committee, conventions, and publications. During
the 1810s the lawyers would complete their ascendancy by seeking and winning electoral office, gradually replacing the old-style Republicans as state
legislators.

The three rising stars of Otsego Republicanism were the young lawyers
Farrand Stranahan (1778–1826), Jabez D. Hammond (1778–1855), and
Ambrose Jordan (1789–1865). They were far better educated, more cosmopolitan, and wealthier than the county's original Republican leaders: the
self-educated farmers Peck, Roseboom, and James Moore. In 1801, at the
age of twenty-three, Stranahan came to Cooperstown, established his law office in the front chamber of a house belonging to Phinney, and quickly developed the largest and most lucrative practice in town. His counterpart in
Cherry Valley was Jabez D. Hammond, who had moved there from Vermont
in 1805 at the age of twenty-seven. Ambrose Jordan was an extraordinarily

charming, well-read, dashing, and handsome young man who migrated to Cooperstown in 1812 at the age of twenty-three. He prospered as Stranahan's legal and political partner. When Peck retired from politics and Stranahan ran into financial difficulties, Jordan became the county's premier power broker during the later 1810s. No Jacobin, he presided over the Cooperstown board of trustees and was master of the Freemasonic lodge.[37]

Like their ally Elihu Phinney, the three new leaders were recent and opportunistic converts to Republicanism. Stranahan had grown rich and influential by exploiting the business provided him by Richard Fenimore Cooper. They dissolved their partnership on January 10, 1807, after Stranahan suddenly espoused Republicanism and joined his friend Phinney in petitioning for a village government and water company. In the election of 1807 Hammond had cooperated with the Federalists, but in 1808 he espoused Republicanism. Until his removal to Cooperstown in 1812, Jordan probably shared the Federalism of his legal mentor, Jacob R. Van Rensselaer of Claverack. Lacking ideological commitment, Stranahan, Hammond, and Jordan simply decided that the Republican party was the most promising vehicle for their considerable ambitions.[38]

Led by the new breed of lawyer-politicians, the Republicans halted the Federalist momentum and restored their party's dominance in New York State in 1810. It helped that in mid-1809 the Jefferson administration recognized political reality and lifted the unpopular and increasingly ineffective embargo. Because the straying Republican voters returned to the fold, Gov. Daniel D. Tompkins won reelection with 54 percent of the statewide vote (52 percent in Otsego), defeating the old-style Federalist Jonas Platt. The Republicans also captured both houses of the state legislature, reinvesting their party with control of the coveted Council of Appointment. In Otsego the Republicans ousted the Federalist assemblymen, capturing all four seats with an average of 53 percent of the vote. In Otsego County both the Federalist and the Republican voters displayed remarkable party discipline. Totals for the Federalists' four assembly candidates fell within a mere 9 votes, from the low man with 2,221 to a high of 2,230. Similarly, the variation among the four Republicans was just 15 votes: from a low of 2,514 to a high of 2,529. The victorious Republicans celebrated by sweeping out the state and county officeholders whom the Federalists had installed before the election.[39]

But the restored Republican party of 1810 was no longer the populist movement of 1800. In their short-term eagerness to stem the Federalist revival, the Republicans turned to entrepreneurial printers and ambitious lawyers for their new champions. At every election the new Republican leaders revived the old populist rhetoric of an ongoing class struggle between common producers (farmers and artisans) and parasitic Federalist aristocrats: "Your old enemies, the Federalists, are now making the most violent, and probably their last efforts to defeat and thwart the wishes of the people." "The Farmers and Mechanics of Otsego, will then decide whether they will be governed by aristocratic lordlings, or whether they will govern themselves by their freely elected representatives." Such rhetoric was more heartfelt when expressed by the county's original Republican leaders, by men of grammar-school educations, plain manners, callused hands, and modest farms. That same rhetoric sounded smoother but more hollow when spoken or written by the newer party leaders. The Republican persuasion had become a stage language, requiring a convincing performance for election but bearing little consequence for domestic policy. It served only to keep Republicans in office and Federalists out. Except in the realm of political organization and style, the electoral revolution of 1800–1801 had faded by 1810 in New York State.[40]

The Republican rivalry with the Federalists remained rancorous and continued to sound significant. Indeed, the electoral rhetoric grew even more heated and personal, and the campaign maneuvers became more cunning as the new breed leaders of each party could look upon one another as morally fallen counterparts. The younger Republican and Federalist leaders saw their rivals as unprincipled gentlemen perverting their comparable educations and opportunities in the service of false political gods. In 1809 the young Federalist lawyer William Dowse publicly denounced the young Republican lawyer Jabez D. Hammond as a political "traitor" who demonstrated "the imbecility and the total depravity of human nature." To a Federalist such as Dowse, Republicanism was far more insidious when adopted by a close counterpart like Hammond than when professed by a common demagogue like Jedediah Peck. As a gentleman Hammond had no excuses; he should have known better than to consort in politics with vulgar populists. Aware that each could easily have chosen the other's side, the young leaders assailed one another with a venom meant to justify and cement their allegiances and reassure themselves and their allies that their own convictions would endure.[41]

Despite the continuing sound and fury, elections mattered little except to determine the particular gentlemen who would hold state and county office. The Federalists had adopted the pose and organization of a democratic party, whereupon the Republicans reacted by empowering young lawyers very much like the new leaders of their rivals. Republican voters settled for the simple notion that keeping the Federalists out of office was sufficient to safeguard the rights and interests of the people. During the 1790s Jedediah Peck had built Otsego Republicanism by denouncing lawyers and Freemasons; during the subsequent decade he found himself cooperating with wealthy and prominent lawyers and Freemasons to defend the Republican party from a resurgent Federalism.

It was in this climate of partisan revitalization, newspaper wars, and village fires that William Cooper was murdered—or so the story goes.

DEATH 🕯

In this century every historical account of Judge William Cooper and every biography of his son the novelist James Fenimore Cooper reports that the judge was killed in Albany in December 1809 by a blow to the head delivered by a political opponent after a heated public meeting. But none of these accounts identifies the murderer. This murder mystery has a special piquancy, because leading literary scholars insist that William Cooper's violent death had a powerful impact on the social attitudes and literary choices of his son. Warren Motley observes, "His father had been murdered by a blow from behind delivered without warning, and Cooper never lost his sense of how swiftly the vestments of civilization could fall to reveal the naked natural brute. . . . Like one of the islands in *The Crater,* society always seemed to him a habitable volcano—dormant, but not extinct." Motley adds, "The veneer of civilization cracked for a moment, and the patriarch of Cooperstown was struck down."[42]

In his Freudian reading of the Leather-Stocking novels, Stephen Railton dwells upon the judge's death as the critical event in shaping James Fenimore Cooper's identity and imagination. He insists that a scene in the twelfth chapter of *The Last of the Mohicans* offers the most intimate insight into the novelist's fundamental psychic conflict: "his ambivalent unconscious attitude toward the figure of his father." Uncas stands over the wrestling, rolling bodies of his father, Chingachgook, and his enemy Magua, but the son cannot strike for fear of hitting his father. Railton equates Chingachgook with William Cooper, who "was in fact murdered by an enemy," and Uncas with James Fenimore Cooper, who "was variously compelled to perceive his father as friend and as foe." Railton similarly analyzes the tavern scene in chapter 14 of *The Pioneers,* where drink arouses the rage that the dispossessed Chingachgook nurtures toward Marmaduke Temple for seizing and settling the land around Otsego Lake. Chingachgook reaches for his tomahawk but is too inebriated to strike the judge. Railton remarks, "Judge Cooper was not so fortunate: as he was leaving an Albany tavern in December 1809, he was fatally wounded by a blow on the head." Referring to the novelist, Railton adds, "Guilt would have been part of his psychic reaction to his father's murder; guilt prompted his haste to marry and to emulate his father's role."[43]

Given the apparent power of historical experience in shaping James Fenimore Cooper's mind and writings, it would be of some moment to identify the judge's killer. What if, for instance, he was a lawless squatter like Aaron Thousandacres of *The Chainbearer,* or a crafty Yankee demagogue rather like Steadfast Dodge of *Home as Found,* or perhaps an embittered Tuscarora Indian very much like Saucy Nick in *Wyandotté?* Think of the speculative possibilities—all the new essays, dissertations, and monographs reinterpreting Cooper's attitudes as shaped by his father's death. But perish the thought if it turns out that the judge was killed by a garrulous old hunter alarmed at the "wasty ways" of the Otsego settlers.

In fact, William Cooper's killer was none of the above, because, I will argue, no one murdered the judge. There is no contemporary evidence to suggest a murder, and the existing evidence gives every reason to believe that the judge died of natural causes. Given William Cooper's rough-hewn, boisterous, and partisan personality, the legend that he fell victim to political violence is all too tempting. Indeed, it is too good to be true. If, as some literary critics insist, James Fenimore Cooper rushed into marriage or nurtured a dread of social collapse into anarchy, it was not because his father was murdered.

What is the source of the Cooper scholars' confidence that the judge was murdered by a political opponent as he left an Albany tavern one evening in December 1809? They rely upon *The Letters and Journals of James Fenimore Cooper,* edited for publication by the late James Franklin Beard. In an editorial note Beard records the family tradition that William Cooper "contracted pneumonia after an opponent struck him on the head from behind as he left a heated political discussion." The legend of the murdered judge also appears in the biographies of James Fenimore Cooper written earlier in this century by William Brandford Shubrick Clymer (1900), Mary E. Phillips (1913), Robert E. Spiller (1931), Henry Walcott Boynton (1931), and James Grossman (1949).[44]

Literary scholars can also find confirmation for the tradition in the works of prominent historians. In *The Revolution of American Conservatism,* David Hackett Fischer describes the judge's vigorous partisanship for the Federalist party and concludes that he "met an appropriate end in a tavern brawl, struck down by a democrat." Fischer based his account primarily on two essays published in 1949 and 1954 in *New York History* by Lyman H. Butterfield, a scrupulous scholar best known for his work as editor of the papers of John Adams and Benjamin Rush. Butterfield insists, "Judge Cooper was to meet his death in consequence of a later scuffle, which took place outside Lewis' Tavern in Albany after a political meeting late in 1809." Given the prestige of Beard, Spiller, Boynton, Grossman, Fischer, and Butterfield, it is small wonder that literary critics have felt free to read James Fenimore Cooper's texts for signs of his father's violent death.[45]

All the biographers of William and James Cooper ultimately rest their case for the judge's murder on the same source: a family tradition first recorded in print by James Fenimore Cooper (1858–1938), a grandson of the novelist and a great-grandson of the judge. This James Fenimore Cooper was a successful lawyer and a zealous caretaker of the family reputation and history. He first published the family tradition in 1897 in his introduction to the republication of William Cooper's *A Guide in the Wilderness.* The younger James Fenimore Cooper repeated that tradition in two eclectic collections of family papers and antiquarian observations: *The Legends and Traditions of a Northern County* (1921) and *Reminiscences of Mid-Victorian Cooperstown* (1936). In the latter he prints the fullest statement of the legend:

> *William Cooper . . . died with his political boots on and in the Federalist cause. He was killed by a blow on the head struck from behind as he was leaving a political meeting in Albany where he had made a speech in a heated debate. In those days, murder and death in the cause of one's political party, were looked upon as among the fortunes of political warfare. No punishment followed such assaults and no legal investigations were made. His assailant was known to all.*[46]

James Fenimore Cooper the younger shared this tradition with Mary E. Phillips, Henry Walcott Boynton, and Robert E. Spiller to record in their biographies of the novelist. In a letter to Phillips, Cooper insisted, "I feel as you have received more assistance from the family than anyone who has ever undertaken the life of Cooper, that the book in these details should be made as nearly satisfactory to me as possible." One of those details concerned William Cooper's death. On the galley proofs the younger J. F. Cooper added that the judge "was killed while leaving a political meeting in the City of Albany as the result of a blow on the head struck by a political opponent from behind. He died the next day." Phillips dutifully accommodated him on this point.[47]

James Fenimore Cooper the younger provided no source, no documentation for his account of the judge's death. He relied on a nebulous family tradition, and an entire century separated him from his great-grandfather's death—sufficient time for a recollected event to evolve into a myth. It is striking that Susan Fenimore Cooper did not mention a violent death for her grandfather in her family reminiscences written in the mid–nineteenth century. Nor did her father, the novelist, ever state that the judge was murdered. In his *Chronicles of Cooperstown* the novelist reported his father's death without any reference to violence: "He died in Albany, and was interred in the burying ground of his family, in Christ Church Yard." Nor did the novelist mention violence when he referred to his father's death in a fond letter or remembrance that he wrote in 1831 about his family's ties to Albany:

> *To me Albany has always been a place of agreeable and friendly recollection. It was the only outlet we had, in my childhood, to the world, and many a merry*

week have I passed there with boys of my own age, while my father has waited
for the opening of the river to go south. . . . My father died in Albany, at the inn
of Stewart Lewis, in 1808 [sic], and my eldest brother Richard Fenimore
Cooper, in his own house. So you see, dear Sir, that Albany is a name I love for
a multitude of associations that are connected with my earliest years.

Would James Fenimore Cooper have nurtured such a loving memory of Albany if it had been the scene of his father's sudden murder?[48]

In the voluminous papers of William Cooper and of his executors, his
sons Isaac and Richard Fenimore Cooper, every clue suggests that the judge
died of natural causes. Surviving bills from doctors and from the Albany
innkeeper suggest a lingering illness. Cooper checked into Stewart Lewis's
inn on November 22 and began to receive medical attention two days later.
Nonetheless, he continued to eat and drink (Madeira, sangria, brandy, and
gin) heartily until December 3—when he ceased to consume alcohol and
began seeing an additional doctor. By then the judge's unspecified malady
was sufficiently ominous that at least four of his children came from Cooperstown to Albany, lodging at the inn. Isaac and Ann arrived first and stayed
the longest, appearing December 4 and lingering through their father's
death. Ann's husband, George Pomeroy, stayed for fifteen days; James,
seven; and Samuel, four. Richard Fenimore Cooper was in Albany during
this period, but he apparently stayed at another location. The documents do
not indicate whether Cooper's wife, Elizabeth, or their son William Cooper,
Jr., came to watch the judge die. None of the documents specify his illness.
In his financial accounts for the estate, Isaac Cooper referred only to "the illness of W. Cooper in Albany" and "the sickness, &c of W. Cooper"—and not
to any violent assault or fatal wound. Moreover, the pattern of an apparently
moderate illness that took a turn for the worse eleven days later and took another nineteen days to kill the judge ill-fits a sudden, crushing blow to the
skull. By no means did he die the day after an assault.[49]

During the early months of 1810, the brothers received and saved several
letters of condolence from family friends. The correspondents expressed a
moving sense of loss. Anna Hay remarked, "Universal Philanthropy and
Benevolence of Heart, in continual exercize for the welfare of his Fellow
Creatures, were the leading Characteristics of your now Sainted Father. . . .
And had I been deprived of a brother, I cou'd not have felt it more
[keenly]." But none of these letters expresses the shock and anger that they
would have conveyed to the sons of a murdered man. There is also a surviving copy of a letter written by Isaac and Richard to inform a family friend of
their father's death. It says simply, "We presume that ere this you have been
informed that our much lamented Father, *William Cooper,* was consigned to
the silent tomb on last Christmas day."[50]

Finally, the family papers also include the funeral sermon pronounced by the Reverend Daniel Nash over William Cooper's grave beside his late daughter, Hannah, on that Christmas Day. Like the letters of condolence, Nash's sermon expresses sorrow at the loss but none of the outrage at human barbarity that a minister would have inevitably invoked over a murdered corpse. It seems to be a funeral sermon for a man who had died of natural causes.[51]

Moreover, the traditional story of Cooper's death is implausible for three reasons. First, the timing is all wrong for a political meeting in New York State in 1809. Partisan publications and political meetings proliferated during the month before the state and congressional elections held in the last week of April. In an especially important race, particularly the triennial gubernatorial elections, nominating meetings and partisan rhetoric could appear as early as January. But a public political meeting in November or December was unheard of. Neither of the two extant newspapers published in Albany in 1809 announces or reports a political meeting for either political party in November or December. The first public meeting in Albany during that election season was held on the night of January 5, 1810, two weeks *after* William Cooper died. Second, no one was indicted or prosecuted for Cooper's murder, which is especially odd given that, according to the tradition, the assault occurred in a public place, after a crowded meeting, and the "assailant was known to all." Third, the Albany and Cooperstown newspapers from late 1809 do not mention any violent assault on William Cooper. His obituaries report a matter-of-fact death, apparently (but not specifically) of natural causes.[52]

James Fenimore Cooper the younger insisted that there was neither any prosecution nor any published comment because political violence was so routine in the early Republic. It is true that partisan politics were contentious and that violent scuffles frequently erupted during elections. But deaths were rare, and it is not true that political violence escaped either commentary or prosecution. On the contrary, the relentless search for partisan advantage led the rival parties and their newspapers to capitalize on any episode that would discredit the opposition as violent brutes.[53]

One episode is especially relevant because it was so close in time, place, and circumstance to Cooper's alleged murder. On April 17, 1807, a Republican meeting in Albany passed a resolution questioning the honesty of Gen. Solomon Van Rensselaer, a leading Federalist in that city. On April 21, armed with a heavy hickory cane, Van Rensselaer stalked the streets, looking for Elisha Jenkins, the author of the offending resolution. Finding his man in State Street, Van Rensselaer staggered and toppled Jenkins with two violent blows to the head, stomping his fallen and prostrate victim for good measure. The respective friends of Jenkins and Van Rensselaer joined the fray, turning State Street into, in the words of one spectator, "a tumultuous *sea of heads,* over which clattered a forest of canes; the vast body, now surging this way, now that, as the tide of combat ebbed or flowed." In the middle of the pack, and at the peak of the battle, a Republican partisan, Dr. Francis Bloodgood, "with the thick end of a heavy cane, which he held with both his hands, struck Van Rensselaer from behind a blow that felled him." His friends hauled the groggy and bloodied Van Rensselaer to safety, while the governor, the mayor, and other magistrates belatedly restored order to the streets. Nine days later an Albany newspaper welcomed the close of an election campaign that had been "wrought up into commotion but little short of insurrection and blood."[54]

It is significant that the Federalists seized upon the episode for political advantage, printing and circulating an election eve handbill that described the affray in vivid detail. At least one newspaper reprinted the handbill. Meanwhile, private correspondents spread the story through the state in letters to their political allies. It is also revealing that the recuperating Van Rensselaer prosecuted Bloodgood and two other assailants, while Elisha Jenkins sued Van Rensselaer. The general collected $4,500 in damages but had to pay out $2,500 to his victim. The newspapers published accounts of the prosecution and the verdicts. Given the prominent play that the Federalists and the courts gave to the assault on Solomon Van Rensselaer—who had initiated the battle and who survived his wounds—it is beyond belief that an unprovoked and fatal assault on another Federalist leader in the same city thirty-two months later would have passed unnoticed by the courts and the press.[55]

Because none of the contemporary documents specify what William Cooper did die of, the evidence I have cited does not *prove* that William Cooper was *not* murdered. But, given that murder was exceptional and shocking in upstate New York during the early nineteenth century, the burden of proof rests with anyone who asserts the unlikely—that William Cooper was murdered in 1809, although no one is known to have said so until 1897.[56]

OUTRAGE

Still we are left with a family tradition. What can account for the development of such an elaborate and improbable tradition in the Cooper family? There is an important germ of documented fact within the murder story. William Cooper did receive a severe wound to the head in a public street from a political opponent. But that blow did not occur in Albany; it did not occur in December 1809; and it did not kill him. That blow did lead to a prosecution, a conviction, and notoriety in at least one Federalist newspaper.

According to an indictment filed on June 2, 1807, by the grand jury of the Otsego County Court of Oyer and Terminer, on May 21 the Republican lawyer Farrand Stranahan violently assaulted William Cooper in a Cooperstown street: "With a large Cane or Club," Stranahan "did beat, bruise, wound & ill treat, and strike upon the head & body [William Cooper], so that his life was greatly despaired of." Stranahan pled guilty and was fined $30. A writer for the *Hudson Balance*, a Federalist newspaper, seized upon and elaborated the episode for partisan advantage: "The judge was walking with a small cane in his hand, could make no resistance, and indeed had no opportunity of making any; for he was knocked down unawares. For this outrage of a young man upon an old one, of one civil officer upon another, a fine has been imposed of only thirty dollars. . . . How much are the violence and cruelty of democracy to be lamented!" That this assault on Cooper was prosecuted and attracted partisan comment is further evidence of the utter implausibility that his (alleged) political murder in 1809 could have escaped public notice.[57]

The indictment's statement that Cooper's "life was greatly despaired of" is common legalese in indictments for assault and battery, but there is reason to believe that in this case the phrase was meaningful. In May 1807 the Otsego County surrogate of probate began to enter a last will and testament for William Cooper. The surrogate did not complete the entry and crossed out what he had begun. The temporary entry suggests that, for a time in May 1807, the family thought the patriarch's life hung in the balance.[58]

Stranahan attacked Cooper during a week of heated controversy and angry meetings over who would name and control the village (and its water). That spring Stranahan had joined his friend Elihu Phinney in forsaking Federalism and seeking to incorporate and rename Cooperstown as Otsego Village—an insulting provocation to William Cooper. Stranahan struck Cooper two days after the May 19 public meeting, when the village's Federalist majority elected trustees who refused to initiate the village government and water company sought by Phinney and Stranahan. Enraged, Stranahan blamed and stalked William Cooper.[59]

In the political culture of the early Republic, a public caning was a gentleman's means of seeking redress for a public insult to his honor. So it was that Solomon Van Rensselaer had sought out and felled Elisha Jenkins in Albany's State Street a month earlier. Had William Cooper insulted Stranahan in public, perhaps before the courthouse crowd on May 19? Cooper certainly had cause to be agitated, as nothing could have hurt him more than to see his name obliterated from the village that he had labored to found and develop. Moreover, he felt especially aggrieved at the ungrateful Phinney and Stranahan, who had so prospered from his patronage. And it would certainly have been in character for the voluble and excitable judge to have blurted out a diatribe against a political foe. In 1793 William Cooper had been convicted of slandering Gov. George Clinton during the gubernatorial campaign of 1792 (Morgan Lewis, then a state supreme court justice, had presided at that trial).[60]

Indeed, two aspects of Stranahan's trial suggest that he had been provoked. First, although he pled guilty, the brief court record indicates that Stranahan summoned eight witnesses, including some leading village Federalists, who would have been at the public meeting on the nineteenth. The only reason to summon witnesses after a guilty plea was to consider extenuating circumstances before sentencing. Second, the paltry fine indicates that the justices found some mitigating cause.[61]

Over the generations recollection of Stranahan's attack in Cooperstown on May 21, 1807, became confused in the Cooper family memory with the judge's death in Albany two and a half years later. Perhaps the Cooper heirs believed that the judge had never fully recovered and that his death had some connection to the serious injury that he had suffered in May 1807. Perhaps in the retelling of that connection over the generations, the time between the assault and the death became foreshortened and the places of attack and death merged into the latter. But there are grounds to doubt that the assault left William Cooper permanently impaired. Within a few months, Cooper had resumed the vigorous management of his far-flung business interests, traveling repeatedly to Albany, New York City, and his lands in the St. Lawrence valley. In the winter of 1808–9, he made two extended trips to his northern lands; no invalid could have made such a long journey in the dead of winter over horrendous roads to a rough frontier settlement. He returned to St. Lawrence County in June and again in October of 1809, just a few months before his death in Albany.[62]

There is also good reason to doubt that the judge's immediate heirs blamed Stranahan for their father's death. In at least two legal cases, one in 1811, less than two years after William Cooper's death, Isaac and Richard Fenimore Cooper employed Stranahan on behalf of the judge's estate. Would they have retained Stranahan if they held him responsible for their father's murder?[63]

A corollary to the family tradition insists that James Fenimore Cooper sought out his father's killer and "damn near killed him." This twist also seems to be a distortion spun around a germ of truth. There is no evidence that the novelist ever attacked Farrand Stranahan, but in 1815 Cooper did assault Stranahan's law partner, Ambrose Jordan. In 1815 Jordan was a lieutenant in Cooperstown's militia company of light infantry, and his captain was James Cooper (who had not yet added Fenimore to his name). In a letter dated June 22, Elihu Phinney, Jr., reported the Cooperstown news to his fiancée:

We have had a little Square fighting here in consequence of some pieces published in the Watch Tower *&* C[ooperstown] Federalist. *Jordan wrote a* *piece in the* Watch Tower, *which cast some reflection on the memory of Judge Cooper; this offended James Cooper so much, that . . . he thought proper to give the Author a genteel Cow-Hiding. This affray happened so near Jordan's House that Mrs. Jordan was very much alarmed &, it is said, Cried Murder. Jordan gave Cooper a pretty clever thump over the head with a loaded Cane & I believe they parted, So-So.*

Eight years and one month after Farrand Stranahan cracked William Cooper's skull with a loaded cane in Cooperstown's main street, Stranahan's law partner did the same to the judge's son James. Not a resident of Cooperstown until 1812, Ambrose Jordan had not killed or even known William Cooper, but he was closely associated with the man who had severely wounded the judge in 1807. So here too it seems that retelling over the generations simplified and confused events, conflating Jordan with Stranahan, transforming James Cooper from loser to victor, and transmuting his motive from recompense for an insulting newspaper essay into revenge for a murder.[64]

Chapter Fourteen

INHERITANCE LOST

IN THE EARLY AMERICAN REPUBLIC IT was alarmingly common for the richest of men suddenly to collapse into bankruptcy and even debtors' prison. Conspicuous examples included the great financiers Robert Morris and William Duer, who had dealt extensively with Judge Cooper. In an economy where almost every capitalist was deeply indebted, lawsuits by anxious creditors could quickly unravel the estates of families living in the grandest manner. In 1803 John Simpson, a visiting Quaker preacher, marveled at Cooper's worldly riches but warned him that they were an unstable foundation for his children's inheritance: "For the Day in which we Live Shews us the Uncertainty & Little worth of great Riches, for a few years Spent in high Life Consumes Great Estates & Leaves

It is fortunate here, as elsewhere, to be the child of a worthy, or even of an affluent parent. The goods of the latter descend, by process of law, to the offspring, and, by aid of public opinion, the son receives some portion of the renown that has been earned by the merit of the father. . . . It is not enough simply to be the son of a great man; in order to render it of essential advantage, some portion of his merit must become hereditary, or the claim had better be suppressed. Even an honourable name may become [a] matter of reproach, since, when the public esteem is once forfeited, the recollection of the ancestor only serves to heighten the demerit of his delinquent child.

—James Fenimore Cooper,
Notions of the Americans,
vol. 1, 156–57

families in a most trying Situation and we see how Comfortable many [others] by their Industry & prudent Oeconomy brings up their Children & Leave them in a Much better way than those who may have the Name of Being Rich." Simpson predicted troubles to come for the Coopers: "For surely thou hast Set thy Children such an Example in Following the Grandeur of the World in thine House that, if thy Estate is not very Large, they will be Likely to meet with more Difficulty than those who have only their hands to support them."[1]

Probated in late 1809, William Cooper's will described an immense and apparently secure fortune bestowed upon his widow, Elizabeth, and their six surviving children: Richard Fenimore, Isaac, Ann, William Jr., Samuel, and James. Elizabeth Cooper received an annual income of $750 a year and the right to use, for the rest of her life, Otsego Hall with its furniture, supplies, grounds, gardens, and outbuildings. She also obtained the annual

rents from three local farms and the revenues from the sales of five unde-
veloped lots in the Otsego Patent. At her death, Otsego Hall and its outbuildings were to pass to the eldest son then living, provided he would pay
the estate $15,000 (if not, the property was to pass on the same terms to the
next oldest child, and so on until someone paid the $15,000). William
Cooper awarded the rest of his immense property to his six children. He estimated that each heir would receive at least $50,000 in lands and securities.
In 1815 the executors were to settle with all the creditors and divide any
residue of the estate equally among the six heirs.[2]

Despite the apparent great wealth described in William Cooper's will,
within fifteen years his estate collapsed into financial ruin. Beginning in
1819, creditors brought lawsuits, won decrees from the courts, and had the
decrees executed by county sheriffs to seize and auction almost all the assets
of the Cooper estate. Virtually the entire portfolio of lands, bonds, and
mortgages assembled by William Cooper passed into the hands of new speculators, who bought up the properties and securities at a fraction of their
face value. The receipts from the auctions went to satisfy the impatient creditors, leaving most of the Cooper heirs in genteel poverty. Visiting Cooperstown as the Cooper fortune imploded, James Kent remarked, "The
melancholy History of the family of William Cooper, the Father & founder
of the Place, gave a sober & impressive Tinge to our Reflections." The estate
that Cooper had built upon the controversial auction at Mabie's Tavern in
1786 vanished in the forced auctions of the 1820s. Ultimately William
Cooper's vision of entrenching an enduring lineage of wealth and power
proved as evanescent as George Croghan's.[3]

Some Cooper biographers blame the collapse of the estate entirely upon
the judge's feckless heirs, for squandering their immense inheritance on
high living. These biographers draw an overly stark contrast between Judge
Cooper as sound, industrious businessman and his irresponsible, spendthrift heirs. In fact, the Cooper children inherited an estate that was fatally
flawed because of a succession of costly mistakes committed by their father.
Contrary to his reputation as the consummate speculator and developer,
Cooper's post-1800 speculations all failed, as both his luck and his judgment faltered. Unfortunately for Cooper's children, most of their patrimony was in bonds and mortgages from poor homesteads within Cooper's
later, ill-conceived, and ill-fated speculations in more distant and economically marginal lands.[4]

William Cooper's will bestowed an estimated $50,000 on each of his chil-
dren, but those bequests were *not* in cash. Instead, each heir received seventeen rental properties valued at approximately $8,500, with the residue
in a mix of canceled debts owed to the father or, predominately, in bonds
and mortgages given by settlers dwelling in eight far-flung counties:
Broome, Cayuga, Clinton, Herkimer, Oneida, Otsego, St. Lawrence, and

Tioga. "In Bonds and Mortgages . . . I am Rich, in Money Poor," Cooper had reflected in 1804. About two-thirds of the estate's lands, both the unsold and the mortgaged, were in cold, distant, recently settled, and hitherto unprofitable St. Lawrence County. In his will Cooper conceded that most of the bonds and mortgages were for "estates lately sold where the improvements are new and the settlers cannot pay with punctuality for several years." According to the estate accounts, the six children, on average, received $63,430 in property. But each received an average of only $16,501 in cash (26 percent). They obtained much more in securities for land—an average of $43,021 (68 percent), principally in St. Lawrence County (see Table 12).[5]

Because settlers rarely paid much, if any, money down, the Cooper estate hinged upon the uncertain prospects of the farmers and petty speculators who had posted the bonds and mortgages to secure eventual payment. Hindered by frontier hardships, few settlers paid their debts on schedule. Cooper explained to Henry Drinker, "The perplexity of recovering moneys from new Settelments is to me well known as well by Experiance as [by] common reason. Nothing but time and a residence among the Setteléers will make them tollorably Productive. Indeed, it is proverbial that Landed men are not monied men, and we know [that William] *Penn* himselfe was needy in money matters, but those that take our Shoes will be rich *indeed.*" His heirs would, he hoped, reap the thousands of dollars promised by the many bonds and mortgages that filled his strongbox. In fact, the ability of the Cooper heirs to realize cash from their inheritance of bonds and mortgages diminished over the course of the 1810s as their lands lost value.[6]

In addition to suffering from dubious assets, the Cooper estate entailed heavy debts upon the children. Judge Cooper had borrowed much of the money he needed to speculate in lands, villages, and stores—in the overconfidence that his genius as a developer could make the invested money grow at a rate faster than the annual interest on his loans. The fundamental problem facing the Cooper heirs was that, to their surprise, their inherited assets lost value during the 1810s while the debts they inherited grew inexorably as the 7 percent annual interest accumulated. William Cooper had borrowed money in the late 1790s and early in the first decade of the nineteenth century, when New York's frontier land values appreciated steadily. But his heirs had to repay the loans during the 1810s, when rural land values declined and when a depression curtailed the money supply. They became trapped between the descending value of their estate and the compounding interest on their mounting debts.

Cooper raised sons who could not cope with the financial problems that they inherited. He had unwittingly built an illusion of secure wealth which he then conveyed to heirs trained to expect a life of luxury. Apparently enriched by the judge's will, the Cooper heirs lived in a grand style, constructing elegant new mansions and launching costly new ventures, both civic and mercantile. Schooled in gentility, the young Coopers were far better at spending money tastefully but prodigiously than at managing a difficult estate through the severe financial times that prevailed in rural New York during the late 1810s and early 1820s. Until it was too late they spent money in the serene but mistaken belief that their fortunes were as large and as secure as William Cooper's will made them appear. Deceived by that will, the heirs overvalued their assets, underestimated their liabilities, and overspent their legacies. Consequently, the historians who take his will and his *Guide in the Wilderness* at face value perpetuate the illusion that disastrously deceived the Cooper heirs.[7]

GENTRY

Except for William Cooper, Jr., who usually lived in New York City, the Cooper heirs resided in Cooperstown, the better to enjoy and manage their inheritance. Elizabeth Cooper lingered as a recluse in Otsego Hall until her death on September 15, 1817. She shared the house with her son Samuel and his new bride. Slightly built, deemed odd, and nicknamed the Doctor, Samuel was well liked but bore smaller expectations than did the other children. In April of 1812, when he married Elizabeth Bartlett, the daughter of a village hatter of modest means, his family reacted with relief that he had married at all, rather than with concern that he had married so far below his social class.[8]

Ann Cooper Pomeroy and her husband George dwelled around the corner on Water Street in the large stone house built for them in 1804 as a wedding present from her father. Growing up in Hannah's shadow, Ann became the other, lesser, insecure sister in the eyes of family and friends. Hannah's apotheosis in tragic death must have compounded Ann's sense of inferiority. Much like her mother, Ann preferred an inconspicuous life at home as wife and mother, following her marriage in 1803 to Pomeroy, a Yankee emigrant, prosperous apothecary, and Presbyterian deacon. George and Ann were noted for their religious devotion and moral rigor.[9]

Richard Fenimore Cooper and his wife, Ann (or Nancy) Low Cary, resided across Water Street from the Pomeroys in a riverside estate named Apple Hill. She was his opposite: beautiful, vivacious, high-strung, unpredictable, and from a penurious family. She was the daughter of Col. Richard Cary, a Continental Army officer, Otsego land speculator, and old friend of the Coopers who had become bankrupt. Consequently, Ann's marriage to the dull but wealthy Richard Fenimore Cooper rescued her from genteel poverty. The match did not impress Eliza McDonald, who complained to a friend: "Richard, you may have heard, has married one of Col. Cary's Daugh-

ters—Nancy—a young, giddy Girl. I fear she will never supply the place of a
Daughter to Mrs. Cooper." Eliza meant that Ann Cary could never replace
Elizabeth Cooper's beloved daughter Hannah. Indeed, the clashing tem-
peraments of Richard and Ann soon led to infidelity and recrimination.[10]

Isaac Cooper and his wife lived a block away from Otsego Hall in a lakeside estate named Edgewater, a large (sixty-six by forty-five feet) and expensive brick mansion built 1810–1813. Genial, witty, and gregarious, Isaac
was the son most like his father. Determined to make a merchant of him,
the judge had arranged two apprenticeships in urban countinghouses: with
Richard R. Smith in Philadelphia in 1800–1801 and with Daniel Hale in Albany in 1801–1804. To the judge's delight, in December 1804 Isaac married Mary Ann Morris, the genteel daughter of Gen. Jacob Morris, thereby
completing William Cooper's reconciliation with his former political rival
and the county's other great landlord. Thereafter, Isaac operated a village
store and looked after a portfolio of Otsego lands, bonds, and mortgages
bestowed by his father.[11]

James Cooper quickly exploited his inheritance to resign from the U.S.
Navy, where he had found tedium instead of glory and promotion. In May
of 1810 James left the navy and proposed marriage to Susan Augusta De
Lancey, the eighteen-year-old daughter of John Peter De Lancey
(1753–1828) of Mamaroneck in Westchester County. The De Lanceys had
been one of the wealthiest and most powerful families in New York until dispossessed for their Loyalism by the victorious Whigs during the Revolution.
After the war John Peter De Lancey returned to Westchester to rescue a portion of his familial estate, but he could never retrieve the full fortune and
power that had been his under the colonial regime. Consequently, the January 1, 1811, marriage of James Cooper and Susan Augusta De Lancey was
a match of new money with old status welcomed by both families for different reasons. The nouveau riche Coopers got the social boost of a connection to the long-distinguished De Lanceys, who, in turn, believed that their
daughter had married into a far greater fortune than they could provide.
Whatever the class considerations, the marriage proved mutually happy.
The couple remained on the De Lancey estate in Westchester through the
births of their first two children: Elizabeth (September 27, 1811) and Susan
Fenimore (April 17, 1813). In July of 1813 James moved his family and four
servants to Cooperstown. They lived in a comfortable, red-painted farm-
house just north of the village on the lake's western shore, while Cooper supervised the construction nearby of a grand stone mansion, which he
named Fenimore House to honor his mother. By 1816 he had expended at
least $3,500 on the still incomplete house.[12]

Sensitive to the newness of their fortunes and gentility, the Coopers
sought to entrench their wealth and status by constructing grand homes
and a sense of belonging to an enduring aristocratic lineage. On December

4, 1813, when Isaac Cooper first slept in Edgewater, he wrote in his diary: "Moved—Where I hope to end my Days and I pray Heaven to allow this House and this Lot—whereon I this day brought my Family— to descend to my Children and to my *Children's Children* and may they increase in virtue and respectability and become worthy of the blessings of Heaven." To cultivate transgenerational continuity, the Coopers usually named their children after their own mother, father, and lost sister, Hannah. Among the thirty-five grandchildren of William and Elizabeth Cooper, there were four Williams, four Elizabeths, three Hannahs, and two Fenimores. Six grandchildren bore Fenimore as a middle name and seven of the ten Pomeroy children received Cooper as their middle name. The heirs apparently responded to William Cooper's wishes as expressed in his will. He encouraged his descendants to perpetuate his name and that of his wife Elizabeth by stipulating that the two most cherished lakeside properties in his estate should be held by the heirs in common until 1850, when Myrtle Grove would become the private property of his youngest descendant named William Cooper, while Elizabeth Cooper's youngest namesake would receive "the fishing point called Shad Cam."[13]

As Judge Cooper intended, his heirs lived in a genteel and genial style dedicated more to leisure than to work. In his diary, Isaac Cooper reported a daily succession of dancing assemblies, backgammon games, tea parties, summer carriage rides through the hills and boating excursions across the lake, winter skating and sleighing, and rich dinners of lakefish, mussels, oysters, and venison as well as occasional performances by visiting theater companies. His brother James was a frequent guest and the life of the party. On August 7, 1813, Isaac recorded, "Mr. [James] C[ooper's] gayety and many eccentric remarks amused us much this evening." On December 23, he recorded: "Dinner parties quite fashionable this season." A day later: "Christmas Eve. St. Nicholas very bountiful." On January 18, 1814, he wrote: "Assembly. 18 Ladies. 23 Gentlemen. Pleasant Enough! Very Pleasant." Forty-four people attended the tea party at Mr. Prevost's house on January 21: "Gay times for Cooperstown." Neglecting any reference to business, he defined himself through a steady succession of social activities meant to sustain a mood of genial gaiety.[14]

Cooperstown's growth created an increasingly cosmopolitan social context for the Coopers' performances as gentlemen and ladies. The village population more than doubled from 349 in 1803 to 826 in 1816. In 1803 Cooperstown had been a modest village of 4 stores, 34 barns, and 75 houses. By 1816 it had grown into a more crowded and complex community comprising 13 stores, 68 barns, and 176 houses (see Table 13). No longer a crude village of log cabins and stumpy pastures, Cooperstown featured two dressmakers, a bookstore, three newspapers, two fine hotels (Joseph Munn's and Francis Henry's), two church buildings, a young man's debating club (known as the Cooperstown Ciceronian Association), a Young Ladies Benevolent Society ("for the support and encouragement of indigent and pious young men intended for the gospel ministry"), a dozen elegant mansions, and a new academy and seminary in adjoining Hartwick. In 1806–1808, at a cost of nearly $7,000, the county supervisors had built a substantial new brick courthouse, 56 by 50 feet and two stories tall. Located beside the turnpike on the west side of Cooperstown, it replaced the ramshackle wooden structure hastily erected by Judge Cooper in 1791 and deemed "deplorable and miserable" by the supervisors in 1805. In 1813 a visitor from New Jersey extolled Cooperstown: "This Town resembles our largest Cities more than any other that I have seen since I left home. It makes a better appearance, because the buildings are new, & perhaps as neatly finished. The Taverns and Stores are large & well filled." Three years later a gentleman visitor "felt equal astonishment and pleasure at the various and rapid improvements that in the lapse of a few years had taken place." He especially admired the "elegance of the Churches" and "the neat, the commodious, and often elegant mansions embosomed or surrounded with the fragrant garden and the thrifty rising orchard."[15]

During the 1810s, an exclusive, genteel social circle developed in Cooperstown as the leading villagers mimicked the fashions, mores, and manners of the upper class in the eastern cities. During the winter of 1812–13 Isaac Cooper was one of four managers for the Cooperstown Assembly, a club that held balls every other Thursday "through the season." By limiting attendance to those formally invited, the managers involved only those deemed sufficiently genteel. The assembly created a demand for itinerant dance instructors, who taught "the newest and most fashionable" dances "now in practice in the City of New York and Albany." Traveling theater companies occasionally visited to perform plays, usually comedies, at the courthouse. In July of 1817 a young law clerk confessed to his friend William Holt Averell that, "[along] with walking, riding, sailing, tea parties, bower building, and dancing, the ladies have engrossed a good share of attention and the Law has been rather neglected." Another friend assured Averell, "Never was Cooperstown more gay or dissipated than it has been this summer." By tastefully arranging "brilliant illumination" and a "profusion of ornament," the local ladies converted the ballroom at Henry's hotel "into a sort of fairy chamber." After attending a genteel dance at the "Lakelands" estate of John M. Bowers in Cooperstown, Sarah Amelia Fairman gushed, "The girls were all in high glee and animation; conversation was kept up on all sides. The young ladies in Cooperstown are all as gay as larks in a pleasant sunshine morning, thinking only of the present hour." A month later, she returned home to her country town with a new discontent: "Butternuts appears now to me like a secluded place divested of society—

that which enlivens, and renders the lives of individuals so pleasing and alluring."[16]

FRICTIONS

However, the local common folk failed to provide the deference that the village gentility needed to complete their aristocratic pretensions. The Cooper heirs were especially sensitive to perceived slights from rude commoners. Taking very seriously their aristocratic obligations, the Coopers, especially Isaac, were renowned for their generous charity to the deferential poor. But they felt threatened by any display of egalitarian independence, especially by their servants.[17]

They had difficulty finding dutiful and modest servants among Yankees who prided themselves on their aggressive assertion of social equality. When Esther Cummings departed after only five months' service, Mary Ann Morris Cooper recorded in her diary: "An impudent, unsteady Girl." Betsey Walby was an exception, singled out for extraordinary praise from Isaac when she stayed a full year: "By One Years Services, faithfully and orderly performed—free from Yankee dignity and ideas of Liberty—which is insolence only." James Cooper's family bitterly resented a Methodist deacon who persuaded their nanny to depart their household to marry a local farmer and Methodist brother. Susan Fenimore Cooper denounced the deacon as a "busy-body" who "aimed a deadly blow at the peace of our household" as part of his "nefarious plot against our peace." Yankee servants could be so insubordinate and mobile because they were white and free. Consequently, the Coopers preferred to employ enslaved Blacks. In 1811 James Cooper paid $50 to buy from his brother Richard a seven-year-old "mulatto Boy called Frederic" (who like other young New York slaves would not become free until 1827). However, Frederic seized his freedom by running away, probably in 1817.[18]

The Coopers also felt under attack from the rude folk dwelling beyond the fences surrounding their estates. In 1808 Isaac Cooper charged Susan Johnson, identified as a "laborer," with stealing $52 worth of handkerchiefs, petticoats, stockings, jackets, and gowns from his store, but a jury found her not guilty. On January 11, 1817, Isaac wrote, "Hickory Tree cut down by some Rascal a few days since—expect to find out who. I doubt it!" However, two days later, he identified a suspect and prepared a lawsuit for trespass. In an October 1819 newspaper notice, William Cooper, Jr., offered a reward to anyone who would help him convict the "many persons" who had been "in the habit of committing trespasses on the estate of the late *William Cooper*."[19]

James Cooper suffered a series of nocturnal thefts in early 1815. On January 19 someone broke into his stable, stealing a "bright bay color" horse with saddle and bridle. A month later Isaac wrote in his diary, "James C[ooper]'s Barn plundered last night. Sharp times." He suffered a third break-in on May 26, 1815, when a thief stole another horse with saddle and bridle. The suspect was Daniel Chapin of Burlington, a poor and hard-drinking Yankee farmer who was fifty years old. His prior involvement with the Coopers had been extensive but unhappy: he bought land from Judge William Cooper but failed to pay for it. Chapin become a tenant, paying Isaac Cooper an annual rent of thirty-six bushels of wheat. By stealing the horse Chapin apparently expressed his resentment and defiance. Arrested, he struck the deputy across the face with a stick and fled into the woods. "Horse Thief eloped—all the world after him," Isaac Cooper wrote in his diary on June 12, just before joining the manhunt that retook Chapin on the 22nd. Thrown into the Cooperstown jail, he nearly escaped again "by taking up a plank in the floor of his prison and digging underneath," until detected and foiled by the jailer. Tried in late August, Chapin was convicted and sentenced to seven years at hard labor in the state prison. If James Fenimore Cooper's dread of anarchy originated in personal experience, the thefts of 1815 were a basis far more real than the alleged murder of his father.[20]

Arrogant and prickly, Cooper also clashed with other prominent villagers who declined to follow his lead. On October 20, 1814, during the War of 1812, the village's leading Republicans and Federalists held a public meeting in Cooperstown, choosing the Republican Elijah H. Metcalf to chair and the Federalist James Cooper as secretary. They came together at a moment of national crisis, in the wake of a British invasion that had captured Washington, D.C., destroying the Capitol and White House. Around the country, the pro-war Republicans called upon the antiwar Federalists to cease their opposition. The Cooperstown meeting seemed to succeed, passing a spirited resolve: "That the situation to which our country has been reduced in consequence of the present war, requires the active and united exertions of every American in its *defence;* and to that object, this meeting pledge their undivided support." However, Cooper quickly and publicly disavowed the resolve:

> *The subscriber cannot permit his signature to appear to the foregoing resolutions, at a time like the present, without stating that he disapproved of them, and he feels it due to himself to add, that had not the object of the meeting (agreeable to his view of it) been perverted, and a resolution of a number of his respectable fellow-citizens compelled him to appear before the public—it would not have been troubled with his individual dissent.*

Although he had chosen to attend the meeting, Cooper refused to abide by its decision—an early manifestation of his career as a contrarian. This newspaper notice is also of special interest as the first known publication by the future novelist; already he had perfected his peculiarly convoluted style.[21]

IMPROVEMENT 🌿

At the same time that the village gentility dined, danced, and conversed in pursuit of elevation and sociability, they nursed a sense of impending chaos. They dreaded every act of petty vandalism, nocturnal burglary, purloined tree, and stolen woodpile as pregnant with looming anarchy. In 1822 the *Freeman's Journal* luridly warned:

> *A gang of villains infest this village, depredating upon private property in the dead of night, and committing acts that would hardly be expected at the hands of the veriest wretch who inhabits our penitentiaries. Even the sanctuaries of our holy religion are polluted, and the tenants of the grave are not left unmolested. It is the duty of our citizens to be on the look out, or before another sun beams upon them the torch of the incendiary may light their dwellings.*

The leading villagers' principal fears—of fire and of crime—united in their greatest nightmare: that insidious arsonists were conspiring to destroy the village.[22]

Gentility necessarily existed in tension with commonality. The essence of gentility was the perfection of self-control, its performance to the applause of onlookers, and its projection outward to control the disorderly. Although gentility demanded an unruffled demeanor, it was impelled by a nagging dread that society was innately vulgar, chaotic, and threatening. To subdue their anxiety and perfect their outward calm, the genteel sought greater mastery over their neighbors. The leading villagers believed that only constant action could contain the forces of anarchy that chronically imperiled property and civility. In turn those efforts at control provoked resentment and resistance, which confirmed to the gentility that they lived on the dangerous brink of anarchy.[23]

As the leaders of four new institutions—the Cooperstown Episcopal Church (Christ Church), the Otsego County Bible Society, the village's Board of Trustees, and the Otsego County Agricultural Society—the Coopers strove to bring greater decorum and order to their expanding village and its rustic hinterland. Frustrated and marginalized by democratic politics, the Coopers and fellow Federalists invested their energies and monies in new voluntary associations dedicated to reforming the appearance, morality, and discipline of the common people. Conceding their impotence at the ballot box, the Federalist gentry became moral and aesthetic reformers, hoping that an improved people would eventually recognize the folly of electing demagogues. The reforming gentry also longed to draw into their new, ostensibly nonpolitical associations the most wealthy and moderate Republicans, who coveted genteel acceptance and who disliked perpetual partisanship.

Most leading villagers, including George and Ann Pomeroy, belonged to the local Presbyterian church organized in 1800, but Isaac and James Cooper championed the Episcopalian church established in the village by the Reverend Daniel Nash with financial assistance from Judge Cooper. Neither Isaac nor James had strong religious convictions until they married devout Episcopalian women. The combined influence of Susan Augusta De Lancey Cooper and, especially, of Mary Ann Morris Cooper, led their husbands to commit authority, energy, and money to sustaining Christ Church. Daniel Nash recalled, "Mrs. [Mary Ann Morris] Cooper was young, pious, and sensible. From the evening [when] I received and gave her hand to Mr. [Isaac] Cooper, I entertained the idea that she would be the Instrument in the hand of Providence of establishing the [Episcopal] Church in the County Town—a Place most carefully guarded by the Presbyterians." The Coopers sought a religion that reinforced their gentility, a religion that was aesthetically pleasing to the eye and ear as well as morally reassuring to their souls. Nash slyly observed to his bishop, "I have by accident found out that the Cooper family design to do more for the Church—but they wish to adorn and beautify the Building. I judge the best way to induce them to be liberal is to meet their request. We ought to be as wise as serpents and [as] harmless as Doves." With their financial assistance, Nash completed a fine little brick church building in the summer of 1815.[24]

During the 1810s the Coopers also played a leading role in the Otsego County Bible Society, an ecumenical association dedicated to buying Bibles and Christian testaments for free distribution to the poor. Organized in Cooperstown in 1813 by the county's leading Episcopalians and Presbyterians, the association belonged to a national movement that spawned Bible societies in 128 counties by 1816. In Otsego the society's officers included George Pomeroy (treasurer), Isaac Cooper (manager), and James Cooper (delegate to the national convention). Although not an officer, William Cooper, Jr., was the Otsego society's most generous donor in 1814, when he paid for thirty Bibles. During its first five years the Otsego Bible Society distributed 1,302 Bibles and 519 testaments to the poor.[25]

The Bible societies revitalized the hierarchical ideal that the benevolent rich could earn popular gratitude and improve public discipline by uniting to offer systematic charity. The Otsego Bible Society insisted that the poor would forsake "the most profligate practices, and become meek, active and useful Christians and citizens. . . . Families, where discord and misery dwelt have become the seat of peace and happiness upon the introduction of a Bible." The reformers also meant to rescue society from "innumerable vices and disorders," by mandating daily readings from the Bible in the common schools. The leaders of the Otsego Bible Society were almost all staunch Federalists, including the Coopers, Robert Campbell, James Averell, Jr., Dr. Thomas Fuller, John H. Prentiss, and Gen. Jacob Morris. Conversely, most local Republicans stayed away because they profoundly distrusted private associations of wealthy men out to reshape public thought and behavior.[26]

The Coopers also dominated Cooperstown's new village government, organized in 1812: an annually elected board of five trustees aided by a clerk-treasurer. George Pomeroy served as the clerk and treasurer from 1812 through 1819, and Robert Campbell, the Coopers' lawyer and political ally, was a trustee during that same period. Isaac Cooper presided over the trustees from 1813 until his death in early 1818. Samuel Cooper replaced Isaac as a trustee (but not as president)—as if the board could not be without a Cooper, no matter how eccentric.[27]

The village trustees framed ordinances intended to impose order and decorum upon the village streets. In 1812 and 1813 they mandated fines for anyone who heaped wood, or who rode his horse or drove any wagon, cart, sleigh, or sled up onto the new, plank sidewalks. Similar fines awaited anyone who left firewood for more than a day in any street or alley between April 30 and December 1 or who failed to remove, by May 1, "all chips and rubbish" made by cutting wood. Above all, the trustees ordered the villagers to pen their geese, swine, and cows. The poorer villagers had let their animals run loose to forage in the streets for grass and rubbish, obliging the more prosperous folk to fence their gardens in to keep the roaming livestock out. Determined to reverse that custom, the trustees threatened to seize, impound, and sell "the swine with which the streets are infested." When the friends of pig freedom responded with nocturnal acts of vandalism and swine-liberation, the trustees imposed a $5 fine on anyone who damaged "any building, pump, pound, or other property belonging to the trustees of this village." And they threatened a $10 fine against those who forcibly rescued an impounded pig. In subsequent years the trustees had to reiterate their swine ordinance, suggesting that it remained much resented, resisted, and ineffective.[28]

The trustees also tried to drive from the village streets those sporting activities that enthused the common sort but alarmed the genteel. In 1813 the trustees banned horse racing within the village bounds. In June of 1816 the board enacted its most momentous ordinance: "Be it ordained, that no person shall play at Ball in Second or West street, in this village, under a penalty of one dollar, for each and every offence." Led by Isaac Cooper the trustees acted against townball, a bat-and-ball game that later evolved into baseball. In *Home as Found,* James Fenimore Cooper conveyed the genteel distaste for

public ballplaying. When "a party of apprentice-boys" led by "a notorious
street-brawler" begin to play ball on the lawn of his mansion, Edward Effingham (Cooper's alter ego) complains to his lawyer: "As I cannot permit the
ears of the ladies to be offended with these rude brawls, and shall never consent to have grounds that are so limited, and which so properly belong to
the very privacy of my dwelling, invaded in this coarse manner, I beg, Mr.
Bragg, that you will, at once, desire these young men to pursue their sports
somewhere else."[29]

In recent years sports historians have discredited the myth that Abner
Doubleday invented baseball in Cooperstown one day in 1839. In fact, baseball neither originated in Cooperstown nor had a single inventor. Instead,
it evolved gradually in the early and mid-nineteenth century, primarily
around New York City during the 1840s in association with the Knicker-
bocker Baseball Club organized by Alexander Cartwright. Indeed, because
of its 1816 ban on ballplaying in the village center, Cooperstown can better
claim to have tried to prevent the invention of baseball.[30]

Beginning in 1817 the leading villagers, including James Cooper, extended their crusade for greater order out into the countryside, uniting
with their hinterland counterparts to form the Otsego County Agricultural
Society. Inspired and guided by Elkanah Watson of Albany, Otsego's leading men organized New York's first county agricultural society (January)
and conducted the state's first county fair (October). Following Otsego's
lead, fifty-one other New York counties established their own agricultural
societies and fairs during the late 1810s. The Otsego society promised to replace rude log cabins and their vulgar inhabitants with "comfortable and elegant habitations, and a happy community." To that end, the members
exhorted the farmer to improve the appearance of his fields and buildings
by working harder throughout the year: to "carry off stones and make walls,
cut up and subdue groves of bushes and briars, make ditches and drain his
wet grounds and swamps."[31]

Most of the members were wealthy and influential gentlemen with little
practical experience in farming. They were great landlords, newspaper editors, village lawyers, gentleman farmers, mercantile entrepreneurs, and
state politicians, rather than common farmers—most of whom were skeptical of, if not hostile to, the movement to reform them. As with the Otsego
Bible Society, most of the leading agricultural reformers were Federalists,
including the first president, Jacob Morris, recording secretary, John H.
Prentiss, and corresponding secretary, James Cooper. Through both societies the defeated and discredited Federalists sought political rehabilitation
and a new vehicle for promoting their vision of social harmony achieved
through the benevolent supervision of a unitary elite distinguished by superior wealth, education, and talent. Prentiss lauded his fellow members as

"Men of the first standing for wealth and talents" out to reform common farmers, who seemed perversely "resolved to plod on in the old way, disregarding all attempts at improvement."[32]

The society denounced common people who nurtured unfitting ambitions to transcend their proper role as laborious cultivators and farm wives. General Morris blamed young men who forsook the farm to engage in commerce for "the multitude of vices and crimes that abound in our country, which create an enormous list of insolvents and bankrupts, and fill our State-Prisons with malefactors." He urged their return "to the steady habits of our revered ancestors, in an honest and diligent cultivation of the earth." The members of the society especially dreaded that common women were becoming too independent as imported consumer goods, especially cloth and clothing, alleviated some of their time-consuming drudgery. The society's second president, Arunah Metcalf, urged all members to wear only homespun "wrought by the fair hands of our wives and daughters, and let them not deem it either menial or disrespectful." While promoting scientific advances in farming techniques, the agricultural societies resisted cultural changes that challenged patriarchy and deference. Seeking technical progress within a traditional culture, the reformers tried to manage social change: accelerating agricultural innovation while reclaiming a lost, golden age of superior harmony, morality, and hierarchy presumed to have existed in the New England past.[33]

The county agricultural societies failed to lull the deep popular suspicion of any private association dominated by wealthy and prominent Federalists. The dirt farmers resented and resisted any institution that tried to centralize in Cooperstown, and to consolidate in an elite, the dispensation of information, honors, and influence. In 1817 a member of the Otsego agricultural society conceded that the common people suspected "that all societies, or combinations of this kind, are bodies not organized for their good, but for the express purpose of debasing and oppressing them." Three years later another member lamented "that by far the most numerous part of the Farmers of this county" manifested an "active hostility against" the society. Heeding public opinion, in early 1821 the Republican state assemblymen from Otsego began voting against further state funding for the county agricultural societies. When the state legislature eliminated the subsidies in 1825, the Otsego agricultural reformers canceled their fair and ceased meeting. Ultimately, the agricultural society failed because common farmers and voters recognized that it attempted, in a new guise, to rehabilitate the Federalist social model that they had rejected in 1799–1801. James Cooper and his compatriots neglected the insight that William Cooper had recorded in *A Guide in the Wilderness:* that common farmers knew "their interest better than strangers can instruct them."[34]

HARD TIMES 🔥

During the later 1810s, while the Cooper heirs spent lavishly and lived grandly, prolonged economic hard times steadily consumed their financial foundation. Before 1807 Otsego had grown rapidly in population and property largely because of the rising European demand for American potash and grains, especially wheat. That foreign trade boom dissipated with the embargo of 1807–1809, the War of 1812–15, and the subsequent commercial depression that culminated in the Panic of 1819. Between 1815 and 1820 the aggregate value of property in Otsego County declined by 13 percent, and the wealth per resident taxpayer fell by 18 percent from $1,013 in 1815 to $832 in 1820 (see Table 10). At this worst of economic times, the climate turned temporarily colder, curtailing the growing seasons of 1815–17. The New York farmers suffered greatly reduced crops at the very moment when their nervous creditors increased their demands for payment, producing a wave of bankruptcies and lawsuits. During the 1790s William Cooper had benefited from the artificial economic stimulus to American development generated by the wars and famines in Europe. During the later 1810s Cooper's heirs doubly suffered from the loss of that stimulus and the substitution of depression at home.[35]

Otsego was no longer a promising, frontier county, but an aging rural district transformed by twenty to thirty years of hard labor with axes, saws, oxen, and fire. By 1820 two-fifths of the county's land had been cleared and improved, primarily for agriculture. Two of the three most deforested towns were Otsego Township (63 percent improved) and Hartwick (55 percent), both located at the county core. The least cleared townships lay on the county's southern and western periphery (for example, Pittsfield, 14 percent, and Otego, 19 percent).[36]

Although new workshops and textile manufactories had proliferated during the early 1810s on the upper Susquehanna and its Oaks Creek tributary (in the towns of Otsego, Hartwick, and Middlefield), the county remained overwhelmingly rural and agricultural. According to the 1820 federal census, 80 percent of the county's men worked in agriculture, 19 percent in manufacturing, and 1 percent in commerce. The adjoining towns of Hartwick and Otsego had the highest proportion of nonagricultural workers: 33 and 31 percent respectively. Despite the growth of the new manufactories, most of the county's mills remained small and traditional: primarily sawmills and gristmills with a sprinkling of fulling and carding mills. These water-powered mills were dispersed throughout the county, with at least nine, as many as thirty-eight, and an average of twenty per township.[37]

Otsego had become a densely settled county, with an 1810 population of 38,425 (37 people per square mile). As a mature county Otsego discharged more emigrants to the more western counties than it received in newcomers from the east. After 1810 natural increase by the residents continued to push up the Otsego population, but at a markedly slower rate, owing to the growing outmigration. Between 1810 and 1820 Otsego's population grew by 16 percent, down from the 81 percent of the preceding decade (see Table 14).[38]

Shifts in the gender ratio and fertility ratio confirm that by 1820 Otsego was no longer a frontier county. The gender ratio is the number of males divided by females (100 represents parity; a higher number indicates a male surplus; a lower figure demonstrates a female majority). The fertility ratio is the number of children under the age of ten divided by the number of women of childbearing age (16 to 44 years). Frontier counties had large numbers of young children (a fertility ratio in excess of 2.0) and a surfeit of men over women (a gender ratio above 100) because early settlement was selective: single men and new families with many young children predominated among the first arrivals. In 1800 Otsego still had the demographic profile of a frontier county: a gender ratio of 112 and a fertility ratio of 2.3. However, by 1820 Otsego had matured demographically as the gender ratio had fallen to parity (100) and the fertility ratio to 1.6.[39]

As Otsego became an older, more crowded county, the opportunities to acquire a freehold farm waned. Growing numbers of Otsego farmers rented, rather than owned, their lands. The proportion of tenant farmers grew steadily from 23 percent in 1795 to 39 percent in 1814. In six of the county's twenty-one townships, a majority of the citizens were tenants. Contrary to William Cooper's initial hopes, Otsego had a high and rising proportion of tenant farmers very much like the older counties of eastern New York (see Table 15).[40]

During the 1810s agricultural productivity declined in upstate New York as the many counties settled during the 1790s, including Otsego, began to show their age. The early settlers had benefited from the "virgin soil," the nutrient-rich humus that had accumulated over the centuries from rotting vegetation. That initial fertility helped compensate the settlers for the intensive labor required to make new farms in a heavily forested landscape. However, on the uplands, cropping for grain steadily depleted the humus, revealing nutrient-poor subsoils that yielded paltry crops. At first, upland farmers coped by shifting their cultivation onto newly cleared fields. But after about twenty years, the small farmer ran out of uncleared, arable land—and their original fields had not yet recovered their virgin fertility.[41]

As fields expanded and the forest constricted, soils became more exposed to water erosion in the spring and fall and to the sun's heat in the summer, further depleting nutrients. Moreover, as the forest barriers came down, pursuing weeds, crop blights, and pests arrived from the east to afflict the Otsego farms. In 1821 a Butternuts farmer warned that "the noxious weeds, such as all sorts of Daisies, Johnsworth, and now and then a patch of Canada Thistles" had made "such progress within a few years" that "the whole county will be overrun by these intruders." By the middle of the nineteenth century, European weeds—including chickweed, purslane, dock, burdock, pigweed, goosefoot, common nettles, burweed, common thistles, doorweed, mulleins, plantains, and dandelions—competed with crops and crowded out native wild plants.[42]

Adapted to extensive agriculture, many New York farmers, especially younger men and women, preferred to perpetuate their frontier way of life by moving on. They headed west, seeking new homesteads where they could once again clear the forest to mine the virgin soil. By opening so many new farms on the more fertile soils in western New York and northern Ohio, the emigrants worsened the lot of those they left behind, for the swelling volume of cheap western produce glutted eastern markets, depressing the grain and livestock prices received by older farmers. In turn, that depressed market encouraged still more young people to head west, creating yet more homesteads, adding to the economic pressure on the older, more eastern farms.[43]

In 1817 the hard times in rural New York helped spawn the agricultural reform movement. The new societies sought to accelerate the transition away from frontier farming, away from a land-extensive to a more labor- and capital-intensive agriculture. A president of the Otsego County Agricultural Society explained:

> Thirty years ago and upwards, when we cleared up our farms, our system of cultivation consisted in sowing the grain, & scratching it in, and we had luxuriant crops, and that because the earth was covered with vegetable manure formed by the yearly putrefacation of the leaves of the forest, accumulated for ages past on its surface. By a succession of crops of grain, many of us exhausted our lands.

To restore the fertility of the increasingly limited and fragile stock of farmland the reformers urged a greater use of manure and other fertilizers, the substitution of beans and turnips for wheat, and of sheep for cattle, and a crop rotation through time that alternated nutrient-restoring plants such as clover and legumes with the nutrient-exhaustive grains.[44]

Although wary of the elite reformers (whose society collapsed in 1825), Otsego's common farmers gradually accepted many of their proposals. In general, during the 1820s and 1830s Otsego farmers cut back on their corn and wheat cultivation, shifting their lands and energies toward raising grasses and grazers, especially sheep and dairy cattle. Unable to compete with the many new grain farms to the west, Otsego farmers took advantage of the two great comparative advantages derived from their new position as a mature county. First, their elimination of wild predators—bears, wolves, and panthers—made Otsego safer for sheep than the frontier counties to the west. Second, Otsego farmers could better produce the relatively bulky, labor-intensive, and perishable dairy products (milk, butter, and cheese) because they enjoyed greater proximity to the growing domestic markets in the cities and towns along the Mohawk and Hudson. Soil-exhausting grain fields shrank in favor of enlarged pastures and meadows, often planted with soil-enriching clovers. The soil also benefited from the increased manure deposited by the swelling herds of livestock. Moreover, many (but by no means all) farmers took new pains to cultivate appearances of neatness, regularity, and beauty in their fences, fields, orchards, buildings, furniture, and clothing. Sensitive to village ridicule, the prosperous farmers meant to prove that they too belonged to the respectable middle class. By the mid-nineteenth century most of rural Otsego County approximated the look sought by the agricultural reformers of the 1810s. Neither especially fertile nor barren, Otsego settled into the midrange among New York counties for agricultural productivity and prosperity. But that resolution of Otsego's difficult agro-ecological transition came too late for the Cooper estate.[45]

DEBACLE 🔥

The economic and climactic hardships of the 1810s were especially devastating for the newer, more marginal settlements of the St. Lawrence valley, where most of the Cooper estate had been invested. The War of 1812 disrupted trade in the north country and exposed the settlements to military incursions from nearby Canada. Many DeKalb settlers became refugees, fleeing south from the danger. Already laggard, payments from the DeKalb settlers for land and for store goods ground to a halt during the war. In a letter to Isaac Cooper written in early 1815, David Goff pleaded the cause of his two sons who had settled in DeKalb:

> *So many difficulties taking place that I fear that they will never be able to pay you & git their Land Clear from the mortgage—especially my youngest Son— So much money on interest—hard times & a large family of Small Children to Support—not able to help him any—that I fear the interest will eat him out. . . . We have done too much already to lose. He seems to have Courrage & says he intends to pay for it yet—but for my part it looks dark to me.*

Indeed, almost all of the settlers who had purchased DeKalb lands in 1803–1804 from William Cooper defaulted on their contracts when they became due in 1813–14. They not only failed to pay off the principal, but remained deeply in arrears for the annual interest.[46]

Lawsuits would only depopulate the settlement without reaping money from settlers without cash reserves. Because their debts exceeded the value of their farms, wiping out their property through forced auctions would realize only a fraction of their worth and would further blight DeKalb's reputation. Who would come to settle where the proprietors were known to have ruined their previous settlers? The Cooper heirs also felt inhibited by an injunction in their father's will to perpetuate his reputation as a Father of the People:

> And as I have influenced many families to settle in new places on my land where numerous difficulties do, and for several years to come must, prevent their paying with that punctuality that is reasonably expected from older settlements where all the conveniencies of living are easily obtained, I therefore wish that my heirs will deal tenderly with all such infant settlements. I wish and advise this mode of proceeding because by experience I have found it the most advantageous and satisfactory to myself.

Nor were the settlers slow to remind the heirs of their father's benevolence and patience. Seeking yet another extension for his overdue debt, a settler assured Isaac Cooper, "[My farm] is about all I have in the world and I have done a great many hard Days work on it and numeris Misfortunes and sickness has Prevented me from paying something towards it. I am very loath to loose all I have done on the land. . . . I know your father did not distress those that was on his land and I do not beleave you will."[47]

Instead of suing, the heirs agreed to take back most of the land that William Cooper had sold, leaving the DeKalb settlers with much smaller, more manageable homesteads. The Coopers and their New York City partners had to write off the unpaid interest due on the surrendered lands. In effect, Cooper's superficially impressive sales of 1803–1804 had all come to naught; his mass sales to impecunious petty speculators had simply tied up most of the township's lands to no good end for over a decade.[48]

Disgruntled by the debacle, the New York City partners lost faith in the ability of the Cooper heirs to manage the DeKalb lands. "We never had received any money from Dekalb," Frederick De Peyster complained. Lacking their father's energy and charisma, the heirs could not reassure the impatient partners with his stories of great exertions or his promises of the immense and imminent profits awaiting the patient. In 1815 the partners obliged the Coopers to divide the reclaimed lands and the new bonds and mortgages among the individual investors. The New York partners also persuaded the Cooper heirs to accept a new agent for DeKalb: John Fine, a young lawyer from New York City.[49]

Neither the reorganization of 1815 nor the return of peace that year could halt the continuing economic stagnation in the north country. Few settlers could buy land or pay their debts to either landlord or storekeeper.

In July 1815 the DeKalb storekeeper Thomas B. Benedict became bankrupt, unable to pay the $3,000 he owed to the Cooper heirs. Thereafter, Courtland C. Cooper, the son of James Cooper (the late judge's brother), managed the store on behalf of its new owner, his first cousin James [Fenimore] Cooper. In 1817 John Fine lamented, "The times for Landholders & Farmers can't be worse. They must & no doubt will be better." They got worse. In 1819 Courtland C. Cooper complained, "I have had nothing but disappointment in every way that I have tryed to get money. To collect it here is utterly imposable except in small sums." He begged for his cousin's patience: "Consider that I have a hard set to deal with who are very poor and [I] am doing all in my power to collect my debts. I do not think it the quickest nor the surest way to sue every man, but I have sued a great many of them."[50]

DeKalb's continued stagnation renewed the recriminations between the Cooper heirs and their New York City partners. Caught in the middle was their mutual agent, John Fine. In late 1816, the Coopers summarily fired Fine as their representative, charging him with bias in favor of their partners. Fine refused to turn over his records until the Coopers paid their overdue share of his annual salary and expenses. Determined to compel Fine to return the papers without compensation, the Coopers threatened a suit in the Court of Chancery.[51]

In the course of the consequent, prolonged stalemate, Fine characterized the Coopers as erratic, selfish, and narcissistic. After announcing Seth Pomeroy as their new agent for DeKalb, the Coopers suddenly changed their minds and refused to empower him. Pressed by Fine to explain their reversal, "James said it was enough for him that P[omeroy] was a Yankee; he wasn't prompt; and the opposite objection he had found with me, that I was not enough of a Yankee." To Fine's further confusion, Isaac and James Cooper alternated accusations with politeness; threats with friendly overtures:

> They gave me to understand [that] it is their way of business. They will have all they can get. And [they] close it all, by saying [that] they repose fully in the integrity of my character, and do not believe I have erred in judgment, and if they have any Law business in St. Lawrence C[ount]y, they shall commit it to my charge. I have written so many inconsistencies, that I forget whether I have ate dinner & indeed am ready to believe or disbelieve any thing.

The dispute lingered into late 1818 when the Coopers apparently paid Fine and received their DeKalb records back.[52]

Those records revealed the continuing erosion of the Cooper estate. The heirs had counted on the interest and the principal on their DeKalb bonds and mortgages to redeem the debts they inherited from their father, as well as the large, new debts they incurred during the 1810s. Consequently, the failure of the settlers to pay doomed the Cooper estate. To paraphrase William Cooper, without money to swim in, the heirs ran aground. In the mid-nineteenth century, long after the Cooper heirs had lost possession, DeKalb enjoyed a brief spurt of prosperity and growth thanks to the iron ore that had so entranced the judge. Founded in 1848, the DeKalb iron-works thrived during the Civil War but collapsed in the economic panic of 1873. After that failure, the village rapidly declined and became a ruined ghost town in the early twentieth century, completing the failure of William Cooper's northern town.[53]

THE LAST OF THE EXECUTORS 🔥

During the 1810s the Cooper heirs also confronted an ominous legal threat to their estate: a lawsuit brought against their title to the Otsego Patent by the brothers, George W. Prevost (1767–1840) and James Augustine Prevost (1769–1822). Both were retired British army officers, the sons of Maj. Augustine Prevost and Susannah Croghan, and so the grandsons of Col. George Croghan, the original proprietor of the Otsego Patent. The Prevosts meant to overturn William Cooper's 1786 purchase, which was the foundation for his entire estate. They enjoyed the assistance of legal documents provided by William Franklin, still an expatriate in London, who hoped to share in their spoils. As William Cooper grew so conspicuously wealthy from the Otsego lands, Franklin and the Prevosts became increasingly envious and resentful.[54]

Before the judge's death the Prevosts were preoccupied with prolonged and costly lawsuits to reclaim from other speculators the McKee's Patent on the eastern edge of Otsego County (including parts of Worcester, Decatur, Maryland, and Cherry Valley townships). Their success in recovering McKee's Patent emboldened the Prevosts in 1814 to begin litigation meant to recover legal possession of the Otsego Patent. If the Prevosts prevailed the settlers would have to repurchase their farms. In turn, the Cooper heirs would be liable to compensate the settlers because Judge Cooper had warranted his original deeds. Because that liability would far exceed the Coopers' dwindling net worth, a Prevost victory would utterly dissolve their estate. Motions by the Cooper lawyers strung out the controversy into 1821 when the financially exhausted Prevosts dropped their suits. It was a hollow victory because the prolonged and complex litigation had added legal expenses that the heirs could ill afford. Moreover, the Prevost threat had a chilling effect on the Coopers' ability to sell Otsego lands and to collect rents or land payments from their settlers, who developed new doubts about the validity of the Cooper title and a new excuse for delaying their payments.[55]

Over the course of the 1810s, it became harder and harder for the Coopers to sustain their genteel merriment. In addition to the balky servants and village contentions, the Prevost suit and DeKalb failures, roaming pigs, ballplaying boys, agricultural stagnation, and farmer resentment, a steady succession of early deaths and funerals repeatedly punctured the Coopers' efforts to live in the grand, airy, sociable, and pleasurable style of gentility. In 1811 Miss Elizabeth Cooper, the seven-year-old daughter of Richard Fenimore Cooper, burned to death when her dress caught fire from a candle. In 1813 James and Susan Augusta De Lancey Cooper lost their tiny daughter Elizabeth during their trip from Mamaroneck to Cooperstown when she sickened and died after eating overripe strawberries. Four years later another daughter of Richard Fenimore Cooper, sixteen-year-old Hannah, died suddenly, to the further distress of her family and friends. Ann Cooper Pomeroy gave birth to a succession of short-lived children, burying infants in 1805, 1811, 1817, 1819, and 1820 (during the same period she bore four other children, who did live to adulthood).[56]

During the 1810s most of the Cooper heirs also died prematurely, worn out by some combination of high living and financial stress. Each death complicated the estate by adding new widows and orphans needing financial support from the surviving heirs. Each death also rearranged fiduciary responsibility for the estate. Initially, the two eldest sons, Richard Fenimore and Isaac Cooper, served as the executors. Their early deaths shifted that responsibility onto, in succession, William Jr. and James.

The first to go was the eldest, Richard Fenimore Cooper, who died in Albany on March 5, 1813, at the age of thirty-seven. His death brought to a head the long-festering scandal involving his beautiful but reckless wife, Ann Low Cary Cooper. By late 1808 she had become notorious for cuckolding her husband. In a letter written December 19, 1808, James Cooper taunted his eldest brother: "I hope we shan't take the lady of Apple Hill in the *straw*. I write plain." Lest Richard miss the innuendo, James thoughtfully drew a crude haystack around the word *straw*. Apparently, James did not consider her child born eleven days earlier to be Richard's son. Resentful of Richard's exercise of paternal authority, James seized the opportunity to add to his considerable chagrin over his wife's conduct. Nine months later a political enemy tried to expose the scandal in the *Otsego Herald*. Although the Republican editor Elihu Phinney had broken politically with the Federalist Coopers, he refused to publish the attack and privately sent a copy to Richard. Apparently, Richard and Ann separated in the spring of 1811, when he published a newspaper notice forbidding anyone from advancing her money or goods on his credit without his written order. Although they both had removed to Albany, they lived apart and she ignored Richard during his prolonged and fatal illness, preferring the company of George Hyde Clarke. An English-born gentleman with vast landholdings throughout New

York State, Clarke had met Ann upon hiring Richard as his agent to collect the rents due from his tenants in Cherry Valley and Middlefield. Instead of mourning her husband, she almost immediately married Clarke, although rumor insisted that he still had a wife living in England. Later in 1813 the scandal was compounded when Ann gave birth to a boy, Alfred, conceived before her remarriage and ostensibly Richard's son. However, given Richard's poor health and separation from Ann, the father must have been Clarke.[57]

Despite her infidelity and her remarriage to the wealthy Clarke, Ann Clarke audaciously billed the Cooper estate for the expensive clothing and education lavished on her teenage daughter, Hannah. When Isaac angrily refused to pay the "extravagant" debits because they were so far "beyond the ability of the Estate to support," she bitterly charged the Cooper heirs with "persecution." Fed up, Isaac wrote her a blistering reply on October 24, 1817:

> *I know not in what manner has your late Husband's family persecuted you. (I presume you mean my late Brother Richard when you allude to your late Husband). . . . What obligations are your late Husband's Family under to you? Why mention the word Delicacy? Does not almost every act of your life contradict the very term? You yourself cannot effect ignorance of the common conversation of everyone, even the Children in the streets of Albany of your neglect to your late Husband during his long death bed confinement and the total Disrespect to his memory immediately after. Your suffering Hannah to go to the ball on [the] Tuesday eve [after Richard's death] struck every virtuous person with horror. You may say, as I have heard many of your family say, "I do not care for the world's oppinion a Fig. ". . . Good God! Can a mortal suppose that by dashing and braving, all vices are to be received as virtues, that do what you please, a bold face is sufficient?*

In a dig at Clarke, Isaac added, "It is unfortunately too true that some part of the Higher Classes of England are notorious for their vices and depravity. Are they not held up to the scorn of the world?"[58]

Isaac died shortly after this explosion. In August of 1815 Isaac and his wife had visited her parental family, the Morrises, at Butternuts. After dinner Isaac engaged in a playful wrestling match with his brother-in-law, Richard Morris. The match ended badly when Richard accidentally hurled Isaac against the piazza, injuring his spine. (Richard Morris seemed to visit tragedy upon the Coopers; he had been with Hannah when she died in 1800.) Never fully recovering, Isaac suffered a series of debilitating complications that left him "sick, very sick" for most of the ensuing two and a half years. Unable to concentrate on business, Isaac was helpless as the Cooper heirs' assets dwindled and their debts mounted. He died on January 1, 1818, mourned by "a numerous assemblage of citizens." Like his older brother, Isaac was only thirty-seven when he died.[59]

His death accelerated the collapse of the Cooper estate for two reasons. First, Isaac had been critical to holding the heirs together under their worsening financial pressures. Gregarious, affectionate, and generous, he was the most mutually beloved by his brothers and sisters. His death dissolved a bond that freed the survivors to bicker over, and thereby hasten, the impending collapse. Second, creditors had been relatively patient so long as Isaac was alive and the chief executor for the Cooper estate. Having far less respect for the business acumen of his widow and three surviving brothers, the creditors resorted to lawsuits after Isaac's death.[60]

They quickly discovered that Isaac was at least as disorganized and careless as his brothers. He had foolishly cosigned notes on behalf of a friend who became bankrupt, leaving Isaac's widow liable for the full $8,400. When Mary Ann Morris Cooper desperately tried to collect the many debts owed to her husband, she could not find the documentation amidst his chaotic records. Forced into genteel poverty, she had to sell off the cherished possessions essential to high status. On November 8, 1818, she recorded, "Sold our horse. Necessity compelled us." In July of 1819 she sent her slave Lizzy to Albany to "find a purchaser."[61]

In 1819 death claimed two more heirs: Samuel, on February 15 at age thirty-two, and William, on October 19 at age thirty-seven (the preferred age at death for Cooper sons). After Samuel's death, his widow and children moved out of Otsego Hall, and the estate rented the mansion to the Reverend John Molther as a boarding school for young ladies. The school quickly failed, and William Cooper's mansion lay empty, gathering dust and cobwebs. The family had never entertained high hopes for Samuel, but William Jr.'s death terminated a life of early promise and prolonged disappointment. By early 1819 he was a bankrupt and broken man, too sick in body and mind to participate any longer in the estate that he had helped to entangle. On August 23, 1819, Robert Campbell informed his client James Cooper: "[William] is in very bad health, & I think will not live long. . . . He will do nothing towards settling the estate—& those who are interested here are desirous that he should not do any thing further [because] . . . whatever goes into his hands is so much sunk, & you & the other heirs will have to pay the debts." His death in late 1819 left only two living heirs, Ann Cooper Pomeroy and James Cooper, less than a decade after their father's demise.[62]

As the lone surviving son of Judge Cooper and the last executor of his estate, James bore the brunt of the collapsing fortune. Like a latter-day George Croghan, James Cooper fled from his responsibilities in Otsego and DeKalb, moving in late 1817 to Scarsdale in Westchester County. There he could continue to live in a genteel style, thanks to 216 acres overlooking Long Island Sound, given to his wife by her father, John Peter De Lancey. While hired hands worked the farm and built a small but precious chateau called Angevine, James Cooper attended the local Episcopal Church,

joined the county Bible and agricultural reform societies, dabbled in electioneering, and served as a militia officer, becoming aide-de-camp to his
new friend, Gov. DeWitt Clinton. In 1820 Cooper zealously campaigned for
Clinton's successful reelection over Daniel D. Tompkins, the candidate of
the democratic wing of the Republican party.[63]

Cooper refused to concede that he no longer enjoyed the income to support his active and refined way of life, especially as the severe commercial
depression of 1819 deepened. Unable to pay his debts, Cooper faced lawsuits from the unpaid contractors who had constructed Fenimore House,
his unoccupied lakeside mansion in Otsego. Rather than retrench to live
more frugally, he gambled his sinking estate on an especially risky investment, buying with borrowed money a whaling ship, the *Union*. To secure his
$9,723 in loans, Cooper encumbered his few remaining properties in
Scarsdale and Otsego Township with mortgages. In 1823, when the *Union*
proved a disappointment, Cooper had to sell those properties, including
Fenimore House.[64]

John Peter De Lancey was shocked by his son-in-law's fiscal mismanagement and dwindling fortune. To prevent Cooper from selling or mortgag-
ing his lone remaining Scarsdale property, De Lancey maintained the
Angevine Farm in a trusteeship. Offended by that restriction, James Cooper
angrily removed his family in late 1822 to a rented house on Broadway in
New York City. Cooper might flee from the De Lanceys, but he could not escape his debts. Acting on behalf of a creditor, in 1823 the New York City
sheriff impounded and inventoried James Cooper's household goods. However, the creditor decided to release the goods when his agent in the city reported that they would fetch very little if auctioned: "I have seen his
household goods. They are of no very great value; they are few and of a
cheap kind." This dismissive judgment must have infuriated James Cooper,
who took such pride in his exquisite taste and who resented his ebbing
fortunes.[65]

COLLAPSE

The final unraveling of the Cooper estate began in 1821 with a court decision in favor of Thomas Bridgen of Albany. In 1794 his father had entrusted William Cooper with about 3,600 acres in the Military Tract of
central New York. As Bridgen's agent, Cooper sold the land but paid very
little of the proceeds to the Bridgen estate—probably because the purchasers defaulted, as did most in the ill-fated Military Tract. At Cooper's
death he still owed Bridgen $3,515. Because his heirs failed to pay any of
the annual interest, the debt ballooned to $11,101 by late 1818. Bridgen
brought suit in the Court of Chancery, winning a decree authorizing the

Otsego County sheriff to seize and auction any real estate belonging to the Cooper estate.[66]

At the Cooperstown courthouse on October 22, 1821, Bridgen's decree began the auctions that would wipe out the Cooper estate. Because, by law, the auctions required immediate payment in the cash that was so scarce during the prevailing depression, the properties fetched only a fraction of their worth. The eleven parcels auctioned on October 22 included Otsego Hall, which fetched only $1,650—a ninth of the value estimated for it by William Cooper in 1808. The debtor—James Cooper, as the surviving executor— had fifteen months to redeem the properties by refunding the bids paid, plus 10 percent annual interest. When he failed to do so, Otsego Hall passed to the bidder, a Cooperstown lawyer named William Holt Averell. Because this first auction of Otsego properties netted only $3,059, less than a quarter of the debt owed Thomas Bridgen, in early 1822 he applied his chancery decree to other Cooper lands lying farther afield. On January 16, 1822, an auction in Broome County consumed 3,969 acres but netted only $1,232 (a mere 31 cents per acre, about a tenth of their value in more prosperous times).[67]

The cheap and rapid rate at which Bridgen's decree ate up the estate alarmed the other creditors and heirs, who feared that soon nothing would be left to satisfy their claims. As the lawyer for the children of Ann Low Cary Cooper Clarke and Richard Fenimore Cooper, Ambrose L. Jordan showed a new solicitude for the estate held by James Cooper—with whom he had previously exchanged blows in a village street. In March of 1822 Jordan insisted, "The precipice upon which the concerns of the Cooper Estate stands at present seems to be a dangerous one, and the state of the concern demands most imperiously that something should be done without delay." He proposed a cooperative effort by the heirs to raise the funds to redeem the auctioned properties for gradual resale at better prices. The lawyer Robert Campbell urged his client James Cooper to exert himself in cooperation with Jordan before it was too late: "If things are permitted to go on thus, utter ruin must be the fate of all concerned. Cannot something be done to arrest this career of destruction?"[68]

Jordan, Cooper, and Campbell framed a proposal meant to persuade Bridgen to delay a further round of auctions. But he refused. At an April 15 auction in St. Lawrence County, the Cooper estate lost another 25,155 acres for a mere $1,634. The average price of 6 cents per acre was a fraction of the $1 per acre that William Cooper had paid for DeKalb in 1803. The paltry price revealed both the depression of the land market in the north country and the utter failure of the expensive Cooper investments there. The properties sold included the sawmill and gristmill built by the judge at a cost of $9,049; they fetched only $480 at the auction. On July 29, 1822, Bridgen and his devouring decree returned to Otsego County to consume forty-two more Cooper properties: eight village lots and 2,260 rural acres for $5,464 in receipts (See Table 16).[69]

Tottering from Bridgen's attacks, the Cooper estate received its mortal blow later in 1822. It came not from another creditor but from fellow heirs: James's sister and brother-in-law, Ann and George Pomeroy. To safeguard their share in the crumbling estate from James's mismanagement, they brought suit in 1820 against his executorship. After James failed to respond to repeated subpoenas, on April 6, 1822, the chancellor, James Kent, referred the Pomeroy suit to James King, a master of chancery. He was to ascertain all the debts owed to the Cooper estate; determine whether James Cooper had "wasted, misapplied or otherwise disposed of" the estate's assets; and discover what remained to satisfy the Pomeroys and the creditors. Cooper refused to cooperate with the investigation, apparently indifferent to the further losses created by his stubbornness. Although repeatedly summoned, he appeared in King's office for only "a few minutes" on one day and declined to participate in any of the proceedings. On October 16 King filed his report, which Chancellor Kent endorsed and promulgated on November 26, 1822. King determined that the Cooper estate owed $15,628 to creditors and a further $4,487 to the Pomeroys as the balance due on Ann's bequest in William Cooper's will. Worse still, the chancellor ruled that the estate had to pay the Pomeroys and creditors in cash, rather than in lands, or bonds and mortgages. If James Cooper failed to pay the Pomeroys within sixty days and the other creditors within five months, they could present their chancery decrees to empower the county sheriff to seize and auction real estate until the bids paid their demands in full.[70]

The largest single outstanding debt was $10,407, owed to Rufus King as executor for the estate of John Alsop of New York City. That sum was the residue of $17,000 that William Cooper and Richard R. Smith had borrowed from Alsop in 1793 to invest in land speculation. Judge Cooper eventually bought Smith's share in the lands and became solely responsible for the debt. He paid off over half the debt but, after his death, his heirs neglected the interest payments, swelling the debt back to $10,407.[71]

On December 28, 1822, Ann and George Pomeroy struck a deal with William Holt Averell, a Cooperstown lawyer and speculator who seemed bent on buying up most of the crumbling estate. In return for their chancery decree, he promised to pay them their full $4,487 with interest by May 1, 1823, and to bear all of the legal costs to collect the monies through auctions. The Pomeroys also agreed to redeem those properties "as the said William shall direct, he the said William furnishing the funds necessary for such redemption, and all the right, title & interest acquired by such redemption, [we will] convey to the said William." In other words, the Pomeroys would collude with Averell's plan to scoop up the Cooper estate properties at fire-sale prices. By exercising their right of redemption as

Cooper heirs, the Pomeroys could prevent James Cooper from rescuing the property by redeeming in his own name. Moreover, in the spring of 1823 the Pomeroys helped Averell acquire the chancery decree issued to Rufus King for the $10,407 (with continuing interest) owed him by the Cooper estate. And they provided details about the locations and dimensions of specific parcels belonging to the estate, information that Averell needed to direct the county sheriffs.[72]

A deacon in the Presbyterian Church, George Pomeroy was conspicuous for his piety and morality, as was his wife—but that did not preclude their unholy alliance with the ruthless speculator William Holt Averell. Determined to have their $4,487 without delay and without compromise, the Pomeroys sacrificed the interests of their brother, nieces, nephews, and sisters-in-law. In May of 1823 Robert Campbell glumly informed James Cooper, "The sale of all the property in this county belonging to the children of R. F. Cooper, Isaac Cooper, and Samuel Cooper is advertised to take place on the first day of July next. It will strip them, it is to be feared, entirely." Indeed, the July 1, 1823, auction at the Cooperstown courthouse wiped out most of the remaining Cooper assets in Otsego County. The sales netted $11,639 for the Pomeroys and the creditors at a cost of seventeen village lots and seventy-two rural properties (see Table 16). On average, the 4,916 rural acres sold for $1.64—less than one-fourth of their value in better times.[73]

The collusion of the Pomeroys with William Holt Averell disgusted Robert Campbell, who explained the operation to his distant client James Cooper:

> *Executions have been issued on these decrees into this county & others, & all the tangible property belonging to your father's estate and of all the branches thereof has been sold. But at these sales [Averell] will not bid any thing near [one] quarter the value of the property, & when the time of redemption (15 months) has nearly expired, he then comes in and redeems the good purchases, & thus takes the property without satisfying the debts. Mr. Pomeroy redeemed some of the sales on Bridgen's execution, which he has however since conveyed to Averell so that Averell has the sale & exclusive right & power of speculating on the ruins of your father's estate. . . . His object [is] to get as much as he can from the property of every branch of the family.*

Averell took a great and grim pleasure in so thoroughly frustrating Robert Campbell, who had severely cost and bitterly offended Averell's father in a past business dispute. Wrenching the Cooper estate away from the helpless Campbell was a sweet measure of revenge for the Averell family. Campbell sighed that he "would be the last person that Averell" would deign to compromise with.[74]

Averell and other speculators mopped up the rest of the Cooper estate in 1824 and 1825, when the auctions found fewer and smaller parcels that generated diminishing returns (see Table 16). Tireless in pursuit of Cooper properties, Averell dispatched an agent to investigate the value of James Cooper's real estate in Westchester and his household goods in New York City, but found the former untouchable (because of the De Lanceys' control) and the latter not worth the effort. Because the decrees held by Averell remained only partially satisfied by all the auctions, Robert Campbell had to keep secret the few village lots still possessed by James Cooper.[75]

Throughout the prolonged and agonizing liquidation, James Cooper remained strangely detached and passive, never bothering any return to Cooperstown to negotiate with the Pomeroys and Averell or to rescue some properties by bidding at the auctions. After departing Cooperstown in 1817, he stayed away for seventeen years. During the crisis of 1822–1824, he remained in New York City, writing novels and entrusting his affairs in Otsego to Robert Campbell, who was hampered by his client's diffidence. In June 1826 Cooper departed America to spend seven years in Europe, largely because of the continuing threat posed by the decrees to any property he held or acquired in New York State. In 1826 Cooper also tried to change his legal name to James Cooper Fenimore, but the state legislature would only permit him to add Fenimore as a middle name. Ostensibly Cooper sought the change to honor his late mother, but another reason may have been to complicate further litigation by Averell. Although James Cooper rarely forgot or forgave an affront, he seems not to have resented the Pomeroys. During his European sojourn, he sustained a regular and friendly correspondence with Ann Cooper Pomeroy; he stayed with them upon returning to Cooperstown in 1834; and he lobbied for George Pomeroy's application to become the village postmaster in 1836. Determined to maintain family amity, Cooper preferred to absolve the Pomeroys and heap all the blame for the lost estate on outsiders, especially Averell.[76]

James Cooper may have behaved so diffidently and forgiven the Pomeroys so readily because he had found a silver lining in the collapse: a liberation from the painful responsibilities of running an estate that was so hopelessly tangled and encumbered. And the loss of the paternal estate freed James Cooper to craft his own identity and expertise in other, newer realms as novelist, diplomat, and foreign traveler. He signaled his new identity in 1826 by changing his name.

During James Cooper's prolonged absence from America, Averell's decree continued to accumulate interest and to threaten the novelist's property until September 1834, when the two men reached an understanding. Despite all the property auctioned in 1821–1825, James Fenimore Cooper remained liable to Averell for $13,060, thanks primarily to the continued accumulation of annual interest. Cooper wanted to live in Cooperstown and own property there, but he could not do so in legal safety without coming to terms with Averell. Having exhausted Cooper's visible properties, in 1834 Averell agreed to waive all further claims in return for a lot in the Military Tract and $4,031 in bonds and mortgages that the novelist had inherited from his father. This legal settlement completed the dissolution of William Cooper's estate and freed James Cooper, at last, to return home.[77]

THE MONEY-CHANGER

Even by the volatile standards of economic life in the early Republic, the collapse of the Cooper estate shocked observers, including William Leete Stone, a New York City editor and publisher who had grown up in Otsego County and had served as a printer's apprentice in Cooperstown. Returning in 1829 after an absence of fifteen years, Stone marveled that "the changes most obvious in this place . . . were in the situation and prospects of the family of the late Judge Cooper." The judge's six heirs had been alive "and in affluent circumstances—when I was last in the village. Now, four of the sons [are] dead, and their families left all but destitute!" Stone was especially moved by the decay of Otsego Hall (after Averell's purchase in 1822 the mansion lay unoccupied most of the time, becoming sadly dilapidated and much vandalized):

> *The grounds and the orchards are the same; but the shrubs and the flowers; the long rows of green-house plants, indigenous and exotic, which rendered the noble corridor at all seasons redolent of spring, are no more! The busts of Franklin, Shakespeare, and Queen Dido, have disappeared; and on the remnants of the dark, lead-colored paper which yet adhere to the walls of the stairway, Britannia has to weep not only over the cruelly amputated arms of the Hero of the Plains of Abraham, but likewise over diverse sad mutilations of her own sacred person. Added to all [of] which, the edifice is ruinous, and some Goth or Vandal has converted the smooth gravel walks and beautiful lawn into a receptacle of planks and scantling, clapboards and shingles!*

The commodities of mundane commerce had obliterated the decorations of genteel seclusion, especially the carefully cultivated plants that had been Elizabeth Fenimore Cooper's special delight.[78]

The mansion's lapse into a lumberyard symbolized the unpredictability of fortune and reputation in the American Republic. The very perfection of extraordinary wealth and power in the eyes of a settler's son had been inverted into a sign of their chronic instability. Commerce and gentility were simultaneously intertwined and at odds: commercial success permitted the pursuit of a gentility that masked social mobility by claiming possession of a timeless aristocratic legacy, but only continued financial success could underwrite the genteel illusion; when it dissolved, the lumber of the latest arriviste reclaimed the mansion lawn.[79]

Although the auctions broke up the extensive Cooper estate, they did not have any egalitarian effect on the distribution of property in Otsego. There were a few men of modest means among the successful bidders; for example, the Hartwick farmer Stephen Holden obtained 61 acres for $116. But as a rule common farmers could not participate in the auctions for want of the requisite cash payment in full on the spot. Instead, seven prominent speculators dominated the bidding, acquiring about two-thirds of the property (see Table 17). The preeminent purchasers were William Holt Averell, George Clarke, Thomas Bridgen of Albany, the Cooperstown lawyers Samuel Starkweather and Robert Campbell, the village doctor Thomas Fuller, and the merchant Lawrence McNamee. Of the eighty-one leasehold farms, only four passed to the tenant, while fifty rental farms passed to the seven leading speculators.

Instead of marking the advent of an egalitarian age, Averell's purchases marked the triumph of a new elite in Cooperstown and America. The substitution of the lawyer-speculator Averell for the Cooper heirs signaled the ultimate failure of Judge Cooper's vision: the perpetuation of a wealthy and powerful estate in the hands of his lineage. The lawyer and businessman had smashed the hollow pretensions of would-be aristocrats practicing an old-fashioned version of gentility.[80]

William Holt Averell came by his relentless drive to accumulate capital from his formidable father. James Averell, Jr., was a man of grave competence and shrewd determination—the epitome of the hard-driving, ever-calculating Yankee entrepreneur. A 1787 emigrant from Massachusetts to Cooperstown, he began modestly as a farmer and shoemaker. According to a 1792 bill, Averell made shoes for William Cooper's young sons James, Richard, Samuel, and William Jr., for daughter Ann, and for the enslaved "wench" Rachel. During the 1790s Averell steadily accumulated property, developing a lake-front tannery, operating a saddlery and harness shop, obtaining a dry goods store, and speculating in local farms. Except for his shares in a cotton textile factory built on the Susquehanna during the 1810s, everything he managed made money, which he spent sparingly, preferring to reinvest every possible penny. By 1811 his Cooperstown tannery was the largest in the state. Punctilious about paying his debts, he never suffered a legal judgment in the county court of common pleas—a remarkable record given his extensive business interests. Renowned for his thrift, intelligence, and integrity, Averell was routinely chosen to manage public monies, including the fund for a new village schoolhouse, the subscriptions for the local Presbyterian church, and the treasury of the Second Company of the Great Western Turnpike. According to his friend, the lawyer Samuel Starkweather, Averell paid a heavy price for "his constant concern" over business. In 1816, Starkweather informed William Holt Averell of his father's recent turn for the worse: "He has sunk rather faster than most persons would with the same pain. His great anxiety about his business is the cause to which I attribute his rapid failure. It had worn him down before its effects appeared in the shape of a regular disease."[81]

James Averell, Jr., raised his sons with far more rigor than did Judge Cooper. Averell stressed the bourgeois virtues of frugality, industry, and the constant calculation of economic advantage. Reversing the judge's priorities, Averell trained his sons as businessmen first and as gentlemen a distant second. Instead of encouraging his sons to consume money gracefully, Averell taught them to delay gratification in favor of accumulating ever more capital. His sons began as their father had, working manually in the tannery and saddle shop (conversely, no son of William Cooper ever made wagon wheels). He sent William Holt Averell off, first to Fairfield Academy in Herkimer County in 1810, and then to Union College in Schenectady in 1812. Upon graduating in 1816, young Averell spent three years as a lawyer's apprentice, at first in the Cooperstown office of Samuel Starkweather and subsequently at the Litchfield, Connecticut, law school run by Tapping Reeve. In 1817, after exhausting all his money, Averell asked his father for more. He received a stinging reply:

> It apears to me that Litchfield is a very extravigant place or you must be rather extravigant. These [are] hard times. Money never was more difficult to be had than at this time. I have never calculated to furnish you with more than four hundred Dollars for your expences while in Litchfield & when you have expended that some [sic], you must get into the Stage & come home & go to work & earn something to support yourself.

Ominously, James Averell, Jr., added that, because William's brother Lewis had behaved so badly in school, "I have put him into the Tanworks & [now] he is tolarable Steddy." Preferring thrift in Litchfield to labor in the Cooperstown tanworks, William Holt Averell completed his studies without significant further cost.[82]

His father's son, William Holt Averell managed his newly acquired Cooper properties without the paternalism practiced by the judge and his heirs. Not giving a damn for popularity or gratitude, he preferred to maximize his profits. Averell never aimed to be a Father of the People. In foreclosing on Cooper properties in Broome County, he directed the sheriff to auction everything, including a lot that the Coopers had set aside for a local church. In St. Lawrence County, Averell refused to exempt settler-occupied lots from his auction purchases, and he demanded that the settlers pay off their debts within four years or face eviction. When he found it difficult to prevent settlers from trespassing onto his lands to cut oak timber for market, Averell hired crews to clear-cut the trees, so that he alone might sell and benefit from that commodity. On the other hand, Averell had a far more sober view of his properties' true worth. He slashed his prices for DeKalb land from the unrealistic $3 to $5 per acre sought, largely in vain, by the Coopers to a more reasonable $2. As a result, in 1826 John Fine reported, "In DeKalb the property of the Coopers has passed into the hands of the Averells. They offer their lands at very low prices and are selling them rapidly."[83]

William Holt Averell's conquest of James Cooper's estate reads like a nineteenth-century bourgeois morality play: the industrious, frugal, and disciplined young businessman bests the diffident dilettante and pampered scion of inherited riches. Confined to a strict budget, one young man graduates from college and triumphs over the indolent and dissipated spendthrift who had been summarily expelled from Yale. Once upon a time, an industrious wheelwright wrenched away the frontier lands of a royal governor, but, in turn, the former wheelwright's own children became idle aristocrats and eventually lost their patrimony to the Yankee son of an early settler. In 1792 a shoemaker made shoes for the family of the rich Judge Cooper; thirty years later the shoemaker's thrifty son wrests away the judge's mansion from his unworthy heirs. Ignoring the warning of a visiting Quaker preacher, the Coopers persisted in mismanagement and luxury until they fulfilled his grim prophecy.[84]

Naturally, James Fenimore Cooper balked at this tale and attempted a rewrite by repurchasing Otsego Hall from Averell. In 1832 Cooper explained to his agent and nephew, Richard (the son of Richard Fenimore Cooper), "If we can succeed in this purchase, the Jews shall be driven from the Temple, dear Dick, and your name will occupy its old station in Otsego." In Cooper's telling, Averell was a sordid, parochial Yankee who valued nothing but money and who despoiled the mansion that was properly the residence of gentility, rather than a den of commerce. By driving Averell from "the Temple," the novelist would restore his family's proper preeminence in Otsego. Cooper probably had this metaphor in mind when he wrote of Judge Temple and the village of Templeton in *The Pioneers*. In 1834 James Cooper succeeded in buying back Otsego Hall, and, after making extensive renovations, he returned with his family to reside in Cooperstown, but his wealth never matched that of William Holt Averell.[85]

Both tellings of the decline and fall of the Cooper estate symbolize the shifting nature of wealth and power in the early nineteenth century. William Cooper had hoped that his sons could redeem his ideal: an entrenched lineage exercising in unity the political, social, cultural, and economic power once enjoyed by the colonial elite. During the late 1810s and early 1820s, that hope vanished in the wreckage of his estate, reiterating the judgment suffered by Judge Cooper in the politics of 1799–1801. Contrary to popular myth, the collapse of old visions and (relatively) old wealth did not inaugurate an egalitarian distribution of wealth and power in either Cooperstown or the American Republic in general. The substitution of

William Holt Averell for James Cooper certainly marked no diminution in the growing gap between the rich and the poor in Otsego County. In 1829 William Leete Stone watched a militia muster in Cooperstown; the lawyer-officers were "brilliantly arrayed" but many of the farmer-soldiers were "ragged as Lazarus." In 1850 Susan Fenimore Cooper noted that Cooperstown included "many persons in want . . . who may be called regular beggars." They lived by a mix of public and private charity supplemented by picking wild berries for summer sale and by petty thefts from gardens and orchards. Although there was considerable turnover at the top rung of the American social order, inequality endured and deepened.[86]

Instead, the essential changes were in the subdivision and specialization of public forms of power and in the popularization of electioneering performances. Although wealthy and well educated, Averell neither sought nor enjoyed political popularity and office. But he exercised formidable economic power as a great landlord and as the director of new corporations, especially the Cooperstown bank. Like his many counterparts in the new economic elite, Averell left overt electioneering and formal governance to the new breed of political specialists, chiefly lawyers and newspaper editors. He recognized that most public power had passed quietly to the conservative judiciary and to the corporations of private wealth, especially banks. The transfer insulated economic power from democratic control. Paradoxically, as common white men became the essential audience for aspiring officeholders, the power of those offices diminished. During the first half of the nineteenth century, the substantive meaning of democratic participation became diluted by the divorce of economic from political power. Unlike his predecessor Judge Cooper, Averell had little cause to lament his lack of political office because, as politics became more democratic (for white men) and professionalized (primarily by lawyers and editors), the authority of state government shrank.[87]

Chapter Fifteen

THE NOVELIST

J AMES COOPER BECAME A NOVELIST
during the early 1820s, at the same time
that his familial estate crumbled into
ruins. Despite a boyish love for "reading
novels and amusing tales," he did not
begin to write fiction until he was thirty
and only after the frustration of his ambitions as a gentleman farmer, landlord, and
investor. In 1829 his friend William Leete
Stone linked Cooper's sudden and unlikely venture into fiction to his financial
downfall: Cooper's "loss of property called
forth the slumbering energies of his
mind." Certainly none of his previous writings—neither his prosaic newspaper notices nor his usually terse letters—indicate
much imagination; they are the matter-of-
fact expressions of a conventional gentle-
man. It seems that the shock of his collapsing fortunes and the novelty of
writing fiction combined to jar James Cooper's mind into new powers.
Crafting fictional worlds filled a need prompted by his decaying property
and status. By creating characters, scenes, and plots, he discovered a reassuring power to control that was especially intoxicating because he was so
impotent to preserve his cherished position as a landed gentleman.[1]

*The youth took the paper, which his
first glance told him was the will of the
Judge. . . . The tears fell from the eyes of
the young man, as he read this unde-
niable testimony of the good faith of
Marmaduke. . . .*

*"I thank thee, my son," said the
Judge, exchanging a warm pressure of
the hand with the youth; "but we have
both erred; thou hast been too hasty
and I have been too slow. One half of
my estates shall be thine as soon as they
can be conveyed to thee; and if what my
suspicions tell me, be true, I suppose the
other must follow speedily." He took the
hand which he held, and united it with
that of his daughter. . . .*

—James Fenimore Cooper,
The Pioneers, *442–44*

NOVELS

According to Susan Fenimore Cooper, her father began his first novel in response to a challenge from his wife:

*He always read a great deal, in a desultory way. Military works, travels, Bi-
ographies, History—and novels! He frequently read aloud at that time to my*

Mother, in the quiet evenings at Angevine. Of course the books were all English.
A new novel had been brought from England in the last monthly packet; *it*
was, I think, one of Mrs. Opie's, or one of that school. My Mother was not well;
she was lying on the sofa, and he was reading this newly imported novel to her;
it must have been very trashy; after a chapter or two he threw it aside, exclaim-
ing, "I could write you a better book than that myself!" *Our Mother*
laughed at the idea, as the height of absurdity—he who disliked writing even a
letter, that he should write a book!! He persisted in his declaration, however,
and almost immediately wrote the first pages of a tale, not yet named, the scene
laid in England, as a matter of course.

The story is plausible, especially in the claim that Cooper turned to fiction
as a lark rather than as a career decision. Because no previous American
novelist had sustained commercial success, James Cooper could not have
begun a novel with any expectation that he would make money. Before
1820 American readers and publishers preferred to import or pirate their
books from England, because English texts were at once less expensive and
more fashionable. For want of copyright protection for imported works, it
was cheaper for American publishers to reprint English works than to pay
native authors. Indeed, although Susanna Rowson's *Charlotte Temple* (1791)
sold phenomenally well, she reaped almost none of the profits, because
it was originally published in London and then pirated in America. Moreover, English novels offered more romantic characters and exotic settings—
lords and ladies in castles or grand estates—than seemed possible in
common and commercial America. Professing themselves a people of
equality and common sense, Americans doubted that their society could
ever inspire a novelist. So doubting, they continued to read the imports.
Consequently, the most promising American novelist of the previous generation, Charles Brockden Brown, had failed to support or sustain himself.[2]

In early 1820, after one false start, James Cooper enthusiastically and
rapidly fabricated a novel of manners set in England and entitled *Precaution,*
but he balked at publishing it for fear of embarrassment. Because women
prevailed among both the writers and readers of novels, many gentlemen
did not respect the genre. They considered novels to be trivial, feminine,
and vaguely dishonorable, because they appealed to the emotions and
aroused the imagination—impulses profoundly distrusted by gentlemen
dedicated to self-control. Because James Cooper took his gentility and masculinity so very seriously, he feared that publishing a novel would be unbe-
coming his dignity and station. Before launching into print Cooper sought
approval from the gentleman he most admired: former governor John Jay,
who lived nearby, within Westchester County. Pretending to present the
work of an anonymous friend, Cooper read his manuscript to a small group
of ladies and gentlemen gathered in Jay's parlor. Pleasantly surprised by
their interest and approval, Cooper hired a New York City publisher and

bookseller who, at the novelist's expense and risk, produced *Precaution* in
November. Still not daring to hazard his name and reputation on a novel,
he published anonymously, but the secret did not keep. In July of 1821 a
Cooperstown newspaper reported as common knowledge that *Precaution*
came "from the pen of James Cooper, Esq., late of this Village, now a resident of Westchester Co., youngest son of the Hon. William Cooper,
deceased."[3]

Badly edited and inferior to its English models, *Precaution* sold poorly in
the United States, and Cooper probably lost money on its publication—as
he was losing money on everything else in 1820 and 1821. But he had fallen
in love with writing—with crafting and controlling characters, plots, and
morals in an imagined world. And he delighted in the gamesmanship and
business of publishing and promoting a novel. In submitting *Precaution*,
Cooper assured his publisher:

> *No book was ever written with less thought and more rapidity. I can make a*
> *much better one—am making a much better one. I send this out as a pilot*
> *baloon. I made it English to impose on the public—and merely wish'd to see my-*
> *self in print—and honestly own [that] I am pleased with my appearance—con-*
> *sidering that from 14 to 28 pages of the book were written between 9 o'clock in*
> *the Morning and 9 at night.*

Cooper took to the genre so readily because its prevailing conventions perfectly served his own concerns and needs. As the victim of a collapsing estate, he shared with other novelists a dread of the economic dislocations of
their commercial society and a longing to stabilize wealth and status. Because his wife was his last and truest token of gentility, he subscribed to the
novel's preoccupation with the critical importance of an appropriate marriage to safeguard a genteel reputation and inheritance. Distrusted and
scorned by his De Lancey in-laws, Cooper also felt drawn to novels because
they tended to vindicate a mysterious and misunderstood protagonist by ultimately revealing his hidden but true nobility of breeding and spirit,
thereby dumbfounding rivals and critics. Determined to instruct his countrymen and women, he reveled in the moral platitudes and civic didacticism
of the most earnest novels.[4]

Upon completing (and before publishing) *Precaution*, Cooper began a
new, more innovative and ambitious novel with an American setting and a
patriotic theme: *The Spy*. Assuming the daunting "task of making American
manners and American scenes interesting to an American reader," Cooper
elaborated upon a story John Jay told of a selfless American spy active in bitterly contested Westchester County during the Revolutionary War. Published in December, Cooper's second novel proved instantly and
phenomenally popular. Although highly priced at $2 apiece, the first 1,000
copies sold out within a month. By the end of the year, bookstores had or-

dered and retailed at least 6,000 copies, and Cooper had reaped royalties worth nearly $4,000—an extraordinary success for an American novelist. A popular play based on *The Spy* began a long run in New York City in March 1822.[5]

Cooper discovered that there was a great new public demand for an adventure tale derived from memories of the American Revolution. In the early 1820s, as the revolutionary generation relinquished public control and life, their heirs sought, by reading *The Spy*, a vicarious participation in their Revolution. Cooper also benefited from the examples provided by the English historical romances written by Sir Walter Scott, which proved so immensely popular on both sides of the Atlantic. Scott's novels were sufficiently "manly" and moral to disarm the opposition to the genre by leading Americans like John Jay. The publication in 1819 of *Ivanhoe* established the new popularity and respectability of the historical romance in America as well as England. In effect, Scott convened the American audience that greeted Cooper's similar works. Moreover, those readers responded so enthusiastically to Cooper because they longed for an American who could compete with Scott. They cherished *The Spy* in the belief that Cooper had so precisely and patriotically captured American manners, character, and setting.[6]

Addicted to writing and heady with success, James Cooper quickly launched a third novel, already entitled *The Pioneers, or the Sources of the Susquehanna*. Primed by the sensational popularity of *The Spy* and by a steady succession of newspaper teasers for the new novel, readers keenly anticipated its publication. In October 1822, after a brief return to Cooperstown, Moss Kent, Jr., remarked, "The Situation of the Village is most beautiful & romantic & I anticipate that the Author of the *Spy* in his next Novel, which is to appear in January, will do ample justice in his description of the Cooperstown Scenery." If known to the novelist, this particular eagerness for *The Pioneers* was especially gratifying because Kent had been Cooper's boyhood hero. The yearlong promotion and expectation paid off in an unprecedented first-day sale of 3,500 copies. Although sales later slowed and never quite matched the remarkable commercial success of *The Spy*, Cooper made a substantial profit and reaped widespread critical acclaim for *The Pioneers*.[7]

In combination, *The Spy* and *The Pioneers* persuaded American readers that at last their Republic had produced a novelist who could refute the British scoff that no one bothered to read an American book. The popularity of Cooper's novels reassured anxious publishers, painters, and writers that there was a public for American arts. Most of the American cultural elite considered Cooper not merely as a successful novelist but as their great champion in a struggle for domestic self-respect and international regard. He suddenly became *the* American novelist, the new nation's counterpart to the celebrated Sir Walter Scott. A grateful reader in Charleston, South Carolina, wrote to Charles Wiley, Cooper's publisher, "My eyes are scarcely yet sufficiently dry to enable me to write you, requesting that you will convey to the author of the Pioneers my heartiest thanks for the pleasure he has given me. The book is certainly the greatest literary honour yet conferred on the country." So read, Cooper's novels became freighted with patriotic significance as vindications of the new Republic's cultural worth and potential. Warming to the role, Cooper grandly announced that he meant to "rouse the sleeping talents of the nation, and in some measure clear us from the odium of dulness."[8]

There were a few dissidents among the New York City literati, who envied Cooper's extraordinary success and resented his formidable pride. Claiming loftier aesthetic and moral ground, these critics disdained *The Pioneers* for including so many common characters and so much colloquial dialect. They dismissed the novel as unsuitable for ladies of delicacy and taste—the presumptive audience for fiction. In a February 1823 review for the *New York Minerva*, George Houston insisted, "Perhaps we may be deemed fastidious; but we do think that no page of any novel that lays claim to reputation, ought to have the slightest indelicacy either of thought or expression, directly or indirectly; and in this the author of *The Pioneers* has offended." In the spring of 1823 the frustrated playwright Samuel B. H. Judah published a vicious satire, *Gotham and the Gothamites,* assailing prominent New Yorkers including

> *a certain conceited signior, of the name of C[oope]r; a chap, who prides himself wonderfully, on being the manufacturer of divers mawkish sentimentalities of little pleasantry, and less grammar, called novels, but which we believe, is all he has to pride himself on, and even these are so filled with incongruous absurdities and execrable poaching, that it required much exertion to cram them down the public mouth.*

The struggling and hypersensitive young poet James Gates Percival hated Cooper as "a literary *parasitic animal"* and detested *The Pioneers*:

> *It might do well enough to amuse the select society of a barber's shop or a porterhouse. But to have the author step forward on such stilts and claim to be the lion of our national literature, and fall to roaring himself and set all his jackals howling (S[tone], C[arter], & Co.) to put better folks out of countenance, — why, it is pitiful, 'tis wondrous pitiful, at least for the country that not only suffers it, but encourages it.*

Bitter with frustration, Percival concluded, "I ask nothing of a people who will lavish their patronage on such a vulgar book as the Pioneers. They and I are well quit. They neglect me, and I despise them."[9]

The dissidents were so disgruntled because they were so few and so ineffectual in a republic suddenly infatuated with a new literary champion.

Cooper had become a national celebrity, especially in New York City, where he was lionized by the readers and writers associated with Wiley's bookstore, with Charles K. Gardner's literary quarterly, and with William Leete Stone's newspaper. Moving there in late 1822, James Cooper arrived in the most populous, prosperous, vibrant, ambitious, and cosmopolitan city in the nation: a bustling center of 20,000 houses, 110,000 people, ten daily newspapers, nine theaters, and Columbia College. In April of 1823 the American Philosophical Society (in Philadelphia) honored Cooper with election to membership, and in August of 1824 he received an honorary degree from Columbia—vindication for his ouster from Yale. In 1824 Cooper gathered his growing circle of prestigious and talented admirers into the Bread and Cheese Club. The members included Chancellor James Kent, the artists Asher B. Durand, John Wesley Jarvis, and Samuel F. B. Morse, and the poets Fitz-Greene Halleck and William Cullen Bryant. Although he was surrounded by talent, Cooper's lively, witty, forceful, and boastful conversation usually dominated their gatherings. After a dinner party Bryant grumbled, "Mr. Cooper engrossed the whole conversation, and seems a little giddy with the great success his works have met with." A more indulgent friend observed, "Mr. Cooper was in person solid, robust, athletic: in voice, manly; in manner, earnest, emphatic, almost dictatorial—with something of self-assertion, bordering on egotism. The first effect was unpleasant, indeed repulsive, but there shone through all this a heartiness, a frankness, which excited confidence, respect, and at last affection." Never bashful, his personality fed on new praise to grow more overpowering. Long frustrated in his dreams of playing the influential landed gentleman, Cooper exuberantly wallowed in his newfound prestige and fame as a popular novelist and literary statesman.[10]

Cooper's prestige and purpose as a writer gradually took shape in the early 1820s as a consequence of three interacting processes: the practice of writing, feedback from his audience and peers, and the collapse of his inherited estate. First, by writing three novels, he became steadily more intrigued by, skilled at, and ambitious for his craft as a novelist. Second, popularity and critical applause combined to offer Cooper the role of patriotic spokesman as the new nation's premier novelist. Third, that role helped him cope with his failure as a landlord and investor. The utter collapse of his inheritance and the simultaneous triumph of *The Spy* and *The Pioneers* determined that Cooper would rely on his pen for a living and for self-esteem. No longer able to play the landed gentleman, he withdrew to the city and threw himself into his new identity. Consequently, although Cooper did not begin writing as a conscious bid for public authority, he reached that station in 1823 after publishing *The Spy* and *The Pioneers*. He found writing so entrancing and fulfilling because, to his initial surprise, it fulfilled his deep but long frustrated hunger for public influence and power. Unable to replicate his father's success as a politician and developer, Cooper found his own prestige and primacy as a popular novelist and literary spokesman for the nation.[11]

After a long string of failures—as a college student, naval officer, agricultural reformer, political operative, shipowner, mercantile investor, and landlord—Cooper finally prospered in the role of novelist. Despite the advantages of a polished education, elite connections, and inherited wealth, Cooper had failed as a conventional gentleman and capitalist only to succeed, beyond anyone's wildest imagination, at the most implausible and risky of ventures: writing and publishing novels set in America. Indeed, he was the only American author before 1850 to support his family primarily from his royalties.

He became the single most influential American writer of the early nineteenth century. In particular, Cooper created the stock characters—the noble but doomed Indian, the resourceful frontiersman, and the loyal slave—as well as the favorite settings, especially the violent frontier, that characterized most historical romances through the nineteenth century and into the twentieth. In Harvey Birch of *The Spy* and Natty Bumppo of *The Pioneers,* James Fenimore Cooper created the essential American hero of innumerable novels, stories, and films: the socially marginal and rootless loner operating in a violent no-man's-land beyond the rule of law but guided by his own superior code of justice. Whether imitating or deriding Cooper, his rivals and successors could never escape the long shadow of his most popular romances, could never fully transcend the expectations that he planted in the minds of their readers.[12]

AN IMAGINARY VILLAGE

In 1823 reviewers almost universally praised *The Pioneers* as a remarkably faithful portrait of frontier life in general and of the Otsego region in particular. If they found any fault, it was that the novel was insufficiently imaginative, insufficiently romantic. In the early nineteenth century Anglo-American reviewers tried to enforce conformity to the prevailing Common-Sense philosophy, which demanded the intelligible and disdained the obscure and fantastic. These reviewers concluded, with relief and pleasure, that Cooper had cleaved to the accepted verities of American rural life. A typical review, republished in a Cooperstown newspaper, applauded Cooper's allegiance to fact:

> *Nothing . . . that [Cooper] presents is fictitious; . . . he is imaginative, but it is only within the bounds of real existence. It adds to the value . . . of his work, that he does but copy scenes amidst which he spent several years of his youth;*

> *that most of his characters are drawn from originals familiar to his memory. . . .*
> *We understand that the Yankee Doctor, the Village Attorney (Lippet), the Ger-*
> *man guest of the Judge, and others of the personages, have been recognized at*
> *once by those who have resided at or near the theatre of the story.*

Excited by the novel, Richard Henry Dana, Sr., boldly wrote to introduce himself to Cooper and to effuse, "What a full and true description you have given of a newly settled village in a new country." Similarly, the *North American Review* extolled the characters in *The Pioneers* as "precisely such a collection as we uniformly meet when we visit a young, thriving village in the interior of our country."[13]

Reviewers who had visited or lived in Otsego County were especially impressed by the accuracy of the novel's depictions of the local settlers and landscape. The reviewer for *Port Folio* remarked that *The Pioneers* "might, indeed, be called historical; for the historian can scarcely find a more just and vivid delineation of the first settlements of our wilderness." In the *New York Spectator,* William Leete Stone—who had grown up in Otsego County—extolled: "The scenes to which he leads the reader, are those of his boyhood, and are endeared to him by all the pleasing associations of youth and many of riper age. [Cooper's] design was *description* of animals and inanimate objects; and he has succeeded in a wonderful manner."[14]

The inhabitants of Cooperstown immediately and proudly detected their village and many former residents in the scenes and characters of *The Pioneers.* In February and March 1823 both Cooperstown newspapers published excerpts from *The Pioneers* along with their editors' ringing endorsement of the scenes as literal and exact. For example, John H. Prentiss of the *Freeman's Journal* (the renamed *Cooperstown Federalist*) insisted that the pigeon shoot on Mount Vision "is painted to the life, as we can vouch, having witnessed similar sport upon the same favoured spot." Matching village and villager counterparts to the fictional buildings and characters became a favorite activity in Cooperstown. The inhabitants quickly associated Judge Marmaduke Temple, founder, landlord, and early ruler of Templeton with Judge William Cooper, the founder, landlord, and early ruler of Cooperstown. They also recognized Judge Cooper's daughter Hannah as the model for Temple's daughter Elizabeth. In local minds the fictional text and the actual place became blended. In April of 1823 the lawyer Robert Campbell wrote to his client James Cooper, "It has been said [that] you intended to visit 'Templeton' before sailing for England." In October a Cooperstown newspaper advertised for sale "a correct view of the Village of Cooperstown, and the Otsego Lake, taken by the help of a *Camera Obscura*. . . . It also embraces some of the most important places described in the *PIONEERS.*" During an 1828 visit to Cooperstown, William Leete Stone adopted the persona of "Hiram Doolittle, Jun," to write an essay for a local newspaper. Further blending fact with fiction, he casually referred to Judge Cooper's mansion as "the spacious hall of the lamented Judge Templeton [*sic*]." In 1832 William Holt Averell took out a policy "for the purpose of Insuring on the Old Mansion of the Late Judge Cooper, or in other words, 'Templeton Hall' in the Village of Cooperstown."[15]

For fifteen years following the publication in 1823, James Fenimore Cooper did not challenge the ubiquitous assertions that Templeton was a close approximation of Cooperstown during the 1790s. In *Notions of the Americans* (1828), Cooper imagined visiting Cooperstown, where he played coy about the authenticity of *The Pioneers:*

> *There resided formerly near this village a gentleman who is the reputed author of a series of tales, which were intended to elucidate the history, manners, usages, and scenery, of his native country. . . . One of them (the "Pioneers") is said to contain some pretty faithful sketches of certain habits, and even of some individuals who were known among the earlier settlers of this very spot. I cannot pledge myself for the accuracy of this opinion, nor could any one be found here who appeared to possess sufficient information on the subject to confirm it.*

After dining with James Fenimore Cooper in Cooperstown in 1836, the English traveler Charles A. Murray reported that "many of the characters [in *The Pioneers*] are family portraits. Its heroine was drawn from a very near relative, the memory of whose beauty and graces, both mental and personal, is still fresh in the neighbourhood. She died early in consequence of a fall from a spirited horse."[16]

Indeed, at first Cooper readily contributed to the easy equation of Templeton with Cooperstown. His subtitle specified that *The Pioneers* was "A Descriptive Tale"—rather than a romance. In the 1823 preface he explained that the novel was written "exclusively, to please myself," and he confessed that it lacked adventure and romance because he had succumbed to the "constant temptation to delineate that which he had known rather than that which he might have imagined." In a letter to his English publisher on the eve of publication, Cooper confided that he had "confined" himself "too much to describing the scenes of my youth. . . . If there be any value in truth, the [descriptions] are very faithful." In 1827 Cooper prepared a map of Otsego Lake and vicinity to illustrate the French edition of *The Pioneers;* he informed his French publisher, "The name of the village is actually *Cooperstown,* though called Templeton in the book." Four years later he observed, "*The Pioneers* contains a pretty faithful description of Cooperstown in its infancy, and as I knew it when a child." In the 1832 edition of *The Pioneers,* Cooper added footnotes confirming the factual basis of several episodes and characters. Following Marmaduke Temple's recounting of his purchase and development of the Otsego Patent (derived from William Cooper's *A Guide in the Wilderness*), a new footnote insists, "All this was literally true." Another footnote in the same chapter encouraged readers to identify Judge Temple's daughter Elizabeth with Judge Cooper's daughter Hannah. After narrating Elizabeth's impulsive and aggressive riding through the forest, James Fenimore Cooper explained, "The author has no better apology for . . . these desultory dialogues, than that they have reference to facts. . . . More than thirty years since, a very near and dear relative of the writer, an elder sister and a second mother, was killed by a fall from a horse, in a ride among the very mountains mentioned in this tale."[17]

However, after publishing the novel *Home as Found* in 1838, Cooper reversed himself emphatically to deny that *The Pioneers* derived from the Cooperstown of his youth. A vitriolic satire set in the 1830s, *Home as Found* depicts Templeton as a sink of vulgarity, hypocrisy, and demagoguery. The genteel protagonists—the heirs of Elizabeth Temple and Oliver Effingham—must defend a cherished lakeside point of land from the trespass of presumptuous villagers: just as James Fenimore Cooper had recently reasserted legal control of Three Mile Point, antagonizing the Cooperstowners, who regarded the point as their common picnic grounds. In the late 1830s several hostile newspaper editors assailed *Home as Found* as a self-serving set of calumnies by Cooper at the expense of his native village. Cooper responded with libel suits and a spate of newspaper essays that vehemently denied any specific connection between Templeton and Cooperstown, and between the Effingham/Temple and Cooper families. To refute those two equations in *Home as Found*, the novelist also had to deny them in *The Pioneers*.[18]

Although obliged to concede that certain details derived from real counterparts, Cooper argued that *The Pioneers* as a whole was larger than the sum of its many parts—that by modifying people, places, and events, and by shuffling them in with inventions, he had rendered them all fictional: "Not an incident of *The Pioneers*, that I can recall, ever occurred. Deer have been taken on the lake; trees have fallen; panthers prowled through the woods, and men have been put in the stocks, certainly, but no scenes, or events strictly like those of *The Pioneers* ever had a real existence to my knowledge." He explained that the novel was not "a literal account of persons and things; but descriptive as regards general characteristics, usages, and the state of a new country." Cooper argued that any deviation from fact rendered a character, place, or event fundamentally fictional rather than historical: "The moment *perfect* identity ceases in these resemblances, the reader has no right to infer that perfect identity was intended." In the terms of present-day literary criticism, Cooper meant to monopolize the assignment of the signified to signifiers. He conceded that he had described the landscape and seasons of Otsego, but he insisted,

> *In the real valley of the Susquehannah, I placed an imaginary village called Templeton. I say imaginary, for after going critically through the book, I find*

> *but one building in it, that ought to be mistaken for any thing in the village of*
> *Cooperstown, and scarcely any conformity in the dates and other similar pecu-*
> *liarities. This village I peopled with imaginary characters. I know this is not the*
> *popular notion of either the village, or the characters, but I do not hold myself*
> *responsible for popular errors.*

Contemptuous of local public opinion, he denounced readers who dared to appropriate the text for themselves by giving it meanings at odds with his revised understanding of his intentions in 1823. William Cullen Bryant aptly observed, "[Cooper] seems to think his own works his own property, instead of being the property of the public, to whom he has given them." In effect Cooper felt as aggrieved at independent readers of *The Pioneers* and *Home as Found* as at the aggressive trespassers on his lakeside land; he demanded the same exclusive property rights in the interpretation of his novel that he claimed for Three Mile Point.[19]

The novelist had particular cause—and took particular pains—to refute the identification of his family with the characters in *The Pioneers* and *Home as Found*. He denied the common equation of Marmaduke Temple with William Cooper:

> *It has been supposed—nay, it has been openly asserted—that Judge Temple is*
> *Judge Cooper, and that the history and character of one, are substantially the*
> *history and character of the other. Nothing can be farther from the truth. There*
> *is not a particle of distinctive resemblance between the personal history of Judge*
> *Temple and that of my father; so far as I know anything of the latter. . . . It is*
> *true the parties filled similar stations in a new country; this was generally*
> characteristic, *and as applicable to fifty other landed proprietors in New York,*
> *half a century since, as it was to Judge Cooper. To give his name to his village,*
> *to be the judge of his county, and a member of the national or of the state legis-*
> *lature, were facts so common among men of his stamp, as to be descriptive of so-*
> ciety, *as it then existed, and not of individuals.*

He conceded, "Now I am ready to admit that tempted by the opportunity, a few *personal peculiarities* of my father are introduced in the character of Marmaduke Temple, but a close resemblance was not even attempted."[20]

The novelist became even more outraged at the universal assumption that his late sister Hannah had been the model for Elizabeth Temple. He insisted that Elizabeth was a thorough fiction because she differed in detail from Hannah:

> *[Elizabeth] is described as having* raven locks, *a* full rounded form, *a nose*
> *approaching to Roman, with a high color, &c. My unfortunate sister was as*
> *little like this as possible. Her features were different, her cheeks were usually col-*
> *orless, her hair was almost* flaxen, *and her form was the extreme of lightness*
> *and delicacy. In a word, it would not be easy to imagine two physiques less*
> *alike than those of the real and the fictitious personages. In the* morale *I know*

of no traits common to both, that may not be supposed to be common to most young women of the same class in life.

Claiming complete proprietorship over both his sister's memory and his character Elizabeth, Cooper felt insulted that anyone would dare to equate the two, labeling such an association "a species of profanity." Describing his sister as "a sort of second mother to me," the novelist insisted that "the image she has left on my mind is any thing but that which would create a desire to disturb her ashes to form a heroine of a novel. A lapse of forty years has not removed the pain with which I allude to this subject at all." In his introduction to the 1851 edition of *The Pioneers,* Cooper asserted that it was excruciatingly "painful to have it believed that one whom he regarded with a reverance that surpassed the love of a brother, was converted by him into the heroine of a work of fiction."[21]

Given that Elizabeth Temple is a paragon of beauty, virtue, taste, piety, and benevolence, it is striking that Cooper thought that such a representation would have disturbed his sister's ashes. He suggested that *any* depiction of a dead and cherished sister in a novel was an act of grave robbery and that those who credited him with such a crime were profaners. Such insensitive readers violated the most sacred and closely guarded recess of Cooper's memory and identity, for he regarded Hannah "with a reverence that surpassed the love of a brother."[22]

REVISION

Although Cooper's post-1838 denials are excessive and often implausible, so are the assertions by the reviewers of 1823 that there was nothing fictional in *The Pioneers.* By diminishing the novel to a reflection of literal experience, the reviewers missed the larger meaning of *The Pioneers*: the ways in which Cooper selectively remembered the past: exaggerating, minimizing, contradicting, and omitting history. The silences, inconsistencies, and infelicities that mark Cooper's novels (and so trouble those critics who evaluate him primarily on aesthetic grounds) are especially interesting and revealing to more recent literary scholars, who read his works as ambivalent dialogues with history. Identifying Cooper's historical distortions serves to reveal the fundamental sources of his personal anxieties, as well as the ideological imperatives of his class, race, and gender during the 1820s.[23]

Because Cooper wrote *The Pioneers* as a mature but troubled man in his thirties, he did not, and could not, offer a simple, straightforward account of the village that he had known as a boy during the 1790s. *The Pioneers* speaks primarily in witness to Cooper's predicament in the 1820s and only secondarily to the Cooperstown of the 1790s. In 1822 Cooper keenly felt the accelerating collapse of his paternal estate, the consequent distrust of his De Lancey in-laws, and the unflattering comparisons of his near bankruptcy to his own father's immense wealth. In fiction he could create an imaginary world where his protagonist and proxy, Oliver Effingham, overcomes adversity and misunderstanding to secure his proper inheritance and esteem. According to the literary scholar Wayne Franklin, Oliver represents Cooper's self-image as "the disregarded heir, a man who is more than he seems to be, and who at last recovers his hidden claims." In his imaginary Otsego, James Fenimore Cooper enjoyed a mastery denied to him in the real world.[24]

The Pioneers offers an especially deep entry into James Cooper's troubles and desires in 1822. Because Cooper wrote rapidly and spontaneously, with minimal revision, his novels express more immediate impulse than careful reconsideration. Susan Fenimore Cooper explained that, when writing, her father "depended in a great measure on the thought and feeling of the moment." In late 1822 Cooper confessed to his English publisher, "I ought in justice to myself to say, that in opposition to a thousand good resolutions, the Pioneers, has been more hastily and carelessly written than any of my books. Not a line has been copied, and it has gone from my desk to the printers. I have not to this moment been able even to *read* it."[25]

In *The Pioneers* Cooper described people, buildings, and the landscape with a vivid, dreamlike intensity. He took inventory of his most powerful memories as if determined to embed and perpetuate them. He lingered lovingly over scenes and characters, indulging in the melancholia of his lost childhood and legacy in Otsego. Indeed, Cooper spent the first fifteen chapters describing the events of a single day. In the words of Wayne Franklin, Cooper re-created such a detailed and intimate recollection of Otsego as "a means of returning to the place . . . and repossessing it with a power more lasting than that provided in the laws of the state of New York."[26]

In *The Pioneers* Cooper reaffirmed his self-worth and reclaimed his legacy by imagining and crafting an improved past, where property and power flow from a well-meaning but flawed patriarch to his perfectly genteel heirs. In the novel's penultimate chapter, Judge Temple flourishes a will that dispels all illusions and assures a just and stable transition of his estate to his heirs—in stark contrast to William Cooper's will, which had proved so deceptive and destabilizing. In the end Oliver Effingham marries Temple's perfect daughter and obtains possession of the Judge's entire estate—the novelist's fondest wish. In Cooper's eyes wealth and power became truly civilized when they passed by inheritance rather than developed from striving ingenuity and open competition. He insisted that superior property and standing should be the prerogatives of birth and breeding.[27]

In *The Pioneers* Cooper also sought to quiet his own fears—and those of other genteel Americans—that the revolutionary upheaval compounded by frontier expansion would prove permanent. He had grown up in a country engaged in the continuing conquest and dispossession of the native peoples, riven with competition to control and own the lands wrested from the Indians, and bitterly divided between Federalists and Republicans contesting for power and competing to control the meaning of the American Revolution. By the 1820s leading Americans hoped for national unity, wished to set aside the bitter political conflicts of the preceding four decades, and longed to consolidate the Revolution into enduring institutions. Cooper succeeded so quickly and spectacularly as a novelist because he was so sensitive to the ideological tensions within America *and* to the powerful desire for consensus. Cooper wrote primarily for the middle and elite classes, for those who could afford the high price of his novels—$2, the equivalent of four days' wages for a laborer.[28]

In *The Pioneers* James Fenimore Cooper first explored the theme central to his frontier novels: the role of a governing patriarch, "the American Abraham," in imposing order on the violent frontier. In Cooper's frontier tales the father initially governs a new settlement as an extended family, exercising almost complete power over his small, isolated, and vulnerable community. Only the patriarch's benevolent power can preserve the settlers from the disorder and danger lurking in the surrounding wilderness. But, as the settlement grows and prospers, the settlers become more numerous, diverse, and restive, ready to forsake their political father and succumb to the insidious flattery of a populist demagogue. As external danger recedes, the subtler but more sinister menace of internal rebellion begins to ferment. Consequently, frontier communities were poised precariously on the verge of either maturing into a stable, prosperous, and just social order or lapsing into a purgatory of deceit, hypocrisy, and turmoil. Cooper insisted that the fate of the American Republic hinged upon the resolution of the contest between law and chaos in the hundreds of new settlements along the expanding frontier arc.[29]

The novelist argued that anarchy could be checked if the community could make a peaceful transition from the personal authority of their patriarch to the civil law uniformly enforced by respected institutions: courts and jails and their officers. In *The Pioneers* Marmaduke Temple is strategically placed to effect that transition because he is both Otsego's founder and its presiding judge. He strives to preserve his authority by shifting its basis from the personal to the legal. To succeed, Temple must prove himself a true gentleman willing and able to put legal principle above personal advantage.[30]

Superficially, *The Pioneers* seems to question the rule of civil law by sympathizing with the plight and arguments of Natty Bumppo. Capable of governing himself in the wilderness free from legal and political institutions,

Natty suffers when surrounded and overpowered by an invasive, crowded, complicated, and commercialized society brought into Otsego by Temple and his settlers. Caught in the trammels of the laws introduced and enforced by the Judge, Natty eloquently denounces the inflexibility of the new system.

The novelist permits Natty a full and sympathetic hearing but ultimately insists that his asocial way of life is doomed and properly so. The novel's glowing opening description of the New York rural landscape and society of the 1820s conveys Cooper's confidence that the triumph of commercial and legal civilization produces the greatest good for the greatest number. Cooper was devoted to the conservative legal philosophy of his friend James Kent, who insisted that English common and equity law were the consummation and distillation of a universal and timeless justice. Kent and Cooper devoutly believed that the pure rule of Anglo-American law was essential to perpetuating property, order, and liberty.[31]

Although the law was perfect, its execution victimized Natty in Templeton, because the officers of that court were unworthy of their noble duties. To function properly the law required well-educated and morally upright gentlemen to serve as judges, sheriffs, and lawyers—and it needed orderly and respectful common men to serve as deputies, jurors, witnesses, and spectators. Indeed, the law's innate power would become inert if entrusted to the incompetent and would become dangerously perverse if usurped by unscrupulous demagogues. *The Pioneers* presents a frontier struggle to possess the power of the law either to protect virtue, industry, property, and liberty or to corrode them. At issue is who possesses the proper dignity, wisdom, integrity, and gentility to compel respect for the law from the settlers.[32]

Natty can make a better case for natural anarchy than he ought because the execution of the law is so flawed in Templeton, because the magistrates and lawyers are not proper gentlemen. The best of the lot, Judge Temple says all the right things, but he is slow and inconsistent in action. The Judge knows the principles of gentility and law but cannot resist fudging them for immediate advantage: determined fraudulently to claim a deer kill, he tries to bribe Natty into cooperating with the lie; seeking an empty consistency with his Quaker principles, Temple puts ownership of his slave in the name of his cousin, Richard Jones. The Judge lacks the learning, dignity, consistency, and integrity necessary to command deference from the settlers. How can they defer to a landlord whose vast property is so morally suspect, so recently fabricated from cunning opportunism? Above all, how can they honor the Judge for legal majesty when he secures the appointment of unprincipled bunglers to the key county posts of sheriff and assistant justice? The Judge seems to redeem himself by presiding at Natty's trial with a firm and judicious hand, but ultimately he squanders his performance by levying an inordinately severe sentence on the convicted hunter. Instead of restoring the dignity of the law, Temple's excessive sentence further discredits the magistracy in Otsego.[33]

Even worse are the other four men who exercise legal power in Templeton: Assistant Justice Hiram Doolittle, Sheriff Richard Jones, and the lawyers Chester Lippett and Dirck Van Der School. Competent only as a clerk, the pedantic, cautious, and obtuse Van Der School is beyond his depth in the courtroom, an easy mark for more cunning competitors. Sheriff Jones is a bombastic and insubordinate fool who exploits his legal authority to gratify his prodigious hunger for attention and power. Squire Doolittle and lawyer Lippett are both driven by insidious greed and sly malevolence to pervert their legal knowledge and popular influence. They accumulate money and power by provoking the conflicts that the law is supposed to restrain. Possessing legal authority without reverence for legal principles, Lippett, Jones, and Doolittle threaten to hijack Otsego's continued development into a stable and just society. Instead of serving as virtuous exemplars engendering popular respect for legal restraint, they pander to the innate greed and ignorance of the common folk. They are virtually unchecked because Judge Temple is not up to his aristocratic responsibilities and because the settlers cannot yet tell true from false law.[34]

Because the officers of the law are so weak or corrupt, chaos impends in Templeton: Natty Bumppo derides the rule of law; Judge Temple seems to abuse his authority and the Revolution to defraud the Effinghams; when drinking, Chingachgook wants to tomahawk the Judge; Sheriff Jones ignores Temple's commands; Lippett and Doolittle foment discontent and dissension; and the people respond with environmental profligacy and populist vigilantism. But Cooper exercises these discontents in the plot so that they can burn out at the conclusion. The last of his tribe, Chingachgook dies in a forest fire, ending his claims forever. By winning his dying benediction and by mourning his demise, Elizabeth and Oliver cheaply legitimate themselves as heirs to the Indians' lands. Similarly, Natty Bumppo voluntarily departs from Otsego for the West after revealing himself to be the Effinghams' tenant, with no legal claims of his own to the land. By finally asserting himself to suppress the militia assault on Natty's cave, Judge Temple discredits Richard Jones and Hiram Doolittle. Exposed as frontier malcontents, they no longer belong in a moral and maturing community. Deprived of their demagogues, the people can see that the genteel Oliver and Elizabeth are their natural rulers. Instead of overthrowing the Judge and democratizing public culture as Jedediah Peck did in the historic Otsego, Hiram Doolittle abandons Otsego to the aristocratic rule of Oliver and Elizabeth. They will exercise a unified authority—at once social, economic, cultural, and political—over an increasingly deferential and harmonious community: the very antithesis of what had actually transpired in postrevolutionary America in general, and in Otsego in particular.[35]

In *The Pioneers* Cooper vividly displayed division and violence only to confine and suffocate them as providence mandates the inevitable triumph of harmony and stability. Concluding with a consoling fiction, he narrated the smooth transition of wealth and power, prestige and authority from the overmatched Judge Temple to his more deserving heirs: Oliver and Elizabeth. Cooper's narrative ultimately suppresses the economic and political conflicts that generated his need to write. By exiling Hiram Doolittle, marginalizing Marmaduke Temple, and empowering Oliver Effingham, Cooper reassured himself and his class that the contentious competition for new wealth and power associated with the revolutionary frontier would quickly pass, giving way to peaceful communities governed by the natural elite at the pinnacle of a stable hierarchy.[36]

By promulgating his will Judge Temple clarifies his enduring fealty to the Effinghams, the Loyalist gentry who had been driven from America by the Revolution. The marriage of Oliver and Elizabeth symbolically binds the Revolution's wounds, reconciling Loyalist and Whig in one reunited American gentry. The reconciliation legitimizes Temple's enterprise and, by extension, the American Republic on conservative terms—by affirming a continuity with the colonial past. Echoing the Federalists of the 1790s and anticipating the consensus historians of the twentieth century, Cooper denied the divisiveness and radicalism of the American Revolution by recasting it as the united effort of a conservative people determined to protect their existing social order. In *Notions of the Americans,* he insisted, "We have ever been reformers rather than revolutionists. Our own struggle for independence was not in its aspect a revolution. We contrived to give it all the dignity of a war, from the first blow."[37]

Cooper denied the Republican upheaval of 1799–1801 that had discredited the association of elitism with political power. Contradicting conventional wisdom, Cooper wishfully insisted that the American gentility enjoyed greater respect and influence than their English counterparts. He reasoned that, because the American people felt secure in their political rights, they did not dread their natural aristocrats. Confident of their sovereignty, the citizens freely bestowed honor and office upon gentlemen distinguished by their good manners, great property, liberal education, and commitment to public service. In turn, the American gentility subtly exercised their calming influence to check popular excesses, to monitor public morals, and to improve the common manners. In sum, during the 1820s Cooper imagined an America where he securely belonged to an honored, ruling class—defying the actual instability of fortune and subdivision of authority in the Republic.[38]

Cooper hoped to hasten the conservative consolidation of the revolutionary frontier by persuading Americans that it was inevitable and just. In

The Pioneers he crafted a reassuring past intended to secure the Republic's future stability. He understood that people sought the future based upon a collective identity derived from narratives that made sense of their past; histories shaped the trajectory of the nation's future. People live out the stories they tell one another. By narrating the memory of their Revolution and frontier expansion in conservative terms, they would make a conservative republic governed by a meritocracy of wealth and gentility. In 1820 he remarked, "Books are, in a great measure, the instruments of controlling the opinions of a nation like ours. They are an engine alike powerful to save or destroy." For Cooper truth was morally didactic; it was what ought to be in a moral universe; and it was what would come to prevail through the influence of moral texts. According to the literary critic W. M. Verhoeven, Cooper substituted myth for history in order "to interfere with and to actively participate in the formation of history's 'official' truth." By cultivating a popular audience, "he was actually able to feed the myth of ideological consensus and national identity back into the historical reality of his day."[39]

Ultimately, Cooper exercised his novelist's power to exorcise Otsego of the travail and conflicts that had troubled his life there during the 1810s. Determined that readers would anticipate this happiest of endings, James Fenimore Cooper opened *The Pioneers* with a glowing description of central New York in the 1820s as the virtual perfection of a social landscape: "neat and comfortable farms, with every indication of wealth about them" surround "beautiful and thriving villages," where the numerous schools, academies, and churches attest to the presence of "a moral and reflecting people." By depicting Otsego as a reassuring land of universal prosperity, social harmony, and civic virtue, Cooper elided many exceptions to the general prosperity: the agricultural stagnation, the surging outmigration westward, the growing uneasiness over crime, and the widespread bankruptcies and foreclosures associated with the Panic of 1819. He willfully forgot his troubles there during the 1810s with horse thieves, street fights, newspaper polemics, dying brothers, forced auctions, roaming pigs, and ballplaying apprentices. But the traumas of the 1810s were too powerful for Cooper to completely suppress; there lingered in his imagination a covert distrust of the social order that he overtly preached. Consequently he invested some of his identity in the outsider Natty Bumppo as well as in the conventional Oliver Effingham. It is telling that in his subsequent novels Cooper felt compelled to revive Natty rather than Oliver as his great protagonist. Originally intended as a minor stock character, Natty became Cooper's preeminent creation—in spite of the author's overt initial intent.[40]

POSTSCRIPT ❧

Both James and William Cooper sought the unity of social, economic, political, and cultural preeminence idealized in colonial America but at odds with the legacy of the American Revolution. Judge Cooper briefly enjoyed power and wealth as the "father" of the real community of Cooperstown. In the wake of his political failure and his heirs' financial debacle, the last son sought to reclaim influence and estate in the imaginary frontier village of Templeton. He hoped that life would then emulate art and restore the authority of an idealized gentry in nineteenth-century America. Templeton would become Cooperstown.

However, to James Fenimore Cooper's disgust, Cooperstown did not become Templeton over time. That is to say, during the 1820s and 1830s Americans did not settle into the stable, rooted, hierarchical communities that he imagined for them in *The Pioneers*. Indeed, during the year that immediately followed publication of that novel, an arsonist (or arsonists) in Cooperstown belied his picture of that village as the complete triumph of civilized order, harmony, and deference. The mysterious arsonist began at midnight on July 12, 1823, by setting a blaze that destroyed the main building of the lakeside tannery belonging to James Averell, Jr.—a loss estimated at $10,000 to $12,000. Both village newspapers attributed the fires to "a wicked incendiary" envious of Averell's wealth.[41]

If Cooper entertained any hopes of reclaiming his Fenimore House, they vanished on the night of July 23–24, 1823, when the incendiary torched the unfinished mansion worth $5,000, leaving "a smoking ruin." Editor John H. Prentiss of the *Freeman's Journal* lamented the fire as a severe blow to the village's gentility and reputation. The loss precluded attracting as purchaser and resident "some gentleman whose society would not only have contributed much to our enjoyment, but whose *means* would have added to the stock of wealth." Prentiss reported the prevailing speculation that the fire was the work of a gang creating a dramatic distraction meant to draw out the villagers, leaving their stores unattended and rife for plundering. However, the "vigilance of the village officers" protected the stores while the people unsuccessfully battled, or avidly watched, the burning mansion, located a mile northwest of Cooperstown. Prentiss conveyed no assurance that Cooperstown was a haven of equality and harmony.[42]

During the next ten months the arsonist or arsonists set at least eight more fires, destroying eight barns in or near Cooperstown and a church and schoolhouse in adjoining Hartwick. The arsonist singled out those barns belonging to the village elite: Horatio Averell, Maj. Joseph Griffin (who lost two barns), Dr. John Russell, Dr. Thomas Fuller, Judge Elisha

Foote, Col. George S. Crofts, and the lawyer and village trustee Farrand Stranahan. Only the exertions of the fire company, assisted by many villagers, contained the barn fires, saving the rest of the crowded village. The *Watch-Tower* especially lauded the women who "principally formed the line for the conveyance of water to the engine!"—while faulting the many men who remained idle spectators. Apparently the incendiary also tried but failed to set fire to Otsego Hall; during the mid-1830s James Fenimore Cooper remodeled that building and discovered signs of the attempted arson.[43]

In 1823–24 dread and anxiety prevailed in Cooperstown—contrary to Cooper's depiction of the peaceful village. In December the *Watch-Tower* observed, "The frequent occurence of these alarms in this village and its vicinity has produced a state of feeling in its inhabitants bordering on what is commonly termed 'the vapours.' No one retires to his pillow with thoughts of security." The *Freeman's Journal* worried, "This village seems fated to destruction." The following March an alarmed James Averell 3d wrote from St. Lawrence County to his brother, William Holt Averell, in Cooperstown: "When will they stop, or rather, what will not next be *Burnt* in your *village.*" In the spring the village trustees offered a $500 reward for the arsonist—but in vain. In April the *Freeman's Journal* expressed the prevailing frustration and anger among the leading villagers: "From these repeated depredations upon property, our citizens have become so much incensed, that they would flay the wretch alive, could they lay their hands upon him." Following the June 12, 1824, destruction of Dr. Fuller's barn, the fires ceased, exactly eleven months after they had begun. The identity of the arsonist or arsonists remained a troubling mystery.[44]

At the same time that the novelist imaginatively reclaimed Cooperstown by writing *The Pioneers,* arson destroyed much of the real village. Years later Susan Fenimore Cooper remembered sitting with her mother when her somber father quietly entered the room and handed a Cooperstown newspaper to his wife. Without speaking Cooper pointed out the passage reporting the incineration of Fenimore House. According to Susan Fenimore Cooper, the fire contributed to her father's resolution to leave America and sojourn in Europe. In effect, the fires of 1823–24 culminated his dispossession and furthered Cooper's alienation from his native village.[45]

In 1833 James Fenimore Cooper returned to America and moved back to Cooperstown. In short order he became profoundly disillusioned with his neighbors. Contrary to the optimistic conclusion of *The Pioneers,* Cooperstown had not matured into his ideal of a country town where a rooted population of modest and deferential commoners took their cues from an enlightened gentility. Indeed, during his seven-year absence in Europe, America had grown more insistently devoted to egalitarian rhetoric, utilitarian ethics, possessive individualism, and social and geographic mobility.

Cooper concluded that greedy and unprincipled demagogues readily manipulated a gullible and volatile public dominated by vulgar and restless newcomers who were mindlessly fond of innovation in the name of republican equality. The villagers ignored the instruction in manners and politics that James Fenimore Cooper so freely offered them, and they defied his authority to bar their access to Myrtle Grove (Three Mile Point) as a picnic ground. Enraged, Cooper blamed the local politicians for "erecting a fabric of conceit and cupidity on a foundation of vulgarity and ignorance." Deemed an un-American aristocrat, Cooper retorted, "In this part of the world, it is thought aristocratic not to frequent taverns, and lounge at corners, squirting tobacco juice."[46]

Struggling to comprehend what had gone wrong, Cooper revised the relatively simple historical sociology of settlement that he had proposed in *The Pioneers*. In that novel he had suggested a relatively quick transition from frontier contention and improvisation to a stable, harmonious, and properly hierarchical maturity. But in *Home as Found*, published in 1838 and set in the Templeton of his own time, Cooper proposed a more complicated three-stage evolution. Nostalgically upgrading his assessment of frontier life, he insisted that "kind feeling and mutual interest" prevailed in a settlement's early years, when "life has much of the reckless gaiety, careless association, and buoyant merriment of childhood." Alas, as a settlement grew in population and complexity, it regressed morally and socially into a contentious and vulgar second stage, where "we see the struggles for place, the heart-burnings and jealousies of contending families, and the influence of mere money." Fortunately, a town could mature into a third stage, where "men and things come within the control of more general and regular laws" and society assumes the proper "division into castes that are more or less rigidly maintained," thereby minimizing competition as everyone keeps to his or her appropriate station.[47]

In Cooper's revised scheme progress toward social perfection is no longer steady and inevitable. Indeed, Cooperstown/Templeton remains stalled in the "equivocal" second stage because there is such a rapid population turnover as old-timers move away and a "nameless multitude" moves in. For want of a rooted majority to preserve cultural continuity, "the birds of passage" substitute "looser sentiment, or the want of sentiment, that so singularly distinguishes the migratory bands." It dismays the Effinghams to find so many "new faces" promoting "new feelings" and "new opinions" in utter "indifference to every thing but the present moment." The rampant geographic mobility so characteristic of nineteenth-century America arrests the proper development of American communities. In Templeton that limbo prolongs the rule of Steadfast Dodge, an unscrupulous newspaper publisher, and Aristabulus Bragg, an unprincipled lawyer. Contrary to the conclusion of *The Pioneers*, the villagers empower the successors of Hiram

Doolittle and Chester Lippett and ignore the heirs of Oliver Effingham and Elizabeth Temple.[48]

Able neither to govern the vulgar masses nor to abide their hideous tribunes, the Effinghams withdraw to the private sanctity of their estate. Publicly ineffectual, they live in genteel seclusion, nurturing the purity of their manners and morals. They await, but do not expect, the possibility that their deluded countrymen will mature into a proper recognition of the Effinghams as their natural aristocracy. By emulating their withdrawal, James Fenimore Cooper belatedly and bitterly accepted the collapse of his father's old dream of uniting all authority in a Father of the People.[49]

Appendix: Tables

Table 1

WILLIAM COOPER'S CIRCULATION RECORD,
LIBRARY COMPANY OF BURLINGTON, 1780–1789

YEAR	VISITS	VOLUMES
1780	5	6
1781	7	10
1782	15	17
1783	28	42
1784	17	31
1785	17	24
1786	31	65
1787	40	74
1788	17	41
1789	5	9
TOTAL	182	319

SOURCE: Circulation Records, 1780–1789, LCB. NOTE: The circulation records for 1789 are incomplete, terminating on March 7.

Table 2

WILLIAM COOPER'S READING BY CATEGORIES IN RELATION TO THE OVERALL
COLLECTION OF THE LIBRARY COMPANY OF BURLINGTON, 1780–1789

	LCB		WC		
CATEGORY	NO. OF VOLS.	%	NO. OF VOLS.	%	WC DIFFERENCE (%)
DIVINITY	192	23	7	2	-21
HISTORY	161	19	71	22	+3
SCIENCES	73	9	1	0	-9
LAW AND POLITICS	62	7	7	2	-5
PHILOSOPHY	60	7	3	1	-6
MISCELLANIES	59	7	0	0	-7
BELLES LETTRES	57	7	103	32	+25
TRAVELS	45	5	51	16	+11
POETRY	37	4	50	16	+12
SCHOOLBOOKS	35	4	1	0	-4
NOVELS	32	4	10	3	-1
COMMERCE	35	4	15	5	+1
TOTAL	848	100	319	100	—

SOURCE: Circulation Records, 1780–1789, LCB; *A Catalogue of Books, Belonging to the Library Company of Burlington* . . . (Burlington, 1792). NOTE: The circulation records for 1789 are incomplete, terminating on March 7. The table categories are composites of the following catalog categories: "Divinity" = "Sermons" and "Divinity"; "History" = "History & Chronology" and "Biography"; "Sciences" = "Physic, Surgery, Chemistry, & Anatomy," "Philology," and "Arts & Sciences"; "Law & Politics" = "Law" and "Politics"; "Philosophy" = "Philosophy" and "Morals & Manners"; "Miscellanies" = "Drama" and "Miscellanies"; "Belles Lettres" = "Letters" and "Polite Literature, or Belles Lettres"; "Travels" = "Voyages & Travels"; "Poetry" = "Poetry"; "Schoolbooks" = "School Books," "Husbandry & Gardening," and "Farriery"; "Novels" = "Novels, Romances, Tales, Fables"; "Commerce" = "Commerce & Navigation," "Geography," and "Natural History." The library holdings in 1792 were virtually unchanged from those in the 1780s.

Table 3

SHIFTS IN WILLIAM COOPER'S READING, 1780–1789

| | 1780–1784 | | 1785–1789 | | |
CATEGORY	NO. OF VOLS	%	NO. OF VOLS.	%	CHANGE %
DIVINITY	1	1	6	3	+2
HISTORY	41	39	30	14	−25
SCIENCES	1	1	0	0	−1
LAW AND POLITICS	4	4	3	1	−3
PHILOSOPHY	1	1	2	1	0
MISCELLANIES	0	0	0	0	0
BELLES LETTRES	13	12	90	42	+30
TRAVELS	24	23	27	13	−10
POETRY	11	10	39	18	+8
SCHOOLBOOKS	0	0	1	0	0
NOVELS	3	3	7	3	0
COMMERCE	7	7	8	4	−3
TOTAL	106	100	213	100	0

SOURCE: Circulation Records, 1780–1789, LCB, *A Catalogue of Books, Belonging to the Library Company of Burlington* . . . (Burlington, 1792). NOTE: The circulation records for 1789 are incomplete, terminating on March 7. See Table 2 for the catalog equivalents of the table categories.

Table 4

SUGAR KETTLES SOLD AND MAPLE SUGAR PRODUCED IN OTSEGO, 1790–1792

	1790	1791	1792
KETTLES SOLD	304	385	140
BUYERS	166	224	86
MAPLE SUGAR (LBS.)	11,180	13,315	1,862
MS PRODUCERS	140	152	42
MS PER PRODUCER (LBS.)	80	88	44

SOURCE: William Cooper and Richard R. Smith, Store Books 1 (1790–91) and 2 (1791–92), WCP, HCA. NOTE: The 1792 figures represent only the first five months of the year.

Table 5

MAPLE SUGAR, ASH, AND POTASH PRODUCTION IN OTSEGO, 1790–1792

	1790	1791	1792	TOTAL
		MAPLE SUGAR		
LBS.	11,180	13,315	1,862	26,357
VALUE (£)	279.10.0	332.17.5	46.11.0	658.18.5
MAKERS	140	152	42	283
		ASHES		
BUSHELS	14,127	21,445	6,766	42,338
VALUE (£)	353.3.6	536.2.6	169.3.0	1,058.9.0
MAKERS	133	218	92	306
		POTASH		
CASKS	22	168	93	283
VALUE (£)	71.6.0	956.19.6	597.19.4	1,626.4.10
MAKERS	12	18	4	22

SOURCE: William Cooper and Richard R. Smith, Store Books 1 (1790–91) and 2 (1791–92), WCP, HCA. NOTE: The 1792 figures represent only the first five months of the year. Cooper measured ashes by the bushel and maple sugar by the pound, and valued each at 6 pence (occasionally he varied the price of maple sugar, depending on quality).

Table 6

RESIDENCE OF COOPER'S POLITICAL FRIENDS
AND FOES, OTSEGO COUNTY, 1792–93

	FRIENDS		FOES		TOTAL	
AREA	N	%	N	%	N	%
COOPER LANDS	119	94	8	6	127	100
REST OF OTSEGO TOWNSHIP	20	56	16	44	36	100
CHERRY VALLEY TOWNSHIP	29	24	91	76	120	100
HARPERSFIELD TOWNSHIP	3	12	22	88	25	100
TOTAL	171	56	137	44	308	100

NOTE: I could not determine the residence for 18 of Cooper's friends and 37 of his foes.

Table 7

ETHNICITY OF COOPER'S POLITICAL FRIENDS
AND FOES, OTSEGO COUNTY, 1792–93

ETHNIC GROUP	FRIENDS		FOES		TOTAL	
	N	%	N	%	N	%
YANKEES	141	75	48	25	189	100
SCOTCH-IRISH	24	21	91	79	115	100
GERMANS/DUTCH	10	27	27	73	37	100
TOTAL	175		166		341	100

NOTE: Fourteen friends and 8 foes were of unknown or other ethnicity. I employed surnames as a surrogate for ethnicity and relied upon Patrick Hanks and Flavia Hodges, *A Dictionary of Surnames* (New York, 1988).

Table 8

AGGREGATE WEALTH (IN DOLLARS), OTSEGO COUNTY TOWNS, 1805–1820

TOWN	1805	1810	1815	1820
BURLINGTON	377,354	295,805	496,642	401,983
BUTTERNUTS	246,397	266,718	388,695	350,710
CHERRY VALLEY	300,901	235,078	419,285	381,917
EXETER	102,968	113,130	168,737	158,735
HARTWICK	174,690	212,507	332,601	303,188
MIDDLEFIELD	227,660	227,790	383,933	285,378
MILFORD	149,748	191,747	337,375	260,950
OTEGO	233,145	216,647	344,254	307,212
OTSEGO	320,612	339,696	663,449	658,758
PITTSFIELD	179,619	215,697	306,274	287,473
PLAINFIELD	112,297	123,879	273,668	165,875
RICHFIELD	191,627	195,426	275,970	212,049
SPRINGFIELD	177,454	205,073	348,614	301,027
UNADILLA	144,182	141,896	261,701	205,927
WORCESTER	304,296	296,354	516,450	501,484
TOTAL	3,242,950	3,277,443	5,517,648	4,782,666
% CHANGE	—	+1	+68	-13

SOURCE: Tax valuation abstracts for 1805, 1810, 1815, and 1820, in Otsego Co. Board of Supervisors, Minute Book, 1804–1823, OCCO. **NOTE:** The Burlington totals for 1810, 1815, and 1820 include Edmeston (incorporated in 1808 out of Burlington); the Otego totals for 1815 and 1820 include Laurens (incorporated in 1810 out of Otego); the Pittsfield figures for 1810, 1815, and 1820 include New Lisbon (incorporated in 1806 out of Pittsfield); the Worcester totals for 1810, 1815, and 1820 include the towns of Decatur, Maryland, and Westford (all incorporated in 1808 out of Worcester).

Table 9

RESIDENT TAXPAYERS, OTSEGO COUNTY TOWNS, 1805–1820

TOWN	1805	1810	1815	1820
BURLINGTON	414	527	558	577
BUTTERNUTS	329	405	453	457
CHERRY VALLEY	325	366	406	450
EXETER	174	174	169	182
HARTWICK	237	307	294	297
MIDDLEFIELD	282	306	288	330
MILFORD	183	273	286	301
OTEGO	271	344	406	423
OTSEGO	470	536	488	534
PITTSFIELD	285	350	348	360
PLAINFIELD	250	234	237	297
RICHFIELD	277	271	286	221
SPRINGFIELD	239	238	248	235
UNADILLA	174	231	302	324
WORCESTER	464	612	679	759
TOTAL	4,374	5,174	5,448	5,747
% CHANGE	—	+18	+5	+5

SOURCE: Tax valuation abstracts for 1805, 1810, 1815, and 1820, in Otsego Co. Board of Supervisors, Minute Book, 1804–1823, OCCO. NOTE: The Burlington totals for 1810, 1815, and 1820 include Edmeston (incorporated in 1808 out of Burlington); the Otego totals for 1815 and 1820 include Laurens (incorporated in 1810 out of Otego); the Pittsfield figures for 1810, 1815, and 1820 include New Lisbon (incorporated in 1806 out of Pittsfield); the Worcester totals for 1810, 1815, and 1820 include the towns of Decatur, Maryland, and Westford (all incorporated in 1808 out of Worcester).

Table 10

PROPERTY (IN DOLLARS) PER RESIDENT TAXPAYER,
OTSEGO COUNTY TOWNS, 1805–1820

TOWN	1805	1810	1815	1820
BURLINGTON	911	561	890	697
BUTTERNUTS	749	659	858	767
CHERRY VALLEY	926	642	1,033	849
EXETER	592	650	998	872
HARTWICK	737	692	1,131	1,021
MIDDLEFIELD	807	744	1,333	865
MILFORD	818	702	1,180	867
OTEGO	860	630	848	726
OTSEGO	682	634	1,360	1,234
PITTSFIELD	630	616	880	799
PLAINFIELD	449	529	1,155	559
RICHFIELD	692	721	965	959
SPRINGFIELD	742	862	1,406	1,281
UNADILLA	829	614	867	636
WORCESTER	656	484	761	661
MEAN	741	633	1,013	832
% CHANGE	—	-15	+60	-8

SOURCE: Tax valuation abstracts for 1805, 1810, 1815, and 1820, in Otsego Co. Board of Supervisors, Minute Book, 1804–1823, OCCO. NOTE: The Burlington totals for 1810, 1815, and 1820 include Edmeston (incorporated in 1808 out of Burlington); the Otego totals for 1815 and 1820 include Laurens (incorporated in 1810 out of Otego); the Pittsfield figures for 1810, 1815, and 1820 include New Lisbon (incorporated in 1806 out of Pittsfield); the Worcester totals for 1810, 1815, and 1820 include the towns of Decatur, Maryland, and Westford (all incorporated in 1808 out of Worcester).

Table 11

FEDERALIST AND REPUBLICAN TOWNS, OTSEGO COUNTY, 1809

TOWN	DOMINANT PARTY	%	1810 POPULATION	YEAR OF INCORPORATION
OTSEGO	FEDERALIST	61	3,840	1788
BUTTERNUTS	FEDERALIST	55	3,074	1796
CHERRY VALLEY	FEDERALIST	59	2,875	1791
OTEGO	FEDERALIST	55	2,712	1796
BURLINGTON	REPUBLICAN	54	2,382	1792
HARTWICK	REPUBLICAN	61	2,139	1802
PLAINFIELD	FEDERALIST	64	2,126	1799
MIDDLEFIELD	FEDERALIST	79	2,087	1797
RICHFIELD	REPUBLICAN	58	2,079	1792
MILFORD	REPUBLICAN	55	2,035	1796
NEW LISBON	REPUBLICAN	56	1,982	1806
SPRINGFIELD	FEDERALIST	80	1,846	1797
UNADILLA	REPUBLICAN	63	1,426	1792
EXETER	REPUBLICAN	52	1,408	1799
EDMESTON	REPUBLICAN	68	1,317	1808
WESTFORD	REPUBLICAN	65	1,212	1808
WORCESTER	REPUBLICAN	78	1,138	1797
MARYLAND	REPUBLICAN	55	1,100	1808
DECATUR	REPUBLICAN	51	902	1808
PITTSFIELD	REPUBLICAN	83	745	1797

SOURCES: U.S. Bureau of the Census, Otsego Co. Census, 1810, series M252, reel 34, National Archives; *Otsego Herald,* May 13, 1809; John Homer French, ed., *Gazetteer of the State of New York* (Syracuse, N.Y., 1860), 530–39.

Table 12

VALUE (IN DOLLARS) OF THE COOPER HEIRS' INHERITANCE, 1810–1815

	JAMES	WILLIAM	SAMUEL	ANNE	ISAAC	RICHARD
MONEY	18,224	12,627	8,791	6,068	35,896	17,398
LEASES	8,644	8,860	8,540	8,476	8,657	8,552
DEKALB	28,957	28,061	28,495	14,698	15,103	27,643
LAND	20,098	14,679	21,420	?	4,635	2,608
WILL	0	11,000	0	?	14,000	15,000
TOTAL	75,923	75,227	67,246	29,242	78,291	71,201
CREDIT	1,139	10,059	0	0	4,084	1,267
NET	74,784	65,168	67,246	29,242	74,207	69,934

SOURCE: Isaac Cooper, Cooper Estate Accounts, 1809–1817, NYSHA. NOTE: The category "Money" consists of all bills drawn on the estate by individual heirs; "Leases" covers the lease-hold properties conveyed in William Cooper's will to each heir; "DeKalb" also includes the value of lands in Bangor, another St. Lawrence Co. town; "Land" includes all other lands, mostly in Otsego Co.; "Will" consists of property received from William Cooper before his death and debited in the will; "Credit" consists of monies and other assets credited by the estate to individual heirs.

Table 13
COOPERSTOWN GROWTH, 1790–1816

	1790	1803	1816
WHITES	33	342	779
BLACKS	2	7	47
HOUSES	7	75	176
BARNS	3	34	68
STORES	1	4	13
TAVERNS	1	4	5

SOURCES: Cooperstown Village Censuses of 1790, 1803, and 1816, Cooper Family Papers, NYSHA.

Table 14
POPULATION GROWTH, OTSEGO COUNTY TOWNS, 1800–1820

TOWNS	1800	1810	1820
BURLINGTON	2,362	3,699	4,275
BUTTERNUTS	1,377	3,074	3,573
CHERRY VALLEY	1,437	2,875	3,658
EXETER	712	1,408	1,427
MIDDLEFIELD	1,042	2,087	2,564
MILFORD	684	2,035	2,500
OTEGO	1,391	2,712	3,487
OTSEGO	4,016	5,979	6,699
PITTSFIELD	1,193	2,727	3,036
PLAINFIELD	1,007	2,126	1,605
RICHFIELD	1,400	2,079	1,765
SPRINGFIELD	1,577	1,846	2,046
UNADILLA	823	1,426	2,175
WORCESTER	2,230	4,352	5,745
COUNTY TOTAL	21,251	38,425	44,555
TOWNSHIP MEAN	1,518	2,745	3,183

SOURCES: U.S. Bureau of the Census, Manuscript Census Returns, Otsego Co., 1800 (series M32, reel 25), 1810 (series M252, reel 34), and 1820 (series M33, reel 74), National Archives.
NOTE: The Burlington totals for 1810 and 1820 include the population of Edmeston (incorporated in 1808 out of Burlington); the Otego total for 1820 includes the population for Laurens (incorporated in 1810 out of Otego); the Pittsfield figures for 1810 and 1820 include New Lisbon (incorporated in 1806 out of Pittsfield); the Worcester totals for 1810 and 1820 include the towns of Decatur, Maryland, and Westford (all incorporated in 1808 out of Worcester); the Otsego Township totals for 1810 and 1820 include Hartwick (incorporated in 1802 out of Otsego Township).

Table 15

TENANCY IN OTSEGO COUNTY, 1795–1814

YEAR	FREEHOLDERS	TENANTS	ALL VOTERS	TENANT %
1795	1,753	530	2,283	23
1807	3,552	1,228	4,780	26
1814	3,897	2,504	6,401	39

SOURCES: *Otsego Herald,* Dec. 17, 1795; New York (State), *A General Account of the Number of Electors in the Several Counties of This State* (Albany, 1808, Shaw-Shoemaker no. 15749); New York (State), *Journal of the Assembly of the State of New-York: At Their Thirty-Eighth Session . . .* (Albany, 1814, Shaw-Shoemaker no. 35462), 257. NOTE: My calculations for 1795 exclude the three towns (Dorlach, Franklin, and Kortright) that became part of Delaware Co. in 1797.

Table 16

COOPER ESTATE PROPERTIES AUCTIONED IN OTSEGO COUNTY, 1821–1825

YEAR	RURAL	VILLAGE	ALL PROP.	PRICE	PRICE PROPERTY
1821	8	3	11	$3,059	$278
1822	34	8	42	5,464	130
1823	72	17	89	11,639	131
1824	17	1	18	900	50
1825	6	13	19	459	24
TOTAL	137	42	179	21,521	120

SOURCES: Otsego Co. Sheriff's Inventories of Oct. 22, 1821, July 29, 1822, July 1, 1823, Oct. 5, 1824, Feb. 15, 1825, and May 10, 1825, all in AFP, box 3, NYSHA.

Table 17

LEADING SPECULATORS IN COOPER ESTATE PROPERTIES,
OTSEGO COUNTY, 1821–1825

SPECULATOR	ACRES	VILLAGE LOTS	ALL PROPERTIES	VALUE ($)
CLARKE	1,439	4	25	3,705
W. AVERELL	1,195	13	35	3,173
STARKWEATHER	839	3	15	2,630
CAMPBELL	807	2	13	1,529
BRIDGEN	767	0	7	1,323
FULLER	422	1	8	899
MCNAMEE	289	7	10	885
SPECULATOR TOTAL	5,758	30	113	14,144
ALL SALES	9,260	42	179	21,521
SPEC. %	62	71	63	66

SOURCES: Otsego Co. Sheriff's Inventories of Oct. 22, 1821, July 29, 1822, July 1, 1823, Oct. 5, 1824, Feb. 15, 1825, and May 10, 1825, all in AFP, box 3, NYSHA. NOTE: "Spec. %" is the proportion of a column acquired by the seven speculators.

Abbreviations

AAS	American Antiquarian Society, Worcester, Mass.
AFP	Averell Family Papers, New York State Historical Association
APS	American Philosophical Society, Philadelphia
BB	Business Box
BJHHP	Bishop John H. Hobart Papers, Protestant Episcopal Church Archives, microfilm edition available at New-York Historical Society
BRP	Benjamin Rush Papers, Library Company of Philadelphia
CB	Correspondence Box
EFP	Ebenezer Foote Papers, Princeton University Library, Library of Congress, and New York State Library
GHCP	George Hyde Clarke Papers, Cornell University Library
GWBWL-MS	G. W. Blunt White Library, Mystic Seaport, Mystic, Conn.
HCA	Hartwick College Archives, Oneonta, N.Y.
HDP	Henry Drinker Papers, Historical Society of Pennsylvania
HSP	Historical Society of Pennsylvania, Philadelphia
JCHP	John Christopher Hartwick Papers, Hartwick College Archives
JFCP	James Fenimore Cooper Papers, American Antiquarian Society
JFP	John Fine Papers, New-York Historical Society
JKP	James Kent Papers, Library of Congress
LC	Library of Congress, Washington, D.C.
LCB	Library Company of Burlington (N.J.)
LCP	Library Company of Philadelphia
MHS	Massachusetts Historical Society, Boston
NJSA	New Jersey State Archives, Trenton, N.J.
NYCHR	New York City Hall of Records
NYHS	New-York Historical Society, New York City
NYPL	New York Public Library, New York City
NYSA	New York State Archives, Albany
NYSHA	New York State Historical Association, Cooperstown, N.Y.
NYSL	New York State Library, Albany
OCCO	Otsego County Clerk's Office, Cooperstown, N.Y.
OC-CCP	Otsego County Court of Common Pleas
OC-CGSP	Otsego County Court of General Sessions of the Peace
OC-CO&T	Otsego County Court of Oyer and Terminer
OCRD	Otsego County Registry of Deeds, Cooperstown, N.Y.
PECA	Protestant Episcopal Church Archives, Austin, Tex.
PHS	Presbyterian Historical Society, Philadelphia
PMHB	*Pennsylvania Magazine of History and Biography*
PVGP	Peter Van Gaasbeck Papers, Senate House Museum, Kingston, N.Y.
SCJ	Superior Court of Judicature
SHM	Senate House Museum, Kingston, N.Y.

STP	Silas Talbot Papers, G. W. Blunt White Library, Mystic Seaport, Mystic, Conn.
SUNY	State University of New York
TCP	Tench Coxe Papers, Historical Society of Pennsylvania
WCP	William Cooper Papers, Hartwick College Archives
WMQ	*William and Mary Quarterly*
WTFEP	William Temple Franklin Estate Papers, New York Public Library

Notes

Introduction

1. Miers Fisher to Isaac Cooper, June 13, 1810, Elk Forest folder, Edward Wanton Smith Coll., HSP. For studies of Cooper's importance as a landlord see Lyman H. Butterfield, "Judge William Cooper (1754–1809): A Sketch of His Character and Accomplishments," *New York History*, 30 (Oct. 1949), 385–408; David Maldwyn Ellis, "The Coopers and the New York State Landholding System," *New York History*, 35 (1954), 412–22; Peter C. Mancall, *Valley of Opportunity: Economic Culture along the Upper Susquehanna, 1700–1800* (Ithaca, N.Y., 1991), 1–2, 10, 171–172, 190–201, 209–10; Alfred F. Young, *The Democratic Republicans of New York: The Origins, 1763–1797* (Chapel Hill, N.C., 1967), 262–67; Lester H. Cohen, "Eden's Constitution: The Paradisiacal Dream and Enlightenment Values in Late Eighteenth-Century Literature of the American Frontier," *Prospects: An Annual of American Cultural Studies*, 3 (1977), 88–90.

2. Miers Fisher to Joseph Pearsall, Feb. 22, 1815, box 16, Fisher Family Papers, HSP.

3. Mancall, *Valley of Opportunity;* 72–159; Anthony F. C. Wallace, *The Death and Rebirth of the Seneca* (New York, 1969), 121–54; Richard H. Schein, "A Historical Geography of Central New York: Patterns and Process of Colonization on the New Military Tract, 1782–1820" (Ph.D. diss., Syracuse Univ., 1989), 52–53; Miers Fisher to Isaac Cooper, June 13, 1810, Elk Forest folder, Edward Wanton Smith Coll., HSP.

4. David Paul Davenport, "The Yankee Settlement of New York, 1783–1820," *Genealogical Journal*, 17 (1988–89), 63–88; David Maldwyn Ellis, "The Rise of the Empire State, 1790–1820," *New York History*, 56 (1975), 5–6; James Macauley, *The Natural, Statistical and Civil History of the State of New-York . . . ,* 3 vols. (New York, 1829), vol. 1, 417–18.

5. Andrew R. L. Cayton, *The Frontier Republic: Ideology and Politics in the Ohio Country, 1780–1825* (Kent, Ohio, 1986); Gregory H. Nobles, "Breaking into the Backcountry: New Approaches to the Early American Frontier, 1750–1800," *WMQ*, 3d ser., 46 (Oct. 1989), 641–70; Peter S. Onuf, "Settlers, Settlements, and New States," in Jack P. Greene, ed., *The American Revolution: Its Character and Limits* (New York, 1987), 171–96; Thomas P. Slaughter, *The Whiskey Rebellion: Frontier Epilogue to the American Revolution* (New York, 1986); Alan Taylor, *Liberty Men and Great Proprietors: The Revolutionary Settlement on the Maine Frontier, 1760–1820* (Chapel Hill, N.C., 1990).

6. Alan Taylor, "From Fathers to Friends of the People: Political Personas in the Early Republic," *Journal of the Early Republic*, 11 (Winter 1991), 465–91; Robert Clark, "Rewriting Revolution: Cooper's War of Independence," in Clark, ed., *James Fenimore Cooper: New Critical Essays* (London, 1985), 187.

7. Gordon S. Wood, *The Radicalism of the American Revolution* (New York, 1992), 229–305; Taylor, "From Fathers to Friends."

8. John P. McWilliams, Jr., *Political Justice in a Republic: James Fenimore Cooper's America* (Berkeley, Calif., 1972), 11–13; Wayne Franklin, *The New World of James Fenimore Cooper* (Chicago, 1982), 4–5, 17–20.

9. For the novel as memory see Warren Motley, *The American Abraham: James Fenimore Cooper and the Frontier Patriarch* (New York, 1987), 75–76; Stephen Railton, *Fenimore Cooper: A*

Study of His Life and Imagination, (Princeton, NJ., 1978), 75–82 (J. F. Cooper's 1850 introduction quoted on p. 80); Franklin, *New World,* 2, 77, 82–85; Robert Emmet Long, *James
Fenimore Cooper,* (New York, 1990), 36–38.

10. James Fenimore Cooper, *The Pioneers, or the Sources of the Susquehanna; A Descriptive Tale,* ed.
James Franklin Beard (Albany, 1980, crit. ed. of New York, 1823). By borrowing the un-
usual name Marmaduke from William Cooper's younger half brother, Marmaduke
Cooper (1781–1863), the novelist provided yet one more hint as to the Cooper family
roots of Judge Temple. See Wayne Wright, "The Cooper Genealogy: Compiled from Ma-
terials in the New York State Historical Association Library" (Typescript, 1983, NYSHA).
For the biographical origins and literary significance of *The Pioneers* see Charles Hansford
Adams, *"The Guardian of the Law": Authority and Identity in James Fenimore Cooper* (University
Park, Pa., 1990), 16; Railton, *Fenimore Cooper,* 36; Motley, *American Abraham,* 1–6, 45–46;
Robert Clark, *History and Myth in American Fiction, 1823–1852* (New York, 1984), 61–64;
Brook Thomas, *Cross-examinations of Law and Literature: Cooper, Hawthorne, Stowe, and
Melville* (New York, 1987), 29–30; William P. Kelly, *Plotting America's Past: Fenimore Cooper
and the Leatherstocking Tales* (Carbondale, Ill., 1983), 35–37; George Dekker, *James Fenimore
Cooper, The Novelist* (London, 1967), 2–8.

11. Butterfield, "Judge William Cooper," 386; John Adams to Francis Adrian Van der Kemp,
Mar. 10, 1824, Van der Kemp Papers, HSP.

12. Michael Warner, *The Letters of the Republic: Publication and the Public Sphere in Eighteenth-Cen-
tury America* (Cambridge, Mass., 1990), 1–33; David Carr, *Time, Narrative, and History*
(Bloomington, Ind., 1986); William Cronon, "A Place for Stories: Nature, History, and
Narrative," *Journal of American History,* 78 (Mar. 1992), 1347–79.

1. FRIEND BILLY

1. Marriage certificate of William Cooper and Elizabeth Fenimore, Nov. 13, 1774, WCP, CB
1704–1793, HCA.

2. Gordon S. Wood, *The Radicalism of the American Revolution* (New York, 1992), 24–42;
Robert Zemsky, *Merchants, Farmers, and River Gods: An Essay on Eighteenth-Century American
Politics* (Boston, 1971), 39–74; Charles S. Sydnor, *Gentlemen Freeholders: Political Practices in
Washington's Virginia* (Chapel Hill, N.C., 1952), 2–8, 39–69.

3. Edmund S. Morgan, *Inventing the People: The Rise of Popular Sovereignty in England and America* (New York, 1988), 174–208; Richard L. Bushman, "American High-Style and Vernacular Cultures," in *Colonial British America: Essays in the New History of the Early Modern Era,* ed.
Jack P. Greene and J. R. Pole (Baltimore, 1984), 353, 356–64.

4. Wood, *Radicalism of the American Revolution,* 76–77, 84–86; Richard L. Bushman, *The Refinement of America: Persons, Houses, Cities* (New York, 1992), 61–99.

5. Wood, *Radicalism of the American Revolution,* 38, 76–77, 85–86; Sheila L. Skemp, *William
Franklin: Son of a Patriot, Servant of a King* (New York, 1990), 8–9, 28–41.

6. Lois Green Carr, Russell R. Menard, and Lorena S. Walsh, *Robert Cole's World: Agriculture
and Society in Early Maryland* (Chapel Hill, N.C., 1991), 151–66; Wood, *Radicalism of the
American Revolution,* 124; Thomas L. Purvis, " 'High-born, Long-recorded Families': Social
Origins of New Jersey Assemblymen, 1703 to 1776," *WMQ,* 3d ser., 37 (Oct. 1980),
592–615; Paul G. E. Clemens and Lucy Simler, "Rural Labor and the Farm Household in
Chester County, Pennsylvania, 1750–1820," and Billy G. Smith, "The Vicissitudes of Fortune: The Careers of Laboring Men in Philadelphia, 1750–1800," both in *Work and Labor
in Early America,* ed. Stephen Innes (Chapel Hill, N.C., 1988), 144–88.

7. Wayne Wright, "The Cooper Genealogy: Compiled from Materials in the Collection of the
New York State Historical Association Library" (Typescript, 1983, NYSHA); Joseph C. Martindale, *A History of the Townships of Byberry and Moreland, in Philadelphia County, Pennsylvania* (Philadelphia, 1901, rev. ed. of 1867), 244; James Fenimore Cooper, *The Pioneers, or
the Sources of the Susquehanna; A Descriptive Tale,* ed. James Franklin Beard (Albany, 1980,
crit. ed. of New York, 1823), 31; William Cooper to Henry Drinker, Feb. 22, 1789, HDP,

CB 1741–1792, HSP. In the novel J. F. Cooper afforded Marmaduke Temple with poor grandparents but with a more prosperous father and a better education than William Cooper enjoyed. For his siblings' better educations but poorer circumstances as adults see the letters to him from Levi Cooper, Feb. 12, 1796, John Breese, Mar. 28, 1796, James Cooper, Jr., Apr. 4, 1796, Benjamin Cooper, Dec. 10, 1796, Letitia [Cooper] Ashton, Sept. 29, 1806, all WCP, HCA.

8. Wright, "Cooper Genealogy"; Martindale, *Byberry*, 245–46 (includes the Cooper quotation); Byberry Township Tax List, 1776, State Tax Assessment Ledger, Philadelphia Co., Philadelphia City Archives. For the family tradition see James Fenimore Cooper (1858–1938, grandson of the novelist), *Reminiscences of Mid-Victorian Cooperstown and a Sketch of William Cooper* (Cooperstown, 1936), 17; Henry W. Boynton, *James Fenimore Cooper* (New York, 1931), 5.

9. Martindale, *Byberry*, 244–46; J. F. Cooper, *Reminiscences of Mid-Victorian Cooperstown*, 17; J. F. Cooper, *Pioneers*, 18; Nathan Field to William Cooper, Jan. 3, 1786, WCP, CB 1704–1793, HCA; W. Cooper to John Porteous, Aug. 2, 1798, Porteous Papers, roll 2A, P-895, Buffalo and Erie Co. Hist. Soc., Buffalo, N.Y.; J. F. Cooper to Susan De Lancey Cooper, June 12, 1834, in James Franklin Beard, ed., *Letters and Journals of James Fenimore Cooper*, 6 vols. (Cambridge, Mass., 1960–1968), vol. 3, 41. John Heise, *Catalogue of Autograph Letters . . .* (Syracuse, N.Y., 1909), offered for sale a "Fine long poetical letter" by William Cooper.

10. J. F. Cooper, *Reminiscences of Mid-Victorian Cooperstown*, 17; William Cooper quoted in Martindale, *Byberry*, 243; Tax ratable list, Willingboro Township, Burlington Co., 1774, NJSA.

11. Burlington Monthly Meeting Minutes, Aug. 7, Sept. 4, Nov. 6, and Dec. 4, 1775, Friends Hist. Lib., Swarthmore College.

12. For the marriage of Rachel to John Heaton see the Women's Minutes, p. 146, Burlington Monthly Meeting, Friends Historical Lib., Swarthmore College. Richard Fenimore, Will, Apr. 3, 1789, in New Jersey (State), *Archives of the State of New Jersey*, 1st ser., 36 (Trenton, 1941), 78.

13. Martindale, *Byberry*, 245–46; E. M. Woodward and J. F. Hageman, *History of Burlington and Mercer Counties, New Jersey . . .* (Philadelphia, 1883), 522b; James Fenimore Cooper to Susan De Lancey Cooper, July 5, 1836, in Beard, *Letters and Journals*, vol. 3, 225; John W. Barber and Henry Howe, *Historical Collections of New Jersey: Past and Present* (Spartanburg, S.C., 1975, repr. of 1868), 122. For the purchase and sale of the city lot see Burlington Co. Deeds, D:217, 220, NJSA. Because of the incompleteness of the deed records for Burlington Co. in the eighteenth century, there is no recorded deed from Richard Fenimore (or anyone else) to William Cooper, but in selling to Andrew Craig a tavern lot of about 3.0 acres in Willingboro on Oct. 8, 1798, William Cooper explained that he had acquired the property by deed from Richard Fenimore. See Burlington Co. Deeds, R:198, NJSA. I assume that the other 165.5 acres in Willingboro that Cooper sold in 1785–86 also came to him from Richard Fenimore. For Cooper's sales see Burlington Co. Mortgages, A:347–51, 392, NJSA. For a time in mid-decade he took on an old Byberry friend, Robert Thomas, as his partner. A Quaker in good standing, Thomas got married in 1784 within the unity to Elizabeth's sister Rachel, who had become a widow upon the death of John Heaton. Two years later Cooper again became the store's sole proprietor by buying out Thomas for £300 (New Jersey currency). See Robert Thomas's receipt, Nov. 13, 1786, WCP, BB 1704–1788, HCA.

14. Skemp, *William Franklin*, 49, 82; Amelia Mott Gummere, "The 'Friendly Institution' of Burlington, New Jersey," *PMHB*, 21 (1897), 347–48; Barber and Howe, *Historical Collections of New Jersey*, 86; Peter O. Wacker, *Land and People: A Cultural Geography of Preindustrial New Jersey: Origins and Settlement Patterns* (New Brunswick, N.J., 1975), 178–83; Jacques Pierre Brissot de Warville, *New Travels in the United States of America, 1788*, ed. Durand Echeverria (Cambridge, Mass., 1964, repr. of 1791), 160.

15. Skemp, *William Franklin*, 49; Carl R. Woodward, *Ploughs and Politicks: Charles Read of New*

Jersey and His Notes on Agriculture, 1715–1774 (New Brunswick, N.J., 1941), 59–61; John H. DeNormandie to Thomas Clifford, May 21, 1790, Pemberton Papers, Clifford subsection, vol. 9, HSP.

16. Records of the Byberry (Pa.) Preparatory Meeting, Abington (Pa.) Monthly Meeting, and Burlington (N.J.) Monthly Meeting, Friends Hist. Lib., Swarthmore College. For the family tradition see Boynton, *James Fenimore Cooper,* 5.

17. Frederick B. Tolles, *Meeting House and Counting House: The Quaker Merchants of Colonial Philadelphia* (Chapel Hill, N.C., 1948), 8–9, 60, 74–75, 137, 141–42, 149, 230, 239; Robert A. Davison, *Isaac Hicks: New York Merchant and Quaker, 1767–1820* (Cambridge, Mass., 1964), 159–66; Brissot de Warville, *New Travels,* 300–305. For William Cooper's business practices see [Trenton] *New-Jersey Gazette,* Feb. 7, 1785; Nathan Field to William Cooper, Jan. 3, 1786, and Kaign & Attmore to W. Cooper, July 27, 1788, WCP, CB 1704–1793, HCA; William Cooper's Ledger Book, 1787–1790, on deposit by Henry Cooper at NYSHA.

18. William Cooper to Benjamin Rush, Oct. 30, 1789, BRP, XXVI, 41, LCP; William Cooper, *A Guide in the Wilderness; or, the History of the First Settlements in the Western Counties of New York, with Useful Instructions to Future Settlers . . .* (Cooperstown, 1986, repr. of Dublin, 1810), 34 ("raise a revenue"), 51 ("awe and reverence"), 52–53.

19. J. F. Cooper, *Pioneers,* 102–3, 154 ("carelessness"); Elaine Forman Crane, ed., *The Diary of Elizabeth Drinker,* 3 vols. (Boston, 1991), vol. 1, 455, 650–51, 758, 761, 764; vol. 2, 768, 770, 772, 777, 782, 806, 861–65, 879, 892, 918, 1267, 1287, 1297 (to meeting, May 4, 1800), 1341, 1447; "A New-England Man," *Whitestown Gazette,,* Dec. 13, 1796.

20. J. F. Cooper, *Pioneers,* 35; Willard V. Huntington, "Old Time Notes Relating to Otsego County and the Upper Susquehanna Valley" (Typescript, NYSHA), 1132; Lyman H. Butterfield, "Judge William Cooper (1754–1809): A Sketch of His Character and Accomplishments," *New York History,* 30 (Oct. 1949), 385–408; William Cooper to Benjamin Rush, Jan. 13, 1792, BRP, XXIV, 45, LCP; Cooper, affidavit, Oct. 5, 1793, in George Clinton v. William Cooper file, Nisi Prius Court, New York SCJ, NYCHR; Cooper to Thomas Fisher, Aug. 9, 1804, Logan-Fisher-Fox Coll., CB 3, HSP. For Cooper's peace testimony see Cooper to Rufus King, Apr. 17, 1794, Rufus King Papers, NYHS. In 1793 William Cooper dropped the Quaker style of letter signing and dating in favor of the fashionable style of gentlemen of the world; see his many letters to Henry Drinker in HDP, CB 1793–1812, HSP.

21. Tolles, *Meeting House and Counting House,* 109, 117–19. For Cooper's business see Joseph Smith's account book, 1786, and George Dillwyn's account book, 1783, both Haverford College Lib.; William Cooper's Ledger Book, 1787–1790, on deposit by Henry Cooper at NYSHA; Nathan Field to Cooper, Jan. 3, 1786, Kaign & Attmore to Cooper, July 27, 1788, Memorandum of Agreement with Wallace & Kisselman, Mar. 12, 1788, and Benjamin Shoemaker to Cooper, Dec. 3, 1788, all WCP, CB 1704–1793, HCA; William Cooper, Advertisement, *New-Jersey Gazette,* Feb. 7, 1785. The six esquires were John Lawrence, John Phillips, Joseph Smith, John Hendry, William Smith, and John Hollinshead (the county sheriff). For Cooper's civic career see Burlington Co. Court of Oyer and Terminer, 1780–1790, Judicial Records Group, NJSA; Woodward and Hageman, *History of Burlington and Mercer Counties,* 128; Burlington Town Meeting Minutes, 1781–1791, Special Collections, Rutgers Univ. Lib.; *Trenton Weekly Mercury,* Aug. 28, 1787. He did not join the Burlington Monthly Meeting, for he does not appear in their Minutes 1775–1788, Friends Hist. Lib., Swarthmore College.

22. Wright, "Cooper Genealogy."

23. Minute Book A, 47–52, LCB; Library Company of Burlington, *A Catalogue of Books, Belonging to the Library Company of Burlington, Taken on the 20th March, 1792* (Burlington, N.J., 1792), 3–4 (quotations). The Library Company's membership included the town's preeminent gentlemen: James Kinsey, Joseph Smith, Richard Smith, John Lawrence, James Verree, Thomas M. Gardiner, Daniel Smith, Bowes Read, Samuel Treat, Joshua M. Wallace, John Hoskins, Abraham Hewling, James Sterling, and Gen. Joseph Bloomfield. For

the ways of gentility see Bushman, *Refinement of America,* 3–203. In working with the circulation records, I greatly benefited from the help and insights provided by Sharon Fitzpatrick of the LCB.

24. Circulation Records, Jan. 8, 1780–Mar. 7, 1789, LCB. The circulation records resume on Jan. 6, 1792, by which time Cooper had moved to Cooperstown and was no longer withdrawing books from the LCB. He remained a member, appearing as such in LCB, *Catalogue of Books,* 5. In 1796 he sold his membership to his friend and business partner Andrew Craig of Burlington.

25. Circulation Records, Jan. 8, 1780, Jan. 20, 1787, LCB; Tobias Smollett, *The Adventures of Roderick Random,* ed. Paul-Gabriel Bouce (New York, 1979), xxvii–xxix, 20 (quotation).

26. Circulation Records, Jan. 8, 1780–Mar. 7, 1789, LCB. The categories and numbers of volumes derive from LCB, *Catalogue of Books,* 9–35.

27. Circulation Records, Jan. 8, 1780–Mar. 7, 1789, LCB. The categories and numbers of volumes derive from LCB, *Catalogue of Books,* 9–35.

28. Circulation Records, Jan. 8, 1780–Mar. 7, 1789, LCB. The categories and numbers of volumes derive from LCB, *Catalogue of Books,* 9–35. To flesh out the brief titles in the circulation records, I relied upon Robert Watt, *Bibliotheca Britannica: or a General Index to British and Foreign Literature* (Edinburgh, 1824). I also benefited from the generous advice of James N. Green, librarian of the LCP.

29. Circulation Records, Jan. 8, 1780–Mar. 7, 1789, LCB. The categories and numbers of volumes derive from LCB, *Catalogue of Books,* 9–35.

30. Circulation Records, June 19 and Aug. 14, 1784, Mar. 5, 12, 19, Apr. 23, July 16, 1785, Feb. 4, Mar. 4 and 25, 1786, LCB.

31. Minute Book A, 47–52, LCB; William Cooper, Ledger Book, 1787–1790, on deposit by Henry Cooper at NYSHA.

32. Minute Book A, 50–52, LCB; Circulation Records, July 26, 1788, LCB.

33. Thomas Purvis, *Proprietors, Patronage, and Paper Money: Legislative Politics in New Jersey, 1703–1776* (New Brunswick, N.J., 1986), 71–72, 98–107, 121–30, 135–37, 239–41; Carl Woodward, *Ploughs and Politicks,* 14, 42, 405.

34. Richard P. McCormick, *Experiment in Independence: New Jersey in the Critical Period, 1781–1789* (New Brunswick, N.J., 1950), 48, 101; Larry R. Gerlach, *New Jersey in the American Revolution, 1763–1783: A Documentary History* (Trenton, N.J., 1975), 160–61, 243–44.

35. McCormick, *Experiment in Independence,* 38–39, 86, 91–93; Burlington Co. petition, Nov. 11, 1782, AM file 1713, NJSA; Captain Curtis and Captain Thomas to the militia, Oct. 9, 1783, and Burlington Co. petitions of Oct. 21 and Nov. 11, 1783, all AM file 1715, NJSA; Burlington Co. petition, Nov. n.d., 1784, AM file 3130, NJSA.

36. Merrill Jensen, ed., *The Documentary History of the Ratification of the Constitution,* 6 vols. (Madison, Wis., 1976–93), vol. 3, 139; Richard P. McCormick, "New Jersey's First Congressional Election, 1789: A Case Study in Political Skulduggery," *WMQ,* 3d ser., 6 (1949), 237–50; Joseph Bloomfield to Jonathan Dayton, Feb. 28, 1789, in Gordon DenBoer, ed., *The Documentary History of the First Federal Elections, 1788–1790,* 4 vols. (Madison, Wis., 1976–89), vol. 3, 89–90 (quotation); McCormick, *Experiment in Independence,,* 90, 297, 302.

37. Burlington Co. Poll List, Oct. 14–15, 1783, and Burlington Co. petition, Nov. 11, 1783, both in AM file 1715, NJSA; H. C. Shinn, "Early New Jersey Poll List [1787]," *PMHB,* 44 (1920), 77–81. For Smith as a clerk see Bloomfield to Dayton, Feb. 28, 1789, in DenBoer, *Documentary History,* vol. 3, 90.

2. VISIONS

1. "Letter from William Sampson, Esq. to Judge Cooper," in William Cooper, *A Guide in the Wilderness; or, the History of the First Settlements in the Western Counties of New York, with Useful Instructions to Future Settlers . . .* (Cooperstown, 1986, repr. of Dublin, 1810), 3.

2. W. Cooper, *Guide in the Wilderness,* 13; Griffith Evans, "Journal of Griffith Evans, 1784–1785," *PMHB,* 65 (April 1941), 218 ("the worst road"); James Fenimore Cooper,

Chronicles of Cooperstown (1838), in Shaw T. Livermore, ed., *A Condensed History of Cooperstown* (Albany, 1862), 13; James Macauley, *The Natural, Statistical and Civil History of the State of New York . . .*, 3 vols. (New York, 1829), vol. 1, 70.

3. James Fenimore Cooper, *The Pioneers, or the Sources of the Susquehanna: A Descriptive Tale*, ed. James Franklin Beard (Albany, 1980, crit. ed. of New York, 1823), 15; James O. Morse, "A Memoir of Otsego County," Dec. 20, 1830, box 1, Albany Inst. Coll., Albany Institute; Susan Fenimore Cooper, *Rural Hours, By a Lady* (New York, 1850), 92, 223–24; William W. Campbell, *Annals of Tryon County, or the Border Warfare of New York, During the Revolution* (New York, 1924, repr. of New York, 1831), 2–3; Nathaniel Edwards, survey field book of Hillington Patent, Nov. 2, 1774, WCP, HCA; Richard Smith, "Notes of a Tour," May 31, 1769 ("whole country"), Du Simitiere Ms., LCP; New York (State) Conservation Department, *A Biological Survey of the Delaware and Susquehanna Watersheds: Supplemental to Twenty-fifth Annual Report, 1935* (Albany, 1936), 11–12; Macauley, *Natural, Statistical and Civil History*, vol. 1, 70–71 ("broad, shoal").

4. Carolyn Merchant, *Ecological Revolutions: Nature, Gender, and Science in New England* (Chapel Hill, N.C., 1989), 33; John H. Thompson, ed., *Geography of New York State* (Syracuse, N.Y., 1966) 107–8; Richard Smith, "Notes of a Tour," May 17, 1769, Du Simitiere Mss., LCP; Ebenezer Emmons, *Agriculture of New-York*, 5 vols. (Albany, 1846–1854), vol. 1, 307; Horatio Gates Spafford, *A Gazetteer of the State of New York* (Albany, 1813, Shaw-Shoemaker no. 29836), 17; John L. Vankat, *The Natural Vegetation of North America: An Introduction* (New York, 1979), 37.

5. Robert Charles McGregor, "Radical Environmental Change: Deforestation in the Upper Delaware River Valley, 1800–1875" (Ph.D. diss., SUNY at Binghamton, 1984), 2–8; Richard Smith, "Notes of a Tour," May 15 and 31, 1769, Du Simitiere Mss., LCP; Robert Piken (surveyor), "A Rough Sketch of a Certain tract of Land on the Susquehanna River Viewed in November 1768," Allinson Family Papers, Haverford College; Vankat, *Natural Vegetation*, 132, 141–44; Campbell, *Annals of Tryon County*, 4; Potter Goff, survey field book of Pittsfield, Dec. 7, 1803, WCP, BB 1802–1804, HCA; Nathaniel Edwards, survey field book of Hillington Patent, Nov. 2, 1774, WCP, HCA; S. F. Cooper, *Rural Hours*, 206–10.

6. W. Cooper, *Guide in the Wilderness*, 13–14; J. F. Cooper, *Chronicles of Cooperstown*, 13. For the novelist's use of Mount Vision see Wayne Franklin, *The New World of James Fenimore Cooper* (Chicago, 1982), 61–63; Robert Emmet Long, *James Fenimore Cooper* (New York, 1990), 37, 41; Warren Motley, *The American Abraham: James Fenimore Cooper and the Frontier Patriarch* (New York, 1987), 12.

7. J. F. Cooper, *The Pioneers*, 235. The novelist told virtually the same story of discovery, except that a deer, rather than a bear, drinks in *Chronicles of Cooperstown*, 13. In the latter the visionary is explicitly William Cooper.

8. W. Cooper, *Guide in the Wilderness*, 17; J. F. Cooper, *Pioneers*, 15; Franklin, *New World*, 61–62.

9. W. Cooper, *Guide in the Wilderness*, 13.

10. Francis Adrian Van der Kemp, *Speech of Fr. Adr. Van der Kemp, at a Meeting the First of June, One Thousand, Seven Hundred and Ninety-Five, at Whitestown for the Institution of a Society of Agriculture* (Whitesboro, N.Y., 1795, Evans no. 29785), 6; [Cooperstown] *Otsego Herald*, Mar. 24, 1796; Peter C. Mancall, *Valley of Opportunity: Economic Culture along the Upper Susquehanna, 1700–1800* (Ithaca, N.Y., 1991), 111; William Cronon, *Changes in the Land: Indians, Colonists, and the Ecology of New England* (New York, 1983), 159–70.

11. William Cronon, "A Place for Stories: Nature, History, and Narrative," *Journal of American History*, 78 (March 1992), 1347–79; Cooper, *Guide in the Wilderness*, 13–14; Lyman H. Butterfield, "Cooper's Inheritance: The Otsego Country and Its Founders," *New York History* 35 (Oct. 1954), 382; Franklin, *New World*, 122–23; Robert Clark, *History and Myth in American Fiction, 1823–1852* (New York, 1984), 61–63; Geoffrey Rans, *Cooper's Leather-Stocking Novels: A Secular Reading* (Chapel Hill, N.C., 1991), 46–101.

12. James A. Tuck, "Northern Iroquoian Prehistory," and Bruce G. Trigger, "Early Iroquoian Contacts with Europeans," in Trigger, ed., *Handbook of North American Indians: Northeast*

(Washington, D.C., 1978), 322–27, 344–61; Anthony F. C. Wallace, *The Death and Rebirth of the Seneca* (New York, 1969), 22; W. Cooper, *Guide in the Wilderness*, 49; Thomas Bard, ed., "Journal of Lieutenant Robert Parker of the Second Continental Artillery, 1779," *PMHB*, 27 (1903), 412; *Otsego Herald*, Sept. 29, 1796; DeWitt Clinton, "A Memoir of the Antiquities of the Western Parts of the State of New-York," Literary and Philosophical Society of New-York, *Transactions*, 2 (1825), 71–84; Macauley, *Natural, Statistical, and Civil History*, vol. 2, 109.

13. Merchant, *Ecological Revolutions*, 74–81.

14. Wallace, *Death and Rebirth of the Seneca*, 25; Mancall, *Valley of Opportunity*, 47–70; Richard White, *The Middle Ground: Indians, Empires, and Republics in the Great Lakes Region, 1650–1815* (New York, 1991), 50–141; Daniel K. Richter, "Ordeals of the Longhouse: The Five Nations in Early American History," in Richter and James H. Merrell, eds., *Beyond the Covenant Chain: The Iroquois and Their Neighbors in Indian North America, 1600–1800* (Syracuse, N.Y., 1987), 11–28; Richard Smith, *A Tour of Four Great Rivers: The Hudson, Mohawk, Susquehanna, and Delaware in 1769*, ed. Francis Whiting Halsey, (New York, 1906), 71.

15. Douglas W. Boyce, " 'As the Wind Scatters the Smoke': The Tuscaroras in the Eighteenth Century," in Richter and Merrell, *Beyond the Covenant Chain*, 155–58; Laurance H. Hauptman, "Refugee Havens: The Iroquois Villages of the Eighteenth Century," in Christopher Vecsey and Robert Venables, eds., *American Indian Environments: Ecological Issues in Native American History* (Syracuse, N.Y., 1980), 130–35; Frances Whiting Halsey, *The Old New York Frontier: Its Wars with Indians and Tories, Its Missionary Schools, Pioneers and Land Titles, 1614–1800* (New York, 1912), 27–29, 76; Mancall, *Valley of Opportunity*, 60–62; Smith, *Tour of Four Great Rivers*, 65–66, 83–87; Samuel Preston, "Journey to Harmony," in Patricia H. Christian and Eleanor H. Keesler, eds., *Samuel Preston, 1789–1989: From Buckingham to Buckingham* (Equinunk, Pa., 1989), 99–100; H. L. Bourdin and S. T. Williams, eds., "Crevecoeur on the Susquehanna, 1774–1776," *The Yale Review* 14 (Apr. 1925), 581.

16. Smith, *Tour of Four Great Rivers*, 82, 88; H. L. Bourdin and S. T. Williams, "Crevecoeur on the Susquehanna," 581; Butler quoted in Barbara Graymont, *The Iroquois in the American Revolution* (Syracuse, N.Y., 1972), 181–82.

17. Eleazar Wheelock, *A Continuation of the Narrative of the State, &c. of the Indian Charity School, at Lebanon, in Connecticut: From Nov. 27th, 1762 to Sept. 3d, 1765* (Boston, 1765), 8, 13–14; Isaac Dakayenensare and Adam Waonwanoron to Wheelock, July 31, 1765, in James Dow McCallum, ed., *The Letters of Eleazar Wheelock's Indians* (Hanover, N.H., 1932), 79–80; Halsey, *The Old New York Frontier*, 76; Adrian A. Pierson, "The Prehistoric Indian in Otsego and His Immediate Successor," NYSHA, *Proceedings* 16 (1917), 113; Campbell, *Annals of Tryon County*, 4.

18. Robert Picken, "A Rough Sketch of a Certain Tract of Land on the Susquehanna River, Viewed in November 1768," Samuel Allinson Papers, Haverford College Archives; Smith, *Tour of Four Great Rivers*, 68; Smith, "Notes of a Tour," May 31, 1769, Du Simitiere Mss., LCP; W. Cooper, *Guide in the Wilderness*, 49; John Tunnecliff to Cooper, Jan. 7, 1789, WCP, CB 1704–1793, HCA; Willard V. Huntington, "Old Time Notes Relating to Otsego County and the Upper Susquehanna Valley" (Typescript, NYSHA), 349 (Smith quoted), 365; Nathaniel Edwards, survey field book of Hillington Patent, Nov. 2, 1774, WCP, HCA; Thomas Bard, ed., "Journal of Lieutenant Robert Parker of the Second Continental Artillery, 1779," *PMHB*, 28 (1904), 411; Levi Beardsley, *Reminiscences: Personal and Other Incidents; Early Settlement of Otsego County . . .* (New York, 1852), 476; Francis Whiting Halsey, *The Pioneers of Unadilla Village, 1784–1840* (Unadilla, 1902), 149.

19. Smith, "Notes of a Tour," May, 21, 30, and 31, June 3, 1769, Du Simitiere Mss., LCP; Alexander Coventry, *Memoirs of an Emigrant: The Journal of Alexander Coventry, M.D.* 2 vols. (Albany, 1978), vol. 1, 560; McGregor, "Radical Environmental Change," 4–7; Vankat, *Natural Vegetation*, 132; Mancall, *Valley of Opportunity*, 220–21; Cronon, *Changes in the Land*, 49–51.

20. William N. Fenton, ed., "The Journal of James Emlen Kept on a Trip to Canandaigua, New York . . . 1794," *Ethnohistory*, 12 (1965), 288; Richard H. Schein, "A Historical Geography

of Central New York: Patterns and Process of Colonization on the New Military Tract, 1782–1820" (Ph.D. diss., Syracuse University, 1989), 62; Mancall, *Valley of Opportunity,* 68–70; Richard Smith, "Notes of a Tour," May 31, 1769, Du Simitiere Mss., LCP; S. F. Cooper, *Rural Hours,* 183–84.

21. Bard, "Journal of Lieutenant Robert Parker," 16. On the effects of projection see Cronon, *Changes in the Land,* 19–33.

22. James Kent, *Commentaries on American Law,* 4 vols. (New York, 1832), vol. 3, 312–13; Van der Kemp, *Speech of Fr. Adr. Van der Kemp,* 7; Benjamin DeWitt, "A Sketch of the Turnpike Roads in the State of New York," Society for the Promotion of Useful Arts, *Transactions* (1807, Shaw-Shoemaker no. 13242), 190.

23. Wallace, *Death and Rebirth of the Seneca,* 196; Henry Clarke Wright, *Human Life, Illustrated in my Individual Experience as a Child, a Youth, and a Man* (Boston, 1849), 112.

24. Bourdin and Williams, "Crevecoeur on the Susquehanna," 582; Book of "Medical Observations," Campbell Family Papers, box 1, NYSHA; Huntington, "Old Time Notes," 752, 1065; Josiah Priest, *Stories of Early Settlers in the Wilderness, Embracing the Life of Mrs. Priest, Late of Otsego County, N.Y.* (Albany, 1837), 37–38; S. F. Cooper, *Rural Hours,* 174–79; Wright, *Human Life,* 112; James Fenimore Cooper, *Notions of the Americans, Picked Up by a Travelling Bachelor,* 2 vols. (New York, 1963, repr. of 1828), vol. 2, 281.

25. John Christopher Hartwick, Last Will and Testament, Hartwick Estate Papers, Lutheran Archive Center, Mount Airy, Pa.; Karl J. R. Arndt, "John Christopher Hartwick: German Pioneer of Central New York," *New York History,* 18 (July 1937), 301; Henry N. Pohlman, ed., *Memorial Volume of the Semi-Centennial Anniversary of Hartwick Seminary, Held August 21, 1866* (Albany, 1867), 27–29, 156–64.

26. John Christopher Hartwick to Dr. Friedrich Wagner, Feb. 19, 1754 ("desperate"), Jan. 31, 1755, in Simon Hart and Harry J. Kreider, eds., *Lutheran Church in New York and New Jersey, 1722–1760: Lutheran Records in the Ministerial Archives of the Staatsarchiv, Hamburg, Germany* (New York, 1962), 371, 385; Hartwick to Rev. Master Pieters, June 26, 1754, Misc. Mss. H, NYHS.

27. John P. Dern, ed., *The Albany Protocol: Wilhelm Christoph Berkenmeyer's Chronicle of Lutheran Affairs in New York Colony, 1731–1750* (Ann Arbor, Mich., 1971), 510 n.1; Harry J. Kreider, *Lutheranism in Colonial New York* (New York, 1942), 109; Charles H. Glatfelter, *Pastors and People: German Lutheran and Reformed Churches in the Pennsylvania Field, 1717–1793,* 2 vols. (Breinigsville, Pa., 1980), vol. 1, 217–18; John Christopher Hartwick to Rev. Master Pieters, June 26, 1754, Misc. Mss. H, NYHS; Hartwick to Friedrich Wagner, Jan. 31, 1755, in Hart and Kreider, *Lutheran Church in New York and New Jersey,* 384.

28. Henry Melchior Muhlenberg, *The Journals of Henry Melchior Muhlenberg,* trans. Theodore G. Tappert and John W. Doberstein, 3 vols. (Philadelphia, 1942–1958), vol. 1, 248, 251, 253, 404.

29. Muhlenberg, *Journals,* vol. 1, 267–68, 403 (magistrate quoted), vol. 3, 177; Pohlman, *Memorial Volume of . . . Hartwick Seminary,* 20–23; Glatfelter, *Pastors and People,* vol. 1, 52. Shortly before his death, a rumor held that Hartwick had married, but his will mentions no wife. See Frederick A. C. Muhlenberg to John Christopher Hartwick, June 5, 1796, JCHP, HCA.

30. John Christopher Hartwick to Dr. Friedrich Wagner, Feb. 19, 1754, and Jan. 31, 1755, in Hart and Kreider, *Lutheran Church in New York and New Jersey,* 371, 384; Hartwick to Rev. Master Pieters, June 26, 1754, Misc. Mss. H, NYHS; "Proposed Address to the King in Favor of the Reverend Mr. Hartwick" [Jan. 1756], in Edmund Bailey O'Callaghan, *The Documentary History of the State of New York,* 4 vols. (Albany, 1849–1851), vol. 4, 298–300.

31. John W. Jordan, "Rev. John Martin Mack's Narrative of a Visit to Onondaga in 1752," *PMHB,* 29 (1905), 344–45; Mohawk Sachems to John Christopher Hartwick, undated, Simon Gratz Coll., case 4, box 5, HSP.

32. John Christopher Hartwick to Sir William Johnson, Jan. 18, 1756, and "Proposed Address to the King in Favor of the Revd. Mr. Hartwick," [Jan. 1756], in O'Callaghan, *Documentary History of the State of New York,* vol. 4, 294, 298–300; Cadwallader Colden to Sir William

Johnson, Mar. 7, 1761, and Johnson to Cadwallader Colden, Mar. 19, 1761, in Milton W. Hamilton and James Sullivan, eds., *The Papers of Sir William Johnson*, 14 vols. (Albany, 1921–1957), vol. 10, 234, and vol. 3, 365; Hartwick to Rev. Master Pieters, June 26, 1754, Misc. Mss. H, NYHS; Pohlman, *Memorial Volume of . . . Hartwick Seminary*, 14–18.

33. Roy L. Butterfield, "The Hartwick Patent," [Cooperstown] *The Otsego Farmer*, Mar. 18, 1955; John Sebastian Stephany's assignment to Hartwick, Mar. 19, 1761, Gottlieb Wolhaupter's assignment to Hartwick, undated, Hartwick's bond to Goldsborough Banyar, Nov. 12, 1761, and William Cooper's memorandum, Dec. 29, 1791, all JCHP, HCA.

34. Sir William Johnson, "Journal of Indian Affairs," Feb. 9, Apr. 6, 1767, and John Tabor Kempe to Johnson, Mar. 11, 1769, in Hamilton and Sullivan, *Papers of Sir William Johnson*, vol. 12, 269, 303, 702–3; J. F. Cooper, *Chronicles of Cooperstown*, 11–12; "Philupnos Philo-Typus," *Otsego Herald*, Apr. 3, 1795.

35. Mary C. Lynn, ed., *An Eyewitness Account of the American Revolution and New England Life: The Journal of J. F. Wasmus, German Company Surgeon, 1776–1783* (New York, 1990), 96–97.

36. Muhlenberg, *Journals*, vol. 3, 273, 291, 315, 453; Huntington, "Old Time Notes," 618; William Ellison to Goldsborough Banyar, Oct. 19, 1787, WCP, CB 1704–94, HCA.

37. Bernard Bailyn, *Voyagers to the West: A Passage in the Peopling of America on the Eve of the Revolution* (New York, 1986), 578–79; Robert Lettis Hooper, Hillington Patent survey field book, Aug. 11, 1770, WCP, Misc. Books box, HCA.

38. Albert T. Volwiler, *George Croghan and the Westward Movement, 1741–1782* (Cleveland, 1926); Nicholas B. Wainwright, *George Croghan, Wilderness Diplomat* (Chapel Hill, N.C., 1959), esp. 3–4, 112–13, 220; Thomas M. Doerflinger, *A Vigorous Spirit of Enterprise: Merchants and Economic Development in Revolutionary Philadelphia* (Chapel Hill, N.C., 1986), 148–51.

39. Doerflinger, *A Vigorous Spirit of Enterprise*, 162–63; Baynton quoted in Wainwright, *George Croghan*, 269, 270.

40. Wainwright, *George Croghan*, 242–44, 248, 253.

41. Julius Goebel, Jr., et al., eds., *The Law Practice of Alexander Hamilton: Documents and Commentary*, 4 vols. (New York, 1964–1981), vol. 4, 79; Wainwright, *George Croghan*, 255–70; Mancall, *Valley of Opportunity*, 90–91; Sheila L. Skemp, *William Franklin: Son of a Patriot, Servant of a King* (New York, 1990), 104; Roy L. Butterfield, *The Land Patents of Otsego County* (Cooperstown, 1955); Ruth L. Higgins, *Expansion in New York, With Especial Reference to the Eighteenth Century* (Columbus, Ohio, 1931), 94–95; Halsey, *Old New York Frontier*, 103.

42. Wainwright, *George Croghan*, 266–70.

43. Wainwright, *George Croghan*, 252, 256, 264; J. F. Cooper, *The Pioneers*, 19; "Philupnos Philo-Typus," *Otsego Herald*, Apr. 3, 1795; Charles A. Hanna, *The Wilderness Trail*, 2 vols. (New York, 1911), vol. 2, 63–64; Smith, *Tour of Four Great Rivers*, 34. For Prevost see Raymond C. Beecher, *Out to Greenville and Beyond: Historical Sketches of Greene County* (Cornwalville, N.Y., 1977), 54–55; Nicholas B. Wainwright, ed., "Turmoil at Pittsburgh: Diary of Augustine Prevost," *PMHB*, 85 (Apr. 1961), 111–14; Edward G. Williams, "The Prevosts of the Royal Americans," *Western Pennsylvania Historical Magazine*, 56 (1973), 1–38.

44. Jay Bloomfield, ed., *Lakes of New York State*, 3 vols. (New York, 1978–1980), vol. 3, 2, 7, 9, 27, 35; Ralph Birdsall, *The Story of Cooperstown* (Cooperstown, 1917), 337–39; Edmund E. Lynch, "Fishing on Otsego Lake," (Master's thesis, SUNY at Oneonta, 1965), 1–11; Smith, *Tour of Four Great Rivers*, 34–36: Macauley, *Natural, Statistical, and Civil History*, vol. 1, 109; Bard, "Journal of Lieutenant Robert Parker," 408; S. F. Cooper, *Rural Hours*, 168 ("here and there"), 376; Evans, "Journal," 218; "Of Lake Otsego and its Productions," *Otsego Herald*, May 28, 1801.

45. Wainwright, *George Croghan*, 264–65; Smith, *Tour of Four Great Rivers*, 36–37, 47.

46. Wainwright, *George Croghan*, 272; Wainwright, "Turmoil at Pittsburgh," 114–15; Augustine Prevost to Sir William Johnson, March 29, 1771, in Hamilton and Sullivan, *The Papers of Sir William Johnson*, vol. 7, 48–49; George Croghan to Barnard and Michael Gratz, Aug. 26, 1771, Simon Gratz Coll., case 4, box 4, HSP.

47. Wainwright, *George Croghan*, 273–79, 284 (Croghan quoted); Doerflinger, *Vigorous Spirit of*

Enterprise, 143; Thomas Perkins Abernethy, *Western Lands and the American Revolution* (New York, 1937), 14–57; Jack M. Sosin, *Whitehall and the Wilderness: The Middle West in British Colonial Policy, 1760–1775* (Lincoln, Neb., 1961), 138–64, 181–210.

48. Volwiler, *George Croghan*, 282–86; Goebel, *Law Practice of Alexander Hamilton*, vol. 4, 84; Receipt from state auditor Peter S. Curtenius to William Cooper and Alexander Craig, Jan. 16, 1788, WCP, BB 1704–88, HCA.

49. Goebel, *Law Practice of Alexander Hamilton*, vol. 4, 81–82; Mary-Jo Kline, ed., *Political Correspondence and Public Papers of Aaron Burr*, 2 vols. (Princeton, N.J., 1983), vol. 2, 20; Larry R. Gerlach, *William Franklin: New Jersey's Last Royal Governor* (Trenton, N.J., 1975), 72–73; Skemp, *William Franklin*, 47–52, 81–82; Burlington Company Meeting, Aug. 9, 1769, Allinson Family Papers, box 7, Haverford College; William Franklin to John Taylor, June 25, 1791, WTFEP, NYPL; William Trent to John Smith, Dec. 28, 1768, Allinson Family Papers, box 7, Haverford College Library ("shall be done"); William Franklin to Trent, Jan. 14, 1771, in *Archives of New Jersey*, 1st. ser., 10 (Newark, 1886), 228. Richard Wells provided £900 and seven other investors—Joseph Fox, Henry Hill, Samuel Preston Moore, James Verree, Richard Smith, his nephew Joseph Smith, and the latter's sister Abigail Smith (who in the spring of 1770 married George Bowne, a Quaker merchant from New York City)—anted up £300 each.

50. Samuel Allinson to William Trent, Aug. 31, 1771, Allinson Family Papers, box 7, Haverford College; Kline, ed., *Papers of Aaron Burr*, vol. 2, 20; Goebel, ed., *Law Practice of Alexander Hamilton*, vol. 4, 84–86; Wainwright, *George Croghan*, 298–99; indenture of William Franklin, Thomas Wharton, and John Morton with Barnard Gratz, April n.d., 1775, WCP, BB 1704–88, HCA; James Fenimore Cooper (1858–1938), "William Cooper and Andrew Craig's Purchase of Croghan's Land," NYSHA, *Quarterly Journal*, 12 (1931), 392.

51. Wainwright, *George Croghan*, 298–99; "New Advertisement," *New London Gazette*, Apr. 21, 1769; Indenture of George Croghan and Joseph Wharton, June 27, 1780, WCP, Oversized I–126, HCA.

52. Augustine Prevost to Barnard Gratz, Nov. 22, 1774, Etting Coll., Croghan-Gratz sec., box 38, HSP; Indenture of George Croghan and Joseph Wharton, June 27, 1780, WCP, Oversized I–126, HCA; Wainwright, "Turmoil at Pittsburgh," 161–62 (includes Croghan to Gratz, Sept. 24, 1774, quoted).

53. Indenture of William Franklin, Thomas Wharton, and John Morton with Barnard Gratz, April n.d., 1775, WCP, BB 1704–88, HCA; Goebel, *Law Practice of Alexander Hamilton*, vol. 4, 85–86; George Croghan to B. Gratz, June 5, 1775, Etting Coll., Gratz-Croghan sec., box 38, HSP; Dr. John Morgan to Croghan, Aug. 12, 1775, Cadwallader Coll., Croghan sec., box 7, HSP.

54. Thompson, *Geography of New York State*, 131; Roy L. Butterfield, *In Old Otsego: A New York County Views Its Past* (Cooperstown, 1959), 5; Campbell, *Annals of Tryon County*, 4–6; Higgins, *Expansion in New York*, 70–76; John Sawyer, *History of Cherry Valley From 1740 to 1898* (Cherry Valley, N.Y., 1898), 2–7; Richard Smith, "Notes of a Tour," May 13 and 14, 1769, Du Simitiere Mss., LCP.

55. James Arthur Frost, *Life on the Upper Susquehanna, 1783–1860* (New York, 1951), 2; Higgins, *Expansion in New York*, 70–76, 95–96; James Fenimore Cooper, *Wyandotté, or The Hutted Knoll, A Tale*, ed. Thomas and Marianne Philbrick, (Albany, 1982, crit. ed. of New York, 1843), 29–30; John W. Brown, *Stanislas Pascal Franchot (1774–1855)* (n.p., 1935), 19; Huntington, "Old Time Notes," 328, 361, 363–64; James H. Pickering, "New York in the Revolution: Cooper's *Wyandotté*," *New York History*, 49 (April 1968), 134; Campbell, *Annals of Tryon County*, 12; R. L. Butterfield, *In Old Otsego*, 5–6; John Hicks to Henry Hill, Oct. 3, 1773, WCP, CB 1704–93, HCA.

56. J. F. Cooper, *Chronicles of Cooperstown*, 28; a settler's son quoted in Duane Hamilton Hurd, *History of Otsego County, New York* (Philadelphia, 1878), 249; James Henry Pickering, "James Fenimore Cooper and the History of New York" (Ph.D. diss., Northwestern Univ., 1964), 198; Susan Fenimore Cooper, ed., *Pages and Pictures, From the Writings of James Fenimore Cooper* (New York, 1861), 51–52. Because neither James Fenimore Cooper nor

Susan Fenimore Cooper identified Shipman's first name (also an omission in the 1792 letters by Hartwick and his agent), some Hoosick antiquarians advanced a claim that one Nathaniel Shipman, who died there in 1809, was the authentic model for Natty Bumppo. Their case rests on the very slender thread of a local family tradition of an utterly implausible conversation in which William Cooper revealed to one John Ryan of Hoosick that his long-lost father-in-law, Nathaniel Shipman, was a lone hunter living in an Otsego cave. There is no contemporary evidence that anyone named Nathaniel Shipman lived in Otsego during William Cooper's lifetime; by contrast, David Shipman is in ample evidence on the 1790 and 1800 censuses, the 1800 tax list, and in Cooper's store book. Consequently, I agree with Pickering's conclusion: "The 'original' Leatherstocking was undoubtedly an old hunter of the Otsego hills named David Shipman." For the Hoosick claim see L. Chandler Ball, "The Real Natty an Elder Brother," NYSHA, *Proceedings*, 16 (1917), 187–92.

57. Floyd M. Shumway, "David and Nathaniel Shipman: The Two Leatherstockings" (Typescript, NYSHA); Birdsall, *Story of Cooperstown*, 167; "Tax List of Hoosack District Pursuant to the Tax Law of the 11th April 1787," G. Lansing Papers, NYSL; "A Very Rough Sketch of Cooper's Patent," n.d., c. 1786, WCP, HCA (this map bears an indication of the magnetic north in 1790 which was probably added years after it was first drawn); Grantee and Grantor indexes, OCRD. For the emigration from Hoosick to Otsego, see Beardsley, *Reminiscences*, 14–21. According to the federal census for 1790, Shipman resided in Otsego with a wife but no children. See U.S. Bureau of the Census, *Heads of Families at the First Census of the United States Taken in the Year 1790: New York* (Baltimore, 1966, repr. of Washington, D.C., 1908), 112. In 1791–1792 Shipman occasionally appeared in William Cooper's store in Cooperstown to buy some cloth, buttons, coating, and tobacco, paying with a few bushels of corn and oats. If he sold animal skins or meat or bought gunpowder or lead at the store, those transactions were on a cash basis, escaping record in the store accounts dedicated to credit sales. See William Cooper and Richard Smith, Store Books, 1 and 2, entries for Jan. 4, and 24, Nov. 21, Dec. 3, 1791, and Mar. 20, 1792, WCP, HCA.

58. Jeremiah Van Rensselaer to William Cooper, Jan. 17, 1792, and John Christopher Hartwick to Cooper, Aug. 20, 1792, both JCHP, HCA. David Shipman appeared on the 1800 tax assessment roll for Otsego township as a poor and landless man with a mere $30 in personal property. See Otsego Co. Tax Assessment Rolls, 1800, Ser. B-0950-85, box 37, NYSA. That year he and his wife also appear on the Federal census roll for Otsego Township. See U.S. Bureau of the Census, 2d Census of the United States, 1800, Otsego County, series M32, reel 25, National Archives. David Shipman died on February 28, 1813, of "the prevailing fever" that claimed many lives in Otsego county in the late winter and early spring of the year. See Shumway, "David and Nathaniel Shipman"; Aaron Hamten, "Notes on a Journey from Kingwood in New Jersey to Lake Erie in the Year 1813," ed. Edna L. Jacobsen, *New York History*, 21 (July 1940), 333.

59. William P. Kelly, *Plotting America's Past: Fenimore Cooper and the Leatherstocking Tales* (Carbondale, Ill., 1983), 29–30.

60. Robert Clark, *History and Myth in American Fiction, 1823–1852* (New York, 1984), 69–72.

61. J. F. Cooper, *Pioneers*, 236–37, 441; Richard Godden, "Pioneer Properties: Or 'What's in a Hut?' " in Robert Clark, ed., *James Fenimore Cooper: New Critical Essays* (London, 1985), 126.

62. J. F. Cooper, *Pioneers*, 112, 266.

63. J. F. Cooper, *Pioneers*, 456; Kelly, *Plotting America's Past*, 24–25; Clark, *History and Myth*, 78; Rans, *Cooper's Leather-Stocking Novels*, 51–52, 99–101; Long, *James Fenimore Cooper*, 44; Brook Thomas, *Cross-examinations of Law and Literature: Cooper, Hawthorne, Stowe, and Melville* (New York, 1987), 43; James D. Wallace, *Early Cooper and His Audience* (New York, 1986), 147–50.

64. Andrew Nelson, "James Cooper and George Croghan," *Philological Quarterly*, 20 (Jan. 1941), 69–73; J. F. Cooper, *Pioneers*, 31–32, 36, 437–38; Clark, *History and Myth*, 69; Franklin, *New World*, 120–21; Kelly, *Plotting America's Past*, 2–5; Thomas, *Cross-examinations of Law and Literature*, 36–37.

3. REVOLUTION

1. John J. McCusker and Russell R. Menard, *The Economy of British America, 1607–1789* (Chapel Hill, N.C. 1985), 361–67; Thomas M. Doerflinger, *A Vigorous Spirit of Enterprise: Merchants and Economic Development in Revolutionary Philadelphia* (Chapel Hill, N.C., 1986), 197–205; Gordon S. Wood, *The Creation of the American Republic, 1776–1787* (Chapel Hill, N.C., 1969), 476–77; Alan Taylor, *Liberty Men and Great Proprietors: The Revolutionary Settlement on the Maine Frontier, 1760–1820* (Chapel Hill, N.C., 1990), 14–18.

2. Doerflinger, *A Vigorous Spirit of Enterprise*, 284–85; Wood, *Creation of the American Republic*, 476–83. James Fenimore Cooper invested Marmaduke Temple with a more heroic role in the Revolution than William Cooper had demonstrated. Temple espouses "the cause of the people" and serves "his country during the struggle, in various civil capacities, and always with dignity and usefulness." James Fenimore Cooper, *The Pioneers, or the Sources of the Susquehanna: A Descriptive Tale*, ed., James Franklin Beard (Albany, 1980, crit. ed. of New York, 1823), 35–36.

3. John C. Guzzardo, "Democracy along the Mohawk: An Election Return, 1773," *New York History*, 57 (Jan. 1976), 31–52; Edward Countryman, *A People in Revolution: The American Revolution and Political Society in New York, 1760–1790* (Baltimore, 1981), 33, 127–28, 146–47; Barbara Graymont, *The Iroquois in the American Revolution* (Syracuse, N.Y., 1972), 50.

4. Richard Bushman, *King and People in Provincial Massachusetts* (Chapel Hill, N.C., 1985), 17–26, 56–60, 74–82, 192–93; Gordon S. Wood, *The Radicalism of the American Revolution* (New York, 1992), 11–76; Augustine Prevost to Sir William Johnson, Mar. 28, 1771, Dreer Coll., XLVI, 21, HSP; Countryman, *A People in Revolution*, 127–30; J. Howard Hanson and Samuel Ludlow Frey, eds., *The Minute Book of the Committee of Safety of Tryon County, the Old New York Frontier* (New York, 1905), 140; Philip Ranlet, *The New York Loyalists* (Knoxville, Tenn., 1986), 161.

5. Wood, *Radicalism of the American Revolution*, 179–80; Isaac Kramnick, *Republicanism and Bourgeois Radicalism: Political Ideology in Late Eighteenth-Century England and America* (Ithaca, N.Y., 1990), 1–18; Countryman, *People in Revolution*, 288, 295–96; Eric Foner, *Tom Paine and Revolutionary America* (New York, 1976), 123–25; Alfred F. Young, *The Democratic Republicans of New York: The Origins, 1763–1797* (Chapel Hill, N.C., 1967), 42–43, 54–55.

6. Edward Countryman, *The American Revolution* (New York, 1985), 106–24; Hanson and Frey, eds., *Minute Book of the Committee of Safety*, 137; Colden quoted in Cynthia A. Kierner, *Traders and Gentlefolk: The Livingstons of New York, 1675–1690* (Ithaca, N.Y., 1992), 207.

7. Countryman, *People in Revolution*, 127–28; Hanson and Frey, eds., *Minute Book of the Committee of Safety*, 15–17, 25–30, 67–68, 85; Graymont, *Iroquois in the American Revolution*, 81–84, 93–94, 146–47, 155–56; William W. Campbell, *Annals of Tryon County, or the Border Warfare of New York, During the Revolution* (New York, 1924, repr. of New York, 1831), 46–51.

8. Graymont, *Iroquois in the American Revolution*, 157–91, 223–58; Hanson and Frey, eds., *Minute Book of the Committee of Safety*, xiii, 111. For the violence, divisions, and destruction wrought by the Revolution see Ronald Hoffman, "The 'Disaffected' in the Revolutionary South," in Alfred F. Young, ed., *The American Revolution: Explorations in the History of American Radicalism* (DeKalb, Ill., 1976), 273–316. For the consensual interpretation see Bernard Bailyn, *Faces of Revolution: Personalities and Themes in the Struggle for American Independence* (New York, 1990), 207–24. James Fenimore Cooper depicted the brutal violence of the frontier revolution in Otsego in his novel *Wyandotté, or The Hutted Knoll, A Tale*, ed., Thomas and Marianne Philbrick (Albany, 1982, crit. ed. of New York, 1843).

9. Campbell, *Annals of Tryon County*, 51, 89–93, 153; Willard V. Huntington, "Old Time Notes Relating to Otsego County and the Upper Susquehanna Valley" (Typescript, NYSHA), 374; John Sawyer, *History of Cherry Valley from 1740 to 1898* (Cherry Valley, N.Y., 1898), 8–11; Association of the People at Unadilla and on the Susquehanna, July 3, 1775, in Maryly B. Penrose, ed., *Mohawk Valley in the Revolution: Committee of Safety Papers and Genealogical Compendium* (Franklin Park, N.J., 1978), 168–69.

10. Richard McGinnis, "A Loyalist Journal," *New York Genealogical and Biographical Record,* 105 (Oct. 1974), 198; Brant quoted in Colin Calloway, *The American Revolution in Indian Country: Crisis and Diversity in Native American Communities* (New York, 1995), Ch. 4. I appreciate Professor Calloway's generosity in sharing a draft copy of this chapter.

11. John Harper to John Frey, June 19, 1776, Tryon County Folder, Misc. Mss. NYHS; Huntington, "Old Time Notes," 383; Graymont, *Iroquois in the American Revolution,* 53, 109–10, 116, 165–68, 175–80; James Henry Pickering, "New York in the Revolution: Cooper's *Wyandotté,*" *New York History,* 49 (April 1968), 135; Ruth L. Higgins, *Expansion in New York, with Especial Reference to the Eighteenth Century* (Columbus, Ohio, 1931), 98; Francis Whiting Halsey, *The Old New York Frontier: Its Wars with Indians and Tories, Its Missionary Schools, Pioneers and Land Titles, 1614–1800* (New York, 1912), 211; Col. Jacob Klock to Gov. George Clinton, June 22, 1778, in *Public Papers of George Clinton,* 10 vols. (Albany, 1899–1914), vol. 3, 475–76.

12. Erkuries Beatty, "Journal of Lt. Erkuries Beatty," Aug. 14, 1779, in Frederick Cook, ed., *Journals of the Military Expedition of Major John Sullivan Against the Six Nations of Indians in 1779* (Albany, 1887), 23; Graymont, *Iroquois in the American Revolution,* 179–82; Samuel Preston, "Journey to Harmony," in Patricia H. Christian and Eleanor H. Keesler, eds., *Samuel Preston, 1789–1989: From Buckingham to Buckingham* (Equinunk, Pa., 1989), 100–101. Appalled by the boast, Preston dismissed Dixon from his service.

13. Graymont, *Iroquois in the American Revolution,* 183–90; Halsey, *Old New York Frontier,* 224, 234–43, 257–58; Sawyer, *History of Cherry Valley,* 22–29; Thomas Bard, ed., "Journal of Lieutenant Robert Parker, of the Second Continental Artillery, 1779," *PMHB,* 27 (1903), 407–11; Beatty, "Journal," July 18, 1779, in Cook, *Journals of the Military Expedition,* 21.

14. J. David Lehman, "The End of the Iroquois Mystique: The Oneida Land Cession Treaties of the 1780s," *WMQ,* 3d. ser., 47 (Oct. 1990), 523–47; Graymont, *Iroquois in the American Revolution,* 264, 286–88; Sawyer, *History of Cherry Valley,* 42–43; Campbell, *Annals of Tryon County,* 186; Huntington, "Old Time Notes," 609–12, 781; Halsey, *Old New York Frontier,* 332–37; Higgins, *Expansion in New York,* 100; Benjamin Lull to Henry Hill, Oct. 11, 1785, WCP, CB 1704–93, HCA; Preston, "Journey to Harmony," 100–101.

15. J. F. Cooper, *Wyandotté,* 8; Josiah Priest, *Stories of Early Settlers in the Wilderness, Embracing the Life of Mrs. Priest, Late of Otsego County, N.Y.* (Albany, 1837), 16, 23; Richard Smith, "Notes of a Tour," Du Simitiere Mss., LCP; Samuel Preston to Hugh Ely, Dec. 23, 1817, Archives Box 2B, HSP; Preston, "Journey to Harmony," 100–101 (quotation).

16. Griffith Evans, "Journal of Griffith Evans, 1784–1785," *PMHB,* 65 (April 1941), 216-21.

17. James Macauley, *The Natural, Statistical and Civil History of the State of New-York . . .,* 3 vols. (New York, 1829), vol. 3, 417–18.

18. Robert Lettis Hooper, Jr., to James Wilson, Sept. 27, 1783, James Wilson Papers, vol. 5, HSP; Thomas Smith to John Taylor, Nov. 30, 1784, WTFEP, NYPL.

19. Nicholas B. Wainwright, *George Croghan, Wilderness Diplomat* (Chapel Hill, N.C., 1959), 300–307; Nicholas B. Wainwright, ed., "Turmoil at Pittsburgh: Diary of Augustine Prevost," *PMHB,* 85 (Apr. 1961), 115–17; Albert T. Volwiler, *George Croghan and the Westward Movement, 1741–1782* (Cleveland, 1926), 327–29; Augustine Prevost, Jr., to Barnard and Michael Gratz, Sept. 30, 1784, Etting Coll., Croghan-Gratz sec., vol. 2, 19, HSP; Prevost to Samuel Stringer, Mar. 29, 1787, Simon Gratz Coll., HSP.

20. Sheila L. Skemp, *William Franklin: Son of a Patriot, Servant of a King* (New York, 1990), 173–246; Julius Goebel, Jr., et al., eds., *The Law Practice of Alexander Hamilton: Documents and Commentary,* 4 vols. (New York, 1964–1981), vol. 4, 82–84; James Fenimore Cooper (1858–1938), "William Cooper and Andrew Craig's Purchase of Croghan's Land," NYSHA *Quarterly Journal,* 12 (Oct. 1931), 392.

21. William Franklin to John Taylor, June 25, 1791, WTFEP, NYPL; Richard Wells to Franklin, May 9, 1806, Jonathan Williams Papers, APS; Richard Bauman, *For the Reputation of Truth: Politics, Religion, and Conflict among the Pennsylvania Quakers, 1750–1800* (Baltimore, 1971), 152; Robert F. Oaks, "Philadelphians in Exile: The Problem of Loyalty during the American Revolution," *PMHB,* 96 (July 1972), 298–325; Doerflinger, *A Vigorous Spirit of Enter-*

prise, 167, 205–6; James to George Bowne, Apr. 20, 1789, Abel James Letterbook for 1785–90, p. 55, HSP; Drinker to Frederick Pigou, Jr., Nov. 3, 1790, HDP, Letter Book 1790–1793, HSP.

22. Oaks, "Philadelphians in Exile," 298–325; Anne H. Wharton, "The Wharton Family," *PMHB,* 1 (1877), 329, 457–58; Wainwright, *George Croghan,* 279; Volwiler, *George Croghan,* 329; Joseph Wharton, Jr., to George Croghan, Sept. 16, 1779, Cadwallader Coll., Croghan sec., box 7, HSP; Croghan's indenture with Joseph Wharton, Jr., June 27, 1780, WCP, Oversized I–126, HCA; Wharton to Thomas Machin, Dec. 24, 1781, Machin Papers, Oneida Co. Hist. Soc., Utica, N.Y.

23. For Morton see Richard A. Harrison, *Princetonians, 1769–1775: A Biographical Dictionary* (Princeton, N.J., 1980), 373–74. For Morgan see James Thomas Flexner, *Doctors on Horseback: Pioneers of American Medicine* (New York, 1937), 26–50; Whitfield J. Bell, Jr., *John Morgan: Continental Doctor* (Philadelphia, 1965), 259–64; Benjamin Rush, *The Autobiography of Benjamin Rush . . .,* ed. George W. Corner (Princeton, N.J., 1948), 180.

24. J. F. Cooper (1858–1938), "William Cooper and Andrew Craig's Purchase," 390–96.

25. On Jan. 26 Cooper and Craig purchased James Verree's share for £617.8.1. On May 7 they obtained George Fox's share for £492.0.0. That same day they reached agreement with Abel James to buy his three shares for £1,876.10.0. See James Verree's assignment to William Cooper and Andrew Craig, Jan. 26, 1785, George Fox's assignment, May 7, 1785, Abel James's assignment, May 7, 1785, Cooper and Craig's receipt to James, May 28, 1785, all in WCP, BB 1704–1788, HCA; William Cooper and Andrew Craig to Alexander Hamilton, May 9, 1785, in Goebel, *Law Practice of Alexander Hamilton,* vol. 4, 123; Cooper and Craig's petition to Chancellor Robert R. Livingston, n.d. [1786], WCP, BB 1704–1788, HCA. Cooper and Craig gave James one bond for £900.0.0 to be paid on June 14, 1786; a second to pay £446.10.0 a year later; and a promise to make good a sum of £530.0.0 that James had received from the Croghan estate but might lose to his own creditors.

26. Richard Wells, "Information," May 9, 1786, William Franklin to Augustine Prevost, Jr., June 24, 1791, Franklin to John Taylor, June 25, 1791, all in WTFEP, NYPL; and Franklin to Jonathan Williams, Nov. 22, 1808, Williams Papers, APS.

27. Cooper had already called upon Hamilton in New York City sometime after buying Verree's share in late January and before purchasing Fox's and James's shares in early May. That Cooper could describe the patent's bounds to Hamilton's clerk early in 1785 suggests that he had already visited Otsego. Perhaps he had first visited Otsego in late 1784, rather than the fall of 1785 (as he stated in *A Guide in the Wilderness*). It makes more sense for Cooper to have scouted the land before, rather than after, he and Craig committed themselves to pay £3,000 for the shares. See Abel James to Alexander Hamilton, Jan. 21, 1785, and William Cooper and Andrew Craig to Hamilton, May 9, 1785, in Goebel, *Law Practice of Alexander Hamilton,* vol. 4, 119–21, 123; W. Cooper, *Guide in the Wilderness, or, the History of the First Settlements in the Western Counties of New York, with Useful Instructions to Future Settlers . . .* (Cooperstown, 1986, repr. of Dublin, 1810), 13–14.

28. Joseph Wharton to Thomas Machin, Dec. 24, 1781, Machin Papers, Oneida Co. Hist. Soc., Utica, N.Y.; Thomas Smith to John Taylor, Nov. 30, 1784, WTFEP, NYPL; William Franklin to Taylor, July 7, 1785, and Franklin to Robert Lettis Hooper, Aug. 4, 1785, Williams Papers, APS; Goebel, *Law Practice of Alexander Hamilton,* vol. 4, 89; Mary-Jo Kline, ed., *Political Correspondence and Public Papers of Aaron Burr,* 2 vols. (Princeton, N.J., 1983), vol. 1, 4, 12.

29. Goebel, *Law Practice of Alexander Hamilton,* vol. 4, 92–93. For a confused account that takes the scire facias role literally see J. F. Cooper (1858–1938), "William Cooper and Andrew Craig's Purchase," 390–96.

30. Barnard Gratz, "Notice," *Pennsylvania Gazette,* May 25, 1786.

31. Sheriff Clyde, "Notice," *Albany Gazette,* Jan. 12, 1786; Goebel, *Law Practice of Alexander Hamilton,* vol. 4, 93–94; William Cooper and Andrew Craig to Alexander Hamilton, May 9, 1785, in ibid., 123; John Morgan, "To the Public," [Philadelphia] *Pennsylvania Gazette,* May 17, 1786.

32. Burr's petition quoted in Goebel, *Law Practice of Alexander Hamilton*, vol. 4, 94–96; John Morgan to Jacob Morton, May 15, 1786, Aaron Burr Papers, Reel 2, NYHS.

33. William Ireson's affidavit, Aug. 10, 1786, in file papers, Augustine Prevost v. William Franklin, file BM P448, NYCHR; John Morgan, "To the Public" and "Reply," *Pennsylvania Gazette*, May 17 and June 7, 1786.

34. Certificate of Christopher P. Yates, et. al., *Pennsylvania Gazette*, May 17, 1786 (the original is in WCP, BB 1704–1788, HCA); John Morgan, "Reply," *Pennsylvania Gazette*, June 7, 1786; William Ireson's affidavit, Aug. 10, 1786, in file papers, Augustine Prevost v. William Franklin, file BM P448, NYCHR.

35. Certificate of Christopher P. Yates, et al., *Pennsylvania Gazette*, May 17, 1786; John Morgan, "To the Public," and "Reply," *ibid.*, May 17 and June 7, 1786; William Ireson's affidavit, Aug. 10, 1786, in file papers, Augustine Prevost v. William Franklin, file BM P448, NYCHR.

36. Certificate of Christopher P. Yates, et. al., *Pennsylvania Gazette*, May 17, 1786; Andrew Craig, "Reply," ibid., May 17, 1786.

37. John Morgan, "To the Public," and "Reply," *Pennsylvania Gazette*, May 17 and June 7, 1786; William Ireson's affidavit, Aug. 10, 1786, in file papers, Augustine Prevost v. William Franklin, file BM P448, NYCHR; Bell, *John Morgan: Continental Doctor*, 257; Samuel Clyde's receipt, Jan. 14, 1786, WCP, BB 1704–1788, HCA. After the vendue Cooper took a special interest in helping Clyde and his family. In 1796 Clyde's widow wrote to Cooper seeking his promised help to avert an impending foreclosure on her Cherry Valley farm: Catharine Clyde to William Cooper, Mar. 28, 1796, WCP, CB 1796–1798, HCA.

38. William Cooper's descendants remained highly sensitive to suggestions that his acquisition of Otsego was irregular and unjust. In his 1926 biography of George Croghan, Albert T. Volwiler insisted that Cooper and Craig used "questionable methods" to procure the Otsego Patent. In 1931 the novelist's grandson and namesake, James Fenimore Cooper (1858–1938), responded with a misleading essay that read historical documents with rigid literalness. He insisted on a number of errors: "that William Franklin himself conducted the proceedings which resulted in the sale"; that Franklin received the £2,700 from the vendue; that neither Burr nor Hamilton appeared in any of the proceedings "or that Hamilton even was employed"; and that Barnard Gratz "deliberately failed to appear in the proceedings in court." See Volwiler, *George Croghan*, 330–31; J. F. Cooper (1858–1938), "William Cooper and Andrew Craig's Purchase," 390–96; Goebel, *Law Practice of Alexander Hamilton*, vol. 4, 92–93.

39. John Morgan, "To the Public," and Andrew Craig, "Reply," *Pennsylvania Gazette*, May 17, 1786; Goebel, *Law Practice of Alexander Hamilton*, vol. 4, 97–103; William Cooper and Andrew Craig petition to Chancellor Robert R. Livingston, n.d. [1786], WCP, BB 1704–1788, HCA; Petition of the heirs and executors of George Croghan to the New York legislature [March 1786], in Kline, *Political Correspondence . . . of Aaron Burr*, vol. 1, 22–25.

40. John Morgan, "To the Public," and Andrew Craig, "Reply," *Pennsylvania Gazette*, May 17, 1786; Aaron Burr to John Morgan, May 6, 1786, Aaron Burr Papers, reel 2, NYHS; William Cooper and Andrew Craig, "Facts in Answer to Doctor John Morgan" (broadside), May 8, 1786, WCP, BB 1704–1788, HCA.

41. Cooper to Burr, May 19, 1786, in Kline, *Political Correspondence . . . of Aaron Burr*, vol. 2, 27; W. Cooper, *A Guide in the Wilderness*, 14. The 54 mortgage deeds are in Mortgage Book A, pp. 118–58, Registry of Deeds, Montgomery Co. Clerk's Office, Fonda, N.Y.

42. Most purchasers were individuals of modest status; only one (Samuel Guthrie) was an esquire; two were physicians; one was a widow; the rest were yeomen farmers (54), artisans (6), or men of unspecified status (10). Mortgage Book A, pp. 118–58, Registry of Deeds, Montgomery Co. Clerk's Office. For New York frontier landlord policies and prices see David Maldwyn Ellis, *Landlords and Farmers in the Hudson-Mohawk Region, 1790–1850* (Ithaca, N.Y., 1946) 45–51. For the free village lots see Andrew Craig and William Cooper, Notice, *Otsego Herald*, Aug. 4, 1796.

43. Mortgage Book A, pp. 118–58, Registry of Deeds, Montgomery Co. Clerk's Office.

44. In 1790 only 33 of the 74 original buyers lived in Otsego according to the first federal census. A somewhat higher number of the buyers (40 of 74) appeared in William Cooper's Cooperstown store book for 1790, suggesting that some sojourned in Otsego without becoming full-time residents. See U.S. Bureau of the Census, *Heads of Families at the First Census of the United States Taken in the Year 1790: New York* (Baltimore, 1966, repr. of Washington, D.C., 1908), 112–13; William Cooper and Richard R. Smith, Store Book 1 (1790–91), WCP, HCA. Recorded deeds and William Cooper's business papers document a total of 14 transactions from 1788 to 1789 in which original purchasers sold some (or all) of their Otsego land. These 14 documented sales represent only some unknown, but undoubtedly small, proportion of the much larger number of actual resales. The new purchasers obtained much smaller tracts (an average of 162 acres) for significantly higher prices (an average markup of £36.2.0 per 100 acres) in addition to assuming the mortgage burden to Cooper and Craig. The 14 transactions are to be found in WCP, BB 1704–1788 and BB 1789–1791, HCA.

45. Mortgage Book A, pp. 118–58, Registry of Deeds, Montgomery Co. Clerk's Office.

46. Andrew Craig, "Notice," *Pennsylvania Gazette*, May 17, 1786; John Morgan, "Notice," ibid., June 7, 1786; George Morgan to John Morgan, Jan. 27, 1787, Morgan Papers, Historical Collection, College of Physicians, Philadelphia (photostat provided through the courtesy of Whitfield J. Bell, Jr.); William Cooper to Jacob Morris, July 29, 1787, WCP, CB 1704–1793, HCA.

47. William Cooper to Aaron Burr, Nov. 19, 1787, in Kline, *Political Correspondence . . . of Aaron Burr*, vol. 1, 32; Goebel, *Law Practice of Alexander Hamilton*, vol. 4, 103–7, 126; Augustine Prevost, Jr., to Cooper, Aug. 20, 1789, and Richard Harrison to Cooper, Sept. 26, 1789, WCP, CB 1704–1793, HCA; Prevost indenture with Aaron Burr, July 30, 1790, BB 1789–1791, WCP, HCA; Cooper to Thomas Rogers, July 22, 1807, WCP, CB 1807–1809, HCA; Burr to John Morgan, May 6, 1786, Aaron Burr Papers, reel 2, NYHS.

48. Andrew Craig to William Cooper, April 26, 1795, WCP, CB 1794–1796, HCA; Craig and Cooper, account, July 27, 1796, WCP, Oversized 7-1, HCA; Craig and Cooper, Articles of Agreement, July 27, 1796, WCP, BB 1796–1798, HCA; Craig to Cooper, Sept. 29, 1797, WCP, CB 1796–1798, HCA.

49. William Cooper and Andrew Craig to Samuel Guthrie, June 9, 1786, Conveyances D:100, OCRD; Cooper and Craig to Hendrick Frey, July 6, 1786 ("Cooper Town") and to William Garratt, July 10, 1786, WCP, BB 1704–1788, HCA; "Philupnos Philo-Typus," *Otsego Herald*, Apr. 3, 1795; James Fenimore Cooper (1789–1851), *Chronicles of Cooperstown* (1838), reprinted in Shaw T. Livermore, ed., *A Condensed History of Cooperstown* (Albany, 1862), 16, 24, 26; James Fenimore Cooper (1789–1851), "Otsego Hall," in James Fenimore Cooper (1858–1938), *The Legends and Traditions of a Northern County* (New York, 1921), 224.

50. J. F. Cooper, "Otsego Hall," 223–24; J. F. Cooper, *Chronicles of Cooperstown*, 26; J. F. Cooper, *Pioneers*, 42; Charles R. Tichy, "Otsego Hall and Its Setting, 1786–1940" (Master's thesis, SUNY at Oneonta, 1973), 2; Daniel Smith's Map of Cooperstown, Sept. 26, 1788, WCP, Map File, HCA. William Cooper secured Andrew Craig's release of the property in May of 1788. See Indenture, Craig with Cooper, May 8, 1788, WCP, BB 1704–1788, HCA. For the move see Cooper to Henry Drinker, Nov. 18, 1790, HDP, CB 1741–1792, HSP; James Fenimore Cooper (1858–1938), *Reminiscences of Mid-Victorian Cooperstown and a Sketch of William Cooper* (Cooperstown, 1936), 44. For continuing work on the house see the entry for Elisha Flint in William Cooper and Richard R. Smith, Store Book 1 (1790–91), Dec. 7, 1790, WCP, HCA.

51. Only 2 of the original 74 buyers (3 percent) received a recorded deed for their entire purchases. It was far more common for the original buyer eventually to obtain a deed for a portion of his original tract (18 of 74 = 24 percent). But it was just as common for all his land to revert to William Cooper, either through foreclosure proceedings or by the settler's relinquishment (19 of 74 = 26 percent). The rest of the original purchasers had sold their lands to newcomers, who made the payments to Cooper and Craig. Those 1786 buyers who eventually received a deed from Cooper for at least part of their purchases had

originally contracted for an average of 350 acres: below the means both of 478 for all purchasers and of 739 for those who later had to relinquish. For reversions, see Indenture,
Thomas Taylor, et al., with William Cooper and Andrew Craig, Jan. 30, 1792, WCP, BB
1789–1791, HCA; 2 Sheriff's deeds, Richard R. Smith to Cooper, June 1, 1792, WCP, BB
1792–1793, HCA; Richard Edwards's Memorandum regarding William Abbott's property,
June 1795, WCP, BB 1794, HCA; Sheriff's deed, Benjamin Gilbert to Cooper, May 1, 1795,
WCP, BB 1795, HCA; Sheriff's deeds, Samuel Dickson to Cooper, Jan. 27 and Mar. 15,
1794, WCP, BB 1794, HCA; Assignment, W. Cooper to Richard Fenimore Cooper, Nov. 8,
1799, WCP, BB 1799–1801, HCA; Sheriff's deed, Richard R. Smith to W. Cooper, May 8,
1792, WCP, BB 1791–1792, HCA.

52. Articles of Agreement, William Cooper with Andrew Craig, Oct. 17, 1790, WCP, Oversized
II, 152, HCA; Piertown Settlement Agreement, Dec. 9, 1790, WCP, Oversized II, 162,
HCA; Cooper to Henry Drinker, Apr. 21, 1792, HDP, CB 1741–1792, HSP.

53. My calculations derive from aggregating the mortgage and conveyance deeds representing Cooper's sales to settlers, 1789–1793, Montgomery Co. Registry of Deeds and OCRD.
For similar, but impressionistic conclusions see Roy Lyman Butterfield, *In Old Otsego: A
New York County Views Its Past* (Cooperstown, 1959), 12–14. The new buyers were much
more successful than the old in paying for their lands and securing complete ownership
(only 12 of the 183 suffered foreclosure, 7 percent).

54. John Tunnecliff to William Cooper, Jan. 7, 1789, WCP, CB 1704–1793, HCA; Articles of
Agreement, Cooper with Andrew Craig, Oct. 17, 1790, WCP, Oversized II, 152, HCA; J. F.
Cooper, *Chronicles of Cooperstown*, 20; Karl J. R. Arndt, "John Christopher Hartwick: Ger-
man Pioneer of Central New York," *New York History*, 18 (July 1937), 293–303.

55. Huntington, "Old Time Notes," 618; William Ellison to Goldsborough Banyar, Oct. 1787,
WCP, CB 1704–1793, HCA; John Christopher Hartwick, undated lease, c. 1787, JCHP,
HCA; Arndt, "John Christopher Hartwick," 301.

56. John Christopher Hartwick, undated lease, c. 1787, JCHP, HCA; Hartwick's last will and
testament, Hartwick Estate Papers, Lutheran Archive Center, Mount Airy, Pa. Hartwick visited Otsego in June and September of 1787, August–September of 1788, Sept. 1789,
Sept.–Oct. 1791, Feb. and May 1792, and Feb.–Mar. and Sept. 1794. See Hartwick's account with Isaac Stacy, June 1787—Sept. 1794, JCHP, HCA.

57. William Cooper to Henry Drinker, Nov. 24, 1789, HDP, CB 1741–1792, HSP; Roy Lyman
Butterfield, "The Hartwick Patent," [Cooperstown] *The Otsego Farmer*, March 18, 1955.

58. John Christopher Hartwick, undated statement, H box, NYSHA; William Cooper, Memorandum, Dec. 29, 1791, JCHP, HCA; Cooper to Hartwick, Sept. 15, 1794, WCP, CB
1794–1796, HCA.

59. John Christopher Hartwick, power of attorney to William Cooper, May 13, 1791, JCHP,
HCA; Cooper to Hartwick, Sept. 15, 1794, WCP, CB 1794–1796, HCA; R. L. Butterfield,
"Hartwick Patent."

60. William Cooper's lease list with Jeremiah Van Rensselaer's receipt, Aug. 14, 1794, WCP,
BB 1794, HCA; R. L. Butterfield, "Hartwick Patent"; Cooper, Memorandum, May 10,
1804, JCHP, HCA. The leaseholders included at least 17 transients, who never before and
never again appeared in the local records, as well as Cooper's friends among the aspiring
entrepreneurs of Cooperstown: James Averell, Jr., John Howard, Samuel Huntington,
Isaac Stacey, Joshua Dewey, and Dr. Thomas Fuller. Only about half of the lessees (28 of
54) were settler-farmers.

61. R. L. Butterfield, "Hartwick Patent."

62. John Christopher Hartwick, undated memorandum, Misc. Coll., H box, NYSHA; Hartwick
to William Cooper, June 22, 1791, WCP, BB 1791–1792, HCA; Hartwick, memorandum,
June 29, 1792, and Jeremiah Van Rensselaer to William Cummings, July 3, 1792, JCHP,
HCA.

63. R. L. Butterfield, "Hartwick Patent"; Hartwick Patent Lease List, 1793, WCP, BB
1792–1793, HCA; John Christopher Hartwick to William Ellison, Mar. 5, 1793, and Ellison to Jeremiah Van Rensselaer, Oct. 15 and Dec. 4, 1793, JCHP, HCA; Arndt, "John

Christopher Hartwick," 298–300. A careful and impartial resurvey in 1810 confirmed the encroachment; see Benjamin Gilbert to Dr. John G. Knauff, Dec. 27, 1810, JCHP, HCA.

64. Jeremiah Van Rensselaer to Frederick A. C. Muhlenburg, Sept. 2, 1796, JCHP, HCA.

65. William Cummings to Jeremiah Van Rensselaer, Oct. 7 and Nov. 4 (Cooper quoted), 1793, JCHP, HCA; John Howard et al., power of attorney to William Cooper, May 10, 1794, JCHP, HCA; Articles of Agreement, Cooper with Noah Adams, June 1, 1794, WCP, BB 1794, HCA; Cooper to John Christopher Hartwick, Sept. 15, 1794, WCP, CB 1794–1796, HCA; Hartwick Patent inhabitants to Hartwick, Oct. 22, 1793, JCHP, HCA; Stephen Holden, *The Holdens of Hartwick* (Cooperstown, 1932), 211. Because half of the original leaseholders (27 of 54) had sold out, the great majority of the Articles went to new men.

66. On August 14, 1794, Cooper delivered to Van Rensselaer £1,729.1.0 in cash—three years' accumulated rent on the leases. Van Rensselaer immediately returned £1,053.10.4 to cancel Hartwick's debts to Cooper for the Banyar mortgage and the commissions due on the leases. Cooper then surrendered the mortgage that had clouded Hartwick's prospects for over thirty years. See John Christopher Hartwick, undated statement, Misc. Coll., H box, NYSHA; Jeremiah Van Rensselaer to Hartwick, Oct. 14, 1793, JCHP, HCA; Hartwick to Van Rensselaer, undated, JCHP, HCA; Van Rensselaer's receipt to William Cooper, Aug. 14, 1794, and Van Rensselaer's account with Hartwick, Aug. 14, 1794, JCHP, HCA.

67. William Cooper to John Christopher Hartwick, Sept. 15, 1794, WCP, CB 1794–96, HCA.

68. Jeremiah Van Rensselaer's receipt to William Cooper, Aug. 14, 1794, JCHP, HCA. For Hillington see Thomas Fitzsimons's indenture to Cooper, Dec. 5, 1796, McAllister Coll., LCP.

69. John Christopher Hartwick, undated statement, Misc. Coll., H box, NYSHA; Hartwick, last will and testament, Hartwick Estate Papers, Lutheran Archive Center, Mount Airy, Pa.; Arndt, "John Christopher Hartwick," 301. After Hartwick's death the management of his rental income and residual lands passed to his executors: Jeremiah Van Rensselaer and Frederick A. C. Muhlenberg (a U.S. congressman from Pennsylvania and the son of Hartwick's old friend and patron, the Reverend Henry M. Muhlenberg). See William Cooper to Van Rensselaer, Aug. 15, 1796, and Mar. 30, 1800, Van Rensselaer to Muhlenberg, Aug. 3 and Sept. 2, 1796, Muhlenberg to Van Rensselaer, Jan. 26, 1797, May 30, and June 2, 1800, all JCHP, HCA; R. L. Butterfield, "Hartwick Patent."

70. John Christopher Hartwick obituary, *Otsego Herald*, Aug. 11, 1796; Hartwick to Anon., Good Friday, 1796, Simon Gratz Autograph Coll., case 8, box 22, HSP; Jeremiah Van Rensselaer to John Cox, July 22, 1796, and to Frederick A. C. Muhlenberg, Aug. 3, 1796 (possessions inventoried), JCHP, HCA.

71. William Franklin to Augustine Prevost, June 24, 1791, WTFEP, NYPL; Goebel, *The Law Practice of Alexander Hamilton*, 107–13.

72. John Morgan, "To the Public," *Pennsylvania Gazette*, May 17, 1786; Morgan to Jacob Morton, May 15, 1786, Aaron Burr Papers, reel 2, NYHS; Flexner, *Doctors on Horseback*, 4–50; Bell, *John Morgan*, 259–64; Rush, *Autobiography*, 180.

73. Joseph Wharton to Miers Fisher, Dec. 15, 1796, Fisher Family Papers, HSP ("Cooper, the hated"); Wharton to William Cooper, Aug. 15, 1797, WCP, CB 1796–1798, HCA; Wharton, "Wharton Family," 455–58.

74. J. F. Cooper, *Pioneers*, 31–35; William P. Kelly, *Plotting America's Past: Fenimore Cooper and the Leatherstocking Tales* (Carbondale, Ill., 1983), 32.

75. J. F. Cooper, *Pioneers*, 36–7, 142–43, 232; Kelly, *Plotting America's Past*, 36.

76. J. F. Cooper, *Pioneers*, 439–45; Kelly, *Plotting America's Past*, 6–7, 14, 25–26, 32–33; John P. McWilliams, Jr., *Political Justice in a Republic: James Fenimore Cooper's America* (Berkeley, Calif., 1972), 33–35; Robert Clark, "Rewriting Revolution: Cooper's War of Independence," in Clark, ed., *James Fenimore Cooper: New Critical Essays* (London, 1985), 195, 201; Thomas Philbrick, "Cooper's *The Pioneers*: Origins and Structure," in Wayne Fields, ed., *James Fenimore Cooper: A Collection of Critical Essays* (Englewood Cliffs, N.J., 1979), 77–79.

4. SETTLEMENT

1. James Fenimore Cooper, *The Pioneers, or the Sources of the Susquehanna; A Descriptive Tale,* ed. James Franklin Beard, (Albany, 1980, crit. ed. of New York, 1823), 22, 135–36, 159, 190–91, 229, 291.

2. Ibid., 244–50; "Miscellaneous," *Freeman's Journal,* March 3, 1823.

3. J. F. Cooper, *Pioneers,* 251–52, 259, 266.

4. Ibid., 248, 260, 266.

5. Ibid., 248, 266.

6. Andrew Craig to Samuel Morris, July 7, 1788, Misc. Coll., box 34, case 19, HSP; George Fox to William Cooper, Sept. 5, 1789, and Feb. 26, 1790, George Fox Letter Book, APS; Cooper to Henry Drinker, Nov. 26, 1789, and May 3, 1792, HDP, CB 1741–1792, HSP. Cooper and Craig did not retire their debts to the Burlington Company bondholders until May of 1792—five years late, but no unusual delay for cash-scarce early American commerce.

7. William Cooper, *A Guide in the Wilderness: or, the History of the First Settlements in the Western Counties of New York, with Useful Instructions to Future Settlers* . . . (Cooperstown, 1986, repr. of Dublin, 1810), 21. There is a mistaken tradition that Cooper had previously speculated in the wilderness lands of northern Pennsylvania. This misunderstanding derives from a letter written by another William Cooper to Benjamin Rush on Sept. 12, 1784 (BRP, LCP). The handwriting and the dating in the non-Quaker style both rule out William Cooper of Burlington and Otsego as the author. For the tradition see Lyman H. Butterfield, "Judge William Cooper (1754–1809): A Sketch of His Character and Accomplishments," *New York History,* 30 (Oct. 1949), 389.

8. W. Cooper, *Guide in the Wilderness,* 17, 60; Horatio Gates Spafford, *A Gazetteer of the State of New York* (Albany, 1824), 416; Carolyn Merchant, *Ecological Revolutions: Nature, Gender, and Science in New England* (Chapel Hill, N.C., 1989), 30, 154–55; Ebenezer Emmons, *Agriculture of New-York,* 5 vols. (Albany, 1846–1854), vol. 1, 229–31, 307, 309, 358; John H. Thompson, ed., *Geography of New York State* (Syracuse, N.Y., 1966), 74–78, 108–9; James O. Morse, "A Memoir of Otsego County," Dec. 20, 1830, Albany Inst. Coll., box 1, Albany Inst.

9. Gurdon Evans, "A General View and Agricultural Survey of the County of Madison," New York State Agricultural Soc., *Transactions,* 11 (1851), 671, 674; Patrick Campbell, *Travels in the Interior Inhabited Parts of North America in the Years 1791 and 1792* (Toronto, 1937, repr. of Edinburgh, 1793), 223; Willard V. Huntington, "Old Time Notes Relating to Otsego County and the Upper Susquehanna Valley" (NYSHA typescript), 640; Robert Piken, "A Rough Sketch of a Certain Tract of Land on the Susquehanna River Viewed in November 1768," Allinson Family Papers, Haverford College; Nahum Jones, Diary, Aug. 15, 1795, AAS.

10. Allen quoted in Dixon Ryan Fox, *Yankees and Yorkers* (New York, 1940), 170. In the town of Hoosick, New York, the Dutch and German families were more likely to persist in town from 1787 to 1790: 52 of 69 (75 percent) with Dutch or German surnames persisted, versus 141 of 217 (65 percent) with Yankee surnames. Another 74 taxpayers on the 1787 list bore surnames of other or indeterminate ethnic origin; their persistence was on a par with that of the Yankees (65 percent). Only a quarter of the Dutch and Germans (17 of 69) bore a surname that was unique in the town, versus almost half the Yankees (96 of 217 = 44 percent). And Dutch and Germans were almost twice as likely as Yankees to live within five entries of someone else with the same surname: 34 of 69 (49 percent) Germans and Dutch, versus 60 of 217 (28 percent) Yankees. The names of taxpayers on the Hoosick tax list are not arranged alphabetically; they seem to be arranged by neighborhood, in the order in which assessors called on households. See "Tax List of Hosack District, Pursuant to the Tax Law of the 11th April 1787," Gilbert Lansing Papers, NYSL. For a discussion of these methods see Dan Scott Smith, " 'All in Some Degree Related to Each Other': A Demographic and Comparative Resolution of the Anomaly of New England Kinship," *American Historical Review,* 94 (Feb. 1989), 44–79.

11. Robert A. Gross, *The Minutemen and Their World* (New York, 1976), 76–81, 210 n. 21; Kenneth Lockridge, "Land, Population, and the Evolution of New England Society,

1630–1790, and an Afterthought," in Stanley N. Katz, ed., *Colonial America: Essays in Politics and Social Development* (Boston, 1971), 466–91; Merchant, *Ecological Revolutions*, 183, 186–87; William Cronon, *Changes in the Land: Indians, Colonists, and the Ecology of New England* (New York, 1983), 127–56; [Elihu Phinney], "Cooperstown," *Otsego Herald*, Sept. 22, 1796; Winifred Barr Rothenberg, *From Marketplaces to Market Economy: The Transformation of Rural Massachusetts, 1750–1850* (Chicago, 1993), 38.

12. Gross, *Minutemen and Their World*, 78–80, 88; Alan Taylor, *Liberty Men and Great Proprietors: The Revolutionary Settlement on the Maine Frontier, 1760–1820* (Chapel Hill, N.C., 1990), 61–63; David Paul Davenport, "The Yankee Settlement of New York, 1783–1820," *Genealogical Journal*, 17 (1988–89), 63–88; Lois Kimball Matthews [Rosenberry], *The Expansion of New England, . . .* (Boston, 1909), 139–46, 153–60; Fox, *Yankees and Yorkers*, 162, 173, 176–98. For the residences of the purchasers see Mortgage Book A, pages 118–58, Registry of Deeds, Montgomery County Clerk's Office, Fonda, New York. For the border country see David J. Goodall, "New Light on the Border: New England Squatter Settlements in New York during the American Revolution" (Ph.D. diss., SUNY at Albany, 1984); Oscar Handlin, "The Eastern Frontier of New York," *New York History*, 18 (Jan. 1937), 50–75; Sung Bok Kim, *Landlord and Tenant in Colonial New York: Manorial Society, 1664–1775* (Chapel Hill, N.C., 1978), 281–415.

13. Doerflinger, *Vigorous Spirit of Enterprise*, 246–47, 265, 286, 314–23; John J. McCusker and Russell R. Menard, *The Economy of British America, 1607–1789* (Chapel Hill, N.C., 1985), 365–74; Douglas S. Robertson, ed., *An Englishman in America, 1785, Being the Diary of Joseph Hadfield* (Toronto, 1973), 26–27; Gov. George Clinton's Address, Jan. 5, 1791, in New York (State), *Journal of the House of Assembly of the State of New-York, Fourteenth Session* (New York, 1791, Evans no. 23615), 4; G. Melvin Herndon, "Agriculture in America in the 1790s: An Englishman's View," *Agricultural History*, 49 (1975), 505–7; Joyce Appleby, *Capitalism and a New Social Order: The Republican Vision of the 1790s* (New York, 1984), 40–45; Joyce Appleby, "Commercial Farming and the Agrarian Myth in the Early Republic," *Journal of American History* 68 (Mar. 1982), 838–44; William Cooper to Benjamin Rush, Mar. 23, 1790, BRP, XXVI, 42, LCP.

14. David Maldwyn Ellis, *Landlords and Farmers in the Hudson-Mohawk Region, 1790–1850* (Ithaca, N.Y., 1946), 14, 77–79; Beardsley, *Reminiscences*, 75–77; Campbell, *Travels in the Interior*, 234; Huntington, "Old Time Notes," 1347; "Philo-Albany," *Albany Register*, July 6, 1795.

15. Jones, "Creative Disruptions," 520–23; Cronon, *Changes in the Land*, 154–55; W. Cooper, *Guide in the Wilderness*, 17, 56; Ellis, *Landlords and Farmers*, 105; Strickland, *Journal of a Tour*, 112, 164; "Seasonable Hints to the Farmers of the United States," *Otsego Herald*, June 12, 1795; J. F. Cooper, *Pioneers*, 229.

16. Doerflinger, *Vigorous Spirit of Enterprise*, 280; Robert A. Davison, *Isaac Hicks: New York Merchant and Quaker, 1767–1820* (Cambridge, Mass., 1964), 1–4; [William Cooper], "A Description of the Country Round the Source of the Susquehanna," *Burlington [N.J.] Advertiser*, May 25, 1790.

17. Edward Countryman, *A People in Revolution: The American Revolution and Political Society in New York, 1760–1790* (Baltimore, 1981), 51–52; Richard L. Bushman, *From Puritan to Yankee: Character and the Social Order in Connecticut, 1690–1765* (Cambridge, Mass., 1967); Watson quoted in Alfred F. Young, *The Democratic Republicans of New York: The Origins, 1763–1797* (Chapel Hill, N.C., 1967), 258; Fox, *Yankees and Yorkers*, 193 ("bees" quotation); Horatio Gates Spafford, *A Gazetteer of the State of New York* (Albany, 1813, Shaw-Shoemaker no. 29836), 36.

18. W. Cooper, *Guide in the Wilderness*, 41–42; Spafford, *Gazetteer* (1813), 36; David M. Ellis, "The Rise of the Empire State, 1790–1820," *New York History*, 56 (Jan. 1975), 10; Fox, *Yankees and Yorkers*, 221; Young, *Democratic Republicans of New York*, 251, 261, 519.

19. Anne (Macvicar) Grant, *Memoirs of an American Lady, with Sketches of Manners and Scenery in America, as they Existed Previous to the Revolution*, 2 vols. (London, 1808), vol. 2, 254; Young, *Democratic Republicans of New York*, 504–5; James Kent, "Western Circuit Journal, 1798," and

"Northern Tour Journal, 1803," JKP, reel 6, LC; Fox, *Yankees and Yorkers,* 200–207 ("jaw" quotation, 200); Nahum Jones, Diary, Aug. 7, 1799, AAS.

20. Grant, *Memoirs of an American Lady,* vol. 2, 219–20, 232, 251–52; Countryman, *A People in Revolution,* 51–52; Fox, *Yankees and Yorkers,* 200–207; Morris quoted in Goodall, "New Light on the Border," 96.

21. J. F. Cooper, *Pioneers,* 16, 158 ("thin, shapeless"), 317 ("that dissatisfied"). Jotham Riddel was probably modeled on Robert Riddle, who bought land from William Cooper in 1786. On Robert Riddle as a troublesome squatter see William Banyar to William Cooper, April 3, 1793, WCP, CB 1704–1793, HCA.

22. Ellis, *Landlords and Farmers,* 7–12, 34–65; Countryman, *A People in Revolution,* 15–29, 154–59; Kim, *Landlord and Tenant,* vii–x, 3–43, 281–415; Handlin, "The Eastern Frontier of New York," 50–75; Staughton Lynd, *Anti-Federalism in Dutchess County, New York* (Chicago, 1962), 37–54; Young, *Democratic Republicans of New York,* 13, 26, 60–61, 203–7, 258–67, 533–35.

23. Frederick B. Tolles, *Meeting House and Counting House: The Quaker Merchants of Colonial Philadelphia* (Chapel Hill, N.C., 1948), 91 n. 15; Richard Bauman, *For the Reputation of Truth: Politics, Religion, and Conflict Among the Pennsylvania Quakers, 1750–1800* (Baltimore, 1971), 115; W. Cooper, *Guide in the Wilderness,* 69.

24. W. Cooper, *Guide in the Wilderness,* 17, 69, 71 ("civil"); William Cooper to Henry Drinker, June 2, 1789, and Cooper to Drinker, Nov. 3, 1791, HDP, CB 1741–1792, HSP; Henry Walcott Boynton, *James Fenimore Cooper* (New York, 1931), 19.

25. Beardsley, *Reminiscences,* 55; W. Cooper, *Guide in the Wilderness,* 14; Huntington, "Old Time Notes," 707; Priest, *Stories of the Early Settlers,* 36; Benjamin Gilbert to Daniel Gilbert, July 18, 1786, in Rebecca D. Symmes, ed., *A Citizen-Soldier in the American Revolution: The Diary of Benjamin Gilbert in Massachusetts and New York* (Cooperstown, 1980), 81; Benjamin Gilbert, Diary, May 12, and 18, 1786, NYSHA; *Otsego Herald,* Aug. 30, 1798. On the wheat blast see Jones, "Creative Disruptions in American Agriculture," 520–21.

26. Beardsley, *Reminiscences,* 19–20; W. Cooper, *Guide in the Wilderness,* 15–16; J. F. Cooper, *Pioneers,* 234.

27. William Cooper to Henry Drinker, May 7, 1789, HDP, CB 1741–1792, HSP. An edited version of the last letter appeared as "Extract of a Letter from Cooper's Town (Otsego Lake) dated 7 May 1789," *New-York Journal,* July 2, 1789.

28. W. Cooper, *Guide in the Wilderness,* 16; J. F. Cooper, *Pioneers,* 234–35; New York (State), *Assembly Journal, Thirteenth Session* (New York, 1789, Evans no. 22009), 3–4, 19–20; Montgomery County Board of Supervisors, Minutes, 1784–1810, July 28, 1789, Montgomery Co. Archives, Fonda, N.Y. For Otsego township's relative population in Montgomery Co., see United States Bureau of the Census, *Heads of Families at the First Census of the United States Taken in the Year 1790: New York* (Baltimore, 1966, reprint of Wash., D.C., 1908), 9. In *Guide in the Wilderness,* Cooper exaggerated when he claimed to have obtained 1,700 bushels of corn from the legislature and to have supervised its distribution. The historical record indicates that Cooper played an auxiliary, rather than a leading, role in procuring and distributing the grain. Cooper probably helped lobby for the aid and may have contributed to its transportation from the Mohawk to Otsego, but the allocation and distribution of the grain fell to the county supervisors, including Jacob Morris of Otsego Township, rather than to Cooper, who held no political office in New York in 1789. Moreover, Otsego's share in the state appropriation could not have purchased the 1,700 bushels claimed by Cooper; at the 1789 price in Albany of 6 shillings per bushel, £30 would have procured only 100 bushels of corn. For the price of corn in 1789, see [William Cooper], "Extract of a Letter from Cooper's Town (Otsego Lake), dated 7 May 1789," *New York Journal,* July 2, 1789.

29. William Cooper to Henry Drinker, July 21, 1790, and Sept. 20, 1791, HDP, CB 1741–1792, HSP.

30. W. Cooper, *Guide in the Wilderness,* 7–8, 10–12; Roy Lyman Butterfield, *In Old Otsego: A New York County Views Its Past* (Cooperstown, 1959), 12–13.

31. William Beaumont to Elkanah Watson, Aug. 13, 1804, Watson Papers, box 2, NYSL; W. Cooper, *Guide in the Wilderness,* 9–10.
32. [William Cooper], "To European Farmers," *Otsego Herald,* Apr. 24, 1795; Cooper to Henry Drinker, Feb. 22, 1789, HDP, CB 1741–1792, HSP.
33. [William Cooper], "To European Farmers," *Otsego Herald,* Apr. 24, 1795; Ephraim Kirby to Tench Coxe, Aug. 17, 1793, in Robert J. Taylor, ed., *The Susquehanna Company Papers,* 11 vols. (Ithaca, N.Y., 1971), vol. 10, 183; Cooper to Aaron Burr, May 19, 1786, in Mary-Jo Kline, ed., *Political Correspondence and Public Papers of Aaron Burr,* 2 vols. (Princeton, N.J., 1983), vol. 2, 27; W. Cooper, *Guide in the Wilderness,* 10.
34. W. Cooper, *Guide in the Wilderness,* 9–12.
35. W. Cooper, *Guide in the Wilderness,* 10–11; [William Cooper], "A Description of the Country Round the Source of the Susquehanna," *Burlington [N.J.] Advertiser,* May 25, 1790.
36. W. Cooper, *Guide in the Wilderness,* 11; Ellis, *Landlords and Farmers,* 43, 71, 77; William Cooper to Gouverneur Morris, Nov. 18, 1804, WCP, CB 1804–1806, HCA.
37. William Cooper to Henry Drinker and Richard Wells, Jan. 29, 1789, and Cooper to Drinker, Feb. 22, 1789, HDP, CB 1741–1792, HSP.
38. W. Cooper, *Guide in the Wilderness,* 9–10.
39. Ibid., 9–12; William Cooper to Henry Drinker, Nov. 24, 1789, HDP, CB 1741–1792, HSP.
40. William Cooper to Henry Drinker, June 8, 1802, HDP, CB 1793–1812, HSP (quotation); Jarvis Bloomfield to Joseph Bloomfield, May 8, 1789, WCP, BB 1789–1791, HC; Cooper to Benjamin Rush, July 14, 1790, BRP, LCP.
41. Goldsborough Banyar, Memorandum, June 30, 1793, Banyar Papers, box 4, NYSL; J. F. Cooper, *Pioneers,* 158; Elijah Hawkins to Cooper, Mar. 15, 1794, WCP, CB 1794–1796, HCA.
42. W. Cooper, *Guide in the Wilderness,* 10, 12.
43. Ibid., 23–25, 250; Richard Godden, "Pioneer Properties: or 'What's in a Hut?' " in Robert Clark, ed., *James Fenimore Cooper: New Critical Essays* (London, 1985), 124. For Temple's "propensity to solve moral issues with money" see Robert A. Ferguson, *Law and Letters in American Culture* (Cambridge, Mass., 1984), 300.
44. J. F. Cooper, *Pioneers,* 108.
45. W. Cooper, *Guide in the Wilderness,* 12; Peter C. Mancall, *Valley of Opportunity: Economic Culture along the Upper Susquehanna, 1700–1800* (Ithaca, N.Y., 1991), 160–216; Ellis, *Landlords and Farmers,* 46–65.
46. On the relationship of household sufficiency and market exchange see Robert A. Gross, "Culture and Cultivation: Agriculture and Society in Thoreau's Concord," *Journal of American History,* 69 (1982), 45–46; Bettye Hobbs Pruitt, "Self-Sufficiency and the Agricultural Economy of Eighteenth-Century Massachusetts," *WMQ,* 3d ser., 41 (1984), 333–64; Rothenberg, *Market-places to Market Economy,* 46–48.
47. Appleby, *Capitalism and a New Social Order,* 44–45; [William Cooper], "To European Farmers," *Otsego Herald,* Apr. 24, 1795; [William Cooper], "A Description of the Country Round the Source of the Susquehanna," *Burlington Advertiser,* May 25, 1790; [William Cooper], "Encouragement for Farmers, Poor Men, &c., &c.," *Albany Gazette,* Mar. 13, 1789; James Fenimore Cooper, *Notions of the Americans, Picked Up by a Travelling Bachelor,* 2 vols. (New York, 1963 repr. of New York, 1828), vol. 2, 246; J. F. Cooper, *Pioneers,* 216.
48. W. Cooper, *Guide in the Wilderness,* 14–15; William Cooper to Henry Drinker, Mar. 24, 1791, HDP, CB 1741–1792, HSP.
49. W. Cooper, *Guide in the Wilderness,* 26, 29; William Cooper and Andrew Craig to Hendrick Frey, July 6, 1786, and to William Garratt, July 10, 1786, WCP, BB 1704–1788, HCA.
50. Jacob Ten Eyck to William Cooper, Sept. 3, 1794, WCP, CB 1794–1796, HCA; Job Gilbert to Cooper, Sept. 26, 1805, WCP, CB 1804–1806, HCA; W. Cooper, *Guide in the Wilderness,* 63. For the rhetoric see William Cooper, "A Letter on the Manufacture of Maple Sugar," in Society Instituted in the State of New-York for the Promotion of Agriculture, Arts, and Manufactures, *Transactions* (1792, Evans no. 24605), 88; Cooper, "To the Public," WCP, HCA.
51. J. F. Cooper, *Pioneers,* 277, 318–321.

52. Ellis, *Landlords and Farmers*, 108; J. Ritchie Garrison, "Farm Dynamics and Regional Exchange: The Connecticut Valley Beef Trade, 1670–1850," *Agricultural History*, 61 (1987), 1–17.

53. For Cooper's cattle drives see *Burlington Advertiser*, Aug. 31, Sept. 28, 1790, and Oct. 11, 1791; Memorandum of Agreement, William Cooper with Nathan Davison, Oct. 1789, WCP, BB 1789–1791, HCA; Account, Cooper with Andrew Craig, 1788–1794, WCP, Oversized, HCA; Tench Coxe to Cooper, Nov. 12, 1789, WCP, CB 1704–1793, HCA. In his account of land payments collected for Craig, cattle amounted to £583.2.8 of the £954.18.9 total (61 percent).

54. Mancall, *Valley of Opportunity*, 206–13; James Macauley, *The Natural, Statistical, and Civil History of the State of New York . . .* , 3 vols. (New York, 1829), vol. 1, 70–78; W. Cooper, *Guide in the Wilderness*, 22–23; *Otsego Herald*, Sept. 29, 1796.

55. Mancall, *Valley of Opportunity*, 210–11; William Cooper, undated note to the Otsego Grand Jury, c. 1791, WCP, Misc. Legal and Land Papers Box, HCA; Cooper, Andrew Craig, Tench Francis, Tench Coxe, and Henry Drinker, Articles of Agreement, March 28, 1789, TCP, reel 53, HSP; Cooper, undated draft petition to the New York State legislature, Cooper Family Papers, NYSHA; New York (State), *Journal of the Senate of the State of New-York, Fourteenth Session* (New York, 1791, Evans no. 23616), 30; Jacob Morris to Cooper, Jan. 9, 1795, Cooper Collection, Burlington Hist. Soc. (N.J.); Morris to Cooper, Feb. 4, 1796, WCP, CB 1794–1796, HCA. For resentment in New York of Pennsylvania's rivalry see *Albany Register*, June 13, 1791. Cooper modeled his dam on the precedent set by Gen. James Clinton's temporary dam built at the foot of the lake during the war. See Ralph Birdsall, *The Story of Cooperstown* (Cooperstown, 1948), 63–66.

56. Gov. George Clinton's speech, Jan. 5, 1791, in New York (State), *Journal of the House of Assembly of the State of New-York, Fourteenth Session* (New York, 1791, Evans no. 23615), 4; New York (State) *Calendar of New York Colonial Manuscripts: Indorsed Land Papers . . . 1643–1803* (Albany, 1864), 814, 835; William Cooper to Aaron Burr, April 9, 1790, in Kline, *Political Correspondence . . . of Aaron Burr*, vol. 1, 57–58; Memorandum of Agreement, Cooper, James Livingston, Eli Parsons, James Horth, and William White, May 12, 1790, WCP, BB 1704–1788, HCA; Cooper and Richard R. Smith, Store Book 1 (1790–91), WCP, HCA; New York State Land Office Papers, vol. 50, 5 (c. Dec. 1790), NYSA.

57. William Cooper to Henry Drinker, Oct. 30, 1789, HDP, CB 1741–1792, HSP; Cooper, Ledger Book, 1790–1791, on deposit by Henry Cooper at NYSHA; William Cooper and Richard R. Smith, Store Book 1 (1790–91), WCP, HCA. For early American storekeeping see Elizabeth A. Perkins, "The Consumer Frontier: Household Consumption in Early Kentucky," *Journal of American History*, 78 (Sept. 1991), 486–510; Gregory H. Nobles, "The Rise of Merchants in Rural Market Towns: A Case Study of Eighteenth-Century Northampton, Massachusetts," *Journal of Social History*, 24 (1990), 5–23; Daniel B. Thorp, "Doing Business in the Backcountry: Retail Trade in Colonial Rowan County, North Carolina," *WMQ*, 3d ser., 48 (July 1991), 387–408.

58. Ruth L. Woodward and Wesley Frank Craven, *Princetonians, 1784–1790* (Princeton, N.J., 1991), 93–94; Richard R. Smith to Tench Coxe, Aug. 29, 1789, TCP, reel 53, HSP; "Notes and Queries," *PMHB*, 17 (1893), 238; William Cooper to Henry Drinker, Feb. 11 and May 22, 1790, HDP, CB 1741–1792, HSP; Cooper and Smith, "Memorandum," Store Book 1 (1790–91), Dec. 2, 1790, WCP, HCA.

59. William Cooper to Henry Drinker, Feb. 11, 1790, HDP, CB 1741–1792, HSP; [William Cooper], "To European Farmers," *Otsego Herald*, April 24, 1795; [William Cooper], "A Description of the Country Round the Source of the Susquehanna," *Burlington Advertiser*, May 25, 1790. Business slowed in the spring, probably because the mud season hindered travel, deterring both teamsters bringing supplies and customers seeking goods. Trade rebounded in the summer, as the roads dried, and peaked in the fall, when the harvest meant that country folk could deliver more produce to replenish their credit. They spent much more on durable goods, especially cloth and finished clothing, in the fall than at any other season.

60. William Cooper and Richard R. Smith, Store Book 1 (1790–91), WCP, HCA; U.S. Bureau of the Census, *Heads of Families at the First Census of the United States Taken in the Year 1790: New York* (Baltimore, 1966, reprint of Washington, D.C., 1908), 9, 112–13; Tax List, Old England District, Montgomery County, October, 1788, Gerrit Y. Lansing Papers, Box 1, Folder 12, NYSL. Land deeds and a separate ledger kept by Cooper identify the settlement of residence for 256 of the 302 heads of household (85 percent) and permit sorting them into two categories: those dwelling within a dozen miles of the store and those living on the fringes of the township. This subdivision reveals that almost two-thirds of those known to live within 12 miles were account customers (101 of 160 = 63 percent) compared to only half of those known to live on the geographic margins of the then immense township (48 of 96 = 50 percent).

61. William Cooper and Richard R. Smith, Store Book 1 (1790–91), WCP, HCA; Perkins, "The Consumer Frontier," 495; Thorp, "Doing Business in the Backcountry," 398. For women's economic activity but legal exclusion see Laurel Thatcher Ulrich, *A Midwife's Tale: The Life of Martha Ballard Based on Her Diary, 1785–1812* (New York, 1990), 29–33, 86–87.

62. Robert Charles McGregor, "Radical Environmental Change: Deforestation in the Upper Delaware River Valley, 1800–1875," (Ph.D. diss., SUNY at Binghamton, 1984), 104; James Wadsworth quoted in Neil Adams McNall, *An Agricultural History of the Genesee Valley, 1790–1860* (Philadelphia, 1952), 89; W. Cooper, *Guide in the Wilderness*, 40, 56; William I. Roberts, "American Potash Manufacture Before the American Revolution," APS, *Proceedings*, 116 (1972), 392–93; John Lincklaen, *Travels in the Years 1791 and 1792 in Pennsylvania, New York, and Vermont*, ed. Helen L. Fairchild (New York, 1897), 71; William Cooper and Richard R. Smith, Store Book 1 (1790–91), WCP, HCA; Thurlow Weed, *The Life of Thurlow Weed*, ed., Harriet A. Weed, 2 vols. (Cambridge, Mass., 1883), vol. 1, 11 ("silver and gold").

63. William Cooper and Richard R. Smith, Store Book 1 (1790–91) and 2 (1791–92), WCP, HCA. See especially the "Memorandum of Agreement" with Daniel Preston entered on Nov. 7, 1791. For the makers' lack of capital see Cooper to Drinker, June 7, 1792, HDP, CB 1741–1792, HSP.

64. William Cooper and Richard R. Smith, Store Book 1 (1790–91), esp. Nov. 24, 1790, Mar. 7, and 28, Apr. 20, and 26, and May 5, 1791, WCP, HCA; Memorandum of Agreement, William Cooper with Leonard Gansevoort & Co., July 21, 1790, WCP, BB 1789–1791, HCA; Glen and Bleecker Co. to William Cooper and Richard R. Smith, June 10, 1793, WCP, BB 1789–1791, HCA.

65. William Cooper, Ledger Book, 1789–1791, on deposit by Henry Cooper at NYSHA; James Fenimore Cooper, *Chronicles of Cooperstown* (1838) in Shaw T. Livermore, ed., *A Condensed History of Cooperstown* (Albany, 1862), 14–16.

66. William Cooper to Henry Drinker, Sep. 20, Nov. 3, 1791, HDP, CB 1741–1792, HSP; Lincklaen, *Travels*, 72–73; James Kent, "Memorandum of My Journey to Lake Otsego," in Edward Porter Alexander, "Judge Kent's 'Jaunt' to Cooperstown in 1792," *New York History*, 22 (Oct. 1941), 454–55; "Philupnos Philo-Typus," *Otsego Herald*, Apr. 3, 1795; "Cooperstown," ibid., Oct. 30, 1795. The identities and occupations of artisans and professionals are derived from advertisements in *Otsego Herald* for the years 1795 and 1796 and from J. F. Cooper, *Chronicles of Cooperstown*, 14–18, 36–37. A close paraphrase of Cooper's Nov. 3, 1791, letter to Drinker appears as [William Cooper], "Burlington," *Burlington Advertiser*, Dec. 6, 1791.

67. Lincklaen, *Travels*, 72–73; Simon Desjardins, "Castorland Journal, 1793–1797," (Typescript trans. Franklin B. Hough, AAS), 22. The U.S. Census for 1790 reported a population of 1,702 for Otsego Township; another 1,000 probably lived in the adjoining settlements of Newtown Martin, Cherry Valley, and Springfield, which were reported as part of Canajoharie township in 1790 but which became part of Otsego County in 1791. For the 1790 figures see U.S. Bureau of the Census, *Heads of Families at the First Census . . .*

New York, 9; U.S. Bureau of the Census, *Return of the Whole Number of Persons Within the Several Districts of the United States* (Washington, D.C., 1802, Shaw-Shoemaker no. 3442), 42.

68. William Cooper to Henry Drinker, Nov. 24, 1789, HDP, CB 1741–1792, HSP; Cadwallader D. Colden to Cooper, Jan. 14, 1790, and Josiah O. Hoffman to Cooper, Feb. 18, 1790, WCP, CB 1704–1793, HCA; L. Butterfield, "Judge William Cooper," 385–408; Richard B. Morris, "Cadwallader David Colden," and Morris, "Josiah Ogden Hoffman," both in Allen Johnson and Dumas Malone, eds., *Dictionary of American Biography,* 20 vols. (New York, 1928–1936), vol. 4, 287–88, vol. 9, 114–15; Thomas Wood Clarke, *Emigres in the Wilderness* (New York, 1941), 19–20, 98–100; Power of Attorney, de la Forest to Cooper, Aug. 4, 1791, Conveyances A, 24, OCRD; Sheila L. Skemp, *William Franklin: Son of a Patriot, Servant of a King* (New York, 1990), 274.

69. Articles of Agreement, William Cooper with Arthur Noble, June 1, 1791, WCP, BB 1789–1791, HCA; John Homer French, *Gazetteer of the State of New York* (Syracuse, N.Y., 1860), 337–39; Goldsborough Banyar, "Day Book, 1786–1793," Aug. 9, Dec. 26, 1792, Banyar Papers, NYHS; Indenture, Cooper with Joseph Pearsall, Nov. 12, 1792, Pearsall Family Papers, NYSL; Cooper to Henry Drinker, Oct. 8, 1794, HDP, CB 1793–1812, HSP; Cooper to Stephen Lush, et al., Dec. 17, 1794, Cooper Misc. Papers, NYHS; Cooper, Memorandum, Jan. 26, 1795, WCP, BB 1795, HCA; Cooper to Richard Harrison, Sept. 10, 1795, WCP, CB 1794–1796, HCA; Benjamin Gilbert to Cooper, May, 4, 1795, and Thomas Fitzsimons to Cooper, Feb. 7, 1797, Otsego Co. Conveyances A:424, B:203, OCRD; Miers Fisher to Richard Fenimore Cooper, Dec. 31, 1810, Fisher Family Papers, HSP.

70. William Cooper to Nicholas Low, Aug. 20, 1792, Nicholas Low Papers, NYHS; Cooper to Stephen Lush, et al., Dec. 17, 1794, Cooper Misc. Papers, NYHS.

71. Ellis, *Landlords and Farmers,* 24; Young, *The Democratic Republicans of New York,* 239–40; Helen I. Cowan, *Charles Williamson: Genesee Promoter, Friend of Anglo-American Rapprochement* (Rochester, N.Y., 1941), 4; William Cooper to Henry Drinker, Sept. 20, 1791, HDP, CB 1741–1792, HSP; Cooper to [?], Dec. 4, 1791, WCP, CB 1704–1793, HCA.

72. Benjamin Rush to Tench Coxe, Sept. 7, 1790, TCP, reel 56, HSP; Cooper to Charles J. Evans, July 3, 1790 ("my Friends"), WCP, CB 1704–1793, HCA.

73. Isaac Smith to William Cooper, July 1, 1796, WCP, CB 1796–1798, HCA.

5. JEWELS OF THE FOREST

1. Thomas M. Doerflinger, *A Vigorous Spirit of Enterprise: Merchants and Economic Development in Revolutionary Philadelphia* (Chapel Hill, N.C., 1986), 155, 321–23.

2. Cecil K. Drinker, *Not So Long Ago: A Chronicle of Medicine and Doctors in Colonial Philadelphia* (New York, 1937), 4–6 (Elizabeth Sandwith Drinker quoted, 6); Elaine Forman Crane, "The World of Elizabeth Drinker," *PMHB,* 107 (Jan. 1983), 3–28; Benjamin Rush, *The Autobiography of Benjamin Rush . . . ,* ed. George Corner (Princeton, N.J., 1948), 316; David W. Maxey, "Of Castles in Stockport and Other Strictures: Samuel Preston's Contentious Agency for Henry Drinker," *PMHB,* 110 (July 1986), 413–46 (Drinker quotation, 430).

3. David W. Maxey, "The Union Farm: Henry Drinker's Experiment in Deriving Profit from Virtue," *PMHB,* 107 (Oct. 1983), 620–28; William Cooper to Henry Drinker, Nov. 24, 1789 ("Greater Lengths"), Dec. 3, 1789 ("contrivance"), HDP, CB 1741–1792, HSP.

4. Benjamin Rush to Tench Coxe, Feb. 26, 1789, TCP, reel 53, HSP; Roy Lyman Butterfield, "The Great Days of Maple Sugar," *New York History,* 39 (1958), 153–56; Maxey, "Union Farm," 612–13; Benjamin Rush, *An Account of the Sugar Maple-Tree of the United States* (Philadelphia, 1792, Shaw-Shoemaker no. 24761), 10–12; Jacob Ernest Cooke, *Tench Coxe and the Early Republic* (Chapel Hill, N.C., 1978).

5. William Cooper to Henry Drinker, Feb. 22, July 27, Dec. 3, 1789, HDP, CB 1741–1792, HSP; Cooper to Benjamin Rush, Mar. 23, 1790, BRP, XXVI, 42, LCP; Cooper, "Encouragement for Farmers, Poor Men, &c., &c.," *Albany Gazette,* Mar. 13, 1789; Cooper, "Information for People who are in Search of Good Lands," *Albany Gazette,* June 11, 1789.

6. Phineas G. Goodrich, *History of Wayne County, Pennsylvania* (Honesdale, Pa., 1880), 32–38;

Joshua Gilpin, "Journey to Bethlehem," *PMHB,* 46 (1922), 15–38, 122–53; Frederick Pursh, *Journal of a Botanical Excursion in the Northeastern Parts of the States of Pennsylvania and New York During the Year 1807,* ed. William M. Beauchamp (Syracuse, N.Y., 1923), 25–26, 30 (quotation); George Colton, "Journal," July 13, 1812, Missionary Society of Connecticut, Papers, reel 3, file 63, Congregational House, Hartford, Conn.

7. Henry Drinker to Samuel Meredith, Nov. 14, 1791, Dreer Coll., New Series, HSP; Drinker to Tench Coxe, Dec. 31, 1788, TCP, reel 52, HSP; Richard Wells and Drinker to William Cooper, Jan. 26, 1789, HDP, Letterbook, 1786–1790, 348, HSP.

8. William Cooper to Henry Drinker and Richard Wells, Jan. 29, 1789, HDP, CB 1741–1792, HSP; Drinker to Tench Coxe, Feb. 16, 1789, TCP, reel 53, HSP; Drinker to Robert Morris, Mar. 20, 1789, HDP, Letterbook, 1786–1790, 363, HSP; Thomas Clifford, Jr., to Cooper, Feb. 14 and 28, 1789, Robert Morris to Cooper, Feb. 28, 1789, and Drinker to Cooper, Mar. 28, 1789, all WCP, CB 1704–1793, HCA.

9. William Cooper to Henry Drinker, May 15, June 28, 1789, HDP, CB 1741–1792, HSP; Samuel Preston, "Journey to Harmony," in Patricia H. Christian and Eleanor H. Keesler, eds., *Samuel Preston, 1789–1989: From Buckingham to Buckingham* (Equinunk, Pa., 1989), 113 (quoting the settler).

10. William Cooper to Henry Drinker, June 2 and 28, 1789, and Drinker to Robert Morris, July 8, 1789, HDP, CB 1741–1792, HSP; Preston, "Journey to Harmony," 83 ("very strange"). For the acreage and commissions see Cooper, Land Record Book, 1789–1790, WCP, HCA; and Drinker, Journal, 1776–1791, Oct. 25, 1790, p. 435, HDP, HSP.

11. Henry Drinker to Robert Morris, July 8, 1789, and William Cooper to Drinker, Aug. 20, 1789, HDP, CB 1741–1792, HSP; Morris to Drinker, July 11, 1789, and Drinker to Morris, Aug. 17 and 23, 1789, HDP, Henry S. Drinker subsection, HSP; Thomas Clifford, Jr., to Cooper, Sept. 10, 1789, Benjamin Rush to Cooper, Sept. 12, 1789, Tench Coxe to Cooper, July 8, Sept. 4 and 12, 1789, John Field to Cooper, Dec. 19, 1789, and Morris to Cooper, Dec. 21, 1789, all WCP, CB 1704–1793, HCA; Cooper to Coxe, Oct. 30, 1789, TCP, reel 53, HSP; Cooper, untitled advertisement, *Albany Gazette,* Apr. 19, 1789. In addition to the above correspondence, my calculation of 90,000 additional acres (and of 51,556 acres actually sold) in the Beech Woods derives from Cooper, Land Record Book, 1789–1790, WCP, HCA.

12. William Cooper to Henry Drinker, June 2, Aug. 31, 1789, HDP, CB 1741–1792, HSP; Maxey, "Union Farm," 612; Doerflinger, *Vigorous Spirit of Enterprise,* 57, 152–53, 321–23.

13. R.L. Butterfield, "Great Days of Maple Sugar," 151–52; Darrell Davis Henning, "The Origins and History of the Maple Products Industry" (Master's thesis, SUNY at Oneonta, 1965), 43–44, 49–52; Donald Culross Peattie, *A Natural History of Trees in Eastern and Central North America,* 2d ed. (Boston, 1966), 453–58; Rush, *Account of the Sugar Maple-Tree,* 3–7; James Fenimore Cooper, *The Pioneers, or the Sources of the Susquehanna; A Descriptive Tale,* ed. James Franklin Beard (Albany, 1980, crit. ed. of New York, 1823), 224; Levi Beardsley, *Reminiscences; Personal and Other Incidents; Early Settlement of Otsego County . . .* (New York, 1852), 31, 60–61; George Peck, *The Life and Times of Rev. George Peck, D.D., Written by Himself* (New York, 1874), 37; Henry Clarke Wright, *Human Life, Illustrated in my Individual Experience as a Child, A Youth, and a Man* (Boston, 1849), 39–40 ("The tapping").

14. William Cooper, "A Letter on the Manufacture of Maple Sugar," in Society, Instituted in the State of New-York, for the Promotion of Agriculture, Arts, and Manufactures, *Transactions* (New York, 1792, Evans no. 24605), 83–88; William Cooper to Henry Drinker, June 2, 1789, HDP, CB 1741–1792, HSP; "Observations," *American Museum,* 6 (1789), 99.

15. Cooper, "Letter on the Manufacture of Maple Sugar," 83–88; [John Hilborn], *Remarks on the Manufacturing of Maple Sugar; with Directions for its Further Improvement* (Philadelphia, 1790, Evans no. 22832); Rush, *Account of the Sugar Maple-Tree,* 8; "Observations," *American Museum,* 6 (1789), 99 ("old enough").

16. William Cooper to Henry Drinker, June 2, 1789, HDP, CB 1741–1792, HSP; William Cooper, "Extract of a Letter from . . . Cooper's-Town," *Universal Asylum and Columbian Magazine,* vol. 5 (July 1790), 134; Cooper, "Letter on the Manufacture of Maple Sugar," 86–87;

R.L. Butterfield, "Great Days of Maple Sugar," 153; Tench Coxe, *A View of the United States of America* (Philadelphia, 1794), 77–81; Rush, *Account of the Sugar Maple-Tree*, 9–10, 13–14; [Hilborn], *Remarks on the Manufacturing of Maple Sugar*, 3–5.

17. William Cooper, "To the Public," *Albany Gazette*, July 22, 1790 (Cooper's quotations); Cooper, "Letter on the Manufacture of Maple Sugar," 87; J. F. Cooper, *Pioneers*, 105–6, 229. For the targeting of sugar maples for destruction see John Lincklaen, *Travels in the Years 1791 and 1792 in Pennsylvania, New York and Vermont: Journals of John Lincklaen, Agent of the Holland Land Company* (New York, 1897), 75; Henry Wansey, *Journal of an Excursion in the United States in the Summer of 1794* (London, 1796), 260; Rush, *Account of the Sugar Maple-Tree*, 4; Michael Williams, *Americans and Their Forests: A Historical Geography* (New York, 1988), 77.

18. Cooper, "Letter on the Manufacture of Maple Sugar," 85; Cooper, "Extract of a Letter," *Universal Asylum and Columbian Magazine*, 5 (July 1790), 133; J. F. Cooper, *Pioneers*, 229.

19. William Cooper, "To the Publick" (draft essay), c. 1790, WCP, BB 1789–1791, HCA; Cooper, "Letter on the Manufacture of Maple Sugar," 84.

20. William Cooper to Henry Drinker, Aug. 31, 1789, HDP, CB 1741–1792, HSP; Cooper, "Letter on the Manufacture of Maple Sugar," 84; William Cooper, "To the Publick" (draft essay), c. 1790, WCP, BB 1789–1791, HCA.

21. William Cooper to Henry Drinker, June 2 and 11, Aug. 20 and 31, ("Spread the flame"), Oct. 1, 1789, HDP, CB 1741–1792, HSP; William Cooper, "Notice," *Albany Gazette*, Oct. 1, 1789 ("set this Valluable Tree"); Drinker to Cooper, Aug. 19, Nov. 14, 1789, HDP, Letter Books, HSP; "American Maple Sugar," *Pennsylvania Gazette* [Philadelphia], Sept. 9, 1789, reprinted in *Albany Gazette*, Sept. 21, 1789; *New-York Journal*, July 16, 1789; Drinker, Journal, 1776–1791, Nov. 19, 1789, p. 346, HDP, HSP; William Cooper, *A Guide in the Wilderness; or, the History of the First Settlements in the Western Counties of New York, with Useful Instructions to Future Settlers . . .* (Cooperstown, 1986, repr. of Dublin, 1810), 15.

22. Rush, *Account of the Sugar Maple-Tree*, 10–12; R.L. Butterfield, "Great Days of Maple Sugar," 153–56; Maxey, "Union Farm," 612–13; Rush, *Autobiography*, 177; Henry Drinker to Robert Morris, Aug. 17, 1789, and Morris to Drinker, Aug. 23, 1789, HDP, Henry S. Drinker subsection, HSP; Drinker to William Cooper, Aug. 19, 1789, HDP, CB 1741–1792, HSP; Maple Sugar Subscription, Sept. 3, 1789, and Tench Coxe to Cooper, Sept. 4, 1789, WCP, CB 1704–1793, HCA. Maxey credits Rush as the prime mover in the scheme and dates it to Aug. of 1789, but Cooper had already won Drinker to the cause by the preceding June. See Cooper to Drinker, June 2 and 11, 1789, HDP, CB 1741–1792, HSP. To interest Coxe, Drinker sent a copy of Cooper's first letter, see TCP, reel 53, HSP. The dozen who had employed Cooper were Tench Coxe, William Coxe, Jr., Henry Drinker, Abraham Dubois, John Field, Miers Fisher, Tench Francis, Thomas Franklin, Isaac Melcher, Samuel Pleasants, Benjamin Rush, and Thomas Shields.

23. William Cooper to Henry Drinker, Mar. 19, 1790, HDP, CB 1741–1792 HSP; Cooper and Richard R. Smith, Store Book 1 (1790–91), WCP, HCA; U.S. Bureau of the Census, *Heads of Families at the First Census of the United States Taken in the Year 1790: New York* (Baltimore, 1966, repr. of Washington, D.C., 1908), 98–116; Tax Assessment List, Old England District, Montgomery Co., Oct. 1788, box 1, folder 12, Gerrit Y. Lansing Papers, NYSL. I supplemented the census list with the occasional notations of residence given for customers in the store book, especially for those who lived at a distance. Three-fifths (98 of 166 = 59 percent) of the buyers lived within Otsego Township—which in 1790 included all the settlements between the Susquehanna (on the east) and the Unadilla (to the west), not just Cooper's Otsego Patent. Most of the other buyers dwelled nearby in Canajoharie Township, which included the settlements of Springfield, Newtown Martin, and Cherry Valley, just to the north and east of Cooperstown (51 of 166 = 31 percent). Fifty-two of the buyers had appeared on the 1788 assessment list, where their mean tax of 28 pence was slightly below the 32 pence average for the entire township.

24. William Cooper to Henry Drinker, Feb. 11, 1790, HDP, CB 1741–1792, HSP; Cooper and Richard R. Smith, Store Book 1 (1790–91), Feb. 11, 1790, WCP, HCA.

25. [William Cooper], "Extract of a Letter from Cooper's Town . . . dated April 8," *Burlington Advertiser,* May 11, 1790; Cooper and Richard R. Smith, Store Book 1 (1790–91), WCP, HC; Cooper to Benjamin Rush, Mar. 23, 1790, BRP, XXVI, 42, LCP; Cooper to Henry Drinker, Mar. 19 and 24, May 22 ("20 yeares"), July 21, 1790, HDP, CB 1741–1792, HSP; William Cooper, "To the Public," *Albany Gazette,* July 22, 1790. Cooper's store book credits the receipt of only 11,180 pounds in 1790—a figure that probably represents only the sugar received in payment for kettles. Apparently, Cooper did not record the sugar taken in payment for other goods. Other sources suggest that the overall production from Otsego shipped by Cooper to market totaled about 20,000 pounds. The front page of the store book itemizes 34 sugar casks totaling 18,193 pounds shipped to Albany, apparently in July of 1790; "Albany," *Albany Gazette,,* July 14, 1791, insists that Cooper had shipped 20,000 pounds to market the year before. W. Cooper, *Guide in the Wilderness,* 15, states that he shipped 43 hogsheads to market in 1790; at an average of 535 pounds that implies a total of 23,005 pounds.

26. William Cooper to Henry Drinker, July 21, 1790, HDP, CB 1741–1792, HSP.

27. Ibid.; "Albany," *Burlington Advertiser,* Aug. 31, 1790; *Albany Gazette,* Sept. 16, 1790.

28. Henry Drinker to George Bowne, Sept. 3, 1790, HDP, Letter Book, 1790–1793, p. 66, HSP; [Benjamin Rush], "Domestic Intelligence," *Universal Asylum and Columbian Magazine,* 5 (1790), 203.

29. Cooper, "Letter on the Manufacture of Maple Sugar," 83–88; William Cooper to Benjamin Rush, n.d., BRP, XXIV, 47, LCP; Robert R. Livingston, Jr., to Cooper, May 28, 1792, WCP, CB 1704–1793, HCA. For the society see George R. Dangerfield, *Chancellor Robert R. Livingston of New York, 1746–1813* (New York, 1960), 282–83.

30. R. L. Butterfield, "Great Days of Maple Sugar," 158; Arthur Noble to William Cooper, May 7, 1791, WCP, CB 1704–1793, HCA; Corner, *Autobiography of Benjamin Rush,* 194; Thomas Jefferson to Benjamin Vaughan, June 27, 1790, and Jefferson to George Washington, May 1, 1791, in Julian P. Boyd et al., eds., *The Papers of Thomas Jefferson,* 28 vols. to date (Princeton, N.J., 1950–), vol. 16, 579–80, and vol. 20, 343, 434–42. The notes were reprinted in the Philadelphia newspapers and in *Albany Register,* Aug. 29, 1791.

31. Henry Drinker to William Cooper, Mar. 29, May 6, June 23, 1791, HDP, Letterbook, 1790–1793, pp. 173, 280, 348, HSP; Benedict Van Pradelles to Drinker, July 15, 1790, HDP, CB 1741–1792, HSP; Jacques Pierre Brissot de Warville, *New Travels in the United States of America, 1788,* ed. Durand Echeverria (Cambridge, Mass., 1964, repr. of 1791), 246–49.

32. William Cooper to Henry Drinker, Aug. 31, 1789, Mar. 19, ("with Boldness") and 24 ("was a Dificulty" and "our Experiment"), 1790, HDP, CB 1741–1792, HSP; Cooper to Benjamin Rush, Mar. 23, 1790, BRP, XXVI, 42, LCP; Cooper to Drinker, Mar. 19, 1790, HDP, CB 1741–1792, HSP; Cooper, "Extract of a Letter . . . ," *Universal Asylum and Columbian Magazine,* 5 (July 1790), 134. For the marks of gentility see Richard L. Bushman, *The Refinement of America: Persons, Houses, Cities* (New York, 1992), 30–60, esp. 41.

33. Edward Pennington to Henry Drinker, Sept. 21, Oct. 27, 1790, HDP, CB 1741–1792, HSP; Drinker to William Cooper, Dec. 25, 1790, Jan. 15, 1791, HDP, Letterbook, 1790–1793, p. 120, HSP; Drinker, Journal, 1776–1791, p. 435 (Oct. 25, 1790), HDP, HSP.

34. Henry Drinker to William Cooper, Feb. 25, 1790, WCP, CB 1704–1793, HCA. At least three of the Beech Woods purchasers—Bill Jarvis, Lewis Moffat, and Adolphus Walbridge—defaulted on their large parcels of Otsego Patent lands bought from Cooper in 1786.

35. William Cooper to Henry Drinker, Nov. 14, 24, 26, 1789, HDP, CB 1741–1792, HSP; William Cooper, "Information for People Who are in Search of Good Lands," *Albany Gazette,* June 11, 1789.

36. Henry Drinker to William Cooper, Feb. 25, 1790, WCP, CB 1704–1793, HCA.

37. William Cooper to Henry Drinker, Nov. 26, 1789 ("Kicks" and "Gantlet"), Mar. 24 ("Those that believe"), May 22, 1790, HDP, CB 1741–1792, HSP; Cooper to Benjamin Rush, Mar. 23, 1790 ("I could wish"), BRP, XXVI, 42, LCP.

38. William Cooper to Benjamin Rush, Mar. 23, 1790, BRP, XXVI, 42, LCP; Cooper to Henry Drinker, Nov. 24, 1789, HDP, CB 1741–1792, HSP.

39. William Cooper to Henry Drinker, Nov. 26, 1789 ("too Young"), May 22, 1790 ("much Paines"), HDP, CB 1741–1792, HSP; Cooper to Benjamin Rush, July 14, 1790, BRP, XXXII, 100, LCP.

40. Henry Drinker to William Cooper, June 23, 1792, HDP, Letterbook, 1790–1793, 348, HSP; Samuel Stanton's enumeration of settlers, Oct. 1, 1793, Dreer Coll., Samuel Meredith folder, HSP; Stanton to Drinker, Aug. 22, 1794, and Drinker to Cooper, Nov. 9, 1800, HDP, CB 1793–1812, HSP.

41. Daniel Johnson to William Cooper, Nov. 30, 1795, WCP, CB 1794–1796, HCA; Gilpin, "Journey to Bethlehem," 30, 134 ("a set"); Miers Fisher to William Fisher, Sept. 10, 1811, Fisher Family Papers, HSP.

42. Henry Drinker to William Cooper, July 30, 1793, Thomas and John Clifford to Cooper, Nov. 11, 1794, WCP, CB 1794–1796, HCA; Drinker to Cooper, July 9, 1794, HDP, Letterbook, 1793–1796, 190, HSP; Cooper to Drinker, Oct. 8, 1794, Samuel Stanton to Drinker, Nov. 25, 1794, and Drinker to Cooper, May 14, 1802, HDP, CB 1793–1812, HSP.

43. Joseph Ellicott to Paul Busti, Jan. 1, 1803, Mar. 20, 1806, in Robert Warwick Bingham, ed., *Reports of Joseph Ellicott As Chief of Survey (1797–1800) And As Agent (1800–1821) Of the Holland Land Company's Purchase in Western New York*, 2 vols. (Buffalo, 1937), vol. 1, 200, 297; Alan Taylor, *Liberty Men and Great Proprietors: The Revolutionary Settlement on the Maine Frontier, 1760–1820* (Chapel Hill, N.C., 1990), 51–53; W. Cooper, *Guide in the Wilderness*, 9–10.

44. William Cooper to Henry Drinker, Nov. 18, Dec. 4, 1790, May 14, 1791, HDP, CB 1741–1792, HSP; Drinker, Journal, 1776–1791, pp. 439 (Oct. 30, 1790), 445 (Oct. 31, 1790), HDP, HSP; Drinker to Edmund Pryor, Aug. 11, 1790, HDP, Letterbook, 1790–1793, p. 56, HSP; Cooper and Richard R. Smith, Store Book 1 (1790–91), WCP, HCA. To determine residence, I relied upon U.S. Bureau of the Census, *Heads of Families at the First Census*, 98–116, and the occasional notations of residence given for customers in the store book, especially for those who lived at a distance.

45. William Cooper to Henry Drinker, Feb. 4, Mar. 24, May 14, 1791, HDP, CB 1741–1792, HSP; Cooper to Benjamin Rush, Mar. 12, 1791, BRP, XXVI, 44, LCP; Maxey, "Union Farm," 613; R. L. Butterfield, "Great Days of Maple Sugar," 154, 158; Cooper and Richard R. Smith, Store Book 1 (1790–91), May 23, 1791, WCP, HCA.

46. William Cooper and Richard R. Smith, Store books 1 (1790–91) and 2 (1791–92), WCP, HCA; "Albany," *Albany Gazette,* July 14, 1791. For the failures see Lincklaen, *Travels in the Years 1791 and 1792*, 41; Arthur Noble to Cooper, May 7, 1791, WCP, CB 1704–1793, HCA; Cooper to Henry Drinker, May 14, 1791 ("The Extrem"), HDP, CB 1741–1792, HSP; Maxey, "Union Farm," 617. Cooper's store book credits 13,315 pounds of maple sugar in 1791, up slightly from the preceding year's 11,180 pounds (see Table 4). Those figures apparently represent only the sugar credited in payment for kettles and therefore exclude that paid for other store goods and the sugar produced by Cooper's own works.

47. William Cooper to Henry Drinker, Feb. 17, Apr. 2 ("Patriotism") and 9 ("not so bad"), May 14, 1791, HDP, CB 1741–1792, HSP; Drinker to Cooper, Mar. 16, Apr. 14, 1791, HDP, Letterbook, 1790–1793, pp. 158, 164, HSP.

48. William Cooper to Henry Drinker, Sept. 20, Nov. 3, 1791, Apr. 21, May 3, 1792, HDP, CB 1741–1792, HSP; Drinker, Journal, 1791–1798, pp. 18 (Apr. 19, 1791), 39 (Aug. 6, 1791), HDP, HSP; Cooper and Richard R. Smith, Store Book 2 (1791–92), WCP, HCA.

49. William Cooper to Henry Drinker, May 3, 1792, HDP, CB 1741–1792, HSP; Cooper and Richard R. Smith, Store Book 2 (1791–92), Apr. 24, 1792, WCP, HCA; Henry François Cenvin de St. Hylair and Jabez White, Agreement, May 15, 1792, WCP, BB 1791–92, HCA; R. L. Butterfield, "Great Days of Maple Sugar," 161–63.

50. Henry Drinker, Journal, 1791–1798, p. 183 (Mar. 30, 1793), HDP, HSP; Maxey, "Union Farm," 619–28; R. L. Butterfield, "Great Days of Maple Sugar," 160–62.

51. For Cooper's potash kettle orders see Henry Drinker, Journal, 1791–1798, 18, 57, 60 (Apr. 16, Oct. 18, Nov. 2, 1791), HDP, HSP. For Cooper's shift from maple sugar to

potash, see also William Cooper to Drinker, Feb. 4, Apr. 9, Sept. 20, Nov. 3, 1791, June 7, 1792, HDP, CB 1741–1792, HSP; Cooper and Richard R. Smith, Store Book 2 (1791–92), May 25 and 26, 1792, WCP, HCA. Hopkins's pearl ash furnace proved just as expensive a failure as the maple sugar works, but Otsego's settlers continued to produce potash the old-fashioned way in vast and growing quantities—with Cooper's encouragement. See Cooper to Drinker, Sept. 1, 1792, HDP, CB 1741–1792, HSP.

52. Carolyn Merchant, *Ecological Revolutions: Nature, Gender, and Science in New England* (Chapel Hill, N.C., 1989), 153–56, 161, 191; John L. Vankat, *The Natural Vegetation of North America: An Introduction* (New York, 1979), 6–21, 34–41.

53. William Cooper and Richard R. Smith, Store Book 2 (1791–92), WCP, HCA.

54. For celebration of Temple/Cooper as the friend of the maple sugar tree see R. L. Butterfield, "Great Days of Maple Sugar," 151–64. For a dissent see Nelson Van Valen, "James Fenimore Cooper and the Conservation Schism," *New York History*, 62 (July 1981), 289–306.

55. J. F. Cooper, *Pioneers*, 221–22; Wayne Franklin, *The New World of James Fenimore Cooper* (Chicago, 1982), 94–103.

56. J. F. Cooper, *Pioneers*, 222.

57. Ibid., 224–30 (quotation, 228).

58. Ibid., 227–28; Richard Godden, "Pioneer Properties: or 'What's in a Hut?' " in Robert Clark, ed., *James Fenimore Cooper: New Critical Essays* (London, 1985), 127–28; Geoffrey Rans, *Cooper's Leather-Stocking Novels: A Secular Reading* (Chapel Hill, N.C., 1991), 79: "Temple expresses his enlightened rationalism convincingly, but he speaks and rides away—and that is the pattern of his behavior throughout."

59. J. F. Cooper, *Pioneers*, 105–6, 228–29.

60. William Strickland, *Journal of a Tour in the United States of America, 1794–1795* (New York, 1971), 138, 170 (quotations).

61. Henry Drinker to William Cooper, July 9, 1794, HDP, Letterbook, 1793–1796, 190, HSP; Elaine Forman Crane, ed., *The Diary of Elizabeth Drinker*, 3 vols. (Boston, 1991), vol. 1, 763; Drinker to Cooper, July 12, 1798, HDP, Letterbook, 1796–1800, 307, HSP.

62. Henry Drinker to William Cooper, June 23, 1792, HDP, Cooper folder, HSP; Drinker to Cooper, June 13, Nov. 19, 1793, Feb. 5, July 9, 1794, Drinker to Richard R. Smith, Aug. 6, Nov. 29 (quotation), 1793, all HDP, Letterbook, 1793–1796, 23, 55, 81, 82, 124, 190–91, HSP; Cooper to Drinker, July 6 and 24, Oct. 8, 1793, HDP, CB 1793–1812, HSP.

63. William Cooper to Henry Drinker, Apr. 20 and 23, 1800, May 4, 1804, HDP, CB 1793–1812, HSP; Drinker to Cooper, May 14, 1803, Apr. 21, 1804, HDP, Letterbook, 1802–1806, 95, 313, HSP.

64. William Cooper to Henry Drinker, May 3, 1792, HDP, CB 1741–1792, HSP.

6. FATHER OF THE PEOPLE

1. William Cooper, "Encouragement for Farmers, Poor Men, &c. &c.," *Albany Gazette*, Mar. 13, 1789; Cooper to Henry Drinker, June 2, 1789, HDP, CB 1741–1792, HSP.

2. William Cooper to Henry Drinker, Jan. 29, May 15, Sept. 24, 1789, and Cooper to Samuel Preston, July 3, 1789, HDP, CB 1741–92, HSP.

3. William Cooper, *A Guide in the Wilderness; or, the History of the First Settlements in the Western Counties of New York, with Useful Instructions to Future Settlers* . . . (Cooperstown, 1986, repr. of Dublin, 1810), 14–16; Cooper to George Bowne and Sons, Apr. 28, 1793, WCP, CB 1704–1793, HCA; New York (State), *Journal of the House of Assembly of the State of New-York, Fourteenth Session* (New York, 1791, Evans no. 23615), 70; Aplin quoted in Duane Hamilton Hurd, *History of Otsego County, New York* . . . (Philadelphia, 1878), 24; Cooper to Tench Coxe, Sept. 8, 1794, TCP, reel 61, HSP; Cooper to Benjamin Rush, Aug. 17, 1795, BRP, XXIV, 46, LCP.

4. John Tunnecliff to William Cooper, Apr. 14, 1788, WCP, CB 1704–1793, HCA; Joseph White, "Address," *Otsego Herald*, Oct. 23, 1795; Ebenezer Averill to Cooper, Jan. 21, 1797, WCP, CB 1796–1798, HCA; Peck quoted in Alfred F. Young, *The Democratic Republicans of*

New York: The Origins, 1763–1797 (Chapel Hill, N.C., 1967), 264; George A. Jarvis et al., *The Jarvis Family* (Hartford, Conn., 1879), 179; James Fenimore Cooper, *Chronicles of Cooperstown* (1838), reprinted in Shaw T. Livermore, ed., *A Condensed History of Cooperstown* (Albany, 1862), 15.

5. Stephen Innes, *Labor in a New Land: Economy and Society in Seventeenth-century Springfield* (Princeton, N.J., 1983), 19–20.

6. Richard L. Bushman, *The Refinement of America: Persons, Houses, Cities* (New York, 1992), xiii–xix, 50–54, 186–87.

7. Ibid., 61–99.

8. Ibid., 43–44; James Fenimore Cooper, *Notions of the Americans, Picked Up by a Travelling Bachelor,* 2 vols. (New York, 1963, repr. of New York, 1828), vol. 1, 80, 88.

9. Daniel Smith, Map of Cooperstown, Sept. 26, 1788, WCP, Map file, HCA; Ralph Birdsall, *The Story of Cooperstown* (Cooperstown, 1917), 1–2; J. F. Cooper, *Chronicles of Cooperstown,* 12, 22. For the carriage see Willard V. Huntington, "Old Time Notes Relating to Otsego County and the Upper Susquehanna Valley" (Typescript, NYSHA), 810. For the library see James Fenimore Cooper (1858–1938), ed., "Correspondence of Judge William Cooper," II, 279, in James Franklin Beard Papers, AAS.

10. Isaac Cooper, "Population of the Town of Coopers-Town in 1790," NYSHA; William Cooper to Henry Drinker, Nov. 3, 1791, WCP, CB 1704–1793, HCA.

11. William Cooper to Henry Drinker, Feb. 22, 1789, HDP, CB 1741–1792, HSP.

12. James Fenimore Cooper (1858–1938), *The Legends and Traditions of a Northern County* (New York, 1921), 223–24; J. F. Cooper, *Chronicles of Cooperstown,* 26; James Fenimore Cooper to Horatio Hastings Weld [for the *Brother Jonathan*], Mar. 22–25 1842, in James Franklin Beard, ed., *The Letters and Journals of James Fenimore Cooper,* 6 vols. (Cambridge, Mass., 1960–1968), vol. 4, 258 ("low and straggling"); Charles R. Tichy, "Otsego Hall and Its Setting, 1786–1940" (Master's thesis, SUNY at Oneonta, 1973, NYSHA copy), 2.

13. Pierre M. Irving, ed., *The Life and Letters of Washington Irving,* 2 vols. (New York, 1862), vol. 1, 51; Levi Beardsley, *Reminiscences; Personal and Other Incidents; Early Settlement of Otsego County . . .* (New York, 1852), 50–51; William Cooper to Joseph Hilbourn, Sept. 6, 1791, HDP, CB 1741–1792, HSP.

14. Robert Troup to William Cooper, June 10, 1800, WCP, CB 1799–1801, HCA ("often heard"); Beardsley, *Reminiscences,* 53–54. For Cooper's wrestling see also J. F. Cooper *Legends and Traditions,* 8–10; James Fenimore Cooper (1858–1938), *Reminiscences of Mid-Victorian Cooperstown and a Sketch of William Cooper* (Cooperstown, 1936), 45–46. For ring wrestling see John Sawyer, *History of Cherry Valley From 1740 to 1898* (Cherry Valley, 1898), 73. Beardsley dated the episode to the time that his father, Obediah, qualified as a justice of the peace; the Council of Appointment named Obediah Beardsley to that post on Mar. 7, 1794; the next court session in Otsego was June 17–20. See Council of Appointment, Record Books (series A1845), III, 83 (Mar. 7, 1794), NYSA; OC-CGSP, Record Book, 1791–1817, OCCO.

15. Charles Hansford Adams, *"The Guardian of the Law": Authority and Identity in James Fenimore Cooper* (University Park, Pa., 1990), 63–64; William P. Kelly, *Plotting America's Past: Fenimore Cooper and the Leatherstocking Tales* (Carbondale, Ill., 1983), 15–22; Geoffrey Rans, *Cooper's Leather-Stocking Novels: A Secular Reading* (Chapel Hill, N.C., 1991), 63–86.

16. Wayne Wright, "The Cooper Genealogy: Compiled from Materials in the Collection of the New York State Historical Association Library," (Typescript, 1983, NYSHA), 4–9. William's seven siblings were Susannah (m. Breese), James, Letitia (m. Woodruff and later Ashton), Levi, Benjamin, Ann (m. Kelley and later Hubbell), and Hannah. Only Hannah (1771–1853) did not receive assistance from William. Their father, James Cooper (1729–1795), remarried in 1778 and had seven more children, none of whom figure in William Cooper's papers or, apparently, in his life. However, one of those half brothers bore the uncommon name Marmaduke, which James Fenimore Cooper borrowed for Judge Temple in *The Pioneers.*

17. For the charity see Henry Drinker, Journal, 1791–1798, 33, 78, 90, 114, HDP, HSP;

William Cooper to Drinker, July 29, 1791, HDP, CB 1741–1792, HSP; Drinker to Cooper, June 13, 1793, HDP, Letterbook, 1793–1796, 23–24, HSP.

18. William Cooper to Henry Drinker, July 6, 1793, Jan. 7, 1794, HDP, CB 1793–1812, HSP; Drinker to Cooper, Feb. 5, 1794, HDP, Letterbook, 1793–1796, HSP; Elaine Forman Crane, ed., *The Diary of Elizabeth Drinker*, 3 vols. (Boston, 1991), vol. 1, 651 (Feb. 20, 1795); Andrew Craig to Cooper, Apr. 26, 1795, and Elihu Phinney to Cooper, Feb. 2, Apr. 7, 1796, WCP, CB 1794–1796, HCA. Letitia and Ann spent most of 1795 in Burlington drawing upon the charity of their brother's friend and partner Andrew Craig. See Cooper's account with Andrew Craig, Nov. 9, 1794–July 1, 1796, WCP, BB 1796–1798, HCA.

19. Letitia Ashton to William Cooper, Sept. 29, 1806, WCP, CB 1804–1806, HCA; Caleb Carmalt to Cooper, Jan. 27, 1807, WCP, CB 1807–1809, HCA. Wright, "Cooper Genealogy," 9, insists that she first married Joseph Ashton on Jan. 1, 1775, but she used the last name Woodruff in the 1790s, and her only know use of the surname Ashton dates to 1806–7.

20. Leven Powell to William Cooper, Jan. 26, Feb. 12, 1796, and John Breese to Cooper, Mar. 28, 1796, WCP, CB 1794–1796, HCA; Powell to Cooper, Dec. 29, 1796, WCP, CB 1796–1798, HCA; Cooper, Memorandum Book, Apr. 1799, WCP, HCA; Otego Tax Assessment List, 1800, series B-0950-85, box 37, NYSA.

21. Lida S. Penfield, "Three Generations of Coopers in Oswego," Oswego Co. Hist. Soc., *Publications* (1941), 3; James Cooper to William Cooper, Apr. 4, 1796, WCP, CB 1794–1796, HCA; J. Cooper to W. Cooper, Feb. 1 and 7, 1797, WCP, CB 1796–1798, HCA; Richard Fenimore Cooper to W. Cooper, Mar. 27, 1800, WCP, CB 1799–1801, HCA; Otsego Township, Tax Assessment List, 1800, series B-0950-85, box 37, NYSA.

22. Montgomery Co. Mortgages, book A, 348 (May 21, 1789), Montgomery County Clerk's office; Levi Cooper to William Cooper, Feb. 12, 1796, and Goldsborough Banyar to W. Cooper, Mar. 21, 1796, WCP, CB 1794–1796, HCA; L. Cooper to W. Cooper, May 19, 1796, WCP, CB 1796–1798, HCA.

23. Benjamin Cooper to William Cooper, Dec. 10, 1796, WCP, CB 1796–1798, HCA. Whether Benjamin got the money is uncertain and unlikely.

24. William Cooper to Henry Drinker, Feb. 11, Mar. 24, 1790, HDP, CB 1741–1792, HSP; Jacob Morris to Cooper, Jan. 9, 1795 [*sic*; actually 1796], Cooper Coll., Burlington Hist. Soc. (N.J.); Andrew Craig to Cooper, Jan. 23, 1797, WCP, CB 1796–1798, HCA; Beard, *Letters and Journals*, vol. 1, 4; Henry Walcott Boynton, *James Fenimore Cooper* (New York, 1931), 16. For examples of her mark see the Cooper leases to William Stoel (Jan. 28, 1793), William Compton (Aug. 28, 1793), and Benjamin Weaver (Dec. 12, 1793), WCP, BB 1792–1793, HCA. For her reading see Hendrick Frey to Cooper, Apr. 1, 1800, WCP, CB 1799–1801, HCA; Susan Fenimore Cooper, "Small Family Memories," in James Fenimore Cooper (1858–1938), ed., *Correspondence of James Fenimore Cooper*, 2 vols. (New Haven, Conn., 1922), vol. 1, 12.

25. William Cooper to Henry Drinker, June 7, 1790, HDP, CB 1741–1792, HSP; James Hibbs to Cooper, Jan. 1, 1808, WCP, CB 1807–1809, HCA.

26. J. F. Cooper, *Reminiscences of Mid-Victorian Cooperstown*, 44; Boynton, *James Fenimore Cooper*, 14–15; William Cooper to Henry Drinker, Nov. 18, 1790, HDP, CB 1741–1792, HSP.

27. William Cooper to Henry Drinker, June 7, 1792, HDP, CB 1741–1792, HSP; Hendrick Frey to Cooper, Apr. 9, 1796, WCP, CB 1794–1796, HCA; Frey to Cooper, Apr. 1, 1800, WCP, CB 1799–1801, HCA; Drinker to Cooper, July 12, 1798, HDP, Letterbook, 1796–1800, 307, HSP.

28. William Cooper to Nicholas Low, Aug. 20, 1792, Low Papers, NYHS.

29. Elihu Phinney to William Cooper, Apr. 7, 1796, and Moss Kent, Jr., to Cooper, Apr. 7, 21, 29, 1796, WCP, CB 1794–1796, HCA; *Otsego Herald*, June 23, 1796.

30. Elihu Phinney to William Cooper, Nov. 22, 1796, Andrew Craig to Cooper, Jan. 23, 1797, and Cooper to Richard Fenimore Cooper, Oct. 8, 1798, WCP, CB 1796–1798, HCA; Henry Drinker to Cooper, July 12, 1798, HDP, Letterbook, 1796–1800, 307, HSP; Cooper and Samuel Huntington, Memorandum of Agreement, Mar. 14, 1798, WCP, Memorandum Book, HCA. James Fenimore Cooper to Isaac Mickle, Dec. 6, 1844, in Beard, *Letters*

and Journals, vol. 4, 498. The novelist misdated Elizabeth's remove to Burlington as 1794 but correctly dated her return to Cooperstown as 1798. For the house purchase (and quick resale at the identical price of £1,500) see Burlington Co. Deeds, E, 417 (Sept. 7, 1798), 420 (Oct. 6, 1798), New Jersey State Archives, Trenton. For Henry Frey Cooper's death in Burlington see James Fenimore Cooper, "Otsego Hall," in J. F. Cooper (1858–1938), *Legends and Traditions,* 228.

31. John Simpson to William Cooper, Oct. 28, 1803, WCP, CB 1802–1803, HCA.

32. Edward M. Cook, Jr., *The Fathers of the Towns: Leadership and Community Structure in Eighteenth-Century New England* (Baltimore, 1976), 95–118, 143–63; Robert Zemsky, *Merchants, Farmers, and River Gods: An Essay on Eighteenth-Century American Politics* (Boston, 1971), 39–74; Edmund S. Morgan, *Inventing the People: The Rise of Popular Sovereignty in England and America* (New York, 1988), 174–208; Richard L. Bushman, "American High-Style and Vernacular Cultures," in *Colonial British America: Essays in the New History of the Early Modern Era,* ed. Jack P. Greene and J. R. Pole (Baltimore, 1984), 353, 356–64; Gordon S. Wood, *The Radicalism of the American Revolution* (New York, 1992), 11–92.

33. Patricia U. Bonomi, *A Factious People: Politics and Society in Colonial New York* (New York, 1971), 34–39, 114–15; Nicholas Varga, "Election Procedures and Practices in Colonial New York," *New York History,* 41 (1960), 249–77; John C. Guzzardo, "Democracy along the Mohawk: An Election Return, 1773," *New York History,* 57 (Jan. 1976), 31–52; Edward Countryman, *A People in Revolution: The American Revolution and Political Society in New York, 1760–1790* (Baltimore, 1981), 76–79, 166–69; Horatio Gates Spafford, *A Gazetteer of the State of New York* (Albany, 1813, Shaw-Shoemaker no. 29836), 25–28; New York State, *Laws of the State of New York . . . From the First to the Fifteenth Sessions, Inclusive,* 2 vols. (New York, 1792, Evans no. 24602), vol. 1, 7–9; Young, *Democratic Republicans of New York,* 8–9, 585–87.

34. Staughton Lynd, *Class Conflict, Slavery, and the United States Constitution: Ten Essays* (New York, 1967), 38; Cynthia Kierner, *Traders and Gentlefolk: The Livingstons of New York, 1675–1790* (Ithaca, N.Y., 1992), 209–10; Countryman, *People in Revolution,* 168–69, 291–92.

35. Gordon S. Wood, *The Creation of the American Republic, 1776–1787* (Chapel Hill, N.C., 1969), 476–80; Michael Kammen, *Colonial New York: A History* (New York, 1975), 342–44.

36. Kierner, *Traders and Gentlefolk,* 201–4, 240–41 (Livingston quotation); Morris quoted in Dixon Ryan Fox, *The Decline of Aristocracy in the Politics of New York, 1801–1840* (New York, 1965), 11.

37. Gordon S. Wood, "Interests and Disinterestedness in the Making of the Constitution," in *Beyond Confederation: Origins of the Constitution and American National Identity,* ed. Richard Beeman, Stephen Botein, and Edward C. Carter II (Chapel Hill, N.C., 1987), 85–89; Jackson Turner Main, *Political Parties before the Constitution* (Chapel Hill, N.C., 1973), 125–26; Douglas S. Robertson, ed., *An Englishman in America, 1785, Being the Diary of Joseph Hadfield* (Toronto, 1973), 33; Young, *Democratic Republicans of New York,* 27–28 (Livingston quotation), 39–42, 51–52, 60 (Schuyler quotation).

38. Countryman, *People in Revolution,* 196–202, 287–88; Kierner, *Traders and Gentlefolk,* 209, 212, 234–35; Young, *Democratic Republicans of New York,* 34–39; E. Wilder Spaulding, *New York in the Critical Period, 1783–1789* (New York, 1932), 96–100.

39. Countryman, *People in Revolution,* 234–38.

40. John Jay to William Vaughan, May 26, 1796, in Henry P. Johnston, ed., *The Correspondence and Public Papers of John Jay,* 4 vols. (New York, 1890–1893), vol. 4, 266; Lewis Morris to Jacob Morris, May 25, 1795, Jacob Morris Papers, box 1, NYHS; Clintonian address quoted in Young, *Democratic Republicans of New York,* 437.

41. Melancton Smith quoted in Young, *Democratic Republicans of New York,* 96.

42. David Hackett Fischer, *The Revolution of American Conservatism: The Federalist Party in the Era of Jeffersonian Democracy* (New York, 1965), 308; Young, *Democratic Republicans of New York,* 14, 16; Countryman, *People in Revolution,* 196–98 (includes the Schuyler quotations); George Metcalfe to Silas Talbot, Feb. 2, 1793, STP, box 3, GWBWL-MS ("Schuyler's misfortune").

43. Fox, *Decline of Aristocracy,* 31–33; Fischer, *Revolution of American Conservatism,* 311; William B. Fink, "Stephen Van Rensselaer: The Last Patroon" (Ph.D. diss., Columbia Univ., 1950), 5–23.

44. Fox, *Decline of Aristocracy,* 8–9; Young, *Democratic Republicans of New York,* 14–15.

45. Fischer, *Revolution of American Conservatism,* 1–17, 250–51; Ronald P. Formisano, *The Transformation of Political Culture: Massachusetts Parties, 1790s–1840s* (New York, 1983), 65–68; David Maldwyn Ellis, "The Rise of the Empire State, 1790–1820," *New York History,* 56 (Jan. 1975), 16; Joyce Appleby, *Capitalism and a New Social Order: The Republican Vision of the 1790s* (New York, 1984), 51–53. Other examples of the nouveau riche Federalist include Washington's Secretary of War Henry Knox—a prewar bookseller in Boston until elevated by service in the Continental Army—and the U.S. senators from Pennsylvania, William Bingham and Robert Morris, middling merchants until enriched by wartime contracts and government offices. See Margaret L. Brown, "William Bingham, Eighteenth-Century Magnate," *PMHB,* 61 (Oct. 1937), 387–434; Wood, "Interests and Disinterestedness," 97–100 (for Morris); Alan Taylor, *Liberty Men and Great Proprietors: The Revolutionary Settlement on the Maine Frontier, 1760–1820* (Chapel Hill, N.C., 1990), 37–47 (for Knox).

46. For the postwar political allegiances of New York Loyalists see Young, *Democratic Republicans of New York,* 66–69; and Robert Troup to Rufus King, Apr. 4, 1809, in Charles R. King, ed., *The Life and Corresponence of Rufus King,* 6 vols. (New York, 1894–1900), vol. 5, 148. For Banyar see Gorham A. Worth, *Random Recollections of Albany from 1800 to 1808* (Albany, 1866), 112–18. For Hoffman see Richard B. Morris, "Josiah Ogden Hoffman," *Dictionary of American Biography,* vol. 9, 114–15. For Frey see James Henry Pickering, "New York in the Revolution: Cooper's *Wyandotté,*" *New York History,* 49 (1968), 123 n. 2; Maryly B. Penrose, ed., *Mohawk Valley in the Revolution: Committee of Safety Papers and Genealogical Compendium* (Franklin Park, N.J., 1978), 127–29, 137; and J. F. Cooper, *Chronicles of Cooperstown,* 13. For Cooper's role in 1789, see "Veritas," *New York Journal and Patriotic Register,* July 25, 1792.

47. E. A. Hartman, "General Jacob Morris Commemorative Address," June 17, 1887, NYSHA; Jacob Morris, "Historical Sketch of the Early Settlement of the Town of Butternuts," 1811, NYSHA; Francis Whiting Halsey, *The Old New York Frontier: Its Wars with Indians and Tories, Its Missionary Schools, Pioneers, and Land Titles, 1614–1800* (New York, 1912), 366–67; Jacob Morris to John Rutherford, June 21, 1787, in Duane Hamilton Hurd, *History of Otsego County, New York . . .* (Philadelphia, 1878), 204–5.

48. William Cooper to Jacob Morris, July 29, 1787, and Morris to Cooper, Apr. 9, 1791, WCP, CB 1704–1793, HCA.

49. Christopher P. Yates to Cooper, Mar. 10, 1790, and Jacob Morris to Cooper, Apr. 9, 1791, WCP, CB 1704–1793, HCA. The voting returns from Montgomery Co. in 1790 do not survive, but it is evident that both Cooper and Morris lost, for neither served in the next session of the assembly. Four members of the Clintonian slate did win Montgomery Co. seats: Abraham Arndt, John Frey, James Livingston, and John T. Vischer. See Franklin B. Hough, *The New York Civil List From 1777 to 1860* (Albany, 1860), 194. For Yates see J. Howard Hanson and Samuel Ludlow Frey, eds., *The Minute Book of the Committee of Safety of Tryon County, the Old New York Frontier* (New York, 1905), 108–10; Young, *Democratic Republicans of New York,* 273; Pickering, "New York in the Revolution," 123 n. 2; and Yates to George Herkimer, Apr. 9, 1788, Herkimer Family Papers, Oneida Co. Hist. Soc., Utica, N.Y.

50. Roy Lyman Butterfield, *In Old Otsego: A New York County Views Its Past* (Cooperstown, 1959), 1–3; Montgomery Co. Board of Supervisors, Minute Book, 1784–1810, and Montgomery Co. Court of General Sessions of the Peace, Record Books, 1 and 2 (1784–1790), Montgomery Co. Historian's Office, Fonda, N.Y.; Council of Appointment, Record Book 2 (1786–1790), 95 (Montgomery Co. civil list for Mar. 27, 1787), 204 (Montgomery Co. civil list for Mar. 27, 1790), NYSA. For Montgomery's assemblymen for the years 1784–1791 (none of them from Otsego) see Hough, *New York Civil List,* 188–94. The four justices of the peace residing in Otsego in 1790 were Witter Johnson, David Culley, Jacob

Morris, and Sluman Wattles, who all lived in the Susquehanna valley on the southern fringe of Otsego.

51. Spafford, *Gazetteer (1813)*, 26; "Cooperstown," *Otsego Herald*, June 19, 1795; *Albany Register*, Jan. 27, 1794; Birdsall, *Story of Cooperstown*, 136; James Fenimore Cooper, *The Pioneers, or the Sources of the Susquehanna; A Descriptive Tale*, ed. James Franklin Beard (Albany, 1980, crit. ed. of New York, 1823), 358–59.

52. William Cooper to Leonard Gansevoort, Nov. 23, 1790, WCP, CB 1704–1793, HCA; Cooper to Henry Drinker, May 3, 1792, HDP, CB 1741–1792, HSP.

53. Joseph Ellicott to Paul Busti, Jan. 1, 1803, in Robert Warwick Bingham, ed., *Reports of Joseph Ellicott As Chief of Survey (1797–1800) and As Agent (1800–1821) Of the Holland Land Company's Purchase in Western New York*, 2 vols. (Buffalo, 1937, 1941), vol. 1, 197. For Cherry Valley's unhappy memory of the competition see Jabez D. Hammond to Martin Van Buren, Jan. 23, 1816, Martin Van Buren Papers, reel 5, LC.

54. Jay Gould, *History of Delaware County and Border Wars of New York* (Roxbury, N.Y., 1856), 11, 30–38; [Anon.], *History of Delaware County, New York* (New York, 1880), 217–18; William W. Campbell, *Annals of Tryon County, or the Border Warfare of New York, During the Revolution* (New York, 1924, repr. of 1831), 12, 153. For the Harpers' Antifederalism see Stephen L. Schecter, ed., *The Reluctant Pillar: New York and the Adoption of the Federal Constitution* (Troy, N.Y., 1985), 186; Abraham Van Vechten to Henry Outhoudt and Jeremiah Van Rensselaer, Jan. 11, 1788, James T. Mitchell Coll., Van Vechten subsection, HSP.

55. For the road controversy see Hendrick Frey to William Cooper, June 21, 1790, WCP, CB 1704–1793, HCA; James Cannan et al. to James Duane, Sept. 3, 1791, James Duane Papers, vol. 3, 99, NYHS; James Fenimore Cooper (1858–1938), *Reminiscences of Mid-Victorian Cooperstown and a Sketch of William Cooper* (Cooperstown, 1936), 51.

56. William Cooper to Henry Drinker, Feb. 4, 1790, Feb. 17, 1791, HDP, CB 1741–1792, HSP; Cooper to Leonard Gansevoort, Nov. 23, 1790, WCP, CB 1704–1793, HCA; *Albany Gazette*, Jan. 10, 1791; "An Act for Dividing Montgomery County," chap. 10 (Feb. 16, 1791), New York (State), *Laws of the State of New-York . . . Fourteenth Session* (New-York, 1791, Evans no. 23617), 7; R. L. Butterfield, *In Old Otsego*, 1–3.

57. Montgomery Co. Caucus, Nominations, Feb. 14, 1791, Council of Appointment Files, box 3, NYSA; Council of Appointment, Record Book 2 (1786–1793), 231 (Feb. 17, 1791); Hugh Hastings, ed., *Military Minutes of the Council of Appointment of the State of New York, 1783–1821*, 4 vols. (Albany, 1901), I, 213 (Feb. 21, 1792); Col. [John] Harper, [Jr.], to the Council of Appointment, n.d. (c. Feb. 15, 1791), Council of Appointment Files, box 3, NYSA. The surrogate, 2 assistant justices, 3 justices of the peace, and a coroner came from Cherry Valley. A judge, 3 assistant justices, 2 justices of the peace, and 2 coroners lived in Harpersfield. Three judges, the sheriff, the county clerk, and 4 justices of the peace hailed from Otsego Township. Harper's slate allocated 1 judge, 2 assistant justices, 4 justices of the peace, 1 coroner, and the county clerk to men from Harpersfield. Cherry Valley would have received 1 judge, 2 assistant justices, and 1 coroner. Otsego was to have 1 judge, 1 justice of the peace, and a single coroner. None of the Otsego nominees came from Cooper's Patent. Indeed, all 3 were Scotch-Irish men with ties to Cherry Valley and dwellings along the Susquehanna on the southern fringes of Otsego, near Harpersfield. I derived the townships of residence for the appointees from Maryly B. Penrose, *Compendium of Early Mohawk Valley Families* (Baltimore, 1990), App. B: 1790 Federal Census, Montgomery Co., N.Y., 1034–1143.

58. For Clinton's political style and his efforts to divide his opponents in 1791 by managing the patronage see Young, *Democratic Republicans of New York*, 34–39, 190–91.

59. William Cooper to Benjamin Rush, Mar. 12, 1791, BRP, XXVI, 44, LCP.

60. Alden Chester and Edwin Melvin Williams, *Courts and Lawyers of New York, a History, 1609–1905* (New York, 1925), vol. 3, 173; J. F. Cooper, *Chronicles of Cooperstown*, 14; William Cooper and Richard R. Smith, Store Book 1 (1790–91), June 2 and 10, 1791, Store Book 2 (1791–92), July 13, Aug. 16, Nov. 3 (specifies yellow ocher paint), Dec. 17, 1791, WCP, HCA; Cooper et al. contract with Seth Tubbs and Robert Blackney, n.d. (c.

Feb. 1791), WCP, Misc. Legal and Land Papers, HCA; Grand Jurors' report, June 17, 1795, Otsego Co. Indictments, OCCO; OC-CGSP, Record Book, June 17, 1795, OCCO. The most detailed description of the courthouse-jail appears in J. F. Cooper, *Pioneers*, 359–60. For the novelist's concession that he described the original courthouse-jail in *The Pioneers* see J. F. Cooper to Horatio Hastings Weld [for the *Brother Jonathan*], Mar. 22–25, 1842, in Beard, *Letters and Journals*, vol. 4, 260.

61. Young, *Democratic Republicans of New York*, 188–89, 274–75; Otsego Co. nominating meeting, Apr. 14, 1791, *Albany Gazette*, Apr. 21, 1791; *Albany Register*, June 13, 1791.

62. New York (State), *Calendar of New York Colonial Manuscripts, Indorsed Land Papers . . . 1643–1803* (Albany, 1864), 854, 856, 857; William Cooper to the Commissioners, Aug. 15, 1791, New York State Land Office Papers, vol. 51, 151, NYSA; Cooper to Henry Drinker, Aug. 18, 1791, HDP, CB 1741–1792, HSP; New York (State), *Journal of the House of Assembly of the State of New-York, Fifteenth Session* (New York, 1792, Evans no. 24600), 196–98; Young, *Democratic Republicans of New York*, 232–43.

63. Young, *Democratic Republicans of New York*, 294–97; Philip Schuyler to Messrs. Billings, Barber, Kent, Radcliff, and Hendrickson, Apr. 16, 1792, PVGP, folder 2836, SHM; William Cooper, Memorandum Book, Aug. 12, 1794, WCP, HCA.

64. Henry C. Van Schaack, ed., *The Life of Peter Van Schaack* (New York, 1842), 438–39; Young, *Democratic Republicans of New York*, 277–82; William Cooper to Henry Drinker, May 3, 1792, HDP, CB 1741–1792, HSP.

65. Young, *Democratic Republicans of New York*, 287–89, 294–97; John P. Kaminski, *George Clinton: Yeoman Politician of the New Republic* (Madison, Wis., 1993), 207–9; "An Elector," *Albany Gazette*, Mar. 22, 1792 (quotations); Joshua Purdy, Ezekiel Halstead, and Daniel Horton, certificate, Apr. 5, 1792, *Albany Gazette*, April 12, 1792; Federalist Committee of Correspondence to Peter Van Gaasbeck, Apr. 13, 1792, PVGP, folder 3026, SHM.

66. Kaminski, *George Clinton*, 203.

67. William Cooper to Stephen Van Rensselaer, Apr. 10, 1792, document 776, NYSL; Cooper to Van Rensselaer, May 2, 1792, WCP, CB 1704–1793, HCA ("Adieu").

68. Abraham C. Ten Broeck to John Sanders, Mar. 16, 1792, Misc. Mss. T, NYHS; Jacob Morris to Philip Schuyler, Leonard Gansevoort, and Stephen Van Rensselaer, Apr. 9, 1792, doc. no. 862, NYSL; Morris, notice, *Albany Gazette*, Apr. 12, 1792; William Cooper to Van Rensselaer, May 2, 1792, WCP, CB 1704–1793, HCA.

69. Stephen Van Rensselaer to William Cooper, Jan. 13, 1793, and Josiah D. Hoffman to Cooper, May 11, 1793, WCP, CB 1704–1793, HCA. For Hoffman see Fox, *Decline of Aristocracy*, 13–14.

70. Alexander Coventry, *Memoirs of an Emigrant: The Journal of Alexander Coventry, M.D.*, 2 vols. (Albany, 1978), vol. 1, 1154; Philip Schuyler to William Cooper, May 7, 1792, WCP, CB 1704–1793, HCA.

7. TRIALS

1. Joseph Whitford, testimony, Feb. 22, 1793, in New York (State), *Journal of the Assembly of the State of New-York . . . Sixteenth Session* (New York, 1793, Evans no. 25900), 199.

2. William Cooper to James [Butterfield], Apr. 6, and 8, 1792, *New-York Journal*, June 16, 1792.

3. Alexander Harper et al., petition, Jan. 1, 1793, WCP, BB 1792–93, HCA: John Cully affidavit, May 18, 1792, and William Cooper to James [Butterfield], Apr. 6, 1792, *New-York Journal*, June 16, 1792; Alfred F. Young, *The Democratic Republicans of New York: The Origins, 1763–1797* (Chapel Hill, N.C., 1967), 295–96.

4. The quotations are from George Clinton v. William Cooper, Judgment Roll, Apr. 21, 1794, parchment 21-L-8, NYCHR. See also William Cooper to James [Butterfield], Apr. 6, 8, 1792, and Joseph Whitford, affidavit, May 17, 1792, both in *New-York Journal*, June 16, 1792.

5. Joseph Whitford, affidavit, May 17, 1792, *New-York Journal*, June 16, 1792; Whitford, testimony, Feb. 22, 1793, New York (State), *Journal of the Assembly . . . Sixteenth Session*, 199.

6. James Moore, testimony, Feb. 21, 1793, in New York (State), *Journal of the Assembly . . . Sixteenth Session,* 193–94.

7. Ibid.

8. Joseph Whitford, testimony, Feb. 22, 1793, and Joseph Tunnecliff, testimony, Feb. 23, 1793, both in New York (State), *Journal of the Assembly . . . Sixteenth Session,* 199, 202.

9. Council of Appointment, Records (series A1845), II, 277 (Feb. 21, 1792), II, 293 (Mar. 30, 1792), NYSA; William Cooper to James [Butterfield], Apr. 8, 1792, *New-York Journal,* June 16, 1792.

10. Affidavits of John Hargrove, Jr., May 10, 1792, Benajah Church, May 17, 1792, Dennis McCafferty, May 17, 1792, and Joseph Whitford, May 17, 1792, in *New-York Journal,* June 16, 1792; Joseph Tunnecliff, testimony, Feb. 23, 1793, in New York (State), *Journal of the Assembly . . . Sixteenth Session,* 202.

11. Alexander Harper et al., petition to the New York assembly, Jan. 1, 1793, WCP, BB 1792–93, HCA; Joseph Hinds, affidavit, Aug. 16, 1792, *Albany Gazette,* Aug. 27, 1792; Jelles A. Fonda, testimony, Feb. 20, 1793, Richard R. Smith, testimony, Feb. 23, 1793, and John Dickens, testimony, Feb. 23, 1793, all in New York (State), *Journal of the Assembly . . . Sixteenth Session,* 189, 203, 204; Ichabod B. Palmer, affidavit, May 25, 1792, WCP, BB 1791–92, HCA.

12. Affidavits of John Hargrove, Jr., May 10, 1792, Phinehas Hill, May 15, 1792, James Abbey, May 16, 1792, Dennis McCafferty, May 17, 1792, James Butterfield, May 17, 1792, and Joseph Mayall, May 18, 1792, all in *New-York Journal,* June 16, 1792. For Clinton's "usurping" see William Cooper to James [Butterfield], Apr. 8, 1792, ibid., June 16, 1792. According to the state's electoral census taken in 1790, Otsego had 190 voters with the £100 freehold required to vote for governor; another 293 qualified to vote for assembly by virtue of a freehold worth £20 and another 57 qualified to vote for assembly by virtue of a leasehold renting for at least £2 a year. See New York (State), *Journal of the House of Assembly of the State of New-York, Fourteenth Session* (New York, 1791, Evans no. 23615), 14.

13. Affidavits of Benajah Church, May 17, 1792, James Butterfield, May 17, 1792, Joseph Mayall, May 18, 1792, and John Cully, May 18, 1792, all in *New-York Journal,* June 16, 1792.

14. Affidavits of Andrew Cannan and John Cully, both May 18, 1792, in *New-York Journal,* June 16, 1792; testimony of Cannan, Feb. 20, 1793, Jacob Morris, Feb. 20, 1793, Jelles A. Fonda, Feb. 20, 1793, Josiah O. Hoffman, Feb. 21, 1793 ("damned Yankees"), James Moore, Feb. 21, 1793 ("rascals"), Butler Gilbert, Feb. 22, 1793, and Joseph Tunnecliff, Feb. 23, 1793, all in New York (State), *Journal of the Assembly . . . Sixteenth Session,* 189, 191, 192, 196, 197, 202. For the law see "An Act for Regulating Elections . . . ," 10th session, Chapter 15, Feb. 13, 1787, in New York (State), *Laws of the State of New York, From the First to the Fifteenth Session, Inclusive,* 2 vols. (New York, 1792, Evans no. 24602), vol. 1, 316–29; "Lucius," *New-York Journal,* June 30, 1792; "An Elector, In Whitestown," *Albany Gazette,* June 4, 1792.

15. William Cooper to Stephen Van Rensselaer, May 2, 1792, WCP, CB 1704–1793, HCA; Cooper to Nicholas Low, May 12, 1792, Nicholas Low Papers, NYHS.

16. William Cooper to Stephen Van Rensselaer, May 2, 1792, WCP, CB 1704–1793, HCA.

17. Stephen Van Rensselaer to William Cooper, Apr. 30, 1792, and Philip Schuyler to Cooper, May 7, 1792, WCP, CB 1704–1792, HCA; Van Rensselaer to Peter Van Gaasback, May 12, 1792, PVGP, folder 2781, SHM; Robert Troup to John Jay, May 6, 1792, in Henry P. Johnston, ed., *The Correspondence and Public Papers of John Jay,* 4 vols. (New York, 1890–1893), vol. 3, 423; John P. Kaminski, *George Clinton: Yeoman Politician of the New Republic* (Madison, Wis., 1993), 211.

18. "An Act for Regulating Elections . . . ," 10th session, Chap. 15, Feb. 13, 1787, in New York (State), *Laws of the State of New York . . . From the First to the Fifteenth Sessions, Inclusive,* 2 vols. (New York, 1792, Evans no. 24602), vol. 1, 316–29; New York (State), *Journal of the House of Assembly of the State of New-York, Fifteenth Session* (New York, 1792, Evans no. 24600), 39, 84; Kaminski, *George Clinton,* 211–12; "Electioneering," *New-York Journal,* June 4, 1789; Christopher P. Yates to William Cooper, Mar. 10, 1790, WCP, CB 1704–1793, HCA; Fed-

eralist Committee of Correspondence to Peter Van Gaasbeck, Apr. 13, 1792, PVGP, folder 3026, SHM; Jelles A. Fonda, testimony, Feb. 23, 1793 ("own hands"), New York (State), *Journal of the Assembly . . . Sixteenth Session*, 203.

19. Ebenezer Foote to Peter Van Gaasbeck, Apr. 3, 1792, PVGP, folder 2696, SHM.
20. Thomas Jefferson to James Monroe, June 23, 1792, in Julian P. Boyd, et al., eds., *The Papers of Thomas Jefferson*, 24 vols. to date (Princeton, 1950–), vol. 24, 114; Robert Troup to John Jay, May 20, 1792, in Johnston, *Correspondence . . . of John Jay*, vol. 3, 423–25; Mary-Jo Kline, ed., *Political Correspondence and Public Papers of Aaron Burr*, 2 vols. (Princeton, N.J., 1983), vol. 1, 106–108; Young, *Democratic Republicans of New York*, 307; Kaminski, *George Clinton*, 213; "A.B.," *New-York Journal*, May 30, 1792 ("shameful arts").
21. Cherry Valley Town Meeting, "Minute Book, 1791–1836," for Apr. 3, and 20, 1792, NYSHA; Samuel Crafts, affidavit, May 12, 1792, WCP, BB 1791–92, HCA; Jonathan Moffatt and William Beekman, affidavit, May 12, 1792, *Albany Gazette*, June 28, 1792; Richard R. Smith, affidavit, May 24, 1792, *Poughkeepsie Country Journal*, July 26, 1792; Otsego Judges and Supervisors ruling, May 1, 1792, WCP, BB 1791–92, HCA; William Cooper to Stephen Van Rensselaer, May 2, 1792, WCP, CB 1704–1793, HCA; "Veritas," and "B," *New-York Journal*, July 4 and 14, 1792.
22. Canvassers' report, June 15, 1792, in New York (State), *Journal of the Assembly . . . Sixteenth Session*, 91; Council of Appointment Records, vol. 2, 293 (Mar. 30, 1793), NYSA; Affidavits of Richard R. Smith and Benjamin Gilbert, both May 24, 1792, *Poughkeepsie Country Journal*, July 26, 1792; Smith, letter, July 4, 1792, in *Albany Gazette*, July 12, 1792; Smith, letter, Aug. 24, 1792, *New-York Journal*, Oct. 17, 1792; Kline, *Political Correspondence . . . of Aaron Burr*, vol. 1, 108.
23. Benjamin Griffin and Nathaniel Wattles, testimony, Dec. 29, 1792, New York (State), *Journal of the Assembly . . . Sixteenth Session*, 96–98; "Portius," "A.B.," and "A Traveller," *New-York Journal*, Aug. 11, Oct. 13, 1792, and Jan. 16, 1793.
24. Affidavits of Richard R. Smith and Benjamin Gilbert, both May 24, 1792, *Poughkeepsie Country Journal*, July 26, 1792; "Portius," and "A.B.," *New-York Journal*, Aug. 11, and Oct. 13, 1792; Smith, letter, Aug. 24, 1792, in ibid., Oct. 17, 1792 ("a matter").
25. Stephen Van Rensselaer to William Cooper, Apr. 30, 1792, WCP, CB 1704–1793, HCA; Van Rensselaer, certificate, Nov. 16, 1792, *Albany Gazette*, Dec. 10, 1792; Thomas Jefferson to James Monroe, June 23, 1792, in Boyd et al., *The Papers of Thomas Jefferson*, vol. 24, 114–15.
26. Kline, *Political Correspondence . . . of Aaron Burr*, vol. 1, 107–11; Thomas Tillotson to Robert R. Livingston, June 3 and 9, 1792, R. R. Livingston Papers, reel 5, NYHS; Robert Troup to John Jay, June 10, 1792, in Johnston, *Correspondence . . . of John Jay*, vol. 3, 427–30; Josiah O. Hoffman to Peter Van Schaack, June 26, 1792, Nicholas Low Papers, NYHS; John Addison to Ebenezer Foote, June 11, 1792, EFP, box 1, Firestone Lib., Princeton Univ.; J. Rutson Van Rensselaer to Peter Van Gaasbeck, June 14, 1792, PVGP, folder 2769, SHM.
27. Lewis A. Scott, testimony, Nov. 23, 1792, and Canvassers' report, June 15, 1792, in New York (State), *Journal of the Assembly . . . Sixteenth Session*, 23–24, 91–92; Young, *Democratic Republicans of New York*, 301–10; Jabez D. Hammond, *The History of Political Parties in the State of New-York . . .*, 2 vols. (Albany, 1842), vol. 1, 63–68; Kline, *Political Correspondence . . . of Aaron Burr*, vol. 1, 107–11; Kaminski, *George Clinton*, 212–13; "Sidney," *Albany Gazette*, Dec. 10, 1792.
28. Young, *Democratic Republicans of New York*, 310–12; Kaminski, *George Clinton*, 219; Sarah Livingston Jay to John Jay, June 11–12, 1792, in Johnston, *Correspondence . . . of John Jay*, vol. 3, 433; Josiah O. Hoffman to Peter Van Schaack, June 26, 1792, Nicholas Low Papers, NYHS; Cooper to [?], July 22, 1792, Document no. 777, NYSL; Ebenezer Foote to [?], June 27, 1792, in Katharine Adelia Foote, ed., *Ebenezer Foote, Founder* (Delhi, N.Y., 1927), 44; William Wheeler to Peter Van Gaasbeck, June 15, 1792, PVGP, folder 2769, SHM.
29. John Addison to Ebenezer Foote, June 11–14, 1792, EFP, box 1, Firestone Lib., Princeton Univ. ("Insult"); John Bogart to Peter Van Gaasbeck, June 21, 1792, PVGP, folder 2985,

SHM; Harold C. Syrett et al., *The Papers of Alexander Hamilton*, 27 vols. (New York, 1961–1987), vol. 12, 31 n. 11.

30. Peter Van Schaack to Theodore Sedgwick, June 19, 1792, Sedgwick Papers, box 2, Massachusetts Historical Society; Rufus King to Alexander Hamilton, July 10, 1792, and Hamilton to King, June 28, and July 25, 1792, in Syrett et al., *Papers of Alexander Hamilton*, vol. 11, 588–9, vol. 12, 20–21, 99–100; John Jay to Sarah Jay, June 18, 1792, in Johnston, *Correspondence . . . of John Jay*, vol. 3, 434–35; Kaminski, *George Clinton*, 225–26.

31. William Cooper to [?], July 22, 1792, doc. no. 777, NYSL; Cooper to Nicholas Low, Aug. 20, 1792, Nicholas Low Papers, NYHS; "A Republican," *New-York Journal*, July 21, 1792.

32. Cooper to Van Rensselaer, Oct. 7, 1792, and Van Rensselaer to Cooper, Oct. 12, 1792 ("Professions"), and Aug. 9, 1793 ("I regret"), WCP, CB 1704–1793, HCA.

33. Pierre Van Cortlandt, Jr., "Narrative respecting a Dispute between Mr. Thomas Tillotson and Stephen V. Rensselaer," [Nov. 11, 1792], in Jacob Judd, ed., *Correspondence of the Van Cortlandt Family of Cortlandt Manor, 1748–1800* (Tarrytown, N.Y., 1977), 527–30.

34. For the Clintonian version see Morgan Lewis to Robert R. Livingston, Jr., July 4, 1792, R. R. Livingston Papers, reel 5, NYHS; Albany meeting, July 19, *Albany Gazette*, July 23, 1792.

35. *New-York Journal*, June 16, 1792; "Lucius," "Veritas," and "A Republican," in ibid., June 30, July 4 and 14, 1792; "Lucius," *Albany Gazette*, Oct. 4, 1792; "Alpha," *Albany Register*, Dec. 17, 1792; Young, *Democratic Republicans of New York*, 315–18.

36. "The Art of Puffing Exemplified," *New-York Journal*, July 14, 1792; "Veritas," *New-York Journal*, July 4, 1792; Henry Parsons, *Parsons Family: Descendants of Cornet Joseph Parsons, Springfield, 1636–Northampton, 1655* (New York, 1912), 133–34; David P. Szatmary, *Shays's Rebellion: The Making of an Agrarian Insurrection* (Amherst, Mass., 1980), 102–7; Robert J. Taylor, *Western Massachusetts in the Revolution* (Providence, R.I., 1954), 160–63; Eli Parsons's proclamation, Feb. 13, 1787, *Albany Gazette*, Mar. 15, 1787. Although he had taken no part in the Regulation (having already settled in Newtown-Martin, near Cooperstown), Benjamin Gilbert, the new sheriff of Otsego County, remained a close friend of his fellow Revolutionary War veteran Capt. Daniel Shays. See Gilbert's Diary, Mar. 30–31, Sept. 25, 1785, NYSHA.

37. For Federalists and the Regulation ("Shays's Rebellion"), see Gordon S. Wood, *The Creation of the American Republic, 1776–1787* (Chapel Hill, N.C., 1969), 465–66. For Clinton's policies toward Vermont and the Regulation see Kaminski, *George Clinton*, 63–77, 107–9; George Clinton, proclamation, Feb. 24, 1787, *Albany Gazette*, Mar. 8, 1787; Benjamin Lincoln to Clinton, Mar. 29, 1787, ibid., Mar. 29, 1787. For Clinton's assistance to Schuyler against the tenants see Young, *Democratic Republicans of New York*, 204–7.

38. Josiah Ogden Hoffman to Stephen Van Rensselaer, June 24, 1792, Misc. Mss. V, NYHS; Affidavits of Jabez Hubbell, May 24, 1792, Ichabod B. Palmer, May 25, 1792, and Joseph Whitford, July 7, 1792, WCP, BB 1791–92, HCA; Affidavit of Palmer, Butler Gilbert, and Timothy Morse, May 29, 1792, *Poughkeepsie Country Journal*, July 26, 1792; John Hargrove, Jr., affidavit, June 6, 1792, *New-York Journal*, Aug. 4, 1792. For the Clintonians' further response see the affidavits of Joseph Hinds, Aug. 16, Jehiel Jackson, Aug. 17, James Butterfield, Aug. 17, and Gerret Staats, Aug. 18, 1792, *Albany Gazette*, Aug. 27, 1792.

39. William Wade, certificate, June 6, 1792, *New-York Journal*, Aug. 4, 1792; Richard R. Smith, letter, July 4, 1792, ibid. July 19, 1792; William Cooper, letter, Aug. 4, 1792 *Poughkeepsie Country Journal*, Sept. 5, 1792; Jacob Morris to Cooper, Jan. 27, 1793, Misc. Mss. M, NYSHA; Cooper et al., petition, Aug. 30, 1792, Council of Appointment Files (series A 1847), box 10, NYSA; Otsego Co. Address, June 30, *Poughkeepsie Country Journal*, July 12, 1792.

40. People v. Whitford, and People v. Cannan, Otsego County Grand Jury, Indictments, June 21, 1792, OCCO; OC-CGSP Records vol. 1, 7 (Jan. 8, 1793), OCCO. There were twenty members of the grand jury, of whom ten can be documented as Cooper's supporters, including the foreman, John Rice; only two grand jurors can be documented as Clintonians (John Campbell and William Dickson, both of Cherry Valley). Harper and McFarland, letter, Aug. 13, 1792, *New-York Journal*, Sept. 1, 1792; OC-CO&T, Minute Book, July 28, 1792,

June 6, 1793, OCCO; William Harper, letter, Aug. 27, 1792, *Albany Gazette,* Aug. 30, 1792. The last warns William Willcocks that Alexander Harper "would wring his snout, as it is said, he did Judge Cooper." From this I infer the assault on Cooper. For snouting see Kenneth S. Greenberg, "The Nose, the Lie, and the Duel in the Antebellum South," *American Historical Review,* 95 (Feb. 1990), 57–74.

41. For the grand jury action see William Cooper, letter, Aug. 4, 1792, *Poughkeepsie Country Journal,* Sept. 5, 1792 ("Although"); William Beekman to Judge Lansing, July 22, 1792 ("only"), *Albany Gazette,* Aug. 6, 1792; Beekman, testimony, Feb. 21, 1793, in New York (State), *Journal of the Assembly . . . Sixteenth Session,* 199. For the liberty pole see Anon. Otsego correspondent, in *Albany Gazette,* Aug. 6, 1792 ("without"); Edward Porter Alexander, "Judge Kent's 'Jaunt' to Cooperstown in 1792," *New York History,* 22 (Oct. 1941), 454. For the special election see Moss Kent, Jr., to James Kent, Sept. 30, 1792, JKP, reel 1, LC; Cooper to Peter Van Schaack, Oct. 1, 1792, WCP, CB 1704–1793, HCA; Jedediah Peck and Peter Lambert, certificate, Oct. 15, 1792, Misc. Mss. P, NYSHA; "An Elector," and "Viator," *Albany Gazette,* Oct. 15, Nov. 1, 1792.

42. Otsego Co. Address, June 30, *Poughkeepsie Country Journal,* July 12, 1792; William Cooper, draft, n.d., but on the reverse of Joseph Whitford, affidavit, July 7, 1792, WCP, BB 1791–92, HCA.

43. Cherry Valley Resolves, Aug. 31, 1792, and Harpersfield Resolves, Sept. 22, 1792, both in *Poughkeepsie Country Journal,* Sept. 26, Oct. 17, 1792.

44. Future Clintonians are conspicuous in the Susquehanna valley whig petitions from 1775 reprinted in Maryly B. Penrose, ed., *Mohawk Valley in the Revolution: Committee of Safety Papers and Genealogical Compendium* (Franklin Park, N.J., 1978), 155, 169. For the wartime sufferings of the future Clintonians see Duane Hamilton Hurd, *History of Otsego County, New York . . .* (Philadelphia, 1878), 192; and the listing of men who lost their farms in Montgomery Co. Conveyances, vol. 2, 287, Montgomery County Registry of Deeds. For their aggrieved sense of the continuing revolution see John Harper, letter, Apr. 12, 1794, in *Albany Register,* Apr. 28, 1794.

45. I garnered the names of Cooper's foes from the affidavits in *New-York Journal,* June 16, 1792; Cherry Valley meeting, Aug. 31, 1792, *Poughkeepsie Country Journal,* Sept. 26, 1792; Harpersfield meeting, Sept. 22, 1792, ibid., Oct. 17, 1792; Alexander Harper et al., petition, Jan. 1, 1793, WCP, BB 1792–93, HCA; and the testimony in New York (State), *Journal of the Assembly . . . Sixteenth Session,* 186–204. I gathered the names of Cooper's friends from *Journal of the Assembly, . . . Sixteenth Session,* 186–204; Cooperstown meetings, June 20 and 30, 1792, *New-York Journal,* June 30, and July 12, 1792; Peter Lambert et al., petition, n.d. [c. Feb. 1793], WCP, Misc. Legal and Land Papers box, HCA; Israel Guild et al., petition, n.d. [c. Feb. 1793], Council of Appointment Files (series A1847), box 12, NYSA. I linked the names to the following sources: William Cooper and Richard R. Smith, Store Books 1 (1790–91) and 2 (1791–92), WCP, HCA; U.S. Bureau of the Census, *Heads of Families at the First Census of the United States Taken in the Year 1790: New York* (Baltimore, 1966, reprint of Washington, D.C., 1908), 98–116; Tax Lists, Old England District (Otsego), Harpersfield, and Canajoharie (Cherry Valley), Montgomery Co., Oct. 1788, Gerrit Y. Lansing Papers, box 1, NYSL; and the pre-1795 conveyances and mortgages in OCRD, OCCO.

46. George Metcalf to Silas Talbot, Jan. 27, 1793, STP, box 3, GWBWL-MS. For the ideal of community unity and the power of ethnic identity in eighteenth-century politics see Patricia U. Bonomi, *A Factious People: Politics and Society in Colonial New York* (New York, 1971); Edward M. Cook, Jr., *The Fathers of the Towns: Leadership and Community Structure in Eighteenth-Century New England* (Baltimore, 1976); Robert A. Gross, *The Minutemen and the World* (New York, 1976).

47. William Cooper and Richard R. Smith, Store Books 1 (1790–91), and 2 (1791–92), WCP, HCA; Mortgage Books, OCRD, OCCO; The statistics refer to the 189 men known to have supported Cooper in 1792–93. Many men who had bought land or who enjoyed store credit appeared in neither camp. For example, 82 men who had bought Cooper's land

and who had settled in Otsego do not appear in the sources listing his friends and foes. But because only a few of the relevant petitions survive, it is not safe to assume that those men remained neutral.

48. Dixon Ryan Fox, *The Decline of Aristocracy in the Politics of New York, 1801–1840* (New York, 1965), 140–41; Kaminski, *George Clinton*, 212; David Hackett Fischer, *The Revolution of American Conservatism: The Federalist Party in the Era of Jeffersonian Democracy* (New York, 1965), 15–16.

49. Otsego County meeting, Nov. 25, 1794, *Albany Gazette*, Dec. 6, 1794.

50. William Beekman, grand jury foreman, to Judge Lansing, July 22, 1792, *Albany Gazette*, Aug. 6, 1792. Cooper made the same point in his letter of Aug. 4, 1792, in *Poughkeepsie Country Journal*, Sept. 5, 1792.

51. OC-CCP, Judgments Book, 1792–1809, OCCO.

52. James Fenimore Cooper, *The Pioneers, or the Sources of the Susquehanna; A Descriptive Tale*, ed. James Franklin Beard (Albany, 1980, crit. ed. of New York, 1823), 122, 225. For Temple's weakness see Robert Clark, *History and Myth in American Fiction, 1823–1852* (New York, 1984), 73–76; William P. Kelly, *Plotting America's Past: Fenimore Cooper and the Leatherstocking Tales* (Carbondale, Ill., 1983), 1–2, 16–25; Geoffrey Rans, *Cooper's Leather-Stocking Novels: A Secular Reading* (Chapel Hill, 1991), 63, 79–91.

53. For the plans see William Cooper to Peter Van Schaack, Oct. 1, 1792, and Cooper to Stephen Van Rensselaer, Oct. 7 ("Pompous Parade") and 12, 1792, all in WCP, CB 1704–1793, HCA. For declining Federalist ardor see Loring Andrews to Van Schaack, Oct. 9, 1792, Peter Van Schaack Papers, LC; Van Rensselaer to Cooper, Oct. 12, 1792, WCP, CB 1704–1792, HCA; Van Schaack to Theodore Sedgwick, Nov. 3, and Nov. 20, 1792, Sedgwick Papers, box 2, Massachusetts Historical Society. For the Clintonian victory see Young, *Democratic Republicans of New York*, 318–21; Kline, *Political Correspondence . . . of Aaron Burr*, vol. 1, 116; New York (State), *Journal of the Assembly . . . Sixteenth Session*, 91–92, 96–98, 102, 121.

54. New York (State), *Journal of the Assembly . . . Sixteenth Session*, 109, 140–41, 145–46, 150, 155–56; Alexander Harper et al., petition, Jan. 1, 1793, WCP, BB 1792–93, HCA; Jacob Morris to William Cooper, Jan. 21, 1793, WCP, CB 1704–1793, HCA; Morris to Cooper, Jan. 27, 1793, Misc. Mss. M, NYSHA; James Kent to Moss Kent, Jr., Jan. 27, 1793, JKP, reel 1, LC.

55. Josiah O. Hoffman to William Cooper, Jan. 28, 1793, WCP, CB 1704–1793, HCA; Jacob Morris to Cooper, Jan. 27, 1793, Misc. Mss. M, NYSHA; Wayne Wright, "The Cooper Genealogy: Compiled from Materials in the Collection of the New York State Historical Association Library" (typescript, NYSHA), 9.

56. Stephen Van Rensselaer to William Cooper, n.d. [Jan. 1793], WCP, Undated Letters box, HCA.

57. Benjamin Gilbert to William Cooper, Feb. 4, 1793, WCP, CB 1704–1793, HCA; Springfield Patent, resolves, Feb. 4, 1793, *Albany Gazette*, Feb. 11, 1793; New York (State), *Journal of the Assembly . . . Sixteenth Session*, 186–87.

58. Young, *Democratic Republicans of New York*, 321–22; Hammond, *History of Political Parties in . . . New York*, vol. 1, 82; New York (State), *Journal of the Assembly . . . Sixteenth Session*, 189–204; "B," *New-York Journal*, July 14, 1792; John Addison to Cornelius Elmendorph, Feb. 27, 1793, PVGP, folder 2997, SHM; James Kent to Moss Kent, Jr., Mar. 4, 1793, JKP, reel 1, LC; James Cochran to William Cooper, Mar. 22, 1793, and John B. Schuyler to Cooper, Apr. 1, 1793, WCP, CB 1704–1793, HCA.

59. Andrew Cannan et al., petition, Feb. 18, 1793, Council of Appointment Files (series A 1847), box 12, NYSA; Hammond, *History of Political Parties in . . . New York*, vol. 1, 83. For the futile efforts by the Otsego Federalists to save Gilbert, see Peter Lambert et al., petition, n.d. [c. Feb. 1793], WCP, Misc. Legal and Land Papers box, HCA.

60. New York (State), *Journal of the Assembly . . . Sixteenth Session*, 246; Young, *Democratic Republicans of New York*, 322–23; Kline, *Political Correspondence . . . of Aaron Burr*, vol. 1, 117; Hammond, *History of Political Parties in . . . New York*, vol. 1, 78; Stephen Van Rensselaer to

William Cooper, May 17, 1793, WCP, CB 1704–1793, HCA; *Daily Advertiser* (New York City), Feb. 21, 1794.

61. Hugh M. Flick, "The Council of Appointment of New York (State): The First Attempt to Regulate Political Patronage, 1777–1822," *New York History*, 15 (July 1934), 263–64; Philip Schuyler to Peter Van Gaasbeck, Feb. 28, 1793 ("Machine"), PVGP, folder 2836, SHM; Young, *Democratic Republicans of New York*, 537; Hammond, *History of Political Parties in . . . New York*, vol. 1, 83–85; Peter Roggen to Van Gaasbeck, Jan. 22, 1794, and John Addison to Van Gaasbeck, Feb. 15, 1794, PVGP, folders 2626, and 2997, SHM.

62. Otsego Co. Meeting, Dec. 21, 1793, Jacob Morris Papers, NYSHA; William Cooper to Benjamin Gilbert, Mar. 8, 1794, Philip Schuyler to Cooper, Mar. 8, 1794, and Cooper to the Council of Appointment, Mar. 9, 1794, WCP, CB 1704–1793, HCA; Council of Appointment, Records (series A 1845), vol. 3, 83 (Mar. 7, 1794), NYSA.

63. William Willcocks to William Cooper, Sept. 1, 1793, WCP, CB 1704–1793, HCA; George Clinton v. William Cooper, SCJ Judgment Roll 21-l-8 (Apr. 21, 1794), and Nisi Prius Court Record Book, p. 351, Harper v. Cooper, SCJ Judgment Roll 67-B-4 (July 27, 1795), Cooper v. Harper, SCJ Judgment Roll 159-H-5 (Oct. 24, 1795), Hudson v. Cooper, SCJ Pleading C-182 (June 6, 1793), H-410 (Nov. 1, 1793), Cannan v. Cooper, SCJ Pleading C-228 (June 6, 1793), all SCJ Files, NYCHR; [New York City] *Columbian Gazetteer*, Nov. 18, 1793; Alexander Harper to John McKesson, July 5, 1794, McKesson Papers, box 1, NYHS; *Otsego Herald*, Oct. 16, 1795. For Cooper's payment to Clinton see Brockholst Livingston, as attorney for Clinton, receipt, Nov. 27, 1795, WCP, BB 1795, HCA. For Harper's payment to Cooper see Cooper, Memorandum Book, Jan. 16, 1796, WCP, HCA; Moss Kent, Jr., to Cooper, Feb. 1, 1796, WCP, CB 1794–1796, HCA.

64. Stephen Van Rensselaer to William Cooper, Jan. 13, 1793, WCP, CB 1704–1793, HCA; George Metcalf to Silas Talbot, Feb. 2, 1793, STP, box 3, GWBWL, MS; Jacob G. Fonda, letter, Jan. 24, 1793, *Albany Register*, Feb. 4, 1793 ("I would advise").

65. George Metcalf to Silas Talbot, Feb. 2, 1793, STP, box 3, GWBWL, MS; Johnstown meeting, Nov. 10, 1792, *Albany Gazette*, Nov. 19, 1792; Cherry Valley meeting, Dec. 24, 1792, and Canajohary meeting, Dec. 26, 1792, *Albany Register*, Dec. 31, 1792; Eli Parsons to Cooper, Jan. 25, 1793, WCP, CB 1704–1793, HCA. For the election returns see *New-York Journal*, Mar. 2, 1793; Young, *Democratic Republicans of New York*, 592. For Winn's life see Maryly B. Penrose, ed., *The Mohawk Valley in the Revolution: Committee of Safety Papers and Genealogical Compendium* (Franklin Park, N.J., 1978), 351. For Talbot's life see Charles G. Paulin, "Silas Talbot," in *Dictionary of American Biography*, vol. 18, 280; Charles R. Schultz, ed., *Inventory of the Silas Talbot Papers, 1767–1867* (Mystic, Conn., 1965), 1–7.

66. "A Correspondent," *Albany Register*, Nov. 10, 1794 ("Let not"); Otsego County meeting, Nov. 25, 1794, *Albany Gazette*, Dec. 6, 1794 ("train"); Young, *Democratic Republicans of New York*, 592.

67. William B. Fink, "Stephen Van Rensselaer: The Last Patroon," (Ph.D. diss., Columbia Univ., 1950), 67; *Otsego Herald*, June 19, 1795; Gaylord Griswold to William Cooper, Aug. 20, 1795, WCP, CB 1794–1796, HCA.

68. For the dinner invitations see George Washington to William Cooper, Feb. 25, 1796, WCP, CB 1794–1796, HCA; Washington to Cooper, Nov. 26, 1796, in James Fenimore Cooper (1858–1938), ed., "Correspondence of Judge William Cooper" (copy in James Franklin Beard Papers, AAS), 20.

69. William Cooper to Richard Harrison, Sept. 10, 1795, WCP, CB 1794–1796, HCA; Stephen Van Rensselaer to Cooper, Feb. 12, 1796, WCP, CB 1794–1796, HCA; Alexander Hamilton to Rufus King, Apr. 15, 1796, in Syrett et al., *Papers of Alexander Hamilton*, vol. 20, 114. According to an analysis of congressional voting, Cooper was an especially partisan Federalist who, during his two terms, voted with his party on 39 of 40 key votes. See Manning J. Dauer, *The Adams Federalists* (Baltimore, 1953), 291.

70. Young, *Democratic Republicans of New York*, 389–91; Rufus King to William Cooper, Mar. 10, 1794, WCP, CB 1794–1796, HCA; Cooper to King, Apr. 17, 1794, Rufus King Papers, CB 1793–1794, NYHS; *Otsego Herald*, May 12, June 16, 1796; Cooper, speeches, Mar. 14 and

Apr. 20, 1796, in [U.S. Congress], *The Debates and Proceedings in the Congress of the United States . . .* , 42 vols. (Washington, D.C., 1834–1856), 4th Congress, 1st session, 541–42; Cooper to Cashier of the Albany Bank, Apr. 13, 1796, Dreer Autograph Coll., III, 45, HSP.

71. Stephen Van Rensselaer to William Cooper, Mar. 21, 1796, Josiah O. Hoffman to Cooper, Mar. 29, 1796, and Robert Troup to Cooper, Apr. 2, 1796, all in WCP, CB 1794–1796, HCA; Ambrose Spencer to Cooper, Mar. 22, [1796], WCP, Undated Letters box, HCA.

72. For his style see the William Cooper quotation in "Diogenes," *Whitestown Gazette,* Dec. 6, 1796; Cooper, speech, Jan. 13, 1797, in [U.S. Congress], *Debates and Proceedings,* 4th Congress, 2nd session, 1864–65; Cooper, "Speech on the Report of the Committee of Ways and Means," *Otsego Herald,* Jan. 26, 1797. For his dispute with Edward Livingston see [U.S. Congress], *Debates and Proceedings,* 4th Congress, 1st session, 949 (Apr. 13, 1796).

8. THE VILLAGE

1. James Fenimore Cooper, *The Pioneers, or the Sources of the Susquehanna; A Descriptive Tale,* ed. James Franklin Beard (Albany, 1980, crit. ed. of New York, 1823), 41–42, 45, 58–59, 146, 183; James Fenimore Cooper, *Notions of the Americans, Picked Up by a Travelling Bachelor,* 2 vols. (New York, 1963, repr. of New York, 1828), vol. 1, 254. Early deeds to Cooperstown lots confirm that painted houses were so uncommon that they were known by their color; James White's house was "commonly known as the yellow house," and Lewis De Villers owned "the red house." See Otsego Conveyances, B:46 (Oct. 8, 1795), B:231 (Aug. 24, 1796), OCRD.

2. William Cooper, Land Book, 21, WCP, HCA; Daniel Smith, Map of Cooperstown, Sept. 26, 1788, WCP, HCA; James Fenimore Cooper, *Chronicles of Cooperstown (1838),* reprinted in Shaw T. Livermore, ed., *A Condensed History of Cooperstown* (Albany, 1862), 26–27; J. F. Cooper, *Pioneers,* 183. In *Chronicles of Cooperstown,* James Fenimore Cooper mistakenly attributed the map to William Ellison. Cooper and Craig rewarded Smith with a town lot valued at £5. See Cooper and Andrew Craig to Daniel Smith, Deed, Mar. 10, 1789, Oversized, WCP, HCA. For frontier promoters' use of maps to impose visions of hierarchy see Gregory H. Nobles, "Straight Lines and Stability: Mapping the Political Order of the Anglo-American Frontier," *Journal of American History,* 80 (June 1993), 9–35.

3. William Cooper, *A Guide in the Wilderness; or, the History of the First Settlements in the Western Counties of New York, with Useful Instructions to Future Settlers . . .* (Cooperstown, 1986, repr. of Dublin, 1810), 26.

4. Ibid., 26–27, 30.

5. Ibid., 27.

6. Ibid., 28.

7. Daniel Smith, Map of Cooperstown, Sept. 26, 1788, WCP, HCA; J. F. Cooper, *Chronicles of Cooperstown,* 26–27.

8. Moss Kent, Jr., to William Cooper, Feb. 1, 1796, Samuel Huntington to Cooper, Feb. 23, 1796, WCP, CB 1794–1796, HCA; Griffin v. Huntington, June 22, 1797, and Cooper v. Huntington, Jan. 1799, OC-CCP Judgments Book, 1793–1809, OCCO; Benjamin Gilbert, sheriff's notice, and Huntington, insolvent's petition, *Otsego Herald,* Nov. 30, 1797, and Apr. 24, 1800.

9. Elihu Phinney to William Cooper, Jan. 4, 1796, WCP, CB 1794–1796, HCA; Cooper and Luke Flint, memorandum of agreement, Mar. 20, 1794, WCP, Memorandum Book, HCA.

10. Thomas Nicholson, Jr., to Moses DeWitt, June 12, 1791, DeWitt Family Papers, box 2, Arents Research Lib., Syracuse Univ.; Jonas Platt to James Kent, Dec. 13, 1796, JKP, reel 1, LC. For the meaning of the Revolution see Joyce Appleby, "The Social Origins of American Revolutionary Ideology," *Journal of American History,* 64 (Dec. 1978), 935–58. For frontier migration and settlement see Peter C. Mancall, *Valley of Opportunity: Economic Culture along the Upper Susquehanna, 1700–1800* (Ithaca, N.Y., 1991), 160–216.

11. Alexander Coventry, *Memoirs of an Emigrant: The Journal of Alexander Coventry, M.D.,* 2 vols. (Albany, 1978) vol. 1, 556; James Fenimore Cooper (1858–1938), *The Legends and Traditions of a Northern County* (New York, 1921), 27–28. The only two references to Powers in

William Cooper and Richard R. Smith, Store Book 1 (1790–91) are occasions when other men permitted him to draw on their credit for very small amounts (9s and 6d respectively).

12. Charles Powers, confession, Oct. 8, 1791, WCP, CB 1704–1793, HCA.

13. W. Cooper, *Guide in the Wilderness*, 28–29 ("a quicker"); [William Cooper], "A Friend to Order," *Otsego Herald*, May 5, 1796; Henry Farnsworth, *An Oration on Music Delivered at the Courthouse in Cooperstown, in Otsego; April 1794 at the Conclusion of a Singing School* (Cooperstown, 1795, Evans no. 28650), 6; "A Farmer," *Otsego Herald*, Nov. 12, 1795. For the widespread efforts to gentrify villages in the early Republic see Richard L. Bushman, *The Refinement of America: Persons, Houses, Cities* (New York, 1992), 370–82.

14. Elihu Phinney to William Cooper, Aug. 1, 1794, WCP, CB 1794–1796, HCA; Madeleine B. Stern, "Books in the Wilderness," *New York History*, 31 (July 1950), 262–64; Elihu Phinney, "To the Public," *Otsego Herald*, Apr. 3, 1795; Clarence S. Brigham, *History and Bibliography of American Newspapers, 1690–1820*, 2 vols. (Worcester, Mass., 1947), vol. 1, 559; Advertisements, *Otsego Herald*, Feb. 16, 1797, and June 24, 1802.

15. Elihu Phinney, "To the Public," *Otsego Herald*, Apr. 3, 1795; Phinney to William Cooper, Apr. 7, 1796, WCP, CB 1796–1798, HCA; *Otsego Herald*, Apr. 7, 1796; Council of Appointment, Records, III, 201 (Mar. 8, 1796), IV, 57 (Mar. 27, 1798), NYSA.

16. Elihu Phinney to John Adams, July 21, 1809, Adams Papers, reel 407, MHS; Phinney poem quoted in Ralph Birdsall, *The Story of Cooperstown* (Cooperstown, 1917), 147; Kathryn Klim Sturrock, "The Phinneys of Cooperstown, 1795–1850" (Master's thesis, SUNY at Oneonta, 1972, NYSHA copy), 2.

17. "To the Public," *Otsego Herald*, June 5, 1795. For the growing importance of voluntary associations as the building blocks of the American social order see Richard D. Brown, "The Emergence of Urban Society in Rural Massachusetts, 1760–1820," *Journal of American History*, 61 (1974–1975), 29–51; Robert A. Gross, *The Minutemen and Their World* (New York, 1976), 173–76; Don Harrison Doyle, *The Social Order of a Frontier Community: Jacksonville, Illinois, 1825–70* (Urbana, Ill., 1983), 156–93.

18. Otsego Academy, subscription list, Apr. 5, 1795, NYSHA. Self-interest also figured in the especially prominent pledges of innkeepers, for an academy promised to bring an increased number of lodgers to Cooperstown.

19. "Anticipation," *Otsego Herald*, Nov. 10, 1796; *Otsego Herald*, Dec. 28, 1797.

20. Conveyances, A:257 (Mar. 7, 1794), OCRD; Robert Troup to William Cooper, June 10, 1800, WCP, HCA; *Otsego Herald*, May 8 ("patriotic"), Oct. 9 ("merry"), and Oct. 30, 1795; Moss Kent to Cooper, Dec. 28, 1795, Apr. 7, 1796, and Samuel Huntington to Cooper, Feb. 23, 1796, WCP, CB 1794–1796, HCA; Stephen Mack to Cooper, Dec. 5, 1796, WCP, CB 1796–1798, HCA. "A Friend to Sobriety," *Burlington [N.J.] Advertiser*, Apr. 27, 1790, made the enlightened case for beer.

21. Abraham C. Ten Broeck to John Sanders, Mar. 16, 1792, Misc. Mss. T, NYHS; Cooperstown Lib., subscription list, 1794, NYSHA; *Otsego Herald*, May 8, 1795, Dec. 15, 1796, Jan. 5, Mar. 9, 1797.

22. "Academy," *Otsego Herald*, May 8, 1795; Otsego Academy, subscription list, Apr. 5, 1795, NYSHA; J. F. Cooper, *Chronicles of Cooperstown*, 19; Jacob Morris et al., petition, n.d. [c. 1795], Cooperstown Coll., box 1, NYSHA; *Otsego Herald*, May 22, 1795, Mar. 24, Aug. 25, 1796; Trustees of Otsego Academy to James Averell, Thomas Fuller, and Norman Landon, Oct. 22, 1796, Conveyances B:298, OCRD; Board of Regents, *Journal of Meetings*, II, 174 (Mar. 5, 1798); J. F. Cooper, *Pioneers*, 99 ("concluded").

23. Otsego Academy, subscription list, Apr. 5, 1795, NYSHA; J. F. Cooper, *Chronicles of Cooperstown*, 19; "Prosper Thrifty," *Otsego Herald*, May 15, 1795. Twenty-three of the 42 subscribers lived in the village, and only 8 lived beyond Otsego Township.

24. Livermore, *Condensed History of Cooperstown*, 108, 196; Trustees of Cherry Valley Academy to the executors of the will of Rev. John Christopher Hartwick, Sept. 29, 1797, Misc. Mss. H, NYHS; J. F. Cooper, *Chronicles of Cooperstown*, 19; J. F. Cooper, *Pioneers*, 99–101. Cooper later explained that he drew upon the Cherry Valley Academy for the particular excesses of decoration ascribed to the Templeton Academy. He said that his description of Tem-

pleton's Academy "might *generally*, but would not *particularly* apply" to the academy in Cooperstown. See James Fenimore Cooper to Horatio Hastings Weld [for the *Brother Jonathan*], Mar. 22–25, 1842, in James Franklin Beard, ed., *The Letters and Journals of James Fenimore Cooper*, 6 vols. (Cambridge, Mass., 1960–1968), vol. 4, 260. Cooper's description of the interior follows that of the academy in Cooperstown rather than that of Cherry Valley.

25. William G. Peacher, "Craft Masonry in Columbia County, New York, 1787–1826," American Lodge of Research of Free and Accepted Masons, *Transactions*, 13 (Jan. 1977), 332; "Masonic Information," *Otsego Herald*, Feb. 25, 1796; Otsego Lodge, Minute Book 1, Mar. 1, 1796, Otsego Lodge, Cooperstown; Elihu Phinney to William Cooper, Mar. 24, 1796, WCP, CB 1794–1796, HCA. The men who joined the Otsego Lodge in 1796 and 1797 included 16 academy subscribers and 4 library subscribers. At least 9 members belonged to all three: William Abbott, James Averell, Jr., Benjamin Gilbert, Joseph Griffin, Francis Hentry, John Howard, Samuel Huntington, Uriah Luce, and Jacob Morris. I culled the members' names from Otsego Lodge, Minute Book 1, Otsego Lodge. For the new hall see *Otsego Herald*, June 29, 1797; Otsego Lodge, Minute Book 1, Mar. 1, Dec. 27, 1796, Mar. 7, June 7, Dec. 25, 1797, June 4, 1798, Otsego Lodge; Jacob Morris to William Cooper, Jan. 2, 1796 [*sic*, should be 1797], WCP, CB 1794–1796, HCA; John Camp, *A Sermon Delivered at the Academy in Cooperstown on the 27 of December 1796, Before the Members of Otsego Lodge*, (Cooperstown, 1797, Evans no. 31910), 13; Allen E. Dages, "The Old Masonic Hall: Cooperstown, New York" (Master's thesis, SUNY at Oneonta, 1975, NYSHA copy), 11–18; Cooper to Otsego Lodge, Deed, Conveyances S:43, OCRD, OCCO.

26. Otsego Lodge, Minute Book 1, esp. Aug. 16 (certificates), Sept. 6, 1796 (loans), Oct. 4, 1796 (money spent), June 7, 1797 (admitting new members), Nov. 5, 1799 (discharge), Otsego Lodge; Bushman, *Refinement of America*, 207–9.

27. Charles T. McClenachan, *History of New York Free Masons*, 2 vols. (New York, 1892), vol. 2, 133–35; Steven C. Bullock, "The Revolutionary Transformation of American Freemasonry, 1752–1792," *WMQ*, 3d ser., 47 (July 1990), 347–69; Bullock, "A Pure and Sublime System: The Appeal of Post-Revolutionary Freemasonry," *Journal of the Early Republic*, 9 (Fall 1989), 359–74.

28. Bullock, "Pure and Sublime System," 359–74; Kathleen Smith Kutolowski, "Freemasonry and Community in the Early Republic: The Case for Antimasonic Anxieties," *American Quarterly*, 34 (Winter 1982), 548–49; "Social Influence of Free Masonry," *Whitestown Gazette*, Sept. 27, 1796 ("to unite"); Camp, *A Sermon Delivered at the Academy in Cooperstown*, 12. For Phinney's song see *Otsego Herald*, June 29, 1797.

29. For disciplinary cases see Otsego Lodge, Minute Book 1, Dec. 6, 1796, Dec. 4, 1798, Apr. 9, May 5, 1801, Otsego Lodge. Kutolowski, "Freemasonry and Community," 543–61; Seth Williston, "Diaries of Reverend Seth Williston, D.D., 1796–1800," Presbyterian Hist. Soc., *Journal*, 7 (1913–14), 182 (July 16–17, 1796); [Elihu Phinney], "Modern Quack Preaching," *Otsego Herald*, Mar. 22, 1798, June 30, 1800; John Frederick Ernst, *Oration with Suitable Prayers, Delivered Before the Grand Royal-Arch Chapter for the State of New York* (Albany, 1800, Shaw-Shoemaker no. 37378), 12 ("nightly revels"). I culled the local Freemasons from the Otsego Lodge Minute Books, 1 and 2, Otsego Lodge; and the church members from Cooperstown Presbyterian Church, Session Records, 1800–1810, NYSHA.

30. *Otsego Herald*, May 8, July 10, 1795; W. Cooper, *Guide in the Wilderness*, 52–53; John McDonald, *The Duty of America Enforced: An Exhortation Delivered at Cooperstown, on the Evening of the National Fast, April 25th, 1799* (Cooperstown, 1799, Evans no. 35757), 6, 13, 15, 20; Philip Wager and Jonathan Newman quoted in George Peck, *Early Methodism Within the Bounds of the Old Genesee Conference From 1788 to 1828* (New York, 1860), 175 ("the people"). My calculations are based on Methodist Episcopal Church, *Journals of the General Conference of the Methodist Episcopal Church, 1796–1836*, 3 vols. (New York, 1855), vol. 1, 42–61; Stephen R. Smith, *Historical Sketches and Incidents Illustrative* (Buffalo, 1843), 89, 99; Ashbel Hosmer, *A View of the Rise and Increase of the Churches Composing the Otsego Baptist Association* (Whitestown, N.Y., 1800, AAS copy), 8, 34–35; George E. DeMille, *A History of the*

Diocese of Albany, 1704–1923 (Philadelphia, 1946), 34; DeMille, *Christ Church, Cooperstown, New York, 1810–1960* (Cooperstown, 1960), 10. For the census totals for Otsego see *Otsego Herald,* Dec. 17, 1795. My calculations omit the four towns of Dorlach, Franklin, Harpersfield, and Kortright, which would be set off into the new counties of Schoharie and Delaware in 1796–97. The evidence suggests 299 Methodists, 261 Baptists, 60 Episcopalians, and 400 Congregational/Presbyterians, for a total of about 1,020 religious members: 22 percent of the adults in Otsego (2,276 families X 2 = 4,552).

31. William Cooper to Henry Drinker, June 2, 1789, HDP, CB 1741–1792, HSP; "A New-England Man," *Whitestown Gazette,* Dec. 13, 1796.

32. "Many" and [Elihu Phinney], "Harmony," *Otsego Herald,* Aug. 28, Oct. 30, 1795; John McDonald to the First Presbyterian Church of Albany, Mar. 19, 1799, Session Records, 1795–1808, entry for Mar. 24, 1799, First Presbyterian Church of Albany; John F. Ernst to William Cooper et al., Apr. 26, 1799, JCHP, HCA; Henry N. Pohlman, ed., *Memorial Volume of the Semi-Centennial Anniversary of Hartwick Seminary, Held August 21, 1866* (Albany, 1867), 27–29, 156–64; Cooper et al. to Jeremiah Van Rensselaer and Frederick A. C. Muhlenberg, Sept. 14, 1797, JCHP, HCA; Cooper to Muhlenberg, Nov. 19, 1797, WCP, CB 1796–1798, HCA.

33. Records of the Executors of the Will of John Christopher Hartwick, Sept. 20, 1797, Lutheran Archives Center, Mount Airy, Pa.; Jeremiah Van Rensselaer to John Cox, July 22, 1796, JCHP, HCA; *Otsego Herald,* Aug. 11, 1796; Charles H. Glatfelter, *Pastors and People: German Lutheran and Reformed Churches in the Pennsylvania Field, 1717–1793,* 2 vols. (Breinigsville, Pa., 1980), vol. 1, 36–37.

34. Henry Melchior Muhlenberg, *The Journal of Henry Melchior Muhlenberg,* trans. Theodore G. Tappert and John W. Doberstein, 3 vols. (Philadelphia, 1942–1958), vol. 3, 291 (Jan. 24, 1780), 335 (July 31, 1780); Glatfelter, *Pastors and People,* vol. 1, 36–37; Edith Von Zemensky, ed., "A Letter from Pastor Johann Friedrich Ernst," *Pennsylvania Folklife,* 26 (Summer 1977), 33–45.

35. Muhlenberg, *Journals,* vol. 3, 335 (July 31, 1780); Glatfelter, *Pastors and People,* vol. 1, 36–37; John Frederick Ernst, "Account of His Removal from Pennsylvania to New York, in November of 1791," *PMHB,* 42 (1918), 172–73; John Frederick Ernst, *An Account of the Performances at the Dedication of Mason-Hall, Hudson, on the Festival of St. John the Evangelist* (Hudson, N.Y., 1797, Evans no. 32287), 6; Ernst to John Arndt, Aug. 24, 1797, Lutheran Archives Center, Mount Airy, Pa. (all quotations); *Documentary History of the Evangelical Lutheran Ministerium of Pennsylvania: Proceedings of the Annual Conventions From 1748 to 1821* (Philadelphia, 1898), 292; Ernst v. Bartle et al., in William Johnson, ed., *Reports of Cases Adjudged in the Supreme Court of Judicature of the State of New-York; From January Term 1799 to January Term 1803,* 3 vols. (New York, 1808–1812, Shaw-Shoemaker no. 15759), vol. 1, 319–26.

36. Hartwick executors, Resolves, Sept. 20, 1797, JCHP, HCA; Ernst v. Bartle et al., in Johnson, *Reports of Cases,* vol. 1, 319–26.

37. Thomas Loomis et al. to John Frederick Ernst, Nov. 20, 1797, JCHP, HCA.

38. Pohlman, *Memorial Volume . . . of Hartwick Seminary,* 27–29, 156–64; William Cooper et al. to Jeremiah Van Rensselaer and Frederick A. C. Muhlenberg, Sept. 14, 1797, JCHP, HCA; Cooper to Muhlenberg, Nov. 19, 1797, WCP, CB 1796–1798, HCA; John Frederick Ernst to Cooper et al. Apr. 26, 1799, JCHP, HCA; Cooper, certificate, Aug. 15, 1799, McAllister Coll., LCP ("instantly gave").

39. Cooperstown Subscription, Dec. 25, 1797, JCHP, HCA; John Frederick Ernst to William Cooper, Dec. 1, 1797, Apr. 23, 1798, WCP, CB 1796–1798, HCA; Ernst, "Outlines of a Plan," Jan. 8, 1798, JCHP, HCA. For the settler reaction see William Cummings to Rev. John C. Kunze, May 24, 1798 ("to mock us"), Hartwick Patent Petition to the Hartwick executors, Aug. 16, 1798, and Ernst to Kunze, Oct. 18, 1798, JCHP, HCA.

40. Trustees of Otsego Academy to John Frederick Ernst, May 8, 1798, McAllister Coll., LCP; Trustees of Otsego Academy, resolve, May 28, 1798, JCHP, HCA; Ernst to Rev. John C. Kunze, July 3, 1798, JCHP, HCA.

41. Richard A. Harrison, *Princetonians: 1776–1783: A Biographical Dictionary* (Princeton, N.J.,

1981), 230; *New Jersey Gazette,* Oct. 10, 1785; J. McCluskey Blayney, *A History of the First Pres-byterian Church of Albany, New York* (Albany, 1877), 18–20; [McDonald], Session Records, 1786–1783, Albany First Presbyterian Church. McDonald described his education in Mc-Donald to the First Presbyterian Church, Mar. 19, 1800, Session Records, 1795–1808, pp. 91–92 (Mar. 24, 1800), First Presbyterian Church, Albany; and McDonald, "To the Friends of Religion, Letter I," *Albany Register,* Dec. 2, 1800.

42. Joel Munsell, *Collections on the History of Albany,* 4 vols. (Albany, 1865–1872), vol. 1, 419 (quotations); *Albany Gazette,* June 4, 1792. In 1794 McDonald visited Otsego; see Pres-bytery of Albany, Records, I, 133 (Aug. 21, 1794), PHS.

43. Presbytery of Albany, Records, I, 2 (Mar. 2, 1791), PHS; John McDonald, "To the Friends of Religion, Letter I," *Albany Register,* Dec. 2, 1800; Jonas Coe, letter, Nov. 28, 1800, *Albany Register,* Dec. 16, 1800; Ernst, *Account of the Performances,* 46.

44. John McDonald to Eliza McDonald, Aug. 6, 1794, Simon Gratz Coll., McDonald file, HSP; Presbytery of Albany, Records, I, 245 (Feb. 23, 1797), PHS; John McDonald, "To the Friends of Religion, Letter II," *Albany Register,* Dec. 5, 1800; Jonas Coe, "To the Public," *Albany Centinel,* Dec. 16, 1800 ("strange").

45. Rev. John Blair Smith to Rev. Ashbel Green, Dec. 19, 1795, Simon Gratz Coll., Smith file, HSP (quotation); Peacher, "Craft Masonry in Columbia County," 323; Stephen Bielinski, comp., Peter W. Yates File, Colonial Albany Social History Project, NYSL; John McDonald to Green, Feb. 9, 1796, Simon Gratz Coll., McDonald file, HSP.

46. Alexander Miller and Jonas Coe, "History of the Presbytery of Albany, 1790–1802," Pres-byterian Hist. Soc., *Journal,* 3 (Mar. 1906), 228; Session Records, 1795–1808, p. 1 (Sept. 11, 1795), Albany First Presbyterian Church; Presbytery of Albany, Records, I, 166–68 (Sept. 24, 1795), PHS, McDonald to the Presbytery of Albany, Sept. 24, 1795, Simon Gratz Coll., McDonald File, HSP.

47. Rev. John Blair Smith to Rev. Ashbel Green, Nov. 24, Dec. 19 (quotations), 1795, Simon Gratz Coll., Smith File, HSP.

48. Rev. John Blair Smith to Rev. Ashbel Green, Feb. 9, 1796, Simon Gratz Coll., Smith File, HSP.

49. John McDonald to Rev. Ashbel Green, Feb. 9, 1796, Gratz Coll., McDonald file, HSP.

50. Rev. John Blair Smith to Rev. Ashbel Green, Feb. 9 and 18, 1796, Simon Gratz Coll., Smith file, HSP; Miller and Coe, "History of the Presbytery of Albany," 231; Presbytery of Albany, Records, I, 244–45 (Feb. 23, 1796), 249 (Apr. 17, 1797), II, 30 (Feb. 21, 1798), PHS; Charles Van Santvoord, *Memoirs of Eliphalet Nott, D.D.,* . . . (New York, 1876), 57–59, 66–67; Codman Hislop, *Eliphalet Nott* (Middletown, Conn., 1971), 37–43.

51. John McDonald to Rev. Ashbel Green, n.d. [c. Feb. 1796], Simon Gratz Coll., McDonald file, HSP; Brigham, *History and Bibliography of American Newspapers,* vol. 1, 531; Elihu Phin-ney, "Fire in Albany," *Otsego Herald,* Nov. 10, 1796; John McDonald, "To the Patrons," *Albany Chronicle,* Jan. 2, 1797; Moss Kent, Jr., to James Kent, Dec. 9, 1798, JKP, reel 1, LC.

52. Jonas Coe, "To the Public," *Albany Centinel,* Dec. 23, 1800; John McDonald to the First Presbyterian Church of Albany, Mar. 19, 1800, Session Records, 1795–1808, pp. 85-86 (Mar. 24, 1800), First Presbyterian Church, Albany.

53. Moss Kent, Jr., to James Kent, Dec. 9, 1798, JKP, reel 1, LC; John McDonald to the First Presbyterian Church of Albany, Mar. 19, 1800, Session Records, 1795–1808, p. 88 (Mar. 24, 1800), First Presbyterian Church, Albany.

54. John Frederick Ernst to Rev. John C. Kunze, July 3, Oct. 18, 1798, JCHP, HCA; Ernst to William Cooper, Oct. 14, 1798, WCP, CB 1796–1798, HCA.

55. John Frederick Ernst to Rev. John C. Kunze, Oct. 18, 1798, Thomas Fuller to Ernst, Dec. 11, 1798, Timothy Barns to Ernst, Dec. 18, 1798, Ernst to Barns, Dec. 27, 1798, and Ernst to Fuller, Dec. 27, 1798, all JCHP, HCA.

56. Frederick A. C. Muhlenberg to Jeremiah Van Rensselaer, Jan. 25, 1799, Van Rensselaer to Muhlenberg, Feb. 4, 1799, John Frederick Ernst to Timothy Barns et al., Mar. 27, 1799, William Cooper et al. to Ernst, Apr. 10, 1799, Ernst to Van Rensselaer, Apr. 17, 1799, JCHP, HCA.

57. John Frederick Ernst to William Cooper et al., Apr. 26, 1799, JCHP, HCA.
58. William Cooper et al. to John Frederick Ernst, Apr. 10, 1799, Ernst to Jeremiah Van Rensselaer, Apr. 17, 1799, and Rev. Daniel Nash to Ernst, Apr. 10, 1799, JCHP, HCA.
59. John McDonald, *The Danger of America Delineated: An Address Delivered at Cooperstown . . . April 25th, the Fast Day Recommended by the President of the United States* (Cooperstown, 1799, Evans no. 35756), 13, 18, 19; McDonald, *Duty of America Enforced,* 14–15.
60. "Interesting Law Case," *Otsego Herald,* Sept. 20, 1798; Otsego Lodge, Minute Book 1, entries for Dec. 5 and 25, 1797, Apr. 2, 9, 16, May 1, July 2, Aug. 6, 1799, Otsego Lodge, Cooperstown.
61. John Frederick Ernst to Timothy Barns et al., Mar. 27, 1799, and Ernst to William Cooper et al., Apr. 26, 1799, JCHP, HCA.
62. Hartwick Executors, Resolves, June 11, 1799, Lutheran Archvies Center, Mount Airy, Pa.; Hartwick Executors, Resolves, Oct. 21, 1801, JCHP, HCA; Ernst v. Bartle et al., in Johnson, *Reports of Cases,* vol. 1, 319–26; John Frederick Ernst to Abraham Lippitt et al., Nov. 14, 1801, Ernst to Jeremiah Van Rensselaer, Dec. 18, 1801, and [Ernst], "Continuation of Patent Matters," Dec. 21, 1801, JCHP, HCA; James Averell and Thomas Fuller to William Cooper, Apr. 30, 1803, WCP, CB 1802–3, HCA; John F. Ernst, Jr., receipt to Thomas Loomis et al., Dec. 9, 1803, AFP, box 1, NYSHA; Glatfelter, *Pastors and People,* vol. 1, 37; *Otsego Herald,* Sept. 16, 1802, Nov. 21, 1805.
63. Presbytery of Albany, Records, II, 100 (Feb. 22, 1798), 143 (Oct. 17, 1799), 147 (Feb. 18, 1800), PHS; First Presbyterian Church to John McDonald, Feb. 11, 1800, and McDonald to First Presbyterian Church of Albany, Mar. 19, 1800, Session Records, 1795–1808, pp. 79 (Mar. 11, 1800), 88 (Mar. 24, 1800), First Presbyterian Church, Albany.
64. John McDonald to First Presbyterian Church of Albany, Mar. 19, 1800, Session Records, 1795–1808, pp. 79 (Mar. 11, 1800), 88 (Mar. 24, 1800), First Presbyterian Church, Albany; Elihu Phinney to William Cooper, Dec. 23, 1799, WCP, CB 1799–1801, HCA. For the debt law see *Otsego Herald,* July 10, 1795.
65. James [Fenimore] Cooper to William Cooper, Mar. 3, 1800, in Beard, *Letters and Journals,* vol. 1, 6–7; Presbytery of Albany, Records, II, 187–91 (Aug. 20–21, 1800), 221–31 (Nov. 11, 1800), PHS; *Albany Register,* Nov. 17, 1800; McDonald, "To the Friends of Religion, Letter III," *Albany Register,* Dec. 12, 1800; Miller and Coes, "History of the Presbytery of Albany," 231; Munsell, *Collections on the History of Albany,* vol. 1, 422. For the exchange see *Albany Register,* Dec. 2, 5, 12 ("the *arts*"), 16, 19, 1800; and *Albany Centinel,* Dec. 16, 23, 26 ("inscrutable mixture"), 30, 1800.
66. Franklin Bowditch Dexter, *Biographical Sketches of the Graduates of Yale College . . . ,* vol. 5 (New York, 1911), 113; Hannah Cooper to Isaac Cooper, Apr. 13, 1800, WCP, CB 1799–1801, HCA; Philemon H. Fowler, *Historical Sketches of Presbyterianism Within the Bounds of the Synod of Central New York* (Utica, N.Y., 1877), 401; Cooperstown Presbyterian Church, Session Records, 1800–1820, p. 3 (June 16, 1800), NYSHA; Presbytery of Albany, Records, II, 184–85 (Aug. 19, 1800), 213 (Oct. 1, 1800), PHS; *Otsego Herald,* Aug. 8, 1805.
67. Cooperstown Presbyterian Church, Session Records, 1800–1810, NYSHA; Ministerial Tax Book for 1804, AFP, box 1, NYSHA; Otsego Lodge, Minute Books 1 and 2, Otsego Lodge. For Cooper's contributions see his undated draft on the reverse of Robert Troup to William Cooper, May 23, 1805, WCP, CB 1804–1806, HCA; and David Mason, as Clerk of the Church, to Cooper, Mar. 12, 1806, Cooperstown Presbyterian Church Records, NYSHA.
68. William Cooper and Walter Morgan, articles of agreement, May 6, 1799, WCP, BB 1799–1801, WCP, HCA; Morgan, advertisements, *Otsego Herald,* Apr. 20, 1797, Jan. 25, 1798, June 26, 1800; "Fire," *Otsego Herald,* Jan. 19, 1804; ibid., Apr. 2, 1807; J. F. Cooper, *Chronicles of Cooperstown,* 20; James Henry Pickering, "James Fenimore Cooper and the History of New York" (Ph.D. diss., Northwestern Univ., 1964), 153. In 1803 there were 39 old Freemasons, 16 new, and 649 nonmembers on the tax assessment list for Otsego Township. See Otsego Co., Tax Assessment Lists, 1803, series B-0950-85, box 38, NYSA.

9. THE POLITICAL WARS

1. James Fenimore Cooper, *The Pioneers, or the Sources of the Susquehanna; A Descriptive Tale*, ed., James Franklin Beard (Albany, 1980, crit. ed. of New York, 1823), 122, 181.

2. William Cooper to Benjamin Walker, Jan. 6, 1802, WCP, CB 1802–1803, HCA. The word snivey in the original was misread and published as snivery by James Fenimore Cooper (the novelist's grandson), misleading those who have relied on J. F. Cooper for the quotation; see James Fenimore Cooper (1858–1938), *The Legends and Traditions of a Northern County* (New York, 1921), 175. For early American elections see Charles S. Sydnor, *Gentlemen Free-holders: Political Practices in Washington's Virginia* (Chapel Hill, N.C., 1952); Robert J. Dinkin, *Voting in Revolutionary America: A Study of Elections in the Original Thirteen States, 1776–1789* (Westport, Conn., 1982); Edmund S. Morgan, *Inventing the People: The Rise of Popular Sovereignty in England and America* (New York, 1988); David Hackett Fischer, *The Revolution of American Conservatism: The Federalist Party in the Era of Jeffersonian Democracy* (New York, 1965), 91–109.

3. John Jay to Judge Lowell, Feb. 29, 1796, in Henry P. Johnston, ed., *The Correspondence and Public Papers of John Jay*, 4 vols. (New York, 1890–1893), vol. 4, 204; "An Elector, In Whitestown," *Albany Gazette*, June 11, 1792; "A Citizen," *Albany Centinel*, Mar. 27, 1798; "Reviewer," ibid., May 23, 1800; Samuel Stringer letter, *Albany Register*, Apr. 17, 1801. In general, I am indebted to Marvin Meyers, *The Jacksonian Persuasion: Politics and Belief* (Stanford, Calif., 1960), 121–41.

4. Gordon S. Wood, *The Radicalism of the American Revolution* (New York, 1992), 88, 189–212; John R. Howe, Jr., "Republican Thought and the Political Violence of the 1790s," *American Quarterly*, vol. 19 (Summer 1967), 147–65; Joyce Appleby, *Capitalism and a New Social Order: The Republican Vision of the 1790s* (New York, 1984), 73–78. The classic work on the development of democratic and partisan politics in New York is Alfred F. Young, *The Democratic Republicans of New York: The Origins, 1763–1797* (Chapel Hill, N.C., 1967). For a greater stress on democratic politics in New York before the Revolution, see Patricia U. Bonomi, *A Factious People: Politics and Society in Colonial New York* (New York, 1971), 240–46, 253–57.

5. David Goff, letter, May 6, 1795, *Otsego Herald*, May 29, 1795; David Paris to William Cooper, Dec. 13, 1794, WCP, CB 1794–1796, HCA ("winning"); "A Farmer," *Albany Register*, Nov. 24, 1794 ("the ambition"). See also Dinkin, *Voting in Revolutionary America*, 58, 74; Gordon S. Wood, *The Creation of the American Republic, 1776–1787* (Chapel Hill, N.C., 1969), 479–80. For Winn's losing margins, see Young, *Democratic Republicans of New York*, 592.

6. "Constantius" and "An Independent Elector," *Albany Gazette*, Feb. 13, 1795, and Mar. 5, 1798; "A Citizen" and "Reviewer," *Albany Centinel*, Mar. 27, 1798, and May 23, 1800. The state law is silent on nominating procedures; see "An Act for Regulating Elections . . . ," 10th session, chap. 15, Feb. 13, 1787, in New York (State), *Laws of the State of New York, First to the Fifteenth Session, Inclusive*, 2 vols. (New York, 1792, Evans no. 24602), vol. 1, 316.

7. On wealth and power in New York see Young, *Democratic Republicans of New York*, 59–82.

8. Theodore Sedgwick to Rufus King, Aug. 24, 1802, quoted in Alvin Kass, *Politics in New York State, 1800–1830* (Syracuse, N.Y., 1965), 17; Wolcott quoted in Lee Benson, *The Concept of Jacksonian Democracy: New York as a Test Case* (Princeton, N.J., 1961), 3; Moss Kent, Jr., to James Kent, May 16, 1798, JKP, reel 1, LC; Dixon Ryan Fox, *Yankees and Yorkers* (New York, 1940), 19–20. For a useful definition of modern political parties and a discussion of how the parties of the early Republic fell short see Ronald P. Formisano, "Deferential-Participant Politics: The Early Republic's Political Culture, 1789–1840," *American Political Science Review*, 68 (June 1974), 474–75.

9. Richard L. Bushman, *King and People in Provincial Massachusetts* (Chapel Hill, N.C., 1985), 3, 6–7; Morgan, *Inventing the People*, 179–81; William Cooper to Stephen Van Rensselaer, Jan. 19, 1792 [*sic*, should be 1793], doc. no. 775, NYSL; Joshua Mersereau to Silas Talbot, Dec. 18, 1792, STP, box 2, GWBWL-MS; William Strickland, *Journal of a Tour in the United States of America, 1794–1795* (New York, 1971), 171.

10. George Metcalf to Silas Talbot, Jan. 18, Feb. 2 ("may produce"), Nov. 16, 1793 (account), Jauncey & Hoyt account with Talbot, Nov. 6, 1793, and Johannes Fryer account with Talbot, Apr. 18, 1793, STP, box 3, GWBWL; Ulster County subscription list, 1794, PVGP, folder 3026, SHM; Sanford Clark to William Cooper, Dec. 12, 1796, WCP, CB 1796–98, HCA; Mr. Mitchell to Morgan Lewis, June 7, 1806, Morgan Lewis Papers, CB 1800–1810, NYHS.

11. Morgan, *Inventing the People*, 174–77; Gordon S. Wood, "Interests and Disinterestedness in the Making of the Constitution," in *Beyond Confederation: Origins of the Constitution and American National Identity*, ed. Richard Beeman, Stephen Botein, and Edward C. Carter II (Chapel Hill, N.C., 1987), 69–109.

12. William Cooper to Peter Smith, Oct. 6, 1794, Peter Smith Papers, box 1, Arents Research Lib., Syracuse Univ.; Goldsborough Banyar, "Day Book, 1793–1796," May 14, 1794, G. Banyar Papers, NYHS; Jonas Platt to Cooper, May 8, 1794, Smith to Cooper, Aug. 25, 1794, Oct. 21, 1794, and Oct. 6, 1795, Thomas R. Gold to Cooper, Dec. 15, 1794 ("P.S."), and Arthur Breese to Cooper, Feb. 5, 1795, all WCP, CB 1794–1796, HCA; Gold to Cooper, n.d. [Jan. 1797], and Apr. 10, 1797, WCP, CB 1796–98, HCA; "A New-England Man," *Whitestown Gazette*, Dec. 13, 1796 ("thro the medium"); Elkanah Watson to Talbot, Feb. 23, 1793, STP, box 3, GWBWL-MS ("Judge M"). For lists of military tract purchasers, see Cooper to Richard Harrison, Sept. 10, 1795, WCP, CB 1794–1796, HCA; Cooper, Memorandum Book, June 19, 1794, WCP, HCA.

13. Josiah Ogden Hoffman to William Cooper, Oct. 6, 1791, WCP, CB 1704–1793, HCA; Joshua Dewey to Cooper, Feb 6, 1797, WCP, CB 1796–98, HCA; Cooper to James [Butterfield], Apr. 8, 1792, in *New-York Journal*, June 16, 1792; Wood, *Radicalism of the American Revolution*, 224.

14. [Jonas Platt], "To the Cataline of the West," *Albany Gazette*, Dec. 2, 1796; Moss Kent, Jr., to James Kent, Dec. 25, 1794, JKP, reel 1, LC; George Metcalf to Silas Talbot, Dec. 8, 1792, STP, box 2, GWBWL-MS.

15. Cooper to [?], Nov. 30, 1794, C. E. French Coll., MHS; Jeremiah Van Rensselaer to Silas Talbot, Dec. 4, 1792, STP, box 2, GWBWL-MS; Elkanah Watson to Talbot, Feb. 10 and 23, 1793, STP, box 3, GWBWL-MS; Talbot to Watson, Feb. 1, 1793, Elkanah Watson Papers, box 9, NYSL; Staughton Lynd, *Class Conflict, Slavery, and the United States Constitution: Ten Essays* (New York, 1967), 39.

16. Ruth L. Woodward and Wesley Frank Craven, *Princetonians, 1784–1790* (Princeton, N.J., 1991), 57; Benjamin W. Dwight, *The History of the Descendants of Elder John Strong of Northampton, Massachusetts*, 2 vols. (Albany, 1871), vol. 1, 671; Harold C. Syrett et al., eds., *The Papers of Alexander Hamilton*, 27 vols. (New York, 1961–1987), vol. 3, 42 n. 92, vol. 20, 303 n. 1, vol. 26, 478; Edward Porter Alexander, "Judge Kent's 'Jaunt' to Cooperstown in 1792," *New York History*, 22 (Oct. 1941), 453 n. 11; John T. Horton, *James Kent, a Study in Conservatism, 1763–1847* (New York, 1939), 45, 47. For the monarchical scheme see Pierre Van Cortlandt, Jr., to [?], Feb. 27, 1804, in Syrett et al., *Papers of Alexander Hamilton*, vol. 26, 198 n. 4. For Hamilton's monarchical views see Gouverneur Morris quoted in ibid., vol. 26, 324 n. 3. For the reputation of Strong and Ten Broeck for wartime Loyalism see David Goff, "To the Pretended Friends to Cooperstown and County," *Otsego Herald*, June 23, 1796. For lawyers' conservatism see Fischer, *Revolution of American Conservatism*, 207; Jackson Turner Main, *Political Parties before the Constitution* (Chapel Hill, N.C., 1973), 362–63, 371–73.

17. William Cooper, grand jury charge [1791], WCP, Misc. Undated Documents box, HCA; Otsego CCP, Records, vol. 1, 7 (June 21, 1791), OCCO; People v. John Bull, June 2, 1791, Oct. 4, 1796, and People v. John McKellup, Oct. 15, 1796, Otsego Co. Indictments, folders 1 and 2, OCCO.

18. Moss Kent, Jr., to James Kent, Nov. 25, Dec. 21, 1793, May 22, June 14, 1794, Dec. 25, 1794, J. Kent to M. Kent, June 2, 1794, Feb. 4, 1795, JKP, reel 1, LC.

19. Moss Kent, Jr., to James Kent, Feb. 16, 1795, JKP, reel 1, LC.

20. For the criminal courts see Otsego CGSP, Records, vol. 1 (1791–1817), OCCO;

OC-CO&T, Minute Book 1 (1792–1809), OCCO. For the civil suits see OC-CCP, Judgments Book 1 (1792–1809), OCCO. For the importance of courts in frontier counties see Michael A. Bellesiles, *Revolutionary Outlaws: Ethan Allen and the Struggle for Independence on the Early American Frontier* (Charlottesville, Va., 1993), 175-79.

21. Stephen West Williams, *American Medical Biography; or, Memoirs of Eminent Physicians* (New York, 1845), 624; Throop Wilder, "Jedediah Peck: Statesman, Soldier, Preacher," *New York History*, 22 (July 1941), 290–94. In 1794–1797 there were two other associate judges, Witter Johnston and Platt Townsend, neither of whom figured prominently in county affairs. Both were removed by the Council of Appointment in the civil list of Mar. 13, 1797, leaving Cooper, Peck, and White alone on the county bench. A year later the council added Elihu Phinney. See Council of Appointment, Records, vol. 3 (1793–1797), 83 (Mar. 7, 1794), 316 (Mar. 13, 1797), and vol. 4, 57 (Mar. 27, 1798), NYSA.

22. Alexander Coventry, *Memoirs of an Emigrant: The Journal of Alexander Coventry, M.D.*, 2 vols. (Albany, 1978), vol. 1, 540 (quotation); Grand Jury Indictment of Benjamin Batchelor et al., June 21, 1791, Otsego Co. Indictments, OCCO; People v. Batchelor et al., June 21 and 23, 1791, OC-CGSP, Records, vol. 1 (1791–1817), 1–3, OCCO.

23. William Cooper, Docket Book, 1799, WCP, HCA; Brigham v. Jewitt, OC-CCP Judgments Book, 1792–1809, OCCO.

24. William Cooper quoted in [Moss Kent, Jr.], "Argus," *Otsego Herald*, Apr. 13, 1797.

25. [Abraham C. Ten Broeck], "By Stander" and "Inquirer, No. I," *Otsego Herald*, June 26, 1795; [Ten Broeck], "Inquirer, No. II," ibid., July 3, 1795; [Ten Broeck], "Inquirer, No. III," ibid., July 10, 1795 (all quotations); [Ten Broeck], "Inquirer, No. IV," ibid., July 17, 1795.

26. Jedediah Peck to Joseph Strong, Apr. 22, 1796, *Otsego Herald*, Apr. 28, 1796; Cooper paraphrased in David Goff, "To the Pretended Friends to Cooperstown and the County," *Otsego Herald*, June 23, 1796. For Strong's reputation for deceit see also Francis Lequoy to William Cooper, Oct. 14, 1796, WCP, CB 1796–98, HCA.

27. [William Cooper], "Philupnos Philo-Typus," and "An Elector," and "A Friend to Consistency," *Otsego Herald*, Apr. 3, 1795; Benjamin Gilbert to Cooper, Mar. 13, 1794, WCP, CB 1794–96, HCA; Jacob Morris to Stephen Van Rensselaer, July 1, 1795, J. Morris Papers, Cornell Univ. Lib. (quotation); [Morris], "A Friend to Truth," *Otsego Herald*, May 8, 1795. For his close association with Joseph Strong, see Morris, "Notice," *Otsego Herald*, Apr. 17, 1795.

28. [Abraham C. Ten Broeck], "Phocion," *Otsego Herald*, Nov. 26, 1795; [Elihu Phinney], "A Friend to Truth," ibid., Dec. 17, 1795; [Ten Broeck], "Aristides," ibid., Dec. 24, 1795; Phinney, "Notice," ibid., Apr. 24, 1795 (policy); ibid., June 26, 1795 (circulation figures); "Philo," ibid., May 5, 1796 (reading aloud); "Terms of the Herald," ibid., Oct. 10, 1805; Richard D. Brown, *Knowledge Is Power: The Diffusion of Information in Early America, 1700–1865* (New York, 1989), 266–80. Phinney encouraged group subscriptions and reported that one such "class" in the town of Exeter had 55 readers. See *Otsego Herald*, Dec. 5, 1807. For Ten Broeck as the author of "Phocion," see Jedediah Peck to Ten Broeck, Apr. 22, 1796, ibid., Apr. 28, 1796.

29. [Jacob Morris], "Information from a Member of Assembly," *Otsego Herald*, Mar. 3, 1796; "To the Electors of the Western District of the State of New York," ibid., Mar. 31, 1796; [Elihu Phinney], "The Friends to Harmony," ibid., Apr. 21, 1796; Stephen Van Rensselaer to William Cooper, Mar. 7, 1796, WCP, CB 1794–1796, HCA. The legislative caucus for the Western District acted extralegally in stipulating certain seats for certain counties. According to the state constitution of 1777, state senators were supposed to be elected at large within the four multicounty senatorial districts—the Southern, Eastern, Middle, and Western. The intent was conservative: to favor the election of prominent and prestigious men with wide name recognition and to discourage the parochial candidacies of populists known only in their home counties. But political practice in New York had defeated the intent as the leading men in every district bowed to popular pressures and informally allocated particular seats to particular counties on the basis of their relative population. Sometimes these ad hoc arrangements produced wrangles between competing counties.

30. Joseph White to William Cooper, Mar. 21, 1796, Benjamin Gilbert to Cooper, Mar. 21, 1796, Moss Kent, Jr., to Cooper, Apr. 7 and 21, 1796, all WCP, CB 1794–1796, HCA.

31. Joseph White to William Cooper, Mar. 21, 1796, Benjamin Gilbert to Cooper, Mar. 21, 1796, WCP, CB 1794–1796, HCA.

32. Benjamin Gilbert to William Cooper, Mar. 21, 1796, and Joseph White to Cooper, Mar. 21, 1796, WCP, CB 1794–1796, HCA.

33. William Cooper, letter to the electors, Mar. 31, 1796, in *Otsego Herald,* Apr. 21, 1796; Moss Kent, Jr., to James Kent, Apr. 21, 1796, and J. Kent to M. Kent, Jr., May 8, 1796, JKP, reel 1, LC; Elihu Phinney to Cooper, Apr. 15, 1796, Benjamin Gilbert to Cooper, Apr. 19, and May 10, 1796, and Stephen Van Rensselaer to Cooper, Apr. 25, 1796, all WCP, CB 1794–1796, HCA. For Kent's reaction see [Moss Kent], "An Independent Elector of the County of Otsego," [Whitestown, N.Y.] *Western Centinel,* undated clipping included in Stephen Van Rensselaer to Cooper, Apr. 30, 1796, WCP, CB 1794–1796, HCA; Hendrick Frey to Cooper, Apr. 26, 1796, WCP, CB 1794–1796, HCA.

34. James Fenimore Cooper (1858–1938), ed., "Correspondence of Judge William Cooper," vol. 1, 174, in the James Franklin Beard Papers, AAS; Jedediah Peck, "Journal of a Voyage," Aug. 15, Sept. 25, Oct. 8, 1771, NYSHA.

35. Jedediah Peck, "The Copy of a Letter from a Son of Liberty, in the Town of Burlington . . .," *Otsego Herald,* Apr. 21, 1796 ("horrors"); Jedediah Peck, "Account of the Peck Family," Misc. Mss. P, NYSHA.

36. Jabez D. Hammond, *The History of Political Parties in the State of New-York . . .,* 2 vols. (Albany, 1842), vol. 1, 123–4 ("Judge Peck"); Levi Beardsley, *Reminiscences; Personal and Other Incidents; Early Settlement of Otsego County* (New York, 1852), 71–72; Wilder, "Jedediah Peck," 290–94; John Lee Frisbee, "The Political Career of Jedediah Peck" (Master's thesis, SUNY at Oneonta, 1966, NYSHA copy), 2–5; [Elihu Phinney], "Liberty of the Press," *Otsego Herald,* Dec. 6, 1798.

37. Jedediah Peck to Stephen Van Rensselaer, Sept. 3, 1792, doc. no. 2160, NYSL; [Peck], "Monarchical and Representative Government Contrasted," *Otsego Herald,* Apr. 21, 1796; [Peck], "J.P. Americus," *Albany Gazette,* Jan. 17, 1793. For his praise for Paine see Jedediah Peck, *The Political Wars of Otsego: or Downfall of Jacobinism and Despotism* (Cooperstown, 1796, Evans no. 30968), 9.

38. Abraham C. Ten Broeck to William Cooper, Jan. 18, 1796, WCP, CB 1794–1796, HCA; [Jedediah Peck], "A Plough-Jogger," *Otsego Herald,* Apr. 14, 1796; Beardsley, *Reminiscences,* 72–3. For the transformation of law in New England see Cornelia Hughes Dayton, "Taking the Trade: Abortion and Gender Relations in an Eighteenth-Century New England Village," *WMQ,* 3d ser., 48 (Jan. 1991), 19–49; and Bruce H. Mann, *Neighbors and Strangers: Law and Community in Early Connecticut* (Chapel Hill, N.C., 1987).

39. Benjamin Gilbert to William Cooper, May 10, 1796, and Joseph White to Cooper, May 10, 1796, WCP, CB 1796–98, HCA.

40. Beardsley, *Reminiscences,* 72 ("saddle bags"); [Jedediah Peck], "Plough-Jogger," *Otsego Herald,* Apr. 14, 1796; [Peck], "The Copy of a Letter from a Son of Liberty, . . ." ibid., Apr. 21, 1796.

41. Jedediah Peck, "To Joseph Strong, Esq.," [Joseph Strong], "Hocus-Pocus," and [Abraham C. Ten Broeck], "To J. Peck, Esq.," all in *Otsego Herald,* Apr. 21, 1796; Peck to Ten Broeck and Strong, Apr. 22, 1796, in ibid., Apr. 28, 1796; Peck to Jacob Morris, Apr. 29, 1796, and Burlington Inspectors of Election to Strong, Apr. 30, 1796, both in ibid., May 12, 1796.

42. [Jedediah Peck], "The Copy of a Letter from a Son of Liberty, in the Town of Burlington to his Friend in Harpersfield," *Otsego Herald,* Apr. 21, 1796 ("Let us"); [Peck], "Advice to Farmers, Mechanics, & Traders" ("These lawyers") and [Peck], "A Plough-Jogger" ("honest lawyer"), *Otsego Herald,* Apr. 14, 1796; Benjamin Gilbert to William Cooper, May 10, 1796, WCP, CB 1796–98, HCA.

43. [Jedediah Peck], "Philo-Virtutus," *Otsego Herald,* Apr. 21, 1796 ("In Representative"); [Peck], "Plough-Jogger," ibid., Apr. 14, 1796; [Peck], "Observer," *Albany Gazette,* Apr. 25, 1796 ("Fellow-citizens").

44. Hugh M. Flick, "The Council of Appointment of New York State: The First Attempt to Regulate Political Patronage, 1777–1822," *New York History*, 15 (July 1934), 265; New York State Assembly proceedings, Feb. 27, 1796, in *Otsego Herald*, Mar. 17, 1796; Hammond, *History of Political Parties*, vol. 1, 95–97, 99–100; Jacob Morris to William Cooper, Jan. 14, 1796, WCP, CB 1794–1796, HCA; Morris to Elihu Phinney, May 6, 1796, *Otsego Herald*, May 12, 1796; [Jedediah Peck], "A Plough Jogger," ibid., Apr. 14, 1796; [Peck], "The Copy of a Letter, from a Son of Liberty . . ." ibid., Apr. 21, 1796; [Peck], "Observer," *Albany Gazette*, Apr. 25, 1796; Peck, *Political Wars of Otsego*, 29–30.

45. [Jedediah Peck], "The Copy of a Letter from a Son of Liberty . . .," Peck, "To Joseph Strong, Esq.," [Joseph Strong], "Hocus-Pocus," and Abraham C. Ten Broeck, "To J. Peck, Esq.," all in *Otsego Herald*, Apr. 21, 1796; Jacob Morris to Elihu Phinney, May 6, 1796, ibid., May 12, 1796; [Ten Broeck], to the editor, Aug. 25, 1796, ibid., Sept. 1, 1796.

46. "Jack-at-all-Trades," *Otsego Herald*, May 4, 1796; David Goff, "To the Pretended Friends to Cooperstown and the County," ibid., June 23, 1796.

47. Jedediah Peck to Jacob Morris, Apr. 29, 1796, and Morris to Elihu Phinney, May 6, 1796, both in *Otsego Herald*, May 12, 1796; Peck to Morris, ibid., May 26, 1796.

48. [Abraham C. Ten Broeck], untitled, first page, *Otsego Herald*, Apr. 21, 1796 ("insinuated"); Ten Broeck to Jedediah Peck, ibid., May 5, 1796 ("Montesquieu").

49. Peck, *Political Wars of Otsego*, 59 ("a Monarchite"), 88; [Abraham C. Ten Broeck] to the editor, Aug. 25, 1796, *Otsego Herald*, Sept. 1, 1796; Jedediah Peck to Ten Broeck, Sept. 8, 1796, ibid., Sept. 8, 1796 ("It is dangerous" and "but as I").

50. *Otsego Herald*, June 9 (assembly returns), July 7 (state senate returns), 1796; "Albany," *Albany Gazette*, June 17, 1796.

51. Moss Kent, Jr., to James Kent, July 8, 1796, JKP, reel 1, LC; Joseph White to William Cooper, May 10, 1796, WCP, CB 1796–98, HCA; Jacob Morris to Elihu Phinney, May 6, 1796, *Otsego Herald*, May 12, 1796; Morris to Jedediah Peck, June 3, 1796, in Peck, *Political Wars of Otsego*, 26; Benjamin Gilbert to "Markwell" [Abraham C. Ten Broeck], May 16, 1796, in *Otsego Herald*, May 16, 1796.

52. Moss Kent, Jr., to James Kent, July 8, 1796, JKP, reel 1, LC.

53. Jedediah Peck, "Proposals for Printing by Subscription," *Otsego Herald*, May 26, 1796; Peck, *Political Wars of Otsego*, 124–26 (list of subscribers).

54. I found a legible list of the subscribers (and their residences) in the copy of Peck, *Political Wars of Otsego* at the Boston Atheneum. I identified their net worth in Otsego Co. towns, assessment rolls, 1800, series B-0950-85, box 37, NYSA. For Freemasonic membership in Otsego in 1796 see Minute Book, vol. 1, Otsego Lodge, Cooperstown. In the April voting Peck got 459 votes in Burlington (237), Otsego Town (169), and Richfield (53). Because the Richfield inspectors of election failed to forward their votes to the county sheriff by the legal deadline, they were not officially counted, reducing Peck's total in Otsego from 526 to 473. See *Otsego Herald*, July 7, 1796.

55. People v. Jacob Morris, Oct. 5, 1796, Otsego Co. Indictments, OCCO; People v. Jacob Morris, Oct. 5, 1796, OC-CO&T, Record Book, OCCO; "Communication," *Otsego Herald*, Oct. 6, 1796.

56. People v. Jacob Morris, and People v. Joseph Strong, both Otsego County Indictments, Oct. 5, 1796, OCCO; People v. Jacob Morris, and People v. Joseph Strong, both OC-CO&T, Record Book, Oct. 5, 1796, OCCO; People v. Joseph Strong, OC-CGSP, Record Book, Oct. 19, 1797, OCCO; Jedediah Peck, "Re-Communication From the Plough-Jogger's Journal," *Otsego Herald*, Oct. 13, 1796. Resenting the heavy and embarrassing fine levied with William Cooper's consent, Jacob Morris refused to help the judge's reelection bid, sullenly sitting out the congressional election. See Morris to Cooper, Jan. 2, 1796 [*sic*, really 1797], WCP, CB 1794–1796, HCA.

57. James Kent to Moss Kent, Jr., June 22, 1796, and M. Kent, Jr., to J. Kent, July 8, 1796, JKP, reel 1, LC; M. Kent, Jr., to William Cooper, July 12, 1796, WCP, CB 1796–98, HCA.

58. Moss Kent, Jr., to James Kent, Sept. 28, 1796, JKP, reel 1, LC.

59. Syrett et al., *Papers of Alexander Hamilton*, vol. 3, 55, 59; Stephen Van Rensselaer to William

Cooper, Sept. 19, 1796, WCP, CB 1796–98, HCA; Moss Kent, Jr., to James Kent, Sept. 28, 1796, J. Kent to M. Kent, Jr., Nov. 27, 1796, and M. Kent, Jr., to J. Kent, Dec. 15, 1796, all in JKP, reel 1, LC.

60. Moss Kent, Jr., to James Kent, Oct. 24, 1796, and Dec. 10, 1796, JKP, reel 1, LC; Joseph White to William Cooper, Dec. 9, 23, 1796, WCP, CB 1796–98, HCA; [Kent], "Hampden," *Otsego Herald*, Sept. 29, 1796 ("pretended Father"); [Kent], "Argus," ibid., Nov. 24, 1796.

61. For Cooper's political assets see P. S. Van Rensselaer to William Cooper, Sept. 9, 1796, Cooper Papers, NYHS; Stephen Van Rensselaer to Cooper, Sept. 19, 1796, WCP, CB 1796–98, HCA. For Cochranite rhetoric see [Moss Kent], "Hamden," *Otsego Herald*, Sept. 29, 1796 ("True liberality"); [Jonas Platt], "Timothy Thistle," *Whitestown Gazette*, Oct. 18, 1796; "T," ibid., Dec. 6, 1796 ("to enlighten"); Thomas Tillotson to Robert R. Livingston, Jan. 20, 1797, R. R. Livingston Papers, reel 6, NYHS.

62. The one newspaper published in the district during the 1794 race was the *Whitestown Western Centinel*. By the fall of 1796, three new newspapers had been established: the *Otsego Herald* in Cooperstown, Otsego Co. (Apr. 3, 1795), the *Johnstown Gazette* in Johnstown, Montgomery Co. (July 15, 1795), and the *Whitestown Gazette* in Whitestown, Herkimer Co. (June 7, 1796). See Clarence S. Brigham, *History and Bibliography of American Newspapers, 1690–1820*, 2 vols. (Worcester, Mass., 1947), vol. 1, 552, 568, 574, 591, 756–57. For Cooperite alarm over the newspaper essays see Elihu Phinney to Cooper, Nov. 22, 1796, and Joseph White to Cooper, Dec. 9, and Dec. 23, 1796, WCP, CB 1796–98, HCA. For the Cochranite lawyers, see Moss Kent, Jr., to James Kent, Sept., 28, JKP, reel 1, LC; White to Cooper, Dec. 9, 1796, and Dec. 23, 1796, WCP, CB 1796–98, HCA; "Bush-Whacker," *Otsego Herald*, Nov. 17, 1796. Cooper enjoyed the support of only two lawyers in Herkimer County: Thomas R. Gold of Whitestown and Gaylord Griswold of Herkimer Township. For the growing influence of lawyers see Gerard W. Gawalt, *The Promise of Power: The Emergence of the Legal Profession in Massachusetts, 1760–1840* (Westport, Conn., 1979).

63. "A Friend to Merit," *Western Centinel*, Dec. 5, 1796; [Moss Kent] "Argus," *Otsego Herald*, Nov. 24, 1796; "T," *Whitestown Gazette*, Dec. 6, 1796; [Jonas Platt], "A Hint," ibid., Dec. 13, 1796; "An Elector," *Albany Gazette*, Aug. 1, 1796 ("Chariot"); James Kent to Moss Kent, Jr., Nov. 27, 1796, JKP, reel 1, LC.

64. "Cooperstown," *Otsego Herald*, June 23, 1796; "An Elector," *Albany Gazette*, Aug. 1, 1796; "Argus," *Otsego Herald*, Nov. 24, 1796; "A Friend to Merit," *Western Centinel*, Dec. 5, 1796.

65. [Elihu Phinney], "Junius," *Otsego Herald*, Sept. 22, 1796; [Thomas R. Gold], "Herkimer Farmer," *Western Centinel*, Dec. 7, 1796; [Jedediah Peck], "A Plough-Jogger," *Whitestown Gazette*, Dec. 13, 1796. Phinney probably wrote "Junius," but Cooper paid for its publication. See his account with Elihu Phinney, Sept. 12, 1796, WCP, BB 1795, HCA.

66. Thomas R. Gold to William Cooper, Dec. 18, 1796, Joseph White to Cooper, Dec. 23, 1796, Joab Griswold to Cooper, Dec. 26, 1796, and Hendrick Frey to Cooper, Dec. 30, 1796, all in WCP, CB 1796–98, HCA.

67. Moss Kent, Jr., to William Cooper, Dec. 18, 1796, Elihu Phinney to Cooper, Jan. 20, 1797, Gaylord Griswold to Cooper, Jan. 22, 1797, Phinney to Cooper, Jan. 31, 1797, Benjamin Gilbert to Cooper, Feb. 6, 1797, and Joshua Dewey to Cooper, Feb. 6, 1797, WCP, CB 1796–98, HCA. For the election returns, see Young, *Democratic Republicans of New York*, 592; *Cooperstown Otsego Herald*, Feb. 2, 1797. In 1796 the electorate exceeded that of 1794 by almost 1,500 votes.

68. Young, *Democratic Republicans of New York*, 592; Joshua Dewey to William Cooper, Feb. 6, 1797, WCP, CB 1796–98, HCA. A stolen ballot box may have cost Cooper the election. One Cooper friend reported that Aaron Wheeler, the election inspector for Harpersfield, then in Otsego Co., took charge of the ballot box but neglected to deliver it to the county sheriff within the five days specified by law. Consequently the canvassers could not count the votes. The friend insisted that Wheeler's delay was intentional and deprived Cooper of a thirty-vote majority in that town—more than Cochran's margin of victory. See Ebenezer Averell to William Cooper, Jan 21, 1797, WCP, CB 1796–98, HCA.

69. Elihu Phinney to William Cooper, Jan. 20, 1797, Cooper to John Jay, Jan. 23, 1797, and

Cooper to [?], June 26, 1797, WCP, CB 1796–98, HCA; James Kent to Moss Kent, Jr., Jan. 8, 1797, JKP, reel 1, LC.

70. *Otsego Herald,* Feb. 2, 1797; Moss Kent, Jr., to James Kent, Mar. 21, 1797, JKP, reel 1, LC.

71. Gaylord Griswold to William Cooper, Jan. 22, 1797, Thomas R. Gold to Cooper, n.d. [Jan. 1797], Benjamin Gilbert to Cooper, Feb. 6, 1797, WCP, CB 1796–98, HCA; [Jonas Platt] "To Cataline under the Muse of Sidney," *Albany Gazette,* Jan. 20, 1797. On politics and masculinity, see John Mack Faragher, *Sugar Creek: Life on the Illinois Prairie* (New Haven, Conn., 1986), 140–42, 154–55, and Alan Taylor, " 'The Art of Hook and Snivey': Political Culture in Upstate New York During the 1790s," *Journal of American History,* 79 (Mar. 1993), 1371–96.

72. Daniel Hale to William Cooper, Jan. 9, 1799, WCP, CB 1799–1801, HCA.

73. Moss Kent, Jr., to James Kent, April 27, 1797, JKP, reel 1, LC; [Phinney], "The First Chap. of the First Book of Chronicles," *Otsego Herald,* Apr. 20, 1797; [Abraham C. Ten Broeck], "Argus," *Otsego Herald,* Apr. 13, 1797. For the Western District voting returns see *Otsego Herald,* June 29, 1797. Cooper's slate (Timothy Hosmer, Michael Myers, and John Richardson) averaged 810 votes in Otsego, to 279 votes for Kent's preferred ticket (George Huntington, Thomas Morris, and Seth Phelps). In Otsego there were also 43 scattered ballots. In the district as a whole, the three victors were Morris (4,917 votes), Myers (4,333), and Phelps (4,097). The three losers were Hosmer (2,609), Huntington (3,982), and Richardson (3,658).

74. Thomas Tillotson to Robert R. Livingston, Feb. 5, 1797, Livingston Papers, reel 6, NYHS; "An Act for Electing Representatives for this State in the House of Representatives of the Congress of the United States of America," Mar. 28, 1797, 20th session, chap. 43, in [New York State], *Laws of the State of New York . . . From the First to the Twentieth session, Inclusive,* 3 vols. (New York, 1797, Evans no. 32555), vol. 1, 442–43.

75. Elihu Phinney to Jacob Morris, Feb. 23, 1798, doc. no. 1018, NYSL; Stephen O. Runyan to Morris, Mar. 7, 1798, Jacob Morris Papers, box 1, NYHS; Jacob Morris to James Morris, Mar. 13, 1798, and Uri Tracy to Jacob Morris, April 16, 1798, Morris Family Papers, box 1, NYHS: [Phinney], "Address to the Electors," Apr. 3, 1798, in *Otsego Herald,* Apr. 12, 1798; Moss Kent, Jr., to James Kent, May 16, 1798, JKP, reel 1, LC. For the voting returns see *Otsego Herald,* June 21, 1798. Cooper outpolled Kent, 473 to 26 in Otsego Township; 1,301 to 404 in Otsego Co. as a whole; and 2,038 to 1,865 in the entire district.

10. FRIENDS OF THE PEOPLE

1. David Hackett Fischer, *The Revolution of American Conservatism: The Federalist Party in the Era of Jeffersonian Democracy* (New York, 1965), 197–99; Alexis de Tocqueville, *Democracy in America,* ed. Phillips Bradley, 2 vols. (New York, 1960), vol. 1, 182–87.

2. Joyce Appleby, *Capitalism and a New Social Order: The Republican Vision of the 1790s* (New York, 1984), 70–78, 90–94; Edward Augustus Kendall, *Travels through the Northern Parts of the United States, in the Years 1807 and 1808,* 3 vols. (New York, 1809), vol. 2, 233.

3. For the rumor see Peter Van Schaack to Abraham Van Vechten, Aug. 5, 1797, C. E. French Coll., MHS.

4. Works that stress the influence of Madison and Jefferson are legion, including Lance Banning, *The Jeffersonian Persuasion: Evolution of a Party Ideology* (Ithaca, N.Y., 1978); James Roger Sharp, *American Politics in the Early Republic: The New Nation in Crisis* (New Haven, Conn., 1993); Stanley Elkins and Eric McKitrick, *The Age of Federalism: The Early American Republic, 1788–1800* (New York, 1993). The local, populist sources of Republicanism are better treated in Richard E. Ellis, *The Jeffersonian Crisis: Courts and Politics in the Young Republic* (New York, 1971).

5. The new stores belonged to James Averell, James Fitch, Jeremiah and Norman Landon, Elijah H. Metcalf, and Rensselaer Williams. The new taverns belonged to William Cook, Joseph Griffin, and Francis Henry. Ellison had lost his tavern to impatient creditors. See advertisements in *Otsego Herald,* Apr. 3, 1795, Dec. 8 and 22, 1796, Nov. 30, 1797, Jan. 11, 1798, Dec. 19, 1799.

6. U.S. Bureau of the Census, *Heads of Families at the First Census of the United States Taken in the Year 1790: New York* (Baltimore, 1966, repr. of Washington, D.C., 1908), 9; federal census returns for Otsego Co., 1800, series M32, reel 25, National Archives. Of the 302 heads of household present in Otsego in 1790, 204 (68 percent) remained in the county in 1800; 28 of the 98 from the 1790 census who did not reappear in the Otsego census for 1800 can be tentatively located in other New York counties; 6 had relocated in a longer-settled and more eastern county (Greene, Montgomery, Rensselaer, Saratoga, and Schoharie) while 22 had moved to a newer and more western county (Cayuga, Chenango, Delaware, Herkimer, Oneida, and Ontario). The most frequent relocation (n = 11) was to Chenango, the county immediately west of Otsego.

7. William Cooper to Elisha Jenkins, Nov. 25, 1803, WCP, CB 1802–1804, HCA; James Fenimore Cooper (1858–1938), *Reminiscences of Mid-Victorian Cooperstown and a Sketch of William Cooper* (Cooperstown, 1936), 44.

8. James Fenimore Cooper, *The Pioneers, or the Sources of the Susquehanna; A Descriptive Tale*, ed. James Franklin Beard (Albany, N.Y., 1980, crit. ed. of New York, 1823), 145; James Fenimore Cooper (1858–1938), *The Legends and Traditions of a Northern County* (New York, 1921), 28–30.

9. Richard L. Bushman, *The Refinement of America: Persons, Houses, Cities* (New York, 1992), 372–75; James Fenimore Cooper, *The Chronicles of Cooperstown* (1838), repr. in Shaw T. Livermore, ed., *A Condensed History of Cooperstown* (Albany, 1862), 22–23; Ralph Birdsall, *The Story of Cooperstown* (Cooperstown, 1917), 96.

10. Stephen Mack to William Cooper, Oct. 24, and Dec. 5, 1796 and Stephen Van Rensselaer to Cooper, Nov. 10, 1797, WCP, CB 1796–1798, HCA; Cooper to John Porteous, Aug. 2, 1798, J. Porteous Papers, reel 2A, Buffalo and Erie Co. Hist. Soc.; James Fenimore Cooper, "Otsego Hall," in J. F. Cooper (1858–1938), *Legends and Traditions,* 224–27; Charles R. Tichy, "Otsego Hall and its Setting, 1786–1940" (Master's thesis, SUNY at Oneonta, 1973, copy at NYSHA), 6–22.

11. Tichy, "Otsego Hall," 7, 17; J. F. Cooper, "Otsego Hall," 224, 227; James Fenimore Cooper (1858–1938) to Mary E. Phillips, Jan. 5, 1911, Phillips Papers, Boston Public Libr.; John Simpson to William Cooper, Oct. 28, 1803, WCP, CB 1802–1803, HCA ("want of"); James Kent, "Western Travel Journal," June 1801, JKP, reel 6, LC.

12. In a December 1797 newspaper advertisement Cooper served notice on his debtors, but he did not actually prosecute until early 1799. See William Cooper, notice, Dec. 26, 1797, *Otsego Herald,* Dec. 28, 1797; OC-CCP, Register of Judgments, 1792–1809, OCCO.

13. [Jedediah Peck], "Cato," and [Peck], "An Elector," *Otsego Herald,* April 20, 1797; Kathleen Smith Kutolowski, "Freemasonry and Community in the Early Republic: The Case for Antimasonic Anxieties," *American Quarterly,* 34 (Winter 1982), 543–61. For the voting returns see *Otsego Herald,* June 29, 1797.

14. For lack of surviving documentation in either the *Otsego Herald* or Cooper's private papers, the evidence for his understanding with Peck is circumstantial. First, the April 3, 1798, meeting in Burlington that nominated Peck for the assembly also endorsed Cooper for Congress. Second, Cooper overwhelmed Kent in Burlington (233 to 9), which also indicates Peck's assistance. Third, Peck finished in the top four in Otsego Township, where Cooper's influence was strongest. Indeed, in contrast to his previous struggles beyond Burlington, Peck polled well in every town in the county except Butternuts (where his old enemy Jacob Morris predominated), suggesting that he benefited from appearing as part of a ticket promoted by someone with influence throughout Otsego. See Burlington nomination meeting, Apr. 3, 1798, *Otsego Herald,* Apr. 12, 1798; Otsego voting returns, ibid., May 31, 1798. Alfred F. Young suggests that Peck won because of popular protest against Cooper's call, in Dec. 1797, for his many debtors to pay up. But this hypothesis does not work because Cooper and Peck both polled well in April 1798 in the same towns—especially Burlington and Otsego Town, where most of Cooper's debtors lived. Moreover, Cooper did not win any lawsuits until 1799. See Alfred F. Young, *The Democratic Republicans of New York: The Origins, 1763–1797* (Chapel Hill, N.C., 1967), 517.

15. [Elihu Phinney], "Cooperstown," *Otsego Herald*, Apr. 7, 1796; Joseph White to William Cooper, Dec. 23, 1796, WCP, CB 1796–1798, HCA; Cadwallader D. Colden to Peter Van Schaack, Jan. 29, 1798, Peter Van Schaack Papers, LC; John C. Miller, *Crisis in Freedom: The Alien and Sedition Acts* (Boston, 1951), 4–7; Manning J. Dauer, *The Adams Federalists* (Baltimore, 1953), 120–51.

16. "An Independent Elector" and "Liberty Poles! No Stamp Act!" *Albany Gazette*, Feb. 19, 1798; "To the Farmers," *Otsego Herald*, Apr. 19, 1798; James Kent, "Western Circuit Journal," 1798, JKP, reel 1, LC; "Communication," *Albany Register*, Nov. 5, 1798; Johannes Miller to Ebenezer Foote, Feb. 21, 1799, EFP, reel 1, LC; Republican orator quoted and denounced in "Federal Creed," Butternuts, Apr. 25, 1798, *Otsego Herald*, May 3, 1798; Jacob Morris to James Morris, Apr. 2, 1797, Morris Family Papers, NYHS.

17. Otsego Co. Address in *A Selection of the Patriotic Addresses, To the President of the United States, Together with the President's Answers, Presented in the Year One Thousand Seven Hundred and Ninety-Eight* (Boston, 1798), 153–54; Otsego Co. Meeting, May 19, 1798, *Otsego Herald*, May 24 ("effeminate spawn"), June 21, 1798; Cooperstown, July 4 celebration, ibid., July 5, 1798.

18. "Characteristics of Jacobin, Electioneering Demagogues," *Albany Centinel*, Apr. 24, 1798; "What is a Democrat?" ibid., Aug. 10, 1798; "A Jacobin," ibid., Sept. 14, 1798; "An Address to the Youthful Citizens of United America," ibid., Nov. 6, 1798; "Albany," ibid., Nov. 16, 1798; "Oration," *Albany Gazette*, July 9, 1798; Miller, *Crisis in Freedom*, 7–15, 30–38.

19. John R. Howe, Jr., "Republican Thought and the Political Violence of the 1790s," *American Quarterly*, 19 (Summer 1967), 147–65; "Marcellus," *Albany Centinel*, Apr. 1, 1800 ("little revolutions").

20. "Benedict Arnold," *Albany Register*, Oct. 12, 1798; "Astronomicus," ibid., Nov. 9, 1798; "A Republican," ibid., Mar. 25, 1799; "Albany," ibid., Mar. 21, 1800; "Address to the Electors of New York," ibid., Mar. 13, 1801 ("war of principles"); *To the Electors of the State of New York* (n.p., 1800, Evans no. 38648).

21. "Marcus Brutus," *Albany Gazette*, May 14, 1798 ("The demagogues"); "A Federalist," *Albany Centinel*, June 29, 1798; "To the Electors of the State of New-York," ibid., Apr. 12, 1799 ("every man"); "Marcellus," ibid., Apr. 22 and 29, 1800; [Alexander Hamilton], "An Address to the Electors of the State of New York," Mar. 21, 1801, in Harold C. Syrett et al., eds., *The Papers of Alexander Hamilton*, 27 vols. (New York, 1961–1987), vol. 25, 370–71.

22. [Jedediah Peck], "Plough-Jogger," *Otsego Herald*, May 17, 1798; Burlington meeting, May 25, 1798, ibid., May 31, 1798; Burlington Address to Pres. John Adams, May 25, 1798, Adams Papers, reel 388, MHS ("to gird").

23. Jedediah Peck to Elihu Phinney, Sept. 1, 1798, *Otsego Herald*, Sept. 6, 1798; Benjamin Gilbert, Joshua Dewey, and Francis Henry to Peck, Sept. 10, 1798, ibid., Sept. 20, 1798; Gilbert to Peck, ibid., Nov. 22, 1798; [Phinney], "Thalia," ibid., Dec. 13, 1798.

24. Joshua Dewey to Jedediah Peck, *Otsego Herald*, Oct. 25, 1798; Francis Henry to Peck, ibid., Nov. 8, 1798; Benjamin Gilbert to Peck, ibid., Nov. 22, 1798; Elihu Phinney addendum to Henry to Peck, ibid., Nov. 8, 1798; [Phinney], "Liberty of the Press!" ibid., Dec. 6, 1798; "Otsegonius," ibid., Jan. 3, 1799 ("No minds").

25. Elihu Phinney, notice, *Otsego Herald*, Nov. 15, 1798; Phinney addendum to Fly Creek Meeting, Nov. 27, ibid., Dec. 6, 1798; Jedediah Peck, notice, Feb. 1, 1799, *Albany Register*, Feb. 1, 1799.

26. Jedediah Peck to Benjamin Gilbert, Joshua Dewey, and Francis Henry, *Otsego Herald*, Oct. 11, 1798; Peck to Dewey, *Albany Register*, Feb. 1, 1799; Peck to Henry, ibid., Feb. 18, 1799; Peck to Gilbert, ibid., Mar. 18, 1799.

27. Jedediah Peck to Joshua Dewey, *Albany Register*, Feb. 1, 1799; Peck to Francis Henry, ibid., Feb. 18, 1799.

28. Jedediah Peck to Francis Henry, *Albany Register*, Feb. 18, 1799; Otsego Lodge Minute Book, vol. 1, Otsego Lodge Vault, Cooperstown. For their convivial style see Elihu Phinney to William Cooper, Jan. 4, 1796, and Dec. 23, 1799, WCP, CB 1796–1798, and CB 1799–1801, HCA.

29. Daniel Hale to William Cooper, Jan. 9, 1799, WCP, CB 1799–1801, HCA; John Jay to Jedediah Morse, Jan. 30, 1799, in Henry P. Johnston, ed., *The Correspondence and Public Papers of John Jay*, 4 vols. (New York, 1890–1893), vol. 4, 252–53.

30. Otsego petition, Feb. 1799, Council of Appointment Files (series A1847), box 5, NYSA; Council of Appointment Records (series A1845), IV, 135 (Mar. 9), 150 (Mar. 16), NYSA; Jedediah Peck to Gov. John Jay, Mar. 14 and 30, 1799, *Albany Register*, Apr. 1, 1799.

31. *Otsego Herald*, Mar. 7, 1799 ("unintelligible"); *Albany Register*, Nov. 9, 1798, Mar. 15, 1799 ("Plough-Joggers").

32. "An Elector," *Albany Register*, Feb. 11, 1799; "Legislature of New York," ibid., Feb. 15, and Mar. 15, 1799; "Assembly Debate," *Otsego Herald*, Feb. 28, 1799; Jabez D. Hammond, *The History of Political Parties in the State of New York*, 2 vols. (Albany, 1842), vol. 1, 123–24; Syrett, *Papers of Alexander Hamilton*, vol. 22, 477 n. 2. For Federalist horror at Peck's proposals see James Kent to Moss Kent, Jr., Feb. 23, 1799, JKP, reel 2, LC; "Extract," *Albany Centinel*, Apr. 30, 1799.

33. Timothy Morse to Jacob Morris, Mar. 5, 1799, Jacob Morris Papers, Cornell Univ. Lib.

34. William Cooper, circular letter, Mar. 14, 1799, *Albany Gazette*, Apr. 5, 1799; Cooper, "Caution!" *Albany Centinel*, Apr. 23, 1799. For the Sedition Act see Miller, *Crisis in Freedom*.

35. *Albany Register*, Apr. 19 and 26, 1799; "Extract of a Letter From a Gentleman in Otsego," ibid., May 13, 1799.

36. Daniel Hale to William Cooper, Jan. 9, 1799, WCP, CB 1799–1801, HCA; James Kent to Moss Kent, Jr., March 8, 1799, and M. Kent, Jr., to J. Kent, May 9, 1799, JKP, reel 2, LC.

37. Otsego Co. meeting, Mar. 27, 1799, *Albany Gazette*, Apr. 5, 1799; Cooperstown meeting, Apr. 8, 1799, and David Mason, letter, Apr. 4, 1799, both in *Albany Centinel*, Apr. 19, 1799; John Russell, affidavit, Apr. 12, 1799, ibid., Apr. 23, 1799. "Elector of Montgomery," ibid., Apr. 23, 1799, hints that Mason delayed at Cooper's dictation.

38. Rensselaer Williams, affidavit, Apr. 12, 1799, *Albany Centinel*, Apr. 26, 1799; David Mason and Thomas Wattels, testimony, Apr. 12, 1799, in William Cooper, Docket Book, WCP, HCA.

39. William Cooper, Docket Book, Apr. 12, 1799, WCP, HCA; People v. Ten Broeck, OC-CO&T, Records, June 13, 1799, OCCO.

40. "To the Public," *Albany Centinel*, Apr. 30, 1799.

41. Hammond, *History of Political Parties*, vol. 1, 130–31; People v. Ten Broeck, OC-CO&T, Records, June 13, 1799, OCCO. For the voting returns see *Albany Register*, May 17, 1799; and *Albany Centinel*, June 14, 1799.

42. "To the Public," *Albany Centinel*, Apr. 30, 1799; "Albany," ibid., May 21, 1799; "Albany," ibid., June 7, 1799; "Albany," ibid., July 2, 1799; John Ostrander, "Address," ibid., July 16, 1799 ("root out"). Unfortunately, it is difficult to document the controversial events of the summer of 1799 because of severe gaps in the two principal sources for Otsego politics. First, virtually no political letters survive in Cooper's papers from 1799, suggesting a subsequent effort to discard painful reminders of a difficult time. Second, there is a gap in the surviving run of the *Otsego Herald*, the principal source for political controversy in the county. It breaks off on Mar. 21, 1799 (issue no. 208), on the eve of the spring election, and does not resume until Sept. 5, 1799 (issue no. 232). When the break begins the *Otsego Herald* is deeply embroiled in political attacks and counterattacks. When the break ends the paper has a remarkably different tone, completely devoid of local political polemics. Something happened in the twenty-three missing issues that seared Phinney into a new policy of stringently avoiding political controversy. I suspect that the events of the spring and summer of 1799 proved so embarrassing and painful to the keeper of the main run now surviving (probably Phinney) that he discarded the embarrassing issues. As a consequence of these twin gaps, my reconstitution of the tangled but critical events of 1799 relies on scattered, mostly external sources (especially the Albany newspapers). For the gap see Clarence S. Brigham, *History and Bibliography of American Newspapers, 1690–1820*, 2 vols. (Worcester, Mass., 1947), vol. 1, 568–9. The main surviving run is now at NYSHA.

43. Charles Giles, *Pioneer: A Narrative of the Nativity, Experience, Travels, and Ministerial Labors of*

Rev. Charles Giles (New York, 1844), 53 ("vault"); "Cooperstown, June 28," *Albany Gazette,* July 5, 1799 ("Spectacle" and "vast damage"). A missing issue of the *Otsego Herald* was probably the source for the newspaper item, and Elihu Phinney was probably its author.

44. Testimony of John Howard, Gustavus Walbridge, Norman Landon, and Charles Mudge, June 27, 1799, in Cooper, Docket Book, WCP, HCA; Court ruling, OC-CCP, Records, vol. 1, June 27, 1799. For Strong's previous legal troubles see People v. Strong, Oct. 5, 1796, and June 19, 1798, OC-CO&T, Indictments, vol. 2, OCCO; People v. Strong, OC-CGSP, Records, vol. 1, June 21, 1798, OCCO.

45. James Morton Smith, "The Sedition Law of 1798 and the Right of Petition: The Attempted Prosecution of Jedidiah Peck," *New York History,* 35 (Jan. 1954), 65; Affidavits of Capt. Jonathan Brown, Capt. Nathan Palmer, and David Goff, June 25–27, 1799, in United States v. Jedediah Peck, Sept. 4, 1799, U.S. Circuit Court, Southern District of New York, record group 21, National Archives; William Cooper to Oliver Wolcott, Aug. 20, 1799, Wolcott Papers, XV, 43, 59, Connecticut Historical Society, Hartford ("dissatisfaction"); Hammond, *History of Political Parties,* vol. 1, 131–32.

46. William Cooper to Oliver Wolcott, Sept. 16, 1799 ("want of Energy"), Wolcott Papers, XV, 43, 59, Connecticut Hist. Soc.; Hammond, *History of Political Parties,* vol. 1, 131–2; James Morton Smith, *Freedom's Fetters: The Alien and Sedition Laws and American Civil Liberties* (Ithaca, N.Y., 1956), 393–95; *Albany Register,* Oct. 1, 1799; Cooper v. Peck, OC-CCP, Records, vol. 1, June 27 and Oct. 17, 1799, OCCO. In Jan. 1795 Peck had bought 90 acres in Burlington from Cooper for £121.14.2. See OCRD, Conveyances A:428, OCCO; and William Cooper, Memorandum Book, Jan. 17, 1795, WCP, HCA. Reflecting Phinney's new policy against covering any local controversy, the *Otsego Herald* did *not* report Peck's arrest; the paper did publish a ringing endorsement of the Sedition Act on Sept. 5, 1799—about the time when the warrant for Peck's arrest reached Otsego.

47. William Cooper, Docket Book, Sept. 28 and Oct. 3, 1799, WCP, HCA; Elihu Phinney to Cooper, Dec. 23, 1799, WCP, CB 1799–1801, HCA; Otsego Co. Indictments of Stephen Scranton, Joshua Scranton, William Scranton, John A. Waterman, Bethel Martin, and Jeremiah Wheeler, Oct. 15, 1799, OCCO. Although there is no surviving indictment for Alexander Truely, Phinney's letter indicates that he had been arrested and incarcerated as one of the suspects.

48. Beardsley, *Reminiscences,* 89–90.

49. John F. Ernst, Sr., to John F. Ernst, Jr., Oct. 20, 1799, Jessie Hyde, deposition, Oct. 16, 1799, and Stephen Ingalls, deposition, Nov. 6, 1799, all in Birdsall, *Story of Cooperstown,* 99–100; Beardsley, *Reminiscences,* 89–90; William Cooper account with Elihu Phinney, Mar. 1, 1798–Jan. 1, 1802, WCP, BB 1802–1804, HCA; J. F. Cooper (1858–1938), *Legends and Traditions,* 36–37. Indicted and convicted in Otsego County for assaulting Cooper, Cochran appealed to the State Supreme Court of Judicature, which, in Oct. 1800, upheld his conviction but reduced his fine to a mere $1. See William Johnson, *Reports of Cases Adjudged in the Supreme Court of Judicature of the State of New-York; From January Term 1799 to January Term 1803,* 3 vols. (New York, 1808–1812, Shaw-Shoemaker no. 15759), vol. 2, 73.

50. Moss Kent, Jr., to James Kent, Aug. 27, 1799, and J. Kent to M. Kent, Jr., Sept. 5, 1799, JKP, reel 1, LC; Elihu Phinney to William Cooper, Dec. 23, 1799, WCP, CB 1799–1801, HCA; The People at the Relation of Joseph Strong v. The judges and Assistant Justices of Otsego, Oct. 25, 1799, New York SCJ, Minutes (series J 0130), NYSA. I am grateful to James Folts of the NYSA for his generous assistance in locating this last source. For Peck see *Albany Register,* Oct. 1, 1799; "Albany," *New London Bee,* Oct. 16, 1799; Hammond, *History of Political Parties,* vol. 1, 132; Richard Harison to Timothy Pickering, Apr. 10, 1800, Pickering Papers, XXVI, 77, MHS; James Arthur Frost, *Life on the Upper Susquehanna, 1783–1860* (New York, 1951), 49; Smith, "Sedition Law of 1798," 66–69.

51. William Cooper to John Jay, Oct. 25, 1799, doc. no. 1550, NYSL; William Cooper, "To the Electors of the Western District," Oct. 30, 1799, *Otsego Herald,* Nov. 7, 1799 (also *Albany Gazette,* Nov. 14, 1799); Cooper account with Elihu Phinney, Mar. 1, 1798–Jan. 1, 1802, WCP, BB 1802–4, HCA. Apparently Cooper was in Albany when the court ruled against him.

52. William Cooper to John Jay, Oct. 25, 1799, doc. no. 1550, NYSL; Council of Appointment, Records (series A1845), vol. 4, 167 (Jan. 8, 1800), 182 (Jan. 21), 184 (Jan. 24), 185 (Jan. 25), 273 (Oct. 29), NYSA; Richard Edwards to William Cooper, Jan. 25, Mar. 14, 1800, Daniel Hale to Cooper, Feb. 14, 1800, and Elihu Phinney to Cooper, Feb. 21, and Mar. 12, 1800, all WCP, CB 1799–1801, HCA.

53. People v. Stephen Scranton, June 3, 1800, OC-COT, Record Book, OCCO; Otsego Co. Indictments of Jacob Cummings, Silas Van Gilder, William Preston, and Moses Wheeler, Jan. 14–16, 1799, OCCO.

54. *Annals of Congress*, 6th Congress, 1st session, 392, 403 (Jan. 22, 1800), 424 (Jan. 23, 1800), 583 (Mar. 3, 1800), 629 (May 5, 1800); J. F. Cooper (1858–1938), *Reminiscences of Mid-Victorian Cooperstown*, 52; William Cooper to John Adams, Feb. 20, Cooper to Adams, May 5, 1800, Adams Papers, reel 397, MHS; John Marshall to Richard Fenimore Cooper, Sept. 24, 1800, WCP, CB 1799–1800, HCA. On January 22, 1800, Cooper was one of only 10 congressmen to vote against reducing the army (82 representatives, including most Federalists, voted in favor).

55. [Moss Kent, Jr.?], "To William Cooper, Esq.," *Albany Centinel*, Nov. 22, 1799; Abraham Van Vechten to Ebenezer Foote, Apr. 22, 1800, Aaron Burr Papers, Mss. Div., Sterling Lib., Yale Univ.

56. Robert Troup to William Cooper, Apr. 4 and May 2, 1800, and Stephen Van Rensselaer to Cooper, Apr. 28, 1800, WCP, CB 1799–1801, HCA; Jedediah Peck to Luther Rich, Mar. 17, 1800, in *Cooperstown Federalist*, Apr. 21, 1810; Hammond, *History of Political Parties*, vol. 1, 134–35; Mary-Jo Kline, ed., *Political Correspondence and Public Papers of Aaron Burr*, 2 vols. (Princeton, N.J., 1983), vol. 1, 419–25.

57. "Philo-Marcellus," *Albany Gazette*, Apr. 10, 1800 ("system of disunion"). For Federalist infighting and intrigue see Peter Colt to James Watson, Jan. 12, 1798, Watson Papers, box 4, Oneida Co. Hist. Soc.; John Williams to Stephen Van Rensselaer, May 10, 1798, Van Rensselaer Family Papers, folder 43, Albany Inst.; Barent Gardner to Peter Van Schaack, Apr. 10, 1799, Van Schaack Papers, LC; Joseph White to John Jay, May 28, 1799, Jay Papers, Columbia Univ.; "Extract of a Letter from Johnstown," *Albany Gazette*, June 10, 1799; Abraham Van Vechten to Ebenezer Foote, Apr. 22, 1800, Aaron Burr Papers, Mss. Div., Sterling Lib., Yale Univ.; Thomas R. Gold to Theodore Sedgwick, Nov. 3, 1800, Sedgwick Papers, box 4, MHS; Jonas Platt to James Kent, Dec. 25, 1800, JKP, reel 2, LC. Much of the Federalist infighting in 1799–1800 resulted from the intrigues by Abraham Van Vechten to manipulate Governor Jay and to control the Council of Appointment. For Van Vechten see Hammond, *History of Political Parties*, vol. 1, 456–57. For the national struggle see Sharp, *American Politics in the Early Republic*, 226–49; Elkins and McKittrick, *Age of Federalism*, 726–43.

58. "Albany," *Albany Centinel*, May 27, 1800; Jacob Morris, "Notice," Feb. 1, 1800, *Albany Gazette*, Feb. 17, 1800; Stephen Van Rensselaer to William Cooper, Apr. 28, 1800, WCP, CB 1798–1801, HCA. For the voting returns see *Otsego Herald*, May 15, 1800.

59. For the voting returns see *Otsego Herald*, May 15, 1800. For the property holding by township see "Abstract of the Valuations and Assessments in the County of Otsego in the Year 1799," series B-0315, NYSA. For the population figures see U.S. Bureau of the Census, 2d Manuscript Census of the United States, 1800, Otsego Co., series M32, reel 25, National Archives.

60. Kline, *Political Correspondence . . . of Aaron Burr*, vol. 1, 430–34; Hammond, *History of Political Parties*, vol. 1, 137–39, 144–45; Alexander Hamilton to John Jay, May 7, 1800, and Philip Schuyler to Jay, May 7, 1800, in Johnston, *Correspondence . . . of John Jay*, vol. 4, 270–73; Dixon Ryan Fox, *The Decline of Aristocracy in the Politics of New York, 1801–1840* (New York, 1965), 2–3; Thomas R. Gold to Theodore Sedgwick, Nov. 3, 1800, T. Sedgwick Papers, box 4, MHS.

61. Hammond, *History of Political Parties*, vol. 1, 143; Jonas Platt to James Kent, Dec. 25, 1800, Platt to Kent, Jan. 16, 1801, JKP, reel 2, LC; Richard Harison to William Cooper, Dec. 27, 1800, Daniel Hale to Cooper, Jan. 5, 1801, Stephen Van Rensselaer to Cooper, Jan. 8,

1801, WCP, CB 1799–1801, HCA; Dumas Malone, *Jefferson and His Time*, vol. 3, *Jefferson and the Ordeal of Liberty* (Boston, 1962), 493–502; William Cooper to Thomas Morris, Feb. 10, 1801, in Matthew L. Davis, ed., *Memoirs of Aaron Burr*, 2 vols. (New York, 1836–37), vol. 2, 113.

62. Jonas Platt to James Kent, Feb. 11, 1801, JKP, reel 2, LC; William Cooper to Thomas Morris, Feb. 13, 1801, in Davis, *Memoirs of Aaron Burr*, vol. 2, 113; Malone, *Jefferson and the Ordeal of Liberty*, 493–505.

63. Levi Lincoln to Richard Fenimore Cooper, Mar. 30, 1801, WCP, CB 1799–1801, HCA; J. F. Cooper (1858–1938), *Reminiscences of Mid-Victorian Cooperstown*, 53.

64. Hammond, *History of Political Parties*, vol. 1, 154–55; William B. Fink, "Stephen Van Rensselaer: The Last Patroon" (Ph.D. diss., Columbia Univ., 1950), 70; John P. Kaminski, *George Clinton: Yeoman Politician of the New Republic* (Madison, Wis., 1993), 256–60; "To the Electors of the State of New York," *Albany Centinel*, Feb. 6, 1801; "To the Electors of the State of New York," *Albany Register*, Mar. 13, 1801; [Jedediah Peck?], "Otsego," *Albany Register*, Apr. 14, 1801; "Extract of a Letter from a Gentleman in Montgomery County," *Albany Gazette*, May 7, 1801.

65. For the voting returns see *Otsego Herald*, May 14, 1801. In Otsego, the Republican assembly candidates averaged 1,406 votes to the Federalists' 1,111, while Clinton obtained 1,186 votes to Van Rensselaer's 1,062. Assuming that the gubernatorial voters cast ballots for the same party in the assembly voting, the Republicans garnered 220 of the 269 (82 percent) ballots for assemblymen cast by men who did not vote for governor. In 1800 the Republicans narrowly prevailed in Otsego by demoralizing the Federalists rather than by expanding the electorate. In 1801 the Republicans won big by drawing unprecedented numbers to the polls. In Otsego the election of 1801, rather than that of 1800, marked the democratic mobilization of the common voters. For Otsego's male population in 1800 see U.S. Bureau of the Census, *Return of the Whole Number of Persons Within the Several Districts of the United States* (Washington, D.C., 1802, Shaw-Shoemaker no. 3442), 46. I calculated the over-21 male population as the 1,063 men in the over-45 category plus the 2,416 men in the 26-to-44 category, plus half of the 1,635 in the 16-to-25 category, for a total of 4,296.

66. "Communication" (quotation), "The Circular Address of the Committee," and "A Sectarian," *Albany Gazette*, Aug. 13 and 17, Sept. 3, 1801.

67. Hammond, *History of Political Parties*, vol. 1, 167–80; Kaminski, *George Clinton*, 261–62; Council of Appointment, Records (series A1845), vol. 4, 255 (Apr. 9, 1800), 273 (Oct. 29, 1800) and vol. 6, 1 (Aug. 14, 1801), 76 (Mar. 2, 1802), 106 (Mar. 29, 1802), NYSA. Comparing the Otsego Civil List of Aug. 14, 1801 (as supplemented on Mar. 2 and 29, 1802), with that of Apr. 9, 1800 (as supplemented on Oct. 29, 1800), indicates who was sacked, who retained, and who newly appointed by the new regime. Twenty-nine of the 38 displaced men can be identified as leading Federalists because they appeared in the proceedings of that party's local nominating meetings. Only 4 of 34 known Federalists on the 1800 civil list survived the Otsego purge of 1801–1802. At least 23 of the 37 new appointees were Republican activists. Most of the holdovers were men of unknown or Republican politics (12 of 17).

68. For the close association of Federalism with Freemasonry see Otsego Lodge proceedings, Dec. 27, 1798, *Otsego Herald*, Jan. 3, 1799. The members of Otsego Lodge were culled from their Minute Book, 1796–1800, Otsego Lodge, Cooperstown, New York. I located the new and the ousted officeholders on the tax returns for their particular township in Otsego County, Tax Assessment Rolls, 1800, series B-0950-85, box 37, NYSA. The two penurious new justices were Christopher Westcott of Richfield and Ezer Windsor of Otego. For the quotation see [Elihu Phinney], "Crito," *Otsego Herald*, Nov. 5, 1801.

69. William Cooper owned property in the towns of Butternuts, Burlington, Milford, Otego, Otsego, and Pittsfield. See their tax assessment lists, 1800, in series B-0950-85, box 37, NYSA.

70. Otsego Co. nominating meeting, Apr. 5, *Albany Gazette*, Apr. 19, 1804; "A Candid Republican," *Otsego Herald*, Apr. 19, 1804; voting returns, ibid., May 10, 1804; Hammond, *History*

of the Political Parties, vol. 1, 218; Council of Appointment proceedings, *Otsego Herald,* Apr. 25, 1805.

71. Beardsley, *Reminiscences,* 71; "Extract from a Learned Traveller," *Hudson Balance,* June 23, 1807.

72. John Lee Frisbee, "The Political Career of Jedediah Peck" (Master's thesis, SUNY at Oneonta, 1966, NYSHA copy), 113–15; Frost, *Life on the Upper Susquehanna,* 55–56, 112; Throop Wilder, "Jedediah Peck: Statesman, Soldier, Preacher," *New York History,* 22 (July 1941), 290–300; "Assembly Proceedings," *Otsego Herald,* Mar. 24, 1803. For the rejected bribes see Jedediah Peck, affidavit, Mar. 27, 1805, in *Albany Register,* Mar. 16, 1807.

73. Wilder, "Jedediah Peck," 298–99; Sherman Williams, "Jedediah Peck, the Father of the Public School System of the State of New York," NYSHA, *Quarterly Journal,* 1 (July 1920), 219–40; Hammond, *History of the Political Parties,* vol. 1, 158–59; [Jedediah Peck], "Thoughts on Public Schools," *Albany Register,* Feb. 18, 1799 ("all countries" and "greedy speculators"); Frisbee, "Political Career of Jedediah Peck," 115, 123; Jedediah Peck, *The Political Wars of Otsego: or Downfall of Jacobinism and Despotism* (Cooperstown, 1796, Evans no. 30968), 10, 91; Codman Hislop, *Eliphalet Nott* (Middletown, Conn., 1971), 87–90.

74. Horatio Gates Spafford, *A Gazetteer of the State of New-York* (Albany, 1824), 69.

75. For the quotation, see Gorham A. Worth, *Random Recollections of Albany From 1800 to 1808* (Albany, 1866), 3.

76. Lee Benson, *The Concept of Jacksonian Democracy: New York as a Test Case* (Princeton, N.J., 1961), 3–32; Harry L. Watson, *Liberty and Power: The Politics of Jacksonian America* (New York, 1990), 66–69.

77. Hammond, *History of the Political Parties,* vol. 1, 162; Richard Hofstadter, *The American Political Tradition and the Men Who Made It* (New York, 1973), 3–21, 56–85; Richard L. Bushman, *King and People in Provincial Massachusetts* (Chapel Hill, N.C., 1985), 248–52; Marvin Meyers, *The Jacksonian Persuasion: Politics and Belief* (Stanford, Calif., 1960), 3–32.

78. Benson J. Lossing, *The Pictorial Field-Book of the Revolution,* 2 vols. (New York, 1860), vol. 1, 221 n. 4.

79. Richard Godden, "Pioneer Properties, or 'What's in a Hut?,' " in Robert Clark, ed., *James Fenimore Cooper: New Critical Essays* (London, 1985), 140; James Henry Pickering, "James Fenimore Cooper and the History of New York" (Ph.D. diss., Northwestern Univ., 1964), 24; Charles Hansford Adams, *'The Guardian of the Law': Authority and Identity in James Fenimore Cooper* (University Park, Pa., 1990), 19–21, 23.

80. James Fenimore Cooper, *The Pioneers, or the Sources of the Susquehanna; A Descriptive Tale,* ed. James Franklin Beard (Albany, 1980, crit. ed. of New York, 1823), xxiv, 347, 389; Pickering, "James Fenimore Cooper and . . . New York," 211, 216–17, 230. Pickering astutely observes that Templeton "represents a telescoping of the early history of Cooperstown as it developed over a period of years, from about 1790 to 1804."

81. J. F. Cooper, *Pioneers,* 151–53, 159, 277, 281, 341.

82. J. F. Cooper, *Pioneers,* 328; William Cooper, *A Guide in the Wilderness* (Cooperstown, 1986, repr. of Dublin, 1810), 58–59.

83. J. F. Cooper, *Pioneers,* 142–43, 328, 345–46.

84. Henry Walcott Boynton, *James Fenimore Cooper* (New York, 1931), 24; Brook Thomas, *Cross-examinations of Law and Literature: Cooper, Hawthorne, Stowe, and Melville* (New York, 1987), 39; James K. Cooper to William Cooper, Mar. 3, 1800, in James Franklin Beard, ed., *The Letters and Journals of James Fenimore Cooper,* 6 vols. (Cambridge, Mass., 1960–1968), vol. 1, 6–7.

85. J. F. Cooper, *Pioneers,* 42–44, 100, 118, 290, 300–301, 317, 321. William Leete Stone, who was a boy in Burlington in 1799 and the novelist's friend in 1823, regarded Ten Broeck as "the original of Cooper's parenthetical lawyer, his compositions having been remarkable for parentheses." Cooperstown historian Ralph Birdsall also identified Van Der School with Ten Broeck, but James Beard offered the incomprehensible equation of the dull Dutch lawyer with the Yankee farmer-preacher-surveyor-carpenter Jedediah Peck, allegedly because Peck wrote political essays with many parenthetical asides. In fact, such

asides are rare in Peck's vivid, colloquial, and direct prose, whereas they abound in the writings by Ten Broeck. Misled by Beard's attribution, James H. Pickering subdues his own caveats to accept Peck as the basis for Van Der School. See Stone quoted in Shaw T. Livermore, ed., *A Condensed History of Cooperstown* (Albany, 1862), 159; Birdsall, *The Story of Cooperstown*, 90; Beard, ed., "Introduction," to J. F. Cooper, *Pioneers*, li-lii n. 30; see Pickering, "James Fenimore Cooper and . . . New York," 323 n. 141.

86. J. F. Cooper, *Pioneers*, 329, 331–33, 382–83.

87. J. F. Cooper, *Pioneers*, 337, 378–79, 434–35. For the assaults on Peck see People v. Garrit Williamson, OC-CGSP, Record Book, Jan. 15, 1795, OCCO; People v. Jacob Morris, Oct. 5, 1796, Otsego County Indictments, OCCO; People v. Jacob Morris, Oct. 5, 1796, OC-CO&T, Record Book, OCCO; "Communication," *Otsego Herald*, Oct. 6, 1796.

88. J. F. Cooper, *Pioneers*, 446–47. For Cooper's practice of displacing conflicts see Robert Clark, *History and Myth in American Fiction, 1823–1852* (New York, 1984), 61–78.

11. HANNAH

1. Otsego Co. Tax Assessment Rolls, 1800, series B-0950-85, box 37, NYSA; Cooper, "List of Lands Unsold, Commencing November 16th 1797," WCP, Land Inventory Book, HCA. For Federalists' expectations that the Republicans would become levelers see Goldsborough Banyar to William Cooper, Apr. 13, 1801, WCP, CB 1799–1801, HCA; Miers Fisher to Cooper, Mar., n.d., 1809, WCP, CB 1807–09, HCA; Richard Harison to Abraham Van Vechten, Mar. 9, 1811, Van Vechten subsection, James T. Mitchell Coll., HSP.

2. Wayne Wright, "The Cooper Genealogy: Compiled from Materials in the Collection of the New York State Historical Association Library" (Typescript, 1983, NYSHA); William Cooper to Isaac Cooper, Feb. 7, 1804, WCP, CB 1802–04, HCA.

3. Warren Motley, *The American Abraham: James Fenimore Cooper and the Frontier Patriarch* (New York, 1987), 38–39; Robert Clark, "Rewriting Revolution: Cooper's War of Independence," in Clark, *James Fenimore Cooper: New Critical Essays* (London, 1985), 195; Stephen Railton, *Fenimore Cooper: A Study of His Life and Imagination* (Princeton, N.J., 1978), 43–45; William P. Kelly, *Plotting America's Past: Fenimore Cooper and the Leatherstocking Tales* (Carbondale, Ill., 1983), 32, 36.

4. James Fenimore Cooper, *The Pioneers, or the Sources of the Susquehanna; A Descriptive Tale*, ed. James Franklin Beard (Albany, 1980, crit. ed. of New York, 1823); Kelly, *Plotting America's Past*, 18–21. Although the novel is ostensibly set in 1793, the novelist described the interior of Otsego Hall, William Cooper's home, built in 1799–1800, rather than its predecessor, the Manor House, built in 1788–1790. The comic exterior description resembles neither mansion. See J. F. Cooper to Horatio Hastings Weld (for the *Brother Jonathan*), Mar. 22–25, 1842, in James Franklin Beard, ed., *Letters and Journals of James Fenimore Cooper*, 6 vols. (Cambridge, Mass., 1960–1968), vol. 4, 257–58.

5. The son exalted himself and diminished his father by, in James Grossman's words, "the private task of treating commerce . . . with amusement and contempt"—in sharp contrast to William Cooper, who had reveled in trade and described the world with commercial metaphors. See James Grossman, *James Fenimore Cooper* (New York, 1949), 73; Richard L. Bushman, *The Refinement of America: Persons, Houses, Cities* (New York, 1992), 417–19.

6. Oliver Corey to William Cooper, Apr. 14, 1802, WCP, CB 1802–03, HCA; unsigned penmanship exercise, 1801, WCP, CB 1799–1801, HCA; James Fenimore Cooper to Charles Kitchel Gardner, May, n.d., 1823, in Beard, *Letters and Journals*, vol. 1, 95; Corey taught James Fenimore Cooper to read. See J. F. Cooper to Richard Cooper, May 25, 1831, in Beard, *Letters and Journals*, vol. 2, 89.

7. James Fenimore Cooper to Susan De Lancey Cooper, June 12, 1834, in Beard, *Letters and Journals*, vol. 3, 41; Hannah Cooper to Catharine Wistar Bache, Sept. 29, 1799, Bache Papers, Firestone Lib., Princeton Univ.; James Fenimore Cooper, *Notions of the Americans, Picked Up by a Travelling Bachelor*, 2 vols. (New York, 1963, repr. of New York, 1828), vol. 2, 131; James Kent, Travel Journal for June 1801, JKP, reel 6, LC.

8. Richard R. Smith to William Cooper, Nov. 10 and Dec. 16 ("I believe"), 1794, Jan. 1, 1795,

WCP, CB 1794–96, HCA; Smith to Cooper, Feb. 22, 1798, WCP, CB 1796–98, HCA; Smith to Cooper, Mar. 15, Apr. 5, June 9, and Dec. 24, 1802, WCP, CB 1802–03, HCA.

9. William Cooper's accounts with Elnathan Osborn, July 5–Oct. 21, 1799; Samuel N. Shove, Aug. 16–Dec. 7, 1799; Elijah H. Metcalf, Aug. 20–Nov. 4, 1799, and May 3–Oct. 23, 1800—all WCP, BB 1799–1801, HCA; Susan Fenimore Cooper, ed., *Pages and Pictures, from the Writings of James Fenimore Cooper* (New York, 1861), 49; Hannah Cooper to William Cooper, Jr., July 12, 1800, WCP, CB 1799–1801, HCA. The organ remains a cherished heirloom in the possession of Henry Cooper, who generously shared a tape recently made of its various tunes; I listened to that tape as I first wrote these words. The organ was made by William Howe of New York City. For Howe see Rita Susswein Gottesman, *The Arts and Crafts in New York, 1777–1799: Advertisements and News Items from New York City Newspapers* (New York, 1954), 363.

10. Susan Fenimore Cooper, "Small Family Memories," in James Fenimore Cooper (1858–1938), ed., *Correspondence of James Fenimore Cooper*, 2 vols. (New Haven, Conn., 1922), vol. 1, 18; Richard R. Smith to William Cooper, June 9, 1802, WCP, CB 1802–03, HCA; James Fenimore Cooper to John H. Prentiss, for the *Freeman's Journal*, Aug. 16, 1837, in Beard, *Letters and Journals*, vol. 3, 277.

11. Cooperstown village census, 1790 and 1803, Cooper Family Papers, NYSHA; James Averell, Jr., to William Cooper, bill, Dec. 1, 1792, WCP, BB 1792–93, HCA; Ralph Birdsall, *The Story of Cooperstown* (Cooperstown, 1917), 305; James Fenimore Cooper, "Otsego Hall," in James Fenimore Cooper (1858–1938), ed., *The Legends and Traditions of a Northern County* (New York, 1921), 230.

12. Abraham C. Ten Broeck receipts, Oct. 21, 1800, May 11, 1801, and July 1, 1802, WCP, BB 1799–1801 and BB 1802–04, HCA; Ten Broeck to Cooper, May, 11, 1801, WCP, CB 1799–1801, HCA; S. F. Cooper, "Small Family Memories," 13; J. F. Cooper (1858–1938), *Legends and Traditions*, 99; Birdsall, *Story of Cooperstown*, 305; Paul S. D'Ambrosio and Charlotte M. Emans, *Folk Art's Many Faces: Portraits in the New York State Historical Association* (Cooperstown, 1987), 83–85.

13. "A Young Wench for Sale," Aug. 19, 1799, *Otsego Herald*, Sept. 5, 12, 19, 26, and Oct. 3, 1799; Hannah Cooper to William Cooper, Jan. 26, 1800, quoted in Clare Benedict, *Five Generations (1785–1923), Being Scattered Chapters From the History of the Cooper, Pomeroy, Woolson and Benedict Families . . .* (London, 1930), 13. The timing of the 1799 advertisement is intriguing: in the midst of Cooper's crusade to suppress political dissent in Otsego (two months after suspending Joseph Strong, a month before arresting Jedediah Peck). Did Cooper fear that the democratic assault on social hierarchy had corrupted the deference of his slaves? Perhaps his attempt to sell the troublesome slave was part of his systematic effort to restore order throughout Otsego.

14. William Wade to William Cooper, Jan. 16, and Sept. 4, 1793, WCP, CB 1704–93, HCA; Richard R. Smith to Cooper, Nov. 6, 10, and 25, 1794, and Andrew Craig to Cooper, June 15, 1795, WCP, CB 1794–96, HCA; Craig's account with Cooper, Nov. 9, 1794–July 1, 1796, WCP, BB 1794, HCA; Ann Cooper to W. Cooper, Nov. 27, 1794, Cooper Family Papers, Rollins College.

15. Ann Cooper to William Cooper, Nov. 27, 1794, Cooper Family Papers, Rollins College; Richard R. Smith to W. Cooper, Nov. 6 and 10, 1794, WCP, CB 1794–96, HCA.

16. Josiah O. Hoffman to William Cooper, Oct. 6, 1791, WCP, CB 1704–93, HCA.

17. [Talleyrand's poem], *Otsego Herald*, Oct. 2, 1795; Hugh Cooke MacDougall, *Cooper's Otsego County* (Cooperstown, 1989), 131; Hannah Cooper to Catharine Wistar Bache, Sept. 29, 1799, Bache Family Papers, Firestone Lib., Princeton Univ. Apparently Hannah did winter in Cooperstown, for she wrote a letter from there on Jan. 5, 1800. See H. Cooper to Chloe Fuller, Jan. 5, 1800, Cooper Family Papers, box 3, NYSHA. MacDougall translates the poem as

> *Cheerful philosopher in the springtime of her life,*
> *Neither time nor place changes her disposition.*

> *Following her own taste, simple and without affectation,*
> *In the midst of the desert she reads—ponders—writes.*
> *Cultivate beautiful Anna, your taste for study;*
> *You cannot here better employ your time;*
> *Otsego is not merry—but habit is everything;*
> *Even Paris would much displease you at first.*
> *One who can be content in a wasteland,*
> *On returning to the world is certain to shine.*

For Talleyrand's visit see Hans Huth and Wilma J. Pugh, "Talleyrand in America," American Historical Association, *Annual Report for 1941* (Washington, D.C., 1942), 5–13.

18. James Fenimore Cooper to Horatio Hastings Weld [for the *Brother Jonathan*], Mar. 22–25, 1842, in Beard, *Letters and Journals,* vol. 4, 256–7; Henry Walcott Boynton, *James Fenimore Cooper* (New York, 1931), 20–22.

19. Stephen Van Rensselaer to William Cooper, Oct. 12, 1792, and William Wade to Cooper, Sept. 4, 1793, WCP, CB 1704–93, HCA; Joseph Pearsall to Cooper, July 18, 1794, S. Van Rensselaer to Cooper, Feb. 12, 1796, WCP, CB 1794–96, HCA; Philip S. Van Rensselaer to Cooper, Sept. 9, 1796, Uriah Tracy to Cooper, Oct. 20, 1796, James H. Imlay to Cooper, Apr. 22, 1797, and Mary Daubeny to Cooper, Apr. 21, [1798], WCP, CB 1796–98, HCA; Birdsall, *Story of Cooperstown,* 117.

20. Hannah Cooper to Chloe Fuller, Jan. 5, 1800, Cooper Family Papers, box 3, NYSHA; Eliza McDonald to Fuller, Jan. 9, 1800, Fuller Family Papers, NYSHA.

21. Hannah Cooper, "Commonplace Book," 31, WCP, HCA; Birdsall, *Story of Cooperstown,* 106; Hannah Cooper to Catharine Wistar Bache, Sept. 29, 1799, Bache Family Papers, Firestone Lib., Princeton Univ.; H. Cooper to Isaac Cooper, Apr. 13, 1800, WCP, CB 1799–1801, HCA.

22. James Fenimore Cooper to Horatio Hastings Weld [for the *Brother Jonathan*], Mar. 22–25, 1842, in Beard, *Letters and Journals,* vol. 4, 256–57; Cooper, "Introduction [1851]," to *Pioneers,* 11; Goldsborough Banyar to William Cooper, Dec. 12, 1796, and Hannah Cooper to Isaac Cooper, June 25, [1798], WCP, CB 1796–98, HCA; Robert E. Spiller, *Fenimore Cooper, Critic of His Times* (New York, 1963, repr. of 1931). For Judge Temple as widower see Railton, *Fenimore Cooper,* 64.

23. Bushman, *Refinement of America,* 289, 309; Cathy N. Davidson, *Revolution and the Word: The Rise of the Novel in America* (New York, 1985), 52–53; Hannah Cooper, "Commonplace Book," WCP, HCA.

24. Davidson, *Revolution and the Word,* 122–23, 139–40; Hannah Cooper, "Commonplace Book," 17, 182, 189.

25. Davidson, *Revolution and the Word,* 140–43; Hannah Cooper, "Commonplace Book," esp. 265 (quotation).

26. Hannah Cooper to William Cooper, Jan. 26, 1800, in Benedict, *Five Generations,* 13; H. Cooper to Isaac Cooper, Apr. 13, 1800, WCP, CB 1799–1801, HCA; James H. Imlay to W. Cooper, Sept. 27, 1800, appended as "Letter the Fourth," in Hannah Cooper, "Commonplace Book," WCP, HCA.

27. James Fenimore Cooper to William Branford Shubrick, Feb. 28, 1841, in Beard, *Letters and Journals,* vol. 4, 124; Boynton, *James Fenimore Cooper,* 21–22.

28. Moss Kent, Jr., to James Kent, July 21, 1792, and Sept. 30, 1792, and J. Kent to M. Kent, Jr., Sept. 17, 1792, JKP, reel 1, LC.

29. Moss Kent, Jr., to James Kent, Sept. 30, 1792, June 14, 1794, Apr. 20, 1795, May 26, 1795, Oct. 24, 1796, and May 1, 1797, and J. Kent to M. Kent, Jr., May 11, 1795, JKP, reel 1, LC. For the Kirkland daughters see Walter Pilkington, ed., *The Journals of Samuel Kirkland: Eighteenth-Century Missionary to the Iroquois, Government Agent, Father of Hamilton College* (Clinton, N.Y., 1980), 223, 285 n. 40, 312.

30. Eliza McDonald to Chloe Fuller, Nov. 28, 1798, Feb. 10, 1799, and June 6, 1799, Fuller Papers, NYSHA.

31. Moss Kent, Jr., to James Kent, July 21, 1795, JKP, reel 1, LC.

32. Ibid.

33. James Kent to Moss Kent, Jr., July 27, 1795, and June 22, 1796, JKP, reel 1, LC.

34. Moss Kent, Jr., to James Kent, Aug. 29, 1800, JKP, reel 2, LC.

35. Moss Kent, Jr., to James Kent, Sept. 12, 1800, JKP, reel 2, LC; Jacob Morris to James Morris, Sept. 15, 1800, Morris Family Papers, NYHS; J. F. Cooper, "Otsego Hall," 227–28. The most detailed account of the ride, based on information from the Morris family, appears in Willard V. Huntington, "Old Time Notes Relating to Otsego County and the Upper Susquehanna Valley" (Typescript, NYSHA), 1075–77. The unlikely legend that Hannah rode the horse reluctantly after her brother Richard teased her for timidity appears in J. F. Cooper (1858–1938), *Legends and Traditions,* 61–62. The version that stresses her insistence on riding aggressively agrees with Elizabeth Temple's behavior in J. F. Cooper *Pioneers,* 231–33.

36. Moss Kent, Jr., to James Kent, Sept. 12, 1800 (with a memorandum appended by J. Kent), JKP, reel 2, LC; J. F. Cooper, "Otsego Hall," 228; "Melancholy Catastrophe," *Otsego Herald,* Sept. 18, 1800; Rev. Daniel Nash, "Funeral Sermon for Miss Hannah Cooper," Sept. 12, 1800, WCP, HCA; "Account of Expences for Miss Cooper's Funeral," WCP, BB 1799–1801, HCA.

37. "Melancholy Catastrophe," *Otsego Herald,* Sept. 18, 1800; James Kent memorandum appended to Moss Kent, Jr., to J. Kent, Sept. 12, 1800, JKP, reel 2, LC; Jacob Morris to James Morris, Sept. 15, 1800, Morris Family Papers, NYHS; [Moss Kent], "Extract of a Letter from a Gentleman in Cooperstown," Sept. 12, 1800, *Albany Centinel,* Sept. 16, 1800; Elaine Forman Crane, ed., *The Diary of Elizabeth Drinker,* 3 vols. (Boston, 1991), vol. 2, 1341; Richard R. Smith to William Cooper, Sept. 20, 1800, Anne Francis to W. Cooper, Oct. 4, 1800, James H. Imlay to W. Cooper, Oct. 10, 1800, Goldsborough Banyar to Richard Fenimore Cooper, Oct. 23, 1800, Mrs. Jephson to W. Cooper, Sept. 22, and Dec. 28, 1800, Catherine [Wistar] Bache to W. Cooper, Dec. 28, 1800, WCP, CB 1799–1801, HCA; Eliza McDonald to Chloe Fuller, Aug. 4, 1801, quoted in Birdsall, *Story of Cooperstown,* 104.

38. J. F. Cooper (1858-1938), *Legends and Traditions,* 61–63; James H. Imlay to William Cooper, Oct. 10, 1800 (Cooper quoted), Mar. 16, Apr. 24, May 30, July 12, and Dec. 23, 1801, Richard R. Smith to Cooper, July 2, 1801, WCP, CB 1799–1801, HCA; Jacob Morris to Cooper, Nov. 4, 1807, WCP, CB 1807–09, HCA.

39. J. F. Cooper (1858–1938), *Legends and Traditions,* 63; Hannah Cooper, "Commonplace Book," 277, WCP, HCA; William Cooper's inscription quoted in Clare Benedict, ed., "Cooper Notebook," 21, Pomeroy Place Coll., NYSHA; William Cooper, Will, Registry of Wills, book B, 239, Otsego Co. Surrogate's Office, Cooperstown; Charles R. Tichy, "Otsego Hall and Its Setting, 1786–1940," (Master's thesis, SUNY at Oneonta, 1973, NYSHA copy), 18.

40. Moss Kent, Jr., to James Kent, Sept. 12, 1800 (with a memorandum appended by J. Kent), and Oct. 26, 1800, JKP, reel 2, LC; Edward Porter Alexander, "Judge Kent's 'Jaunt' to Cooperstown in 1792," *New York History,* 22 (Oct. 1941), 453 n. 11.

41. James H. Imlay to Richard Fenimore Cooper, Jan. 1, and Mar. 29, 1803, WCP, CB 1802–03, HCA; Imlay to William Cooper, June 15, 1805, WCP, CB 1804–06, HCA ("I have not"); Imlay to R. F. Cooper, Mar. 9, 1807, and Apr. 24, 1809, WCP, CB 1807–09, HCA.

42. Alexander Coventry, *Memoirs of an Emigrant: The Journal of Alexander Coventry, M.D.,* 2 vols. (Albany, 1978), vol. 1, 1197–99; Boynton, *James Fenimore Cooper,* 16; Isaac Cooper, diary, Dec. 4, 1813, and June 19, 1814, NYSHA.

43. Susan Fenimore Cooper, "Small Family Memories," in James Fenimore Cooper (1858–1938), ed., *Correspondence of James Fenimore Cooper,* 2 vols. (New Haven, Conn., 1922), vol. 1, 12–13; D'Ambrosio and Emans, *Folk Art's Many Faces,* 83–85.

44. Charlotte Daubeny to William Cooper, Aug. 3, 1803, WCP, CB 1802–03, HCA; Cooper to Mary Daubeny, Dec. 10, 1805, Cooper file, Misc. Mss., NYPL.

45. James Fenimore Cooper to Mrs. Cooper, June 9, 1850, in Beard, *Letters and Journals,* vol.

6, 193; "An Evening with the Spirits," [Cooperstown], *Freeman's Journal,* June 15, 1850. I am indebted to Hugh C. MacDougall for bringing this last source to my attention. Long after the fact, the biographer Clymer conceded, but tried to minimize, Cooper's interest in spiritualism. See William Brandford Shubrick Clymer, *James Fenimore Cooper* (Boston, 1900), 6.

46. James Fenimore Cooper to Sarah Heyward Cruger, Dec. 20, 1849, in Beard, *Letters and Journals,* vol. 6, 99; Lucy B. Maddox, "Susan Fenimore Cooper and the Plain Daughters of America," *American Quarterly,* 40 (June, 1988), 135–37.

47. J. F. Cooper, *Pioneers,* 231–33.

48. Ibid., 239, 309, 408–11; Railton, *Fenimore Cooper,* 82, 107–8.

49. J. F. Cooper, *Pioneers,* 239, 309, 411, 413, 416.

50. Ibid., 411.

51. Ibid., 408, 411, 412. For the function of Elizabeth's adoration see Motley, *American Abraham,* 80; and Richard Godden, "Pioneer Properties: or 'What's in a Hut?' " in Robert Clark, ed., *James Fenimore Cooper: New Critical Essays* (London, 1985), 130.

52. J. F. Cooper, *Pioneers,* 407 ("flowing robes"), 412, 415; "Died," *Otsego Herald,* Oct. 5, 1811.

53. Railton, *Fenimore Cooper,* 87, 110 ("Oliver's"); Motley, *The American Abraham,* 80–81; Wayne Franklin, *The New World of James Fenimore Cooper* (Chicago, 1982), 105–6; Brook Thomas, *Cross-examinations of Law and Literature: Cooper, Hawthorne, Stowe, and Melville* (New York, 1987), 39; J. F. Cooper, "Introduction" (1851) to *Pioneers,* 11.

54. Joy S. Kasson, "Templeton Revisited: Social Criticism in *The Pioneers* and *Home as Found,*" *Studies in the Novel,* 9 (Spring 1977), 56. Franklin, *New World,* 105, aptly notes that Edwards represents Cooper's sense of himself as "the disregarded heir, a man who is more than he seems to be, and who at last recovers his due by revealing his hidden claims."

12. FATHER AND SONS

1. James Kent, Travel Journal, June 1801, JKP, reel 6, LC; John Simpson to William Cooper, Oct. 28, 1803, WCP, CB 1802–3, HCA; Miers Fisher to Thomas and Samuel Fisher, July 25, and Aug. 1, 1808 ("We reach'd"), Fisher Family Papers, box 4, HSP; "Extract from a Letter of a Learned Traveller," *Hudson Balance,* June 23, 1807.

2. Elkanah Watson to William Cooper, Apr. 22, 1803, WCP, CB 1802–3, HC; William Sampson to Cooper, in William Cooper, *A Guide in the Wilderness; or, the History of the First Settlements in the Western Counties of New York, with Useful Instructions to Future Settlers* (Cooperstown, 1986, repr. of Dublin, 1810), 1–4.

3. Edward Conrad Smith, "William Sampson," in *Dictionary of American Biography,* vol. 16, 321; Donald M. Roper, ed., "The Elite of the New York Bar as Seen from the Bench: James Kent's Necrologies," NYHS, *Quarterly,* 56 (July 1972), 225.

4. William Sampson to William Cooper, in W. Cooper, *Guide in the Wilderness,* 1–4, 13, 17; Sampson to Cooper, May 12, 1807, WCP, CB 1807–9, HCA.

5. Of the 682 taxpayers in 1800, 216 (32 percent) did not reappear on the 1803 tax list. Of the 736 on the 1800 federal census for Otsego Township, 359 (49 percent) did not reappear in 1810. See Otsego Township, Tax Assessment List, Otsego Co., 1800, series B-0950-85, box 37, NYSA; Otsego Township, Tax Assessment List, Otsego Co., 1803, series B-0950-85, box 38, NYSA; U.S. Bureau of the Census, Otsego Co., 1800, series M32, reel 25, National Archives; U.S. Bureau of the Census, Otsego Co. Census, 1810, series M252, reel 34, National Archives. For settler mobility see Gurdon Evans, "A General View and Agricultural Survey of the Co. of Madison," New York State Agricultural Soc., *Transactions,* 11 (1851), 682; Isaac Weld, Jr., *Travels Through the States of North America . . . During the Years 1795, 1796, and 1797,* 2 vols. (New York, 1968, repr. of London, 1807), vol. 2, 326; John Lorain, "Account of the Modes Pursued in Clearing Land in Pennsylvania, and on the Fences in New Settlements," Philadelphia Soc. for Promoting Agriculture, *Memoirs,* vol. 3 (1814), 113; François Alexandre Frédéric, Duc de La Rochefoucauld-Liancourt, *Travels Through the United States of North America . . . ,* 2 vols. (London, 1799), vol. 1, 107.

6. Joseph Crafts to Jeremiah Van Rensselaer, May 25, and June 10, 1793, JCHP, HCA; Golds-

borough Banyar, Memorandum, June 30, 1793, G. Banyar Papers, box 4, NYSL; James Fenimore Cooper, *The Pioneers, or the Sources of the Susquehanna; A Descriptive Tale,* ed. James Franklin Beard (Albany, 1980, crit. ed. of New York, 1823), 16, 158, 317; Elijah Hawkins to William Cooper, Mar. 15, 1794, WCP, CB 1794–96, HCA.

7. See the many "Articles of Agreement," in WCP, BB 1794 and BB 1795, HCA, esp. William Cooper to Elisha Fullam, June 1, 1795.

8. William Cooper to [Richard Harison], Sept. 10, 1795, WCP, CB 1794–96, HCA; Cooper, Memorandum Book, Sept. n.d., 1794, WCP, HCA.

9. William Cooper, Notice, *Otsego Herald,* Dec. 28, 1797; Rent Roll, Nov. 1, 1806, WCP, BB 1805–8, HCA; Lease lists, William Cooper, Will, May 13, 1808, Registry of Wills, book B, 244–48, Otsego Co. Surrogate's Office, Cooperstown; Roy Lyman Butterfield, *In Old Otsego: A New York County Views Its Past* (Cooperstown, 1959), 13; William Cooper to Thomas Fisher, Nov. 22, 1807, WCP, CB 1807–9, HCA ("For if"); W. Cooper, *Guide in the Wilderness,* 18–19. For rents elsewhere in New York see David Maldwyn Ellis, *Landlord and Farmers in the Hudson-Mohawk Region, 1790–1850* (Ithaca, N.Y., 1946), 45–51.

10. I culled Cooper's Articles of Agreement for Hartwick Patent land from WCP, BB 1794, BB 1795, BB 1796–98, and BB 1799–1801, HCA.

11. Otsego Township, Tax Assessment List, 1800, series B-0950-85, box 37, NYSA.

12. Rent Roll, Nov. 1, 1806, WCP, BB 1805–8, HCA; New York (State), *A General Account of the Number of Electors in the Several Counties of This State* (Albany, 1808, Shaw-Shoemaker no. 15749), 12. According to the state electoral census in Hartwick and Otsego townships, there were 169 tenants (22 percent) and 608 (78 percent) freeholders.

13. Franklin B. Hough, *A History of St. Lawrence and Franklin Counties, New York* (Albany, 1853), 288–90; W. Cooper, Land Record Book, 1, 59, 61, Cooper Family Papers, NYSHA; Cooper, Memorandum, n.d., c. 1804, and Cooper indenture with Daniel McCormick, May 4, 1804, WCP, BB 1802–4, HCA; Horatio G. Spafford, *A Gazetteer of the State of New York* (Albany, 1813, Shaw-Shoemaker no. 29836), 104, 175; W. Cooper, *Guide in the Wilderness,* 24 ("in my judgment"). Cooper's additional tracts were 15,527 acres in Scriba Township (held in partnership with Frederick De Peyster, a New York City merchant); 7,174 acres in Bangor Township; 6,750 acres in Township No. 5; and 5,463 acres in Edwards Township.

14. W. Cooper, *Guide in the Wilderness,* 24.

15. William Cooper, Land Record Book, 1, 59, 61, Cooper Family Papers, NYSHA; Henry Waddell to Cooper, July 9, 1805, WCP, CB 1804–6, HCA. For the Daubenys see Rufus Wilmot Griswold, *The Republican Court, or American Society in the Days of Washington* (New York, 1846), 31 n.; *Longworth's American Almanac, New-York Register and City Directory* (New York, 1809), 150.

16. Henry Waddell to William Cooper, July 9, 1805, WCP, CB 1804–6, HCA; Frederick De Peyster to Cooper, May 13, 1809, WCP, CB 1807–9, HCA.

17. Hough, *History of St. Lawrence,* 288–90; Jared House quoted in Clare Benedict, *Five Generations (1785–1923), Being Scattered Chapters From the History of the Cooper, Pomeroy, Woolson and Benedict Families . . .* (London, 1930), 2 n.; William Cooper, accounting of DeKalb expenses, June 20, 1803, WCP, BB 1802–4, HCA.

18. Daniel Hale to William Cooper, July 9, 1803, and Richard Harison to Cooper, July 13, 1803, WCP, CB 1802–3, HCA; Cooper's list of DeKalb purchasers, Feb. 2, 1804, WCP, BB 1802–4, HCA; Cooper to Thomas Fisher, Aug. 9, 1804, Logan-Fisher-Fox Papers, box 3, HSP.

19. William Cooper's list of DeKalb purchasers, Feb. 2, 1804, WCP, BB 1802–4, HCA; Hough, *History of St. Lawrence,* 289; Otsego Township, Tax Assessment List, 1803, series B-0950-85, box 38, NYSA; Potter Goff to Cooper, Aug. 6, 1804, WCP, CB 1804–6, HCA; Cooper to William Copley, June 30, 1804, and Cooper to Joseph Plumb, June 30, 1804, WCP, BB 1802–4, HCA. In addition to Stacey, the other leading DeKalb buyers were Salmon Rich (11,798 acres); James Farr (10,576); Alva Sharp (6,482); and Alexander and Andrew McCollom (5,833). For the subsequent survey problems see "An Act to Remedy Mistakes in

the Sale and Location of Certain Lands Granted by the People of this State" (chap. 125), New York (State), *Laws of the State of New-York, Passed at the Thirty-Fourth Session of the Legislature . . .* (Albany, 1811, Shaw-Shoemaker no. 23549), 223; Simeon DeWitt to Isaac Cooper, July 21, 1813, WCP, CB 1810–16, HCA.

20. William Cooper to Henry Drinker, June 8, 1802, HDP, CB 1793–1812, HSP.

21. Hough, *History of St. Lawrence,* 288–90; William Cooper, "Memorandum," undated, WCP, BB 1802–4, HCA; Cooper to Peter Goff and James Cooper, Feb. 16, 1805, and Cooper, memorandum of agreement with Stephen Titus, Jan. 19, 1805, WCP, BB 1805–8, HCA; Alexander McCollom to Cooper, Oct. 27, 1804, Thomas B. Benedict to Cooper, Aug. 15, and Nov. 24, 1805, and Cooper, undated memorandum drafted on the reverse of Robert L. Bowne to Cooper, Oct. 1, 1806, WCP, CB 1804–6, HCA; Spafford, *Gazetteer* (1813), 175. For Cooper's iron mine scheme see Benedict to Cooper, July 18, and 31, 1806, WCP, CB 1804–6, HCA.

22. William Cooper to John Campbell, Oct. 21, 1804, Cooper to Andrew McCollom, June 13, 1804, Cooper to Alexander McCollom, Feb. 5, 1805, Andrew McCollom to Cooper, June 18, 1804, Nathaniel Smith to Cooper, May 14, 1805, and Thomas B. Benedict to Cooper, Aug. 15, 1805, WCP, CB 1804–6, HCA; Articles of agreement, Cooper with Alexander and Andrew McCollom, Oct. 13, 1803, WCP, BB 1802–4, HCA; Cooper to Potter Goff and James Cooper, Feb. 16, 1805, WCP, BB 1805–8, WCP.

23. Hough, *History of St. Lawrence,* 290; William Cooper, undated memorandum, on the reverse side of Robert L. Bowne to Cooper, Oct. 1, 1806, and Thomas B. Benedict to Cooper, Jan. 10, 1806 [*sic,* should be 1807], July 18, and Dec. 22, 1806, all WCP, CB 1804–6, HCA; Moss Kent, Jr., to James Kent, Jan. 10, 1808, JKP, reel 2, LC.

24. Richard P. Casey, "North Country Nemesis: The Potash Rebellion and the Embargo of 1807–9," NYHS, *Quarterly,* 64 (Jan. 1980), 34–45. For the judge's smuggling see Thomas B. Benedict to William Cooper, Dec. 20, 1808, Mar. 21, 1809, and Apr. 24, 1809, and Forsythe, Richardson, and Co., to Benedict, Mar. 2, 1809, and Forsythe, Richardson, and Co., to Cooper, July 10, 1809, and Cooper to Albert Gallatin, Dec. 30, 1808, all in WCP, CB 1807–9, HCA. For his son's duty see James Adams to James Cooper, June 23, 1809, JFCP, box 1, AAS.

25. W. Cooper, *Guide in the Wilderness,* 9–11, 54–55.

26. Washington Irving, *Journals and Notebooks,* ed., Nathalia Wright, 4 vols. (Madison, Wis., 1969–70), vol. 1, 17–26 (Aug. 12–16, 1803); St. Lawrence Co. petition to the state legislature, c. June 1809, WCP, CB 1807–9, HCA.

27. William Cooper to Peter Goff and James Cooper, Feb. 16, 1805, WCP, BB 1805–8, HCA; Spafford, *Gazetteer* (1813), 175. In fact, no church was organized in DeKalb until 1817. See Hough, *History of St. Lawrence,* 291.

28. Cooper to Waddell, Nov. 29, 1804, Cooper to Madame de Stael, Apr. 1, 1805 ("You must not"), Waddell to Cooper, July 9, 1805, and Thomas B. Benedict to Cooper, July 18, 1806, WCP, CB 1804–6, HCA; Cooper to Frederick De Peyster, Mar. 27, 1809, Cooper Family Papers, box 2, NYSHA; Spafford, *Gazetteer of the State of New York* (1813), 175.

29. Miers Fisher to William Milner, Sept. 28, 1808, Fisher Family Papers, box 13, HSP; W. Cooper, *Guide in the Wilderness,* 24; Malcolm J. Rohrbough, *The Land Office Business: The Settlement and Administration of American Public Lands, 1789–1837* (New York, 1968), 23, 48.

30. Lyman H. Butterfield, "Judge William Cooper (1754–1809): A Sketch of His Character and Accomplishments," *New York History* 30 (Oct. 1949), 386, 395, 404. See also David Maldwyn Ellis, "The Coopers and the New York State Landholding System," *New York History,* 35 (Oct. 1954), 412–22; Peter C. Mancall, *The Valley of Opportunity: The Economic Culture of the Upper Susquehanna, 1700–1800* (Ithaca, N.Y., 1991), 1–2, 10, 171–172, 190–201, 209–10; Alfred F. Young, *The Democratic Republicans of New York: The Origins, 1763–1797* (Chapel Hill, N.C., 1967), 262–67; Lester H. Cohen, "Eden's Constitution: The Paradisiacal Dream and Enlightenment Values in Late Eighteenth-Century Literature of the American Frontier," *Prospects: An Annual of American Cultural Studies,* vol. 3 (1977), 88–90.

31. For the celebration of land speculators see Bernard Bailyn, *The Peopling of British North*

America: An Introduction (New York, 1986), 65–85, 154–55; Charles S. Grant, *Democracy in the Connecticut Frontier Town of Kent* (New York, 1961), 12–28; Robert P. Swierenga, "Land Speculation and Its Impact on American Economic Growth and Welfare: A Historiographical Review," *The Western Historical Quarterly,* 18 (July 1977), 283–302; William Wyckoff, *The Developer's Frontier: The Making of the Western New York Landscape* (New Haven, Conn., 1988), 1–23. For the failure of attempts to force development see Helen I. Cowan, *Charles Williamson: Genesee Promoter, Friend of Anglo-American Rapprochement* (Rochester, N.Y., 1941), 177–226.

32. William Cooper to Mary Daubeny, Dec. 10, 1805, Cooper file, Misc. Mss., NYPL.

33. William Cooper to Thomas Fisher, Aug. 9, 1804, Logan-Fisher-Fox Papers, box 3, HSP ("from home"); James Smith, Jr., to W. Cooper, July 27, 1804 ("I knew"), and W. Cooper to Henry Waddell, Nov. 29, 1804, WCP, CB 1804–6, HCA. For Cooper's absences see his account with Stewart Lewis, Albany innkeeper, Feb. 20–Mar. 22, 1805, WCP, BB 1804–6, HCA; W. Cooper to Peter Goff and James Cooper, Feb. 16, 1805, WCP, BB 1805–8, HCA; W. Cooper to Samuel Meredith, Nov. 14, 1805, Clymer-Meredith-Read Papers, box 10, NYPL. For disgruntled creditors see William R. Hart to W. Cooper, May 16, 1805, and Robert L. Bowne to W. Cooper, June 16, 1806, WCP, CB 1804–6, HCA; Bowne to W. Cooper, Apr. 3, and 23, 1807, James Sterling to W. Cooper, Sept. 2, 1807, and Apr. 7, 1808, WCP, CB 1807–9, HCA.

34. James and Henry Shotwell to William Cooper, Sept. 28, 1802, and William Allinson to Cooper, Nov. 9, 1803, WCP, CB 1802–3, HCA; Allinson to Cooper, June 17, 1805, and Mar. 3, 1806, and J. and H. Shotwell to Cooper, Jan. 11, 1806, WCP, CB 1804–6, HCA; J. and H. Shotwell to Cooper, Jan. 15, 1807, James Verree to Cooper, Jan. 20, and Nov. 25, 1807, Feb. 12, and Dec. 13, 1808, and May 25, 1809, and Allinson to Cooper, Jan. 17, Feb. 27, 1807 ("Why William"), and May 17, 1808, WCP, CB 1807–9, HCA.

35. William Cooper to Madame de Stael, Apr. 1, 1805, WCP, CB 1804–6, HCA.

36. Susan Fenimore Cooper, "Small Family Memories," in James Fenimore Cooper (1858–1938), ed., *Correspondence of James Fenimore Cooper,* 2 vols. (New Haven, Conn., 1922), vol. 1, 14 ("handsome man"); Richard Fenimore Cooper to William Cooper, Mar. 14, 1794, WCP, CB 1794–96, HCA; R. F. Cooper, certificate of admission to the Otsego bar, Oct. 10, 1797, WCP, CB 1796–98, HCA; R. F. Cooper to W. Cooper, Jan. 13, Nov. 27, and Dec. 30, 1799, WCP, CB 1799–1801, HCA; Goldsborough Banyar, Jr., to R. F. Cooper, Nov. 10, 1803, WCP, CB 1802–4, HCA; Farrand Stranahan and R. F. Cooper, Articles of Agreement, Dec. 30, 1803, WCP, BB 1802–4, HCA.

37. Goldsborough Banyar, Jr., to Richard Fenimore Cooper, Oct. 12, 1802, Sept. 16, and Oct. 15, 1803, James H. Imlay to R. F. Cooper, June 29, and Nov. 28, 1803, and Robert L. Bowne to R. F. Cooper, Dec. 9, 1803, WCP, CB 1802–3, HCA; Joseph Bloomfield to R. F. Cooper, Oct. 2 and Dec. 27, 1804, Banyar to R.F. Cooper, Oct. 29, 1805, Bowne to R. F. Cooper, Dec. 8, 1804, Feb. 14, Mar. 30, May 8 and May 11, Dec. 20, 1805, and May 8, 1806, and Bloomfield to R. F. Cooper, June 26, 1806, WCP, CB 1804–6, HCA; R. F. Cooper to Bloomfield, Mar. 10, 1808, and Bloomfield to R. F. Cooper, June 25, 1809, WCP, CB 1807–9, HCA; Bloomfield to R. F. Cooper, May 15, 1812, WCP, CB 1810–16, HCA. In 1812 Bloomfield formally severed his relationship with Cooper, and the agency passed to Dr. John Russell of Cooperstown.

38. Daniel Hale to William Cooper, Oct. 24, Dec. 3, 1804, and May 18, 1805 ("truly unfortunate"), and Cooper to Hale, Nov. 11 ("finding fault"), and Dec. 15, 1804, WCP, CB 1804–6, HCA. For the firm's disgruntled creditors see Gilbert and John Aspinwall to Cooper, May 22, and Nov. 14, 1806, WCP, CB 1804–6, HCA.

39. "Great Western Turnpike," *Otsego Herald,* Aug. 13, 1801; [Elihu Phinney], "Western Turnpike," ibid., Dec. 3, 1801; Goldsborough Banyar, Jr., to William Cooper, Dec. 18, 1801, WCP, CB 1799–1801, HCA; Cooper to Jeremiah Van Rensselaer, Aug. 10, 1803, JCHP, HCA; David Mason, notices, *Otsego Herald,* Jan. 19, and July 19, 1804. For the turnpike movement in New York see James Arthur Frost, *Life on the Upper Susquehanna, 1783–1860* (New York, 1951), 61–63; David Maldwyn Ellis, "The Rise of the Empire State,

1790–1820," *New York History,* 56 (Jan. 1975), 5–27; Spafford, *Gazetteer* (1813), 16; Joseph A. Durrenberger, *Turnpikes: A Study of the Toll Road Movement in the Middle Atlantic States and Maryland* (Cos Cob, Conn., 1968), 43, 60–64; Benjamin De Witt, "A Sketch of the Turnpike Roads in the State of New-York," Soc. for the Promotion of Useful Arts, *Transactions* (New York, 1807, Shaw-Shoemaker no. 13242), 199.

40. Stephen North to James Averell, Jr., May 13, 1805, AFP, box 1, NYSHA; David Mason, notices, *Otsego Herald,* July 11, 1805, and July 17, 1806; People v. William Cooper et al., June 1806 and June 1807, OC-CCP, Record Book, OCCO; "Great Western Turnpike Company," *Otsego Herald,* Aug. 20, 1806, and July 23, 1807; Andrew Brown to Cooper, Aug. 21, 1806, WCP, CB 1804–6, HCA; Christian Miller to Cooper, Aug. 11, 1807, WCP, CB 1807–9, HCA. For the widespread problems with New York turnpikes see "Observations on Turnpikes," *Albany Register,* Mar. 6, 1804; Spafford, *Gazetteer* (1813), 16.

41. John Maude, *Visit to the Falls of Niagara in 1800* (London, 1826), 38–41; Richard H. Schein, "A Historical Geography of Central New York: Patterns and Process of Colonization on the New Military Tract, 1782–1820" (Ph.D. diss., Syracuse Univ., 1989), 56–65, 81–92, 104–7, 143–50, 152–55; Joshua H. V. Clark, *Onondaga; or Reminiscences of Earlier and Later Times,* 2 vols. (Syracuse, N.Y., 1849), vol. 1, 359–64; William Cooper to Richard Harison, Sept. 10, 1795, WCP, CB 1794–1796, HCA. Schein calculates that only 14 percent of the soldiers retained their land. For the title problems see Charles Newkirk to Cooper, July 5, 1793, WCP, CB 1704–1793, HCA; Jonas Platt to Cooper, June 25, 1795, and John Richardson to Cooper, June 22, 1795, WCP, CB 1794–1796, HCA; Richardson to Cooper, Aug. 21, 1798, Arthur Breese to Cooper, Aug. 8, 1797, and Richard S. Treat to Cooper, Sept. 27, 1798, all WCP, CB 1796–98, HCA.

42. Peter Ten Broeck to William Cooper, July 19, 1794, WCP, CB 1794–1796, HCA; P. Ten Broeck to Abraham C. Ten Broeck, May 1, 1798, and P. Ten Broeck to Cooper, Aug. 9, 1798, WCP, CB 1796–98, HCA; P. Ten Broeck to Cooper, July 20, 1799, WCP, CB 1799–1801, HCA.

43. Richard Harison to Cooper, Apr. 18, 1801, WCP, CB 1799–1801, HCA; Harison and Troup to Cooper, Oct. 2, 1804, Cooper to Harison and Troup, Nov. 24, 1804, WCP, CB 1804–6, HCA; Harison to Cooper, Dec. 13, 1807, WCP, CB 1807–9, HCA.

44. James Franklin Beard, ed., *Letters and Journals of James Fenimore Cooper,* 6 vols. (Cambridge, Mass., 1960–1968), vol. 1, 27 n. 2; William Wade to William Cooper, Oct. 2, 1792, WCP, CB 1704–1793, HCA; Cooper to Benjamin Rush, Feb. 1, 1800, BRP, vol. 3, 96, LCP.

45. William Cooper to Benjamin Rush, Feb. 1, 1800, BRP, vol. 3, 96, LCP; Samuel Stanhope Smith to Jonathan Dayton, Dec. 22, 1801, Smith Papers, Firestone Lib., Princeton Univ.; Smith to Cooper, Feb. 4, 1800, WCP, CB 1799–1801, HCA.

46. William Cooper to William Cooper, Jr., July 9, 1800, WCP, CB 1799–1801, HCA.

47. William Cooper, Jr., to Isaac Cooper, July 13, 1801, WCP, CB 1799–1801, HCA.

48. Samuel Stanhope Smith to William Cooper, Dec. 19, 1800, and Aug. 13, 1801, WCP, CB 1799–1801, HCA; Smith to Cooper, Feb. 22, 1802, WCP, CB 1802–1803, HCA.

49. William Cooper, Jr.,'s accounts with John Thompson, Nov. 2, 1801–Mar. 18, 1802, and with Robert Voorhees, Sept. 29, 1801–Feb. 26, 1802, and Voorhees to William Cooper, Feb. 26, 1802, WCP, CB 1802–1803, HCA.

50. Richard R. Smith to William Cooper, Mar. 15, 1802, and Samuel Stanhope Smith to Cooper, May 17, 1802, WCP, CB 1802–1803, HCA.

51. Princeton Faculty Minutes, Dec. 31, 1801, Jan. 1, 2, 9, 1802, and Joseph Olden to Mary Middleton, Mar. 7, 1802, Seelye G. Mudd Lib., Princeton Univ.; William Cooper, Jr., to Isaac Cooper, Jan. 2 and 13, 1802, WCP, CB 1802–1803, HCA.

52. Joseph Olden to Mary Middleton, Mar. 7, 1802, Seelye G. Mudd Lib., Princeton Univ.; Mark A. Noll, *Princeton and the Republic, 1768–1822: The Search for a Christian Enlightenment in the Era of Samuel Stanhope Smith* (Princeton, N.J., 1989), 158–59; Rev. William Neill, *A Discourse Reviewing a Ministry of Fifty Years* (Philadelphia, 1857), 10; Samuel Stanhope Smith to Jedediah Morse, Mar. 10, 1802, Morse Family Papers, Sterling Lib., Yale Univ.

53. Princeton Trustees' Minutes, Mar. 19, 1802, Seelye G. Mudd Lib., Princeton Univ.;

Thomas Jefferson Wertenbaker, *Princeton, 1746–1896* (Princeton, N.J., 1946), 127–28. Judge Cooper learned of the fire, but not of his son's apprehension, in Samuel Stanhope Smith to William Cooper, Mar. 8, 1802, WCP, CB 1802–03, HCA. The judge learned of the charges against his son from Richard R. Smith to Cooper, Mar. 15, 1802, and Joseph Bloomfield to Cooper, Mar. 21, 1802, WCP, CB 1802–03, HCA.

54. Joseph Bloomfield to William Cooper, Mar. 21, 1802, Richard R. Smith to Cooper, Apr. 5, 1802, and Samuel Stanhope Smith to Cooper, May 17, 1802, WCP, CB 1802–03, HCA.

55. Joseph Bloomfield to William Cooper, Oct. 2, 1802, WCP, CB 1802–03, HCA. For the accident theory see Wertenbaker, *Princeton,* 127–28. For suspicions of the local slaves see Joseph Olden to Mary Middleton, Mar. 7, 1802, Seelye G. Mudd Lib., Princeton Univ. For charges that students instigated the slaves see Richard R. Smith to Cooper, Mar. 15, 1802, WCP, CB 1802–03, HCA; and Neill, *Discourse,* 10.

56. Princeton Trustees Minutes, Mar. 19, 1802, Seelye G. Mudd Lib., Princeton Univ.; Rev. Ashbel Green, *An Address to the Students and Faculty of the College of New-Jersey, Delivered May 6th 1802* (Trenton, N.J., 1802, Shaw-Shoemaker no. 2355), 7–8. For subsequent student rebellions at Princeton see Augustus John Foster, *Jeffersonian America: Notes on the United States of America Collected in the Years 1805–6–7 and 11–12,* ed., Richard B. Davis (San Marino, Calif., 1954), 284; Noll, *Princeton and the Republic,* 159, 168–69, 227–31, 245, 279–81.

57. S. F. Cooper, "Small Family Memories," 14 ("wonderfully clever"); Richard Harison to William Cooper, May 16 and 28, and July 12, 1803, and William Cooper, Jr., to Isaac Cooper, June 28, 1803, WCP, CB 1802–03, HCA; Harison to W. Cooper, June 24, 1806, and William Cooper, Jr., to W. Cooper, Sept. 8 [1807], WCP, CB 1807–1809, HCA; J. F. Cooper, "Otsego Hall," 230. For the house and library see William Cooper, May 13, 1808, will, Registry of Wills, book B, 241, Otsego Co. Surrogate's Office, Cooperstown. For the balloon venture see Agreement of Elisha C. Tracy and Samuel Fry with William Cooper, Jr., undated [Nov.–Dec. 1818], WCP, BB 1801–34, HCA. For William's marital problems see Richard Fenimore Cooper to Isaac Clason, July 12, 1810, Clason to R. F. Cooper, July 21, 1810, WCP, CB 1810–16, HCA; and John Fine to Luther Bradish, Sept. 29, 1817, JFP, NYHS. For his business failures see William Cooper, Jr., to R. F. Cooper, Mar. 1, 1812, WCP, CB 1810–16, HCA; "Floating Battery," *Otsego Herald,* Aug. 21, 1813; Lida S. Penfield, "Three Generations of Coopers in Oswego," Oswego Hist. Soc., *Publications,* 5 (1941), 2–3; W. Cooper, Jr., to Col. Benjamin Walker, Aug. 31, 1813, Throop-Martin Autograph Coll., Firestone Lib., Princeton Univ. ("I am not").

58. Charles Hansford Adams, *"The Guardian of the Law": Authority and Identity in James Fenimore Cooper* (Univ. Park, Pa., 1990), 16; Warren Motley, *The American Abraham: James Fenimore Cooper and the Frontier Patriarch* (New York, 1987), 1–6, 45–46; Robert Clark, "Rewriting Revolution: Cooper's War of Independence," in Clark, *James Fenimore Cooper: New Critical Essays* (London, 1985), 195; Stephen Railton, *Fenimore Cooper: A Study of His Life and Imagination* (Princeton, N.J., 1978), 36; William P. Kelly, *Plotting America's Past: Fenimore Cooper and the Leatherstocking Tales* (Carbondale, Ill., 1983), 35–37; Robert Clark, *History and Myth in American Fiction, 1823–1852* (New York, 1984), 61–64; Brook Thomas, *Cross-examinations of Law and Literature: Cooper, Hawthorne, Stowe, and Melville* (New York, 1987), 29–30; George Dekker, *James Fenimore Cooper, the Novelist* (London, 1967), 2–8.

59. Railton, *Fenimore Cooper,* 116–20, 274; Motley, *American Abraham,* 46–47; Adams, *Guardian of the Law,* 16–17.

60. Reconstructing James Cooper's troubled adolescence is difficult because so few documents survive about his life before 1810 and because his early years have been obscured by a thick layer of often unreliable family tradition. The family legends were chiefly recorded by his grandson and namesake, James Fenimore Cooper (1858–1938), and usually accepted and perpetuated by James Franklin Beard, Jr., the editor of the novelist's letters and journals. See James Fenimore Cooper (1858–1938), *The Legends and Traditions of a Northern County* (New York, 1921); and James Fenimore Cooper (1858–1938), *Reminiscences of Mid-Victorian Cooperstown and a Sketch of William Cooper* (Cooperstown, 1936).

61. Hannah Cooper to Isaac Cooper, June 25, [1798], WCP, CB 1796–98, HCA; Beard, *Letters and Journals*, vol. 1, 4; James Fenimore Cooper to Richard Cooper, May 25, 1831, in ibid., vol. 2, 89. For the printing office tradition see G. Pomeroy Keese, "Memories," *Harper's Weekly*, July 29, 1871, p. 708.

62. Thomas Ellison to Cooper, Dec. 29 [1796], WCP, Undated box, HCA; Ralph Birdsall, *The Story of Cooperstown* (Cooperstown, 1917), 110; Cooper quoted in Henry Walcott Boynton, *James Fenimore Cooper* (New York, 1931), 26; James H. Pickering, "James Fenimore Cooper and the History of New York" (Ph.D. diss., Northwestern Univ., 1964), 153; J. F. Cooper to William Buell Sprague, Nov. 15, 1831, in Beard, *Letters and Journals*, vol. 2, 155.

63. Charles Tabb Hazelrigg, *American Literary Pioneer: A Biographical Study of James A. Hillhouse* (New York, 1953), 20–26; Anson Phelps Stokes, *Memorials of Eminent Yale Men*, 2 vols. (New Haven, Conn., 1914), vol. 1, 137–39; Jane W. Hill (Librarian, Yale Memorabilia Coll.) to James F. Beard, Jr., Sept. 21, 1953, Beard Papers, AAS; Beard, *Letters and Journals*, vol. 1, 5 n.

64. Boynton, *James Fenimore Cooper*, 29–30; James Fenimore Cooper to Benjamin Silliman, June 10, 1831 ("My misfortune"), and Sept. 16, 1842, in Beard, *Letters and Journals*, vol. 2, 99, and vol. 4, 314; Silliman quoted in ibid., vol. 1, 5. For the debts see Nathan Smith to William Cooper, Mar. 1, 1805, Finn and Sherman to W. Cooper, Sept. 6, 1805, and Feb. 19, 1806, and William Fitch (shoemaker) to W. Cooper, Apr. 30, 1806, WCP, CB 1804–1806, HCA. For James's reputation as a flirt see Daniel Mulford, Diary, Mar. 23, 1805, Sterling Lib., Yale Univ.

65. Nathan Smith to William Cooper, Dec. 21, 1805, WCP, CB 1804–1806, HCA; Jane W. Hill to James F. Beard, Jr., Sept. 21, 1953, Beard Papers, AAS; "John Boyle," in Franklin Bowditch Dexter, *Biographical Sketches of the Graduates of Yale College* (New Haven, Conn., 1911), vol. 6, 96; Cooper v. Boyle, 1805, Superior Court Records, New Haven County, vol. 2, 75, Clerk's Office, New Haven, Conn.; Cooper v. Boyle, 1805, Superior Court Files, Connecticut State Lib.

66. Jane W. Hill to James F. Beard, Jr., Sept. 21, 1953, Beard Papers, AAS; Boynton, *James Fenimore Cooper*, 31–2; Beard, *Letters and Journals*, vol. 1, 5; Pickering, "J. F. Cooper and . . . New York," 114–22.

67. William Neill quoted in Beard, *Letters and Journals*, vol. 1, 5; James Fenimore Cooper to William Buell Sprague, Nov. 15, 1831, in ibid., vol. 2, 157; Neill, *Discourse*, 10–14.

68. Thomas Philbrick, *James Fenimore Cooper and the Development of American Sea Fiction* (Cambridge, Mass., 1961).

69. Railton, *Fenimore Cooper*, 116–20, 274; A. Robert Lee, "Making History, Making Fiction: Cooper's *The Spy*," in W. M. Verhoeven, ed., *James Fenimore Cooper: New Historical and Literary Contexts* (Atlanta, 1993), 36. For the father-and-son collaboration view see Dekker, *James Fenimore Cooper*, 7; Boynton, *James Fenimore Cooper*, 32–34. For the notion that Judge Cooper sent his son to sea as an act of well-meaning and overdue discipline see Robert E. Spiller, *Fenimore Cooper: Critic of His Times* (New York, 1963, repr. of 1931), 47; Beard, *Letters and Journals*, vol. 1, 3, 5; James Grossman, *James Fenimore Cooper* (New York, 1949), 13; Mary E. Phillips, *James Fenimore Cooper* (New York, 1913), 42–43. Ultimately the biographers rely on a family tradition recorded in print by the novelist's grandson and namesake. See J. F. Cooper (1858–1938), *Legends and Traditions*, 256; J. F. Cooper (1858–1938), *Reminiscences of Mid-Victorian Cooperstown*, 51.

70. James Fenimore Cooper, *Afloat and Ashore, A Sea Tale* (New York, 1861, ed. of 1844), 30, 42. For its autobiographical aspect see Philbrick, *James Fenimore Cooper*, 131–32. The two letters are Richard R. Smith to Isaac Cooper, July 18, and Aug. 8, 1806, WCP, CB 1804–1806, HCA. Transcripts of the letters and a fuller discussion appear in Alan Taylor, "James Fenimore Cooper Goes to Sea: Two Unpublished Letters by a Family Friend," in Joel Myerson, ed., *Studies in the American Renaissance: 1993* (Charlottesville, Va., 1993), 43–54. James Beard mistakenly dates the *Stirling*'s departure to Oct. 15–16, 1806; on the basis of papers inherited from the *Stirling*'s captain, Edith Sawyer dates the departure to Sept. 1, 1806, when James Cooper's age was precisely that of Miles Wallingford at em-

barkation. James Cooper was born Sept. 15, 1789. See Beard, *Letters and Journals*, vol. 1, 5; Edith A. Sawyer, "A Year of Cooper's Youth," *New England Magazine*, 37 (Dec. 1907), 500.

71. James Fenimore Cooper, "The Eclipse," *Putnam's Magazine*, 2d ser., 4 (Sept. 1869), 357; Richard R. Smith to Isaac Cooper, July 18 and Aug. 8, 1806, WCP, CB 1804–1806, HCA. Stephen Railton notes that Cooper was in error in claiming to have already been a sailor at the time of the eclipse. Railton plausibly interprets the mistake as "remembered impatience at sixteen to go to sea," and "a heartfelt longing at the time to become a sailor." Given this insight, it is odd that Railton insists that the judge ordered his son to sea as a punishment—hardly a punishment, given the young man's apparent desires. See Railton, *Fenimore Cooper*, 261–62.

72. Smith to Isaac Cooper, Aug. 8, 1806, WCP, CB 1804–1806, HCA; William Spence Robertson, *The Life of Miranda*, 2 vols. (Chapel Hill, N.C.,1929), vol. 1, 299–320; Dumas Malone, *Jefferson and His Time*, vol. 5, *Jefferson the President: Second Term, 1805–1809* (Boston, 1974), 80–82; *Otsego Herald*, Mar. 13 and 27, Apr. 3, 17, and 24, June 19 and 26, 1806; Walter Pilkington, ed., *The Journals of Samuel Kirkland: Eighteenth-Century Missionary to the Iroquois, Government Agent, Father of Hamilton College* (Clinton, N.Y., 1980), 280. For Kirkland's political support of William Cooper, see Nomination meeting, Herkimer Township, Nov. 14, 1796, in *Albany Gazette*, Dec. 2, 1796.

73. Richard R. Smith to Isaac Cooper, Aug. 8, 1806, WCP, CB 1804–6, HCA; J. F. Cooper, *Afloat and Ashore*, 31–32.

74. Richard R. Smith to Isaac Cooper, Aug. 8, 1806, WCP, CB 1804–6, HCA; Robertson, *Life of Miranda*, 306–20. On the impressment of American sailors, see Paul Gilje, *The Road of Mobocracy: Popular Disorder in New York City, 1763–1834*, (Chapel Hill, N.C., 1987), 178–82.

75. *Ned Myers; Or a Life Before the Mast*, ed. James Fenimore Cooper (New York, 1912, repr. of 1843), 16; Sawyer, "Year of Cooper's Youth," 498–504. On Barker, see W. J. Ghent, "Jacob Barker," *Dictionary of American Biography*, vol. 1, 602–3. Unfortunately, Barker's autobiography says nothing about the Coopers or the *Stirling;* see [Jacob Barker], *Incidents in the Life of Jacob Barker of New Orleans, Louisiana* (Washington, D.C., 1855). For the *Stirling* and her captain, John Johnston, Jr., see William Armstrong Fairburn, *Merchant Sail*, 6 vols. (Center Lovell, Me., 1945–55), vol. 5, 3343–46; Fannie S. Chase, *Wiscasset in Pownalborough* (Wiscasset, Me., 1941), 471–73. I am indebted to Robert L. Webb, curator, and Harold E. Brown, curator emeritus, of the Marine Maritime Museum for their bibliographic assistance. For Cooper's subsequent naval career see Beard, *Letters and Journals*, vol. 1, 6, 24–25; James Adams to James Cooper, June 23, 1809, JFCP, AAS.

76. Richard R. Smith to Isaac Cooper, Aug. 8, 1806, WCP, CB 1804–6, HCA; James Cooper to Richard Fenimore Cooper, Dec. 19, 1808, in Beard, *Letters and Journals*, vol. 1, 11–12.

13. MURDER AND BLOODSHED

1. For the Otsego voting returns from the 1802 and 1803 elections see *Otsego Herald*, May 13, 1802, June 9, 1803, and May 10, 1804. In the assembly races each party ran a slate of four candidates who received varying votes; my percentages derive from comparing the average vote for a Republican and a Federalist candidate in each year. For example, in 1802 the four Republican candidates polled 1,213, 1,199, 1,158, and 1,102 votes, for an average of 1,168, while the four Federalists garnered 928, 843, 884, and 870 votes, for an average of 881. Adding 1,168 (57 percent) to 881 (43 percent) yields a total vote of 2,049 (100 percent).

2. Joseph White to Timothy Pickering, Jan. 17, 1815, Pickering Papers, XLIV, 104, MHS; White to Ebenezer Foote, June 28, 1824, Foote Papers, box 7, NYSL; Jacob Morris to James Morris, Dec. 18, 1801, and Mar. 25, 1812, Morris Family Papers, NYHS; Jacob Morris to Ebenezer Foote, May 28, 1814, and Apr. 25, 1815, EFP, box 4, Special Colls., Firestone Lib., Princeton Univ.

3. Stephen West Williams, *American Medical Biography; or, Memoirs of Eminent Physicians* (New York, 1845), 627–29; John Sawyer, *History of Cherry Valley From 1740 to 1898* (Cherry Val-

ley, N.Y., 1898), 95; E. A. Hartman, "General Jacob Morris Commemorative Address," June 17, 1887, NYSHA; Jacob Morris to Major Dix, Dec. 26, 1829, Jacob Morris Papers, Cornell Univ. Lib. White died in 1832 and Morris in 1844.

4. Foote quoted in William B. Fink, "Stephen Van Rensselaer: The Last Patroon" (Ph.D. diss., Columbia Univ., 1950), 74. See also James Kent, Western Circuit Journal, May 25, 1802, JKP, reel 6, LC; Loring Andrews to Ebenezer Foote, May 21, 1801, Josiah Ogden Hoffman to Foote, May 22, 1801, Jacob Rutsen Van Rensselaer to Foote, Nov. 28, 1802, and James Bill to Foote, May 11, 1803, all EFP, box 3, Special Collections, Firestone Lib., Princeton Univ.

5. Jabez D. Hammond, *The History of Political Parties in the State of New-York . . .*, 2 vols. (Albany, 1842), vol. 1, 195, 202–9; Daniel Hale to Richard Fenimore Cooper, Feb. 22 and 29, Mar. 17 ("This my friend") and 19, 1804, and Hale to William Cooper, Apr. 28, 1804, WCP, CB 1804–1806, HCA; Hale to Ebenezer Foote, Mar. 17, 1804, and Jacob Morris to Foote, Mar. 24, 1804, EFP, box 3, Special Colls., Firestone Lib., Princeton Univ.; Isaac Foote to Morris, Apr. 18, 1804, Morris Family Papers, box 1, NYHS. For the Otsego returns see *Otsego Herald,* May 10, 1804.

6. As measured by cases in the Otsego Court of Common Pleas, Strong's law practice fell precipitously from 77 judgments in 1797 to 26 in 1799, and a mere 16 in 1800. Strong died in 1840 in Flatbush, Long Island. Ten Broeck subsequently became a lawyer and distiller in Philadelphia, dying there in obscurity in 1841. Kent also served as the presiding judge in Jefferson Co., 1810–1818. In 1818 he resigned his judicial post and land office and left Jefferson Co. to join his beloved brother in Albany, serving as the register for his court of chancery until 1823. Kent died on June 1, 1838, at his sister's house in Plattsburg, New York. For Strong's travails see OC-CCP, Register of Judgments, 1792–1809, OCCO; grand jury indictments, People v. Richard Edwards, June 3, 1800, and People v. Jacob Kibbey, June 4, 1800, Otsego Indictments, folder 4, OCCO; Joseph Strong, notices, *Otsego Herald,* Mar. 27, Dec. 18, 1800, Feb. 26, Dec. 31, 1801; Eliza McDonald to Chloe Fuller, Aug. 4, 1801, McDonald File, NYSHA; Benjamin W. Dwight, *The History of the Descendants of Elder John Strong of Northampton, Massachusetts,* 2 vols. (Albany, N.Y., 1871), vol. 1, 671. For Ten Broeck see Notice, Nov. 23, 1802, *Otsego Herald,* Nov. 25, 1802; Abraham C. Ten Broeck to John Russell, Dec. 20, 1802, Conveyances, E:71, OCRD, OCCO; Joseph Bloomfield to Richard Fenimore Cooper, Apr. 21, 1804, WCP, CB 1804–1806, HCA; "Abraham Ten Broeck," in Ruth L. Woodward and Wesley Frank Craven, *Princetonians, 1784–1790* (Princeton, N.J., 1991), 57. For Kent see Council of Appointment, Minute Books (series A1845), VI, 291 (Nov. 7, 1804), NYSA; Moss Kent, Jr., to Joseph White, Feb. 1, 1805, Conveyances, F:453, OCRD, OCCO; Edward Porter Alexander, "Judge Kent's 'Jaunt' to Cooperstown in 1792," *New York History,* 22 (Oct. 1941), 453 n. 11; Franklin B. Hough, *A History of Jefferson County in the State of New York* (Albany, 1854), 57; Moss Kent, Jr., to James Kent, May 17, Sept. 5, 1806, JKP, reel 2, LC.

7. William Cooper to Richard Harison, July 13, 1806, WCP, CB 1804–1806, HCA. For the interest in public religion taken by many Federalists after 1800 see David Hackett Fischer, *The Revolution of American Conservatism: The Federalist Party in the Era of Jeffersonian Democracy* (New York, 1965), 48–49.

8. William Cooper, *A Guide in the Wilderness; or, the History of the First Settlements in the Western Counties of New York, with Useful Instructions to Future Settlers . . .* (Cooperstown, 1986, repr. of Dublin, 1810), 53; William Cooper to the Presbyterian Church [March 1806], an undated draft on the backside of Robert Troup to Cooper, May 23, 1805, WCP, CB 1804–1806, HCA. In that draft Cooper replies to a letter from the Presbyterian Church dated March 12, 1806.

9. Daniel Nash to William Cooper, Jan. 29, 1802, WCP, CB 1802–1803, HCA; Henry Chapman to Cooper, Dec. 15, 1806, WCP, CB 1804–1806, HCA; Otsego Co. Conveyances, C:129, K:131, and U:204, OCRD; Duane Hamilton Hurd, *History of Otsego County, New York . . .* (Philadelphia, 1878), 104; David Mason to Cooper, Mar. 12, 1806, Cooperstown Pres-

byterian Church Records, NYSHA; Cooper to the Presbyterian Church, an undated draft on the backside of Robert Troup to Cooper, May 23, 1805, WCP, CB 1804–1806, HCA; Rev. William Neill, *A Discourse Reviewing a Ministry of Fifty Years* (Philadelphia, 1857), 13.

10. For the interplay of religion and politics in the early Republic see Nathan O. Hatch, *The Democratization of American Christianity* (New Haven, Conn., 1989), 17–46; Alan Taylor, *Liberty Men and Great Proprietors: The Revolutionary Settlement on the Maine Frontier, 1760–1820* (Chapel Hill, N.C., 1990), 123–53.

11. Dixon Ryan Fox, *The Decline of Aristocracy in the Politics of New York, 1801–1840* (New York, 1965), 25–29, 137–39; Daniel Nash to William Cooper, Jan. 29, 1802, WCP, CB 1802–1803, HCA; Nash to Bishop John H. Hobart, Aug. 10, 1803, Apr. 23, 1806, BJHHP, PECA (NYHS microfilm copy, reel 8); Nash to W. Cooper, May 8, 1804, and Nash to Richard Fenimore Cooper, Dec. 27, 1806, WCP, CB 1804–1806, HCA. For Nash see Sylvester Nash, *A Portrait of Father Nash, Late Missionary in Otsego* (n.p., n.d., c. 1853), AAS copy; Franklin Bowditch Dexter, *Biographical Sketches of the Graduates of Yale College . . .* vol. 4 (New York, 1907), 431–32.

12. Daniel Nash to Richard Fenimore Cooper, Dec. 27, 1806, WCP, CB 1804–1806, HCA; Nash to Bishop John H. Hobart, Sept. 16, 1807, Jan. 24, 1812, May 29, 1815, BJHHP, PECA (NYHS microfilm copy, reels 9 and 11).

13. William Cooper to Richard Harison, July 13, 1806, and Harison to Cooper, July 21, 1806, WCP, CB 1804–1806, HCA; Fox, *Decline of Aristocracy*, 25–29, 137–39. For the religious views of James and William Cooper see also John Towner Frederick, *The Darkened Sky: Nineteenth-Century American Novelists* (Notre Dame, Ind., 1969), 2–3.

14. John Simpson to William Cooper, Oct. 28, 1803, WCP, CB 1802–3, HCA; Alexander Coventry, *Memoirs of an Emigrant: The Journal of Alexander Coventry, M.D.*, 2 vols. (Albany, 1978), vol. 1, 1196–99; "Memorandum," *Cooperstown Federalist*, Sept. 2, 1809 ("Found houses"). For the political debate over public morality see "Otsego Village," *Otsego Herald*, Sept. 9, 1809; "Clio," *Cooperstown Federalist*, Sept. 16, 1809.

15. Hammond, *History of Political Parties*, vol. 1, 225–27, 237–38; Philip G. Hubert, Jr., *The Merchants' National Bank of the City of New York* (New York, 1903), 52–54, 73–74; James Cheetham, *An Impartial Inquiry Into Certain Parts of the Conduct of Governor Lewis . . .* (New York, 1806, Shaw-Shoemaker no. 10724); Morgan Lewis to Edward Livingston, Apr. 16, 1805, Edward Livingston Papers, box 49, Special Coll., Firestone Lib., Princeton Univ.; Lewis to Cooper, June 5 (quotations), July 26, 1806, WCP, CB 1804–1806, HCA; Jedediah Peck, affidavit, Mar. 27, 1805, *Albany Register*, Mar. 16, 1807.

16. Ray W. Irwin, *Daniel P. Tompkins: Governor of New York and Vice President of the United States* (New York, 1968), 53–55; *Otsego Herald*, Sept. 12 and 19, Nov. 7, 1805, July 24, Sept. 25, 1806, Apr. 2 and 9, 1807. For other Federalists who jumped to Tompkins see Hammond, *History of Political Parties*, vol. 1, 246.

17. "Learned Traveller," *Hudson Balance*, July 28, 1807; "An Act to Vest Certain Powers in the Freeholders and Inhabitants of the Village of Otsego, in the County of Otsego," chap. 121 (Apr. 3, 1807), New York (State), *Laws of the State of New-York . . . [30th-32nd Sessions; 1807–1809]* (Albany, 1809, Shaw-Shoemaker no. 18237), 138–40; "A Number of the Freeholders of the Village of Otsego," *Otsego Herald*, June 11, 1807. For the waterworks company see Otsego Co. Conveyances, book A, 257 (Mar. 7, 1794), OCRD, OCCO. In a letter to William Cooper [June 10, 1800, WCP, CB 1799–1801, HCA], Robert Troup remarked that he had often heard the judge boast of the "pure water . . . brought to your door in logs." In "One of You," *Otsego Herald*, Mar. 13, 1806, Elihu Phinney had urged the incorporation of the village and identified the high cost of water as a prime consideration.

18. For the awkward efforts to keep the collusion quiet see William P. Beers to Ebenezer Foote, Aug. 15, 1805, Abraham Van Vechten to Foote, June 15, 1806, and Thomas Tillotson to Foote, Mar. 28, 1806, Mar. 20, 1807, all EFP, box 3, Special Colls., Firestone Lib., Princeton Univ.; Beers to Richard Fenimore Cooper, Apr. 17, 1807, WCP, CB 1807–1809, HCA. For the Republican glee, see *Albany Register*, Feb. 19, Mar. 2 and 26, 1807; "A Dialogue" and "Election," *Otsego Herald*, Apr. 16 and 23, 1807.

19. T. L. Ogden to William Cooper, Apr. 24, 1807, and Cooper to Mr. Leroy, May 9, 1807, WCP, CB 1807–1809, HCA; *Otsego Herald,* May 14 and 21, 1807; "Learned Traveller," *Hudson Balance,* June 23, 1807.
20. "Otsego Charter Election," *Otsego Herald,* May 14, 1807; "Otsego Village," ibid., May 28, 1807; Cooperstown meeting, May 23, 1807, [Albany] *Republican Crisis,* June 2, 1807; [Elihu Phinney], "A Number of Freeholders of the Village of Otsego," *Otsego Herald,* June 11, 1807. According to the election returns, the town of Otsego (including the village) cast 201 votes for Lewis to 135 for Tompkins, one of only 3 towns among Otsego's 16 to have a majority for Lewis. See *Otsego Herald,* May 14, 1807.
21. Cooperstown Federal Committee resolutions, Mar. 10, 1807, WCP, BB 1805–1808, HCA; *Otsego Herald,* May 28, 1807, May 21, June 18, 1808; William Andrews to William Cooper, May 30, July 20, Aug. 7, and Sept. 1, 1808, Thomas W. Moore to Cooper, Sept. 1, 1808, and Cooperstown Federalist Committee to Moore, Sept. 14, 1808, WCP, CB 1807–1809, HCA; Cooper to Charles and George Webster, Aug. 22, 1808, Simon Gratz Coll., HSP; *Impartial Observer,* Oct. 22, 1808, Dec. 3 and 10, 1808.
22. "The Imp," "A Clodhopper," and "Junius," *Otsego Herald,* Oct. 29, 1808, and Jan. 21, and Feb. 18, 1809; *Impartial Observer,* Mar. 4 and 11, Apr. 22 ("pigmy"), 1809; "Senectus," *Otsego Herald,* Mar. 18, 1809; Elijah H. Metcalf, letter, Mar. 16, 1809, in ibid.
23. *Impartial Observer,* Apr. 1, May 27, 1809; *Otsego Herald,* June 3, 1809. For Prentiss see Shaw T. Livermore, ed., *A Condensed History of Cooperstown* (Albany, 1862), 168.
24. *Impartial Observer,* Apr. 1, 1809; *Otsego Herald,* Apr. 1, 1809.
25. *Impartial Observer,* Apr. 1, 1809 ("The worthy"); *Otsego Herald,* Apr. 1, 1809; "A Villager," *Impartial Observer,* May 13, 1809; "A Looker On," *Otsego Herald,* May 13, 1809; Livermore, *Condensed History of Cooperstown,* 161.
26. "Fire!" *Cooperstown Federalist,* June 8, 1811; "Fire!" *Otsego Herald,* Dec. 5, 1812 ("timely exertions"); "An Act to Vest Certain Powers in the Freeholders and Inhabitants of the Village of Cooperstown, in the County of Otsego," chap. 150 (June 12, 1812), in New York (State), *Laws of the State of New-York, Passed at the Thirty-Fifth Session of the Legislature . . .* (Albany, 1812, Shaw-Shoemaker no. 26279), 266–71; Douglas M. Preston, "The Clang of the Bell, the Wail of the Whistle: A History of the Cooperstown Fire Department" (Master's thesis, SUNY at Oneonta, 1975, NYSHA copy), 10–19; *Otsego Herald,* July 17, 1813; James Fenimore Cooper, *Chronicles of Cooperstown* (1838), reprinted in Livermore, *Condensed History of Cooperstown,* 32.
27. Hammond, *History of Political Parties,* vol. 1, 265, 276; James Arthur Frost, *Life on the Upper Susquehanna, 1783–1860* (New York, 1951), 52. I compiled the petitioners for insolvency from the back pages of the *Otsego Herald* (1806–1809) and *Cooperstown Federalist* (1808–9). I compiled the debt suits from OC-CCP, Judgments Book, 1792–1809, OCCO.
28. Irwin, *Daniel D. Tompkins,* 61–66; Joseph White to Timothy Pickering, Dec. 26, 1808, Pickering Papers, XLIII, MHS. For the election returns see *Otsego Herald,* May 14, 1808, May 13, 1809.
29. U.S. Bureau of the Census, Otsego Co. Census, 1810, series M252, reel 34; *Otsego Herald,* May 13, 1809; John Homer French, ed., *Gazetteer of the State of New York* (Syracuse, N.Y., 1860), 530–39; "An Abstract for the County of Otsego for the Year 1810," in Otsego Co. Board of Supervisors, Minute Book, 1804–1823, OCCO.
30. I culled the names from the partisan notices in the *Otsego Herald,* 1808–1810 and the *Impartial Observer/Cooperstown Federalist,* 1809–10. I could determine the age categories for 53 Federalists and 103 Republicans in the 1810 federal census returns for Otsego towns. In each camp only one leader was less than twenty-six years old. The proportions of men under and over forty-five were virtually identical: 28 of 53 Federalists (53 percent) and 56 of 103 Republicans (54 percent) were under forty-five; 25 of 53 Federalists (47 percent) and 47 of 103 Republicans (46 percent) were over forty-five. See U.S. Bureau of the Census, Otsego Co. Census, 1810, series M252, reel 34. Only minorities in both parties had been activists in Otsego during the campaigns of the 1790s: 19 of 71 Federalists (27 percent) and 18 of 131 Republicans (14 percent). Fifty of the 71 Federalists bore Yankee sur-

names (70 percent), compared with 94 of 131 Republicans (72 percent); 10 of 71 Federalists bore Scotch-Irish surnames (14 percent), compared with 24 of 131 Republicans (18 percent). Men of German or Dutch ancestry were a bit more common among leading Federalists: 6 of 71 (8 percent) versus 5 of 131 Republicans (4 percent). The balances in both parties were men of uncertain patronymics. To sort names into probable ethnic groups, I relied on Patrick Hanks and Flavia Hodges, *A Dictionary of Surnames* (New York, 1988).

31. Otsego Co., Tax Assessment Lists, 1803, series B-0950-85, box 38, NYSA. The gap was greatest at the top of each party—the chairmen, secretaries, and candidates—and a bit narrower at the lower tier: the town delegates and committeemen. The 19 premier Federalists averaged $3,786, compared with $1,428 for the top 18 Republicans. Although narrower, there was also a gap at the second tier of leadership, where the 39 Federalists averaged $1,324, compared with $858 for the 84 Republicans.

32. Leonard Gansevoort et al., Federalist state committee circular letter, Jan. 17, 1809, EFP, reel 1, LC; Fischer, *Revolution of American Conservatism,* 60–61, 69–70, 75. For Federalist committees and conventions in Otsego and the Western District see *Impartial Observer,* Jan. 7, Feb. 25, and Mar. 4, 1809; Benjamin Walker et al., Federalist Western District circular letter, Dec. 10, 1808, WCP, CB 1807–1809, HCA.

33. "Gentlemen, you are Called Upon," Jan. [1809], WCP, Undated folder, Misc. Legal and Land Papers box, HCA; the folksy Federalist writer is quoted in James Fenimore Cooper (1858–1938), *The Legends and Traditions of a Northern County* (New York, 1921), 22; "Peace and no Embargo Nomination," [1809], WCP, Undated folder, Misc. Legal and Land Papers box, HCA; *Impartial Observer,* Apr. 15 and 22, 1809; Erastus Crafts to William B. Campbell, Mar. 30, 1810, Campbell Family Papers, box 1, NYSHA.

34. For young Federalists in general see Fischer, *Revolution of American Conservatism,* 29–49. For Campbell see Rev. E. A. Campbell, *A Sermon on the Death of Robert Campbell, Esq.,* . . . (Cincinnati, 1848), 5. For Dowse see *Otsego Herald,* Feb. 20, 1813. For Prentiss see *Biographical Directory of the American Congress, 1774–1989* (Washington, D.C., 1989), 1671.

35. Jacob Morris to James Morris, Mar. 25, 1812, Morris Family Papers, NYHS; Jacob Morris to Ebenezer Foote, May 28, 1814, EFP, box 4, Special Colls., Firestone Lib., Princeton Univ. For the discontents of the old, in general, see Fischer, *Revolution of American Conservatism,* 33–35.

36. Otsego Co. Federalist Committee, resolves, Apr. 23, 1808, Political Broadside Coll., NYSHA; Ebenezer Foote to William Cooper, June 1, 1808, and Foote to Isaac Cooper, June 5, 1808, WCP, CB 1807–1809, HCA; I. Cooper to Foote, June 3, 1808, EFP, box 1, NYSL. For the voting returns see *Otsego Herald,* May 14, 1808. Upon returning home from DeKalb, Judge Cooper belatedly rebuked William Dowse, who defended his conduct in Dowse to Cooper, Dec. 26, 1808, WCP, CB 1807–1809, HCA. David Hackett Fischer mischaracterizes Foote as "a young Federalist" in *Revolution of American Conservatism,* 313–14.

37. [Anonymous], *Genealogies of the Stranahan, Josselyn, Fitch and Dow Families in North America* (Brooklyn, 1868), 13, 19; Farrand Stranahan's advertisement, *Otsego Herald,* Sept. 10, 1801 (although dated June 24, this advertisement was not published in any previous issue of the *Otsego Herald*); Ralph Birdsall, *The Story of Cooperstown* (Cooperstown, 1917), 141; Dixon Ryan Fox, "Jabez Delano Hammond," *Dictionary of American Biography,* vol. 8, 205; Richard H. Levet, *Ambrose L. (Acqua Fortis) Jordan, Lawyer* (New York, 1973), 42–55. In 1806–7 Stranahan was the prevailing lawyer in 67 cases in the OC-CCP; the second most active lawyer in the county was Robert Campbell with 40 cases during that same period. In 1808–9 Hammond won 69 cases in the OC-CCP, second only to Isaac Seelye (98 cases) among Cherry Valley's lawyers. See OC-CCP, Judgments Book, 1792–1809, OCCO.

38. Articles of Agreement between Farrand Stranahan and Richard Fenimore Cooper, Dec. 30, 1803, WCP, BB 1802–1804, HCA; Levet, *Ambrose L. (Acqua Fortis) Jordan,* 20. For Hammond's political evolution see Jabez D. Hammond to Elihu Phinney, May 3, 1809, *Otsego Herald,* May 6, 1809; William Dowse to John H. Prentiss, May 13, 1809, *Impartial Observer,* May 13, 1809. For Van Rensselaer see Fox, *Decline of Aristocracy,* 44–45.

39. Irwin, *Daniel D. Tompkins*, 76–83. For the voting returns see *Otsego Herald*, May 5, 1810; *Cooperstown Federalist*, May 5, 1810.

40. *Otsego Herald*, Apr. 8 (both quotations) and 15, 1809. See also Jabez D. Hammond, *An Oration Delivered on the Glorious Tenth of June 1809, in the Court-House, in the Village of Otsego* (Cooperstown, 1809, Shaw-Shoemaker no. 17702), 21–22.

41. William Dowse to John H. Prentiss, May 13, 1809, *Impartial Observer*, May 13, 1809. See also James Steere to William Eddy, Jr., Mar. 13, 1810, S box, NYSHA; *Otsego Herald*, May 6, 13, and 27, June 10, 1809; *Impartial Observer*, Apr. 22, 1809.

42. Warren Motley, *The American Abraham: James Fenimore Cooper and the Frontier Patriarch* (New York, 1987), 13, 33; George Dekker, *James Fenimore Cooper, The Novelist* (London, 1967), 7; Frederick, *Darkened Sky*, 5; Hugh Cooke MacDougall, *Cooper's Otsego County* (Cooperstown, 1989), 33; Wayne Franklin, *The New World of James Fenimore Cooper* (Chicago, 1982), 16; Robert Emmet Long, *James Fenimore Cooper* (New York, 1990), 16.

43. Stephen Railton, *Fenimore Cooper: A Study of His Life and Imagination* (Princeton, N.J., 1978), 35–36, 49, 101–2, 120.

44. James Franklin Beard, ed., *The Letters and Journals of James Fenimore Cooper*, 6 vols. (Cambridge, Mass., 1960–1968), vol. 1, 16 n. 1; Beard does not cite his source for the tradition. William Brandford Shubrick Clymer, *James Fenimore Cooper* (Boston, 1900), 13; Mary E. Phillips, *James Fenimore Cooper* (New York, 1913), 62; Robert E. Spiller, *Fenimore Cooper, Critic of His Times* (New York, 1963, repr. of 1931), 25; Henry Walcott Boynton, *James Fenimore Cooper* (New York, 1931), 52; James Grossman, *James Fenimore Cooper* (New York, 1949), 15. Phillips and Boynton are on their own in locating the murder on the Capitol steps. Boynton commits an anachronism in calling the assailant a Whig, a party name from the mid–nineteenth century rather than the early Republic. He seems to have assumed that the son's political foes were also the father's.

45. Fischer, *Revolution of American Conservatism*, 14, 16, 26 (quotation); Lyman H. Butterfield, "Judge William Cooper (1754–1809): A Sketch of His Character and Accomplishments," *New York History*, 30 (Oct. 1949), 385–408 (quotation 402); Butterfield, "Cooper's Inheritance: The Otsego Country and Its Founders," *New York History*, 35 (Oct. 1954), 374–411.

46. W. Cooper, *Guide in the Wilderness*, introduced by James Fenimore Cooper (1858–1938) (Rochester, N.Y., 1897, reprint of Dublin, 1810), v; J. F. Cooper (1858–1938), *Legends and Traditions;* J. F. Cooper (1858–1938), *Reminiscences of Mid-Victorian Cooperstown and a Sketch of William Cooper* (Cooperstown, N.Y., 1936), 56.

47. J. F. Cooper (1858–1938) to Mary E. Phillips, Feb. 12, 1912, and Mary Phillips's galley proofs as amended by J. F. Cooper, Mary E. Phillips Papers, Rare Book and Manuscript Room, Boston Public Lib. For Cooper's assistance to the other biographers, see Beard, *Letters and Journals*, vol. 1, xxxviii–xxxix. Because Thomas R. Lounsbury did not receive any assistance from the Cooper family, his biography of the novelist, first published in 1882, does not subscribe to the legend but simply observes, "His father had died in 1809, and his mother in 1817." Thomas R. Lounsbury, *James Fenimore Cooper* (Boston, 1897), 15.

48. Susan Fenimore Cooper, ed., *Pages and Pictures, From the Writings of James Fenimore Cooper* (New York, 1861); Susan Fenimore Cooper, "Small Family Memories," James Fenimore Cooper (1858–1938), ed., in *Correspondence of James Fenimore Cooper*, 2 vols. (New Haven, Conn., 1922), vol. 1, 7–72; J. F. Cooper, *Chronicles of Cooperstown*, 63; J. F. Cooper to William Buell Sprague, Nov. 15, 1831, in Beard, *Letters and Journals*, vol. 2, 155.

49. McClelland and Low, bill, Dec. 22, 1809, H. Woodruff, bill, Dec. 22, 1809, and Stewart Lewis, account, Nov. 22–Dec. 23, 1809, WCP, BB 1809–1813, HCA; Isaac Cooper, Account Book for the William Cooper Estate, 1809–1817, entries for Jan. 5 and 9, 1810, on deposit from Henry S. Cooper at NYSHA.

50. Isaac and Richard Fenimore Cooper to Lady Anna Hay, Feb. 22, 1810, Isaac Cooper's letter Book, WCP, microfilm roll 2, HCA; Maria Banyar to R. F. Cooper, Jan. 17, 1810, Richard R. Smith to R. F. Cooper, Jan. 22, 1810, James H. Imlay to R. F. Cooper, Feb. 12, 1810, Anna Hay to I. and R. F. Cooper, Mar. 17, 1810, and Miers Fisher to I. Cooper, June

13, 1810, all WCP, CB 1810–1816, HCA. A letter by another Cooper son, William Cooper, Jr., also mentions no violence in informing an old friend of the judge's death; William Cooper, Jr., to Miers Fisher, Jan. 27, 1809 [*sic*], Fisher Family Papers, HSP. An inaccurate transcription of Hay's letter appears in J. F. Cooper, *Legends and Traditions*, 184.

51. Reverend Daniel Nash's funeral sermon for William Cooper, Dec. 25, 1809, WCP, Misc. box 1, HCA.

52. There were three newspapers published in Albany in late 1809 and early 1810: *The Balance* (Federalist), *The Albany Gazette* (Federalist) and *The Albany Register* (Republican). No issues survive from *The Albany Gazette* for the months Nov. 1809–Feb. 1810; a check of the other two Albany papers and the two Cooperstown papers for those months revealed neither a reference to a political meeting in Albany in Dec. nor any mention of an attack on William Cooper. For the Jan. 5 meeting see *The Balance*, Jan. 5, 1810. For the Albany newspapers see Clarence S. Brigham, *History and Bibliography of American Newspapers, 1690–1820*, 2 vols. (Worcester, Mass., 1947), vol. 1, 527–44. For obituaries see *The Balance*, Dec. 26, 1809; *Otsego Herald*, Dec. 30, 1809; *Cooperstown Federalist*, Dec. 30, 1809; [Hudson, N.Y.] *Northern Whig*, Jan. 18, 1810. The *Otsego Herald* is typical: "DIED, In Albany, on the 22d instant, WILLIAM COOPER, Esq. AEt. 55, and his remains, being removed to this place, were interred on Monday last, attended by a large concourse of citizens." Lyman Butterfield observed of Cooper's death, "The details are unrecorded, the Albany and Cooperstown newspapers providing only conventional notices of the death of an eminent citizen." Still, he clung to the story. See L. H. Butterfield, "Judge William Cooper," 402.

53. J. F. Cooper, *Reminiscences of Mid-Victorian Cooperstown*, 56; Boynton, *James Fenimore Cooper*, 52; and L. H. Butterfield, "Judge William Cooper," 402. A noteworthy example of partisan attempts to capitalize on political violence is the furor that Federalist orators and newspapers whipped up in the wake of the fatal duel in July 1804 when the Republican Aaron Burr shot the Federalist Alexander Hamilton. Harold C. Syrett et al., eds., *The Papers of Alexander Hamilton*, 27 vols. (New York, 1961–1989), vol. 26, 255–341.

54. Worth, *Random Recollections of Albany*, 78 ("a tumultuous"); "Affray in Albany," *Hampshire Federalist*, May 14, 1807 ("with the thick end"); William Pitt Beers to Maj. Augustine Prevost, Apr. 22, 1807, Prevost Papers, Rare Book and Manuscript Room, Boston Public Lib.; Elisha Jenkins to Martin Van Buren, Apr. 22, 1807, Van Buren Papers, reel 4, LC; [Albany], *Republican Crisis*, Apr. 30, 1807.

55. "Affray in Albany," *Hampshire Federalist*, May 14, 1807; William Pitt Beers to Maj. Augustine Prevost, Apr. 22, 1807, Prevost Papers, Rare Book and Manuscript Room, Boston Public Lib.; Elisha Jenkins to Martin Van Buren, Apr. 22, 1807, Van Buren Papers, reel 4, LC. For the prosecution see the reprint from *Republican Crisis* in *Otsego Herald*, Sept. 10, 1808.

56. In reviewing 16 years spent riding circuit in upstate New York as a state supreme court justice, James Kent calculated that he had tried 1,755 cases, but only 8 were murder convictions. See John T. Horton, *James Kent, a Study in Conservatism, 1763–1847* (New York, 1939), 135 n. 43.

57. People v. Farrand Stranahan, OC-CO&T, Indictment filed June 2, 1807, and Record Book 1, June 2, 1807, entry, both OCCO; "Extract from a Learned Traveller," *Hudson Balance*, June 23, 1807. The newspaper writer mistakenly identified the assailant as the Otsego Co. clerk (Dr. John Russell). "Corrector," *Hudson Balance*, July 21, 1807, reaffirmed the nature of the assault but correctly identified the assailant as Stranahan.

58. Otsego Co. Wills, book B, 116, Otsego Co. Surrogate's Office.

59. "Otsego Charter Election," *Otsego Herald*, May 14, 1807; J. F. Cooper, *Chronicles of Cooperstown*, 32; "Otsego Village," *Otsego Herald*, May 28, 1807; Cooperstown Meeting, May 23, 1807, *Republican Crisis*, June 2, 1807; "A Number of the Freeholders of the Village of Otsego," *Otsego Herald*, June 11, 1807.

60. George Clinton v. William Cooper, Nov. 15, 1793, Supreme Court of Judicature, Nisi Prius Court Record Book, 1784–1796, p. 351, NYCHR; Birdsall, *Story of Cooperstown*, 99–100.

61. People v. Stranahan, June 2, 1807, OC-CO&T, Record Book 1, OCCO.

62. For William Cooper's vigorous traveling in his last years see Thomas B. Benedict to Cooper, Mar. 16, 1808, and Anna Hay to Cooper, Dec. 18, 1809, WCP, CB 1807–1809, HCA; Cooper to Frederick De Peyster, Mar. 27, 1809, Cooper Family Papers, NYSHA; Cooper to De Peyster, May 29, 1809, De Peyster Papers, II, 66, NYHS.

63. Stranahan was employed as the plaintiffs' lawyer in Executors of William Cooper v. Joseph Griffin, Oct. 31, 1811, and Executors of William Cooper v. Uriah Luce, June 11, 1813, OC-CCP, Docket Book of Judgments, 1809–1817, OCCO.

64. For the corollary tradition see Boynton, *James Fenimore Cooper,* 52 (quotation); Beard, *Letters and Journals,* vol. 1, 16 n. 1. Elihu Phinney, Jr., to Nancy Whiting Tiffany, June 22, 1815, Phinney Family Papers, NYSHA; Levet, *Ambrose L. (Aqua Fortis) Jordan,* 13–49. Recently established as Cooperstown's third newspaper, *The Watch-Tower* was even more partisanly Republican than the old *Otsego Herald,* which had lost a lot of its bite after Elihu Phinney's death in 1813. Unfortunately, no issues of *The Watch-Tower* survive from June 1815, so it is impossible to know what Jordan wrote about Judge Cooper. Old myths die very hard. In a recent essay the literary critic Robert Lawson-Peebles cites my previously published essay "Who Murdered William Cooper?" to support his statement that the judge "died (possibly in odd circumstances)." His statement is odd given that my essay argued that there was nothing unusual about Cooper's death except the myths spun around it a century after the fact by his highly imaginative great-grandson, James Fenimore Cooper the younger. See Robert Lawson-Peebles, "Property, Marriage, Women, and Fenimore Cooper's First Fictions," in W. M. Verhoeven, ed., *James Fenimore Cooper: New Historical and Literary Contexts* (Atlanta, 1993), 59. The latest repetition of the myth is in Michael Davitt Bell, "Conditions of Literary Vocation," in Sacvan Bercovitch, ed., *The Cambridge History of American Literature,* Volume 2: 1820–1865 (New York, 1995), 26.

14. INHERITANCE LOST

1. William Simpson to Cooper, Oct. 28, 1803, WCP, CB 1802–3, HCA. For Morris see Gordon S. Wood, "Interests and Disinterestedness in the Making of the Constitution," in *Beyond Confederation: Origins of the Constitution and American National Identity,* ed. Richard Beeman, Stephen Botein, and Edward C. Carter, II, (Chapel Hill, N.C., 1987), 69–109. For Duer see Cathy Matson, "Public Vices, Private Benefit: William Duer and His Circle, 1776–1792," in William Pencak and Conrad Edick Wright, eds., *New York and the Rise of American Capitalism: Economic Development and the Social and Political History of an American State, 1780–1870* (New York, 1989), 72–123.

2. William Cooper, Will, May 13, 1808, Registry of Wills, book B, 237, Otsego Co. Surrogate's Office.

3. James Henry Pickering, "Fenimore Cooper as Country Gentleman: A New Glimpse at Cooper's Westchester Years," *New York History,* 72 (July 1991), 298–318; James Kent, Travel Journal, July 23, 1819, JKP, reel 6, LC.

4. William Cooper, Will, May 13, 1808, Registry of Wills, book B, 237, Otsego Co. Surrogate's Office. The heirs bear the blame in Henry Walcott Boynton, *James Fenimore Cooper* (New York, 1931), 70; Stephen Railton, *Fenimore Cooper: A Study of His Life and Imagination* (Princeton, N.J., 1978), 46.

5. William Cooper, Will, May 13, 1808, Registry of Wills, book B, 237, Otsego Co. Surrogate's Office; Cooper to Henry Waddell, Nov. 29, 1804, WCP, CB 1804–6, HCA. For the predominance of St. Lawrence Co. properties among the inherited lands see Isaac Cooper, "A Fine Chance for Settlers," *Cooperstown Federalist,* Apr. 4, 1812.

6. William Cooper to Henry Drinker, June 8, 1802, HDP, CB 1793–1812, HSP.

7. For overly optimistic readings of Cooper's record as a developer see Lyman H. Butterfield, "Judge William Cooper (1754–1809): A Sketch of His Character and Accomplishments," *New York History,* 30 (Oct. 1949), 385–408; Lyman H. Butterfield, "Cooper's Inheritance: The Otsego Country and Its Founders," *New York History,* 35 (Oct. 1954), 374–411; David Maldwyn Ellis, "The Coopers and the New York State Landholding System," *New York His-*

tory, 35 (Oct. 1954), 412–22; Lester H. Cohen, "Eden's Constitution: The Paradisiacal Dream and Enlightenment Values in Late Eighteenth-Century Literature of the American Frontier," *Prospects: An Annual of American Cultural Studies,* 3 (1977), 99.

8. James Franklin Beard, ed., *The Letters and Journals of James Fenimore Cooper* 6 vols. (Cambridge, Mass., 1960–1963), vol. 1, 7 n. 3; James Fenimore Cooper to Susan Augusta DeLancey Cooper, Apr. 26, 1812, in ibid., vol. 2, 26; *Cooperstown Federalist,* Apr. 11, 1812; James Fenimore Cooper (1858–1938), *The Legends and Traditions of a Northern County* (New York, 1921), 170–71, 230; Clare Benedict, *Five Generations (1785–1923), Being Scattered Chapters From the History of the Cooper, Pomeroy, Woolson and Benedict Families . . .* (London, 1930), 10; Boynton, *James Fenimore Cooper,* 70–73; Beard, *Letters and Journals,* vol. 1, 23; James Fenimore Cooper, *Chronicles of Cooperstown* (Cooperstown, 1838), reprinted in Shaw T. Livermore, ed., *A Condensed History of Cooperstown* (Albany, 1862), 32.

9. Ralph Birdsall, *The Story of Cooperstown* (Cooperstown, 1917), 124–25; James Fenimore Cooper, "Otsego Hall," in J. F. Cooper (1858–1938), *Legends and Traditions,* 229–30.

10. J. F. Cooper (1858–1938), *Legends and Traditions,* 46; J. F. Cooper, "Otsego Hall," in ibid., 229–30; Eliza McDonald to Chloe Fuller, Aug. 4, 1801, quoted in Birdsall, *Story of Cooperstown,* 104.

11. Susan Fenimore Cooper, "Small Family Memories," in James Fenimore Cooper (1858–1938), ed., *Correspondence of James Fenimore Cooper,* 2 vols. (New Haven, Conn., 1922), vol. 1, 13–14; J. F. Cooper, "Otsego Hall," 229; Isaac Cooper, account with Daniel Hale & Co., Nov. 17, 1801–Apr. 16, 1803, WCP, BB 1802–4, HCA; Hale to W. Cooper, Apr. 29, 1802, W. Cooper to I. Cooper, Feb. 7, 1804, and W. Cooper to Hale, Nov. 11, 1804, WCP, CB 1802–4, HCA.

12. Beard, *Letters and Journals,* vol. 1, 6, 23, 25 n. 1, 26 n. 3; James Cooper to Richard Fenimore Cooper, May 18, 1810, and J. Cooper to Susan Augusta De Lancey Cooper, June 30, 1814, in ibid., vol. 1, 17–18, 32; S. F. Cooper, "Small Family Memories," 9–12; Pickering, "Fenimore Cooper as Country Gentleman," 300–302; George Dekker, *James Fenimore Cooper, The Novelist* (London, 1967), 16–17. The nurse and cook were free white women, a mother and daughter, working for wages. The coachman was also free and white, but the waiter was an enslaved young Black man named Frederic.

13. Isaac Cooper, Diary, Dec. 4, 1813, NYSHA; Wayne Wright, "The Cooper Genealogy: Compiled from Materials in the Collection of the New York State Historical Association Library" (typescript, 1983, NYSHA), 15–17; William Cooper, Will, May 13, 1808, Registry of Wills, book B, 239, Otsego Co. Surrogate's Office. Isaac Cooper realized only one earthly part of his prayer: he would die in Edgewater within five years, leaving an insolvent estate that deprived his children of their home.

14. Isaac Cooper, Diary, 1812–18, NYSHA; "Cooperstown Assembly," invitation, Dec. 26, 1812, Campbell Family Papers, box 1, NYSHA.

15. Cooperstown village censuses of 1803 and 1816, Cooper Family Papers, NYSHA; Otsego Co. Board of Supervisors, Record Book for 1804–1822, entries for Oct. 2, 1805, Apr. 14, Oct. 8, 1806, Oct. 6, 1807, and Oct. 6, 1808, OCCO; Aaron Hamten, "Notes on a Journey from Kingwood in New Jersey to Lake Erie in the Year 1813," ed. Edna L. Jacobsen, *New York History,* 21 (July 1940), 334; "A Friend to Youth," *Otsego Herald,* Feb. 1, 1816; Cooperstown Ciceronian Association Proceedings, 1817, NYSHA; Young Ladies Benevolent Society, Constitution, 1819, Misc. Mss. C, NYSHA; James Kent, Travel Journal, July 23, 1819, JKP, reel 6, LC.

16. "Miscellaneous" and "Education," *Cooperstown Federalist,* Aug. 3, and Nov. 5, 1811; T. Shepherd, "Dancing School," *Otsego Herald,* July 17, 1813, "Theatre, Cooperstown," ibid., Sept. 25, 1813; James Averell 3d to William Holt Averell, May 19, 1813, AFP, box 2, NYSHA; George W. Scott to W. H. Averell, July 25, 1817, and Ebenezer B. Morehouse to W. H. Averell, July 25, 1817, AFP, box 3, NYSHA; Edward P. Alexander, "Cooperstown Society in 1820," *Cooperstown Journal,* Sept. 24, 1941; Sarah Amelia Fairman, Diary, Sept. 22, and Oct. 10, 1820, NYSHA.

17. "[Isaac Cooper] Obituary," *Otsego Herald,* Jan. 5, 1818. For James Fenimore Cooper's pre-

occupation with class distinctions see especially his novel *Home as Found* (New York, 1852).
18. Isaac Cooper, "Notice," *Otsego Herald*, Dec. 5, 1816; Isaac Cooper, Diary, Dec. 31, 1816, NYSHA; Mary Ann Morris Cooper, continuation of the Isaac Cooper, Diary, June 23, 1819, NYSHA; S. F. Cooper, "Small Family Memories," 19; Richard Fenimore Cooper receipt to James Cooper, May 2, 1811, WCP, BB 1801–34, HCA. For a futile attempt to buy a Black woman for Mary Ann Morris Cooper see John V. Henry to R. F. Cooper and Isaac Cooper, July 19, 1810, WCP, CB 1810–16, HCA. Susan Fenimore Cooper wrote that "Fred, a colored boy from Heathcote Hill, was the waiter" mistakenly implying that he came to the Coopers from prior service to the De Lanceys (S. F. Cooper, "Small Family Memories," 10).
19. People v. Susan Johnson, June 28, 1808, Otsego County Indictments, OCCO; Isaac Cooper, Diary, Jan. 11 and 13, 1817, NYSHA; William Cooper, [Jr.,] "Caution to Trespassers," *Freeman's Journal*, Oct. 18, 1819.
20. Isaac Cooper, Diary, Feb. 26, June 12, 13, and 22, 1815, NYSHA; "20 Dollars Reward," *Otsego Herald*, Feb. 9, 1815; "Look Out for Horse Thieves!" ibid., June 15, 1815; "Stop Thief!" ibid., June 22, 1815; "Dan Chapin, the Horse Thief," ibid., Aug. 31, 1815; "People v. Chapin," OC-CGSP, Records, vol. 1, Aug. 31, 1815, OCCO. For Chapin see Duane H. Hurd, *History of Otsego County, New York* . . . (Philadelphia, 1878), 99–100. For his leasehold see William Cooper's Will, May 13, 1808, Registry of Wills, book B, 244–48, Otsego Co. Surrogate's Office. For the suggestion that the novelist's fearful world view derived from his father's murder see Warren Motley, *The American Abraham: James Fenimore Cooper and the Frontier Patriarch* (New York, 1987), 13, 33.
21. Otsego County Citizens' meeting, Oct. 20, 1814, *Otsego Herald*, Nov. 3, 1814.
22. *Freeman's Journal*, Dec. 6, 1819, Dec. 11, 1820, May 23, 1821, Sept. 9, 1822, Jan. 9, 1824; [Cooperstown], *Watch-Tower*, Sept. 16 and Dec. 30, 1822.
23. Richard L. Bushman, *The Refinement of America: Persons, Houses, Cities* (New York, 1992), 420–25.
24. George E. DeMille, *A History of the Diocese of Albany, 1704–1923* (Philadelphia, 1946), 35; G. Pomeroy Keese, ed., *Historic Records of Christ Church, Cooperstown, New York* (Cooperstown, 1899), 3–7; John Towner Frederick, *The Darkened Sky: Nineteenth-Century American Novelists* (Notre Dame, Ind., 1969), 2–5; Rev. Daniel Nash to Bishop John H. Hobart, Jan. 24, 1812, and May. 29, 1815, BJHHP, VIII, 6, and XI, 48, PECA (reels 9 and 11, NYHS). Isaac, James, and Samuel Cooper all served on the vestry; see the Records of Christ Church, Record Book, Jan. 1, 1811, Apr. 12, 1814, and Apr. 8, 1817, Christ Church, Cooperstown.
25. Livermore, *Condensed History of Cooperstown*, 118; Otsego Co. Bible Soc., *Second Annual Report* (Cooperstown, 1814, AAS Copy), 3, 16.
26. Otsego Co. Bible Soc., *Fifth Annual Report of the Board of Managers* (Cooperstown, 1817, Shaw-Shoemaker no. 41713), 10, 16–17; Otsego Co. Bible Soc., *Sixth Annual Report of the Board of Managers* (Cooperstown, 1818, Shaw-Shoemaker no. 45191), 3 ("the most profligate").
27. Bushman, *Refinement of America*, 353–54, 370–82; Hurd, *History of Otsego County*, 260.
28. *Otsego Herald*, Jan. 16, May 29, Oct. 30, and Nov. 13, 1813.
29. *Otsego Herald*, May 29, 1813, and June 6, 1816; J. F. Cooper, *Home as Found*, 174–77.
30. For the Doubleday myth see Birdsall, *Story of Cooperstown*, 247–57. The first assertion of the Doubleday myth came in the reminiscences of Abner Graves, written 68 years after the alleged invention. In 1839 Doubleday was a West Point cadet and not a resident of Cooperstown; he never claimed to have played, much less invented, baseball. For the actual origins of baseball in evolution from townball see Harold Seymour, *Baseball: The Early Years* (New York, 1989), 3–12.
31. "Agricultural Meeting," *Otsego Herald*, Jan. 9, 1817; "Agricultural Society of Otsego County," ibid., Feb. 20, 1817; James Cooper, "To the Freeholders of the County of Otsego," in Beard, *Letters and Journals*, vol. 1, 36–38; Clifford Lord, "Elkanah Watson and New York's First County Fair," *New York History*, 23 (Oct. 1942), 437–45; Elkanah Watson, *History of Agricultural Societies on the Modern Berkshire System* (Albany, 1820), 148–51, 160, 169.

For the aesthetic impulse behind agricultural reform see Bushman, *Refinement of America,*
378–82; Jack Larkin, *The Reshaping of Everyday Life, 1790–1840* (New York, 1988), 127–33;
Jacob Morris, *Address of Gen. Jacob Morris, President of the Otsego County Agricultural Society*
(Cooperstown, 1817, Shaw-Shoemaker no. 41491), 4; Metcalf, address, *Watch-Tower,* Mar.
16, 1818 ("comfortable"); "A Member," *Freeman's Journal,* Dec. 4, 1820 ("carry off"); "February," ibid., Feb. 21, 1821; "Viewing Committee's Report," ibid., Oct. 11, 1819.

32. Otsego Co. Agricultural Soc., Record Book, Oct. 14, 1817, NYSHA; "Agricultural Society," *Freeman's Journal,* Feb. 21, 1820; David Maldwyn Ellis, *Landlords and Farmers in the
Hudson-Mohawk Region, 1790–1850* (Ithaca, N.Y., 1946), 135–40; Elkanah Watson, address, included in Morris, *Address of Gen. Jacob Morris,* 8; "P," *Watch-Tower,* Aug. 24, 1818.
A few conservative Republicans—including the county sheriff, Arunah Metcalf—joined
the Otsego County agricultural society and then broke with their party to support the dissident Republican DeWitt Clinton. In effect, the county agricultural societies served as
way stations for a new conservative political alignment rallying around the increasingly
elitist governor, DeWitt Clinton. See Metcalf, address, *Watch-Tower,* Mar. 16, 1818. The
county's most partisan Republican newspaper, the *Watch-Tower,* initially supported the
agricultural society but later soured on it owing to the increasing power of John H. Prentiss, the Federalist editor of the rival *Freeman's Journal.* See "Agricultural Societies," *Watch-
Tower,* June 15, 1818. For the bolting Republicans see "County Meeting of Independent
Electors," *Otsego Herald,* Apr. 20, 1818. Philip L. White found the same political alignments behind the support for, and the opposition to, the agricultural society in Clinton
County. See White, *Beekmantown, New York: Forest Frontier to Farm Community* (Austin, Tex.,
1979), 58–63.

33. [John H. Prentiss], "Cattle Show and Fair," *Freeman's Journal,* Oct. 4, 1819; [Prentiss],
"Clodhopper," ibid., Dec. 25, 1820; Morris, *Address of Gen. Jacob Morris,* 6; Metcalf, address,
Watch-Tower, Mar. 16, 1818; Metcalf, address, *Freeman's Journal,* Oct. 11, 1819.

34. "A Member," *Otsego Herald,* Sept. 18, 1817; Metcalf, address, *Watch-Tower,* Mar. 16, 1818;
Ellis, *Landlords and Farmers,* 140; Donald B. Marti, "Early Agricultural Societies in New
York: The Foundations of Improvement," *New York History,* 48 (Oct. 1967), 321–24; Geoffrey N. Stein, "The Otsego County Fair in the Nineteenth Century, 1817–1915" (Master's
thesis, SUNY at Oneonta, 1968, NYSHA copy), 23; "A Member," *Freeman's Journal,* Nov. 27,
1820; Paschal Franchot, address, *Watch-Tower,* Oct. 15, 1821; William Cooper, *A Guide in
the Wilderness; or, the History of the First Settlements in the Western Counties of New York, with Useful Instructions to Future Settlers . . .* (Cooperstown, 1986, repr. of Dublin, 1810), 69–70. For
a similar reading of the opposition to the agricultural society in Clinton County, see White,
Beekmantown, 62–63.

35. U.S. Bureau of the Census, 1820 Census of Manufactures, Otsego Co., New York, series
279, reel 8, National Archives; "Public Meeting," *Otsego Herald,* Oct. 10, 1816; Morris, *Address of Gen. Jacob Morris,* 6; Otsego Co. Tax Valuation Abstracts for 1815 and 1820, Otsego
County Board of Supervisors, Minute Book, 1804–1823, Basement Vault, Otsego County
Office Building.

36. Susan Fenimore Cooper, *Rural Hours, By a Lady* (New York, 1850), 144–48, 182, 193,
206–7, 223–25; Otsego Co. Tax Valuation Abstract for 1820, Otsego Co. Board of Supervisors, Minute Book, 1804–1823, OCCO; New York (State) *Journal of the Assembly of the State
of New-York at their Forty-Fifth Session* (Albany, 1822), 37–38.

37. Otsego Co. Tax Valuation Abstract for 1820, Otsego Co. Board of Supervisors, Minute
Book, 1804–1823, OCCO; U.S. Bureau of the Census, 1820 Census of Manufactures, Otsego County, series 279, reel 8, National Archives; U.S. Bureau of the Census, Manuscript
Census Return, Otsego Co., 1820, series M33, reel 74, National Archives; New York (State)
Journal of the Assembly . . . at their Forty-Fifth Session, 37–38.

38. Between 1810 and 1820 Otsego's population grew by only 6,130, down from the previous
decade's increase of 17,174. If the 1810 population had grown at 3 percent annually (the
prevailing rate of natural increase in rural America), Otsego should have had an 1820 population of 51,798; the actual population of 44,555 suggests a net loss to outmigration of

7,243 between 1810 and 1820. See U.S. Bureau of the Census returns from Otsego Co. for 1810 (series M252, reel 34) and 1820 (series M33, reel 74), National Archives.

39. U.S. Bureau of the Census returns from Otsego Co. for 1800 (series M32, reel 25) and 1820 (series M33, reel 74), National Archives.

40. For the electoral census of 1795 see *Otsego Herald*, Dec. 17, 1795. My calculations exclude the three towns (Dorlach, Franklin, and Kortright) that became part of Delaware County in 1797. For the electoral census of 1814 see New York (State), *Journal of the Assembly of the State of New-York: At Their Thirty-Eighth Session* . . . (Albany, 1814, Shaw-Shoemaker no. 35462), 257. For tenancy in eastern New York see David Maldwyn Ellis, "Land Tenure and Tenancy in the Hudson Valley, 1790–1860," *Agricultural History*, 18 (Apr. 1944), 75–82. For an exaggerated notion of the long-term effect of Cooper's land policies see Ellis, "Coopers and the New York State Landholding System," 412–22.

41. Ellis, *Landlords and Farmers*, 136; Clarence H. Danhof, *Change in Agriculture: The Northern U.S., 1820–1870* (Cambridge, Mass., 1969), 121, 251–52; Paul Gates, *The Farmer's Age: Agriculture, 1815–1860* (New York, 1960), 35; Bushman, "Opening the American Countryside," 239–56; Horatio Gates Spafford, *A Gazetteer of the State of New York* (Albany, 1813, Shaw-Shoemaker no. 29836), 17.

42. E. L. Jones, "Creative Disruptions in American Agriculture, 1620–1820," *Agricultural History*, 48 (Oct. 1974), 510–28; Carolyn Merchant, *Ecological Revolutions: Nature, Gender, and Science in New England* (Chapel Hill, N.C., 1989), 163–67; Alfred W. Crosby, *Ecological Imperialism: The Biological Expansion of Europe, 900–1900* (New York, 1986), 145–70; "Agriculture," [Cooperstown], *Watch-Tower*, May 11, 1818; Pascal Franchot, address, ibid., Oct. 15, 1821 ("the noxious"); S. F. Cooper, *Rural Hours*, 81, 105–108.

43. Dan Bradley, "Comments on the Soil and Agriculture of Onondaga County," in Board of Agriculture of the State of New York, *Memoirs*, 3 (Albany, 1826), 94; "Epitome of Agriculture," [Cooperstown], *Freeman's Journal*, Oct. 18, 1819; Harry J. Carman, "Jesse Buel, Albany County Agriculturalist," *New York History*, 14 (July 1933), 244; Ellis, *Landlords and Farmers*, 118–20; Danhof, *Change in Agriculture*, 121; John Nicholson, *The Farmer's Assistant* (Albany, 1814), 55.

44. "Agricultural Meeting," *Otsego Herald*, Jan. 9, 1817; Paschal Franchot, presidential address, *Watch-Tower*, Oct. 7, 1822 ("Thirty years ago"); Morris, *Address of Gen. Jacob Morris*, 3–4; Ellis, *Landlords and Farmers*, 139; "Epitome of Agriculture," *Freeman's Journal*, Oct. 18, 1819; Franchot, address, *Watch-Tower*, Oct. 15, 1821.

45. S. F. Cooper, *Rural Hours*, 156, 225–26, 381–83; Ellis, *Landlords and Farmers*, 150; Bushman, "Opening the American Countryside," 245, 253.

46. James Averell 3d, to William H. Averell, July 4, 1812, and Dec. 19, 1812, AFP, box 3, NYSHA; Potter Goff to Isaac Cooper, Feb. 24, 1814, and Jan. 18, 1815, David Goff to I. Cooper, Mar. 20, 1815, and John Garvin to I. Cooper, Aug. 22, 1815, WCP, CB 1810–16, HCA. For the defaults see Frederick De Peyster to I. Cooper, Apr. 18, 1815, and John Fine to I. Cooper, May 19, 1815, WCP, CB 1810–16, HCA; Fine to Luther Bradish, Aug. 25, 1817, JFP, NYHS. DeKalb's population declined from 541 in 1810 to 487 in 1814. See Horatio Gates Spafford, *A Gazetteer of the State of New York* (Albany, 1824), 104; New York (State), *Journal of the Assembly . . . Thirty-Eighth Session*, 263.

47. Robert Campbell to Philip S. Parker, Aug. 4, 1819, WCP, CB 1817–25, HCA; William Cooper, Will, May 13, 1808, Registry of Wills, book B, 237, Otsego Co. Surrogate's Office; Pickering, "Fenimore Cooper as Country Gentleman," 304–5. For settler appeals see William Foxe et al. to Richard Fenimore Cooper and Isaac Cooper, Feb. 7, 1810, David Goff to I. Cooper, Mar. 20, 1815, John Garvin to I. Cooper, Aug. 22, 1815 ("is about all"), and Simeon Gold to I. Cooper, Jan. 2, 1815, WCP, CB 1810–16, HCA.

48. Frederick De Peyster to Isaac Cooper, Apr. 18, 1815, and John Fine to I. Cooper, May 19, 1815, WCP, CB 1810–16, HCA; Fine to Luther Bradish, Aug. 25, 1817, JFP, NYHS.

49. Frederick De Peyster to Isaac Cooper, Feb. 6, 1815, and Apr. 18, 1815 ("we never"), William Ogden to I. Cooper, June 21, 1815, WCP, CB 1810–16, HCA; Isaac Cooper et al., indenture with Lloyd Daubeny et al., June 1, 1815, AFP, box 3, NYSHA.

50. John Fine to Frederick De Peyster, Mar. 18, 1816, and Fine to Luther Bradish, June 28, 1817, JFP, NYHS; Courtland C. Cooper to James [Fenimore] Cooper, Mar. 11, June 5, and Nov. 20, 1817, May 5 and June 24, 1818, Apr. 1, June 1 ("Consider that"), July 15, and Dec. 1, 1819 ("nothing but disappointment"), JFCP, box 2, AAS; Fine to Isaac Cooper, May 30, July 5, and Dec. 20, 1815, and Seth Pomeroy to I. Cooper, Dec. 19, 1817, WCP, CB 1817–25, HCA; Foreclosure notice, [Ogdensburgh, N.Y.] *St. Lawrence Gazette,* Dec. 30, 1817.

51. John Fine to Isaac Cooper, Nov. 11 and 23, 1816, Seth Pomeroy to I. Cooper, Dec. 25, 1816, WCP, CB 1810–16, HCA; I. Cooper to William Ogden, Jan. 24, 1817, WCP, Isaac Cooper Letter Book, HCA; Fine to Luther Bradish, Nov. 11, 1816, and Mar. 3, 1817, JFP, NYHS; Fine to James [Fenimore] Cooper, Dec. 23, 1816, James Fenimore Cooper Papers, Sterling Lib., Yale Univ. A reference to a legal difficulty involving "the *Fine,*" in J. [F.] Cooper's letter of Dec. 15, 1816, to his lawyer, John V. Henry, is probably an allusion to this controversy with John Fine (in Beard, *Letters and Journals,* vol. 1, 35).

52. John Fine to Luther Bradish, Mar. 3 and 7, 1817, JFP, NYHS; Seth Pomeroy to Isaac Cooper, Dec. 19, 1817, and Fine to Robert Campbell, June 15, 1818, WCP, CB 1817–1825, HCA.

53. Atwood Manley, "Our Most Notable Ghost Town: Cooper's Falls," St. Lawrence Hist. Assoc., *Quarterly,* 5 (July 1960), 9–11.

54. Edward G. Williams, "The Prevosts of the Royal Americans," *Western Pennsylvania Historical Magazine,* 56 (1973), 2; Augustine Prevost to Jonathan Williams, Jan. 6, 1808, Williams to William Franklin, Jan. 22, 1809, and Franklin to Williams, Nov. 1, 1811, Jonathan Williams Papers, Indiana Univ. (microfilm copy at the APS); J. Augustine Prevost to Phineas Bond, Mar. 15, 1812, and George W. Prevost to Thomas Cadwallader, Aug. 2, 1811, Cadwallader Coll., George Croghan sec., box 4, HSP; A. Prevost to Franklin, Dec. 31, 1812, WTFEP, box 2, NYPL.

55. George W. Prevost to Augustine Prevost, Feb. 22, 1814, Prevost Family Papers, Albany Inst.; David Wright to Isaac Cooper, Jan. 2 and 20, 1815, WCP, CB 1810–16, HCA; Robert Campbell to James Cooper, Nov. 2, 1818, Apr. 29 and June 2, 1819, Apr. 5, 1820, and Sept. 18, 1821, JFCP, box 2, AAS.

56. *Otsego Herald,* Oct. 5, 1811; S. F. Cooper, "Small Family Memories," 17; James Fenimore Cooper to William Jay, Aug. 29, 1813, in Beard, *Letters and Journals,* vol. 1, 29; [Cooperstown], *Watch-tower,* Dec. 11, 1817; Wayne Wright, "The Cooper Genealogy: Compiled from Materials in the Collection of the New York State Historical Association Library" (typescript, 1983, NYSHA), 15–17.

57. "Obituary," *Otsego Herald,* Mar. 13, 1813; James Cooper to Richard Fenimore Cooper, Dec. 19, 1808, in Beard, *Letters and Journals,* vol. 1, 12; "Amicus" [Elihu Phinney] to R. F. Cooper, Aug. 4, 1809, and John V. Henry to R. F. Cooper, Sept. 6, 1809, WCP, CB 1807–9, HCA; R. F. Cooper, "To the Public," Apr. 20, 1811; Barry L. Wold, *The George Hyde Clarke Family Papers: A Guide to the Collection at Cornell University* (Ithaca, N.Y., 1977), 19; J. F. Cooper (1858–1938), *Legends and Traditions,* 76–77. Because George Clarke treated Alfred as an adopted son in his will, Wold, Beard, and J. F. Cooper (1858–1938) regard Alfred Cooper Clarke as Richard Fenimore Cooper's son, in contrast to my judgment that George Clarke was the father.

58. Isaac Cooper to Ann Clarke, Oct. 24, 1817, WCP, Isaac Cooper Letter Book, HCA.

59. S. F. Cooper, "Small Family Memories," 13–14; Courtland C. Cooper to James Cooper, Jan. 27, 1816, WCP, CB 1810–16, HCA; Isaac Cooper to William Allinson, July 14, 1817, WCP, Isaac Cooper, Letter Book, HCA; I. Cooper, Diary, Aug. 14, 1815–Jan. 1, 1818, NYSHA; "Obituary," *Otsego Herald,* Jan. 5, 1818.

60. S. F. Cooper, "Small Family Memories," 13–14.

61. John M. Leake to Mary Ann Cooper, Jan. 15, 1818, and John Thorne to M. A. Cooper, Mar. 10, 1818, WCP, BB 1801–34, HCA; Isaac Cooper, Diary, continued by M. A. Cooper, Nov. 8, 1818, NYSHA; M. A. Cooper to James Cooper, Nov. 4, 1818, and Robert Campbell to J. Cooper, July 7, 1819, and Sept. 18, 1821, JFCP, box 2, AAS; Peter Kean to Campbell,

Apr. 4, 1820, Robert Campbell Papers, box 2, NYSHA; Ambrose L. Jordan to George Clarke, Apr. 22, 1824, GHCP, box 26, Cornell Univ. Lib.

62. "[Samuel Cooper] Obituary," *Watch-Tower*, Feb. 23, 1819; "Boarding School," *Freeman's Journal*, Dec. 20, 1819; Campbell to J. Cooper, Aug. 23, 1819, JFCP, box 2, AAS.

63. Robert Campbell to James Cooper, Feb. 15 and Aug. 23, 1819, Feb. 21, 1821, JFCP, box 2, AAS; James Pickering, "Fenimore Cooper as Country Gentleman," 305–6; S. F. Cooper, "Small Family Memories," 21–37.

64. Pickering, "Fenimore Cooper as Country Gentleman," 307–11; Beard, *Letters and Journals*, vol. 1, 23–24.

65. Beard, *Letters and Journals*, vol. 1, 84, 87 n. 1, 88 n. 1; Pickering, "Fenimore Cooper as Country Gentleman," 312–18; Dudley Selden to William Holt Averell, Nov. 27, 1823, JFCP, box 2, AAS.

66. Thomas Bridgen to Robert Campbell, Oct. 28, 1818, WCP, BB 1801–34, HCA; Campbell to James [Fenimore] Cooper, Sept. 10, 1821, JFCP, box 2, AAS.

67. Otsego Co. Sheriff's Inventory of Sales, Oct. 22, 1821, Sheriff's certificate of sale to William Holt Averell, Oct. 22, 1821, Broome Co. Sheriff's Inventory of Sales, Jan. 16, 1822, AFP, box 3, NYSHA; W. A. Duer to Averell, Mar. 31, 1822, AFP, box 8, NYSHA; Robert Campbell to James Cooper, Oct. 23, 1821, JFCP, box 2, AAS.

68. Ambrose L. Jordan to Robert Campbell, Mar. 6, 1822, Robert Campbell Papers, box 2, NYSHA; Campbell to James Cooper, Mar. 15, 1822, JFCP, box 2, AAS.

69. Ambrose L. Jordan to Robert Campbell, Apr. 6, 1822, Robert Campbell Papers, box 2, NYSHA; Campbell to James Cooper, Apr. 5, 1822, JFCP, box 2, AAS; St. Lawrence Co. Sheriff's Inventory of Sales, Apr. 15, 1822, and Otsego Co. Sheriff's Inventory of Sales, July 29, 1822, AFP, box 3, NYSHA.

70. Robert Campbell to James Cooper, Mar. 15, 1822, and Oct. 28, 1823, JFCP, box 2, AAS; *Watch-Tower*, June 17, 1822; Ann and George Pomeroy v. James Cooper, Chancery Court Decree, Nov. 26, 1822, AFP, box 3, NYSHA.

71. Rufus King to William Cooper, June 6, 1805, Misc. Mss. K, NYHS; King to Richard Fenimore Cooper and Isaac Cooper, May 10 and July 26, 1810, WCP, CB 1810–16, HCA; King to William Cooper, Jr., May 21, 1819, and Robert Campbell to Ann L. Clarke, July 31, 1822, WCP, BB 1801–34, HCA; King to George Pomeroy, June 8, 1822, Mar. 18 and Apr. 2, 1823, AFP, box 3, NYSHA.

72. Ann and George Pomeroy to William H. Averell, indenture of agreement, Dec. 28, 1822, G. Pomeroy to Averell, Apr. 21, 1823, and Averell to Thomas G. Waterman, Aug. 28, 1823, AFP, box 3, NYSHA.

73. Otsego Co. Sheriff's Inventories of July 1, 1823, auction sales, and John V. Henry to William H. Averell, July 12, 1823, AFP, box 3, NYSHA; Robert Campbell to James Cooper, May 26, and Oct. 28, 1823, JFCP, box 3, AAS.

74. James Averell, Jr., to John H. Prentiss, June 18, 1821, AFP, box 1, NYSHA; Robert Campbell to James [Fenimore] Cooper, Oct. 28, 1823, JFCP, box 2, AAS.

75. Otsego Co. Sheriff's Inventories of Vendue Sales, Oct. 5, 1824, Feb. 15 and May 10, 1825, AFP, box 3, NYSHA; Dudley Selden to William H. Averell, Nov. 27, 1823, and Robert Campbell to James [Fenimore] Cooper, May 24, 1826, JFCP, box 2, AAS; Donald Osgood De Mers, Jr., "William Holt Averell: His Business and Political Career in Relation to Otsego County, New York" (Master's thesis, SUNY at Oneonta, 1972), 16.

76. James Fenimore Cooper to Ann Cooper Pomeroy, July 24, 1826, J. F. Cooper to Richard Cooper, May 25, 1831, and Aug. 5, 1832, J. F. Cooper to A. C. Pomeroy, Nov. 14, 1833, J. F. Cooper to Susan Augusta De Lancey Cooper, June 15, 1834, and J. F. Cooper to A. C. Pomeroy, July 5, 1836, in Beard, *Letters and Journals*, vol. 1, 147–53, vol. 2, 86–90, 296, vol. 3, 33, 43–44. In his May 25, 1831, letter to Richard Cooper, J. F. Cooper noted that he had not been to Cooperstown since his departure in 1817. In his Aug. 5, 1832, letter to R. Cooper, J. F. Cooper explained that he did not know W. H. Averell. For the name change see J. F. Cooper to Philander Benjamin Prindle, Mar. 30, 1847, ibid., vol. 5, 200. In this letter he insisted, incorrectly, that by 1826 he had become "extricated" from his debts and

legal problems and therefore was at last at liberty to change his name. In *Letters and Journals*, vol. 1, 86, James F. Beard, Jr., states that Cooper did not leave America until "the end of the debts was in sight"—which is mistaken.

77. James Fenimore Cooper to Mrs. Cooper, June 15 and 26, 1834, and J. F. Cooper to Richard Cooper, May 14, 1835, in Beard, *Letters and Journals*, vol. 3, 43, 45, 152–53; Articles of Agreement, J. F. Cooper with William H. Averell, Sept. 1, 1834, JFCP, box 2, AAS.

78. Julian P. Boyd, "William Leete Stone," *Dictionary of American Biography*, 18 (New York, 1936), 89–90; William Leete Stone, "From New York to Niagara, Journal of a Tour . . . in the Year 1829," Buffalo Hist. Soc., *Publications*, 14 (1910), 214; [W. L. Stone], "Hiram Doolittle, Jun.," *Freeman's Journal*, Sept. 21, 1829 ("The grounds").

79. Bushman, *Refinement of America*, 406–9.

80. For the transformation of the American elite see Gordon S. Wood, *The Radicalism of The American Revolution* (New York, 1992), 347–69; Marvin Meyers, *The Jacksonian Persuasion: Politics and Belief* (Stanford, Calif., 1960), 3–15.

81. De Mers, "William Holt Averell," 1–20; James Averell, Jr., to William Cooper, bill, Dec. 1, 1792, WCP, BB 1792–93, HCA; J. Averell, advertisement, *Otsego Herald*, Dec. 8, 1796; Cooperstown Presbyterian Church, Session Book, 1800–1820, NYSHA; Ministerial Tax Book for 1804, J. Averell to Noah Crane, Mar. 2, 1806, and "Tax to Pay for the Schoolhouse, 1809," AFP, box 1, NYSHA; Isaac Cooper, Cooperstown Businesses, [1811], WCP, Undated box, HCA; Samuel Starkweather to William H. Averell, Mar. 18, 1816, AFP, box 3, NYSHA.

82. De Mers, "William Holt Averell," 1–11; James Averell, Jr., to William H. Averell, Sept. 26, 1817, AFP, box 1, NYSHA.

83. William H. Averell to Captain Joseph Plumb, July 21, 1823, W. H. Averell to Thomas G. Waterman, Aug. 28, 1823, AFP, box 3, NYSHA; John Fine to Frederick De Peyster, Sept. 19, 1823, De Peyster Papers, V, 28, NYHS; Fine to Luther Bradish, Jan. 13, 1826, and Nov. 25, 1829, JFP, NYHS; Hurd, *History of Otsego County*, 280.

84. For stories of industry triumphant over inherited wealth see Stephen Thernstrom, *Poverty and Progress: Social Mobility in a Nineteenth Century City* (Cambridge, Mass., 1964), 57–79.

85. James Fenimore Cooper to Richard Cooper, Aug. 5, 1832, in Beard, *Letters and Journals*, vol. 2, 96. For Cooper's animus against Yankees see Kay Seymour House, *Cooper's Americans* (Columbus, Ohio, 1965), 117–45; James Henry Pickering, "James Fenimore Cooper and the History of New York" (Ph.D. diss., Northwestern Univ., 1964), 114–21; Boynton, *James Fenimore Cooper*, 19.

86. S. F. Cooper, *Rural Hours*, 130, 142–43, 254–55. For the growing inequality in early-nineteenth-century America see Edward Pessen, *Riches, Class, and Power before the Civil War* (Lexington, Mass., 1973). For the subdivision of power see Lee Benson, *The Concept of Jacksonian Democracy: New York as a Test Case* (Princeton, N.J., 1961).

87. L. Ray Gunn, *The Decline of Authority: Public Economic Policy and Political Development in New York, 1800–1860* (Ithaca, N.Y., 1988).

15. THE NOVELIST

1. James Franklin Beard, ed., *The Letters and Journals of James Fenimore Cooper*, 6 vols. (Cambridge, Mass., 1960–1968), vol. 1, xxi, 5; William Leete Stone, "From New York to Niagara, Journal of a Tour . . . in the Year 1829," in Buffalo Hist. Soc., *Publications*, 14 (1910), 214; Wayne Franklin, *The New World of James Fenimore Cooper* (Chicago, 1982), 21. Later in their careers Stone and Cooper became bitter enemies.

2. Susan Fenimore Cooper, "Small Family Memories," in James Fenimore Cooper (1858–1938), ed., *Correspondence of James Fenimore Cooper*, 2 vols. (New Haven, Conn., 1922), vol. 1, 38; Robert E. Spiller, *Fenimore Cooper: Critic of His Times* (New York, 1963, repr. of 1931), 72–73; Cathy N. Davidson, *Revolution and the Word: The Rise of the Novel in America* (New York, 1986), 15–37; James D. Wallace, *Early Cooper and His Audience* (New York, 1986), 29–62, 86–87; James Fenimore Cooper, *Notions of the Americans, Picked Up by a Travelling Bachelor*, 2 vols. (New York, 1963, repr. of 1828), vol. 2, 106–12; Michael T.

Gilmore, "The Literature of the Revolutionary and Early National Periods," in Sacvan Bercovitch, ed., *The Cambridge History of American Literature, Volume 1: 1590–1820* (New York, 1994), 625, 626, 644, 676.

3. S. F. Cooper, "Small Family Memories," 39; James Cooper to Andrew Thompson Goodrich, Oct. 19–20, 1820, in Beard, *Letters and Journals,* vol. 1, 66; *Freeman's Journal,* July 23, 1821; Davidson, *Revolution and the Word,* 38–53; Wallace, *Early Cooper,* 79; George Dekker, *James Fenimore Cooper: The American Scott* (New York, 1967), 10–13; Warren Motley, *The American Abraham: James Fenimore Cooper and the Frontier Patriarch* (New York, 1987), 55–57.

4. James Cooper to Andrew Thompson Goodrich, Oct. 19–20, 1820, in Beard, *Letters and Journals,* vol. 1, 66; S. F. Cooper, "Small Family Memories," 42–43; Dekker, *James Fenimore Cooper,* 18–19; Wallace, *Early Cooper,* 67–72, 83–85, 100–101, 172. For Cooper's enduring preoccupation with marriage and inheritance see Robert Lawson-Peebles, "Property, Marriage, Women, and Fenimore Cooper's First Fictions," in W. M. Verhoeven, ed., *James Fenimore Cooper: New Historical and Literary Contexts* (Atlanta, 1993), 47–70; Franklin, *New World,* 26–28; Joy S. Kasson, "Templeton Revisited: Social Criticism in *The Pioneers* and *Home as Found,*" *Studies in the Novel,* 9 (Spring 1977), 54–64. For the prevailing conventions see Gilmore, "Literature of the Revolutionary and Early National Periods," 623–35.

5. James Cooper to Andrew Thompson Goodrich, June 28, 1820, in Beard, *Letters and Journals,* vol. 1, 44; Cooper to Rufus Wilmot Griswold, Jan. 10–18, 1843, in ibid., vol. 4, 342; Wallace, *Early Cooper,* 108–9; Charles Wiley to Cooper, Jan. 7, 1821 [*sic:* 1822], JFCP, box 2, AAS; Michael Kammen, *A Season of Youth: The American Revolution and the Historical Imagination* (New York, 1978), 21, 130.

6. George Dekker, "James Fenimore Cooper and the American Romance Tradition," and Susan Scheckel, "'In the Land of His Fathers': Cooper, Land Rights, and the Legitimation of American National Identity," both in Verhoeven, *James Fenimore Cooper,* 24, 138; Charles Hansford Adams, *"The Guardian of the Law": Authority and Identity in James Fenimore Cooper* (University Park, Pa., 1990), 25–28; James Franklin Beard, "Cooper and the Revolutionary Mythos," *Early American Literature,* 11 (Spring 1976), 84–104; Kammen, *Season of Youth,* 21, 130; Franklin, *New World,* 41–42.

7. James Franklin Beard, "Historical Introduction," to James Fenimore Cooper, *The Pioneers, or the Sources of the Susquehanna; A Descriptive Tale* (Albany, 1980, crit. ed. of New York, 1823), xl–xlii; Beard, *Letters and Journals,* vol. 1, xx, xliv–xlvi, 84; Charles Wiley to James Cooper, Jan. 7, 1821 [*sic:* 1822], JFCP, box 2, AAS; *Watch-Tower,* Feb. 4, July 15, 1822; *Freeman's Journal,* Feb. 4, 1822, Jan. 13 and 27, 1823; Cooper to John Murray, Nov. 29, 1822, Jan. 15, 1823, in Beard, *Letters and Journals,* vol. 1, 85–86, 91–92; Moss Kent, Jr., to Nathan Williams, Oct. 15, 1822, Nathan Williams Papers, box 2, Oneida Co. Hist. Soc.; "The Pioneers," *New York Spectator,* Jan. 17, Feb. 4 and 14, 1823.

8. Samuel G. Goodrich, *Recollections of a Lifetime, or Men and Things I Have Seen,* 2 vols. (New York, 1856), vol. 2, 110; Beard, "Historical Introduction," to J. F. Cooper, *Pioneers,* xlvii; Anon. to Charles Wiley, Feb. 20, 1823, JFCP, box 2, AAS; James Cooper to Richard Henry Dana, Apr. 14, 1823, in Beard, *Letters and Journals,* vol. 1, 93–95; Spiller, *Fenimore Cooper,* 92–94; W. M. Verhoeven, "Introduction: Reconsidering Cooper," in Verhoeven, *James Fenimore Cooper,* 10–11.

9. George Houston, Review of *The Pioneers,* in *New York Minerva,* Feb. 23, 1823; Samuel B. H. Judah, *Gotham and the Gothamites—A Medley* (New York, 1823), xlvii; James Gates Percival to James Lawrence Yvonnet, Apr. 17, July 18, 1823, in Julius H. Ward, *The Life and Letters of James Gates Percival* (Boston, 1866), 154–55, 170–71.

10. Beard, "Historical Introduction," to J. F. Cooper, *Pioneers,* xxxviii; Beard, *Letters and Journals,* vol. 1, 24–25, 83–84 (includes the Bryant quotation); S. F. Cooper, "Small Family Memories," 50; Spiller, *Fenimore Cooper,* 76–86; Goodrich, *Recollections of a Lifetime,* vol. 2, 134 ("Mr. Cooper"); Motley, *American Abraham,* 60–64.

11. Motley, *American Abraham,* 42–43, 56–61; Stephen Railton, *Fenimore Cooper: A Study of His Life and Imagination* (Princeton, N.J., 1978), 59–61; Verhoeven, "Introduction: Reconsid-

ering Cooper," 12–15. Unfairly criticizing Motley, Verhoeven takes excessive pains to insist that Cooper did not "*consciously* set out to seek a sense of self through the authority of his writing." My point (and Motley's) is that, whatever Cooper's original intent, within three years he achieved a new self-assurance and authority as a writer.

12. Wallace, *Early Cooper*, 84–116, 171–84; Kammen, *Season of Youth*, 149; W. M. Verhoeven, "Neutralizing the Land: The Myth of Authority, and the Authority of Myth in Fenimore Cooper's *The Spy,*" in Verhoeven, *James Fenimore Cooper*, 77; John P. McWilliams, Jr., *Political Justice in a Republic: James Fenimore Cooper's America* (Berkeley, Calif., 1972), 60–61.

13. Dorothy Waples, *The Whig Myth of James Fenimore Cooper* (New Haven, Conn., 1938), 67–68; review from the *National Gazette* reprinted in *Freeman's Journal*, Mar. 10, 1823; Richard Henry Dana to James Cooper, Apr. 2, 1823, in Beard, *Letters and Journals*, vol. 1, 92; W. H. Gardiner review for *North American Review*, reprinted in George Dekker and John P. McWilliams, Jr., eds., *Fenimore Cooper: The Critical Heritage* (Boston, 1973), 118. For the role of reviewers see Wallace, *Early Cooper*, 19–22.

14. *Port Folio* review reprinted in Dekker and McWilliams, *Fenimore Cooper: The Critical Heritage*, 69–70; William Leete Stone, "The Pioneers," *New York Spectator*, Feb. 4, 1823; "The Wilderness and the Pioneers," *New York Mirror*, Aug. 2, and 16, 1823.

15. James Henry Pickering, "James Fenimore Cooper and the History of New York" (Ph.D. diss., Northwestern Univ., 1964), 225; Ralph Birdsall, *The Story of Cooperstown* (Cooperstown, 1917), 79, 90, 96; *Watch-Tower*, Feb. 3, 1823; *Freeman's Journal*, Feb. 17 and 24, Mar. 3, 1823; Robert Campbell to James Cooper, Apr. 10, 1823, JFCP, box 2, AAS; Abel and Henry Bowen, "Proposals," *Freeman's Journal*, Oct. 13, 1823; [William Leete Stone], "Hiram Doolittle, Jun," *Freeman's Journal*, Sept. 21, 1829; Stone, "From New York to Niagara," 214; Insurance Policy, Oct. 23, 1832, AFP, box 6, NYSHA.

16. J. F. Cooper, *Notions of the Americans*, vol. 1, 254; Charles A. Murray, *Travels in North America During the Years, 1834, 1835, & 1836 . . .* (New York, 1839), vol. 2, 235–36.

17. J. F. Cooper, "Preface [1823]," *Pioneers*, 3–5; J. F. Cooper to John Murray, Nov. 29, 1822, in Beard, *Letters and Journals*, vol. 1, 85; J. F. Cooper to Charles Gosselin, Sept. 8, 1827, in ibid., vol. 6, 294–95; J. F. Cooper to Samuel Carter Hall, Mar. n.d., 1831, in ibid., vol. 2, 59; J. F. Cooper, *Pioneers*, 233, 235.

18. Franklin, *New World*, 77–80; Pickering, "J. F. Cooper and . . . New York," 13–16; Richard H. Levet, *Ambrose L. (Aqua Fortis) Jordan, Lawyer* (New York, 1973), 95–99; Eric J. Sundquist, *Home as Found: Authority and Genealogy in Nineteenth Century American Literature* (Baltimore, 1979), 1–5, 19–20; James Fenimore Cooper to William M. Swain, Sept. 27, 1840, and J. F. Cooper to Horatio Hastings Weld [for *Brother Jonathan*], Mar. 22–25, 1842, in Beard, *Letters and Journals*, vol. 4, 76, 252–59.

19. James Fenimore Cooper to Horatio Hastings Weld [for the *Brother Jonathan*], Mar. 22–25, 1842, in Beard, *Letters and Journals*, vol. 4, 252–59; Bryant quoted in Spiller, *Fenimore Cooper*, 79.

20. James Fenimore Cooper to Horatio Hastings Weld [for the *Brother Jonathan*], Mar. 22–25, 1842, in Beard, *Letters and Journals*, vol. 4, 254–55; J. F. Cooper to William M. Swain, Sept. 27–Oct. 10, 1840, in Beard, *Letters and Journals*, vol. 4, 75.

21. James Fenimore Cooper to Horatio Hastings Weld [for the *Brother Jonathan*], Mar. 22–25, 1842, in Beard, *Letters and Journals*, vol. 4, 256–57; J. F. Cooper, *Pioneers*, 11.

22. J. F. Cooper, "Introduction" (1851) to *Pioneers*, 11.

23. For some of the new historicist readings of Cooper see Robert Clark, ed., *James Fenimore Cooper: New Critical Essays* (New York, 1985), 7–13; William P. Kelly, *Plotting America's Past: Fenimore Cooper and the Leatherstocking Tales* (Carbondale, Ill., 1983), vii–ix, 9–13, 27, 43; Motley, *American Abraham;* Geoffrey Rans, *Cooper's Leather-Stocking Novels: A Secular Reading* (Chapel Hill, N.C., 1991), x–xi, 3–4; and Verhoeven, *James Fenimore Cooper.*

24. James H. Pickering has determined "that the world of Templeton as a whole is but a thinly disguised version of the world of Cooperstown which Cooper knew as a boy." Concurring, Stephen Railton dismisses Cooper's special pleading of post-1838 as "specious and unconvincing." See Pickering, "J. F. Cooper and . . . New York," 216; Railton, *Fenimore Cooper,*

80; Spiller, *Fenimore Cooper*, 26; Beard, "Historical Introduction," to J. F. Cooper, *Pioneers*, xxiv–xxviii. For *The Pioneers* as paternal displacement, see Kelly, *Plotting America's Past*, 36; Motley, *American Abraham*, 38–39; Railton, *Fenimore Cooper*, 112–13. For Cooper's repossession through imagination see Franklin, *New World*, 106–7; Robert Clark, *History and Myth in American Fiction, 1823–1852* (New York, 1984), 61–64; Richard Godden, "Pioneer Properties, or 'What's in a Hut?' " in Clark, *James Fenimore Cooper*, 137–40; Kelly, *Plotting America's Past*, 15–19; Robert Emmet Long, *James Fenimore Cooper* (New York, 1990), 37, 44.

25. Railton, *Fenimore Cooper*, 21–30, 75–76; Susan Fenimore Cooper quoted in Henry Walcott Boynton, *James Fenimore Cooper* (New York, 1931), 100; James Fenimore Cooper to John Murray, Nov. 29, 1822, in Beard, *Letters and Journals*, vol. 1, 86.

26. Franklin, *New World*, 2–5, 82–87; Long, *James Fenimore Cooper*, 36; Rans, *Cooper's Leather-Stocking Novels*, 70.

27. Rans, *Cooper's Leather-Stocking Novels*, 63, 79–91; Brook Thomas, *Cross-examinations of Law and Literature: Cooper, Hawthorne, Stowe, and Melville* (New York, 1987), 39; Wallace, *Early Cooper*, 155, 160; Adams, *"Guardian of the Law,"* 72–73; Motley, *American Abraham*, 50–54.

28. Adams, *"Guardian of the Law,"* 74–75; Verhoeven, "Introduction: Reconsidering Cooper," 15–16; Verhoeven, "Neutralizing the Land," 73–87; Kelly, *Plotting America's Past*, 11–13; McWilliams, *Political Justice*, 1–31; Thomas, *Cross-examinations of Law and Literature*, 44; Gilmore, "Literature of the Revolutionary and Early National Periods," 628.

29. Motley, *American Abraham*, 1–2, 11–13, 20–21, 29–33, 100; Rans, *Cooper's Leather-Stocking Novels*, 9; Robert A. Ferguson, *Law and Letters in American Culture* (Cambridge, Mass., 1984), 297–303.

30. Kelly, *Plotting America's Past*, 4; Allan Axelrad, *History and Utopia: A Study of the World View of James Fenimore Cooper* (Norwood, Pa., 1974), 90–91, 97, 123–24. Motley notes, "The familial relationship between community and leader remained Cooper's primary model of good government." See Motley, *American Abraham*, 29.

31. Adams, *"Guardian of the Law,"* 19, 56–58; McWilliams, *Political Justice*, 108–13; Robert Barton, "Natty's Trial, or the Triumph of Hiram Doolittle," *Cimmaron Review*, 36 (July 1976), 29–37; Gilmore, "Literature of the Revolutionary and Early National Periods," 691–92; Thomas, *Cross-examinations of Law and Literature*, 21–44.

32. Ferguson, *Law and Letters*, 11–12, 26–28, 297–303; Thomas, *Cross-examinations of Law and Literature*, 21–44; Adams, *"Guardian of the Law,"* 1–23, 58; McWilliams, *Political Justice*, 1–31.

33. Kelly, *Plotting America's Past*, 15–18, 24–25; Adams, *"Guardian of the Law,"* 64–65; Wallace, *Early Cooper*, 155; Rans, *Cooper's Leather-Stocking Novels*, 83.

34. Franklin, *New World*, 94–100; McWilliams, *Political Justice*, 106, 114–15, 125; Adams, *"Guardian of the Law,"* 60, 64; Thomas, *Cross-examinations of Law and Literature*, 30; Kay Seymour House, *Cooper's Americans* (Columbus, Ohio, 1965), 271–73.

35. J. F. Cooper, *Pioneers*, 446–47. For Cooper's practice of displacing conflicts see Clark, *History and Myth in American Fiction*, 61–78.

36. Kelly, *Plotting America's Past*, 1–6, 12, 15–18, 23, 26, 30–34; Thomas, *Cross-examinations of Law and Literature*, 43; Thomas Philbrick, "Cooper's *The Pioneers*: Origins and Structure," in Wayne Fields, ed., *James Fenimore Cooper: A Collection of Critical Essays* (Englewood Cliffs, N.J., 1979), 70–79; Marvin Meyers, *The Jacksonian Persuasion: Politics and Belief* (Stanford, Calif., 1960), 60–63. For a dissenting view, insisting that Cooper could not bring himself to suppress the conflicts that he forthrightly mustered in his text, see Rans, *Cooper's Leather-Stocking Novels*, 21–24, 40–46.

37. Verhoeven, "Neutralizing the Land," 87; Adams, *"Guardian of the Law,"* 80; Robert Clark, "Introduction," in Clark, *James Fenimore Cooper*, 8; McWilliams, *Political Justice*, 1–7, 10; Scheckel, " 'In the Land of His Fathers,' " 125–50; J. F. Cooper, *Notions of the Americans*, vol. 1, 269 ("reformers"), vol. 2, 108–9.

38. J. F. Cooper, *Notions of the Americans*, vol. 1, 81, vol. 2, 293–94.

39. Dekker, "James Fenimore Cooper," 24–25; Wallace, *Early Cooper*, 120–21; Cooper quoted in Beard, *Letters and Journals*, vol. 1, xxii; Verhoeven, "Neutralizing the Land," 73–74. For

the nature of narrative see David Carr, *Time, Narrative, and History* (Bloomington, Ind., 1986).

40. J. F. Cooper, *Pioneers*, 15–16. For my concluding point I am indebted to a letter from Wayne Franklin, who would put a greater emphasis on Cooper's divided loyalties to society than I do in this discussion.

41. "Fire," *Watch-Tower*, July 14, 1823; "Fire," *Freeman's Journal*, July 14, 1823; Douglas Preston, "The Clang of the Bell, the Wail of the Whistle: A History of the Cooperstown Fire Department" (Master's thesis, SUNY at Oneonta, 1975, NYSHA copy), 24.

42. James Fenimore Cooper, *Chronicles of Cooperstown* (1838), reprinted in Shaw T. Livermore, ed., *A Condensed History of Cooperstown* (Albany, 1862), 35; "Fire," *Watch-Tower*, July 28, 1823; "Fire," *Freeman's Journal*, July 28, 1823; Preston, "Clang of the Bell," 24–25.

43. Preston, "Clang of the Bell," 25–29; *Watch-Tower*, Sept. 8, Nov. 24 ("principally formed"), Dec. 8, 1823, Jan. 26, Feb. 23, Apr. 26, 1824; *Freeman's Journal*, Sept. 8, Dec. 8, 1823, Apr. 26, June 14, 1824; J. F. Cooper, *Chronicles of Cooperstown*, 35. Another fire, which consumed a tannery on Aug. 26, was deemed accidental. See "Fire!" *Watch-Tower*, Sept. 1, 1823.

44. "Fire!" *Watch-Tower*, Dec. 8, 1823; "Another Fire!" *Freeman's Journal*, Dec. 8, 1823; James Averell 3d to William H. Averell, Mar. 6, 1824, AFP, box 2, NYSHA; "Yet Another Fire!" *Freeman's Journal*, Apr. 26, 1824; Cooper, *Chronicles of Cooperstown*, 35.

45. S. F. Cooper, "Small Family Memories," 52.

46. James Fenimore Cooper to John Holmes Prentiss [for *Freeman's Journal*], Aug. 16, 1837, in Beard, *Letters and Journals*, vol. 3, 276–83; Meyers, *Jacksonian Persuasion*, 74–100; McWilliams, *Political Justice*, 185–236; Sundquist, *Home as Found*, 4–9; Kasson, "Templeton Revisited," 54–64; Cooper quoted in Ralph Birdsall, "Fenimore Cooper in Cooperstown," NYSHA, *Proceedings*, 16 (1917), 143 ("In this part").

47. James Fenimore Cooper, *Home as Found* (New York, 1852, repr. of New York, 1838), 180–83; Kasson, "Templeton Revisited," 60–62.

48. J. F. Cooper, *Home as Found*, 133, 184–85.

49. Meyers, *Jacksonian Persuasion*, 94–95; McWilliams, *Political Justice*, 227–36; Sundquist, *Home as Found*, 31–33.

Acknowledgments

Preparing these acknowledgments reminds me of the many people whose expertise and kindness made researching and writing this book possible and enjoyable. Like the Cooper heirs, I have incurred debts, which I can only gratefully acknowledge and never repay in full. Fortunately, I have more gracious creditors than did James Fenimore Cooper.

My first debt is to the late Paul Fenimore Cooper, Jr., who in 1988 welcomed me to his home outside Cooperstown and shared with me his extraordinary collection of the correspondence and business records of Judge William Cooper. I could not have begun this project without his encouragement and assistance. I found myself in the historian's fondest dream: a substantial private archive virtually untapped by scholars but carefully preserved, systematically organized, and thoroughly cataloged by a man who devoted the last decade of his life to caring for his ancestors' papers. He opened up his vault filled with records and letters, cleared a nineteenth-century desk for me to work at, and taught me to use the index he had painstakingly created and entered into his personal computer. As I read through the papers, he would often stop by to offer keen observations and raise intriguing questions. I've found that those comments and queries shaped much of my subsequent research and writing. Paul and his mother, Babbie, were wonderfully generous in making me feel at home, even sharing with me a bottle of Madeira that dated to James Fenimore Cooper's lifetime. Unfortunately my acquaintance with Paul Cooper was cut short by his untimely death just six months after we met. Fortunately for my project and for other scholars, he had the foresight and public spirit to donate the William Cooper papers to the Hartwick College Archives and the James Fenimore Cooper papers to the American Antiquarian Society. I have received continuing encouragement, advice, and assistance from Paul's cousin, Henry S. F. Cooper, Jr., who as a writer and environmentalist has carried on his family's traditions. I am especially grateful to Henry for sharing with me a tape made of the music played on the mechanical organ from Otsego Hall which James Fenimore Cooper listened to as a child. Playing that tape has often helped me imagine his household as I wrote.

It was my great good fortune that the William Cooper papers passed into the stewardship of Shelley Wallace, the archivist at Hartwick College. She accelerated my work by years with her extraordinary efficiency and enormous goodwill. Best of all, she and her husband, Peter, and sons, Erik and Evan, befriended me, making their home a welcome haven after my days of research. I especially cherish the invitation to give the official historical address dedicating the model train layout built by Peter and Erik. In gratitude for their many acts of friendship, I have dedicated this book to them (and to the memory of Paul Fenimore Cooper, Jr.). My research at Hartwick College also benefited from the generous support extended by Philip Wilder, then the president of the college, and by Bob Danford, the director of the library.

For much of my supplementary research I relied upon the collections and staff of the New York State Historical Association in Cooperstown. Paul S. D'Ambrosio, the curator of the art collection, introduced me to the wonders of townball (the precursor game to baseball) as well as to the mysteries of Cooperstown past and present. During my research trips I frequently had the good fortune to enjoy the hospitality extended by Paul and his wife, Anna. I also received generous assistance from the librarian, Amy Barnum, the special collections librarian, Eileen O'Brien, and from Wayne Wright and Gib Vincent. Publishing an essay in *New York History* was an especially rewarding experience because of my opportunity to work with the editor, Wendell Tripp.

I also spent many days researching at the New York State Archives and State Library in Albany. Despite severe state budget cuts, the staffs there were remarkably efficient and resourceful. I am particularly grateful to Stefan Bielinski, Bill Evans, Bill Gorman, and James Folts—who all went out of their way to be helpful. My many stays in Albany were especially pleasant because of the wise guidance and generous hospitality provided by my friend, student, and archival adviser Martha Shattuck, who took so much time out from her own scholarship on the New Netherlands to help mine on a later century.

At the Massachusetts Historical Society in Boston the staff was always helpful and friendly. I am especially grateful to Peter Drummey, Richard A. Ryerson, and Celeste Walker. At the G. W. Blunt White Library of the Mystic Seaport Museum I benefited from the assistance extended by Douglas Stein, curator of manuscripts. At the McKinney Library of the Albany Institute of History and Art Prudence Backman was resourceful and helpful. At the Montgomery County Historical Society, the archivist, Violet Fallone, provided valuable guidance. I was able to delve into Otsego's county records thanks to the understanding of the county clerk, Charlotte Koniuto, and to the assistance of her thoughtful assistant Marion Brophy. At the county clerk's office or at NYSHA I frequently ran into Connie Ulrich, who shared her expertise on the genealogy of Otsego County families. Father Douglas

Smith, rector of Christ Church in Cooperstown, made available his church's historical records. Arthur Jenkins, Jr., secretary of Otsego Lodge No. 138, kindly permitted me to work with that lodge's documents. I consulted two private collections of historical papers, belonging to G. McMurtrie Godley of Morris, New York, and to Michael Moffat of Cooperstown. I thank them for their consideration. The staff at the New York City Hall of Records, the New York Public Library, and the New-York Historical Society were immensely patient and helpful. I especially enjoyed my research trips to New York City because of the generous hospitality and good company provided by Barbara Brooks and David Jaffee.

My research also took me to the American Antiquarian Society, where I spent six wonderful months in early 1990 on a fellowship funded by the National Endowment for the Humanities. I am grateful for the support afforded my research by Nancy H. Burkett, librarian, John B. Hench, the director of research and publications, and Marcus McCorison, then the director. My stay was enriched by exchanges with the other fellows, especially William W. Freehling, Lee Heller, and Mark and Lynn Valeri. Stephen Bullock of Worcester Polytechnic Institute was a genial presence in the reading room and an invaluable guide to understanding Freemasonry. The rich holdings and extraordinary staff render the AAS the ideal library for research scholars working on early American history and literature. Thomas G. Knoles, Dennis Leary, Joyce Ann Tracy, Marie Lamoroux, and Joanne D. Chaison made working at the AAS a great pleasure and a fond memory.

The most productive summer of my research was that spent in 1990 at the Library Company of Philadelphia and the Historical Society of Pennsylvania. My sojourn in Philadelphia was especially memorable for the advice and friendship provided by Rosalind Remer and by James N. Green, the librarian at the LCP. At the Library Company of Burlington (New Jersey) I benefited from the assistance of Sharon Fitzpatrick.

In the winter and spring of 1991, a fellowship at the Center for the History of Freedom of Washington University enabled me to pursue my research and take in a few St. Louis Cardinals games. Despite being a National League fan and Astroturf apologist, David "El Jefe" Konig proved a wonderful friend and inspirational leader/editor of our band of amigos, who included Paul Gilje, Jan Lewis, and the famous Peter Onuf. For their warm good friendship during and after the St. Louis interlude, I am also grateful to Kristen Onuf and Judy Mann.

I spent the fall of 1993 at the National Humanities Center, where I was the Tri-Delta fellow, thanks to the commitment of that sorority to promoting scholarship. I wrote much of this book at the NHC, thanks largely to the environment created by its talented and dedicated staff. I am especially grateful to Kent Mulliken, the assistant director, who did so much to make the fellows feel at home. I learned much from my fellow fellows, especially

Christopher Baswell, Philip J. Benedict, Shepherd Krech III, Laurie Mafflie-Kipp, John Scott, and Katharine Tachau.

I largely completed this book during the winter and spring of 1994, when I enjoyed a Mead fellowship at the Huntington Library, a scholar's paradise and my refuge from the Northeast's worst winter in fifty years. One of my greatest treats was the chance to work with Frederick Jackson Turner's signed copy of Jabez D. Hammond's classic *History of Political Parties in the State of New-York.* Barring the occasional earthquake, I had a blissful time in Southern California, thanks primarily to the guidance and generosity of the director of research, Roy Ritchie. I learned much from the other fellows, Michael and Carol Kammen. I also benefited from the advice and friendship of Jennie Watts, Bill Deverell, Louise Nocas, Amy and Jack Myers, and Peter and Sue Blodgett. Will Jacobs and Mark Roosa kept me honest on the local tennis courts. Margaret Cunningham graciously permitted me to stay in her family's home, beautifully set at the foot of the San Gabriel Mountains.

Several scholars generously responded to my written queries: Whitfield J. Bell, Jr., John Brooke, Patricia Christian, Craig Hanyan, William A. Kearns, David W. Maxey, and James H. Pickering. The members of the James Fenimore Cooper Society shared their enthusiasm and insights. In particular, I wish to thank Allan Axelrad, Kay House, John P. McWilliams, Jr., Robert D. Madison, Thomas Philbrick, Geoffrey Rans, and George Test. My footnotes often convey my debts to their scholarship. The society's secretary, Hugh MacDougall, very kindly shared his fund of information about the life and writings of James Fenimore Cooper. I never met James F. Beard, but, like all other Cooper scholars, I am greatly indebted to his immense work in editing and publishing the novelist's letters and journals and a critical edition of *The Pioneers.* Although Beard never completed his biography of James Fenimore Cooper, his notes, deposited at the AAS, provided many valuable leads. I also benefited greatly from reading an unpublished paper by Lissa Gifford on James Fenimore Cooper and the environmental history of Otsego Lake. My debt to Alfred F. Young for his classic study of New York politics in the early Republic grew with every chapter of this book.

I also wish to thank Richard Dunn and Wayne Bodle for the opportunity to present a chapter to the Philadelphia Center for Early American History—where I learned much from the freewheeling interchange. In particular, comments that day gave shape to this book's discussion of Elizabeth Cooper. Another chapter benefited from the close scrutiny of the American history faculty and graduate students at the University of Virginia, a presentation arranged and moderated, with characteristic élan, by Peter Onuf. Peter Mancall and Wayne Franklin closely read, and astutely commented upon, several draft chapters to my immense benefit. By their kind support for my scholarship, Richard Bushman, David Hall, Linda Kerber, and Laurel Thatcher Ulrich helped make possible my several fellowships.

I was especially fortunate that Jane Garrett of Alfred A. Knopf took a special interest in this project. I eventually learned that years ago she had helped her friend Paul Fenimore Cooper, Jr., organize the papers that are at the core of this book. In the past six years she has been a thoughtful and nurturing editor whose sage advice has repeatedly smoothed my path.

I researched and wrote most of this book as a member of the faculty at Boston University. The dean, Dennis Berkey, the history department chair, Bill Keylor, and my departmental colleagues were remarkably supportive. Jim McCann was an ideal colleague: funny, supportive, thoughtful, and challenging (but unrelenting in his powerful first serve). And I was especially fortunate in the bright and wonderful people who were my graduate students at BU. I leave my friends there with great regret. But I am also grateful to my new colleagues and administrators at UC Davis for the opportunity and encouragement they have so generously provided.

Above all, I am thankful that Emily Albu has been my very best friend and more.

Index

A Note About the Author

Born in Portland, Maine, Alan Taylor received his B.A. degree from Colby College in 1977 and his Ph.D. from Brandeis University in 1986. He has taught at Colby College, the College of William and Mary, Boston University, and the University of California at Davis, where he is Professor of History. He has been the recipient of Best Annual Article Prizes from *American Quarterly* (1986), *New York History* (1991), and *Journal of the Early Republic* (1991), and fellowships from the National Endowment for the Humanities/Institute of Early American History and Culture, NEH/American Antiquarian Society, the National Humanities Center, and the Huntington Library. He is vice president for the Northern Hemisphere of the Peripheral Studies Association and the author of *Liberty Men and Great Proprietors: The Revolutionary Settlement on the Maine Frontier, 1760–1820.*

A Note on the Type

This book was set in a type called Baskerville. The face itself is a facsimile reproduction of types cast from the molds made for John Baskerville (1706–1775) from his designs. Baskerville's original face was one of the forerunners of the type style known to printers as "modern face"—a "modern" of the period A.D. 1800.

Composed by ComCom, an R. R. Donnelley & Sons company, Allentown, Pennsylvania
Printed and bound by R. R. Donnelley & Sons, Harrisonburg, Virginia
Maps by Russell Jones
Designed by Anthea Lingeman